Pro JavaFX 2

A Definitive Guide to Rich Clients with Java Technology

James L. Weaver
Weiqi Gao, Ph.D.
Stephen Chin
Dean Iverson
with Johan Vos, Ph.D.

Apress®

Pro JavaFX 2: A Definitive Guide to Rich Clients with Java Technology

ISBN-13 (pbk): 978-1-4302-6872-7

ISBN-13 (electronic): 978-1-4302-6873-4

President and Publisher: Paul Manning
Lead Editor: Richard Carey
Technical Reviewer: Carl Dea
Editorial Board: Steve Anglin, Ewan Buckingham, Gary Cornell, Louise Corrigan, Morgan Ertel,
    Jonathan Gennick, Jonathan Hassell, Robert Hutchinson, Michelle Lowman, James Markham,
    Matthew Moodie, Jeff Olson, Jeffrey Pepper, Douglas Pundick, Ben Renow-Clarke,
    Dominic Shakeshaft, Gwenan Spearing, Matt Wade, Tom Welsh
Coordinating Editors: Stephen Moles and Annie Beck
Copy Editor: Valerie Greco and Heather Lang
Production Support: Patrick Cunningham
Indexer: SPi Global
Artist: SPi Global
Cover Designer: Anna Ishchenko

Distributed to the book trade worldwide by Springer Science+Business Media New York, 233 Spring Street, 6th Floor, New York, NY 10013. Phone 1-800-SPRINGER, fax (201) 348-4505, e-mail orders-ny@springer-sbm.com, or visit www.springeronline.com.

For information on translations, please e-mail rights@apress.com, or visit www.apress.com.

Apress and friends of ED books may be purchased in bulk for academic, corporate, or promotional use. eBook versions and licenses are also available for most titles. For more information, reference our Special Bulk Sales–eBook Licensing web page at www.apress.com/bulk-sales.

Any source code or other supplementary materials referenced by the author in this text is available to readers at www.apress.com. For detailed information about how to locate your book's source code, go to http://www.apress.com/source-code/.

Contents at a Glance

iii

Contents

Foreword

I remember it distinctly, like it was yesterday. Standing center stage at Moscone Center when we launched JavaFX at JavaOne 2007. We promised to build a world-class client platform for Java. With the world watching with skeptical eyes and in a crowded client arena, we set out to build the dream. In hindsight, it was a rather ambitious goal.

Fast forward four years, with the release of JavaFX 2, we have taken a huge leap forward in fulfilling that promise. As the vision unfolded, our product plans have shifted to match the evolving RIA market and what developers and the Java community told us they were looking for. As someone who was there at the inception of JavaFX and has watched it mature over the last four years to this current release, my feelings are akin to a parent watching a toddler blossom.

Jim Weaver and Stephen Chin have been traveling through the evolution of JavaFX with me. They have both presented on JavaFX at numerous international conferences and have been developing with and blogging about JavaFX since 2007. Jim is a 30-year software veteran and has authored several books on Java, as well as articles for *Java Magazine* and *Oracle Technology Network*. He has also developed numerous JavaFX applications for a wide variety of customers.

Stephen is passionate about open source technologies and is the the founder of WidgetFX and JFXtras. He also has a deep passion for improving development technologies and processes, as well as agile development methodologies.

Johan Vos is co-founder of LodgOn and holds a PhD in applied physics. His interest lies in the enterprise communication aspects of JavaFX, combining the world of large servers with end-user devices. Johan's analogy to physics: The grand unified theory combines quantum mechanics (small) with relativity theory (large); similarly in software, Java combines JavaFX with Java EE. Dean Iverson is a longtime client developer with a great eye for creating elegant user interfaces. He develops GroovyFX libraries and is a contributor to the JFXtras project. He has been developing and blogging about JavaFX since 2007. Weiqi Gao holds a PhD in mathematics. His expertise is in the language aspects of JavaFX as is reflected in the chapters on Properties and Bindings and Collections and Concurrency.

Today, the core JavaFX team at Oracle still has several of the developers who were part of the early versions of JavaFX and we also have new engineers who have joined us. As we move ahead and open source JavaFX, we are looking forward to having more developers and experts from the extended Java community join us in making JavaFX the number one choice for client development.

I am proud and honored to be part of this key software technology. Given the length of experience and depth of expertise in all aspects of JavaFX and across the Java platform, I cannot think of a better group of authors to bring you JavaFX 2. I hope you will enjoy this book and find JavaFX as satisfying as I have found it over the years. I hope it piques your interest sufficiently to join the JavaFX community in making JavaFX the platform of choice for clients.

Nandini Ramani
Vice President, Fusion Middleware Group
Oracle Corporation

About the Authors

**James L. (Jim) Weaver** is a Java and JavaFX developer, author, and speaker with a passion for helping rich-client Java and JavaFX become preferred technologies for new application development. Books that Jim has authored include *Inside Java, Beginning J2EE,* and *Pro JavaFX Platform,* with the latter being updated to cover JavaFX 2. His professional background includes 15 years as a systems architect at EDS, and the same number of years as an independent developer. Jim is an international speaker at software technology conferences, including the JavaOne conferences in San Francisco and São Paulo. Jim blogs at http://javafxpert.com, tweets @javafxpert, and may be reached at jim.weaver @javafxpert.com.

**Weiqi Gao** is a principal software engineer with Object Computing, Inc., in St. Louis, MO. He has more than 18 years of software development experience and has been using Java technology since 1998. He is interested in programming languages, object-oriented systems, distributed computing, and graphical user interfaces. He is a presenter and a member of the steering committee of the St. Louis Java Users Group. Weiqi holds a PhD in mathematics.

**Stephen Chin** is chief agile methodologist at GXS and a technical expert in client UI technologies. He is lead author on the Pro Android Flash title and coauthored the Pro JavaFX Platform title, which is the leading technical reference for JavaFX. In addition, Stephen runs the very successful Silicon Valley JavaFX User Group, which has hundreds of members and tens of thousands of online viewers. Finally, he is a Java Champion, chair of the OSCON Java conference, and an internationally recognized speaker featured at Devoxx, Codemash, AnDevCon, Jazoon, and JavaOne, where he received a Rock Star Award. Stephen can be followed on twitter @steveonjava and reached via his blog: http://steveonjava.com.

■**Dean Iverson** has been writing software professionally for more than 15 years. He is employed by the Virginia Tech Transportation Institute, where he is a rich client application developer. He also has a small software consultancy called Pleasing Software Solutions, which he cofounded with his wife.

■**Johan Vos** started to work with Java in 1995. As part of the Blackdown team, he helped port Java to Linux. With LodgON, the company he cofounded, he has been mainly working on Java-based solutions for social networking software. Because he can't make a choice between embedded development and enterprise development, his main focus is on end-to-end Java, combining the strengths of backend systems and embedded devices. His favorite technologies are currently Java EE/Glassfish at the backend and JavaFX at the frontend. Johan's blog can be followed at http://blogs.lodgon.com/johan, he tweets at http://twitter.com/johanvos, and can be reached at johan@lodgon.com.

About the Technical Reviewer

 **Carl P. Dea** is a currently a senior software engineer working for BCT-LLC on projects with high performance computing (HPC) architectures. He has been developing software for over 15 years with many clients from Fortune 500 companies to nonprofit organizations. He has written software ranging from mission-critical applications to Web applications. Carl has been using Java since the very beginning and he also is a huge JavaFX enthusiast dating back when it used to be called F3. His passion for software development started when his middle-school science teacher showed him the TRS-80 computer. His current software development interests are: rich-client applications, Groovy, game programming, Arduino, mobile phones, and tablet computers. Carl's blog can be found at http://carlfx.wordpress.com, and he tweets at @carldea.

Acknowledgments

This book is dedicated to my wife, Julie, daughters Lori and Kelli, son, Marty, and grandchildren, Kaleb and Jillian. Thanks to Merrill and Barbara Bishir, Marilyn Prater, and Walter Weaver for being such wonderful examples. A very special thanks to Weiqi Gao, Stephen Chin, Dean Iverson, Johan Vos, and Carl Dea, with whom I had the privilege of writing this book. Thanks also to the amazing JavaFX teams at Oracle and the talented editors at Apress. *"I have told you all this so that you may have peace in me. Here on earth you will have many trials and sorrows. But take heart, because I have overcome the world." (John 16:33)*

Jim Weaver

I would like to thank my wife, Youhong Gong, for her support, understanding, and encouragement during the writing process. My thanks also go to the author and technical review team: Jim Weaver, Stephen Chin, Dean Iverson, Johan Vos, and Carl Dea for making this book a fun project. I share with my coauthors the appreciation to the JavaFX team at Oracle and the editorial team at Apress.

Weiqi Gao

To my wife, Justine, and daughter, Cassandra, who supported me in writing this book on top of all my other responsibilities. Also, a huge thanks to the entire author team, including our newest members, Johan Vos and Carl Dea, who both went above and beyond in their contributions to this title. Finally, a great debt of gratitude to the JavaFX team and JVM language designers who have produced technology that will profoundly change the way we design and code UIs going forward.

Stephen Chin

I would like to thank my family, Sondra, Alex, and Matt, for their support and understanding during yet another writing project You guys make this possible. I would also like to thank the writing and review team of Jim Weaver, Stephen Chin, Weiqi Gao, Johan Vos, and Carl Dea for their dedication and their patience. The editorial team at Apress was, as usual, first rate and utterly professional. And of course none of this would be possible without the hard work of an extremely talented team of engineers on the JavaFX team at Oracle.

Dean Iverson

Writing a book is often done in spare time. I want to thank my wife, Kathleen, and our son, Merlijn, for allowing me to spend evening and weekend time in front of my computer. I'm very pleased to be involved in this JavaFX book, and I want to thank authors Jim Weaver, Weiqi Gao, Stephen Chin, and Dean Iverson, technical reviewer Carl Dea, and the Apress team for their trust in me. A special thanks to my colleagues Joeri Sykora and Erwin Morrhey for helping me with the examples. The JavaFX team at Oracle did a great job releasing JavaFX 2. The combination of their efforts and those of the Java community makes Java an excellent platform for an increasing number of clients.

Johan Vos

I would like to thank my wife, Tracey, and my daughters, Caitlin and Gillian, for their loving support and sacrifices. A big thanks to Jim Weaver for recommending me to this project. I also want to thank the amazing authors Jim Weaver, Weiqi Gao, Stephen Chin, Dean Iverson, and Johan Vos. Thanks to the wonderful people at Apress for their professionalism especially Stephen Moles for keeping the team laser focused. Lastly, I want to give a big kudos and acknowledgment to the people at Oracle involved with moving Java and JavaFX forward by growing the community. *"Iron sharpeneth iron; so a man sharpeneth the countenance of his friend." (Proverbs 27:17)*

Carl Dea

Getting a Jump Start in JavaFX

Don't ask what the world needs. Ask what makes you come alive, and go do it. Because what the world needs is people who have come alive.

—Howard Thurman

At the annual JavaOne conference in May 2007, Sun Microsystems announced a new product family named JavaFX. Its stated purpose includes enabling the development and deployment of content-rich applications on consumer devices such as cell phones, televisions, in-dash car systems, and browsers. Josh Marinacci, a software engineer at Sun, made the following statement very appropriately in a recent Java Posse interview: "JavaFX is sort of a code word for reinventing client Java and fixing the sins of the past." Josh was referring to the fact that Java Swing and Java 2D have lots of capability, but are also very complex. JavaFX allows us to simply and elegantly express user interfaces (UIs) with a declarative programming style. It also leverages the full power of Java, because you can instantiate and use the millions of Java classes that exist today. Add features such as binding the UI to properties in a model and change listeners that reduce the need for setter methods, and you have a combination that will help restore Java to the client side of the RIA equation.

In this chapter, we give you a jump start in developing JavaFX applications. After bringing you up to date on the brief history of JavaFX, we show you how to get the JavaFX software development kit (SDK). We also explore some great JavaFX resources and walk you through the process of compiling and running JavaFX applications. In the process you'll learn a lot about the JavaFX API as we walk through application code together. First, however, we point out a related technology that is enabling the rise of rich-client Java.

JavaFX Can't Bring Rich-Client Java Back by Itself

When Java was first introduced in 1995, the hope was that the Java Runtime Environment (JRE) would become the common client platform on which the UI portion of client–server applications could be deployed. Although the JRE became ubiquitous on the server side of the equation, factors such as the browser wars of the late 1990s delayed the prospect of achieving a consistent JRE on client machines. The result has been that web browser technologies such as HTML and JavaScript have stepped in to fill the gap, which we feel has proven suboptimal at best. The software development industry and the users we serve need to have the JRE on all client machines so that we can break free from browser technologies and enable graphically rich, fast-performing applications. Fortunately, the technology known as Java SE 6 Update 10 is solving that problem.

■ **Note** What has come to be known as Java SE 6 Update 10 has actually had several names. It started life as the Consumer JRE, and then Java SE 6 Update N. Then it became known as Java SE 6 Update 10. As of this writing, Java SE 7 has been released, but we just refer to this technology as Java SE 6 Update 10.

Java SE 6 Update 10 consists of several technologies that improve the user experience related to installing the JRE, and to deploying and running rich-client Java (and JavaFX) programs:

- *Java Kernel Online Installer*—The JRE is now divided into small bundles. If the user's machine doesn't have the JRE installed when a Java program is invoked, the online installer will ascertain which of the bundles are needed to run the program. Those bundles will be installed first and the program will begin executing as soon as this takes place.

- *Java Auto-Updater:* This provides a faster and more reliable process for updating the JRE by using a *patch-in-place* mechanism.

- *Java Quick Starter:* After a cold boot of the system, portions of the JRE are prefetched into memory. This enables a Java program to start more quickly.

- *Pack200 Format:* Pack200 is a highly compressed format that enables Java libraries and resources, for example, to download more quickly than traditional JAR files.

- *Java Deployment Toolkit:* This includes a simple JavaScript interface with which to deploy Java applets and applications. The JavaScript library is located at a well-known URL, and is engineered to make the right deployment decisions based on the detected JRE environment on the user's machine.

- *Next Generation Java Plug-In:* This Java plug-in is much more reliable and versatile than its predecessor. For example, you now have the ability to specify large heap sizes, and per-applet command-line arguments. Also, it has built-in Java Network Launching Protocol (JNLP) support as well as improved Java/JavaScript communications.

- *Hardware Acceleration Support:* In a media-rich environment, it is crucial to take advantage of the graphics capabilities on the underlying hardware. For example, Java SE 6 Update 10 currently has a hardware accelerated graphics pipeline based on the Microsoft Direct3D API. This is a predecessor to the new Prism pipeline that JavaFX uses.

The net result is that we are now at a point in software development history when two technologies (JavaFX and Java SE 6 Update 10) are working together to restore rich client Java. We feel that sanity is in the process of being restored to Internet software development, and we want you to join us in this RIA revolution. But first, a brief history lesson about JavaFX.

A Brief History of JavaFX

JavaFX started life as the brainchild of Chris Oliver when he worked for a company named SeeBeyond. They had the need for richer user interfaces, so Chris created a language that he dubbed F3 (Form

Follows Function) for that purpose. In the article, "Mind-Bendingly Cool Innovation" (cited in the Resources section at the end of this chapter) Chris is quoted as follows. "When it comes to integrating people into business processes, you need graphical user interfaces for them to interact with, so there was a use case for graphics in the enterprise application space, and there was an interest at SeeBeyond in having richer user interfaces."

SeeBeyond was acquired by Sun, who subsequently changed the name of F3 to JavaFX, and announced it at JavaOne 2007. Chris joined Sun during the acquisition and continued to lead the development of JavaFX.

The first version of JavaFX Script was an interpreted language, and was considered a prototype of the compiled JavaFX Script language that was to come later. Interpreted JavaFX Script was very robust, and there were two JavaFX books published in the latter part of 2007 based on that version. One was written in Japanese, and the other was written in English and published by Apress (*JavaFX Script: Dynamic Java Scripting for Rich Internet/Client-Side Applications*, Apress, 2007).

While developers were experimenting with JavaFX and providing feedback for improvement, the JavaFX Script compiler team at Sun was busy creating a compiled version of the language. This included a new set of runtime API libraries. The JavaFX Script compiler project reached a tipping point in early December 2007, which was commemorated in a blog post entitled "Congratulations to the JavaFX Script Compiler Team—The Elephant Is Through the Door." That phrase came from the JavaFX Script compiler project leader Tom Ball in a blog post, which contained the following excerpt.

> *An elephant analogy came to me when I was recently grilled about exactly when the JavaFX Script compiler team will deliver our first milestone release. "I can't give you an accurate date," I said. "It's like pushing an elephant through a door; until a critical mass makes it past the threshold you just don't know when you'll be finished. Once you pass that threshold, though, the rest happens quickly and in a manner that can be more accurately predicted."*

A screenshot of the silly, compiled JavaFX application written by one of the authors, Jim Weaver, for that post is shown in Figure 1-1, demonstrating that the project had in fact reached the critical mass to which Tom Ball referred.

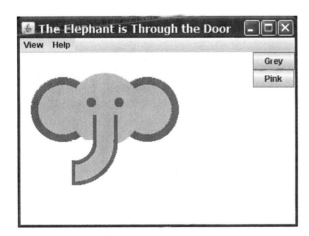

Figure 1-1. *Screenshot for the "Elephant Is Through the Door" program*

Much progress continued to be made on JavaFX in 2008:

- The NetBeans JavaFX plug-in became available for the compiled version in March 2008.

- Many of the JavaFX runtime libraries (mostly focusing on the UI aspects of JavaFX) were rewritten by a team that included some very talented developers from the Java Swing team.

- In July 2008, the JavaFX Preview SDK was released, and at JavaOne 2008 Sun announced that the JavaFX 1.0 SDK would be released in fall 2008.

- On December 4, 2008, the JavaFX 1.0 SDK was released. This event increased the adoption rate of JavaFX by developers and IT managers because it represented a stable codebase.

- In April 2009, Oracle and Sun announced that Oracle would be acquiring Sun. The JavaFX 1.2 SDK was released at JavaOne 2009.

- In January 2010, Oracle completed its acquisition of Sun. JavaFX 1.3 SDK was released in April 2010, with JavaFX 1.3.1 being the last of the 1.3 releases.

At JavaOne 2010, JavaFX 2.0 was announced. The JavaFX 2.0 roadmap was published by Oracle on the Web page noted in the Resources section below, and includes items such as the following.

- Deprecate the JavaFX Script language in favor of using Java and the JavaFX 2.0 API. This brings JavaFX into the mainstream by making it available to any language (such as Java, Groovy, and JRuby) that runs on the JVM.

- Make the compelling features of JavaFX Script, including binding to expressions, available in the JavaFX 2.0 API.

- Offer an increasingly rich set of UI components, building on the components already available in JavaFX 1.3.

- Provide a Web component for embedding HTML and JavaScript content into JavaFX applications.

- Enable JavaFX interoperability with Swing.

- Rewrite the media stack from the ground up.

JavaFX 2.0 was released at JavaOne 2011, and has enjoyed a greatly increased adoption rate due to the innovative features articulated previously. Now that you've had the obligatory history lesson in JavaFX, let's get one step closer to writing code by showing you where some examples, tools, and other resources are.

Going to the Source: Oracle's JavaFX Web Site

Oracle's JavaFX.com site is a great resource for seeing example JavaFX programs, downloading the JavaFX SDK and tools, taking tutorials on JavaFX, and linking to other resources. See Figure 1-2 for a screenshot of this web site.

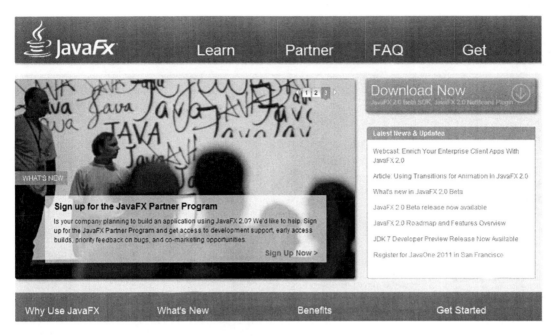

Figure 1-2. *Oracle's official JavaFX web site*

In addition, blogs maintained by JavaFX engineers and developers are great resources for up-to-the-minute technical information on JavaFX. For example, Oracle JavaFX Engineers Richard Bair, Jasper Potts, and Jonathan Giles keep the developer community apprised of the latest JavaFX innovations at http://fxexperience.com. In addition, the Resources section at the end of this chapter contains the URLs of the blogs that the authors of this book use to engage the JavaFX developer community.

Take a few minutes to explore these sites. Next we point out some more valuable resources that are helpful.

Accessing the JavaFX SDK API

A useful resource available from the JavaFX sites is the SDK API JavaDoc documentation, shown in Figure 1-3.

<u>Overview</u> <u>Package</u> **Class** <u>Use</u> <u>Tree</u> <u>Deprecated</u> <u>Index</u> <u>Help</u>
<u>PREV CLASS</u> <u>NEXT CLASS</u>   <u>FRAMES</u> <u>NO FRAMES</u>
SUMMARY: NESTED | FIELD | <u>CONSTR</u> | <u>METHOD</u>   DETAIL: FIELD | <u>CONSTR</u> | <u>METHOD</u>

javafx.scene.shape

Class Rectangle

```
java.lang.Object
  └ javafx.scene.Node
      └ javafx.scene.shape.Shape
          └ javafx.scene.shape.Rectangle
```

All Implemented Interfaces:
> <u>EventTarget</u>

```
public class Rectangle
extends Shape
```

The `Rectangle` class defines a rectangle with the specified size and location. By default the rectangle has sharp corners. Rounded corners can be specified using the arcWidth and arcHeight variables.

Example code: the following code creates a rectangle with 20 pixel rounded corners.

```
import javafx.scene.shape.*;

Rectangle r = new Rectangle();
r.setX(50);
```

Figure 1-3. *JavaFX SDK API Javadoc*

The API documentation in Figure 1-3, for example, shows how to use the Rectangle class, located in the javafx.scene.shape package. Scrolling down this web page shows the properties, constructors, methods, and other helpful information about the Rectangle class. By the way, this API documentation is available in the JavaFX SDK that you'll download shortly, but we wanted you to know how to find it online as well.

Now that you've explored Oracle's JavaFX web site and available resources, it's time to obtain the JavaFX SDK and related tools so that you can begin developing JavaFX programs.

Obtaining the JavaFX SDK

You can get the JavaFX SDK from Oracles's JavaFX web site mentioned earlier. Currently you have the choice of downloading the JavaFX SDK, the JavaFX Runtime, and the JavaFX Plugin for NetBeans IDE. To develop JavaFX applications you'll need the JavaFX SDK. In addition, we recommend that you download the JavaFX Plugin for NetBeans IDE as it contains modules that will help you develop and package JavaFX 2.0 applications. The instructions for the examples in this first chapter assume that you have the NetBeans Plugin installed.

Go ahead and download the JavaFX SDK, and the JavaFX Plugin for NetBeans, following the installation instructions. In addition, so that you can compile and run the JavaFX application from the command-line, the JAR file that contains the JavaFX runtime must be on the classpath. The name of this file is jfxrt.jar, and it is located in the rt/lib directory subordinate to the directory in which the JavaFX SDK is installed.

Other Available Tools

There are other tools available for developing JavaFX applications. For example, there is a JavaFX plug-in being developed by Tom Schindl for the Eclipse IDE, but at the time of this writing it isn't as mature as the NetBeans plugin. The URL for the Eclipse plugin is listed in the Resources section.

Now that you have the tools installed, we show you how to create a simple JavaFX program, and then we walk through it in detail. The first program that we've chosen for you is called "Hello Earthrise," which demonstrates more features than the typical beginning "Hello World" program.

Developing Your First JavaFX Program: "Hello Earthrise"

On Christmas Eve in 1968 the crew of Apollo 8 entered lunar orbit for the first time in history. They were the first humans to witness an "Earthrise," taking the magnificent picture shown in Figure 1-4. This image is dynamically loaded from this book's web site when the program starts, so you'll need to be connected to the Internet to view it.

Figure 1-4. *The Hello Earthrise program*

In addition to demonstrating how to dynamically load images over the Internet, this example shows you how to use animation in JavaFX. Now it's time for you to compile and run the program. We show you two ways to do this: from the command-line, and using NetBeans with the JavaFX plug-in.

Compiling and Running from the Command-Line

We usually use an IDE to build and run JavaFX programs, but to take all of the mystery out of the process we use the command-line tools first.

▨ **Note** For this exercise, as with most others in the book, you need the source code. If you prefer not to type the source code into a text editor, you can obtain the source code for all of the examples in this book from the code download site. See the Resources section at the end of this chapter for the location of this site.

Assuming that you've downloaded and extracted the source code for this book into a directory, follow the directions in this exercise, performing all of the steps as instructed. We dissect the source code after the exercise.

COMPILING AND RUNNING THE HELLO EARTHRISE PROGRAM FROM THE COMMAND

You'll use the javafxc and javafx command-line tools to compile and run the program in this exercise. From the command-line prompt on your machine:

1. Navigate to the Chapter01/Hello directory.

2. Execute the following command to compile the HelloEarthRiseMain.java file.

   ```
   javac -d . HelloEarthRiseMain.java
   ```

3. Because the –d option was used in this command, the class files generated are placed in directories matching the package statements in the source files. The roots of those directories are specified by the argument given for the –d option, in this case the current directory.

4. To run the program, execute the following command. Note that we use the fully qualified name of the class that will be executed, which entails specifying the nodes of the path name and the name of the class, all separated by periods.

   ```
   java projavafx.helloearthrise.ui.HelloEarthRiseMain
   ```

The program should appear as shown in Figure 1-4 earlier, with the text scrolling slowly upward, reminiscent of the Star Wars opening crawls.

Congratulations on completing your first exercise as you explore JavaFX!

Understanding the Hello Earthrise Program

Now that you've run the application, let's walk through the program listing together. The code for the Hello Earthrise application is shown in Listing 1-1.

Listing 1-1. *The HelloEarthRiseMain.java Program*

```java
/*
 *  HelloEarthRiseMain.java - A JavaFX "Hello World" style example
 *
 *  Developed 2011 by James L. Weaver jim.weaver [at] javafxpert.com
 *  as a JavaFX SDK 2.0 example for the Pro JavaFX book.
 */
package projavafx.helloearthrise.ui;

import javafx.animation.Interpolator;
import javafx.animation.Timeline;
import javafx.animation.TranslateTransition;
import javafx.application.Application;
import javafx.builders.GroupBuilder;
import javafx.builders.ImageViewBuilder;
import javafx.builders.RectangleBuilder;
import javafx.builders.SceneBuilder;
import javafx.builders.TextBuilder;
import javafx.builders.TranslateTransitionBuilder;
import javafx.geometry.VPos;
import javafx.scene.Scene;
import javafx.scene.image.Image;
import javafx.scene.paint.Color;
import javafx.scene.text.Font;
import javafx.scene.text.FontWeight;
import javafx.scene.text.Text;
import javafx.scene.text.TextAlignment;
import javafx.stage.Stage;
import javafx.util.Duration;

/**
 *  Main class for the "Hello World" style example
 */
public class HelloEarthRiseMain extends Application {

  /**
   * @param args the command-line arguments
   */
  public static void main(String[] args) {
    Application.launch(args);
  }

  @Override
  public void start(Stage stage) {

    String message =
      "Earthrise at Christmas: " +
      "[Forty] years ago this Christmas, a turbulent world " +
      "looked to the heavens for a unique view of our home  " +
      "planet. This photo of Earthrise over the lunar horizon " +
      "was taken by the Apollo 8 crew in December 1968, showing " +
```

```
        "Earth for the first time as it appears from deep space. " +
        "Astronauts Frank Borman, Jim Lovell and William Anders " +
        "had become the first humans to leave Earth orbit, " +
        "entering lunar orbit on Christmas Eve. In a historic live " +
        "broadcast that night, the crew took turns reading from " +
        "the Book of Genesis, closing with a holiday wish from " +
        "Commander Borman: \"We close with good night, good luck, " +
        "a Merry Christmas, and God bless all of you -- all of " +
        "you on the good Earth.\"";

// Reference to the Text
Text textRef = TextBuilder.create()
    .layoutY(100)
    .textOrigin(VPos.TOP)
    .textAlignment(TextAlignment.JUSTIFY)
    .wrappingWidth(400)
    .text(message)
    .fill(Color.rgb(187, 195, 107))
    .font(Font.font("SansSerif", FontWeight.BOLD, 24))
    .build();

// Provides the animated scrolling behavior for the text
TranslateTransition transTransition = TranslateTransitionBuilder.create()
    .duration(new Duration(75000))
    .node(textRef)
    .toY(-820)
    .interpolator(Interpolator.LINEAR)
    .cycleCount(Timeline.INDEFINITE)
    .build();

Scene scene  = SceneBuilder.create()
    .width(516)
    .height(387)
    .root(
      GroupBuilder.create()
        .children(
          ImageViewBuilder.create()
            .image(new Image("http://projavafx.com/images/earthrise.jpg"))
            .build(),
          GroupBuilder.create()
            .layoutX(50)
            .layoutY(180)
            .children(
              textRef
            )
            .clip(
              RectangleBuilder.create()
                .width(430)
                .height(85)
                .build()
            )
```

```
            .build()
        )
        .build()
    )
    .build();

stage.setScene(scene);
stage.setTitle("Hello Earthrise");
stage.show();

// Start the text animation
transTransition.play();
  }
}
```

Now that you've seen the code, let's take a look at its constructs and concepts in detail.

Declarative Code That Defines the User Interface

One of the most exciting features of JavaFX is its ability to express a graphical user interface (GUI) using simple, consistent, and powerful builder classes.

▧ **Note**   As we show a little later, JavaFX supports data binding, which is characterized by binding the value of a property (such as the height of a rectangle) to an expression. Data binding is a major enabler of using declarative code.

In this example, some of the program is declarative in that it contains a large expression. This expression begins by defining a Scene object with the SceneBuilder class. Nested within that are properties of the Scene object, such as its width and height. A Scene also has a property named root that holds the graphical elements that are displayed in the Scene, in this case a Group instance that contains an ImageView instance (which displays an image) and a Group instance. Nested within the latter Group is a Text instance (which is a graphical element, usually called a *graphical node*, or simply *node*).

The build() method of builder classes creates an instance (also known as an object) of the Java class it is responsible for building.

Using the Stage Class

A Stage contains the user interface of a JavaFX app, whether it is deployed on the desktop, within a browser, or on other devices. On the desktop, for example, a Stage has its own top-level window, which typically includes a border and title bar. In the browser the Stage doesn't have a window, but is rendered as an applet within a rectangular area of the browser.

The Stage class has a set of properties and methods. Some of these properties and methods, as shown in the following code snippet from the listing, are as follows.

- A scene that contains the graphical nodes in the user interface

- A title that appears in the title bar of the window (when deployed on the desktop)

- The visibility of the Stage

```
stage.setScene(scene);
stage.setTitle("Hello Earthrise");
stage.show();
```

Using the Scene Class

As mentioned previously, a Scene holds the graphical elements that are displayed on the Stage. Every element in a Scene is a graphical node, which is any class that extends the javafx.scene.Node. Take another look at the declarative code that creates the Scene in our example program:

```
Scene scene = SceneBuilder.create()
  .width(516)
  .height(387)
  .root(
    GroupBuilder.create()
      .children(
        ImageViewBuilder.create()
          .image(new Image("http://projavafx.com/images/earthrise.jpg"))
          .build(),
        GroupBuilder.create()
          .layoutX(50)
          .layoutY(180)
          .children(
            textRef
          )
          .clip(
            RectangleBuilder.create()
              .width(430)
              .height(85)
              .build()
          )
          .build()
      )
      .build()
  )
  .build();
```

Notice that the root property of the Scene contains an instance of the Group class, created by the build() method of the GroupBuilder class. The root property may contain any subclass of javafx.scene.Node, and typically contains a subclass that is capable of holding its own set of Node instances. Take a look at the JavaFX API documentation that we showed you how to access in the "Accessing the JavaFX SDK API" section earlier and check out the Node class to see the properties and methods available to any graphical node. Also, take a look at the ImageView class in the javafx.scene.image package and the Group class in the javafx.scene package. In both cases, they inherit from the Node class.

■ **Tip**   We can't emphasize enough the importance of having the JavaFX API documentation handy while reading this book. As classes, variables, and functions are mentioned, it's often a good idea to look at the documentation to get more information. In addition, this habit helps you become more familiar with what is available to you in the API.

Displaying Images

As shown in the following code, displaying an image entails using an ImageView instance in conjunction with an Image instance.

```
ImageViewBuilder.create()
  .image(new Image("http://projavafx.com/images/earthrise.jpg"))
  .build(),
```

The Image instance identifies the image resource and loads it from the URL assigned to its URL variable. Both of these classes are located in the javafx.scene.image package.

Working with Graphical Nodes as a Group

One powerful graphical feature of JavaFX is the ability to create scene graphs, which consist of a tree of graphical nodes. You can then assign values to properties of a Group located in the hierarchy, and the nodes contained in the Group will be affected. In our current example from Listing 1-1, we're using a Group to contain a Text node and to clip a specific rectangular region within the Group so that the text doesn't appear on the moon or the Earth as it animates upward. Here's the relevant code snippet:

```
GroupBuilder.create()
  .layoutX(50)
  .layoutY(180)
  .children(
    textRef
  )
  .clip(
    RectangleBuilder.create()
      .width(430)
      .height(85)
      .build()
  )
  .build()
```

Notice that the Group is located 50 pixels to the right and 180 pixels down, from where it would have been located by default. This is due to the values assigned to the layoutX and layoutY variables of the Group instance. Because this Group is contained directly by the Scene, its upper-left corner's location is

50 pixels to the right and 180 pixels down from the upper-left corner of the Scene. Take a look at Figure 1-5 to see this example illustrated as you read the rest of the explanation.

Figure 1-5. *The Scene, Group, Text, and clip illustrated*

A Group instance contains instances of Node subclasses by assigning a collection of them to itself via the children() method. In the previous code snippet, the Group contains a Text instance that has a value assigned to its layoutY property. Because this Text is contained by a Group, it assumes the two-dimensional space (also called the *co-ordinate space*) of the Group, with the origin of the Text node (0,0) coincident with the top-left corner of the Group. Assigning a value of 100 to the layoutY property causes the Text to be located 100 pixels down from the top of the Group, which is just below the bottom of the clip region, thus causing it to be out of view until the animation begins. Because a value isn't assigned to the layoutX variable, its value is 0 (the default).

The layoutX and layoutY properties of the Group just described are examples of our earlier statement that nodes contained in a Group will be affected by values assigned to properties of the Group. Another example is setting the opacity property of a Group instance to 0.5, which causes all of the nodes contained in that Group to become translucent. If the JavaFX API documentation is handy, look at the properties available in the javafx.scene.Group class. Then look at the properties available in the javafx.scene.Node class properties, which is where you'll find the layoutX, layoutY, and opacity variables that are inherited by the Group class.

Drawing Text

In the previous snippet, notice that several variables are available in the Text class. This particular example is a little more complicated than the normal use of the Text class. Let's first look at a typical case, shown in the following snippet, in which you simply want to draw a string of text characters somewhere in the scene.

```
TextBuilder.create()
  .layoutX(65)
  .layoutY(12)
  .textOrigin(VPos.TOP)
  .fill(Color.WHITE)
  .text("Audio Configuration")
  .font(Font.font("SansSerif", FontWeight.BOLD, 20))
  .build(),
```

This snippet, borrowed from the Audio Configuration example in Figure 1-7 and Listing 1-3 later in this chapter, draws the graphical Text string "Audio Configuration" in a bold Sans Serif font. The font size is 20, and the color of the text is white.

Referring again to the JavaFX API documentation, notice that the VPos enum (in the javafx.geometry package) has fields that serve as constants, for example, BASELINE, BOTTOM, and TOP. These control the origin of the text with respect to vertical locations on the displayed Text:

- The TOP origin, as we're using it in the previous code snippet, places the top of the text (including ascenders) at the layoutY position, relative to the co-ordinate space in which the Text is located.

- The BOTTOM origin would place the bottom of the text, including descenders (located in a lowercase "g", for example) at the layoutY position.

- The BASELINE origin would place the baseline of the text (excluding descenders) at the layoutY position. This is the default value for the textOrigin property of a Text instance.

While you're looking at the javafx.scene.text package in the API documentation, take a look at the font function of the Font class, which is used in the previous snippet to define the font family, weight, and size of the Text.

Turning back again to the Hello Earthrise example in Listing 1-1, we're using some additional properties of the Text class that enable it to flow from one line to the next:

- The wrappingWidth property enables you to specify at what number of pixels the text will wrap.

- The textAlignment property enables you to control how the text will be justified. In our example, TextAlignment.JUSTIFY aligns the text on both the left and right sides, expanding the space between words to achieve that.

The text that we're displaying is sufficiently long to wrap and be drawn on the Earth, so we need to define a rectangular region outside of which that text can't be seen.

Clipping Graphical Areas

To define a clipping area, we assign a Node subclass to the clip property that defines the clipping shape, in this case a Rectangle that is 430 pixels wide and 85 pixels high. In addition to keeping the Text from covering the moon, when the Text scrolls up as a result of animation the clipping area keeps the Text from covering the earth.

Animating the Text to Make It Scroll Up

When the HelloEarthriseMain program is invoked, the Text begins scrolling up slowly. To achieve this animation, we're using the TranslateTransition class located in the javafx.animation package, as shown in the following snippet from Listing 1-1.

```
TranslateTransition  transTransition = TranslateTransitionBuilder.create()
    .duration(new Duration(75000))
    .node(textRef)
    .toY(-820)
    .interpolator(Interpolator.LINEAR)
    .cycleCount(Timeline.INDEFINITE)
    .build();
    ...code omitted...
    // Start the text animation
    transTransition.play();
```

The javafx.animation package contains convenience classes for animating nodes. This TranslateTransition instance (created by the TranslateTransitionBuilder class) translates the Text node referenced by the textRef variable from its original Y position of 100 pixels to a Y position of –820 pixels, over a duration of 75 seconds. The Interpolator.LINEAR constant is assigned to the interpolator property, which causes the animation to proceed in a linear fashion. A look at the API docs for the Interpolator class in the javafx.animation package reveals that there are other forms of interpolation available, one of which is EASE_OUT, which slows down the animation toward the end of the specified duration.

■ **Note** *Interpolation* in this context is the process of calculating the value at any point in time, given a beginning value, an ending value, and a duration.

The last line in the previous snippet begins executing the play method of the TranslateTransition instance created earlier in the program. This makes the Text begin scrolling upward. Because of the value assigned to the cycleCount variable, this transition will repeat indefinitely.

Now that you've compiled and run this example using the command-line tools and we've walked through the code together, it is time to begin using the NetBeans IDE with the JavaFX plug-in to make the development and deployment process faster and easier.

Building and Running the Program with NetBeans

Assuming that you've downloaded and extracted the source code for this book into a directory, follow the directions in this exercise to build and run the Hello Earthrise program in NetBeans with the JavaFX plug-in. If you haven't yet downloaded the JavaFX SDK and the JavaFX plug-in for NetBeans, please do so from Oracle's JavaFX site listed in the Resources section at the end of this chapter.

BUILDING AND RUNNING HELLO EARTHRISE WITH NETBEANS

To build and run the Hello Earthrise program, perform the following steps.

1. Start up NetBeans containing the JavaFX 2.0 plug-in.

2. Choose File ➤ New Project from the menu bar. The first window of the New Project Wizard will appear:

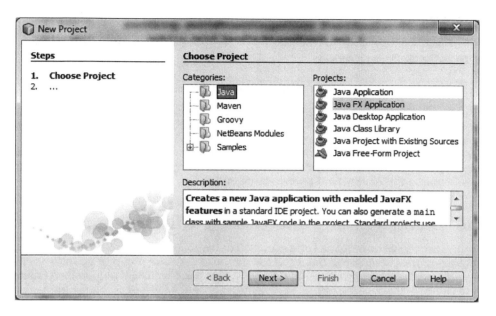

3. Choose Java in the Categories pane and JavaFX Application in the Projects pane,
   and click the Next button. The next page in the New Project Wizard should appear:

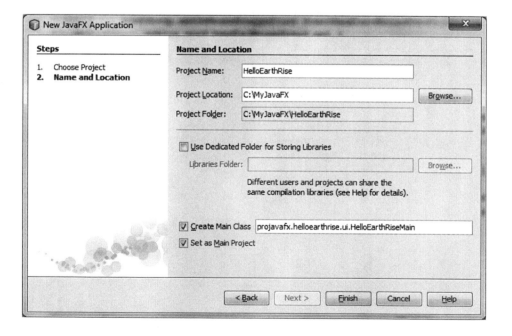

4. On this screen, type the project name (we used HelloEarthRise) and click the Browse button.

5. On the Select Project Location screen, navigate to the directory in which you'd like to create this project (we used C:\MyJavaFX), and click the Open button.

6. Select the Create Main Class check box, and change the supplied package/class name to: projavafx.helloearthrise.ui.HelloEarthRiseMain

7. Select the Set as Main Project check box.

8. Click the Finish button. The HelloEarthrise project with a default main class created by the JavaFX Plugin for NetBeans should now be created. If you'd like to run this default program, right-click on the HelloEarthRise project in the Projects pane and select Run Project from the context menu.

9. Enter the code from Listing 1-1 above into the HelloEarthRiseMain.java code window. You can type it in, or cut and paste it from the HelloEarthRiseMain.java file located in the Chapter01/HelloEarthRise/src/projavafx/helloearthrise/ui directory of this book's source code download.

10. Right-click on the HelloEarthrise project in the Projects pane and select Run Project from the context menu.

The HelloEarthRise program should begin executing, as you saw in Figure 1-4 earlier in the chapter.

At this point, you've built and run the "Hello Earthrise" program application, both from the command-line and using NetBeans. Before leaving this example, we show you another way to achieve the scrolling Text node. There is a class in the javafx.scene.control package named ScrollPane whose purpose is to provide a scrollable view of a node that is typically larger than the view. In addition, the user can drag the node being viewed within the scrollable area. Figure 1-6 shows the Hello Earthrise program after being modified to use the ScrollPane control.

Figure 1-6. *Using the ScrollPane control to provide a scrollable view of the Text node*

Notice that the *move* cursor is visible, signifying that the user can drag the node around the clipped area. Note that the screenshot in Figure 1-6 is of the program running on Windows, and the *move* cursor has a different appearance on other platforms. Listing 1-2 contains the code for this example, named HelloScrollPaneMain.java.

Listing 1-2. *The HelloScrollPaneMain.java Program*

```
...code omitted...
    Text  textRef = TextBuilder.create()
        .layoutY(100)
        .textOrigin(VPos.TOP)
        .textAlignment(TextAlignment.JUSTIFY)
        .wrappingWidth(400)
        .text(message)
        .fill(Color.rgb(187, 195, 107))
        .font(Font.font("SansSerif", FontWeight.BOLD, 24))
        .build();

    TranslateTransition  transTransition = TranslateTransitionBuilder.create()
        .duration(new Duration(75000))
        .node(textRef)
        .toY(-820)
        .interpolator(Interpolator.LINEAR)
        .cycleCount(Timeline.INDEFINITE)
        .build();

    Scene scene  = SceneBuilder.create()
        .width(516)
        .height(387)
        .root(
          GroupBuilder.create()
            .children(
              ImageViewBuilder.create()
                .image(new Image("http://projavafx.com/images/earthrise.jpg"))
                .build(),
              ScrollPaneBuilder.create()
                .layoutX(50)
                .layoutY(180)
                .prefWidth(440)
                .prefHeight(85)
                .hbarPolicy(ScrollBarPolicy.NEVER)
                .vbarPolicy(ScrollBarPolicy.NEVER)
                .pannable(true)
                .content(textRef)
                .style("-fx-background-color: transparent;")
                .build()
            )
            .build()
        )
        .build();
...code omitted...
```

Now that you've learned some of the basics of JavaFX application development, let's examine another JavaFX example application to help you learn more JavaFX Script concepts and constructs.

Developing Your Second JavaFX Program: "More Cowbell!"

If you're familiar with the Saturday Night Live television show, you may have seen the More Cowbell sketch, in which Christopher Walken's character keeps asking for "more cowbell" during a Blue Oyster Cult recording session. The following JavaFX example program covers some of the simple but powerful concepts of JavaFX in the context of an imaginary application that lets you select a music genre and control the volume. Of course, "Cowbell Metal," shortened to "Cowbell," is one of the available genres. Figure 1-7 shows a screenshot of this application, which has a sort of retro iPhone application look.

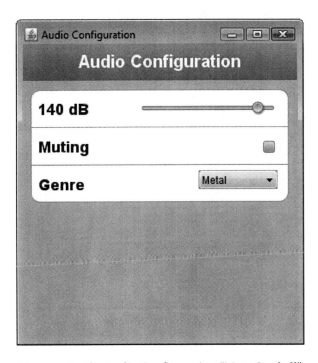

Figure 1-7. *The Audio Configuration "More Cowbell" program*

Building and Running the Audio Configuration Program

Earlier in the chapter, we showed you how to create a new JavaFX project in NetBeans, and how to add a folder that contains source code files to the project.

For this example (and the rest of the examples in the book), we take advantage of the fact that the code download bundle for the book contains both NetBeans and Eclipse project files for each example. Follow the instructions in this exercise to build and run the Audio Configuration application.

**BUILDING AND RUNNING THE AUDIO CONFIGURATION PROGRAM
USING NETBEANS**

To build and execute this program using NetBeans, perform the following steps.

1. From the File menu, select the Open Project menu item. In the Open Project dialog box, navigate to the Chapter01 directory where you extracted the book's code download bundle, as shown here:

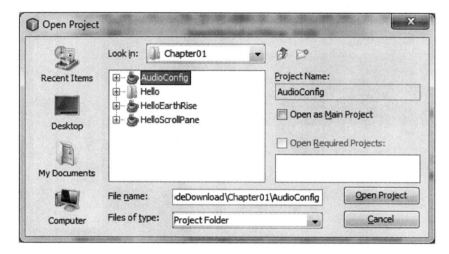

2. Select the AudioConfig project in the pane on the left, and click the Open Project button.

3. Run the project as discussed previously.

The application should appear as shown in Figure 1-7.

The Behavior of the Audio Configuration Program

When you run the application, notice that adjusting the volume slider changes the associated decibel (dB) level displayed. Also, selecting the Muting check box disables the slider, and selecting various genres changes the volume slider. This behavior is enabled by concepts that are shown in the code that follows, such as

- Binding to a class that contains a model

- Using change listeners

- Creating observable lists

Understanding the Audio Configuration Program

The Audio Configuration program contains two source code files, shown in Listing 1-3 and Listing 1-4 (which appear in the section "The Model Class for the Audio Configuration Example" in just a moment):

- The AudioConfigMain.java file in Listing 1-3 contains the main class, and expresses the UI in a manner that you are familiar with from the Hello Earthrise example in Listing 1-1.

- The AudioConfigModel.java file in Listing 1-4 contains a model for this program, which holds the state of the application, to which the UI is *bound*.

Take a look at the AudioConfigMain.java source code in Listing 1-3, after which we examine it together, focusing on concepts not covered in the previous example.

Listing 1-3. *The AudioConfigMain.java Program*

```
package projavafx.audioconfig.ui;

import javafx.application.Application;
import javafx.builders.CheckBoxBuilder;
import javafx.builders.ChoiceBoxBuilder;
import javafx.builders.GroupBuilder;
import javafx.builders.LineBuilder;
import javafx.builders.LinearGradientBuilder;
import javafx.builders.RectangleBuilder;
import javafx.builders.SceneBuilder;
import javafx.builders.SliderBuilder;
import javafx.builders.TextBuilder;
import javafx.geometry.VPos;
import javafx.scene.Scene;
import javafx.scene.control.CheckBox;
import javafx.scene.control.ChoiceBox;
import javafx.scene.control.Slider;
import javafx.scene.paint.Color;
import javafx.scene.paint.Stop;
import javafx.scene.text.Font;
import javafx.scene.text.FontWeight;
import javafx.scene.text.Text;
import javafx.stage.Stage;
import projavafx.audioconfig.model.AudioConfigModel;

public class AudioConfigMain extends Application {

  // A reference to the model
  AudioConfigModel acModel = new AudioConfigModel();

  Text textDb;
  Slider slider;
  CheckBox mutingCheckBox;
  ChoiceBox genreChoiceBox;
```

```java
public static void main(String[] args) {
  Application.launch(args);
}

@Override
public void start(Stage stage) {
  Scene scene = SceneBuilder.create()
    .width(320)
    .height(343)
    .root(
      GroupBuilder.create()
        .children(
          RectangleBuilder.create()
            .width(320)
            .height(45)
            .fill(
              LinearGradientBuilder.create()
                .endX(0.0)
                .endY(1.0)
                .stops(
                  new Stop(0, Color.web("0xAEBBCC")),
                  new Stop(1, Color.web("0x6D84A3")))
                )
                .build()
            )
            .build(),
          TextBuilder.create()
            .layoutX(65)
            .layoutY(12)
            .textOrigin(VPos.TOP)
            .fill(Color.WHITE)
            .text("Audio Configuration")
            .font(Font.font("SansSerif", FontWeight.BOLD, 20))
            .build(),
          RectangleBuilder.create()
            .x(0)
            .y(43)
            .width(320)
            .height(300)
            .fill(Color.rgb(199, 206, 213))
            .build(),
          RectangleBuilder.create()
            .x(9)
            .y(54)
            .width(300)
            .height(130)
            .arcWidth(20)
            .arcHeight(20)
            .fill(Color.WHITE)
            .stroke(Color.color(0.66, 0.67, 0.69))
            .build(),
```

```
textDb = TextBuilder.create()
  .layoutX(18)
  .layoutY(69)
  .textOrigin(VPos.TOP)
  .fill(Color.web("#131021"))
  .font(Font.font("SansSerif", FontWeight.BOLD, 18))
  .build(),
slider = SliderBuilder.create()
  .layoutX(135)
  .layoutY(69)
  .prefWidth(162)
  .min(acModel.minDecibels)
  .max(acModel.maxDecibels)
  .build(),
LineBuilder.create()
  .startX(9)
  .startY(97)
  .endX(309)
  .endY(97)
  .stroke(Color.color(0.66, 0.67, 0.69))
  .build(),
TextBuilder.create()
  .layoutX(18)
  .layoutY(113)
  .textOrigin(VPos.TOP)
  .fill(Color.web("#131021"))
  .text("Muting")
  .font(Font.font("SanSerif", FontWeight.BOLD, 18))
  .build(),
mutingCheckBox = CheckBoxBuilder.create()
  .layoutX(280)
  .layoutY(113)
  .build(),
LineBuilder.create()
  .startX(9)
  .startY(141)
  .endX(309)
  .endY(141)
  .stroke(Color.color(0.66, 0.67, 0.69))
  .build(),
TextBuilder.create()
  .layoutX(18)
  .layoutY(154)
  .textOrigin(VPos.TOP)
  .fill(Color.web("#131021"))
  .text("Genre")
  .font(Font.font("SanSerif", FontWeight.BOLD, 18))
  .build(),
genreChoiceBox = ChoiceBoxBuilder.create()
  .layoutX(204)
  .layoutY(154)
  .prefWidth(93)
```

```
                .items(acModel.genres)
                .build()
            )
            .build()
        )
        .build();

    textDb.textProperty().bind(acModel.selectedDBs.asString().concat(" dB"));
    slider.valueProperty().bindBidirectional(acModel.selectedDBs);
    slider.disableProperty().bind(acModel.muting);
    mutingCheckBox.selectedProperty().bindBidirectional(acModel.muting);
    acModel.genreSelectionModel = genreChoiceBox.getSelectionModel();
    acModel.addListenerToGenreSelectionModel();
    acModel.genreSelectionModel.selectFirst();

    stage.setScene(scene);
    stage.setTitle("Audio Configuration");
    stage.show();
  }
}
```

Now that you've seen the main class in this application, let's walk through the new concepts.

Creating an Instance of the Model, and the Magic of Binding

One of the powerful aspects of JavaFX is binding, which enables the application's UI to easily stay in sync with the state, or model, of the application. The model for a JavaFX application is typically held in one or more classes, in this case the AudioConfigModel class. Look at the following snippet, taken from Listing 1-3, in which we create an instance of this model class.

```
AudioConfigModel acModel = new AudioConfigModel();
```

There are several graphical node instances in the scene of this UI (recall that a scene consists of a sequence of nodes). Skipping past several of them, we come to the graphical nodes shown in the following snippet that have a property bound to the selectedDBs property in the model.

```
            textDb = TextBuilder.create()
              .layoutX(18)
              .layoutY(69)
              .textOrigin(VPos.TOP)
              .fill(Color.web("#131021"))
              .font(Font.font("SansSerif", FontWeight.BOLD, 18))
              .build(),
            slider = SliderBuilder.create()
              .layoutX(135)
              .layoutY(69)
              .prefWidth(162)
              .min(acModel.minDecibels)
              .max(acModel.maxDecibels)
              .build(),
```

```
...code omitted...
textDb.textProperty().bind(acModel.selectedDBs.asString().concat(" dB"));
slider.valueProperty().bindBidirectional(acModel.selectedDBs);
```

As shown in this snippet, the text property of the Text object is bound to an expression. The bind function contains an expression (that includes the selectedDBs property), which is evaluated and becomes the value of the text property. Look at Figure 1-7 (or check the running application) to see the content value of the Text node displayed to the left of the slider.

Notice also in the snippet that the value property of the Slider node is bound to the selectedDBs property in the model as well, but that it uses the bindBidirectional() method. This causes the bind to be bidirectional, so in this case when the slider is moved, the selectedDBs property in the model changes. Conversely, when the selectedDBs property changes (as a result of changing the genre), the slider moves.

Go ahead and move the slider to demonstrate the effects of the bind expressions in the snippet. The number of decibels displayed at the left of the slider should change as the slider is adjusted.

There are other bound properties in Listing 1-3 that we point out when we walk through the model class. Before leaving the UI, we point out some color-related concepts in this example.

Colors and Gradients

The following snippet from Listing 1-3 contains an example of defining a color gradient pattern, as well as defining colors.

```
RectangleBuilder.create()
  .width(320)
  .height(45)
  .fill(
    LinearGradientBuilder.create()
      .endX(0.0)
      .endY(1.0)
      .stops(
        new Stop(0, Color.web("0xAEBBCC")),
        new Stop(1, Color.web("0x6D84A3"))
      )
      .build()
  )
  .build(),
```

If the JavaFX API docs are handy, first take a look at the javafx.scene.shape.Rectangle class and notice that it inherits a property named fill that is of type javafx.scene.paint.Paint. Looking at the JavaFX API docs for the Paint class, you'll see that the Color, LinearGradient, and RadialGradient classes are subclasses of Paint. This means that the fill of any shape can be assigned a color or a gradient.

To create a LinearGradient, as shown in the snippet, you need to define at least two stops, which define the location and color at that location. In this example the offset value of the first stop is 0.0, and the offset value of the second stop is 1.0. These are the values at both extremes of the *unit square*, the result being that the gradient will span the entire node (in this case a Rectangle). The direction of the LinearGradient is controlled by its startX, startY, endX, and endY values. In this case, the direction is only vertical because the startY value is 0.0 and the endY value is 1.0, whereas the startX and endX values are both 0.0.

Note that in the Hello Earthrise example in Listing 1-1, the constant named Color.WHITE was used to represent the color white. In the previous snippet, the web function of the Color class is used to define a color from a hexadecimal value.

The Model Class for the Audio Configuration Example

Take a look at the source code for the AudioConfigModel class in Listing 1-4.

Listing 1-4. The Source Code for AudioConfigModel.java

```java
package projavafx.audioconfig.model;

import javafx.beans.property.BooleanProperty;
import javafx.beans.property.IntegerProperty;
import javafx.beans.property.SimpleBooleanProperty;
import javafx.beans.property.SimpleIntegerProperty;
import javafx.beans.value.ChangeListener;
import javafx.beans.value.ObservableValue;
import javafx.collections.FXCollections;
import javafx.collections.ObservableList;
import javafx.scene.control.SingleSelectionModel;

/**
 * The model class that the AudioConfigMain class uses
 */
public class AudioConfigModel {
  /**
   * The minimum audio volume in decibels
   */
  public double minDecibels = 0.0;

  /**
   * The maximum audio volume in decibels
   */
  public double maxDecibels = 160.0;

  /**
   * The selected audio volume in decibels
   */
  public IntegerProperty selectedDBs = new SimpleIntegerProperty(0);

  /**
   * Indicates whether audio is muted
   */
  public BooleanProperty muting = new SimpleBooleanProperty(false);

  /**
   * List of some musical genres
   */
```

```java
public ObservableList genres = FXCollections.observableArrayList(
  "Chamber",
  "Country",
  "Cowbell",
  "Metal",
  "Polka",
  "Rock"
);

/**
 * A reference to the selection model used by the Slider
 */
public SingleSelectionModel genreSelectionModel;

/**
 * Adds a change listener to the selection model of the ChoiceBox, and contains
 * code that executes when the selection in the ChoiceBox changes.
 */
public void addListenerToGenreSelectionModel() {
  genreSelectionModel.selectedIndexProperty().addListener(new ChangeListener() {
    public void changed(ObservableValue ov, Object oldValue, Object newValue) {
      int selectedIndex = genreSelectionModel.selectedIndexProperty().getValue();
      switch(selectedIndex) {
        case 0: selectedDBs.setValue(80);
          break;
        case 1: selectedDBs.setValue(100);
          break;
        case 2: selectedDBs.setValue(150);
          break;
        case 3: selectedDBs.setValue(140);
          break;
        case 4: selectedDBs.setValue(120);
          break;
        case 5: selectedDBs.setValue(130);
      }
    }
  });
}
}
```

Defining Change Listeners in the Model class

Change listeners are a construct that helps enable declarative programming. For example, the change listener shown in this snippet executes whenever the selected index property of the selection model associated with the ChoiceBox changes:

```java
genreSelectionModel.selectedIndexProperty().addListener(new ChangeListener() {
    public void changed(ObservableValue ov, Object oldValue, Object newValue) {
        int selectedIndex = genreSelectionModel.selectedIndexProperty().getValue();
```

```
        switch(selectedIndex) {
          case 0: selectedDBs.setValue(80);
            break;
          case 1: selectedDBs.setValue(100);
            break;
          case 2: selectedDBs.setValue(150);
            break;
          case 3: selectedDBs.setValue(140);
            break;
          case 4: selectedDBs.setValue(120);
            break;
          case 5: selectedDBs.setValue(130);
        }
      }
    });
```

What causes selectedIndexProperty of the genreSelectionModel to change, though? To see the answer to this, we have to revisit some code in Listing 1-3. In the following code snippet, the items method of the ChoiceBoxBuilder is used to populate the ChoiceBox with items that each contain a genre.

```
        genreChoiceBox = ChoiceBoxBuilder.create()
            .layoutX(204)
            .layoutY(154)
            .prefWidth(93)
            .items(acModel.genres)
            .build()
```

This snippet from the model code in Listing 1-4 contains the collection to which the ComboBox items are bound:

```
    /**
     * List of some musical genres
     */
    public ObservableList genres = FXCollections.observableArrayList(
        "Chamber",
        "Country",
        "Cowbell",
        "Metal",
        "Polka",
        "Rock"
    );
```

When the user chooses a different item in the ChoiceBox, the change listener is invoked. Looking again at the code in the change listener, you'll see that the value of the selectedDBs property changes, which as you may recall, is bidirectionally bound to the slider. This is why the slider moves when you select a genre in the combo box. Go ahead and test this out by running the Audio Config program.

■ **Note** Associating the items property of the ChoiceBox with an ObservableList causes the items in the ChoiceBox to be automatically updated when the elements in the underlying collection are modified.

Surveying JavaFX Features

We close this chapter by surveying many of the features of JavaFX, some of which are a review for you. We do this by describing several of the more commonly used packages and classes in the JavaFX SDK API.

The javafx.stage package contains:

- The Stage class, which is the top level of the UI containment hierarchy for any JavaFX application, regardless of where it is deployed (such as the desktop, a browser, or a cell phone).

- The Screen class, which represents the displays on the machine in which a JavaFX program is running. This enables you to get information about the screens, such as size and resolution.

The javafx.scene package contains some classes that you'll use often:

- The Scene class is the second level of the UI containment hierarchy for JavaFX applications. It includes all of the UI elements contained in the application. These elements are called graphical nodes, or simply nodes.

- The Node class is the base class of all of the graphical nodes in JavaFX, UI elements such as text, images, media, shapes, and controls (such as text boxes and buttons) are all subclasses of Node. Take a moment to look at the variables and functions in the Node class to appreciate the capabilities provided to all of its subclasses, including bounds calculation and mouse and keyboard event handling.

- The Group class is a subclass of the Node class whose purpose includes grouping nodes together into a single co-ordinate space and allowing transforms (such as rotate) to be applied to the whole group. Also, attributes of the group that are changed (such as opacity) apply to all of the nodes contained within the group.

Several packages begin with javafx.scene that contain subclasses of Node of various types. For example:

- The javafx.scene.image package contains the Image and ImageView classes, which enable images to be displayed in the Scene. The ImageView class is a subclass of Node.

- The javafx.scene.shape package contains several classes for drawing shapes such as Circle, Rectangle, Line, Polygon, and Arc. The base class of the shapes, named Shape, contains an attribute named fill that enables you to specify a color or gradient with which to fill the shape.

- The javafx.scene.text package contains the Text class for drawing text in the scene. The Font class enables you to specify the font name and size of the text.

- The javafx.scene.media package has classes that enable you to play media. The MediaView class is a subclass of Node that displays the media.

- The javafx.scene.chart package has classes that help you easily create *area, bar, bubble, line, pie,* and *scatter* charts. The corresponding UI classes in this package are AreaChart, BarChart, BubbleChart, LineChart, PieChart, and ScatterChart.

Here are some other packages in the JavaFX 1.2 API.

- The javafx.scene.control package contains several UI controls, each one having the ability to be skinned and styled via CSS.

- The javafx.scene.transform package enables you to transform nodes (scale, rotate, translate, shear, and affine).

- The javafx.scene.input package contains classes such as MouseEvent and KeyEvent that provide information about these events from within an event handler function such as the Node class's onMouseClicked event.

- The javafx.scene.layout package contains several layout containers, including HBox, VBox, BorderPane, FlowPane, StackPane, and TilePane.

- The javafx.scene.effect and javafx.scene.effect.light packages contain easy-to-use effects such as Reflection, Glow, Shadow, BoxBlur, and Lighting.

- The javafx.scene.web package contains classes for easily embedding a web browser in your JavaFX applications.

- The javafx.animation package contains time-based interpolations typically used for animation, and convenience classes for common transitions, respectively.

- The javafx.beans, javafx.beans.binding, javafx.beans.property, and javafx.beans.value packages contain classes that implement properties and binding.

- The javafx.fxml package contains classes that implement a very powerful facility known as FXML, a markup language for expressing JavaFX user interfaces in XML.

- The javafx.builder package contains builder classes such as the ones demonstrated in earlier in this chapter.

- The javafx.util package contains utility classes such as the Duration class used in the HelloEarthRise example earlier in this chapter.

Take a look at the JavaFX API docs again in light of the information to get a deeper sense of how you can use its capabilities.

Summary

Congratulations, you learned a lot about JavaFX in this chapter, including:

- JavaFX is rich-client Java, and is needed by the software development industry.

- Java SE 6 Update 10 is a technology by Sun that solves the deployment problems that have prevented the Java Runtime Environment (JRE) from being ubiquitous on client machines. Java SE 6 Update 10 also addresses the ease and speed of deploying Java/JavaFX applications.

- Some of the high points of the history of JavaFX.

- Where to find JavaFX resources, including the JavaFX SDK, the JavaFX plug-in for NetBeans, and the API documentation.

- How to compile and run a JavaFX program from the command-line.

- How to declaratively express a user interface in JavaFX, using builder classes.

- How to build and run a JavaFX program using NetBeans.

- How to use several of the classes in the JavaFX API.

- How to create a class in JavaFX and use it as a model contains the state of a JavaFX application.

- How to use property binding to keep the UI easily in sync with the model.

We also looked at many of the available API packages and classes, and you learned how you can leverage their capabilities. Now that you have a jump start in JavaFX, you can begin examining the details of JavaFX in Chapter 2.

Resources

For some background information on JavaFX, you can consult the following resources.

- *This book's code examples:* The Source Code/Download section at the Apress web site (www.apress.com).

- *Java Posse #163: Newscast for February 8, 2008:* This is a podcast of a Java Posse interview with Josh Marinacci and Richard Bair on the subject of JavaFX. The URL is www.javaposse.com/index.php?post_id=305735.

- "Mind-Bendingly Cool Innovation": This article contains an interview with Chris Oliver, the founder of JavaFX The URL is http://research.sun.com/minds/2008-1202/.

- *"Congratulations to the JavaFX Script Compiler Team—The Elephant Is Through the Door":* A blog post by one of this book's authors, Jim Weaver, that congratulated the JavaFX compiler team for reaching a tipping point in the project. The URL is http://learnjavafx.typepad.com/weblog/2007/12/congratulations.html.

- *"Development and Deployment of Java Web Apps (Applets and Java Web Start Applications) for JavaSE 6u10":* This set of web pages from Sun discusses the features of Java SE 6 Update 10 and how to use them. The URL is http://java.sun.eom/javase/6/docs/technotes/guides/jweb/index.html.

- *Oracles's JavaFX.com site:* The home page for JavaFX where you can download the JavaFX SDK and other resource for JavaFX. The URL is http://www.javafx.com.

- *FX Experience:* A blog maintained by Oracle JavaFX Engineers Richard Bair, Jasper Potts, and Jonathan Giles. The URL is http://fxexperience.com.

- *Jim Weaver's JavaFX Blog:* A blog, started in October 2007, whose stated purpose is to help the reader become a "JavaFXpert." The URL is http://javafxpert.com.

- *Weiqi Gao's Observation:* A blog in which Weiqi Gao shares his experience in software development. The URL is `http://www.weiqigao.com/blog`.

- *Dean Iverson's Pleasing Software Blog:* A blog in which Dean Iverson shares his innovations in JavaFX and GroovyFX. The URL is `http://pleasing software.blogspot.com`.

- *Steve on Java:* A blog in which Stephen Chin keeps the world updated on his tireless exploits in the areas of JavaFX, Java, and Agile development. The URL is `http://steveonjava.com`.

- *JavaFX Eclipse Plugin:* Eclipse tooling for JavaFX 2.0, being developed by Tom Shindl. The URL for the announcement is `http://tomsondev.bestsolution .at/2011/06/24/introducing-efxclipse/`.

- *JavaFX 2.0 Roadmap:* The roadmap and associated milestones published by Oracle for JavaFX 2.0.

Creating a User Interface in JavaFX

Life is the art of drawing without an eraser.

—John W. Gardner

Chapter 1 gave you a jump start using JavaFX by covering the basics in developing and executing JavaFX programs. Now we cover many of the details about creating a user interface in JavaFX that were glossed over in Chapter 1. First on the agenda is to get you acquainted with the *theater* metaphor used by JavaFX to express user interfaces and to cover the significance of what we call *a node-centric UI*.

Introduction to Node-Centric UIs

Creating a user interface in JavaFX is like creating a theater play in that it typically consists of these very simple steps:

1. *Create a* stage *on which your program will perform*: The realization of your stage will depend on the platform on which it is deployed (e.g., a web page, the desktop, or a tablet).

2. *Create a scene in which the actors and props (nodes) will visually interact with each other and the audience (the users of your program):* Like any good set designer in the theater business, good JavaFX developers endeavor to make their scenes visually appealing. To this end, it is often a good idea to collaborate with a graphic designer on your "theater play."

3. *Create* nodes *in the scene*: These nodes are subclasses of the javafx.scene.Node class, which include UI controls, shapes, Text (a type of shape), images, media players, embedded browsers, and *custom UI components* that you create. Nodes may also be containers for other nodes, often providing cross-platform layout capabilities. A scene has a *scene graph* that contains a directed graph of nodes. Individual nodes and groups of nodes can be manipulated in many ways (such as moving, scaling, and setting opacity) by changing the values of a very rich set of Node properties.

4. *Create variables and classes that represent the* model *for the nodes in the scene:* As discussed in Chapter 1, one of the very powerful aspects of JavaFX is binding, which enables the application's UI to stay in sync easily with the state, or model, of the application.

■ **Note**   Most of the examples in this chapter are small programs intended to demonstrate UI concepts. For this reason, the model in many of these examples consists of variables appearing in the main program, rather than being contained by separate Java classes (such as the AudioConfigModel class in Chapter 1).

---

5. *Create* event handlers, *such as* onMousePressed, *that allow the user to interact with your program:* Often these event handlers manipulate instance variables in the model.

6. *Create* timelines *and* transitions *that animate your scene:* For example, you may want the thumbnail images of a list of books to move smoothly across the scene or a page in the UI to fade into view. You may simply want a ping-pong ball to move across the scene, bouncing off walls and paddles, which is demonstrated later in this chapter in the section, "The Zen of Node Collision Detection."

Let's get started with a closer look at Step 1, in which we examine the capabilities of the stage.

Setting the Stage

The appearance and functionality of your stage will depend on the platform on which it is deployed. For example, if deployed in a web browser, your stage will be a rectangular area, called an *applet*, within a web page. The stage for a JavaFX program deployed via Java Web Start will be a window.

Understanding the Stage Class

The Stage class is the top-level container for any JavaFX program that has a graphical UI. It has several properties and methods that allow it, for example, to be positioned, sized, given a title, made invisible, or given some degree of opacity. The two best ways that we know of to learn the capabilities of a class are to study the JavaFX API documentation and to examine (and write) programs that use it. In this section, we ask you to do both, beginning with looking at the API docs.

The JavaFX API docs may be found in the docs/api directory subordinate to where you installed the JavaFX SDK. Also, they are available online at the URL given in the Resources section at the end of this chapter. Open the index.html file in your browser, navigate to the javafx.stage package, and select the Stage class. That page should contain tables of Properties, Constructors, and Methods as shown in the excerpt in Figure 2-1.

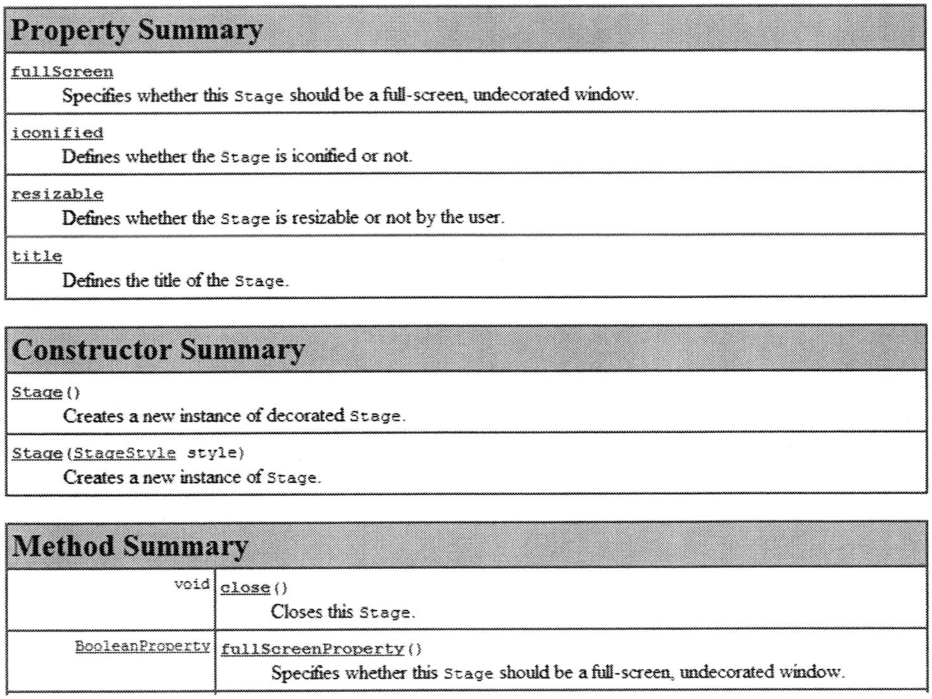

Property Summary		
`fullScreen`		
Specifies whether this `Stage` should be a full-screen, undecorated window.		
`iconified`		
Defines whether the `Stage` is iconified or not.		
`resizable`		
Defines whether the `Stage` is resizable or not by the user.		
`title`		
Defines the title of the `Stage`.		

Constructor Summary
`Stage()`
Creates a new instance of decorated `Stage`.
`Stage(StageStyle style)`
Creates a new instance of `Stage`.

Method Summary		
void	`close()`	
	Closes this `Stage`.	
`BooleanProperty`	`fullScreenProperty()`	
	Specifies whether this `Stage` should be a full-screen, undecorated window.	

Figure 2-1. *A portion of the Stage class documentation in the JavaFX API*

Go ahead and explore the documentation for each of the properties and methods in the Stage class, remembering to click the links to reveal more detailed information. When you're finished, come back and we show you a program that demonstrates many of the properties and methods available in the Stage class.

Using the Stage Class: The StageCoach Example

A screenshot of the unassuming, purposely ill-fitting StageCoach example program is shown in Figure 2-2.

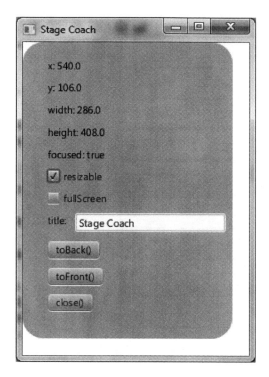

Figure 2-2. A screenshot of the StageCoach example

The StageCoach program was created to coach you through the finer points of using the Stage class and related classes such as StageStyle and Screen. Also, we use this program to show you how to get arguments passed into the program. Before walking through the behavior of the program, go ahead and open the project and execute it by following the instructions for building and executing the Audio-Config project in Chapter 1. The project file is located in the Chapter02 directory subordinate to where you extracted the book's code download bundle.

EXAMINING THE BEHAVIOR OF THE STAGECOACH PROGRAM

When the program starts, its appearance should be similar to the screenshot in Figure 2-2. To fully examine its behavior, perform the following steps. Note that for instructional purposes, the property and method names on the UI correspond to the properties and methods in the Stage instance.

1. Notice that the StageCoach program's window is initially displayed near the top of the screen, with its horizontal position in the center of the screen. Drag the program's window and observe that the x and y values near the top of the UI are dynamically updated to reflect its position on the screen.

2. Resize the program's window and observe that the width and height values change to reflect the width and height of the Stage. Note that this size includes the decorations (title bar and borders) of the window.

3. Click the program (or cause it to be in focus some other way) and notice that the focused value is true. Cause the window to lose focus, perhaps by clicking somewhere else on the screen, and notice that the focused value becomes false.

4. Deselect the resizable check box and then notice that the resizable value becomes false. Then try to resize the window and note that it is not permitted. Select the resizable check box again to make the window resizable.

5. Select the fullScreen check box. Notice that the program occupies the full screen and that the window decorations are not visible. Deselect the fullScreen check box to restore the program to its former size.

6. Edit the text in the text field beside the title label, noticing that the text in the window's title bar is changed to reflect the new value.

7. Drag the window to partially cover another window, and click the toBack() button. Notice that this places the program behind the other window, therefore causing the z-order to change.

8. With a portion of the program's window behind another window, but with the toFront() button visible, click that button. Notice that the program's window is placed in front of the other window.

9. Click the close() button, noticing that the program exits.

10. Invoke the program again, passing in the string "undecorated". If invoking from NetBeans, use the Project Properties dialog to pass this argument as shown In Figure 2-3. See the Hello Earthrise example in Chapter 1 for instructions on accessing this dialog.

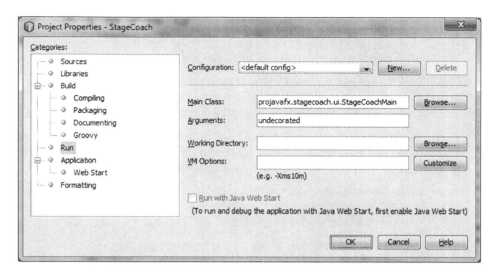

Figure 2-3. *Using NetBeans' Project Properties dialog to pass an argument into the program*

11. Notice that this time the program appears without any window decorations, but that the white background of the program includes the background of the window. The black outline in the screenshot shown in Figure 2-4 is part of the desktop background.

12. Exit the program again by clicking the close() button, and then run the program again, passing in the string "transparent" as the argument. Notice that the program appears in the shape of a rounded rectangle, as shown in Figure 2-5.

Figure 2-4. *The StageCoach program after being invoked with the undecorated argument*

■ **Note** You may have noticed that the screenshots in Figures 2-4 and 2-5 have y values that are negative. This is because the application was positioned on the secondary monitor, logically above the primary monitor, when the screenshots were taken.

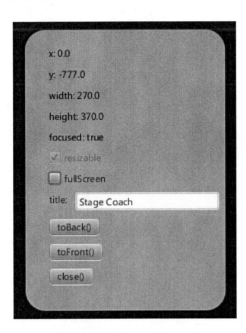

Figure 2-5. *The StageCoach program after being invoked with the transparent argument*

13. Click the application's UI, drag it around the screen, and click the close() button when finished. Congratulations on sticking with this 13-step exercise! Performing this exercise has prepared you to relate to the code behind it, which we now walk through together.

Understanding the StageCoach Program

Take a look at the code for the StageCoach program in Listing 2-1, and after that we point out new and relevant concepts.

Listing 2-1. *StageCoachMain.java*

```java
package projavafx.stagecoach.ui;

import java.util.List;
import javafx.application.Application;
import javafx.beans.property.SimpleStringProperty;
import javafx.beans.property.StringProperty;
import javafx.event.EventHandler;
import javafx.geometry.Rectangle2D;
import javafx.geometry.VPos;
import javafx.scene.Group;
import javafx.scene.GroupBuilder;
import javafx.scene.Scene;
import javafx.scene.SceneBuilder;
import javafx.scene.control.ButtonBuilder;
import javafx.scene.control.CheckBox;
import javafx.scene.control.CheckBoxBuilder;
import javafx.scene.control.Label;
import javafx.scene.control.TextField;
import javafx.scene.control.TextFieldBuilder;
import javafx.scene.input.MouseEvent;
import javafx.scene.layout.HBoxBuilder;
import javafx.scene.layout.VBoxBuilder;
import javafx.scene.paint.Color;
import javafx.scene.shape.RectangleBuilder;
import javafx.scene.text.Text;
import javafx.scene.text.TextBuilder;
import javafx.stage.Screen;
import javafx.stage.Stage;
import javafx.stage.StageStyle;
import javafx.stage.WindowEvent;

public class StageCoachMain extends Application {
  StringProperty title = new SimpleStringProperty();

  Text textStageX;
  Text textStageY;
  Text textStageW;
  Text textStageH;
  Text textStageF;
  CheckBox checkBoxResizable;
  CheckBox checkBoxFullScreen;

  double dragAnchorX;
  double dragAnchorY;

  public static void main(String[] args) {
    Application.launch(args);
  }
```

```
@Override
public void start(Stage stage) {
  StageStyle stageStyle = StageStyle.DECORATED;
  List<String> unnamedParams = getParameters().getUnnamed();
  if (unnamedParams.size() > 0) {
    String stageStyleParam = unnamedParams.get(0);
    if (stageStyleParam.equalsIgnoreCase("transparent")) {
      stageStyle = StageStyle.TRANSPARENT;
    }
    else if (stageStyleParam.equalsIgnoreCase("undecorated")) {
      stageStyle = StageStyle.UNDECORATED;
    }
    else if (stageStyleParam.equalsIgnoreCase("utility")) {
      stageStyle = StageStyle.UTILITY;
    }
  }
  final Stage stageRef = stage;
  Group rootGroup;
  TextField titleTextField;
  Scene scene  = SceneBuilder.create()
    .width(270)
    .height(370)
    .fill(Color.TRANSPARENT)
    .root(
      rootGroup = GroupBuilder.create()
        .children(
          RectangleBuilder.create()
            .width(250)
            .height(350)
            .arcWidth(50)
            .arcHeight(50)
            .fill(Color.SKYBLUE)
            .build(),
          VBoxBuilder.create()
            .layoutX(30)
            .layoutY(20)
            .spacing(10)
            .children(
              textStageX = TextBuilder.create()
                .textOrigin(VPos.TOP)
                .build(),
              textStageY = TextBuilder.create()
                .textOrigin(VPos.TOP)
                .build(),
              textStageW = TextBuilder.create()
                .textOrigin(VPos.TOP)
                .build(),
              textStageH = TextBuilder.create()
                .textOrigin(VPos.TOP)
                .build(),
```

43

```java
                textStageF = TextBuilder.create()
                  .textOrigin(VPos.TOP)
                  .build(),
                checkBoxResizable = CheckBoxBuilder.create()
                  .text("resizable")
                  .disable(stageStyle == StageStyle.TRANSPARENT ||
                           stageStyle == StageStyle.UNDECORATED)
                  .build(),
                checkBoxFullScreen = CheckBoxBuilder.create()
                  .text("fullScreen")
                  .build(),
                HBoxBuilder.create()
                  .spacing(10)
                  .children(
                    new Label("title:"),
                    titleTextField = TextFieldBuilder.create()
                      .text("Stage Coach")
                      .prefColumnCount(15)
                      .build()
                  )
                  .build(),
                ButtonBuilder.create()
                  .text("toBack()")
                  .onAction(new EventHandler<javafx.event.ActionEvent>() {
                    @Override public void handle(javafx.event.ActionEvent e) {
                      stageRef.toBack();
                    }
                  })
                  .build(),
                ButtonBuilder.create()
                  .text("toFront()")
                  .onAction(new EventHandler<javafx.event.ActionEvent>() {
                    @Override public void handle(javafx.event.ActionEvent e) {
                      stageRef.toFront();
                    }
                  })
                  .build(),
                ButtonBuilder.create()
                  .text("close()")
                  .onAction(new EventHandler<javafx.event.ActionEvent>() {
                    @Override public void handle(javafx.event.ActionEvent e) {
                      stageRef.close();
                    }
                  })
                  .build()
              )
              .build()
          )
          .build()
      )
      .build();
```

```java
        // When mouse button is pressed, save the initial position of screen
        rootGroup.setOnMousePressed(new EventHandler<MouseEvent>() {
            public void handle(MouseEvent me) {
                dragAnchorX = me.getScreenX() - stageRef.getX();
                dragAnchorY = me.getScreenY() - stageRef.getY();
            }
        });

        // When screen is dragged, translate it accordingly
        rootGroup.setOnMouseDragged(new EventHandler<MouseEvent>() {
            public void handle(MouseEvent me) {
                stageRef.setX(me.getScreenX() - dragAnchorX);
                stageRef.setY(me.getScreenY() - dragAnchorY);
            }
        });

        textStageX.textProperty().bind(new SimpleStringProperty("x: ")
                .concat(stageRef.xProperty().asString()));
        textStageY.textProperty().bind(new SimpleStringProperty("y: ")
                .concat(stageRef.yProperty().asString()));
        textStageW.textProperty().bind(new SimpleStringProperty("width: ")
                .concat(stageRef.widthProperty().asString()));
        textStageH.textProperty().bind(new SimpleStringProperty("height: ")
                .concat(stageRef.heightProperty().asString()));
        textStageF.textProperty().bind(new SimpleStringProperty("focused: ")
                .concat(stageRef.focusedProperty().asString()));
        stage.setResizable(true);
        checkBoxResizable.selectedProperty()
                .bindBidirectional(stage.resizableProperty());
        checkBoxFullScreen.selectedProperty().addListener(new ChangeListener() {
          public void changed(ObservableValue ov, Object oldValue, Object newValue) {
            stageRef.setFullScreen(checkBoxFullScreen.selectedProperty().getValue());
          }
        });
        title.bind(titleTextField.textProperty());

        stage.setScene(scene);
        stage.titleProperty().bind(title);
        stage.initStyle(stageStyle);
        stage.setOnCloseRequest(new EventHandler<WindowEvent>() {
            public void handle(WindowEvent we) {
                System.out.println("Stage is closing");
            }
        });
        stage.show();
        Rectangle2D primScreenBounds = Screen.getPrimary().getVisualBounds();
        stage.setX((primScreenBounds.getWidth() - stage.getWidth()) / 2);
        stage.setY((primScreenBounds.getHeight() - stage.getHeight()) / 4);
    }
}
```

Obtaining Program Arguments

The first new concept introduced by this program is the ability to read the arguments passed into a JavaFX program. The javafx.application package includes a class named Application that has application lifecycle related methods such as launch(), init(), start(), and stop(). Another method in the Application class is getParameters(), which gives the application access to the arguments passed on the command-line, as well as unnamed parameters and <name,value> pairs specified in a JNLP file. Here's the relevant code snippet from Listing 2-1 for your convenience:

```
StageStyle stageStyle = StageStyle.DECORATED;
List<String> unnamedParams = getParameters().getUnnamed();
if (unnamedParams.size() > 0) {
  String stageStyleParam = unnamedParams.get(0);
  if (stageStyleParam.equalsIgnoreCase("transparent")) {
    stageStyle = StageStyle.TRANSPARENT;
  }
  else if (stageStyleParam.equalsIgnoreCase("undecorated")) {
    stageStyle = StageStyle.UNDECORATED;
  }
  else if (stageStyleParam.equalsIgnoreCase("utility")) {
    stageStyle = StageStyle.UTILITY;
  }
}
...code omitted...
stage.initStyle(stageStyle);
```

Setting the Style of the Stage

We're using the getParameters() method described previously to get an argument that tells us whether the stage style of the Stage instance should be its default (StageStyle.DECORATED), StageStyle.UNDECORATED, or StageStyle.TRANSPARENT. You saw the effects of each in the preceding exercise, specifically in Figures 2-2, 2-4, and 2-5.

Controlling Whether a Stage Is Resizable

As shown in the snippet below from Listing 2-1, to make this application's window initially resizable we're calling the setResizable() method of the Stage instance. To keep the resizable property of the Stage and the state of the resizable check box synchronized, the check box is bidirectionally bound to the resizable property of the Stage instance.

```
stage.setResizable(true);
checkBoxResizable.selectedProperty()
        .bindBidirectional(stage.resizableProperty());
```

■ **Tip**   A property that is bound cannot be explicitly set. In the code preceding the snippet, the resizable property is set with the setResizable() method *before* the property is bound in the next line.

Making a Stage Full Screen

Making the Stage show in full-screen mode is done by setting the fullScreen property of the Stage instance to true. As shown in the snippet below from Listing 2-1, to keep the fullScreen property of the Stage and the state of the fullScreen check box synchronized, the fullScreen property of the Stage instance is updated whenever the selected property of the checkBox changes.

```
checkBoxFullScreen.selectedProperty().addListener(new ChangeListener() {
  public void changed(ObservableValue ov, Object oldValue, Object newValue) {
    stageRef.setFullScreen(checkBoxFullScreen.selectedProperty().getValue());
  }
});
```

Working with the Bounds of the Stage

The bounds of the Stage are represented by its x, y, width, and height properties whose values can be changed at will. This is demonstrated in the following snippet from Listing 2-1 where the Stage is placed near the top and centered horizontally on the primary screen after the Stage has been initialized.

```
Rectangle2D primScreenBounds = Screen.getPrimary().getVisualBounds();
stage.setX((primScreenBounds.getWidth() - stage.getWidth()) / 2);
stage.setY((primScreenBounds.getHeight() - stage.getHeight()) / 4);
```

We're using the Screen class of the javafx.stage package to get the dimensions of the primary screen so that the desired position may be calculated.

▓ **Note**　We intentionally made the Stage in Figure 2-2 larger than the Scene contained within to make the following point. The width and height of a Stage include its decorations (title bar and border), which vary on different platforms. It is therefore usually better to control the width and height of the Scene (we show you how in a bit) and let the Stage conform to that size.

Drawing Rounded Rectangles

As pointed out in Chapter 1, you can put rounded corners on a Rectangle by specifying the arcWidth and arcHeight for the corners. The following snippet from Listing 2-1 draws the sky-blue rounded rectangle that becomes the background for the transparent window example in Figure 2-5.

```
RectangleBuilder.create()
  .width(250)
  .height(350)
  .arcWidth(50)
  .arcHeight(50)
  .fill(Color.SKYBLUE)
  .build(),
```

Dragging the Stage on the Desktop When a Title Bar Isn't Available

The Stage may be dragged on the desktop using its title bar, but in the case where its StageStyle is UNDECORATED or TRANSPARENT, the title bar isn't available. To allow dragging in this circumstance, we added the code shown in the following code snippet from Listing 2-1.

```
// When mouse button is pressed, save the initial position of screen
rootGroup.setOnMousePressed(new EventHandler<MouseEvent>() {
    public void handle(MouseEvent me) {
        dragAnchorX = me.getScreenX() - stageRef.getX();
        dragAnchorY = me.getScreenY() - stageRef.getY();
    }
});

// When screen is dragged, translate it accordingly
rootGroup.setOnMouseDragged(new EventHandler<MouseEvent>() {
    public void handle(MouseEvent me) {
        stageRef.setX(me.getScreenX() - dragAnchorX);
        stageRef.setY(me.getScreenY() - dragAnchorY);
    }
});
```

Event handlers are covered a little later in the chapter, but as a preview, the handle() method of the anonymous class that is supplied to the onMouseDragged() method is called when the mouse is dragged. As a result, the values of the x and y properties are altered by the number of pixels that the mouse was dragged, which moves the Stage as the mouse is dragged.

Using UI Layout Containers

When developing applications that will be deployed in a cross-platform environment or are internationalized, it is good to use *layout containers*. One advantage of using layout containers is that when the node sizes change, their visual relationships with each other are predictable. Another advantage is that you don't have to calculate the location of each node that you place in the UI.

The following snippet from Listing 2-1 shows how the VBox layout class, located in the javafx.scene.layout package, is used to arrange the Text, CheckBox, HBox, and Button nodes in a column. This snippet also shows that layout containers may be nested, as demonstrated by the HBox that arranges the Label and TextField nodes horizontally. Note that several lines of code are omitted from this snippet in order to see the layout nesting clearly:

```
VBoxBuilder.create()
  .spacing(10)
  .children(
    textStageX = TextBuilder.create()
      .build(),
    checkBoxResizable = CheckBoxBuilder.create()
      .text("resizable")
      .build(),
```

```
            HBoxBuilder.create()
              .spacing(10)
              .children(
                new Label("title:"),
                titleTextField = TextFieldBuilder.create()
                  .text("Stage Coach")
                  .build()
              )
              .build(),
            ButtonBuilder.create()
              .text("toBack()")
              .build(),
          )
          .build()
```

The VBox layout class is similar to the Group class discussed in the Hello Earthrise example in Chapter 1, in that it contains a collection of nodes within it. Unlike the Group class, the VBox class arranges its contained nodes vertically, spacing them apart from each other by the number of pixels specified in the spacing property.

Ascertaining Whether the Stage Is in Focus

To know whether your JavaFX application is the one that currently is in focus (e.g., keys pressed are delivered to the application), simply consult the focused property of the Stage instance. The following snippet from Listing 2-1 demonstrates this.

```
textStageF.textProperty().bind(new SimpleStringProperty("focused: ")
        .concat(stageRef.focusedProperty().asString()));
```

Controlling the Z-Order of the Stage

In the event that you want your JavaFX application to appear on top of other windows or behind other windows onscreen, you can use the toFront() and toBack() methods, respectively. The following snippet from Listing 2-1 shows how this is accomplished.

```
            ButtonBuilder.create()
              .text("toFront()")
              .onAction(new EventHandler<javafx.event.ActionEvent>() {
                @Override public void handle(javafx.event.ActionEvent e) {
                  stageRef.toFront();
                }
              })
              .build(),
            ButtonBuilder.create()
              .text("close()")
              .onAction(new EventHandler<javafx.event.ActionEvent>() {
                @Override public void handle(javafx.event.ActionEvent e) {
                  stageRef.close();
                }
              })
              .build()
```

Closing the Stage and Detecting When It Is closed

As shown in the following code snippet from Listing 2-1, you can programmatically close the Stage with its close() method. This is important when the stageStyle is undecorated or transparent, because the close button supplied by the windowing system is not present.

```
ButtonBuilder.create()
  .text("close()")
  .onAction(new EventHandler<javafx.event.ActionEvent>() {
    @Override public void handle(javafx.event.ActionEvent e) {
      stageRef.close();
    }
  })
  .build()
```

By the way, you can detect when there is an external request to close the Stage by using the onCloseRequest event handler as shown in the following code snippet from Listing 2-1.

```
stage.setOnCloseRequest(new EventHandler<WindowEvent>() {
    public void handle(WindowEvent we) {
        System.out.println("Stage is closing");
    }
});
```

To see this in action, run the application without any arguments so that it has the appearance of Figure 2-2 shown previously, and then click the close button on the decoration of the window.

■ **Tip**   The onCloseRequest event handler is only called when there is an external request to close the window. This is why the "Stage is closing" message doesn't appear in this example when you click the button labeled "close()".

Making a Scene

Continuing on with our theater metaphor for creating JavaFX applications, we now discuss putting a Scene on the Stage. The Scene, as you recall, is the place in which the actors and props (nodes) visually interact with each other and the audience (the users of your program).

Using the Scene Class: The OnTheScene Example

As with the Stage class, we're going to use a contrived example application whose purpose is to demonstrate and teach the details of the available capabilities in the Scene class. See Figure 2-6 for a screenshot of the OnTheScene program.

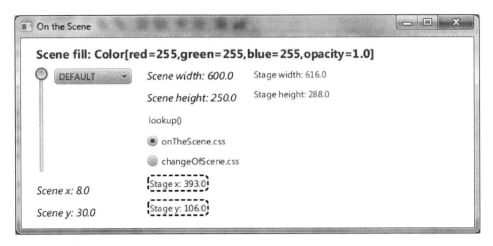

Figure 2-6. The OnTheScene program when first invoked

Go ahead and run the OnTheScene program, putting it through its paces as instructed in the following exercise. We follow up with a walkthrough of the code so that you can associate the behavior with the code behind it.

EXAMINING THE BEHAVIOR OF THE ONTHESCENE PROGRAM

When the OnTheScene program starts, its appearance should be similar to the screenshot in Figure 2-6. To fully examine its behavior, perform the following steps. Note that the property and method names on the UI correspond to the property and methods in the Scene, Stage, and Cursor classes, as well as CSS (Cascading Style Sheets) file names.

1. Drag the application around, noticing that although the Stage x and y values are relative to the screen, the Scene's x and y values are relative to the upper-left corner of the exterior of the Stage (including decorations). Similarly, the width and height of the Scene are the dimensions of the interior of the Stage (which doesn't include decorations). As noted earlier, it is best to set the Scene width and height explicitly (or let it be set implicitly by assuming the size of the contained nodes), rather than setting the width and height of a decorated Stage.

2. Resize the program's window and observe that the width and height values change to reflect the width and height of the Scene. Also notice that the position of much of the content in the scene changes as you change the height of the window.

3. Click the lookup() hyperlink and notice that the string "Scene height: XXX.X" prints in the console, where XXX.X is the Scene's height.

4. Hover the mouse over the choice box dropdown and notice that it becomes slightly larger. Click the choice box and choose a cursor style in the list, noticing that the cursor changes to that style. Be careful with choosing NONE, as the cursor may disappear, and you'll need to use the keyboard (or psychic powers while moving the mouse) to make it visible.

5. Drag the slider on the left, noticing that the fill color of the Scene changes and that the string at the top of the Scene reflects the red-green-blue (RGB) and opacity values of the current fill color.

6. Notice the appearance and content of the text on the Scene. Then click the changeOfScene.css button, noticing that the color and font and content characteristics for some of the text on the Scene changes as shown in the screenshot in Figure 2-7.

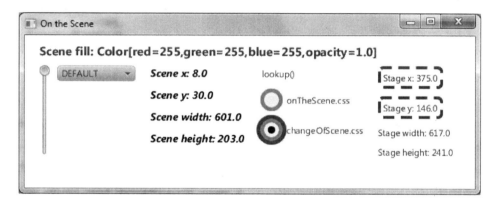

Figure 2-7. *The OnTheScene program with the changeOfScene CSS style sheet applied*

7. Click the OnTheScene.css button, noticing that the color and font characteristics return to their previous state.

Now that you've explored this example program that demonstrates features of the Scene, let's walk through the code!

Understanding the OnTheScene Program

Take a look at the code for the OnTheScene program in Listing 2-2, and after that we point out new and relevant concepts.

Listing 2-2. *OnTheSceneMain.fx*

```
package projavafx.onthescene.ui;

import javafx.application.Application;
import javafx.beans.property.DoubleProperty;
import javafx.beans.property.SimpleDoubleProperty;
import javafx.beans.property.SimpleStringProperty;
import javafx.beans.value.ChangeListener;
import javafx.beans.value.ObservableValue;
import javafx.collections.FXCollections;
import javafx.collections.ObservableList;
import javafx.event.EventHandler;
import javafx.geometry.HPos;
import javafx.geometry.Insets;
import javafx.geometry.Orientation;
import javafx.geometry.VPos;
import javafx.scene.Cursor;
import javafx.scene.Scene;
import javafx.scene.SceneBuilder;
import javafx.scene.control.ChoiceBox;
import javafx.scene.control.ChoiceBoxBuilder;
import javafx.scene.control.HyperlinkBuilder;
import javafx.scene.control.Label;
import javafx.scene.control.LabelBuilder;
import javafx.scene.control.RadioButton;
import javafx.scene.control.RadioButtonBuilder;
import javafx.scene.control.Slider;
import javafx.scene.control.SliderBuilder;
import javafx.scene.control.ToggleGroup;
import javafx.scene.layout.FlowPane;
import javafx.scene.layout.FlowPaneBuilder;
import javafx.scene.layout.HBoxBuilder;
import javafx.scene.paint.Color;
import javafx.scene.text.Font;
import javafx.scene.text.FontWeight;
import javafx.scene.text.Text;
import javafx.scene.text.TextBuilder;
import javafx.stage.Stage;

public class OnTheSceneMain extends Application {
  DoubleProperty fillVals = new SimpleDoubleProperty(255.0);

  Scene sceneRef;

  ObservableList cursors = FXCollections.observableArrayList(
      Cursor.DEFAULT,
      Cursor.CROSSHAIR,
      Cursor.WAIT,
      Cursor.TEXT,
      Cursor.HAND,
      Cursor.MOVE,
```

```
      Cursor.N_RESIZE,
      Cursor.NE_RESIZE,
      Cursor.E_RESIZE,
      Cursor.SE_RESIZE,
      Cursor.S_RESIZE,
      Cursor.SW_RESIZE,
      Cursor.W_RESIZE,
      Cursor.NW_RESIZE,
      Cursor.NONE
    );

  public static void main(String[] args) {
    Application.launch(args);
  }

  @Override
  public void start(Stage stage) {
    Slider sliderRef;
    ChoiceBox choiceBoxRef;
    Text textSceneX;
    Text textSceneY;
    Text textSceneW;
    Text textSceneH;
    Label labelStageX;
    Label labelStageY;
    Label labelStageW;
    Label labelStageH;

    final ToggleGroup toggleGrp = new ToggleGroup();

    FlowPane sceneRoot = FlowPaneBuilder.create()
      .layoutX(20)
      .layoutY(40)
      .padding(new Insets(0, 20, 40, 0))
      .orientation(Orientation.VERTICAL)
      .vgap(10)
      .hgap(20)
      .columnHalignment(HPos.LEFT)
      .children(
        HBoxBuilder.create()
          .spacing(10)
          .children(
            sliderRef = SliderBuilder.create()
              .min(0)
              .max(255)
              .value(255)
              .orientation(Orientation.VERTICAL)
              .build(),
            choiceBoxRef = ChoiceBoxBuilder.create()
              .items(cursors)
              .build()
          )
```

```
          .build(),
      textSceneX = TextBuilder.create()
        .styleClass("emphasized-text")
        .build(),
      textSceneY = TextBuilder.create()
        .styleClass("emphasized-text")
        .build(),
      textSceneW = TextBuilder.create()
        .styleClass("emphasized-text")
        .build(),
      textSceneH = TextBuilder.create()
        .styleClass("emphasized-text")
        .id("sceneHeightText")
        .build(),
      HyperlinkBuilder.create()
        .text("lookup()")
        .onAction(new EventHandler<javafx.event.ActionEvent>() {
          @Override public void handle(javafx.event.ActionEvent e) {
            System.out.println("sceneRef:" + sceneRef);
            Text textRef = (Text)sceneRef.lookup("#sceneHeightText");
            System.out.println(textRef.getText());
          }
        })
        .build(),
      RadioButtonBuilder.create()
        .text("onTheScene.css")
        .toggleGroup(toggleGrp)
        .selected(true)
        .build(),
      RadioButtonBuilder.create()
        .text("changeOfScene.css")
        .toggleGroup(toggleGrp)
        .build(),
      labelStageX = LabelBuilder.create()
        .id("stageX")
        .build(),
      labelStageY = LabelBuilder.create()
        .id("stageY")
        .build(),
      labelStageW = new Label(),
      labelStageH = new Label()
    )
    .build();

sceneRef = SceneBuilder.create()
  .width(600)
  .height(250)
  .root(sceneRoot)
  .build();
```

```
        sceneRef.getStylesheets().addAll(OnTheSceneMain.class
                .getResource("onTheScene.css").toExternalForm());
        stage.setScene(sceneRef);

        choiceBoxRef.getSelectionModel().selectFirst();

        // Setup various property binding
        textSceneX.textProperty().bind(new SimpleStringProperty("Scene x: ")
                .concat(sceneRef.xProperty().asString()));
        textSceneY.textProperty().bind(new SimpleStringProperty("Scene y: ")
                .concat(sceneRef.yProperty().asString()));
        textSceneW.textProperty().bind(new SimpleStringProperty("Scene width: ")
                .concat(sceneRef.widthProperty().asString()));
        textSceneH.textProperty().bind(new SimpleStringProperty("Scene height: ")
                .concat(sceneRef.heightProperty().asString()));
        labelStageX.textProperty().bind(new SimpleStringProperty("Stage x: ")
                .concat(sceneRef.getWindow().xProperty().asString()));
        labelStageY.textProperty().bind(new SimpleStringProperty("Stage y: ")
                .concat(sceneRef.getWindow().yProperty().asString()));
        labelStageW.textProperty().bind(new SimpleStringProperty("Stage width: ")
                .concat(sceneRef.getWindow().widthProperty().asString()));
        labelStageH.textProperty().bind(new SimpleStringProperty("Stage height: ")
                .concat(sceneRef.getWindow().heightProperty().asString()));
        sceneRef.cursorProperty().bind(choiceBoxRef.getSelectionModel()
                .selectedItemProperty());
        fillVals.bind(sliderRef.valueProperty());

        // When fillVals changes, use that value as the RGB to fill the scene
        fillVals.addListener(new ChangeListener() {
          public void changed(ObservableValue ov, Object oldValue, Object newValue) {
            Double fillValue = fillVals.getValue() / 256.0;
            sceneRef.setFill(new Color(fillValue, fillValue, fillValue, 1.0));
          }
        });

        // When the selected radio button changes, set the appropriate stylesheet
        toggleGrp.selectedToggleProperty().addListener(new ChangeListener() {
          public void changed(ObservableValue ov, Object oldValue, Object newValue) {
            String radioButtonText = ((RadioButton)toggleGrp.getSelectedToggle())
                    .getText();
            sceneRef.getStylesheets().addAll(OnTheSceneMain.class
                    .getResource(radioButtonText).toExternalForm());
          }
        });

        stage.setTitle("On the Scene");
        stage.show();
```

```
    // Define an unmanaged node that will display Text
    Text addedTextRef = TextBuilder.create()
      .layoutX(0)
      .layoutY(-30)
      .textOrigin(VPos.TOP)
      .fill(Color.BLUE)
      .font(Font.font("Sans Serif", FontWeight.BOLD, 16))
      .managed(false)
      .build();

    // Bind the text of the added Text node to the fill property of the Scene
    addedTextRef.textProperty().bind(new SimpleStringProperty("Scene fill: ").
           concat(sceneRef.fillProperty()));

    // Add to the Text node to the FlowPane
    ((FlowPane)sceneRef.getRoot()).getChildren().add(addedTextRef);
  }
}
```

Setting the Cursor for the Scene

The cursor can be set for a given node and/or for the entire scene. To do the latter, set the cursor property of the Scene instance to one of the constant values in the Cursor class, as shown in the following snippet from Listing 2-2.

```
    sceneRef.cursorProperty().bind(choiceBoxRef.getSelectionModel()
           .selectedItemProperty());
```

These cursor values can be seen by looking at the javafx.scene.Cursor class in the JavaFX API docs; we've created a collection of these constants in Listing 2-2.

Painting the Scene's Background

The Scene class has a fill property whose type is javafx.scene.paint.Paint. Looking at the JavaFX API will reveal that the known subclasses of Paint are Color, LinearGradient, and RadialGradient. Therefore, a Scene's background may be filled with solid colors and gradients. If you don't set the fill property of the Scene, the default color (white) will be used.

▓ **Tip**   One of the Color constants is Color.TRANSPARENT, so you may make the Scene's background completely transparent if desired. In fact, the reason that the Scene behind the rounded-cornered rectangle in the StageCoach screenshot in Figure 2-5 isn't white is that its fill property is set to Color.TRANSPARENT. (See Listing 2-1 again.)

To set the fill property in the OnTheScene example, instead of using one of the constants in the Color class (such as Color.BLUE), we're using an RGB formula to create the color. Take a look at the javafx.scene.paint.Color class in the JavaFX API docs and scroll down past the constants such as ALICEBLUE and WHITESMOKE to see the constructors and methods. We're using a constructor of the Color class, setting the fill property to it, as shown in the following snippet from Listing 2-2.

```
sceneRef.setFill(new Color(fillValue, fillValue, fillValue, 1.0));
```

As you move the Slider, to which the fillVals property is bound, each of the arguments to the Color() constructor are set to a value from 0 to 255, as indicated in the following code snippet from Listing 2-2.

```
fillVals.bind(sliderRef.valueProperty());
```

Populating the Scene with Nodes

As covered in Chapter 1, you can populate a Scene with nodes by instantiating them using builder classes. We've also discussed that some nodes (such as Group and VBox) can contain other nodes. These capabilities enable you to construct complex *scene graphs* containing nodes. In the current example, the root property of the Scene contains a Flow layout container, which causes its contents to flow either vertically or horizontally, wrapping as necessary. The Flow container in our example contains an HBox (which contains a Slider and a ChoiceBox) and several other nodes (instances of Text, Hyperlink, and RadioButton classes).

Finding a Scene Node by ID

Each node in a Scene can be assigned an ID in the id property of the node. For example, in the following snippet from Listing 2-2, the id property of a Text node is assigned the String "sceneHeightText". When the action event handler in the Hyperlink control is called, the lookup() method of the Scene instance is used to obtain a reference to the node whose id is "sceneHeightText". The event handler then prints the content of the Text node to the console.

■ **Note** The Hyperlink control is essentially a button that has the appearance of hyperlink text. It has an action event handler in which you could place code that opens a browser page or any other desired functionality.

```
textSceneH = TextBuilder.create()
  .styleClass("emphasized-text")
  .id("sceneHeightText")
  .build(),
HyperlinkBuilder.create()
  .text("lookup()")
  .onAction(new EventHandler<javafx.event.ActionEvent>() {
```

```
@Override public void handle(javafx.event.ActionEvent e) {
    System.out.println("sceneRef:" + sceneRef);
    Text textRef = (Text)sceneRef.lookup("#sceneHeightText");
    System.out.println(textRef.getText());
}
})
.build(),
```

A close examination of the action event handler reveals that the lookup() method returns a Node, but the actual type of object returned in this snippet is a Text object. Because we need to access a property of the Text class (text) that isn't in the Node class, it is necessary to coerce the compiler into trusting that at runtime the object will be an instance of the Text class.

Accessing the Stage from the Scene

To obtain a reference to the Stage instance from the Scene, we use a property in the Scene class named window. The accessor method for this property appears in the following snippet from Listing 2-2 to get the x and y co-ordinates of the Stage on the screen.

```
labelStageX.textProperty().bind(new SimpleStringProperty("Stage x: ")
        .concat(sceneRef.getWindow().xProperty().asString()));
labelStageY.textProperty().bind(new SimpleStringProperty("Stage y: ")
        .concat(sceneRef.getWindow().yProperty().asString()));
```

Inserting a Node into the Scene's Content Sequence

Sometimes it is useful to add a node dynamically to the children of a UI container class. The code snippet shown below from Listing 2-2 demonstrates how this may be accomplished by dynamically adding a Text node to the children of the FlowPane instance:

```
// Define an unmanaged node that will display Text
Text addedTextRef = TextBuilder.create()
    .layoutX(0)
    .layoutY(-30)
    .textOrigin(VPos.TOP)
    .fill(Color.BLUE)
    .font(Font.font("Sans Serif", FontWeight.BOLD, 16))
    .managed(false)
    .build();

// Bind the text of the added Text node to the fill property of the Scene
addedTextRef.textProperty().bind(new SimpleStringProperty("Scene fill: ").
        concat(sceneRef.fillProperty()));

// Add to the Text node to the FlowPane
((FlowPane)sceneRef.getRoot()).getChildren().add(addedTextRef);
```

This particular Text node is the one at the top of the Scene shown in Figures 2-6 and 2-7, in which the value of the Scene's fill property is displayed. Note that in this example the managed property of the addedTextRef instance is set to false, so its position isn't governed by the FlowPane.

CSS Styling the Nodes in a Scene

A very powerful aspect of JavaFX is the ability to use CSS to style the nodes in a Scene dynamically. You used this capability in Step 6 of the previous exercise when you clicked the changeOfScene.css button to change the appearance of the UI from what you saw in Figure 2-6 to what was shown in Figure 2-7. Also, in Step 7 of the exercise, the appearance of the UI changed back to what was shown in Figure 2-6 when you clicked the onTheScene.css radio button. The relevant code snippet from Listing 2-2 is shown here:

```
sceneRef.getStylesheets().addAll(OnTheSceneMain.class
        .getResource("onTheScene.css").toExternalForm());
...code omitted...
// When the selected radio button changes, set the appropriate stylesheet
toggleGrp.selectedToggleProperty().addListener(new ChangeListener() {
  public void changed(ObservableValue ov, Object oldValue, Object newValue) {
    String radioButtonText = ((RadioButton)toggleGrp.getSelectedToggle())
            .getText();
    sceneRef.getStylesheets().addAll(OnTheSceneMain.class
            .getResource(radioButtonText).toExternalForm());
  }
});
```

In this snippet, the stylesheets property of the Scene is initialized to the location of the onTheScene.css file, which in this case is the same directory as the OnTheSceneMain class. Also shown in the snippet is the assignment of the CSS files to the Scene as the appropriate buttons are clicked. Take a look at Listing 2-3 to see the style sheet that corresponds to the screenshot in Figure 2-6.

Some of the CSS *selectors* in this style sheet represent the nodes whose id property is either "stageX" or "stageY". There is also a selector in this style sheet that represents nodes whose styleClass property is "emphasized-text". In addition, there is a selector in this style sheet that maps to the ChoiceBox UI control by substituting the camel-case name of the control to a lowercase hyphenated name (choice-box). The *properties* in this style sheet begin with "-fx-", and correspond to the type of node with which they are associated. The *values* in this style sheet (such as black, italic, and 14pt) are expressed as standard CSS values.

Listing 2-3. onTheScene.css

```
#stageX, #stageY {
  -fx-padding: 1;
  -fx-border-color: black;
  -fx-border-style: dashed;
  -fx-border-width: 2;
  -fx-border-radius: 5;
}

.emphasized-text {
  -fx-font-size: 14pt;
  -fx-font-weight: normal;
  -fx-font-style: italic;
}
```

```
.choice-box:hover {
    -fx-scale-x: 1.1;
    -fx-scale-y: 1.1;
}

.radio-button .radio  {
   -fx-background-color: -fx-shadow-highlight-color, -fx-outer-border,
                         -fx-inner-border, -fx-body-color;
   -fx-background-insets: 0 0 -1 0,  0,  1,  2;
   -fx-background-radius: 1.0em;
   -fx-padding: 0.333333em;
}

.radio-button:focused .radio {
    -fx-background-color: -fx-focus-color, -fx-outer-border,
                          -fx-inner-border, -fx-body-color;
    -fx-background-radius: 1.0em;
    -fx-background-insets: -1.4, 0, 1, 2;
}
```

Listing 2-4 is the style sheet that corresponds to the screenshot in Figure 2-7. For more information on CSS style sheets, see the Resources section at the end of this chapter.

Listing 2-4. *changeOfScene.css*

```
#stageX, #stageY {
  -fx-padding: 3;
  -fx-border-color: blue;
  -fx-stroke-dash-array: 12 2 4 2;
  -fx-border-width: 4;
  -fx-border-radius: 5;
}

.emphasized-text {
  -fx-font-size: 14pt;
  -fx-font-weight: bold;
  -fx-font-style: normal;
}

.radio-button *.radio  {
    -fx-padding: 10;
    -fx-background-color: red, yellow;
    -fx-background-insets: 0, 5;
    -fx-background-radius: 30, 20;
}

.radio-button:focused *.radio {
    -fx-background-color: blue, red, yellow;
    -fx-background-insets: -5, 0, 5;
    -fx-background-radius: 40, 30, 20;
}
```

Now that you've had some experience with using the Stage and Scene classes, several of the Node subclasses, and CSS styling, we show you how to handle events that can occur when your JavaFX program is running.

Handling Input Events

So far we've shown you a couple of examples of event handling. For example, we used the onAction event handler to execute code when a button is clicked. We also used the onCloseRequest event handler of the Stage class to execute code when the Stage has been requested externally to close. In this section, we explore more of the event handlers available in JavaFX.

Surveying Mouse and Keyboard Events and Handlers

Most of the events that occur in JavaFX programs are related to the user manipulating input devices such as a mouse and keyboard. To see the available event handlers and their associated event objects, we take yet another look at the JavaFX API documentation. First, navigate to the javafx.scene.Node class and look for the properties that begin with the letters "on". These properties represent the event handlers common to all nodes in JavaFX. Here is a list of these event handlers in the JavaFX 2.0 API:

- Key event handlers: onKeyPressed, onKeyReleased, onKeyTyped

- Mouse event handlers: onMouseClicked, onMouseDragged, onMouseEntered, onMouseExited, onMouseMoved, onMousePressed, onMouseReleased

- Drag and drop handlers: onDragDetected, onDragDone, onDragDropped, onDragEntered, onDragExited, onDragOver

Each of these is a property that defines a method to be called when particular input events occur. In the case of the key event handlers, as shown in the JavaFX API docs, the method's parameter is a javafx.scene.input.KeyEvent instance. The method's parameter for the mouse event handlers is a javafx.scene.input.MouseEvent.

Understanding the KeyEvent Class

Take a look at the JavaFX API docs for the KeyEvent class, and you'll see that it contains several methods, a commonly used one being getCode(). The getCode() method returns a KeyCode instance representing the key that caused the event when pressed. Looking at the javafx.scene.input.KeyCode class in the JavaFX API docs reveals that a multitude of constants exist that represent keys on an international set of keyboards. Another way to find out what key was pressed is to call the getCharacter() method, which returns a string that represents the unicode character associated with the key pressed.

The KeyEvent class also enables you to see whether the Alt, Ctrl, Meta, and/or Shift keys were down at the time of the event by calling the isAltDown(), isControlDown(), isMetaDown(), or isShiftDown() methods, respectively.

Understanding the MouseEvent Class

Take a look at the MouseEvent class in the JavaFX API docs, and you see that significantly more methods are available than in KeyEvent. Like KeyEvent, MouseEvent has the isAltDown(), isControlDown(), isMetaDown(), and isShiftDown() methods, as well as the source field, which is a reference to the object in which the event originated. In addition, it has several methods that pinpoint various co-ordinate spaces where the mouse event occurred, all expressed in pixels:

- getX() and getY() return the horizontal and vertical position of the mouse event, relative to the origin of the node in which the mouse event occurred.

- getSceneX() and getSceneY() return the horizontal and vertical position of the mouse event, relative to the Scene.

- getScreenX() and getScreenY() return the horizontal and vertical position of the mouse event, relative to the screen.

Here are a few other commonly useful methods:

- isDragDetect() returns true if a drag event is detected.

- getButton(), isPrimaryButtonDown(), isSecondaryButtonDown(), isMiddleButtonDown(), and getClickCount() contain information about what button was clicked, and how many times it was clicked.

A little later in this chapter you get some experience with creating key and mouse event handlers in the ZenPong example program. To continue preparing you for the ZenPong example, we now give you a look at how you can animate the nodes that you put in your scene.

Animating Nodes in the Scene

One of the strengths of JavaFX is the ease with which you can create graphically rich user interfaces. Part of that richness is the ability to animate nodes that live in the Scene. At its core, animating a node involves changing the value of its properties over a period of time. Examples of animating a node include the following.

- Gradually increasing the size of a node when the mouse enters its bounds, and gradually decreasing the size when the mouse exits its bounds. Note that this requires scaling the node, which is referred to as a transform.

- Gradually increasing or decreasing the opacity of a node to provide a fade-in or fade-out effect, respectively.

- Gradually altering values of properties in a node that change its location, causing it to move from one location to another. This is useful, for example, when creating a game such as Pong. A related capability is detecting when a node has collided with another node.

Animating a node involves the use of the Timeline class, located in the javafx.animation package. Depending on the requirements of an animation and personal preference, use one of two general techniques:

- Create an instance of the Timeline class directly and supply key frames that specify values and actions at specific points in time.

- Use the javafx.animation.Transition subclasses to define and associate specific transitions with a node. Examples of transitions include causing a node to move along a defined path over a period of time, and rotating a node over a period of time. Each of these transition classes extends the Timeline class.

We now cover these techniques, showing examples of each, beginning with the first one listed.

Using a Timeline for Animation

Take a look at the javafx.animation package in the JavaFX API docs, and you see three of the classes that are used when directly creating a timeline: Timeline, KeyFrame, and Interpolator. Peruse the docs for these classes, and then come back so we can show you some examples of using them.

■ **Tip**   Remember to consult the JavaFX API docs for any new packages, classes, properties, and methods that you encounter.

The Metronome1 Example

We use a simple metronome example to demonstrate how to create a timeline.

As the screenshot in Figure 2-8 shows, the Metronome1 program has a pendulum as well as four buttons that start, pause, resume, and stop the animation. The pendulum in this example is a Line node, and we're going to animate that node by *interpolating* its startX property over the period of one second. Go ahead and take this example for a spin by doing the following exercise.

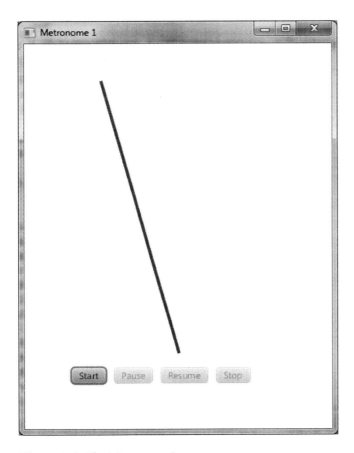

Figure 2-8. *The Metronome1 program*

EXAMINING THE BEHAVIOR OF THE METRONOME1 PROGRAM

When the Metronome1 program starts, its appearance should be similar to the screenshot in Figure 2-8. To fully examine its behavior, perform the following steps.

1. Observe that of the four buttons on the scene, only the Start button is enabled.

2. Click the Start button. Notice that the top of the line moves back and forth, taking one second to travel each direction. Also, observe that the Start and Resume buttons are disabled and that the Pause and Stop buttons are enabled.

3. Click the Pause button, noticing that the animation pauses. Also, observe that the Start and Pause buttons are disabled and that the Resume and Stop buttons are enabled.

4. Click the Resume button, noticing that the animation resumes from where it was paused.

5. Click the Stop button, noticing that the animation stops and that the button states are the same as they were when the program was first started (see Step 1).

6. Click the Start button again, noticing that the line jumps back to its starting point before beginning the animation (rather than simply resuming as it did in Step 4).

7. Click the Stop button.

Now that you've experienced the behavior of the Metronome1 program, we walk through the code behind it.

Understanding the Metronome1 program

Take a look at the code for the Metronome1 program in Listing 2-5, and then we point out relevant concepts.

Listing 2-5. *Metronome1Main.java*

```
package projavafx.metronome1.ui;

import javafx.animation.Animation;
import javafx.animation.Interpolator;
import javafx.animation.KeyFrame;
import javafx.animation.KeyValue;
import javafx.animation.Timeline;
import javafx.animation.TimelineBuilder;
import javafx.application.Application;
import javafx.beans.property.DoubleProperty;
import javafx.beans.property.SimpleDoubleProperty;
import javafx.event.EventHandler;
import javafx.scene.GroupBuilder;
import javafx.scene.Scene;
import javafx.scene.SceneBuilder;
import javafx.scene.control.Button;
import javafx.scene.control.ButtonBuilder;
import javafx.scene.layout.HBoxBuilder;
import javafx.scene.paint.Color;
import javafx.scene.shape.Line;
import javafx.scene.shape.LineBuilder;
import javafx.stage.Stage;
import javafx.util.Duration;

public class Metronome1Main extends Application {
  DoubleProperty startXVal = new SimpleDoubleProperty(100.0);
```

```java
Button startButton;
Button pauseButton;
Button resumeButton;
Button stopButton;
Line line;

Timeline anim = TimelineBuilder.create()
  .autoReverse(true)
  .keyFrames(
    new KeyFrame(
      new Duration(0.0),
      new KeyValue(startXVal, 100.0)
    ),
    new KeyFrame(
      new Duration(1000.0),
      new KeyValue(startXVal, 300.0, Interpolator.LINEAR)
    )
  )
  .cycleCount(Timeline.INDEFINITE)
  .build();

public static void main(String[] args) {
  Application.launch(args);
}

@Override
public void start(Stage stage) {
  Scene scene  = SceneBuilder.create()
    .width(400)
    .height(500)
    .root(
      GroupBuilder.create()
        .children(
          line = LineBuilder.create()
            .startY(50)
            .endX(200)
            .endY(400)
            .strokeWidth(4)
            .stroke(Color.BLUE)
            .build(),
          HBoxBuilder.create()
            .layoutX(60)
            .layoutY(420)
            .spacing(10)
            .children(
              startButton = ButtonBuilder.create()
                .text("Start")
                .onAction(new EventHandler<javafx.event.ActionEvent>() {
                  @Override public void handle(javafx.event.ActionEvent e) {
                    anim.playFromStart();
                  }
                })
```

```
                        .build(),
                  pauseButton = ButtonBuilder.create()
                    .text("Pause")
                    .onAction(new EventHandler<javafx.event.ActionEvent>() {
                      @Override public void handle(javafx.event.ActionEvent e) {
                        anim.pause();
                      }
                    })
                    .build(),
                  resumeButton = ButtonBuilder.create()
                    .text("Resume")
                    .onAction(new EventHandler<javafx.event.ActionEvent>() {
                      @Override public void handle(javafx.event.ActionEvent e) {
                        anim.play();
                      }
                    })
                    .build(),
                  stopButton = ButtonBuilder.create()
                    .text("Stop")
                    .onAction(new EventHandler<javafx.event.ActionEvent>() {
                      @Override public void handle(javafx.event.ActionEvent e) {
                        anim.stop();
                      }
                    })
                    .build()
                )
                .build()
            )
          .build()
        )
      .build();

    line.startXProperty().bind(startXVal);
    startButton.disableProperty().bind(anim.statusProperty()
            .isNotEqualTo(Animation.Status.STOPPED));
    pauseButton.disableProperty().bind(anim.statusProperty()
            .isNotEqualTo(Animation.Status.RUNNING));
    resumeButton.disableProperty().bind(anim.statusProperty()
            .isNotEqualTo(Animation.Status.PAUSED));
    stopButton.disableProperty().bind(anim.statusProperty()
            .isEqualTo(Animation.Status.STOPPED));

    stage.setScene(scene);
    stage.setTitle("Metronome 1");
    stage.show();
  }
}
```

Understanding the Timeline Class

The main purpose for the Timeline class is to provide the ability to change the values of properties in a gradual fashion over given periods of time. Take a look at the following snippet from Listing 2-5 to see the timeline being created, along with some of its commonly used properties.

```
DoubleProperty startXVal = new SimpleDoubleProperty(100.0);
```

...code omitted...

```
Timeline anim = TimelineBuilder.create()
  .autoReverse(true)
  .keyFrames(
    new KeyFrame(
      new Duration(0.0),
      new KeyValue(startXVal, 100.0)
    ),
    new KeyFrame(
      new Duration(1000.0),
      new KeyValue(startXVal, 300.0, Interpolator.LINEAR)
    )
  )
  .cycleCount(Timeline.INDEFINITE)
  .build();
```

...code omitted...

```
  line = LineBuilder.create()
    .startY(50)
    .endX(200)
    .endY(400)
    .strokeWidth(4)
    .stroke(Color.BLUE)
    .build(),
```

...code omitted...

```
  line.startXProperty().bind(startXVal);
```

Inserting Key Frames into the Timeline

Our timeline contains a collection of two KeyFrame instances. Using the KeyValue constructor, one of these instances assigns 100 to the startXVal property at the beginning of the timeline, and the other assigns 300 to the startXVal property when the timeline has been running for one second. Because the startX property of the Line is bound to the value of the startXVal property, the net result is that the top of the line moves 200 pixels horizontally over the course of one second.

In the second KeyFrame of the timeline, the KeyValue constructor is passed a third argument that specifies that the interpolation from 100 to 300 will occur in a linear fashion over the one-second duration. Other Interpolation constants include EASEIN, EASEOUT, and EASEBOTH. These cause the interpolation in a KeyFrame to be slower in the beginning, ending, or both, respectively.

Following are the other Timeline properties, inherited from the Animation class, used in this example:

- autoReverse, which we're initializing to true. This causes the timeline to automatically reverse when it reaches the last KeyFrame. When reversed, the interpolation goes from 300 to 100 over the course of one second.

- cycleCount, which we're initializing to Timeline.INDEFINITE. This causes the timeline to repeat indefinitely until stopped by the stop() method of the Timeline class.

Speaking of the methods of the Timeline class, now is a good time to show you how to control the timeline and monitor its state.

Controlling and Monitoring the Timeline

As you observed when using the Metronome1 program, clicking the buttons causes the animation to start, pause, resume, and stop. This in turn has an effect on the states of the animation (running, paused, or stopped). Those states are reflected in the buttons in the form of being enabled/disabled. The following snippet from Listing 2-5 shows how to start, pause, resume, and stop the timeline, as well as how to tell whether the timeline is running and/or paused.

```
startButton = ButtonBuilder.create()
  .text("Start")
  .onAction(new EventHandler<javafx.event.ActionEvent>() {
    @Override public void handle(javafx.event.ActionEvent e) {
      anim.playFromStart();
    }
  })
  .build(),
pauseButton = ButtonBuilder.create()
  .text("Pause")
  .onAction(new EventHandler<javafx.event.ActionEvent>() {
    @Override public void handle(javafx.event.ActionEvent e) {
      anim.pause();
    }
  })
  .build(),
resumeButton = ButtonBuilder.create()
  .text("Resume")
  .onAction(new EventHandler<javafx.event.ActionEvent>() {
    @Override public void handle(javafx.event.ActionEvent e) {
      anim.play();
    }
  })
```

```
        .build(),
   stopButton = ButtonBuilder.create()
    .text("Stop")
    .onAction(new FventHandler<javafx.event.ActionEvent>() {
      @Override public void handle(javafx.event.ActionEvent e) {
        anim.stop();
      }
    })
    .build()
```

...code omitted...

```
startButton.disableProperty().bind(anim.statusProperty()
        .isNotEqualTo(Animation.Status.STOPPED));
pauseButton.disableProperty().bind(anim.statusProperty()
        .isNotEqualTo(Animation.Status.RUNNING));
resumeButton.disableProperty().bind(anim.statusProperty()
        .isNotEqualTo(Animation.Status.PAUSED));
stopButton.disableProperty().bind(anim.statusProperty()
        .isEqualTo(Animation.Status.STOPPED));
```

As shown here in the action event handler of the Start button, the playFromStart() method of the Timeline instance is called, which begins playing the timeline from the beginning. In addition, the disable property of that Button is bound to an expression that evaluates whether the status property of the timeline is not equal to Animation.Status.STOPPED. This causes the button to be disabled when the timeline is not stopped (in which case it must be either running or paused).

When the user clicks the Pause button, the action event handler calls the timeline's pause() method, which pauses the animation. The disable property of that Button is bound to an expression that evaluates whether the timeline is not running.

The Resume button is only disabled when the timeline is not paused. To resume the timeline from where it was paused, the action event handler calls the play() method of the timeline.

Finally, the Stop button is disabled when the timeline is stopped. To stop the timeline, the action event handler calls the stop() method of the timeline.

Now that you know how to animate nodes by creating a Timeline class and creating KeyFrame instances, it's time to learn how to use the transition classes to animate nodes.

Using the Transition Classes for Animation

The javafx.transition package contains several classes whose purpose is to provide convenient ways to do commonly used animation tasks. For example, Table 2-1 contains a list of transition classes in that package.

71

Table 2-1. *Transition Classes in the javafx.transition Package for Animating Nodes*

Transition Class Name	Description
TranslateTransition	Translates (moves) a node from one location to another over a given period of time. This was employed in the Hello Earthrise example program in Chapter 1.
RotateTransition	Rotates a node over a given period of time.
ScaleTransition	Scales (increases or decreases the size of) a node over a given period of time.
FadeTransition	Fades (increases or decreases the opacity of) a node over a given period of time.
FillTransition	Changes the fill of a shape over a given period of time.
StrokeTransition	Changes the stroke color of a shape over a given period of time.
PauseTransition	Executes an action at the end of its duration; designed mainly to be used in a SequentialTransition as a means to wait for a period of time.
SequentialTransition	Allows you to define a series of transitions that execute sequentially.
ParallelTransition	Allows you to define a series of transitions that execute in parallel.

Let's take a look at a variation on the metronome theme in which we create a metronome using TranslateTransition for the animation.

The MetronomeTransition Example

When using the transition classes, we take a different approach toward animation than when using the Timeline class directly:

- In the timeline-based Metronome1 program, we bound a property of a node (specifically, startX) to a property in the model (startXVal), and then used the timeline to interpolate the value of the property in the model.

- When using a transition class, however, we assign values to the properties of the Transition subclass, one of which is a node. The net result is that the node itself is affected, rather than just a bound attribute of the node being affected.

The distinction between these two approaches becomes clear as we walk through the MetronomeTransition example. Figure 2-9 shows a screenshot of this program when it is first invoked.

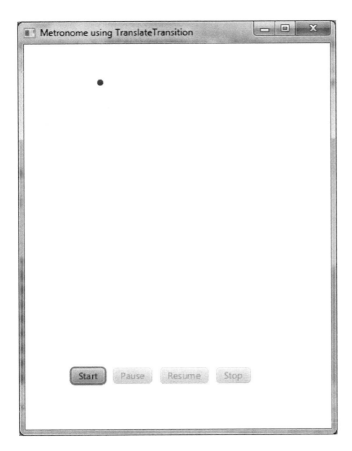

Figure 2-9. *The MetronomeTransition program*

The first noticeable difference between this example and the previous (Metronome1) example is that instead of one end of a line moving back and forth, we're going to make a Circle node move back and forth.

The Behavior of the MetronomeTransition Program

Go ahead and run the program, and perform the same steps that you did in the previous "Examining the Behavior of the Metronome1 Program" exercise. Everything should function the same, except for the visual difference pointed out previously.

Understanding the MetronomeTransition Program

Take a look at the code for the MetronomeTransition program in Listing 2-6, and then we point out relevant concepts.

Listing 2-6. *MetronomeTransitionMain.fx*

```
package projavafx.metronometransition.ui;

import javafx.animation.Animation;
import javafx.animation.Interpolator;
import javafx.animation.Timeline;
import javafx.animation.TranslateTransition;
import javafx.animation.TranslateTransitionBuilder;
import javafx.application.Application;
import javafx.event.EventHandler;
import javafx.scene.GroupBuilder;
import javafx.scene.Scene;
import javafx.scene.SceneBuilder;
import javafx.scene.control.Button;
import javafx.scene.control.ButtonBuilder;
import javafx.scene.layout.HBoxBuilder;
import javafx.scene.paint.Color;
import javafx.scene.shape.Circle;
import javafx.scene.shape.CircleBuilder;
import javafx.stage.Stage;
import javafx.util.Duration;

public class MetronomeTransitionMain extends Application {
  Button startButton;
  Button pauseButton;
  Button resumeButton;
  Button stopButton;
  Circle circle = CircleBuilder.create()
    .centerX(100)
    .centerY(50)
    .radius(4)
    .fill(Color.BLUE)
    .build();

  TranslateTransition anim = TranslateTransitionBuilder.create()
    .duration(new Duration(1000.0))
    .node(circle)
    .fromX(0)
    .toX(200)
    .interpolator(Interpolator.LINEAR)
    .autoReverse(true)
    .cycleCount(Timeline.INDEFINITE)
    .build();

  public static void main(String[] args) {
    Application.launch(args);
  }
```

```java
@Override
public void start(Stage stage) {
  Scene scene  = SceneBuilder.create()
    .width(400)
    .height(500)
    .root(
      GroupBuilder.create()
        .children(
          circle,
          HBoxBuilder.create()
            .layoutX(60)
            .layoutY(420)
            .spacing(10)
            .children(
              startButton = ButtonBuilder.create()
                .text("Start")
                .onAction(new EventHandler<javafx.event.ActionEvent>() {
                  @Override public void handle(javafx.event.ActionEvent e) {
                    anim.playFromStart();
                  }
                })
                .build(),
              pauseButton = ButtonBuilder.create()
                .text("Pause")
                .onAction(new EventHandler<javafx.event.ActionEvent>() {
                  @Override public void handle(javafx.event.ActionEvent e) {
                    anim.pause();
                  }
                })
                .build(),
              resumeButton = ButtonBuilder.create()
                .text("Resume")
                .onAction(new EventHandler<javafx.event.ActionEvent>() {
                  @Override public void handle(javafx.event.ActionEvent e) {
                    anim.play();
                  }
                })
                .build(),
              stopButton = ButtonBuilder.create()
                .text("Stop")
                .onAction(new EventHandler<javafx.event.ActionEvent>() {
                  @Override public void handle(javafx.event.ActionEvent e) {
                    anim.stop();
                  }
                })
                .build()
            )
            .build()
        )
        .build()
    )
    .build();
```

```
    startButton.disableProperty().bind(anim.statusProperty()
            .isNotEqualTo(Animation.Status.STOPPED));
    pauseButton.disableProperty().bind(anim.statusProperty()
            .isNotEqualTo(Animation.Status.RUNNING));
    resumeButton.disableProperty().bind(anim.statusProperty()
            .isNotEqualTo(Animation.Status.PAUSED));
    stopButton.disableProperty().bind(anim.statusProperty()
            .isEqualTo(Animation.Status.STOPPED));

    stage.setScene(scene);
    stage.setTitle("Metronome using TranslateTransition");
    stage.show();
  }
}
```

Using the TranslateTransition Class

As shown in the following snippet from Listing 2-6, to create a TranslateTransition we're supplying values that are reminiscent of the values that we used when creating a timeline in the previous example. For example, we're setting autoReverse to true and cycleCount to Timeline.INDEFINITE. Also, just as when creating a KeyFrame for a timeline, we're supplying a duration and an interpolation type here as well.

In addition, we're supplying some values to properties that are specific to a TranslateTransition, namely fromX and toX. These values are interpolated over the requested duration and assigned to the layoutX property of the node controlled by the transition (in this case, the circle). If we also wanted to cause vertical movement, assigning values to fromY and toY would cause interpolated values between them to be assigned to the layoutY property.

An alternative to supplying toX and toY values is to provide values to the byX and byY properties, which enables you to specify the distance to travel in each direction rather than start and end points. Also, if you don't supply a value for fromX, the interpolation will begin with the current value of the node's layoutX property. The same holds true for fromY (if not supplied, the interpolation will begin with the value of layoutY).

```
Circle circle = CircleBuilder.create()
   .centerX(100)
   .centerY(50)
   .radius(4)
   .fill(Color.BLUE)
   .build();

TranslateTransition anim = TranslateTransitionBuilder.create()
   .duration(new Duration(1000.0))
   .node(circle)
   .fromX(0)
   .toX(200)
   .interpolator(Interpolator.LINEAR)
   .autoReverse(true)
   .cycleCount(Timeline.INDEFINITE)
   .build();
```

Controlling and Monitoring the Transition

The TranslateTransition class, as do all of the classes in Table 2-1 earlier, extends the javafx.animation.Transition class, which in turn extends the Animation class. Because the Timeline class extends the Animation class, as you can see by comparing Listings 2-5 and 2-6, all of the code for the buttons in this example are identical to that in the previous example.

The MetronomePathTransition Example

As shown in Table 2-1 earlier, PathTransition is a transition class that enables you to move a node along a defined geometric path. Figure 2-10 shows a screenshot of a version of the metronome example, named MetronomePathTransition, that demonstrates how to use the PathTransition class.

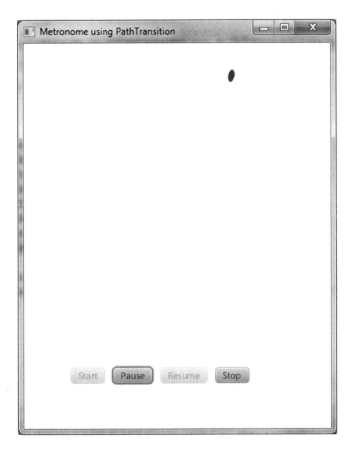

Figure 2-10. *The MetronomePathTransition program*

The Behavior of the MetronomePathTransition Program

Go ahead and run the program, performing once again the same steps that you did in the "Examining the Behavior of the Metronome1 Program" exercise. Everything should function the same as it did in the MetronomeTransition example, except that the node is an ellipse instead of a circle, and the node moves along the path of an arc.

Understanding the MetronomePathTransition Program

Listing 2-7 contains code snippets from the MetronomePathTransition program that highlight the differences from the preceding (MetronomeTransition) program. Take a look at the code, and we point out relevant concepts.

Listing 2-7. Portions of MetronomePathTransitionMain.java

```
package projavafx.metronomepathtransition.ui;
...imports omitted...
public class MetronomePathTransitionMain extends Application {
  Button startButton;
  Button pauseButton;
  Button resumeButton;
  Button stopButton;
  Ellipse ellipse = EllipseBuilder.create()
    .centerX(100)
    .centerY(50)
    .radiusX(4)
    .radiusY(8)
    .fill(Color.BLUE)
    .build();

  Path path = PathBuilder.create()
    .elements(
      new MoveTo(100, 50),
      ArcToBuilder.create()
        .x(300)
        .y(50)
        .radiusX(350)
        .radiusY(350)
        .sweepFlag(true)
        .build()
    )
    .build();

  PathTransition anim = PathTransitionBuilder.create()
    .duration(new Duration(1000.0))
    .node(ellipse)
    .path(path)
    .orientation(OrientationType.ORTHOGONAL_TO_TANGENT)
    .interpolator(Interpolator.LINEAR)
    .autoReverse(true)
```

```
      .cycleCount(Timeline.INDEFINITE)
      .build();

  public static void main(String[] args) {
    Application.launch(args);
  }

  @Override
  public void start(Stage stage) {
    Scene scene  = SceneBuilder.create()
      .width(400)
      .height(500)
      .root(
        GroupBuilder.create()
          .children(
            ellipse,
            ...HBox and Button instances omitted...
          )
          .build()
      )
      .build();
    ...property bindings omitted...
    stage.setScene(scene);
    stage.setTitle("Metronome using PathTransition");
    stage.show();
  }
}
```

Using the PathTransition Class

As shown in Listing 2-7, defining a PathTransition includes supplying an instance of type Path to the path property that represents the geometric path that the node is to travel. Here we're creating a Path instance that defines an arc beginning at 100 pixels on the x axis and 50 pixels on the y axis, ending at 300 pixels on the x axis and 50 pixels on the y axis, with 350 pixel horizontal and vertical radii. This is accomplished by using the PathBuilder to create elements in the Path that contain the MoveTo and ArcTo path elements shown previously. Take a look at the javafx.scene.shapes package in the JavaFX API docs for more information on the PathElement class and its subclasses, which are used for creating a path.

■ **Tip**   The properties in the ArcTo class are fairly intuitive except for sweepFlag. If sweepFlag is true, the line joining the center of the arc to the arc itself sweeps through increasing angles. Otherwise, it sweeps through decreasing angles.

Another property of the PathTransition class is orientation, which controls whether the node's orientation remains unchanged or stays perpendicular to the path's tangent as it moves along the path. Listing 2-7 uses the OrientationType.ORTHOGONAL_TO_TANGENT constant to accomplish the latter, as the former is the default.

Drawing an Ellipse

As shown in Listing 2-7, drawing an Ellipse is similar to drawing a Circle, the difference being that an additional radius is required (radiusX and radiusY instead of just radius).

Now that you've learned how to animate nodes by creating a timeline and by creating transitions, we create a very simple Pong-style game that requires animating a ping-pong ball. In the process, you learn how to detect when the ball has hit a paddle or wall in the game.

The Zen of Node Collision Detection

When animating a node, you sometimes need to know when the node has collided with another node. To demonstrate this capability, our colleague Chris Wright developed a simple version of the Pong-style game that we call ZenPong. Originally we asked him to build the game with only one paddle, which brought the famous Zen koan (philosophical riddle), "What is the sound of one hand clapping," to mind. Chris had so much fun developing the game that he snuck a second paddle in, but we're still calling this example ZenPong. Figure 2-11 shows this very simple form of the game when first invoked.

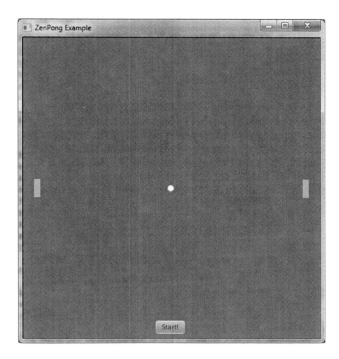

Figure 2-11. *The initial state of the ZenPong game*

Try out the game by following the instructions in the upcoming exercise, remembering that you control both paddles (unless you can get a colleague to share your keyboard and play).

EXAMINING THE BEHAVIOR OF THE ZENPONG GAME

When the program starts, its appearance should be similar to the screenshot in Figure 2-11. To fully examine its behavior, perform the following steps.

1. Before clicking the Start button, drag each of the paddles vertically to other positions. One game cheat is to drag the left paddle up and the right paddle down, which will put them in good positions to respond to the ball after being served.

2. Practice using the A key to move the left paddle up, the Z key to move the left paddle down, the L key to move the right paddle up, and the comma (,) key to move the right paddle down.

3. Click the Start button to begin playing the game. Notice that the Start button disappears and the ball begins moving at a 45° angle, bouncing off paddles and the top and bottom walls. The screen should look similar to Figure 2-12.

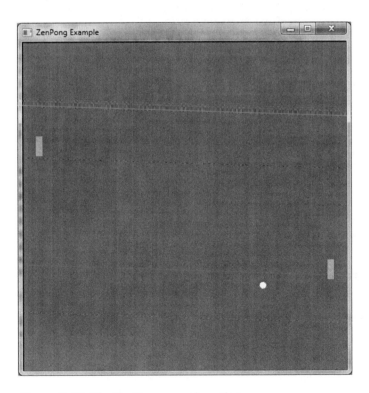

Figure 2-12. *The ZenPong game in action*

4. If the ball hits the left or right wall, one of your hands has lost the game. Notice that the game resets, looking again like the screenshot in Figure 2-11.

Now that you've experienced the behavior of the ZenPong program, we walk through the code behind it.

Understanding the ZenPong Program

Examine the code for the ZenPong program in Listing 2-8, and then we highlight some concepts demonstrated within.

Listing 2-8. ZenPongMain.java

```java
package projavafx.zenpong.ui;
...imports omitted...
public class ZenPongMain extends Application {
  /**
   * The center points of the moving ball
   */
  DoubleProperty centerX = new SimpleDoubleProperty();
  DoubleProperty centerY = new SimpleDoubleProperty();

  /**
   * The Y coordinate of the left paddle
   */
  DoubleProperty leftPaddleY = new SimpleDoubleProperty();

  /**
   * The Y coordinate of the right paddle
   */
  DoubleProperty rightPaddleY = new SimpleDoubleProperty();

  /**
   * The drag anchor for left and right paddles
   */
  double leftPaddleDragAnchorY;
  double rightPaddleDragAnchorY;

  /**
   * The initial translateY property for the left and right paddles
   */
  double initLeftPaddleTranslateY;
  double initRightPaddleTranslateY;
```

```java
/**
 * The moving ball
 */
Circle ball;

/**
 * The Group containing all of the walls, paddles, and ball.  This also allows
 * us to requestFocus for KeyEvents on the Group
 */
Group pongComponents;

/**
 * The left and right paddles
 */
Rectangle leftPaddle;
Rectangle rightPaddle;

/**
 * The walls
 */
Rectangle topWall;
Rectangle rightWall;
Rectangle leftWall;
Rectangle bottomWall;

Button startButton;

/**
 * Controls whether the startButton is visible
 */
BooleanProperty startVisible = new SimpleBooleanProperty(true);

/**
 * The animation of the ball
 */
Timeline pongAnimation = TimelineBuilder.create()
  .keyFrames(
    new KeyFrame(
      new Duration(10.0),
      new EventHandler<ActionEvent>() {
        public void handle(javafx.event.ActionEvent t) {
          checkForCollision();
          int horzPixels = movingRight ? 1 : -1;
          int vertPixels = movingDown ? 1 : -1;
          centerX.setValue(centerX.getValue() + horzPixels);
          centerY.setValue(centerY.getValue() + vertPixels);
        }
      }
    )
  )
```

```java
    .cycleCount(Timeline.INDEFINITE)
    .build();

/**
 * Controls whether the ball is moving right
 */
boolean movingRight = true;

/**
 * Controls whether the ball is moving down
 */
boolean movingDown = true;

/**
 * Sets the initial starting positions of the ball and paddles
 */
void initialize() {
  centerX.setValue(250);
  centerY.setValue(250);
  leftPaddleY.setValue(235);
  rightPaddleY.setValue(235);
  startVisible.set(true);
  pongComponents.requestFocus();
}

/**
 * Checks whether or not the ball has collided with either the paddles,
 * topWall, or bottomWall.  If the ball hits the wall behind the paddles,
 * the game is over.
 */
void checkForCollision() {
  if (ball.intersects(rightWall.getBoundsInLocal()) ||
      ball.intersects(leftWall.getBoundsInLocal())) {
    pongAnimation.stop();
    initialize();
  }
  else if (ball.intersects(bottomWall.getBoundsInLocal()) ||
           ball.intersects(topWall.getBoundsInLocal())) {
    movingDown = !movingDown;
  }
  else if (ball.intersects(leftPaddle.getBoundsInParent()) && !movingRight) {
    movingRight = !movingRight;
  }
  else if (ball.intersects(rightPaddle.getBoundsInParent()) && movingRight) {
    movingRight = !movingRight;
  }
}
```

```java
/**
 * @param args the command line arguments
 */
public static void main(String[] args) {
  Application.launch(args);
}

@Override
public void start(Stage stage) {
  Scene scene  = SceneBuilder.create()
    .width(500)
    .height(500)
    .fill(
      LinearGradientBuilder.create()
        .startX(0.0)
        .startY(0.0)
        .endX(0.0)
        .endY(1.0)
        .stops(
          new Stop(0.0, Color.BLACK),
          new Stop(0.0, Color.GRAY)
          )
        .build()
    )
    .root(
      pongComponents = GroupBuilder.create()
        .focusTraversable(true)
        .children(
          ball = CircleBuilder.create()
            .radius(5.0)
            .fill(Color.WHITE)
            .build(),
          topWall = RectangleBuilder.create()
            .x(0)
            .y(0)
            .width(500)
            .height(1)
            .build(),
          leftWall = RectangleBuilder.create()
            .x(0)
            .y(0)
            .width(1)
            .height(500)
            .build(),
          rightWall = RectangleBuilder.create()
            .x(500)
            .y(0)
            .width(1)
            .height(500)
            .build(),
```

85

```java
        bottomWall = RectangleBuilder.create()
          .x(0)
          .y(500)
          .width(500)
          .height(1)
          .build(),
        leftPaddle = RectangleBuilder.create()
          .x(20)
          .width(10)
          .height(30)
          .fill(Color.LIGHTBLUE)
          .cursor(Cursor.HAND)
          .onMousePressed(new EventHandler<MouseEvent>() {
            public void handle(MouseEvent me) {
              initLeftPaddleTranslateY = leftPaddle.getTranslateY();
              leftPaddleDragAnchorY = me.getSceneY();
            }
          })
          .onMouseDragged(new EventHandler<MouseEvent>() {
            public void handle(MouseEvent me) {
              double dragY = me.getSceneY() - leftPaddleDragAnchorY;
              leftPaddleY.setValue(initLeftPaddleTranslateY + dragY);
            }
          })
          .build(),
        rightPaddle = RectangleBuilder.create()
          .x(470)
          .width(10)
          .height(30)
          .fill(Color.LIGHTBLUE)
          .cursor(Cursor.HAND)
          .onMousePressed(new EventHandler<MouseEvent>() {
            public void handle(MouseEvent me) {
              initRightPaddleTranslateY = rightPaddle.getTranslateY();
              rightPaddleDragAnchorY = me.getSceneY();
            }
          })
          .onMouseDragged(new EventHandler<MouseEvent>() {
            public void handle(MouseEvent me) {
              double dragY = me.getSceneY() - rightPaddleDragAnchorY;
              rightPaddleY.setValue(initRightPaddleTranslateY + dragY);
            }
          })
          .build(),
        startButton = ButtonBuilder.create()
          .layoutX(225)
          .layoutY(470)
          .text("Start!")
          .onAction(new EventHandler<javafx.event.ActionEvent>() {
            @Override public void handle(javafx.event.ActionEvent e) {
              startVisible.set(false);
              pongAnimation.playFromStart();
```

```
                         pongComponents.requestFocus();
                     }
                 })
               .build()
          )
          .onKeyPressed(new EventHandler<KeyEvent>() {
            @Override public void handle(KeyEvent k) {
              if (k.getCode() == KeyCode.SPACE &&
                  pongAnimation.statusProperty()
                      .equals(Animation.Status.STOPPED)) {
                rightPaddleY.setValue(rightPaddleY.getValue() - 6);
              }
              else if (k.getCode() == KeyCode.L &&
                  !rightPaddle.getBoundsInParent().intersects(topWall.getBoundsInLocal())) {
                rightPaddleY.setValue(rightPaddleY.getValue() - 6);
              }
              else if (k.getCode() == KeyCode.COMMA &&
                  !rightPaddle.getBoundsInParent().intersects(bottomWall.getBoundsInLocal()))
{
                rightPaddleY.setValue(rightPaddleY.getValue() + 6);
              }
              else if (k.getCode() == KeyCode.A &&
                  !leftPaddle.getBoundsInParent().intersects(topWall.getBoundsInLocal())) {
                leftPaddleY.setValue(leftPaddleY.getValue() - 6);
              }
              else if (k.getCode() == KeyCode.Z &&
                  !leftPaddle.getBoundsInParent().intersects(bottomWall.getBoundsInLocal())) {
                leftPaddleY.setValue(leftPaddleY.getValue() + 6);
              }
            }
          })
        .build()
    )
  .build();

ball.centerXProperty().bind(centerX);
ball.centerYProperty().bind(centerY);
leftPaddle.translateYProperty().bind(leftPaddleY);
rightPaddle.translateYProperty().bind(rightPaddleY);
startButton.visibleProperty().bind(startVisible);

stage.setScene(scene);
initialize();
stage.setTitle("ZenPong Example");
stage.show();
  }
}
```

Using the KeyFrame Action Event Handler

We're using a different technique in the timeline than demonstrated in the Metronome1 program earlier in the chapter (see Figure 2-8 and Listing 2-5). Instead of interpolating two values over a period of time, we're using the action event handler of the KeyFrame instance in our timeline. Take a look at the following snippet from Listing 2-8 to see this technique in use.

```
Timeline pongAnimation = TimelineBuilder.create()
  .keyFrames(
    new KeyFrame(
      new Duration(10.0),
      new EventHandler<ActionEvent>() {
        public void handle(javafx.event.ActionEvent t) {
          checkForCollision();
          int horzPixels = movingRight ? 1 : -1;
          int vertPixels = movingDown ? 1 : -1;
          centerX.setValue(centerX.getValue() + horzPixels);
          centerY.setValue(centerY.getValue() + vertPixels);
        }
      }
    )
  )
  .cycleCount(Timeline.INDEFINITE)
  .build();
```

As shown in the snippet, we use only one KeyFrame, and it has a very short time (10 milliseconds). When a KeyFrame has an action event handler, the code in that handler is executed when the time for that KeyFrame is reached. Because the cycleCount of this timeline is indefinite, the action event handler will be executed every 10 milliseconds. The code in this event handler does two things:

- Calls a method named checkForCollision() which is defined in this program, whose purpose is to see whether the ball has collided with either paddle or any of the walls

- Updates the properties in the model to which the position of the ball is bound, taking into account the direction in which the ball is already moving

Using the Node intersects() Method to Detect Collisions

Take a look inside the checkForCollision() method in the following snippet from Listing 2-8 to see how we check for collisions by detecting when two nodes intersect (share any of the same pixels).

```
void checkForCollision() {
  if (ball.intersects(rightWall.getBoundsInLocal()) ||
      ball.intersects(leftWall.getBoundsInLocal())) {
    pongAnimation.stop();
    initialize();
  }
  else if (ball.intersects(bottomWall.getBoundsInLocal()) ||
           ball.intersects(topWall.getBoundsInLocal())) {
    movingDown = !movingDown;
  }
```

```
    else if (ball.intersects(leftPaddle.getBoundsInParent()) && !movingRight) {
      movingRight = !movingRight;
    }
    else if (ball.intersects(rightPaddle.getBoundsInParent()) && movingRight) {
      movingRight = !movingRight;
    }
}
```

The intersects() method of the Node class shown here takes an argument of type Bounds, located in the javafx.geometry package. It represents the rectangular bounds of a node, for example, the leftPaddle node shown in the preceding code snippet. Notice that to get the position of the left paddle in the Group that contains it, we're using the boundsInParent property that the leftPaddle (a Rectangle) inherited from the Node class.

The net results of the intersect method invocations in the preceding snippet are as follows.

- If the ball intersects with the bounds of the rightWall or leftWall, the pongAnimation Timeline is stopped and the game is initialized for the next play. Note that the rightWall and left Wall nodes are one-pixel-wide rectangles on the left and right sides of the Scene. Take a peek at Listing 2-8 to see where these are defined.

- If the ball intersects with the bounds of the bottomWall or topWall, the vertical direction of the ball will be changed by negating the program's Boolean movingDown variable.

- If the ball intersects with the bounds of the leftPaddle or rightPaddle, the horizontal direction of the ball will be changed by negating the program's Boolean movingRight variable.

■ **Tip**   For more information on boundsInParent and its related properties, layoutBounds and boundsInLocal, see the "Bounding Rectangles" discussion at the beginning of the javafx.scene.Node class in the JavaFX API docs. For example, it is a common practice to find out the width or height of a node by using the expression myNode.getLayoutBounds().getWidth() or myNode.getLayoutBounds().getHeight().

Dragging a Node

As you experienced previously, the paddles of the ZenPong application may be dragged with the mouse. The following snippet from Listing 2-8 shows how this capability is implemented in ZenPong.

```
DoubleProperty rightPaddleY = new SimpleDoubleProperty();
...code omitted...
double rightPaddleDragStartY;
double rightPaddleDragAnchorY;
...code omitted...
void initialize() {
  centerX.setValue(250);
  centerY.setValue(250);
```

```
      leftPaddleY.setValue(235);
      rightPaddleY.setValue(235);
      startVisible.set(true);
      pongComponents.requestFocus();
    }
    ...code omitted...
    rightPaddle = RectangleBuilder.create()
      .x(470)
      .width(10)
      .height(30)
      .fill(Color.LIGHTBLUE)
      .cursor(Cursor.HAND)
      .onMousePressed(new EventHandler<MouseEvent>() {
        public void handle(MouseEvent me) {
          initRightPaddleTranslateY =  rightPaddle.getTranslateY();
          rightPaddleDragAnchorY = me.getSceneY();
        }
      })
      .onMouseDragged(new EventHandler<MouseEvent>() {
        public void handle(MouseEvent me) {
          double dragY = me.getSceneY() - rightPaddleDragAnchorY;
          rightPaddleY.setValue(initRightPaddleTranslateY + dragY);
        }
      })
      .build(),
```

Note that in this ZenPong example, we're dragging the paddles only vertically, not horizontally Therefore, the code snippet only deals with dragging on the y axis.

Giving Keyboard Input Focus to a Node

In order for a node to receive key events, it has to have keyboard focus. This is accomplished in the ZenPong example by doing these two things, as shown in the snippet below from Listing 2-8:

- Assigning true to the focusTraversable property of the Group node. This allows the node to accept keyboard focus.

- Calling the requestFocus() method of the Group node (referred to by the pongComponents variable). This requests that the node obtain focus.

■ **Tip**   You cannot directly set the value of the focused property of a Stage. Consulting the API docs also reveals that neither can you set the value of the focused property of a Node (e.g., the Group that we're discussing now). However, as discussed in the second bullet point above, you can call requestFocus() on the node, which if granted (and focusTraversable is true) sets the focused property to true. By the way, Stage doesn't have a requestFocus() method, but it does have a toFront() method, which should give it keyboard focus.

```
...code omitted...
        pongComponents = GroupBuilder.create()
          .focusTraversable(true)
        ...code omitted...
        pongComponents.requestFocus();
        ...code omitted...
          .onKeyPressed(new EventHandler<KeyEvent>() {
            @Override public void handle(KeyEvent k) {
              if (k.getCode() == KeyCode.SPACE &&
                  pongAnimation.statusProperty()
                      .equals(Animation.Status.STOPPED)) {
                rightPaddleY.setValue(rightPaddleY.getValue() - 6);
              }
              else if (k.getCode() == KeyCode.L &&
                  !rightPaddle.getBoundsInParent().intersects(topWall.getBoundsInLocal())) {
                rightPaddleY.setValue(rightPaddleY.getValue() - 6);
              }
              else if (k.getCode() == KeyCode.COMMA &&
                  !rightPaddle.getBoundsInParent().intersects(bottomWall↩
.getBoundsInLocal())) {
                rightPaddleY.setValue(rightPaddleY.getValue() + 6);
              }
              else if (k.getCode() == KeyCode.A &&
                  !leftPaddle.getBoundsInParent().intersects(topWall.getBoundsInLocal())) {
                leftPaddleY.setValue(leftPaddleY.getValue() - 6);
              }
              else if (k.getCode() == KeyCode.Z &&
                  !leftPaddle.getBoundsInParent().intersects(bottomWall.getBoundsInLocal())) {
                leftPaddleY.setValue(leftPaddleY.getValue() + 6);
              }
            }
          }
        })
```

Now that the node has focus, when the user interacts with the keyboard, the appropriate event handlers will be invoked. In this example, we're interested in whenever certain keys are pressed, as discussed next.

Using the onKeyPressed Event Handler

When the user presses a key, the handle() method of the anonymous class supplied to the onKeyPressed method is invoked, passing a KeyEvent instance that contains information about the event. This handle method, shown in the preceding snippet from Listing 2-8, compares the getCode() method of the KeyEvent instance to the KeyCode constants that represent the arrow keys to ascertain which key was pressed.

Summary

Congratulations, you have learned a lot in this chapter about creating UIs in JavaFX, including the following.

- Creating a user interface in JavaFX, which we loosely based on the metaphor of creating a theater play and typically consists of creating a stage, a scene, nodes, a model, and event handlers, and animating some of the nodes

- The details about using most of the properties and methods of the Stage class, including how to create a Stage that is transparent with no window decorations

- How to use the HBox and VBox layout containers to organize nodes horizontally and vertically, respectively

- The details about using many of the properties and methods of the Scene class

- How to create and apply CSS styles to nodes in your program by associating one or more style sheets with the Scene

- How to handle keyboard and mouse input events

- How to animate nodes in the scene, both with the Timeline class and the transition classes

- How to detect when nodes in the scene have collided

Now that you have learned more about JavaFX user interface development, it is time to move on to Chapter 3 to take a deeper dive into the areas of Properties and Binding.

Resources

For some additional information on creating JavaFX user interfaces, you can consult the following resources.

- JavaFX 2.0 SDK documentation online: `http://download.oracle.com/javafx/2.0/api/index.html`

- JavaFX 2.0 CSS Reference Guide: `http://download.oracle.com/javafx/2.0/api/javafx/scene/doc-files/cssref.html`

- The w3schools.com CSS Tutorial: `http://www.w3schools.com/css`

CHAPTER 3

Properties and Bindings

Heaven acts with vitality and persistence.
In correspondence with this
The superior person keeps himself vital without ceasing.

—I Ching

In Chapters 1 and 2, we introduced you to the JavaFX 2.0 platform. You downloaded the JavaFX 2.0 SDK and the JavaFX plugin for Netbeans. You wrote and ran your first JavaFX 2.0 GUI programs. You learned the fundamental building blocks of JavaFX 2.0: the Stage and Scene classes, and the Nodes that go into the Scene. And you have no doubt noticed the use of user-defined model classes to represent the application state and have that state communicated to the UI through properties and bindings.

In this chapter, we give you a guided tour of the JavaFX 2.0 properties and bindings framework. After recalling a little bit of history and presenting a motivating example that shows various ways that a JavaFX 2.0 Property can be used, we cover key concepts of the framework: Observable, ObservableValue, WritableValue, ReadOnlyProperty, Property, and Binding. We show you the capabilities offered by these fundamental interfaces of the framework. We then show you how Property objects are bound together, how Binding objects are built out of properties and other bindings—using the factory methods in the Bindings utility class, the fluent interface API, or going low-level by directly extending abstract classes that implement the Binding interface—and how they are used to easily propagate changes in one part of a program to other parts of the program without too much coding. We finish this chapter by introducing the JavaFX Beans naming convention, an extension of the original JavaBeans naming convention that makes organizing your data into encapsulated components an orderly affair.

Because the JavaFX 2.0 properties and bindings framework is a nonvisual part of the JavaFX 2.0 platform, the example programs in this chapter are also nonvisual in nature. We deal with Boolean, Integer, Long, Float, Double, String, and Object typed properties and bindings as these are the types in which the JavaFX 2.0 binding framework specializes. Your GUI building fun resumes in the next and further chapters.

Forerunners of JavaFX 2.0 Binding

The need for exposing attributes of Java components directly to client code, allowing them to observe and to manipulate such attributes and to take action when their values change, is recognized early in Java's life. The JavaBeans framework in Java 1.1 provided support for properties through the now familiar getter and setter convention. It also supported the propagations of property changes through its

PropertyChangeEvent and PropertyChangeListener mechanism. Although the JavaBeans framework is used in many Swing applications, its use is quite cumbersome and requires quite a bit of boilerplate code. Several higher-level data binding frameworks were created over the years with various levels of success. The heritage of the JavaBeans in the JavaFX 2.0 properties and bindings framework lies mainly in the JavaFX Beans getter, setter, and property getter naming convention when defining JavaFX 2.0 components. We talk about the JavaFX Beans getter, setter, and property getter naming convention later in this chapter, after we have covered the key concepts and interfaces of the JavaFX 2.0 properties and bindings framework.

Another strand of heritage of the JavaFX 2.0 properties and bindings framework comes from the JavaFX Script language that was part of the JavaFX 1.x platform. Although the JavaFX Script language was deprecated in the JavaFX 2.0 platform in favor of a Java-based API, one of the goals of the transition was to preserve most of the powers of the JavaFX Script's bind keyword, whose expressive power has delighted many JavaFX enthusiasts. As an example, JavaFX Script supports the binding to complex expressions:

```
var a = 1;
var b = 10;
var m = 4;
def c = bind for (x in [a..b] where x < m) { x * x };
```

This code will automatically recalculate the value of c whenever the values of a, b, or m are changed.

Although the JavaFX 2.0 properties and bindings framework does not support all of the binding constructs of JavaFX Script, it supports the binding of many useful expressions. We talk more about constructing compound binding expressions after we cover the key concepts and interfaces of the framework.

A Motivating Example

Let's start with an example that shows off the capabilities of the Property interface through the use of a couple of instances of the SimpleIntegerProperty class.

Listing 3-1. *MotivatingExample.java*

```java
import javafx.beans.InvalidationListener;
import javafx.beans.Observable;
import javafx.beans.property.IntegerProperty;
import javafx.beans.property.SimpleIntegerProperty;
import javafx.beans.value.ChangeListener;
import javafx.beans.value.ObservableValue;

public class MotivatingExample {
    private static IntegerProperty intProperty;

    public static void main(String[] args) {
        createProperty();
        addAndRemoveInvalidationListener();
        addAndRemoveChangeListener();
        bindAndUnbindOnePropertyToAnother();
    }
```

```java
    private static void createProperty() {
        System.out.println();
        intProperty = new SimpleIntegerProperty(1024);
        System.out.println("intProperty = " + intProperty);
        System.out.println("intProperty.get() = " + intProperty.get());
        System.out.println("intProperty.getValue() = " + intProperty.getValue().intValue());
    }

    private static void addAndRemoveInvalidationListener() {
        System.out.println();
        final InvalidationListener invalidationListener =
                new InvalidationListener() {
                    @Override
                    public void invalidated(Observable observable) {
                        System.out.println("The observable has been invalidated: " +↵
observable + ".");
                    }
                };

        intProperty.addListener(invalidationListener);
        System.out.println("Added invalidation listener.");

        System.out.println("Calling intProperty.set(2048).");
        intProperty.set(2048);

        System.out.println("Calling intProperty.setValue(3072).");
        intProperty.setValue(Integer.valueOf(3072));

        intProperty.removeListener(invalidationListener);
        System.out.println("Removed invalidation listener.");

        System.out.println("Calling intProperty.set(4096).");
        intProperty.set(4096);
    }

    private static void addAndRemoveChangeListener() {
        System.out.println();
        final ChangeListener changeListener = new ChangeListener() {
            @Override
            public void changed(ObservableValue observableValue, Object oldValue, Object↵
newValue) {
                System.out.println("The observableValue has changed: oldValue = " +↵
oldValue + ", newValue = " + newValue);
            }
        };

        intProperty.addListener(changeListener);
        System.out.println("Added change listener.");

        System.out.println("Calling intProperty.set(5120).");
        intProperty.set(5120);
```

```
            intProperty.removeListener(changeListener);
            System.out.println("Removed change listener.");

            System.out.println("Calling intProperty.set(6144).");
            intProperty.set(6144);
        }

    private static void bindAndUnbindOnePropertyToAnother() {
        System.out.println();
        IntegerProperty otherProperty = new SimpleIntegerProperty(0);
        System.out.println("otherProperty.get() = " + otherProperty.get());

        System.out.println("Binding otherProperty to intProperty.");
        otherProperty.bind(intProperty);
        System.out.println("otherProperty.get() = " + otherProperty.get());

        System.out.println("Calling intProperty.set(7168).");
        intProperty.set(7168);
        System.out.println("otherProperty.get() = " + otherProperty.get());

        System.out.println("Unbinding otherProperty from intProperty.");
        otherProperty.unbind();
        System.out.println("otherProperty.get() = " + otherProperty.get());

        System.out.println("Calling intProperty.set(8192).");
        intProperty.set(8192);
        System.out.println("otherProperty.get() = " + otherProperty.get());
    }
}
```

In this example we created a SimpleIntegerProperty object called intProperty with an initial value of 1024. We then updated its value through a series of different integers while we added and then removed an InvalidationListener, added and then removed a ChangeListener, and finally created another SimpleIntegerProperty named otherProperty, bound it to and then unbound it from intProperty. The sample program used a generous amount of println calls to show what is happening inside the program.

When we run the program in Listing 3-1, the following output is printed to the console:

```
intProperty = IntegerProperty [value: 1024]

intProperty.get() = 1024

intProperty.getValue() = 1024
```

Added invalidation listener.

Calling intProperty.set(2048).

The observable has been invalidated: IntegerProperty [value: 2048].

Calling intProperty.setValue(3072).

The observable has been invalidated: IntegerProperty [value: 3072].

Removed invalidation listener.

Calling intProperty.set(4096).

Added change listener.

Calling intProperty.set(5120).

The observableValue has changed: oldValue = 4096, newValue = 5120

Removed change listener.

Calling intProperty.set(6144).

otherProperty.get() = 0

Binding otherProperty to intProperty.

otherProperty.get() = 6144

Calling intProperty.set(7168).

otherProperty.get() = 7168

Unbinding otherProperty from intProperty.

otherProperty.get() = 7168

Calling intProperty.set(8192).

otherProperty.get() = 7168

By correlating the output lines with the program source code (or by stepping through the code in the debugger of your favorite IDE), we can draw the following conclusions.

- A SimpleIntegerProperty object such as intProperty and otherProperty holds an int value. The value can be manipulated with the get(), set(), getValue(), and setValue() methods. The get() and set() methods perform their operation with the primitive int type. The getValue() and setValue() methods use the Integer wrapper type.

- You can add and remove InvalidationListener objects to and from intProperty.

- You can add and remove ChangeListener objects to and from intProperty.

- Another Property object such as otherProperty can bind itself to intProperty. When that happens, otherProperty receives the value of intProperty.

- When a new value is set on intProperty, whatever object that is attached to it is notified. The notification is not sent if the object is removed.

- When notified, InvalidationListener objects are only informed of which object is sending out the notification and that object is only known as an Observable.

- When notified, ChangeListener objects are informed on two more pieces of information—the oldValue and the newValue—in addition to the object sending the notification. The sending object is known as an ObservableValue.

- In the case of a binding property such as otherProperty, we cannot tell from the output when or how it is notified of the change of value in intProperty. However, we can infer that it must have known of the change because when we asked otherProperty for its value we get back the latest value of intProperty.

■ **Note** Even though this motivating example uses an Integer property, similar examples can be made to use properties based on the Boolean, Long, Float, Double, String, and Object types. In the JavaFX 2.0 properties and bindings framework, when interfaces are extended or implemented for concrete types, they are always done for the Boolean, Integer, Long, Float, Double, String, and Object types.

This example brings to our attention some of the key interfaces and concepts of the JavaFX 2.0 properties and bindings framework: including the Observable and the associated InvalidationListener interfaces, the ObservableValue and the associated ChangeListener interfaces, the get(), set(), getValue(), and setValue() methods that allow us to manipulate the values of a SimpleIntegerProperty object directly, and the bind() method that allows us to relinquish direct manipulation of the value of a SimpleIntegerProperty object by subordinating it to another SimpleIntegerProperty object.

In the next section we show you these and some other key interfaces and concepts of the JavaFX 2.0 properties and bindings framework in more detail.

Understanding Key Interfaces and Concepts

Figure 3-1 is an UML diagram showing the key interfaces of the JavaFX 2.0 properties and bindings framework. It includes some interfaces that you have seen in the last section, and some that you haven't seen.

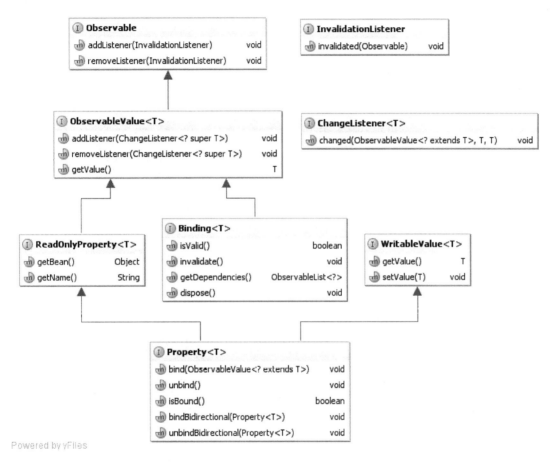

Figure 3-1. Key interfaces of the JavaFX 2.0 properties and bindings framework

---

■ **Note** We did not show you the fully qualified names of the interfaces in the UML diagram. These interfaces are spread out in four packages: javafx.beans, javafx.beans.binding, javafx.beans.property, and javafx.beans.value. You can easily figure out which interface belongs to which package by examining the JavaFX API documentation or by the "find class" feature of your favorite IDE.

Understanding the Observable Interface

At the root of the hierarchy is the Observable interface. You can register InvalidationListener objects to an Observable object to receive *invalidation* events. You have already seen invalidation events fired from one kind of Observable object, the SimpleIntegerProperty object intProperty in the motivating example in the last section. It is fired when the set() or setValue() methods are called to change the underlying value from one int to a different int.

■ **Note**   An invalidation event is fired only once by any of the implementations of the Property interface in the JavaFX 2.0 properties and bindings framework if you call the setter with the same value several times in a row.

Another place where invalidation events are fired is from Binding objects. You haven't seen an example of a Binding object yet. But there are plenty of Binding objects in the second half of this chapter. For now we just note that Binding objects may become invalid, for example, when its invalidate() method is called or, as we show later in this chapter, when one of its dependencies fires an invalidation event.

■ **Note**   An invalidation event is fired only once by any of the implementations of the Binding interface in the JavaFX 2.0 properties and bindings framework if it becomes invalid several times in a row.

Understanding the ObservableValue Interface

Next up in the hierarchy is the ObservableValue interface. It's simply an Observable that has a value. Its getValue() method returns its value. The getValue() method that we called on the SimpleIntegerProperty objects in the motivating example can be considered to have come from this interface. You can register ChangeListener objects to an ObservableValue object to receive *change* events.

You have seen change events being fired in the motivating example in the last section. When the change event fires, the ChangeListener receives two more pieces of information: the old value and the new value of the ObservableValue object.

■ **Note**   A change event is fired only once by any of the implementations of the ObservableValue interface in the JavaFX 2.0 properties and bindings framework if you call the setter with the same value several times in a row.

The distinction between an invalidation event and a change event is made so that the JavaFX 2.0 properties and bindings framework may support *lazy evaluations*. We show an example of this by looking at three lines of code from the motivating example:

```
otherProperty.bind(intProperty);
intProperty.set(7168);
System.out.println("otherProperty.get() = " + otherProperty.get());
```

When `intProperty.set(7168)` is called, it fires an invalidation event to `otherProperty`. Upon receiving this invalidation event, `otherProperty` simply makes a note of the fact that its value is no longer valid. It does not immediately perform a recalculation of its value by querying `intProperty` for its value. The recalculation is performed later when `otherProperty.get()` is called. Imagine if instead of calling `intProperty.set()` only once as in the above code we call `intProperty.set()` multiple times; `otherProperty` still recalculates its value only once.

■ **Note** The `ObservableValue` interface is not the only direct subinterface of `Observable`. There are two other direct subinterfaces of `Observable` that live in the `javafx.collections` package: `ObservableList` and `ObservableMap` with corresponding `ListChangeListener` and `MapChangeListener` as callback mechanisms. These JavaFX 2.0 observable collections are covered in Chapter 6, "Collections and Concurrency."

Understanding the WritableValue Interface

This may be the simplest subsection in the entire chapter, for the `WritableValue` interface is truly as simple as it looks. Its purpose is to inject the `getValue()` and `setValue()` methods into implementations of this interface. All implementation classes of `WritableValue` in the JavaFX 2.0 properties and bindings framework also implement `ObservableValue`, therefore you can make an argument that the value of `WritableValue` is only to provide the `setValue()` method.

You have seen the `setValue()` method at work in the motivating example.

Understanding the ReadOnlyProperty Interface

The `ReadOnlyProperty` interface injects two methods into its implementations. The `getBean()` method should return the `Object` that contains the `ReadOnlyRroperty` or null if it is not contained in an `Object`. The `getName()` method should return the name of the `ReadOnlyProperty` or the empty string if the `ReadOnlyProperty` does not have a name.

The containing object and the name provide *contextual* information about a `ReadOnlyProperty`. The contextual information of a property does not play any direct role in the propagation of invalidation events or the recalculation of values. However, if provided, it will be taken into account in some peripheral calculations.

In our motivating example, the `intProperty` is constructed without any contextual information. Had we used the full constructor to supply it a name:

```
intProperty = new SimpleIntegerProperty(null, "intProperty", 1024);
```

the output would have contained the property name:

```
intProperty = IntegerProperty [name: intProperty, value: 1024]
```

Understanding the Property Interface

Now we come to the bottom of our key interfaces hierarchy. The Property interface has as its superinterfaces all four interfaces we have examined thus far: Observable, ObservableValue, ReadOnlyProperty, and WritableValue. Therefore it inherits all the methods from these interfaces. It also provides five methods of its own:

```
void bind(ObservableValue<? extends T> observableValue);
void unbind();
boolean isBound();
void bindBidirectional(Property<T> tProperty);
void unbindBidirectional(Property<T> tProperty);
```

You have seen two of the methods at work in the motivating example in the last section: bind() and unbind().

Calling bind() creates a *unidirectional binding* or a dependency between the Property object and the ObservableValue argument. Once they enter this relationship, calling the set() or setValue() methods on the Property object will cause a RuntimeException to be thrown. Calling the get() or getValue() methods on the Property object will return the value of the ObservableValue object. And, of course, changing the value of the ObservableValue object will invalidate the Property object. Calling unbind() releases any existing unidirectional binding the Property object may have. If a unidirectional binding is in effect, the isBound() method returns true; otherwise it returns false.

Calling bindBidirectional() creates a *bidirectional binding* between the Property caller and the Property argument. Notice that unlike the bind() method, which takes an ObservableValue argument, the bindBidirectional() method takes a Property argument. Only two Property objects can be bound together bidirectionally. Once they enter this relationship, calling the set() or setValue() methods on either Property object will cause both objects' values to be updated. Calling unbindBidirectional() releases any existing bidirectional binding the caller and the argument may have. The program in Listing 3-2 shows a simple bidirectional binding at work.

Listing 3-2. *BidirectionalBindingExample.java*

```java
import javafx.beans.property.SimpleStringProperty;
import javafx.beans.property.StringProperty;

public class BidirectionalBindingExample {
    public static void main(String[] args) {
        System.out.println("Constructing two StringProperty objects.");
        StringProperty prop1 = new SimpleStringProperty("");
        StringProperty prop2 = new SimpleStringProperty("");

        System.out.println("Calling bindBidirectional.");
        prop2.bindBidirectional(prop1);

        System.out.println("prop1.isBound() = " + prop1.isBound());
        System.out.println("prop2.isBound() = " + prop2.isBound());

        System.out.println("Calling prop1.set(\"prop1 says: Hi!\")");
        prop1.set("prop1 says: Hi!");
        System.out.println("prop2.get() returned:");
        System.out.println(prop2.get());
```

```
        System.out.println("Calling prop2.set(prop2.get() + \"\\nprop2 says: Bye!\")");
        prop2.set(prop2.get() + "\nprop2 says: Bye!");
        System.out.println("prop1.get() returned:");
        System.out.println(prop1.get());
    }
}
```

In this example we created two SimpleStringProperty objects called prop1 and prop2, created a bidirectional binding between them, and then called set() and get() on both properties.

When we run the program in Listing 3-2, the following output is printed to the console:

```
Constructing two StringProperty objects.

Calling bindBidirectional.

prop1.isBound() = false

prop2.isBound() = false

Calling prop1.set("prop1 says: Hi!")

prop2.get() returned:

prop1 says: Hi!

Calling prop2.set(prop2.get() + "\nprop2 says: Bye!")

prop1.get() returned:

prop1 says: Hi!

prop2 says: Bye!
```

▪ **Caution**   Each Property object may have at most one active unidirectional binding at a time. It may have as many bidirectional bindings as you want. The isBound() method pertains only to unidirectional bindings. Calling bind() a second time with a different ObservableValue argument while a unidirectional binding is already in effect will unbind the existing one and replace it with the new one.

Understanding the Binding Interface

The Binding interface defines four methods that reveal the intentions of the interface. A Binding object is an ObservableValue whose validity can be queried with the isValid() method and set with the invalidate() method. It has a list of dependencies that can be obtained with the getDependencies()

method. And finally a dispose() method signals that the binding will not be used anymore and resources used by it can be cleaned up.

From this brief description of the Binding interface, we can infer that it represents a *unidirectional binding with multiple dependencies*. Each dependency, we imagine, could be an ObservableValue to which the Binding is registered to receive invalidation events. When the get() or getValue() method is called, if the binding is invalidated, its value is recalculated.

The JavaFX 2.0 properties and bindings framework does not provide any concrete classes that implement the Binding interface. However, it provides multiple ways to create your own Binding objects easily: you can extend the abstract base classes in the framework; you can use a set of static methods in the utility class Bindings to create new bindings out of existing regular Java values (i.e., unobservable values), properties, and bindings; you can also use a set of methods that are provided in the various properties and bindings classes and form a fluent interface API to create new bindings. We go through the utility methods and the fluent interface API in the Creating Bindings section later in this chapter. For now, we show you the first example of a binding by extending the DoubleBinding abstract class. The program in Listing 3-3 uses a binding to calculate the area of a rectangle.

Listing 3-3. *RectangleAreaExample.java*

```java
import javafx.beans.binding.DoubleBinding;
import javafx.beans.property.DoubleProperty;
import javafx.beans.property.SimpleDoubleProperty;

public class RectangleAreaExample {
    public static void main(String[] args) {
        System.out.println("Constructing x with initial value of 2.0.");
        final DoubleProperty x = new SimpleDoubleProperty(null, "x", 2.0);
        System.out.println("Constructing y with initial value of 3.0.");
        final DoubleProperty y = new SimpleDoubleProperty(null, "y", 3.0);
        System.out.println("Creating binding area with dependencies x and y.");
        DoubleBinding area = new DoubleBinding() {
            private double value;

            {
                super.bind(x, y);
            }

            @Override
            protected double computeValue() {
                System.out.println("computeValue() is called.");
                return x.get() * y.get();
            }
        };
        System.out.println("area.get() = " + area.get());
        System.out.println("area.get() = " + area.get());
        System.out.println("Setting x to 5");
        x.set(5);
        System.out.println("Setting y to 7");
        y.set(7);
        System.out.println("area.get() = " + area.get());
    }
}
```

In the anonymous inner class, we called the protected bind() method in the superclass DoubleBinding, informing the superclass that we would like to listen to invalidation events from the DoubleProperty objects x and y. We finally implemented the protected abstract computeValue() method in the superclass DoubleBinding to do the actual calculation when a recalculation is needed.

When we run the program in Listing 3-3, the following output is printed to the console:

```
Constructing x with initial value of 2.0.

Constructing y with initial value of 3.0.

Creating binding area with dependencies x and y.

computeValue() is called.

area.get() = 6.0

area.get() = 6.0

Setting x to 5

Setting y to 7

computeValue() is called.

area.get() = 35.0
```

Notice that computeValue() is called only once when we call area.get() twice in a row.

▓ **Caution**   The DoubleBinding abstract class contains a default implementation of dispose() that is empty and a default implementation of getDependencies() that returns an empty list. To make this example a correct Binding implementation we should override these two methods to behave correctly.

Now that you have a firm grasp of the key interfaces and concepts of the JavaFX 2.0 properties and bindings framework, we show you how these generic interfaces are specialized to type-specific interfaces and implemented in type-specific abstract and concrete classes.

Type-Specific Specializations of Key Interfaces

We did not emphasize this fact in the last section because we believe its omission does not hurt the explanations there, but except for Observable and InvalidationListener, the rest of the interfaces are generic interfaces with a type parameter <T>. In this section we examine how these generic interfaces are specialized to the specific types of interest: Boolean, Integer, Long, Float, Double, String, and Object. We also examine some of the abstract and concrete classes of the framework and explore typical usage scenarios of each class.

A Common Theme for Type-Specific Interfaces

Although the generic interfaces are not all specialized in exactly the same way, a common theme exists:

- The Boolean type is specialized directly.
- The Integer, Long, Float, and Double types are specialized through the Number supertype.
- The String type is specialized through the Object type.

This theme exists in the type-specific specializations of all the key interfaces. As an example, we examine the subinterfaces of the ObservableValue<T> interface:

- ObservableBooleanValue extends ObservableValue<Boolean>, and it offers one additional method.
    - boolean get();
- ObservableNumberValue extends ObservableValue<Number>, and it offers four additional methods.
    - int intValue();
    - long longValue();
    - float floatValue();
    - double doubleValue();
- ObservableObjectValue<T> extends ObservableValue<t>, and it offers one additional method.
    - T get();
- ObservableIntegerValue, ObservableLongValue, ObservableFloatValue, and ObservableDoubleValue extend ObservableNumberValue and each offers an additional get() method that returns the appropriate primitive type value.
- ObservableStringValue extends ObservableObjectValue<String> and inherits its get() method that returns String.

Notice that the get() method that we have been using in the examples is defined in the type-specific ObservableValue subinterfaces. A similar examination reveals that the set() method that we have been using in the examples is defined in the type-specific WritableValue subinterfaces.

A practical consequence of this derivation hierarchy is that any numerical property can call bind() on any other numerical property or binding. Indeed, the signature of the bind() method on any numerical property is

```
void bind(ObservableValue<? extends Number>  observable);
```

and any numerical property and binding is assignable to the generic parameter type. The program in Listing 3-2 shows that any numerical properties of different specific types can be bound to each other.

Listing 3-4. NumericPropertiesExample.java

```java
import javafx.beans.property.DoubleProperty;
import javafx.beans.property.FloatProperty;
import javafx.beans.property.IntegerProperty;
import javafx.beans.property.LongProperty;
import javafx.beans.property.SimpleDoubleProperty;
import javafx.beans.property.SimpleFloatProperty;
import javafx.beans.property.SimpleIntegerProperty;
import javafx.beans.property.SimpleLongProperty;

public class NumericPropertiesExample {
    public static void main(String[] args) {
        IntegerProperty i = new SimpleIntegerProperty(null, "i", 1024);
        LongProperty l = new SimpleLongProperty(null, "l", 0L);
        FloatProperty f = new SimpleFloatProperty(null, "f", 0.0F);
        DoubleProperty d = new SimpleDoubleProperty(null, "d", 0.0);
        System.out.println("Constructed numerical properties i, l, f, d.");

        System.out.println("i.get() = " + i.get());
        System.out.println("l.get() = " + l.get());
        System.out.println("f.get() = " + f.get());
        System.out.println("d.get() = " + d.get());

        l.bind(i);
        f.bind(l);
        d.bind(f);
        System.out.println("Bound l to i, f to l, d to f.");

        System.out.println("i.get() = " + i.get());
        System.out.println("l.get() = " + l.get());
        System.out.println("f.get() = " + f.get());
        System.out.println("d.get() = " + d.get());

        System.out.println("Calling i.set(2048).");
        i.set(2048);

        System.out.println("i.get() = " + i.get());
        System.out.println("l.get() = " + l.get());
        System.out.println("f.get() = " + f.get());
        System.out.println("d.get() = " + d.get());

        d.unbind();
        f.unbind();
        l.unbind();
        System.out.println("Unbound l to i, f to l, d to f.");

        f.bind(d);
        l.bind(f);
```

```
        i.bind(l);
        System.out.println("Bound f to d, l to f, i to l.");

        System.out.println("Calling d.set(10000000000L).");
        d.set(10000000000L);

        System.out.println("d.get() = " + d.get());
        System.out.println("f.get() = " + f.get());
        System.out.println("l.get() = " + l.get());
        System.out.println("i.get() = " + i.get());
    }
}
```

In this example we created four numeric properties and bound them into a chain in decreasing size to demonstrate that the bindings work as expected. We then reversed the order of the chain and set the double property's value to a number that would overflow the integer property to highlight the fact that even though you can bind different sizes of numeric properties together, when the value of the dependent property is outside the range of the binding property, normal Java numeric conversion applies.

When we run the program in Listing 3-4, the following is printed to the console:

```
Constructed numerical properties i, l, f, d.

i.get() = 1024

l.get() = 0

f.get() = 0.0

d.get() = 0.0

Bound l to i, f to l, d to f.

i.get() = 1024

l.get() = 1024

f.get() = 1024.0

d.get() = 1024.0

Calling i.set(2048).

i.get() = 2048

l.get() = 2048

f.get() = 2048.0
```

```
d.get() = 2048.0

Unbound l to i, f to l, d to f.

Bound f to d, l to f, i to l.

Calling d.set(10000000000L).

d.get() = 1.0E10

f.get() = 1.0E10

l.get() = 10000000000

i.get() = 1410065408
```

Commonly Used Classes

We now give a survey of the content of the four packages javafx.beans, javafx.beans.binding, javafx.beans.property, and javafx.beans.value. In this section, "the SimpleIntegerProperty series of classes" refers to the classes extrapolated over the Boolean, Integer, Long, Float, Double, String, and Object types. Therefore what is said also applies to SimpleBooleanProperty, and so on.

- The most often used classes in the JavaFX 2.0 properties and bindings framework are the SimpleIntegerProperty series of classes. They provide all the functionalities of the Property interface including lazy evaluation. They are used in all the examples of this chapter up to this point.

- Another set of concrete classes in the JavaFX 2.0 properties and bindings framework is the ReadOnlyIntegerWrapper series of classes. These classes implement the Property interface but also have a getReadOnlyProperty() method that returns a ReadOnlyProperty that is synchronized with the main Property. They are very handy to use when you need a full-blown Property for the implementation of a component but you only want to hand out a ReadOnlyProperty to the client of the component.

- The IntegerPropertyBase series of abstract classes can be extended to provide implementations of full Property classes, although in practice the SimpleIntegerProperty series of classes is easier to use. The only abstract methods in the IntegerPropertyBase series of classes are getBean() and getName().

- The ReadOnlyIntegerPropertyBase series of abstract classes can be extended to provide implementations of ReadOnlyProperty classes. This is rarely necessary. The only abstract methods in the ReadOnlyIntegerPropertyBase series of classes are get(), getBean(), and getName().

- The WeakInvalidationListener and WeakChangeListener classes can be used to wrap InvalidationListener and ChangeListener instances before addListener() is called. They hold weak references of the wrapped listener instances. As long as you hold a reference to the wrapped listener on your side, the weak references will be kept alive and you will receive events. When you are done with the wrapped listener and have unreferenced it from your side, the weak references will be eligible for garbage collection and later garbage collected. All the JavaFX 2.0 properties and bindings framework Observable objects know how to clean up a weak listener after its weak reference has been garbage collected. This prevents memory leaks when the listeners are not removed after use.

That covers all the JavaFX 2.0 properties and bindings API that reside in the javafx.beans, javafx.beans.property, and javafx.beans.value packages and some but not all of the APIs in the javafx.beans.binding package. The remaining classes of the javafx.beans.binding package are APIs that help you to create new bindings out of existing properties and bindings. That is the focus of the next section.

Creating Bindings

We now turn our focus to the creation of new bindings out of existing properties and bindings. You learned in the "Understanding Key Interfaces and Concepts" section earlier in this chapter that a binding is an observable value that has a list of dependencies which are also observable values.

The JavaFX 2.0 properties and bindings framework offers three ways of creating new bindings:

- Extending the IntegerBinding series of abstract classes

- Using the bindings creating static methods in the utilities class Bindings

- Using the fluent interface API provided by the IntegerExpression series of abstract classes

You saw the direct extension approach in the "Understanding the Binding Interface" section earlier in this chapter. We explore the Bindings utility class next.

Understanding the Bindings Utility Class

The Bindings class contains 163 factory methods that make new bindings out of existing observable values and regular values. Most of the methods are overloaded to take into account that both observable values and regular Java (unobservable) values can be used to build new bindings. At least one of the parameters must be an observable value. Here are the signatures of the nine overloaded add() methods:

```
public static NumberBinding add(ObservableNumberValue n1, ObservableNumberValue n2)
public static DoubleBinding add(ObservableNumberValue n, double d)
public static DoubleBinding add(double d, ObservableNumberValue n)
public static NumberBinding add(ObservableNumberValue n, float f)
public static NumberBinding add(float f, ObservableNumberValue n)
public static NumberBinding add(ObservableNumberValue n, long l)
public static NumberBinding add(long l, ObservableNumberValue n)
public static NumberBinding add(ObservableNumberValue n, int i)
public static NumberBinding add(int i, ObservableNumberValue n)
```

When the add() method is called, it returns a NumberBinding whose dependencies include all the observable value parameters, and whose value is the sum of the value of its two parameters. Similarly overloaded methods exist for subtract(), multiply(), and divide().

■ **Note** Recall from the last section that ObservableIntegerValue, ObservableLongValue, ObservableFloatValue, and ObservableDoubleValue are subclasses of ObservableNumberValue. Therefore the four arithmetic methods mentioned above can take any combinations of these observable numeric values as well as any unobservable values.

The program in Listing 3-5 uses the arithmetic methods in Bindings to calculate the area of a triangle in the Cartesian plane with vertices (x1, y1), (x2, y2), (x3, y3) using this formula:

Area = (x1*y2 + x2*y3 + x3*y1 - x1*y3 - x2*y1 - x3*y2) / 2

Listing 3-5. TriangleAreaExample.java

```java
import javafx.beans.binding.Bindings;
import javafx.beans.binding.NumberBinding;
import javafx.beans.property.IntegerProperty;
import javafx.beans.property.SimpleIntegerProperty;

public class TriangleAreaExample {
    public static void main(String[] args) {
        IntegerProperty x1 = new SimpleIntegerProperty(0);
        IntegerProperty y1 = new SimpleIntegerProperty(0);
        IntegerProperty x2 = new SimpleIntegerProperty(0);
        IntegerProperty y2 = new SimpleIntegerProperty(0);
        IntegerProperty x3 = new SimpleIntegerProperty(0);
        IntegerProperty y3 = new SimpleIntegerProperty(0);

        final NumberBinding x1y2 = Bindings.multiply(x1, y2);
        final NumberBinding x2y3 = Bindings.multiply(x2, y3);
        final NumberBinding x3y1 = Bindings.multiply(x3, y1);
        final NumberBinding x1y3 = Bindings.multiply(x1, y3);
        final NumberBinding x2y1 = Bindings.multiply(x2, y1);
        final NumberBinding x3y2 = Bindings.multiply(x3, y2);

        final NumberBinding sum1 = Bindings.add(x1y2, x2y3);
        final NumberBinding sum2 = Bindings.add(sum1, x3y1);
        final NumberBinding sum3 = Bindings.add(sum2, x3y1);
        final NumberBinding diff1 = Bindings.subtract(sum3, x1y3);
        final NumberBinding diff2 = Bindings.subtract(diff1, x2y1);
        final NumberBinding determinant = Bindings.subtract(diff2, x3y2);
        final NumberBinding area = Bindings.divide(determinant, 2.0D);
```

```
        x1.set(0); y1.set(0);
        x2.set(6); y2.set(0);
        x3.set(4); y3.set(3);

        printResult(x1, y1, x2, y2, x3, y3, area);

        x1.set(1); y1.set(0);
        x2.set(2); y2.set(2);
        x3.set(0); y3.set(1);

        printResult(x1, y1, x2, y2, x3, y3, area);
    }

    private static void printResult(IntegerProperty x1, IntegerProperty y1,
                                    IntegerProperty x2, IntegerProperty y2,
                                    IntegerProperty x3, IntegerProperty y3,
                                    NumberBinding area) {
        System.out.println("For A(" +
                x1.get() + "," + y1.get() + "), B(" +
                x2.get() + "," + y2.get() + "), C(" +
                x3.get() + "," + y3.get() + "), the area of triangle ABC is " +
area.getValue());
    }
}
```

We used IntegerProperty to represent the co-ordinates. The building up of the NumberBinding area uses all four arithmetic factory methods of Bindings. Because we started with IntegerProperty objects, even though the return type from the arithmetic factory methods of Bindings are NumberBinding, the actual object that is returned, up to determinant, are IntegerBinding objects. We used 2.0D rather than a mere 2 in the divide() call to force the division to be done as a double division, not as int division. All the properties and bindings that we build up form a tree structure with area as the root, the intermediate bindings as internal nodes, and the properties x1, y1, x2, y2, x3, y3 as leaves. This tree is similar to the parse tree we will get if we parse the mathematical expression for the area formula using grammar for the regular arithmetic expressions.

When we run the program in Listing 3-5, the following output is printed to the console:

```
For A(0,0), B(6,0), C(4,3), the area of triangle ABC is 9.0

For A(1,0), B(2,2), C(0,1), the area of triangle ABC is 1.5
```

Aside from the arithmetic methods, the Bindings class also has the following factory methods.

- Logical operators: and, or, not

- Numeric operators: min, max, negate

- Object operators: isNull, isNotNull

- Relational operators:

  - equal

  - equalIgnoreCase

  - greaterThan

  - greaterThanOrEqual

  - lessThan

  - lessThanOrEqual

  - notEqual

  - notEqualIgnoreCase

- Selection operators:

  - select

  - selectBoolean

  - selectInteger

  - selectLong

  - selectFloat

  - selectDouble

  - selectString

Except for the selection operators, the preceding operators all do what you think they will do. The object operators are meaningful only for observable string values and observable object values. All relational operators except for the IgnoreCase ones apply to numeric values. There are versions of the equal and notEqual operators for numeric values that have a third double parameter for the tolerance when comparing float or double values. The equal and notEqual operators also apply to boolean, string, and object values. For string and object values, the equal and notEqual operator compares their values using the equals() method.

The selection operators operate on what are called *JavaFX beans*, Java classes constructed according to the JavaFX Beans specification. We talk about JavaFX Beans in the "Understanding JavaFX Beans" section later in this chapter.

That covers all methods in Bindings that return a binding object. There are seven methods in Bindings that do not return a binding object. The bindBidirectional() and unbindBidirectional() methods create bidirectional bindings. As a matter of fact, the bindBidirectional() and unbindBidirectional() methods in the various properties classes simply call the corresponding ones in the Bindings class. Four of the other five methods, convert(), concat(), and a pair of overloaded format(), return StringExpression objects. And finally the when() method returns a When object.

The When and the StringExpression classes are part of the fluent interface API for creating bindings, which we cover in the next subsection.

Understanding the Fluent Interface API

If you asked the question: "Why would anybody name a method when()? And what kind of information would the When class encapsulate?" Welcome to the club. While you were not looking, the object-oriented programming community invented a brand new way of API design that totally disregards the decades-old principles of object-oriented practices. Instead of encapsulating data and distributing business logic into relevant domain objects, this new methodology produces a style of API that encourages method chaining and uses the return type of one method to determine what methods are available for the next car of the choo-choo train. Method names are chosen not to convey complete meaning but to make the entire method chain read like a fluent sentence. This style of APIs is called *fluent interface APIs.*

■ **Note** You can find a more through exposition of fluent interfaces on Martin Fowler's web site, referenced at the end of this chapter.

The fluent interface APIs for creating bindings are defined in the IntegerExpression series of classes. IntegerExpression is a superclass of both IntegerProperty and IntegerBinding, making the methods of IntegerExpression also available in the IntegerProperty and IntegerBinding classes. The four numeric expression classes share a common superinterface NumberExpression, where all the methods are defined. The type-specific expression classes override some of the methods that yield a NumberBinding to return a more appropriate type of binding.

The methods thus made available for the seven kinds of properties and bindings are listed here:

- For BooleanProperty and BooleanBinding

    - BooleanBinding and(ObservableBooleanValue b)

    - BooleanBinding or(ObservableBooleanValue b)

    - BooleanBinding not()

    - BooleanBinding isEqualTo(ObservableBooleanValue b)

    - BooleanBinding isNotEqualTo(ObservableBooleanValue b)

    - StringBinding asString()

- Common for all numeric properties and bindings

    - BooleanBinding isEqualTo(ObservableNumberValue m)

    - BooleanBinding isEqualTo(ObservableNumberValue m, double err)

    - BooleanBinding isEqualTo(double d, double err)

    - BooleanBinding isEqualTo(float f, double err)

    - BooleanBinding isEqualTo(long l)

    - BooleanBinding isEqualTo(long l, double err)

- BooleanBinding isEqualTo(int i)

- BooleanBinding isEqualTo(int i, double err)

- BooleanBinding isNotEqualTo(ObservableNumberValue m)

- BooleanBinding isNotEqualTo(ObservableNumberValue m, double err)

- BooleanBinding isNotEqualTo(double d, double err)

- BooleanBinding isNotEqualTo(float f, double err)

- BooleanBinding isNotEqualTo(long l)

- BooleanBinding isNotEqualTo(long l, double err)

- BooleanBinding isNotEqualTo(int i)

- BooleanBinding isNotEqualTo(int i, double err)

- BooleanBinding greaterThan(ObservableNumberValue m)

- BooleanBinding greaterThan(double d)

- BooleanBinding greaterThan(float f)

- BooleanBinding greaterThan(long l)

- BooleanBinding greaterThan(int i)

- BooleanBinding lessThan(ObservableNumberValue m)

- BooleanBinding lessThan(double d)

- BooleanBinding lessThan(float f)

- BooleanBinding lessThan(long l)

- BooleanBinding lessThan(int i)

- BooleanBinding greaterThanOrEqualTo(ObservableNumberValue m)

- BooleanBinding greaterThanOrEqualTo(double d)

- BooleanBinding greaterThanOrEqualTo(float f)

- BooleanBinding greaterThanOrEqualTo(long l)

- BooleanBinding greaterThanOrEqualTo(int i)

- BooleanBinding lessThanOrEqualTo(ObservableNumberValue m)

- BooleanBinding lessThanOrEqualTo(double d)

- BooleanBinding lessThanOrEqualTo(float f)

- BooleanBinding lessThanOrEqualTo(long l)

- BooleanBinding lessThanOrEqualTo(int i)

- StringBinding asString()
- StringBinding asString(String str)
- StringBinding asString(Locale locale, String str)
- For IntegerProperty and IntegerBinding
  - IntegerBinding negate()
  - NumberBinding add(ObservableNumberValue n)
  - DoubleBinding add(double d)
  - FloatBinding add(float f)
  - LongBinding add(long l)
  - IntegerBinding add(int i)
  - NumberBinding subtract(ObservableNumberValue n)
  - DoubleBinding subtract(double d)
  - FloatBinding subtract(float f)
  - LongBinding subtract(long l)
  - IntegerBinding subtract(int i)
  - NumberBinding multiply(ObservableNumberValue n)
  - DoubleBinding multiply(double d)
  - FloatBinding multiply(float f)
  - LongBinding multiply(long l)
  - IntegerBinding multiply(int i)
  - NumberBinding divide(ObservableNumberValue n)
  - DoubleBinding divide(double d)
  - FloatBinding divide(float f)
  - LongBinding divide(long l)
  - IntegerBinding divide(int i)
- For LongProperty and LongBinding
  - LongBinding negate()
  - NumberBinding add(ObservableNumberValue n)
  - DoubleBinding add(double d)
  - FloatBinding add(float f)

- LongBinding add(long l)
- LongBinding add(int i)
- NumberBinding subtract(ObservableNumberValue n)
- DoubleBinding subtract(double d)
- FloatBinding subtract(float f)
- LongBinding subtract(long l)
- LongBinding subtract(int i)
- NumberBinding multiply(ObservableNumberValue n)
- DoubleBinding multiply(double d)
- FloatBinding multiply(float f)
- LongBinding multiply(long l)
- LongBinding multiply(int i)
- NumberBinding divide(ObservableNumberValue n)
- DoubleBinding divide(double d)
- FloatBinding divide(float f)
- LongBinding divide(long l)
- LongBinding divide(int i)

- For FloatProperty and FloatBinding
  - FloatBinding negate()
  - NumberBinding add(ObservableNumberValue n)
  - DoubleBinding add(double d)
  - FloatBinding add(float g)
  - FloatBinding add(long l)
  - FloatBinding add(int i)
  - NumberBinding subtract(ObservableNumberValue n)
  - DoubleBinding subtract(double d)
  - FloatBinding subtract(float g)
  - FloatBinding subtract(long l)
  - FloatBinding subtract(int i)
  - NumberBinding multiply(ObservableNumberValue n)

117

- DoubleBinding multiply(double d)
- FloatBinding multiply(float g)
- FloatBinding multiply(long l)
- FloatBinding multiply(int i)
- NumberBinding divide(ObservableNumberValue n)
- DoubleBinding divide(double d)
- FloatBinding divide(float g)
- FloatBinding divide(long l)
- FloatBinding divide(int i)
- For DoubleProperty and DoubleBinding
    - DoubleBinding negate()
    - DoubleBinding add(ObservableNumberValue n)
    - DoubleBinding add(double d)
    - DoubleBinding add(float f)
    - DoubleBinding add(long l)
    - DoubleBinding add(int i)
    - DoubleBinding subtract(ObservableNumberValue n)
    - DoubleBinding subtract(double d)
    - DoubleBinding subtract(float f)
    - DoubleBinding subtract(long l)
    - DoubleBinding subtract(int i)
    - DoubleBinding multiply(ObservableNumberValue n)
    - DoubleBinding multiply(double d)
    - DoubleBinding multiply(float f)
    - DoubleBinding multiply(long l)
    - DoubleBinding multiply(int i)
    - DoubleBinding divide(ObservableNumberValue n)
    - DoubleBinding divide(double d)
    - DoubleBinding divide(float f)

- - DoubleBinding divide(long l)
  - DoubleBinding divide(int i)
- For StringProperty and StringBinding
  - StringExpression concat(Object obj)
  - BooleanBinding isEqualTo(ObservableStringValue str)
  - BooleanBinding isEqualTo(String str)
  - BooleanBinding isNotEqualTo(ObservableStringValue str)
  - BooleanBinding isNotEqualTo(String str)
  - BooleanBinding isEqualToIgnoreCase(ObservableStringValue str)
  - BooleanBinding isEqualToIgnoreCase(String str)
  - BooleanBinding isNotEqualToIgnoreCase(ObservableStringValue str)
  - BooleanBinding isNotEqualToIgnoreCase(String str)
  - BooleanBinding greaterThan(ObservableStringValue str)
  - BooleanBinding greaterThan(String str)
  - BooleanBinding lessThan(ObservableStringValue str)
  - BooleanBinding lessThan(String str)
  - BooleanBinding greaterThanOrEqualTo(ObservableStringValue str)
  - BooleanBinding greaterThanOrEqualTo(String str)
  - BooleanBinding lessThanOrEqualTo(ObservableStringValue str)
  - BooleanBinding lessThanOrEqualTo(String str)
  - BooleanBinding isNull()
  - BooleanBinding isNotNull()
- For ObjectProperty and ObjectBinding
  - BooleanBinding isEqualTo(ObservableObjectValue<?> obj)
  - BooleanBinding isEqualTo(Object obj)
  - BooleanBinding isNotEqualTo(ObservableObjectValue<?> obj)
  - BooleanBinding isNotEqualTo(Object obj)
  - BooleanBinding isNull()
  - BooleanBinding isNotNull()

With these methods, you can create an infinite variety of bindings by starting with a property and calling one of the methods that is appropriate for the type of the property to get a binding, and calling one of the methods that is appropriate for the type of the binding to get another binding, and so on. One fact that is worth pointing out here is that all the methods for the type-specific numeric expressions are defined in the NumberExpression base interface with a return type of NumberBinding, and are overridden in the type-specific expression classes with an identical parameter signature but a more specific return type. This way of overriding a method in a subclass with an identical parameter signature but a more specific return type is called *covariant return-type overriding,* and has been a Java language feature since Java 5. One of the consequences of this fact is that numeric bindings built with the fluent interface API have more specific types than those built with factory methods in the Bindings class.

The program in Listing 3-6 is a modification of the triangle area example in Listing 3-5 that uses the fluent interface API instead of calling factory methods in the Bindings class.

Listing 3-6. *TriangleAreaFluentExample.java*

```java
import javafx.beans.binding.Bindings;
import javafx.beans.binding.NumberBinding;
import javafx.beans.binding.StringExpression;
import javafx.beans.property.IntegerProperty;
import javafx.beans.property.SimpleIntegerProperty;

public class TriangleAreaFluentExample {
    public static void main(String[] args) {
        IntegerProperty x1 = new SimpleIntegerProperty(0);
        IntegerProperty y1 = new SimpleIntegerProperty(0);
        IntegerProperty x2 = new SimpleIntegerProperty(0);
        IntegerProperty y2 = new SimpleIntegerProperty(0);
        IntegerProperty x3 = new SimpleIntegerProperty(0);
        IntegerProperty y3 = new SimpleIntegerProperty(0);

        final NumberBinding area = x1.multiply(y2)
                .add(x2.multiply(y3))
                .add(x3.multiply(y1))
                .subtract(x1.multiply(y3))
                .subtract(x2.multiply(y1))
                .subtract(x3.multiply(y2))
                .divide(2.0D);

        StringExpression output = Bindings.format(
                "For A(%d,%d), B(%d,%d), C(%d,%d), the area of triangle ABC is %3.1f",
                x1, y1, x2, y2, x3, y3, area);

        x1.set(0); y1.set(0);
        x2.set(6); y2.set(0);
        x3.set(4); y3.set(3);

        System.out.println(output.get());
```

```
        x1.set(1); y1.set(0);
        x2.set(2); y2.set(2);
        x3.set(0); y3.set(1);

        System.out.println(output.get());
    }
}
```

Notice how the 13 lines of code and 12 intermediate variables used in Listing 3-5 to build up the area binding are reduced to the 7 lines of code with no intermediate variables used in Listing 3-6. We also used the Bindings.format() method to build up a StringExpression object called output. There are two overloaded Bindings.format() methods with signatures:

```
StringExpression format(Locale locale, String format, Object... args)
StringExpression format(String format, Object... args)
```

They work similarly to the corresponding String.format() methods in that they format the values args according to the format specification format and the Locale locale, or the default Locale. If any of the args is an ObservableValue, its change is reflected in the StringExpression.

When we run the program in Listing 3-6, the following output is printed to the console:

```
For A(0,0), B(6,0), C(4,3), the area of triangle ABC is 9.0

For A(1,0), B(2,2), C(0,1), the area of triangle ABC is 1.5
```

Next we unravel the mystery of the When class and the role it plays in constructing bindings that are essentially if/then/else expressions. The When class has a constructor that takes an ObservableBooleanValue argument:

```
public When(ObservableBooleanValue b)
```

It has the following 11 overloaded then() methods.

```
When.NumberConditionBuilder then(ObservableNumberValue n)
When.NumberConditionBuilder then(double d)
When.NumberConditionBuilder then(float f)
When.NumberConditionBuilder then(long l)
When.NumberConditionBuilder then(int i)
When.BooleanConditionBuilder then(ObservableBooleanValue b)
When.BooleanConditionBuilder then(boolean b)
When.StringConditionBuilder then(ObservableStringValue str)
When.StringConditionBuilder then(String str)
When.ObjectConditionBuilder<T> then(ObservableObjectValue<T> obj)
When.ObjectConditionBuilder<T> then(T obj)
```

The type of object returned from the then() method depends on the type of the argument. If the argument is a numeric type, either observable or unobservable, the return type is a nested class When.NumberConditionBuilder. Similarly, for Boolean arguments, the return type is When.BooleanConditionBuilder; for string arguments, When.StringConditionBuilder; and for object arguments, When.ObjectConditionBuilder.

These condition builders in turn have the following otherwise() methods.

- For When.NumberConditionBuilder

  - NumberBinding otherwise(ObservableNumberValue n)

  - DoubleBinding otherwise(double d)

  - NumberBinding otherwise(float f)

  - NumberBinding otherwise(long l)

  - NumberBinding otherwise(int i)

- For When.BooleanConditionBuilder

  - BooleanBinding otherwise(ObservableBooleanValue b)

  - BooleanBinding otherwise(boolean b)

- For When.StringConditionBuilder

  - StringBinding otherwise(ObservableStringValue str)

  - StringBinding otherwise(String str)

- For When.ObjectConditionBuilder

  - ObjectBinding<T> otherwise(ObservableObjectValue<T> obj)

  - ObjectBinding<T> otherwise(T obj)

The net effect of these method signatures is that you can build up a binding that resembles an if/then/else expression this way:

```
new When(b).then(x).otherwise(y)
```

where b is an ObservableBooleanValue, and x and y are of similar types and can be either observable or unobservable. The resulting binding will be of a type similar to that of x and y.

The program in Listing 3-7 uses the fluent interface API from the When class to calculate the area of a triangle with given sides a, b, and c. Recall that to form a triangle, the three sides must satisfy the following conditions.

```
a + b > c, b + c > a, c + a > b,
```

When the preceding conditions are satisfied, the area of the triangle can be calculated using Heron's formula:

```
Area = sqrt(s * (s - a) * (s - b) * (s - c))
```

where s is the semiperimeter:

```
s = (a + b + c) / 2.
```

Listing 3-7. *HeronsFormulaExample.java*

```
import javafx.beans.binding.DoubleBinding;
import javafx.beans.binding.When;
import javafx.beans.property.DoubleProperty;
import javafx.beans.property.SimpleDoubleProperty;
```

```
public class HeronsFormulaExample {
    public static void main(String[] args) {
        DoubleProperty a = new SimpleDoubleProperty(0);
        DoubleProperty b = new SimpleDoubleProperty(0);
        DoubleProperty c = new SimpleDoubleProperty(0);

        DoubleBinding s = a.add(b).add(c).divide(2.0D);

        final DoubleBinding areaSquared = new When(
                        a.add(b).greaterThan(c)
                        .and(b.add(c).greaterThan(a))
                        .and(c.add(a).greaterThan(b)))
                    .then(s.multiply(s.subtract(a))
                            .multiply(s.subtract(b))
                            .multiply(s.subtract(c)))
                    .otherwise(0.0D);

        a.set(3);
        b.set(4);
        c.set(5);
        System.out.printf("Given sides a = %1.0f, b = %1.0f, and c = %1.0f," +
                " the area of the triangle is %3.2f\n", a.get(), b.get(), c.get(),
                Math.sqrt(areaSquared.get()));

        a.set(2);
        b.set(2);
        c.set(2);
        System.out.printf("Given sides a = %1.0f, b = %1.0f, and c = %1.0f," +
                " the area of the triangle is %3.2f\n", a.get(), b.get(), c.get(),
                Math.sqrt(areaSquared.get()));
    }
}
```

Inasmuch as there is no ready-made binding method in DoubleExpression that calculates the square root, we create a DoubleBinding for areaSquared instead. The constructor argument for When() is a BooleanBinding built out of the three conditions on a, b, and c. The argument for the then() method is a DoubleBinding that calculates the square of the area of the triangle. And because the then() argument is numeric, the otherwise() argument also has to be numeric. We choose to use 0.0D to signal that an invalid triangle is encountered.

▦ **Note** Instead of using the When() constructor, you can also use the factory method when() in the Bindings utility class to create the When object.

When we run the program in Listing 3-7, the following output is printed to the console:

Given sides a = 3, b = 4, and c = 5, the area of the triangle is 6.00.

Given sides a = 2, b = 2, and c = 2, the area of the triangle is 1.73.

If the binding defined in Listing 3-7 makes your head spin a little, you are not alone. We choose this example simply to illustrate the use of the fluent interface API offered by the When class. As a matter of fact, this example may be better served with a direct subclassing approach we first introduced in the "Understanding the Binding Interface" section earlier in this chapter.

The program in Listing 3-8 solves the same problem as Listing 3-7 by using the direct extension method.

Listing 3-8. *HeronsFormulaDirectExtensionExample.java*

```java
import javafx.beans.binding.DoubleBinding;
import javafx.beans.property.DoubleProperty;
import javafx.beans.property.SimpleDoubleProperty;

public class HeronsFormulaDirectExtensionExample {
    public static void main(String[] args) {
        final DoubleProperty a = new SimpleDoubleProperty(0);
        final DoubleProperty b = new SimpleDoubleProperty(0);
        final DoubleProperty c = new SimpleDoubleProperty(0);

        DoubleBinding area = new DoubleBinding() {
            {
                super.bind(a, b, c);
            }
            @Override
            protected double computeValue() {
                double a0 = a.get();
                double b0 = b.get();
                double c0 = c.get();

                if ((a0 + b0 > c0) && (b0 + c0 > a0) && (c0 + a0 > b0)) {
                    double s = (a0 + b0 + c0) / 2.0D;
                    return Math.sqrt(s * (s - a0) * (s - b0) * (s - c0));
                } else {
                    return 0.0D;
                }
            }
        };

        a.set(3);
        b.set(4);
        c.set(5);
```

```
        System.out.printf("Given sides a = %1.0f, b = %1.0f, and c = %1.0f," +
                " the area of the triangle is %3.2f\n", a.get(), b.get(), c.get(),
                area.get());

        a.set(2);
        b.set(2);
        c.set(2);
        System.out.printf("Given sides a = %1.0f, b = %1.0f, and c = %1.0f," +
                " the area of the triangle is %3.2f\n", a.get(), b.get(), c.get(),
                area.get());
    }
}
```

The direct extension method is preferred for complicated expressions and for expressions that go beyond the available operators.

Now that you have mastered all the APIs in the javafx.beans, javafx.beans.binding, javafx.beans.property, and javafx.beans.value packages, you are ready step beyond the details of the JavaFX 2.0 properties and bindings framework and learn how these properties are organized into bigger components called JavaFX Beans.

Understanding the JavaFX Beans Convention

JavaFX 2.0 introduces the concept of JavaFX Beans, a set of conventions that provide properties support for Java objects. In this section, we talk about the naming conventions for specifying JavaFX Beans properties, several ways of implementing JavaFX Beans properties, and finally the use of selection bindings.

The JavaFX Beans Specification

For many years Java has used the JavaBeans API to represent a property of an object. A JavaBeans property is represented by a pair of getter and setter methods. Property changes are propagated to property change listeners through the firing of property change events in the setter code.

JavaFX 2.0 introduces the JavaFX Beans specification that adds properties support to Java objects through the help of the properties classes from the JavaFX 2.0 properties and bindings framework.

▩ **Caution**   The word *property* is used here with two distinct meanings. When we say JavaFX Beans properties, it should be understood to mean a higher-level concept similar to JavaBeans properties. When we say JavaFX 2.0 properties and bindings framework properties, it should be understood to mean the various implementations of the Property or ReadOnlyProperty interfaces, such as IntegerProperty, StringProperty, and so on. JavaFX Beans properties are specified using JavaFX 2.0 properties and bindings framework properties.

Like its JavaBeans counterparts, *JavaFX Beans properties* are specified by a set of methods in a Java class. To define a JavaFX Beans property in a Java class, you provide three methods: the getter, the setter, and the property getter. For a property named height of type double, the three methods are:

```
public final double getHeight();
public final void setHeight(double h);
public DoubleProperty heightProperty();
```

The names of the getter and setter methods follow the JavaBeans convention. They are obtained by concatenating "get" and "set" with the name of the property with the first character capitalized. For boolean type properties, the getter name can also start with "is". The name of the property getter is obtained by concatenating the name of the property with "Property". To define a *read only JavaFX Beans property*, you can either remove the setter method or change it to a private method and change the return type of the property getter to be a ReadOnlyProperty.

This specification speaks only about the interface of JavaFX Beans properties and does not impose any implementation constraints. Depending on the number of properties a JavaFX Bean may have, and the usage patterns of these properties, there are several implementation strategies. Not surprisingly, all of them use the JavaFX 2.0 properties and bindings framework properties as the backing store for the values of the JavaFX Beans properties. We show you these strategies in the next two subsections.

Understanding the Eagerly Instantiated Properties Strategy

The *eagerly instantiated properties* strategy is the simplest way to implement JavaFX Beans properties. For every JavaFX Beans property you want to define in an object, you introduce a private field in the class that is of the appropriate JavaFX 2.0 properties and bindings framework property type. These private fields are instantiated at bean construction time. The getter and setter methods simply call the private field's get() and set() methods. The property getter simply returns the private field itself.

The program in Listing 3-9 defines a JavaFX Bean with an int property i, a String property str, and a Color property color.

Listing 3-9. *JavaFXBeanModelExample.java*

```java
import javafx.beans.property.IntegerProperty;
import javafx.beans.property.ObjectProperty;
import javafx.beans.property.SimpleIntegerProperty;
import javafx.beans.property.SimpleObjectProperty;
import javafx.beans.property.SimpleStringProperty;
import javafx.beans.property.StringProperty;
import javafx.scene.paint.Color;

public class JavaFXBeanModelExample {
    private IntegerProperty i = new SimpleIntegerProperty(this, "i", 0);
    private StringProperty str = new SimpleStringProperty(this, "str", "Hello");
    private ObjectProperty<Color> color = new SimpleObjectProperty<Color>(this, "color",↵
Color.BLACK);

    public final int getI() {
        return i.get();
    }

    public final void setI(int i) {
        this.i.set(i);
    }
```

```java
    public IntegerProperty iProperty() {
        return i;
    }

    public final String getStr() {
        return str.get();
    }

    public final void setStr(String str) {
        this.str.set(str);
    }

    public StringProperty strProperty() {
        return str;
    }

    public final Color getColor() {
        return color.get();
    }

    public final void setColor(Color color) {
        this.color.set(color);
    }

    public ObjectProperty<Color> colorProperty() {
        return color;
    }
}
```

This is a straightforward Java class. There are only two things we want to point out in this implementation. First, the getter and setter methods are declared final by convention. Secondly, when the private fields are initialized, we called the simple properties constructors with the full context information, supplying them with this as the first parameter. In all of our previous examples in this chapter, we used null as the first parameter for the simple properties constructors because those properties are not part of a higher-level JavaFX Bean object.

The program in Listing 3-10 defines a view class that watches over an instance of the JavaFX Bean defined in Listing 3-9. It observes changes to the i, str, and color properties of the bean by hooking up change listeners that print out any changes to the console.

Listing 3-10. JavaFXBeanViewExample.java

```java
import javafx.beans.value.ChangeListener;
import javafx.beans.value.ObservableValue;
import javafx.scene.paint.Color;

public class JavaFXBeanViewExample {
    private JavaFXBeanModelExample model;
```

```java
    public JavaFXBeanViewExample(JavaFXBeanModelExample model) {
        this.model = model;
        hookupChangeListeners();
    }

    private void hookupChangeListeners() {
        model.iProperty().addListener(new ChangeListener<Number>() {
            @Override
            public void changed(ObservableValue<? extends Number> observableValue, Number↵
oldValue, Number newValue) {
                System.out.println("Property i changed: old value = " + oldValue + ", new↵
value = " + newValue);
            }
        });

        model.strProperty().addListener(new ChangeListener<String>() {
            @Override
            public void changed(ObservableValue<? extends String> observableValue, String↵
oldValue, String newValue) {
                System.out.println("Property str changed: old value = " + oldValue + ", new↵
value = " + newValue);
            }
        });

        model.colorProperty().addListener(new ChangeListener<Color>() {
            @Override
            public void changed(ObservableValue<? extends Color> observableValue, Color↵
oldValue, Color newValue) {
                System.out.println("Property color changed: old value = " + oldValue + ",↵
new value = " + newValue);
            }
        });
    }
}
```

The program in Listing 3-11 defines a controller that can modify a model object.

Listing 3-11. *JavaFXBeanControllerExample.java*

```java
import javafx.scene.paint.Color;

public class JavaFXBeanControllerExample {
    private JavaFXBeanModelExample model;
    private JavaFXBeanViewExample view;

    public JavaFXBeanControllerExample(JavaFXBeanModelExample model, JavaFXBeanViewExample↵
view) {
        this.model = model;
        this.view = view;
    }
```

```
    public void incrementIPropertyOnModel() {
        model.setI(model.getI() + 1);
    }

    public void changeStrPropertyOnModel() {
        final String str = model.getStr();
        if (str.equals("Hello")) {
            model.setStr("World");
        } else {
            model.setStr("Hello");
        }
    }

    public void switchColorPropertyOnModel() {
        final Color color = model.getColor();
        if (color.equals(Color.BLACK)) {
            model.setColor(Color.WHITE);
        } else {
            model.setColor(Color.BLACK);
        }
    }
}
```

Notice that this is not a full-blown controller and does not do anything with its reference to the view object. The program in Listing 3-12 provides a main program that assembles and test drives the classes in Listings 3-9 to 3-11 in a typical model–view–controller pattern.

Listing 3-12. *JavaFXbeanMainExample.java*

```
public class JavaFXBeanMainExample {
    public static void main(String[] args) {
        JavaFXBeanModelExample model = new JavaFXBeanModelExample();
        JavaFXBeanViewExample view = new JavaFXBeanViewExample(model);
        JavaFXBeanControllerExample controller = new JavaFXBeanControllerExample(model, view);

        controller.incrementIPropertyOnModel();
        controller.changeStrPropertyOnModel();
        controller.switchColorPropertyOnModel();
        controller.incrementIPropertyOnModel();
        controller.changeStrPropertyOnModel();
        controller.switchColorPropertyOnModel();
    }
}
```

When we run the program in Listings 3-9 to 3-12, the following output is printed to the console:

```
Property i changed: old value = 0, new value = 1

Property str changed: old value = Hello, new value = World

Property color changed: old value = Color[red=0,green=0,blue=0,opacity=1.0], new value =
Color[red=255,green=255,blue=255,opacity=1.0]

Property i changed: old value = 1, new value = 2

Property str changed: old value = World, new value = Hello

Property color changed: old value = Color[red=255,green=255,blue=255,opacity=1.0], new value
= Color[red=0,green=0,blue=0,opacity=1.0]
```

Understanding the Lazily Instantiated Properties Strategy

If your JavaFX Bean has many properties, instantiating all the properties objects up front at bean creation time may be too heavy an approach. The memory for all the properties objects is truly wasted if only a few of the properties are actually used. In such situations, you can use one of several lazily instantiated properties strategies. Two typical such strategies are the *half-lazy instantiation* strategy and the *full-lazy instantiation* strategy.

In the half-lazy strategy, the property object is instantiated only if the setter is called with a value that is different from the default value, or if the property getter is called. The program in Listing 3-13 illustrates how this strategy is implemented.

Listing 3-13. *JavaFXBeanModelHalfLazyExample.java*

```java
import javafx.beans.property.SimpleStringProperty;
import javafx.beans.property.StringProperty;

public class JavaFXBeanModelHalfLazyExample {
    private static final String DEFAULT_STR = "Hello";
    private StringProperty str;

    public final String getStr() {
        if (str != null) {
            return str.get();
        } else {
            return DEFAULT_STR;
        }
    }
}
```

```
    public final void setStr(String str) {
        if ((this.str != null) || !(str.equals(DEFAULT_STR))) {
            strProperty().set(str);
        }
    }

    public StringProperty strProperty() {
        if (str == null) {
            str = new SimpleStringProperty(this, "str", DEFAULT_STR);
        }
        return str;
    }
}
```

In this strategy, the client code can call the getter many times without the property object being instantiated. If the property object is null, the getter simply returns the default value. As soon as the setter is called with a value that is different from the default value, it will call the property getter which lazily instantiates the property object. The property object is also instantiated if the client code calls the property getter directly.

In the full-lazy strategy, the property object is instantiated only if the property getter is called. The getter and setter go through the property object only if it is already instantiated. Otherwise they go through a separate field.

The program in Listing 3-14 shows an example of a full-lazy property.

Listing 3-14. *JavaFXBeanModelFullLazyExample.java*

```
import javafx.beans.property.SimpleStringProperty;
import javafx.beans.property.StringProperty;

public class JavaFXBeanModelFullLazyExample {
    private static final String DEFAULT_STR = "Hello";
    private StringProperty str;
    private String _str = DEFAULT_STR;

    public final String getStr() {
        if (str != null) {
            return str.get();
        } else {
            return _str;
        }
    }

    public final void setStr(String str) {
        if (this.str != null) {
            this.str.set(str);
        } else {
            _str = str;
        }
    }
```

```
    public StringProperty strProperty() {
        if (str == null) {
            str = new SimpleStringProperty(this, "str", DEFAULT_STR);
        }
        return str;
    }
}
```

■ **Caution**   The full-lazy instantiation strategy incurs the cost of an extra field in order to stave off the need for property instantiation a little longer. Similarly, both the half-lazy and the full-lazy instantiation strategies incur costs of implementation complexity and runtime performance to gain the benefit of a potentially reduced runtime memory footprint. This is a classical trade-off situation in software engineering. Which strategy you choose will depend on the circumstance of your application. Our advice is to introduce optimization only if there is a need.

Using Selection Bindings

As you have seen in the "Understanding the Bindings Utility Class" subsection of the "Creating Bindings" section, the Bindings utility class contains seven selection operators. The method signatures of these operators are:

- select(ObservableValue<?> root, String... steps)

- selectBoolean(ObservableValue<?> root, String... steps)

- selectDouble(ObservableValue<?> root, String... steps)

- selectFloat(ObservableValue<?> root, String... steps)

- selectInteger(ObservableValue<?> root, String... steps)

- selectLong(ObservableValue<?> root, String... steps)

- selectString(ObservableValue<?> root, String... steps)

These selection operators allow you to create bindings that observe deeply nested JavaFX Beans properties. Suppose that you have a JavaFX bean that has a property, whose type is a JavaFX bean that has a property, whose type is a JavaFX bean that has a property, and so on. Suppose also that you are observing the root of this properties chain through an ObjectProperty. Then you can create a binding that observes the deeply nested JavaFX Beans property by calling one of the select methods whose type matches the type of the deeply nested JavaFX Beans property with the ObjectProperty as the root, and the successive JavaFX Beans property names that reach into the deeply nested JavaFX Beans property as the rest of the arguments.

In the following example, we use a few classes from the javafx.scene.effect package—Lighting and Light—to illustrate how the selection operator works. We teach you how to apply lighting to a JavaFX scene graph in a later chapter of the book. For now, our interest lies in the fact that Lighting is a JavaFX bean that has a property named light whose type is Light, and that Light is also a JavaFX bean that has a property named color whose type is Color (in javafx.scene.paint).

The program in Listing 3-15 illustrates how to observe the color of the light of the lighting.

Listing 3-15. *SelectBindingExample.java*

```java
import javafx.beans.binding.Bindings;
import javafx.beans.binding.ObjectBinding;
import javafx.beans.property.ObjectProperty;
import javafx.beans.property.SimpleObjectProperty;
import javafx.beans.value.ChangeListener;
import javafx.beans.value.ObservableValue;
import javafx.scene.effect.Light;
import javafx.scene.effect.Lighting;
import javafx.scene.paint.Color;

public class SelectBindingExample {
    public static void main(String[] args) {
        ObjectProperty<Lighting> root = new SimpleObjectProperty<>();
        final ObjectBinding<Color> selectBinding = Bindings.select(root, "light", "color");
        selectBinding.addListener(new ChangeListener<Color>() {
            @Override
            public void changed(ObservableValue<? extends Color> observableValue, Color⏎
 oldValue, Color newValue) {
                System.out.println("\tThe color changed:\n\t\told color = " +
                        oldValue + ",\n\t\tnew color = " + newValue);
            }
        });

        System.out.println("firstLight is black.");
        Light firstLight = new Light.Point();
        firstLight.setColor(Color.BLACK);

        System.out.println("secondLight is white.");
        Light secondLight = new Light.Point();
        secondLight.setColor(Color.WHITE);

        System.out.println("firstLighting has firstLight.");
        Lighting firstLighting = new Lighting();
        firstLighting.setLight(firstLight);

        System.out.println("secondLighting has secondLight.");
        Lighting secondLighting = new Lighting();
        secondLighting.setLight(secondLight);

        System.out.println("Making root observe firstLighting.");
        root.set(firstLighting);

        System.out.println("Making root observe secondLighting.");
        root.set(secondLighting);

        System.out.println("Changing secondLighting's light to firstLight");
        secondLighting.setLight(firstLight);
```

```
            System.out.println("Changing firstLight's color to red");
            firstLight.setColor(Color.RED);
        }
    }
```

In this example, the root is an `ObjectProperty` that observes `Lighting` objects. The binding `colorBinding` observes the color property of the `light` property of the `Lighting` object that is the value of root. We then created some Light and Lighting objects and changed their configuration in various ways.

When we run the program in Listing 3-15, the following output is printed to the console:

```
firstLight is black.

secondLight is white.

firstLighting has firstLight.

secondLighting has secondLight.

Making root observe firstLighting.

        The color changed:

                old color = null,

                new color = Color[red=0,green=0,blue=0,opacity=1.0]

Making root observe secondLighting.

        The color changed:

                old color = Color[red=0,green=0,blue=0,opacity=1.0],

                new color = Color[red=255,green=255,blue=255,opacity=1.0]

Changing secondLighting's light to firstLight

        The color changed:

                old color = Color[red=255,green=255,blue=255,opacity=1.0],

                new color = Color[red=0,green=0,blue=0,opacity=1.0]
```

Changing firstLight's color to red

    The color changed:

            old color = Color[red=0,green=0,blue=0,opacity=1.0],

            new color = Color[red=255,green=0,blue=0,opacity=1.0]

As expected, a change event is fired for every change in the configuration of the object being observed by root; and the value of colorBinding always reflects the color of the light of the current Lighting object in root.

▓ **Caution**   The JavaFX 2.0 properties and bindings framework does not issue any warnings if the supplied property names do not match any property names in a JavaFX bean. It will simply have the default value for the type: null for object type, zero for numeric types, false for boolean type, and the empty string for string type.

Summary

In this chapter, you learned the fundamentals of the JavaFX 2.0 properties and bindings framework and the JavaFX Beans specification. You now understand the following important principles.

- JavaFX 2.0 properties and bindings framework properties and bindings are the fundamental workhorses of the framework.

- They conform to the key interfaces of the framework.

- They fire two kinds of events: invalidation event and change event.

- All properties and bindings provided by the JavaFX 2.0 properties and bindings framework recalculate their values lazily, only when a value is requested. To force them into eager re-evaluation, attach a ChangeListener to them.

- New bindings are created out of existing properties and bindings in one of three ways: using the factory methods of the Bindings utility class, using the fluent interface API, or directly extending the IntegerBinding series of abstract classes.

- The JavaFX Beans specification uses three methods to define a property: the getter, the setter, and the property getter.

- JavaFX Beans properties can be implemented through the eager, half-lazy, and full-lazy strategies.

Resources

Here are some useful resources for understanding properties and bindings:

- *Martin Fowler's write up on fluent interface APIs:*
  http://www.martinfowler.com/bliki/FluentInterface.html

- *The Properties and Binding tutorial at Oracle's JavaFX.com site:*
  http://download.oracle.com/javafx/2.0/binding/jfxpub-binding.htm

- *Michael Heinrichs's blog includes entries on JavaFX properties and bindings:*
  http://blog.netopyr.com/

CHAPTER 4

Building Dynamic UI Layouts in JavaFX

When I am working on a problem, I never think about beauty. I think only of how to solve the problem. But when I have finished, if the solution is not beautiful, I know it is wrong.

—Buckminster Fuller

JavaFX has facilities for creating dynamic layouts that allow you to easily create beautiful-looking user interfaces (UIs) that scale to any resolution and are backed by clean code. At your disposal you have the simple, yet elegant, binding facility; powerful custom layouts built on top of the Pane and Region classes; and the built-in layouts that include HBox, VBox, AnchorPane, BorderPane, FlowPane, TilePane, StackPane, and GridPane.

In this chapter we show how you can leverage these dynamic layout mechanisms to build complicated user interfaces with zero static positioning.

Introducing JavaFX Reversi

To demonstrate the power of dynamic layout in JavaFX, the goal of this chapter is to build a fully functional version of the popular Reversi game. Reversi is a game of strategy where players take turns on an eight-by-eight game board placing black and white pieces. The objective of the game is to have the most pieces on the board by surrounding your opponent's pieces and flipping them over to your color.

Originally invented in 1880 by Lewis Waterman and James Mollett, Reversi gained considerable popularity in nineteenth-century England, and was one of the first titles published by German game manufacturer Ravensburger. It is more commonly known today as Othello, which is trademarked and sold by Pressman.

The rules of Reversi are extremely simple, which lets us focus on the JavaFX layout. To make things a little more challenging, we are going to bring Reversi into the twenty-first century with a modern RIA-style interface, pseudo-3D game board, and fully resizable layout.

Board Layout and Basic Rules

Reversi is a turn-based game where two players choose white and black sides. Each player gets 32 pieces to play; the first player is black.

The initial board setup has four pieces placed in alternating cells in the center of the board (see Figure 4-1).

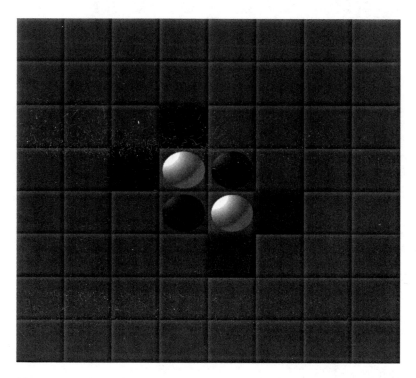

Figure 4-1. *This is the starting board position for Reversi.*

Black gets the first turn and can place a piece anywhere adjacent to one of white's pieces where there is a matching black piece on the same line (vertical, horizontal, or diagonal). From the starting position, there are only four legal moves, which are highlighted in blue. All moves are equal positionwise, so let's assume that black goes in the uppermost position. This allows black to flip the upper white piece, taking that entire column (see Figure 4-2).

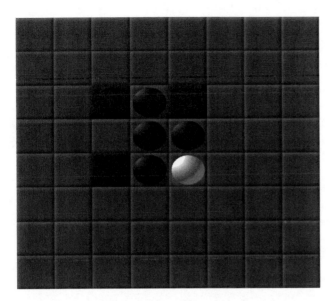

Figure 4-2. This shows the board position after black's first move.

White gets the second turn and has three available options highlighted in blue. Let's assume white goes in the lowermost position, flipping one black piece. Now it is black's turn again with five available positions (shown in Figure 4-3).

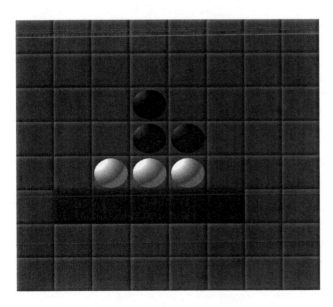

Figure 4-3. This shows the board position after the next move by white.

Play continues this way, alternating between black and white unless one player has no moves, in which case they pass on that turn. The game is over when both players have no moves, and the winner is the player with the most pieces on the final board.

Building a JavaFX Model for Reversi

Now that you are armed with knowledge of how Reversi works, it is time to translate that into a set of Java classes that represent the game model.

Your ReversiModel class needs to contain two primary pieces of information: the current board position and the player whose turn it is. Listing 4-1 shows a basic model class to get you started.

Listing 4-1. ReversiModel Class for the Reversi Application

```
public class ReversiModel {
  public static int BOARD_SIZE = 8;

  public ObjectProperty<Owner> turn = new SimpleObjectProperty<Owner>(Owner.BLACK);

  public ObjectProperty<Owner>[][] board = new ObjectProperty[BOARD_SIZE][BOARD_SIZE];

  private ReversiModel() {
    for (int i = 0; i < BOARD_SIZE; i++) {
      for (int j = 0; j < BOARD_SIZE; j++) {
        board[i][j] = new SimpleObjectProperty<Owner>(Owner.NONE);
      }
    }
    initBoard();
  }

  public static ReversiModel getInstance() {
    return ReversiModelHolder.INSTANCE;
  }

  private static class ReversiModelHolder {
    private static final ReversiModel INSTANCE = new ReversiModel();
  }
}
```

Some things to point out about this model are:

- It uses the Java singleton pattern for creating and providing access to an instance.

- The board size is defined via a constant, which makes it easy to adjust the dimensions in the future.

- The turn variable is declared as an observable object property so that we can make use of it in bind statements.

- The board is declared as a two-dimensional array containing observable object properties, allowing binding to the current game state.

- The model references an Owner class for both the board contents and the current turn.

Next we need to define the Owner enumeration that is used in the ReversiModel. As shown in the following code, you can define the Owner class as a Java enum that contains states for WHITE, BLACK, and, in the case of empty cells, NONE.

```java
public enum Owner {
  NONE,
  WHITE,
  BLACK;

  public Owner opposite() {
    return this == WHITE ? BLACK : this == BLACK ? WHITE : NONE;
  }

  public Color getColor() {
    return this == Owner.WHITE ? Color.WHITE : Color.BLACK;
  }

  public String getColorStyle() {
    return this == Owner.WHITE ? "white" : "black";
  }
}
```

This enumeration class contains a few extra helper functions that we make use of later. The first is called opposite() and can be used to convert from black to white and vice versa, which is very useful for swapping turns and implementing the game algorithm later. The next two methods return a color as either a JavaFX Color object or a style String for use within style properties in the UI.

The final step is to initialize our model to the starting position for a Reversi game. The following implementation of the initBoard() method places the first four pieces in the center of the board.

```java
private void initBoard() {
  int center1 = BOARD_SIZE / 2 - 1;
  int center2 = BOARD_SIZE /2;
  board[center1][center1].setValue(Owner.WHITE);
  board[center1][center2].setValue(Owner.BLACK);
  board[center2][center1].setValue(Owner.BLACK);
  board[center2][center2].setValue(Owner.WHITE);
}
```

We come back to the model later, but let's switch over to building out the Reversi user interface by using some of the basic dynamic layout mechanisms in JavaFX.

Dynamic Layout Techniques

JavaFX provides a wide variety of layouts that are suitable for different tasks. They range from the versatile bind to the freeform Pane and Region, which allow you to create an entirely new layout on the fly. There is also a large set of built-in layouts, including HBox, VBox, AnchorPane, BorderPane,

StackPane, TilePane, FlowPane, and GridPane, that can be composed to accomplish sophisticated layouts.

To demonstrate this, we show how you can build a UI shell for the Reversi application that has absolutely no static positioned components and that supports dynamic resizing.

Centering Text Using Bind

One of the most powerful facilities in JavaFX is the ability to bind variables. Earlier we showed how binding could be used to keep the UI and model in sync with no complicated events or listeners.

Another very powerful use of binding is to keep UI components in alignment by binding to their location and size. This technique can be used to align components to the edges of a window, keep nodes in relative alignment with each other, or center them inside a container, which is what we show in this example.

To accomplish this, you need to make use of several properties and methods of the Node class in combination with bind. The common Node members that you need to use when creating bound layouts are listed in Table 4-1.

Table 4-1. *Node Variables Commonly Used in Bind Layouts*

Access	Name	Type/Return	Description
public	layoutXProperty	DoubleProperty	Horizontal offset of the Node for layout positioning
public	layoutYProperty	DoubleProperty	Vertical offset of the Node for layout positioning
public	prefWidth(double)	Double	Preferred width of the Node (when given the passed- in height for nodes with a vertical content bias)
public	prefHeight(double)	Double	Preferred height of the Node (when given the passed-in width for nodes with a horizontal content bias)

To demonstrate, Listing 4-2 is a simple code example that shows how to center the "JavaFX Reversi" title within a Scene.

Listing 4-2. *Example of Centering Text in a Scene*

```
public class CenterUsingBind extends Application {

  public static void main(String[] args) {
    launch(args);
  }
```

```
    @Override
    public void start(Stage primaryStage) {
        Text text = new Text("JavaFX Reversi");
        text.setTextOrigin(VPos.TOP);
        text.setFont(Font.font(null, FontWeight.BOLD, 18));
        Scene scene = new Scene(new Group(text), 400, 100);
        text.layoutXProperty().bind(scene.widthProperty().subtract(text.prefWidth(-1)).divide(2));
        text.layoutYProperty().bind(scene.heightProperty().subtract(text.prefHeight(-
1)).divide(2));
        primaryStage.setScene(scene);
        primaryStage.show();
    }
}
```

Some specific points to highlight about Listing 4-2 are:

- The default value for the textOrigin property of Text is BASELINE, which aligns to the bottom of the letters, not including descenders. We chose to use TOP instead, which makes the origin line up with the top of the letters. This makes Text behave similarly to most other Nodes, and is much easier to center.

- We have to add the Text node to a Group in order to add it to the Scene, which expects a container of type Parent. There are better options than using a Group, as we show in the next section, because this disables any automatic resizing.

- When getting the prefWidth and prefHeight we pass in a parameter of –1 for the counterdimension, because this does not affect the returned dimensions for Text nodes. (Text nodes have no content bias.)

Running this program produces a window where the title stays centered even if you resize the frame, as shown in Figure 4-4.

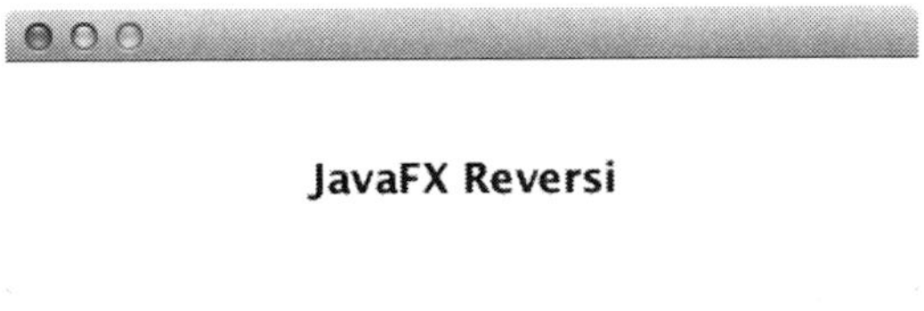

Figure 4-4. A Text node centered within a Scene using bind

Centering Revisited Using a StackPane

In the previous section you saw how to center text using the bind operator. That is one way to center text, however, we show you an alternative approach using the StackPane class, which has built-in capabilities for aligning nodes.

The StackPane class is a layout container that allows you to layer nodes on top of each other to create composite effects. For all the nodes in a StackPane to be visible, the upper nodes must be shaped or transparent so that it is possible to see through them. Table 4-2 lists some of the functions that you can use to add and align nodes in a StackPane.

Table 4-2. Functions on the StackPane Layout Class

Name	Defined In	Description
setAlignment(Node)	StackPane	Sets the default alignment of nodes added to a StackPane
setAlignment(Node, Pos)	StackPane	Static function to set the alignment for a given node when added to a StackPane
getChildren():ObservableList<Node>	Pane	A sequence of children that will be stacked from back to front

The order of the children in the content sequence controls the z-order of the StackPane, with the first element (index 0) appearing on the bottom and the last (index size –1) on the top. The setAlignment functions can be used to control the alignment of nodes that do not fill all the available space in the StackPane. When the node alignment is set, that gets precedence, otherwise the default alignment for the StackPane is used. Finally, if neither is set, a default value of CENTER is used to align nodes.

To build on the previous example, we invert the text and background by adding a black Ellipse to the scene that covers most of the background and by changing the color of the Text node to white. Also, to simplify the alignment and allow layering of nodes, we use a StackPane instead of bind to lay out the nodes as shown in Listing 4-3.

Listing 4-3. Example of Using a StackPane to Overlay and Align Nodes

```
public class CenterUsingStack extends Application {

  public static void main(String[] args) {
    launch(args);
  }

  @Override
  public void start(Stage primaryStage) {
    Text text = new Text("JavaFX Reversi");
    text.setFont(Font.font(null, FontWeight.BOLD, 18));
    text.setFill(Color.WHITE);
    Ellipse ellipse = new Ellipse();
    StackPane stack = new StackPane();
    stack.getChildren().addAll(ellipse, text);
    Scene scene = new Scene(stack, 400, 100);
    ellipse.radiusXProperty().bind(scene.widthProperty().divide(2));
    ellipse.radiusYProperty().bind(scene.heightProperty().divide(2));
    primaryStage.setScene(scene);
    primaryStage.show();
  }
}
```

Notice that there is nothing special that we needed to do to align the Text in the window. The default alignment for nodes in a StackPane is to center them, which is exactly what we wanted to happen. Later we show how you can override this behavior on a per-layout or per-node basis.

Because a StackPane extends Parent, there is no need to wrap it in a Group when adding it to the Scene. Also, when adding a resizable container such as a StackPane to a Scene, it will automatically get resized when the window size changes. Some bindings were still required to keep the Ellipse properly sized. It is common to use bind together with layouts in this fashion.

The completed example is shown running in Figure 4-5.

Figure 4-5. *Inverted JavaFX Reversi logo using a StackPane*

Aligning to Edges Using StackPanes and TilePanes

Using edge alignment, you can improve the title program to fit in with the Reversi theme. To emphasize the black and white contrast of the Reversi pieces, let's create a design where the words are alternating colors on an alternating background.

To accomplish this visual effect, you need to do the following.

1. Create a Scene that has a white background (the default).

2. Add a TilePane to the Scene to split it into a left and right half.

3. On the right side, add a Text node with "Reversi" aligned to the left.

4. On the left side, add a StackPane with a black background.

5. Add a Text node to the StackPane with "JavaFX" in white text aligned to the right.

One way of looking at this problem is that you are creating two equal size tiles that will contain text aligned towards the center of the window. The right side is simply a Text node that is aligned to the left edge, and the left side can be accomplished using a StackPane with right-aligned Text. Rather than using a Rectangle object, which would require binding to set its dimensions, we make use of the background-color style that is a feature of the Region class that all layouts extend.

To create equal size tiles, we use the built-in TilePane layout. This layout divides its content into equal-sized areas to fit all of its nodes. The available layout methods on TilePane are shown in Table 4-3.

Table 4-3. *Layout Methods on the TilePane Class*

Name	Default	Description
setPrefRows(int)		Number of rows used to calculate the preferred height of the TilePane
setPrefColumns(int)		Number of columns used to calculate the preferred width of the TilePane
setHGap(double)	0	Horizontal gap between the columns
setVGap(double)	0	Vertical gap between the rows
setAlignment(Pos)	TOP_LEFT	Alignment of the TilePane contents
setAlignment(Node, Pos)		Alignment of nodes added to the TilePane
setMargin(Node, Insets)		Margin used around nodes added to the TilePane
setTileAlignment(Pos)	CENTER	Default alignment of nodes added to the TilePane
setPrefTileWidth(double)	USE_COMPUTED_SIZE	Sets the preferred tile width (can be reset by setting it back to the default)
setPrefTileHeight(double)	USE_COMPUTED_SIZE	Sets the preferred tile height (can be reset by setting it back to the default)
setOrientation(Orientation)	HORIZONTAL	Direction in which the tiles should be laid out. Can be either HORIZONTAL or VERTICAL.
setSnapToPixel(boolean)	True	Whether or not the layout will align tiles to the pixel boundaries or use fractional tile widths

TilePane is a very versatile class with lots of options for setting the preferred tile width and height, preferred number of rows and columns, gaps between rows and columns, and the horizontal and vertical position. Most of these have reasonable defaults, such as preferredTileWidth and preferredTileHeight, that use the largest preferred width/height of all its children. Similarly, rows and columns are set automatically based on the number of tiles that fit the width and height of the TilePane.

Just like the StackPane class, TilePane also has variables for setting the default alignment and also the alignment of each individual node added. We use the latter, because we want the text aligned to the right on one side and the left on the other.

Rather than using separate horizontal and vertical positions like JavaFX 1.3, JavaFX 2.0 uses a single Pos enumeration that contains all the combinations. Table 4-4 lists all the possible values you can pass in where a Pos is expected.

Table 4-4. *Different Combinations for the Pos Enumeration*

Name	Description
TOP_LEFT	Aligns to the top-left of the container
TOP_CENTER	Aligns to the top-center of the container
TOP_RIGHT	Aligns to the top-right of the container
CENTER_LEFT	Aligns to the middle of the left side of the container
CENTER	Aligns to the center of the container
CENTER_RIGHT	Aligns to the middle of the right side of the container
BOTTOM_LEFT	Aligns to the bottom-left of the container
BOTTOM_CENTER	Aligns to the bottom-center of the container
BOTTOM_RIGHT	Aligns to the bottom-right of the container
BASELINE_LEFT	Aligns to the left side along the baseline (bottom of text and components)
BASELINE_CENTER	Aligns to the center along the baseline (bottom of text and components)
BASELINE_RIGHT	Aligns to the right along the baseline (bottom of text and components)

We take advantage of the Pos constants of BASELINE_LEFT and BASELINE_RIGHT to align half the text to the right and the other half to the left, as shown in Listing 4-4.

Listing 4-4. *Example Showing How to Use a TilePane and StackPane to Align Nodes*

```java
public class AlignUsingStackAndTile extends Application {

  public static void main(String[] args) {
    launch(args);
  }

  @Override
  public void start(Stage primaryStage) {
    StackPane left = new StackPane();
    left.setStyle("-fx-background-color: black");
    Text text = new Text("JavaFX");
    text.setFont(Font.font(null, FontWeight.BOLD, 18));
    text.setFill(Color.WHITE);
    StackPane.setAlignment(text, Pos.BASELINE_RIGHT);
    left.getChildren().add(text);
```

```
        Text right = new Text("Reversi");
        right.setFont(Font.font(null, FontWeight.BOLD, 18));
        TilePane tiles = new TilePane();
        tiles.setSnapToPixel(false);
        TilePane.setAlignment(right, Pos.BASELINE_LEFT);
        tiles.getChildren().addAll(left, right);
        Scene scene = new Scene(tiles, 400, 100);
        left.prefWidthProperty().bind(scene.widthProperty().divide(2));
        left.prefHeightProperty().bind(scene.heightProperty());
        primaryStage.setScene(scene);
        primaryStage.show();
    }
}
```

The completed layout makes use of a TilePane for splitting the background, a StackPane for layering nodes, and binding to make the contents resize with the Scene. To prevent wrapping artifacts on fractional tile sizes, we set the snapToPixels property to false. This allows fractional tile widths and prevents rounding errors from causing our layout to wrap to the next line.

The end result is that the layout resizes correctly when the size of the Scene is changed, including the StackPane with a black background, which always occupies half the area, as shown in Figure 4-6.

Figure 4-6. Result of running the node alignment example

Using FlowPane and Boxes for Directional Alignment

In the previous sections we showed how you can use StackPane and TilePane to create dynamic nested user interfaces, but what if you simply want to arrange nodes along a vertical or horizontal line? This is where the directional layouts, HBox, VBox, and FlowPane, come in. They allow you to lay out a string of nodes at their preferred size with or without wrapping.

To demonstrate directional node alignment, we show you how to implement the next piece of the Reversi UI: the player score box. There are two score boxes for the players, each with very similar content:

- *Score:* The number of pieces of the player's color on the board

- *Player Color:* The color of the player's pieces

- *Turns Remaining:* The number of turns remaining

Before starting on the UI, this is a good time to flush out the model with additional methods to capture these requirements. Listing 4-5 shows an example implementation of getScore and getTurnsRemaining that returns exactly what we need to populate the player score box UI.

Listing 4-5. Additional Model Methods to Implement Player Score Backend

```java
public NumberExpression getScore(Owner owner) {
  NumberExpression score = new SimpleIntegerProperty();
  for (int i = 0; i < BOARD_SIZE; i++) {
    for (int j = 0; j < BOARD_SIZE; j++) {
      score = score.add(Bindings.when(board[i][j].isEqualTo(owner)).then(1).otherwise(0));
    }
  }
  return score;
}

public NumberBinding getTurnsRemaining(Owner owner) {
  NumberExpression emptyCellCount = getScore(Owner.NONE);
  return Bindings.when(turn.isEqualTo(owner))
    .then(emptyCellCount.add(1).divide(2))
    .otherwise(emptyCellCount.divide(2));
}
```

Some points to highlight about Listing 4-5 include:

- Both getScore and getTurnsRemaining return bindings that will automatically recalculate their values when the turn and board state change.

- The getScore method uses a SimpleIntegerProperty as a bound aggregator to sum the total number of cells belonging to the owner.

- The getTurnsRemainingMethod uses a conditional binding and bound arithmetic to calculate the number of remaining turns for a given owner.

Now that we have the model functions created, we can use them to build a JavaFX UI class that shows each player's score. Because we need to create the same UI components twice, this is a good time to raise the abstraction level of the UI by creating functions that create portions of the UI. This lets us reuse the same score box for both players.

Listing 4-6 has the first half of the code and shows how to set up a simple two-column TilePane layout that contains the player score boxes.

Listing 4-6. First Half of Player Score Implementation

```java
@Override
public void start(Stage primaryStage) {
  Scene scene;
  TilePane tiles;
  primaryStage.setScene(scene = SceneBuilder.create()
    .width(600)
    .height(120)
    .root(
      tiles = TilePaneBuilder.create()
        .children(
          createScore(Owner.BLACK),
          createScore(Owner.WHITE))
        .build()
    )
```

```
        .build());
    tiles.prefTileWidthProperty().bind(scene.widthProperty().divide(2));
    tiles.prefTileHeightProperty().bind(scene.heightProperty());
    primaryStage.show();
}
```

Notice that we have explicitly bound the tileWidth and tileHeight. This ensures that the tiles resize together with the window. Also notice that we have bound against the scene's width and height rather than the tile's dimensions. Binding against the parent's width works properly, because the bind update happens synchronously, whereas binding against your own width and height will happen after layout is complete and produce artifacts.

For the second half, you need to use the HBox, VBox, and FlowPane classes. Table 4-5 shows a list of all the variables available, and to which layouts they apply.

Table 4-5. *List of Variables for HBox, VBox, and FlowPane*

Name	Type	Default	Found in	Description
hpos	HPos	HPos.LEFT	HBox, VBox, FlowPane	Horizontal position of the entire layout
vpos	VPos	VPos.TOP	HBox, VBox, FlowPane	Vertical position of the entire layout
nodeHPos	HPos	HPos.LEFT, HPos.CENTER	VBox, FlowPane	Default horizontal alignment of nodes
nodeVPos	VPos	HPos.TOP, HPos.CENTER	HBox, FlowPane	Default vertical alignment of nodes
spacing	Number	0	HBox, VBox	Space between nodes in the direction of layout
hgap	Number	0	FlowPane	Horizontal gap between the rows
vgap	Number	0	FlowPane	Vertical gap between the columns
vertical	Boolean	false	FlowPane	True if this FlowPane runs top-to-bottom, false for left-to-right

The main difference between HBox/VBox and FlowPane is that the FlowPane layout will wrap when it reaches the container width for horizontal layouts and container height for vertical layouts, whereas HBox and VBox always retain their orientation.

Listing 4-7 shows the implementation of the createScore method, which takes the model functions you wrote earlier and turns them into a visual representation. It also makes use of the alternate builder style of developing JavaFX applications. All the same properties are available on the layout builder classes, and you can often make your code shorter and more readable by using this syntax, especially for complicated layouts.

Listing 4-7. Implementation of createScore Method Using Directional Alignment

```java
private StackPane createScore(Owner owner) {
  Region background;
  Ellipse piece;
  Text score;
  Text remaining;
  ReversiModel model = ReversiModel.getInstance();
  StackPane stack = StackPaneBuilder.create()
    .prefHeight(1000)
    .children(
      background = RegionBuilder.create()
        .style("-fx-background-color: " + owner.opposite().getColorStyle())
        .build(),
      FlowPaneBuilder.create()
        .hgap(20)
        .vgap(10)
        .alignment(Pos.CENTER)
        .children(
          score = TextBuilder.create()
            .font(Font.font(null, FontWeight.BOLD, 100))
            .fill(owner.getColor())
            .build(),
          VBoxBuilder.create()
            .alignment(Pos.CENTER)
            .spacing(10)
            .children(
              piece = EllipseBuilder.create()
.effect(DropShadowBuilder.create().color(Color.DODGERBLUE).spread(0.2).build())
                .radiusX(32)
                .radiusY(20)
                .fill(owner.getColor())
                .build(),
              remaining = TextBuilder.create()
                .font(Font.font(null, FontWeight.BOLD, 12))
                .fill(owner.getColor())
                .build()
            )
            .build()
        )
        .build()
    )
    .build();
  InnerShadow innerShadow = InnerShadowBuilder.create()
    .color(Color.DODGERBLUE)
    .choke(0.5)
    .build();
  background.effectProperty().bind(Bindings.when(model.turn.isEqualTo(owner))
    .then(innerShadow)
    .otherwise((InnerShadow) null));
```

```
DropShadow dropShadow = DropShadowBuilder.create()
  .color(Color.DODGERBLUE)
  .spread(0.2)
  .build();
piece.effectProperty().bind(Bindings.when(model.turn.isEqualTo(owner))
  .then(dropShadow)
  .otherwise((DropShadow) null));
score.textProperty().bind(model.getScore(owner).asString());
remaining.textProperty().bind(model.getTurnsRemaining(owner).asString().concat(" turns
remaining"));
  return stack;
}
```

Notice that we used a FlowPane as the outer layout and a VBox inside to keep the Ellipse and Text vertically aligned. This ensures that the Ellipse will always stay on top of the Text but still allows the display to wrap into a vertical layout if horizontal screen real estate is limited.

We use binding both to enable and disable the special effects (DropShadow and InnerShadow) that highlight the current player's turn, as well as to dynamically update the text based on the model. This is a very powerful use of binding that keeps the user interface in sync with the game state without requiring the use of event listeners or imperative callbacks. However, binding is not compatible with the builder syntax, so the best way to use them together is to declare the nodes you want to bind against outside the builder clause, as we have done in Listing 4-7.

The result of running the program for a horizontal layout is shown in Figure 4-7, and the resized vertical layout is shown in Figure 4-8.

Figure 4-7. Output of running the Player Score Example in a horizontally sized window

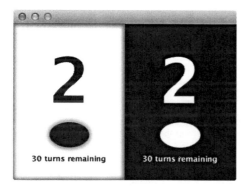

Figure 4-8. Output of running the Player Score Example in a vertically sized window

Although it may be surprising that the starting score is not zero, if you remember the Reversi starting position, there are four pieces in the center of the board, which gives each player two points. Also, the sum of all the scores and turns remaining should always add up to 64, which is true in this case.

The next step is to combine the logo and score using a BorderPane to build the minimal shell for the Reversi application.

Composing a Layout Using BorderPane

We have built up several elements of the Reversi UI, and now we need to tie them together into a single composition. In this section we demonstrate how you can use the BorderPane class to quickly put together other components in a common layout pattern. Unlike the layouts used earlier in this chapter, you should not modify the BorderPanel's list of children, but instead use the properties for each of the content areas listed in Table 4-6.

Table 4-6. Properties Available on the BorderPanel Class

Name	Type	Description
top	Node	Element placed at the top edge of the BorderPanel area. Will be resized to its preferred height and extended to fill the full width.
bottom	Node	Element placed at the bottom edge of the BorderPanel area. Will be resized to its preferred height and extended to fill the full width.
left	Node	Element placed at the left edge of the BorderPanel area. Will be resized to its preferred width and extended to fill the full height between the top and bottom nodes.
right	Node	Element placed at the right edge of the BorderPanel area. Will be resized to its preferred width and extended to fill the full height between the top and bottom nodes.
center	Node	Element placed in the center of the BorderPanel area. Will be extended to fill the full space between the top, bottom, right, and left nodes.

The BorderPanel's top and bottom areas get positioned first, followed by the left and right, which can extend up to the height minus the top and bottom. Finally the center resizes to take any remaining space in the layout.

For our use in the Reversi application, we require only the top, center, and bottom content areas. The layout code to set up the BorderPanel with these three content areas is shown in Listing 4-8.

Listing 4-8. Reversi Root Stage Declaration Using a BorderPanel for Layout

```
@Override
public void start(Stage primaryStage) {
  primaryStage.setScene(SceneBuilder.create()
    .width(600)
    .height(400)
```

```
    .root(BorderPaneBuilder.create()
      .top(createTitle())
      .center(createBackground())
      .bottom(createScoreBoxes())
      .build())
    .build());
  primaryStage.show();
}
```

We are using this to create a docklike behavior where the title is aligned to the top with a fixed height and the score boxes are aligned to the bottom, also with a fixed height. All remaining space in the center is occupied by the grid. This could also have been done using bind expressions, but using a BorderPanel guarantees that the layout function will be called once per layout cycle, yielding higher performance and artifact-free layout.

Listing 4-9 shows a simple abstraction of a createScoreBoxes() function from "Using FlowPane and Boxes for Directional Alignment," earlier in this chapter. Notice that the tileWidth is dynamically bound to the parent width using the Bindings.selectDouble() function, which breaks the dependency on the scene.

Listing 4-9. Create Score Boxes Function

```
private Node createScoreBoxes() {
  TilePane tiles = TilePaneBuilder.create()
    .snapToPixel(false)
    .prefColumns(2)
    .children(
      createScore(Owner.BLACK),
      createScore(Owner.WHITE))
    .build();
  tiles.prefTileWidthProperty().bind(Bindings.selectDouble(tiles.parentProperty(),
"width").divide(2));
  return tiles;
}
```

Implementing createTitle is a similar modification of the Scene definition from the earlier section "Aligning to Edges Using Tiles." In this case we have also increased the preferred height of the title to give it a little padding around the text. The additional changes required are highlighted in bold in Listing 4-10.

Listing 4-10. Changes Required to the Title Creation Code to Turn It into a Function

```
private Node createTitle() {
  StackPane left = new StackPane();
  left.setStyle("-fx-background-color: black");
  Text text = new Text("JavaFX");
  text.setFont(Font.font(null, FontWeight.BOLD, 18));
  text.setFill(Color.WHITE);
  StackPane.setAlignment(text, Pos.CENTER_RIGHT);
  left.getChildren().add(text);
  Text right = new Text("Reversi");
  right.setFont(Font.font(null, FontWeight.BOLD, 18));
  TilePane tiles = new TilePane();
```

```
  tiles.setSnapToPixel(false);
  TilePane.setAlignment(right, Pos.CENTER_LEFT);
  tiles.getChildren().addAll(left, right);
  tiles.setPrefTileHeight(40);
  tiles.prefTileWidthProperty().bind(Bindings.selectDouble(tiles.parentProperty(),
"width").divide(2));
  return tiles;
}
```

The final task is to create the board background by implementing createBackground(). In "The Grid Layout Algorithm" section later in this chapter, we show you how to use a GridLayout to implement the Reversi board, but for now you can simply create a Region and fill it with a RadialGradient. RadialGradients are very similar to the LinearGradients you have created in past exercises, but will render the colors in an ellipse from the center outward. Because we are using the Region to create the background, we need to configure the RadialGradient using the style property, as shown in Listing 4-11.

Listing 4-11. *Bound Function to Create the Reversi Board Background*

```
private Node createBackground() {
  return RegionBuilder.create()
    .style("-fx-background-color: radial-gradient(radius 100%, white, gray)")
    .build();
}
```

When you run the complete program, you should see a window that looks like Figure 4-9.

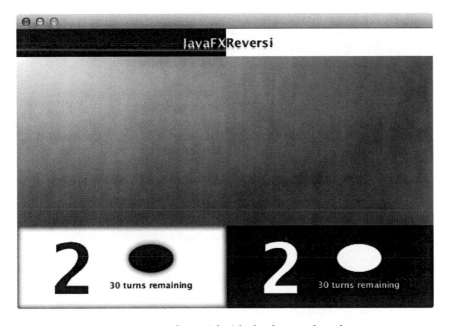

Figure 4-9. *Reversi user interface with title, background, and scores*

Try resizing the window and notice that the BorderPanel keeps the components edge aligned and automatically resizes them to fill all available space. This combined example demonstrates how bind and the built-in layouts can be used to compose dynamic layouts in JavaFX easily.

Creating Custom Regions

In previous sections we have made use of the Region class to provide simple styled backgrounds for our application, but the Region class underlies all of the JavaFX layouts and is capable of much more than just this.

In this section we show you how to create custom Regions in JavaFX that are fully resizable to build the Reversi playing pieces and squares that make up the game board. In the following section we show you how to build dynamic containers from scratch to take these resizable nodes and use the final layout, GridPane, to construct a dynamic playing board that resizes both the squares and the playing pieces.

Building a Custom Square Region

The foundation class of all the JavaFX layouts is the Region. It has standard functions on it to get bounds preferences for layout and also variables to set the width and height of the Node. In this section we show you how you can build a Reversi board square that dynamically responds to height and width changes by extending Region. The Region class has 10 properties that you can use to control the dimensions and layout, as shown in Table 4-7.

Table 4-7. *Properties of the Region Class*

Name	Access	Type	Default	Description
width	Read-only	Double		The width of the Node, set by the Parent container
height	Read-only	Double		The height of the Node, set by the Parent container
minWidth	Read/write	Double	USE_COMPUTED_SIZE	The overridden minimum width of this Region
maxHeight	Read/write	Double	USE_COMPUTED_SIZE	The overridden minimum height of this Region
prefWidth	Read/write	Double	USE_COMPUTED_SIZE	The overridden preferred width of this Region
prefHeight	Read/write	Double	USE_COMPUTED_SIZE	The overridden preferred height of this Region
maxWidth	Read/write	Double	USE_COMPUTED_SIZE	The overridden maximum width of this Region

Name	Access	Type	Default	Description
maxHeight	Read/write	Double	USE_COMPUTED_SIZE	The overridden maximum height of this Region
padding	Read/write	Insets	Insets.EMPTY	The amount of space requested on the top, bottom, left, and right of this Region
snapToPixel	Read/write	Boolean	True	If true, will round off the position and size of the Region to integral values

The width and height of a Region are read-only properties that you can use to get the size after layout is complete. Be careful binding directly to the width and height, because any changes that affect the size of this node or its children will not be updated until the next layout cycle, causing artifacts.

The padding property lets you set the amount of space to surround the content of the region during layout. Again, we use the snapToPixel property before to make sure the TilePane fits within the scene boundaries with no rounding errors. It is defined on the Region class and the default value of true will help reduce artifacts caused by pixel misalignment.

The remaining properties let you override the min, max, and pref width and height of this Region. They are hints to the Parent about how it should allocate space, and default to the calculated value for this Region. Once set, these properties can be reset to their calculated values by giving them a value of Region.USE_COMPUTED_SIZE. Also, the min and max properties can be assigned to the same value as the respective pref property by giving them a value of Region.USE_PREF_SIZE.

To define the calculated values for these, override the calculate* functions defined on the Region class as listed in Table 4-8.

Table 4-8. Functions of the Region Class

Name	Access	Returns	Description
computeMinWidth(height)	Protected	Double	Returns the computed minimum width of this Region. The default is the sum of the left and right insets.
computeMinHeight(width)	Protected	Double	Returns the computed minimum height of the Region. The default is the sum of the top and bottom insets.
computePrefWidth(height)	Protected	Double	Returns the computed preferred width of the Region. The default is the sum of the left and right insets plus the width needed to hold the children when given their preferred location and size.

Continued

Name	Access	Returns	Description
computePrefHeight(width)	Protected	Double	Returns the computed preferred height of this Region. The default is the sum of the top and bottom insets plus the height needed to hold the children when given their preferred location and size.
computeMaxWidth(height)	Protected	Double	Returns the computed maximum width of this Region. The default is Double.MAX_VALUE.
computeMaxHeight(width)	Protected	Double	Returns the computed maximum height of this Region. The default is Double.MAX_VALUE.

The defaults returned by the compute functions are fine, except for the preferred width and height, which both return 0 because we have no children and no insets. To get a nonzero preferred size, we can either override the computerPrefWidth/Height methods or simply call one of the setters for the preferredWidth/Height properties. The following implementation does the latter.

```
public class ReversiSquare extends Region {
  public ReversiSquare() {
    setStyle("-fx-background-color: burlywood");
    Light.Distant light = new Light.Distant();
    light.setAzimuth(-135);
    light.setElevation(30);
    setEffect(LightingBuilder.create().light(light).build());
    setPrefSize(200, 200);
  }
}
```

To provide styling to the squares in the above code, we set the style property, which accepts CSS properties for the background and borders. Because you cannot specify JavaFX lighting effects in CSS, we use the LightingBuilder to create a distant lighting effect and set it on the Region.

■ **Caution**   On platforms without hardware acceleration of effects, the Lighting effect may significantly affect performance.

To exercise this class, we create a quick StackPane wrapper holding a single ReversiSquare that resizes with the scene, as shown in Listing 4-12.

Listing 4-12. Wrapper Script to Show a ReversiSquare That Resizes with the Scene

```
public class ReversiSquareTest extends Application {
  public static void main(String[] args) {
    launch(args);
  }

  @Override
  public void start(Stage primaryStage) {
    primaryStage.setScene(SceneBuilder.create()
      .root(StackPaneBuilder.create()
        .children(new ReversiSquare()).build())
      .build());
    primaryStage.show();
  }
}
```

Running the completed class produces a distinctive board square that dynamically resizes with the window, as shown in Figure 4-10.

Figure 4-10. Single Reversi square that resizes with the window

Building a Resizable Reversi Piece

Creating a Reversi playing piece is done very similarly to how you created a square in the previous section. Your class should extend Region and have a public owner property that can be set to change the color of the playing piece to either WHITE or BLACK:

```
public class ReversiPiece extends Region {
  private ObjectProperty<Owner> ownerProperty = new SimpleObjectProperty<Owner>(this, "owner"
, Owner.BLACK.NONE);
  public ObjectProperty<Owner> ownerProperty() {
    return ownerProperty;
  }
  public Owner getOwner() {
    return ownerProperty.get();
  }
```

```
public void setOwner(Owner owner) {
  ownerProperty.set(owner);
}
```

We used the simplified property format in this example, with a SimpleObjectProperty of generic type Owner that gets created upon object initialization. It has public methods to get the property or get and set the value and default to Owner.NONE, which should show no playing piece.

To create the style of the playing piece, we make use of a conditional bind in the constructor to change the style whenever the owner changes. In the case of a WHITE playing piece, we use a radial gradient that goes from white to gray to black (simulating a shadow). In the case of a BLACK playing piece, we use a radial gradient that goes from white quickly to black (simulating a highlight).

We can also hide the playing piece when the owner is NONE by using a second conditional bind to set the radius to 0. Finally to give the Region a circular shape, we set the background radius to a very large value (1,000 em), which gives us a rounded rectangle with zero length sides (or an oval) as shown in the following code at the beginning of the constructor.

```
public ReversiPiece() {
  styleProperty().bind(Bindings.when(ownerProperty.isEqualTo(Owner.NONE))
    .then("radius 0")
    .otherwise(Bindings.when(ownerProperty.isEqualTo(Owner.WHITE))
      .then("-fx-background-color: radial-gradient(radius 100%, white .4, gray .9, darkgray
1)")
      .otherwise("-fx-background-color: radial-gradient(radius 100%, white 0, black .6)"))
    .concat("; -fx-background-radius: 1000em; -fx-background-insets: 5"));
  …
```

The constructor code continues on to set up a reflection effect that will make the playing surface seem glossy, and also sets a preferred size with enough room around the edges to match the preferred size of the square minus a five-pixel background inset. The last step is to set the playing piece to be transparent to mouse events, so that the square underneath can pick them up instead:

```
  …
  Reflection reflection = new Reflection();
  reflection.setFraction(1);
  reflection.topOffsetProperty().bind(heightProperty().multiply(-.75));
  setEffect(reflection);
  setPrefSize(180, 180);
  setMouseTransparent(true);
}
```

For convenience we also include a constructor version that takes an initial value for the owner property:

```
public ReversiPiece(Owner owner) {
  this();
  ownerProperty.setValue(owner);
}
```

To demonstrate the finished product, you need to make a few additions to the previous sample application to overlay the Reversi piece. The easiest way to accomplish this is to refactor the Scene to use a StackPane layout to place the Reversi piece on top of the square, and put it inside an HBox so you can have side-by-side playing pieces.

We also make use of a new constraint on HBox and VBox called grow. Setting hgrow on an element added to an HBox, or vgrow on an element added to a VBox lets the element expand from its preferred size to take additional space as it becomes available. For a more detailed discussion of grow and priority, see the next section on the GridPane where it is used heavily.

The completed wrapper code using stacks, boxes, and grow constraint is shown in Listing 4-13.

Listing 4-13. *Wrapper Application That Displays Two Reversi Squarses Side-by-Side with Playing Pieces on Top*

```java
public class ReversiPieceTest extends Application {
  public static void main(String[] args) {
    launch(args);
  }

  @Override
  public void start(Stage primaryStage) {
    Node white, black;
    primaryStage.setScene(SceneBuilder.create()
      .root(HBoxBuilder.create()
        .snapToPixel(false)
        .children(
          white = StackPaneBuilder.create()
            .children(
              new ReversiSquare(),
              new ReversiPiece(Owner.WHITE)
            )
            .build(),
          black = StackPaneBuilder.create()
            .children(
              new ReversiSquare(),
              new ReversiPiece(Owner.BLACK)
            )
            .build()
        )
        .build())
      .build());
    HBox.setHgrow(white, Priority.ALWAYS);
    HBox.setHgrow(black, Priority.ALWAYS);
    primaryStage.show();
  }
}
```

Figure 4-11 shows the completed application with both white and black pieces displayed side by side.

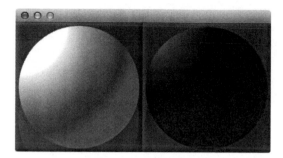

Figure 4-11. *One Reversi square with a white playing piece on it, and another with a black piece*

Laying Out the Tiles Using a GridPane

One of the most flexible and powerful layouts contained in JavaFX is the GridPane. It lets you arrange the children in a grid composed of rows and columns, optionally assigning constraints such as alignment, grow, and margin to individual nodes or an entire row/column. You can also do advanced layouts that will span rows and/or columns, giving you a layout container that is truly a superset of all the other containers discussed so far.

Table 4-9 lists the different properties on GridPane that you can set either per-Node or on an entire column or row (with the exception of margin).

Table 4-9. *Properties Available on Nodes in a GridPane Layout*

Name	Type	Description
halignment	HPos	Horizontal alignment of nodes in GridPane cell. Can be one of LEFT, CENTER, or RIGHT.
valignment	VPos	Vertical alignment of nodes in a GridPane cell. Can be one of TOP, CENTER, BASELINE, or BOTTOM.
hgrow	Priority	Priority for the GridPane cell growing horizontally beyond its preferred side.
vgrow	Priority	Priority for the GridPane cell growing vertically beyond its preferred size.
margin	Insets	Margin surrounding the element in the GridPane cell, specified as an Inset with a top, left, bottom, and right stand-off.

Just as with earlier layouts, these constraints can be set via a series of like-named static methods on the GridPane class that accept a node and constraint value. The first two constraints for alignment are similar to the alignment on StackPane, except they are constrained to be in either the horizontal or vertical direction. However, the cross-product of using horizontal and vertical alignment together gives you the same 12 combinations.

Margin is similar to the like-name constraint first described in the earlier section entitled, "Aligning Edges Using StackPane and TilePane." It is also the only constraint that can be applied solely to individual nodes, but not an entire row or column.

Both hgrow and vgrow take a value of type Priority, similar to the like-name constraints on HBox and VBox, respectively. These can be given one of three possible values:

- NEVER: Will never grow beyond the preferred dimensions of the node.

- SOMETIMES: Will only grow if there is still available space after all nodes with grow priority "ALWAYS" are taken into account.

- ALWAYS: Will grow up to the maximum dimensions of the node, sharing space equally with other nodes that have a grow priority of "ALWAYS."

Setting the grow constraint property can greatly simplify the job of laying out complex user interfaces. For example, you could use a grow constraint of NEVER on a button and ALWAYS on a TextField to ensure that the text field fills the form width, and the button is sized perfectly for the contained text.

We take advantage of the flexible capabilities of the GridPane to lay out the grid of squares and pieces for the Reversi application. The default alignment, grow policy, and margin work perfectly for the needs of our playing board, so the only thing we need to update as we add in squares is the x and y position. We don't even need to set the size of the grid, because it will automatically scale to fit the number and position of components that get added in.

To start with, we need to update the start method in the Reversi application to put the tiles on top of the background. To accomplish this we make use of a StackPane to compose the center region of the BorderLayout as shown in Listing 4-14.

Listing 4-14. *Changes to the Reversi Application to Overlay a List of Tiles (Highlighted in Bold)*

```
@Override
public void start(Stage primaryStage) {
  primaryStage.setScene(SceneBuilder.create()
    .width(600)
    .height(400)
    .root(BorderPaneBuilder.create()
      .top(createTitle())
      .center(StackPaneBuilder.create().children(
        createBackground(),
        tiles()
      ).build())
      .bottom(createScoreBoxes())
      .build())
    .build());
  primaryStage.show();
}
```

The implementation of the tiles method is a direct application of what we have learned about the GridPane layout. We simply create a new GridPane using the default constructor, and then go in a couple of loops across columns and then rows to populate each of the game cells as shown in Listing 4-15.

Listing 4-15. Implementation of the Tiles Method Using a GridPane

```
private Node tiles() {
  GridPane board = new GridPane();
  for (int i = 0; i < ReversiModel.BOARD_SIZE; i++) {
    for (int j = 0; j < ReversiModel.BOARD_SIZE; j++) {
      ReversiSquare square = new ReversiSquare();
      ReversiPiece piece = new ReversiPiece();
      piece.ownerProperty().bind(model.board[i][j]);
      board.add(StackPaneBuilder.create().children(
        square,
        piece
      ).build(), i, j);
    }
  }
  return board;
}
```

Notice that we are using the GridPane add method that takes a node first, and then the x, y co-ordinates second for convenience. Also, we are making use of a nested StackPane to hold the ReversiSquare on the bottom and the ReversiPiece on top.

The single binding from model.board to each playing piece is all that is needed to have the UI reflect the current board state and update whenever the model is changed. With these simple changes, the Reversi application shows us our starting position with two black and two white pieces played, as shown in Figure 4-12.

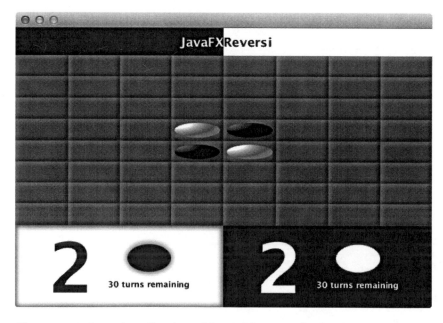

Figure 4-12. Reversi application with a GridPane to display the board and pieces

Aligning and Stretching with AnchorPane

The last built-in layout is the AnchorPane. It is a fairly specialized layout that serves two related purposes. When used with one or two nonopposing constraints, it can be used to align the child to a particular corner of the layout with a set stand-off. The other purpose is to stretch the child horizontally and/or vertically by setting opposing constraints, again with an optional stand-off from the parent edges as shown in Figure 4-13.

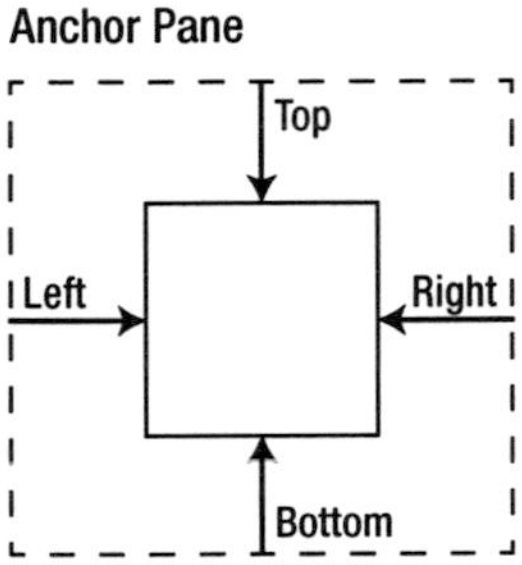

Anchor Pane

Figure 4-13. AnchorPane constraints for a child Node (solid line) in a Parent (dashed line)

The AnchorPane works by accepting a list of children that are displayed in stack order, each of which can optionally specify constraints for left, right, top, and bottom anchors. If no anchors are specified, it will position children at the top/left of the container. Once an anchor is set, it will align to a set distance away from that edge and get the minimum of the preferred size and the container size.

If opposing anchors are set on the left and right or top and bottom, the sizing behavior changes to stretching where the child width will be equal to the parent width minus the left and right anchor distances or the parent high minus the top and bottom anchor distances, respectively. It is also possible to set all four anchors, in which case the child will resize together with the parent.

With a few modifications to the Reversi application we make use of both the alignment and stretching properties of an AnchorPane to add in a new "Restart" button to the UI. The first step is to refactor the Reversi constructor to extract the existing game view into a variable and add in an AnchorPane as the root node:

```
@Override
public void start(Stage primaryStage) {
  Node game = BorderPaneBuilder.create()
    .top(createTitle())
    .center(StackPaneBuilder.create().children(
      createBackground(),
      tiles()
    ).build())
    .bottom(createScoreBoxes())
    .build();
  Node restart = restart();
```

```
primaryStage.setScene(SceneBuilder.create()
  .width(600)
  .height(400)
  .root(AnchorPaneBuilder.create().children(
    game,
    restart
  ).build()
).build());
...
```

Notice that we have also added in a second component to the AnchorPane for the restart button that we define later. The rest of the constructor goes on to set the AnchorPane constraints for the game and restart nodes so that the former scales together with the scene, and the latter is aligned 10 pixels off the top-right corner:

```
...
AnchorPane.setTopAnchor(game, 0d);
AnchorPane.setBottomAnchor(game, 0d);
AnchorPane.setLeftAnchor(game, 0d);
AnchorPane.setRightAnchor(game, 0d);
AnchorPane.setRightAnchor(restart, 10d);
AnchorPane.setTopAnchor(restart, 10d);
}
```

The next step is to create the restart() method that builds the restart button and wires up an ActionEvent handler that will reset the model:

```
private Node restart() {
  return ButtonBuilder.create().text("Restart").onAction(new EventHandler<ActionEvent>() {
    public void handle(ActionEvent t) {
      model.restart();
    }
  }).build();
}
```

Finally, you need to implement the restart model function that will restart all the squares to their initial values and set the turn back to black:

```
public void restart() {
  for (int i = 0; i < BOARD_SIZE; i++) {
    for (int j = 0; j < BOARD_SIZE; j++) {
      board[i][j].setValue(Owner.NONE);
    }
  }
  initBoard();
  turn.setValue(Owner.BLACK);
}
```

Upon running the completed application you will have a fully functional restart button that is anchored to the top-right corner, as shown in Figure 4-14.

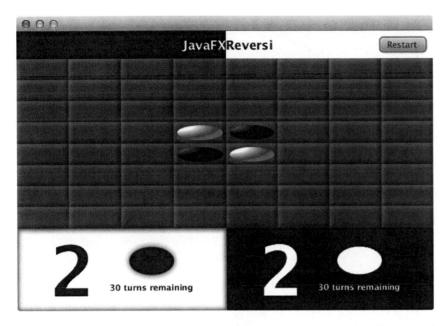

Figure 4-14. Reversi application with a restart button anchored to the top-right corner

When to Use Different Layouts

The combination of different layout techniques discussed throughout this chapter creates a very powerful capability for creating dynamic layouts. However, inasmuch as there are so many ways to accomplish the same results, it can often be confusing as to what the best practice is when creating new layouts. In this section, we discuss the benefits and disadvantages of each layout in different situations to help you more easily ascertain which best suits your application needs.

Binding was the first technique described, and is powerful enough to construct virtually any dynamic UI you can imagine. However, bind has two primary drawbacks:

- *Complexity:* The more nodes in the user interface, the more edges and constraints each one must adhere to in order to show up in the right location.

- *Performance:* Although JavaFX is very efficient about how it evaluates bind statements, too many bound variables will result in reduced performance, and also display artifacts on resizing.

That is where the built-in layouts, HBox, VBox, FlowPane, StackPane, TilePane, GridPane, and AnchorPane, come in. For the common case where a series of Nodes are stacked horizontally or vertically, using a box layout will result in less complex code than the equivalent bind. Also, unlike bind, layout containers are evaluated only once per display cycle, so you are guaranteed consistent performance regardless of the complexity of your user interface.

In practice, you usually need to use both layouts and bind together to create a dynamic layout. Table 4-10 explains for what situations each type of layout is most suitable.

Table 4-10. *When to Use Bind Versus Layouts*

Technique	Applicability
bind	Use for resizing fixed Shapes, such as Rectangles, Ellipses, and Lines.
	Easy to create layouts where Nodes overlap (also see StackPane and AnchorPane).
	Overuse can reduce performance or cause rendering artifacts.
HBox/VBox	Use for vertical or horizontal alignment of nodes.
	High performance; can be used for large number of Nodes.
	Make use of alignment and grow constraints for more complex use cases.
FlowPane	Similar to HBox/VBox in usage.
	Useful in situations where the layout should wrap lines to fit.
StackPane	Allows composition through overlapping of Nodes.
	Very useful to create layered effects such as placing text over a background.
	Be careful when stacking nodes where mouse events need to pass through. Use the mouseTransparent property on nodes or consider an AnchorPane instead.
TilePane	Creates a tiled effect where all nodes are equally sized.
	Can be forced to fill the parent via binding (make sure to snapToPixel to false).
	Is not a replacement for a general purpose Grid (see GridPane).
GridPane	Provides the most flexible layout container available.
	Should be used wherever components need pixel-perfect row and column alignment.
	Cannot be used to overlap components, except in conjunction with another layout.
AnchorPane	Highly specialized layout that can be used either for edge alignment or stretching.
	Best layout for overlapping components (passes through mouse events cleanly).
	Some use cases better accomplished with margins/padding or other constraints.

A New Perspective on Reversi: The JavaFX 3D Scene Graph

The Reversi application is starting to shape up, but is in need of a little perspective to make it more visually appealing. JavaFX comes with 3D capabilities that let you do transformations on your scene graph objects to create more advanced visual effects. We take advantage of these 3D capabilities to make the Reversi application more visually appealing.

You cannot import full 3D models into a JavaFX application today, however, you can manipulate your 2D scene graph objects in three dimensions, allowing you to give your application a 3D look and feel. The 3D Scene Graph capabilities are available only if you have a supported graphics card, so it is important to have a 2D UI to fall back on if the client machine does not have the right hardware.

To find out if you are running a machine that supports 3D transformations, you can check the Scene 3D conditional property using the Platform class using the following code fragment.

```
Platform.isSupported(ConditionalFeature.SCENE3D)
```

If you are on a computer that supports 3D transformations, this method call will return true. Otherwise, you will get a result of false and will not be able to take advantage of 3D Scene Graph capabilities. Even in the case where it returns false, you will not get an exception when using the 3D transforms; they will simply have no effect in the appearance of the application.

Once you know that your computer supports 3D effects, you can then manipulate your scene graph objects in three dimensions. The methods and transforms that support a third dimension are listed in Table 4-11.

Table 4-11. Classes and Methods That Support 3D Transforms

Class	Methods	Description
ScaleTransition	fromZ, byZ	Starting and relative z values for a scale transition
TranslateTransition	fromZ, byZ	Starting and relative z values for a translate transition
Bounds	minZ, maxZ	The minimum and maximum bounding values in the z coordinate direction
Affine	mxz, myz, mzz, tz	xz co-ordinate, yz co-ordinate, z scaling, and z translation, respectively
Rotate	pivotZ, Z_AXIS	The z pivot co-ordinate for rotation, and axis for z-based rotation, respectively
Scale	z, pivotZ	The z scale factor and z pivot co-ordinate, respectively
Translate	z	The relative z translation distance
Light.Spot	pointsAtZ	The z coordinate of the light point

Continued

Class	Methods	Description
Node	scaleZ, translateZ	The z scale and translation factors for a node
Point3D	Z	Z component of a co-ordinate in 3D space

Whenever you apply a 3D translation or rotation to one of the scene graph elements, it alters the displayed graphics by applying a matrix transformation on all graphics from source to destination co-ordinates. This translation is done in graphics hardware and optimized for high performance even when dealing with animations, complex graphics, or media. For example, a rectangular region that is rotated and translated in three dimensions would have a transformed co-ordinate space like one of the mappings shown in Figure 4-15.

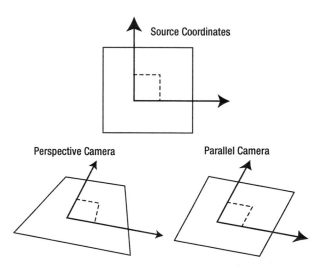

Figure 4-15. Mapping from source co-ordinates to either a perspective or parallel camera

In addition to graphics being translated into three dimensions, input and events from pointing devices get the reverse transformation from destination to source co-ordinates. This makes it possible to interact with the transformed components and controls just as you would normally do in a 2D application.

You can choose from either a ParallelCamera or a PerspectiveCamera. A ParallelCamera always displays objects at the same size regardless of distance to the camera. This is called orthographic projection, and although much easier to calculate, does not look realistic. For example Figure 4-15 on the right uses a parallel camera, where the destination co-ordinates form a perfect diamond with sides of equal length, giving it a flat look. In contrast, when using a PerspectiveCamera objects in the distance are smaller than objects in the foreground, which gives a realistic 3D effect like the example shown on the left in Figure 4-15.

The first step to using 3D capabilities in your application is to set the Camera used on the Scene. We are going to use a PerspectiveCamera to transform the Reversi board, and also supply a fieldOfView property value to control how distorted objects get as they get closer to the camera. To create the feeling of the board reaching out to the viewer, we set it to a relatively high value as shown in Listing 4-16.

Listing 4-16. Additions to the Reversi Constructor to Set the Camera Used for 3D Perspective

```
if (SCENE3D) {
  primaryStage.getScene().setCamera(PerspectiveCameraBuilder.create()
    .fieldOfView(60).build());
}
```

The other change we need to make to control the transformation of the Reversi board is to set the transforms property with a few transformations that affect the z distance. Just as in the camera code sample, we first check to make sure that 3D Scene Graph capabilities are available before applying the transformations so that we gracefully degrade to the same 2D behavior on a computer without 3D support. The code for the 3D transforms is shown in Listing 4-17.

Listing 4-17. Additions to the Tiles() Method in Order to Transform the Board in 3D Space

```
if (Platform.isSupported(ConditionalFeature.SCENE3D)) {
  Transform scale = new Scale(.45, .8, 1, 300, 60, 0);
  Transform translate = new Translate(75, -2, -150);
  Transform xRot = new Rotate(-40, 300, 150, 0, Rotate.X_AXIS);
  Transform yRot = new Rotate(-5, 300, 150, 0, Rotate.Y_AXIS);
  Transform zRot = new Rotate(-6, 300, 150, 0, Rotate.Z_AXIS);
  board.getTransforms().addAll(scale, translate, xRot, yRot, zRot);
}
```

In this code we are using a mixture of translation, rotation, and scaling to achieve the 3D perspective look that we want. When run, the new Reversi application will display a very slick-looking perspective transformed board, as shown in Figure 4-16.

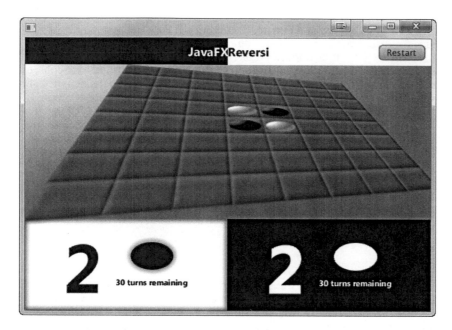

Figure 4-16. *The Reversi application using a perspective transform layout*

Notice that the application remains fully resizable even though you have significantly changed the layout and design of the grid. This is the advantage of using Containers to lay out complex user interfaces that need to be very dynamic.

Bringing Reversi to Life

Up to this point we have been singularly focused on layouts, which is important but doesn't make for a very interesting game. However, the beauty of using dynamic layouts is that with a few enhancements to the game algorithm, we can turn this static application into a dynamic playable game.

Highlighting Legal Moves

The first step of a playable game algorithm is to make sure that pieces can be placed only on legal squares. Rather than simply implement an algorithm in the backend, we take this as an opportunity to add a feature to the application where it shows you all of the next available moves.

Going back to the Reversi game rules, a move is valid only in the following circumstances.

- There is not already another piece at the same location.

- The piece is placed adjacent to a piece of the opposite color, and on that same line, there is another piece of the same color on the opposite end that would allow a flip of one or more of the opposing player's pieces.

To start with, you need to add a legalMove function to the model class that checks whether the cell is empty and then verifies all eight directions around a given Cell:

```
public BooleanBinding legalMove(int x, int y) {
  return board[x][y].isEqualTo(Owner.NONE).and(
    canFlip(x, y, 0, -1, turn).or(
    canFlip(x, y, -1, -1, turn).or(
    canFlip(x, y, -1, 0, turn).or(
    canFlip(x, y, -1, 1, turn).or(
    canFlip(x, y, 0, 1, turn).or(
    canFlip(x, y, 1, 1, turn).or(
    canFlip(x, y, 1, 0, turn).or(
    canFlip(x, y, 1, -1, turn))))))))
  );
}
```

■ **Note**   We have chosen to make all the public model functions return bindings. This makes it possible to use property binding to update the UI and will efficiently defer updates until the playing board changes.

The canFlip method validates the second condition for the given direction indicated by the cellX, cellY arguments and the player whose turn is indicated. Because it would be more complicated and less efficient to use the fluent binding interface, we chose to create a custom binding instead.

Creating a custom binding involves the following.

- First override the binding class (in this case BooleanBinding) with an inner class.

- To set up the bound variables, use a static initializer that calls the bind function for each variable on which the algorithm depends.

- Override the computeValue method, and return the new calculated value of the binding.

The basic algorithm for calculating whether this is a legal move is to check the first cell in the given direction to make sure it is a different color, and if it is, continue walking cells until you find one that is the same color. If you do find one that is the same color, it is a legal move with pieces to flip, but if the next cell is the same color or there is no opposite color piece at the other end, it is not a legal move.

This means that the static initializer needs to add a property binding for every cell in the given direction, and the algorithm needs to use a loop to go through all of the cells, checking their owner, as shown in the following code.

```
public BooleanBinding canFlip(final int cellX, final int cellY, final int directionX, final
int directionY, final ObjectProperty<Owner> turn) {
  return new BooleanBinding() {
    {
      bind(turn);
      int x = cellX + directionX;
      int y = cellY + directionY;
```

```
        while (x >= 0 && x < BOARD_SIZE && y >= 0 && y < BOARD_SIZE) {
          bind(board[x][y]);
          x += directionX;
          y += directionY;
        }
      }
      @Override
      protected boolean computeValue() {
        Owner turnVal = turn.get();
        int x = cellX + directionX;
        int y = cellY + directionY;
        boolean first = true;
        while (x >= 0 && x < BOARD_SIZE && y >= 0 && y < BOARD_SIZE && board[x][y].get() !=
Owner.NONE) {
          if (board[x][y].get() == turnVal) {
            return !first;
          }
          first = false;
          x += directionX;
          y += directionY;
        }
        return false;
      }
    };
}
```

The last step in highlighting legal moves is to wire the legalMove model function up to the squares. This involves binding the style property of the ReversiSquare class to the legalMove method (changes in bold).

```
public ReversiSquare(final int x, final int y) {
  styleProperty().bind(Bindings.when(model.legalMove(x, y))
    .then("-fx-background-color: derive(dodgerblue, -60%)")
    .otherwise("-fx-background-color: burlywood"));
  Light.Distant light = new Light.Distant();
```

■ **Tip** The derive function used is a JavaFX-specific CSS function that lets you create a new color based on an existing one. The second parameter is brightness, which can range from −100% (black) to 100% white.

Also, don't forget to add in the static model variable on which this code depends:

```
private static ReversiModel model = ReversiModel.getInstance();
```

And also to update the ReversiSquare construction in the tiles() method to pass in the x and y board co-ordinates:

```
ReversiSquare square = new ReversiSquare(i, j);
```

Now upon running the application, it correctly highlights the same four moves for black that were described in the "Board Layout and Basic Rules" section, as shown in Figure 4-17.

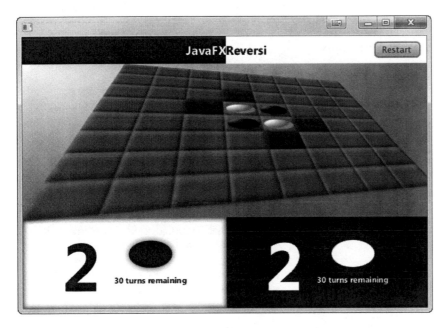

Figure 4-17. *Reversi application highlighting the available moves for black's first turn*

Highlighting the Active Cell

The simplest example of board interaction is to highlight the current cell that the user has moused over. Rather than highlighting cells that are not playable, you can take advantage of the legalMove() function you defined in the last section to highlight only cells that are active.

For the highlight we are going to use a nested Region with a blue stroke to outline the cell the cursor is over. Although we could simply add a stroke to our existing Region, creating a separate Region makes it easier to isolate the highlight and animate it independently.

The highlight region can be quickly created as a variable in the ReversiSquare class using CSS styling and the builder pattern as shown in Listing 4-18.

Listing 4-18. *Additions to the ReversiSquare create() Method to Enable Highlighting*

```
private Region highlight = RegionBuilder.create()
  .opacity(0)
  .style("-fx-border-width: 3; -fx-border-color: dodgerblue")
  .build();
```

Then to add it in to the scenegraph, you can append the following line in the constructor.

```
getChildren().add(highlight);
```

175

The default layout of the Region class simply sets children to their preferred size, but does not position them or allow them to fill the content area. We want the highlight to match the size of the square, therefore we need to override the layout algorithm and supply our own. Table 4-12 lists several additional functions on Region that allow us to override the layout algorithm and help with sizing and positioning of child nodes.

Table 4-12. *Layout Functions of the Region Class*

Name	Access	Returns	Description
layoutChildren()	Protected	Void	Method that is called to perform layout on the child nodes. Can be overridden to supply a custom algorithm.
layoutInArea(node, x, y, width, height, baseline, halign, valign)	Protected	Void	Helper method that will position the given Node at the specified co-ordinates and scale resizable nodes to fit the given width and height. If the node is resizable or the node's maximum dimensions prevent it from being resized, it will be positioned according to the given baseline, halign, and valign.
layoutInArea(node, x, y, width, height, baseline, margin, halign, valign)	Protected	Void	Same as the previous layoutInArea method, except that the given margin will be applied to the edges of the node.
layoutInArea(node, x, y, width, height, baseline, margin, fillWidth, fillHeight, halign, valign)	Protected	Void	Same as the previous layoutInArea method, except that if fillWidth or fillHeight are set to false, the node will only scale up to the preferred width or height, respectively.

To make sure the size and position of the contained region match the parent, we are going to override the layoutChildren method and supply our own algorithm. The first variant of the layoutInArea helper method allows us to position and scale in one shot, which is ideal for our use case:

```
@Override
protected void layoutChildren() {
  layoutInArea(highlight, 0, 0, getWidth(), getHeight(), getBaselineOffset(), HPos.CENTER,
VPos.CENTER);
}
```

To create the animation highlight, we make use of a FadeTransition that animates the opacity of the highlight created in Listing 4-18 from 0.0 to 1.0. This is used to produce a fade-in effect when the user mouses over the Node and a fade-out effect when the user mouses out. The following code shows the FadeTransition to accomplish this.

```
private FadeTransition highlightTransition = FadeTransitionBuilder.create()
  .node(highlight)
  .duration(Duration.millis(200))
  .fromValue(0)
  .toValue(1)
  .build();
```

▓ **Note** Even though the starting value of the opacity was set to 0, you still need to set the fromValue property of the transition to 0 explicitly for it to work correctly in reverse.

The last step is to add in the event listeners that will fire when the user mouses over the Node. These can be added by calling the addEventHandler method with an EventHandler inner class that accepts MouseEvents:

```
addEventHandler(MouseEvent.MOUSE_ENTERED_TARGET, new EventHandler<MouseEvent>() {
  public void handle(MouseEvent t) {
    if (model.legalMove(x, y).get()) {
      highlightTransition.setRate(1);
      highlightTransition.play();
    }
  }
});
addEventHandler(MouseEvent.MOUSE_EXITED_TARGET, new EventHandler<MouseEvent>() {
  public void handle(MouseEvent t) {
    highlightTransition.setRate(-1);
    highlightTransition.play();
  }
});
```

Notice that the code plays the same animation in either case, but changes the rate of the animation based on whether it should be played forwards (1) or backwards –1). This ensures that the animation will seamlessly transition even if it is in progress.

When run, the Reversi application now animates a subtle blue outline over the highlighted Node under the cursor, as shown in Figure 4-18.

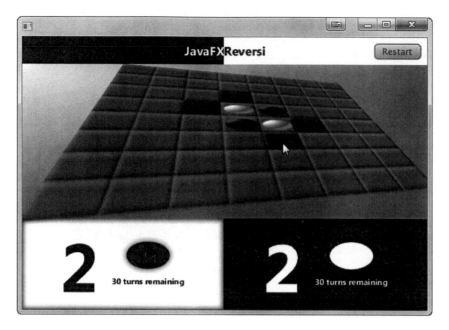

Figure 4-18. *The Reversi application with a highlight animation over the active cell*

Taking Turns

The last bit of missing functionality in the Reversi application is the ability for players to take turns placing pieces on the board. We already have all the infrastructure needed to accept mouse input and display pieces. All that is needed is a little glue code, plus some model enhancements to finish the game play.

Picking up where we left off in the previous section, the first step is to add an onMouseClicked event handler to the ReversiSquare init method:

```
addEventHandler(MouseEvent.MOUSE_CLICKED, new EventHandler<MouseEvent>() {
  public void handle(MouseEvent t) {
    model.play(x, y);
    highlightTransition.setRate(1);
    highlightTransition.play();
  }
});
```

This method both calls the model function to play the current turn, and also removes the highlight from the current cell, similar to the mouse exited event handler.

The play() function in the model class needs to perform several activities for each legal move:

- Set the clicked cell to be owned by the current player.

- Flip over captured pieces in any of eight possible directions.

- Change the turn to be the opposite player's.

An example implementation of the play() method is shown in Listing 4-19.

Listing 4-19. Example play() Method That Flips Cells in Eight Directions

```
public void play(int cellX, int cellY) {
  if (legalMove(cellX, cellY).get()) {
    board[cellX][cellY].setValue(turn.get());
    flip(cellX, cellY, 0, -1, turn);
    flip(cellX, cellY, -1, -1, turn);
    flip(cellX, cellY, -1, 0, turn);
    flip(cellX, cellY, -1, 1, turn);
    flip(cellX, cellY, 0, 1, turn);
    flip(cellX, cellY, 1, 1, turn);
    flip(cellX, cellY, 1, 0, turn);
    flip(cellX, cellY, 1, -1, turn);
    turn.setValue(turn.getValue().opposite());
  }
}
```

Notice that it follows the same pattern as the legalMove() function we defined earlier to determine whether any pieces can be flipped, with the main difference being that it does not make use of binding. The implementation of the flip method also shares many similarities to the algorithm used in the canFlip() method, but again does not need to bother with creating a binding:

```
public void flip(int cellX, int cellY, int directionX, int directionY, ObjectProperty<Owner>
turn) {
  if (canFlip(cellX, cellY, directionX, directionY, turn).get()) {
    int x = cellX + directionX;
    int y = cellY + directionY;
    while (x >= 0 && x < BOARD_SIZE && y >= 0 && y < BOARD SIZE && board[x][y].get() !=
turn.get()) {
      board[x][y].setValue(turn.get());
      x += directionX;
      y += directionY;
    }
  }
}
```

With a completed game algorithm, you can now play a full game with two players at the same computer, as shown in Figure 4-19. Notice that even the turn indicator that you set up at the beginning of the chapter is now properly flipping and indicating the current player.

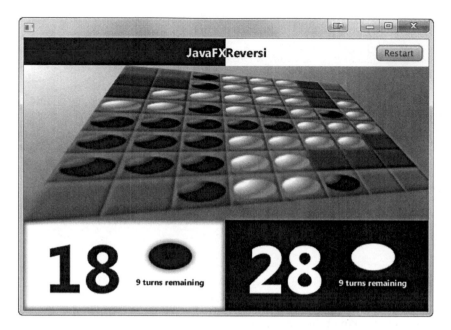

Figure 4-19. *Black's turn in the Final 2006 World Othello Championship*

Besides being a great example of the game in action, Figure 4-19 is also a replay of the famous 2006 World Othello Championship between Caroline Sandberg Odsell (black) and Hideshi Tamenori (white). What should black's next move be to win 37–27? See the Resources section for the answer.

Additional Game Enhancements

The Reversi application that was developed in this chapter is completely dynamic and flexible both in layout and structure, so it is time to take advantage of this and push the limits of your coding skills.

Here are some coding challenges that you can use to take the Reversi application from a well-designed tutorial into a full-fledged application.

- There is one rule that we neglected to implement, which is skipping turns. If, and only if, a player has no available options to play, the next player can go. Try implementing a facility that automatically detects whether there are no legal moves and skips a turn.

- Although the 3D effect is very dynamic, other than setting the rotation of the playing board we do not take advantage of this characteristic. Try implementing a start-up animation that tilts the board as the application opens.

- Playing against another player on the same computer is not nearly as interesting as playing against a remote opponent. After reading some of the later chapters on backend integration with JavaFX, try implementing a network-capable version of the Reversi application.

- Wouldn't it be great to have a JavaFX AI for playing Reversi? Give it a try, and see if you can create an unbeatable opponent!

Summary

In this chapter you were able to fully leverage the JavaFX layout capabilities to do dynamic layout of a complex application. Along the way, you learned how to

- Align Nodes using bind.

- Use StackPane to layer Nodes and create composite layouts.

- Use TilePane to do fixed-size layouts.

- Use FlowPane, HBox, and VBox to do directional layouts with and without wrapping.

- Create a dynamic game board using binding and GridPane.

- Use AnchorPane to align and stretch overlapping nodes.

- Create custom components using Regions and CSS.

- Use 3D Scene Graph capabilities to add perspective.

- Build a rich user interface backed by a game model.

- Apply JavaFX effects and transitions.

After experiencing the advantages of dynamic layout, you will be hard-pressed to go back to static positioning of components with fixed sizes. In the next chapter we show you how to create custom UI components and charts that you can use to create even more impressive business-centric applications!

Resources

For more information about dynamic layouts, consult the following resources.

- JavaFX 2.0 Layout: A Class Tour:
  `http://amyfowlersblog.wordpress.com/2011/06/02/javafx2-0-layout-a-class-tour/`

- Working with Layouts in JavaFX:
  `http://docs.oracle.com/javafx/2.0/layout/jfxpub-layout.htm`

To learn more about the game of Reversi, please refer to the following resources.

- Wikipedia, "Reversi." URL: `http://en.wikipedia.org/wiki/Reversi`

- The Othello Wiki Book Project. URL:
  `http://www.othello.dk/book/index.php/Main_Page`

- The solution for the Reversi challenge shown in Figure 4-19 can be found at the following URL: `http://www.othello.dk/book/index.php/Solution_solitaire`

CHAPTER 5

Using the JavaFX UI Controls

Miracles are a retelling in small letters of the very same story which is written across the whole world in letters too large for some of us to see.

—C. S. Lewis

In Chapter 2 you learned how to create user interfaces (UIs) in JavaFX by creating a stage, putting a scene on the stage, and putting nodes in the scene. You also learned how to handle mouse and keyboard events, as well as how to animate nodes in the scene.

In this chapter we pick up the UI discussion from Chapter 2 by showing you how to use the UI controls available in JavaFX. The knowledge you've gained about property binding in Chapter 3 and layouts in Chapter 4 will serve you well in this chapter, as it builds upon those concepts.

Trying Out the JavaFX UI Controls

JavaFX has a rich set of UI controls for creating your applications. These range from relatively simple controls such as `TextField` to more complex controls such as `WebView`. To get you up to speed quickly on these controls, we've created an example application named StarterApp. This application has an example of most of the UI controls available in JavaFX, and it also serves as a starting point from which you can modify to create an application.

Before walking through the behavior of the program, go ahead and open the project and execute it by following the instructions for building and executing the AudioConfig project in Chapter 1. The project file is located in the Chapter05 directory subordinate to which you extracted the book's code download bundle.

EXAMINING THE BEHAVIOR OF THE STARTERAPP PROGRAM

When the program starts, its appearance should be similar to the screenshot in Figure 5-1.

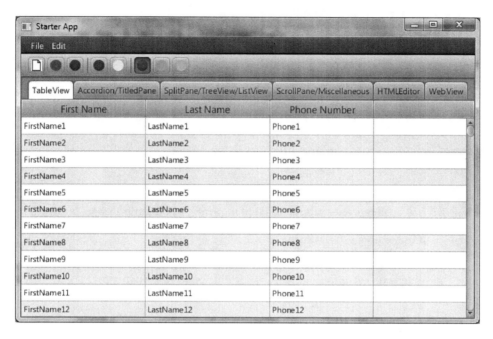

Figure 5-1. The StarterApp program when first invoked

To fully examine its behavior, perform the following steps.

1. Click the File menu, noticing that the dropdown menu contains a menu item named New, with an image and the Ctrl+N shortcut key combination as shown in Figure 5-2.

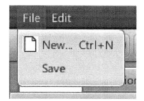

Figure 5-2. The File menu of the StarterApp program

2. Select the New menu item by clicking it or pressing the shortcut key combination, noticing that the following message appears in the Java console: "ACTION occurred on MenuItem New".

3. Examine the toolbar under the menu bar, shown in Figure 5-3, clicking the leftmost button that has the same image that is on the New menu item. Notice that the following message appears in the Java console: "New toolbar button clicked".

Figure 5-3. *The toolbar of the StarterApp program*

4. Hover the mouse cursor over the leftmost button in the toolbar, noticing that a tooltip appears with the message: "New Document... Ctrl+N".

5. Click the fourth and fifth buttons on the toolbar, located between the vertical separator bars. Note that the buttons have two states, independent of each other.

6. Click the three rightmost buttons on the toolbar, located to the right of the last vertical separator bar. Note that the buttons have two states, but that only one button at a time is in the selected (depressed) state.

7. Drag the thumb on the vertical scroll bar on the right side of the TableView, noting that there are 10,000 rows in the table containing FirstName, LastName, and Phone data in each row. Click on one of the rows, noting that a message like "Person: FirstNameX LastNameX chosen in TableView" prints to the Java console.

8. Drag the TableView column headers horizontally to rearrange them. Drag the right and left sides of the column headers to resize them.

9. Click the tab labeled Accordion/TitledPane, noting that the tab contains an Accordion control with three expandable titled panes as shown in Figure 5-4. Click each TitledPane, noting that they expand and collapse.

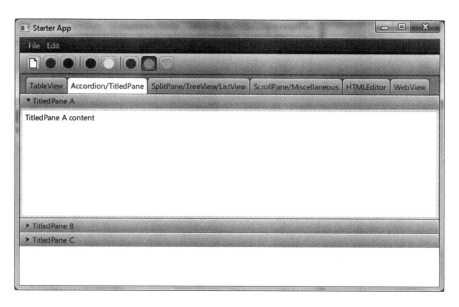

Figure 5-4. *The Accordion/TitledPane tab of the StarterApp program*

10. Click the tab labeled SplitPane/TreeView/ListView, noting that the tab contains a split pane with a tree control on the left and an empty list view on the right as shown in Figure 5-5.

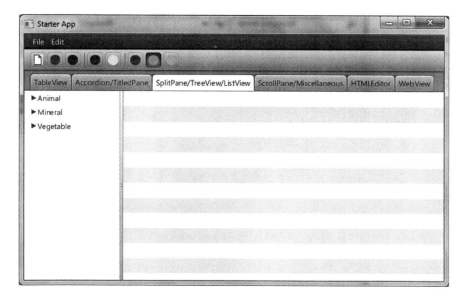

Figure 5-5. *The SplitPane/TreeView/ListView tab of the StarterApp program*

11. Expand the nodes in the TreeView on the left, clicking on various leaf nodes. Note that the ListView on the right is populated with 10,000 rows containing the same name as the node clicked.

12. Drag the divider of the SplitPane to the right, resulting in the application having the appearance shown in Figure 5-6. Drag the divider of the SplitPane to the left, noting that it is prevented from hiding the TreeView.

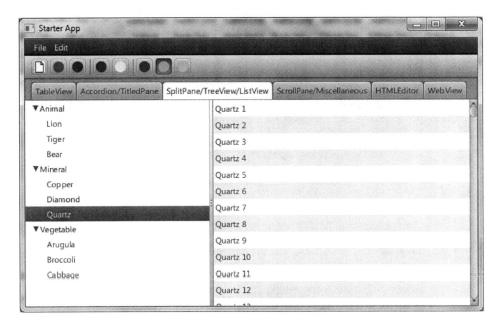

Figure 5-6. *After expanding the nodes on the TreeView and selecting one of the leaf nodes*

13. Click the tab labeled ScrollPane/Miscellaneous, noting that the tab contains a variety of UI controls in a scrollable pane, as shown in Figure 5-7.

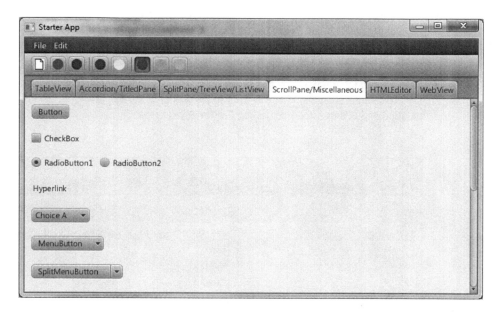

Figure 5-7. *The ScrollPane/Miscellaneous tab of the StarterApp program*

14. Click the `Button` (labeled "Button"), noting that the following message is output to the Java console: "ACTION occurred on Button".

15. Click the `CheckBox`, noting that the following message is output to the Java console: "ACTION occurred on CheckBox, and selectedProperty is: true".

16. Select each radio button, noting that a message such as "RadioButton2 selected" is output to the Java console when a given `RadioButton` is selected.

17. Click the `Hyperlink` control, noting that the following message is output to the Java console: "ACTION occurred on Hyperlink".

18. Select various items (e.g., "Choice B") in the `ChoiceBox`, noting that a message such as "Choice B chosen in ChoiceBox" is output to the Java console when a given item is selected.

19. Select the "MenuItem A" option in the `MenuButton` (labeled "MenuButton"), noting that the message "ACTION occurred on Menu Item A" is output to the Java console.

20. Click on the area of the `SplitMenuButton` (labeled "SplitMenuButton"), noting that the following message is output to the Java console: "ACTION occurred on SplitMenuButton".

21. Click the down arrow on the right side of the `SplitMenuButton` and select the "MenuItem A" option, noting that the message "ACTION occurred on Menu Item A" is output to the Java console.

22. Scroll down as necessary in the `ScrollPane` to see the controls shown in Figure 5-8.

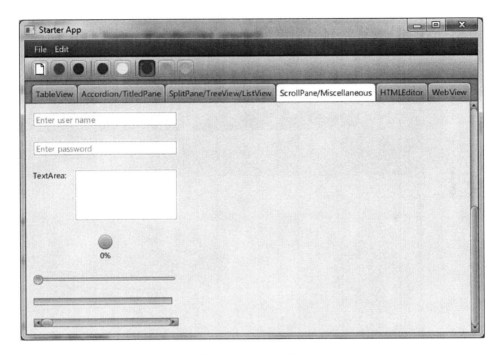

Figure 5-8. The ScrollPane/Miscellaneous tab scrolled to the bottom

23. Enter some text into the `TextField` that has the prompt text "Enter user name", noting that each time the text is modified the contents of the TextField are output to the Java console.

24. Enter some text into the `PasswordField` that has the prompt text "Enter password", noting that a mask character is displayed instead of the characters that you typed. Click on anything other than the `PasswordField`, causing it to lose focus, noting that the contents of the `PasswordField` are output to the Java console.

25. Enter some text into the `TextArea` (labeled "TextArea"). Click on anything other than the `TextArea`, causing it to lose focus, noting that the contents of the `TextArea` are output to the Java console.

26. Slide the thumb of the horizontal `Slider` to the right, noticing that the `ProgressIndicator` above it displays from 0% through 99%, and then Done. Slide it all the way to the left, noticing that `ProgressIndicator` changes in appearance to its spinning indeterminate state.

27. Slide the thumb of the horizontal ScrollBar to the right, noticing that the ProgressBar above it represents the same value. Slide it all the way to the left, noticing that ProgressBar changes in appearance to its indeterminate state.

28. Click the secondary (usually the right) button on your mouse somewhere in the blank area of the ScrollPane, noting that a ContextMenu appears as shown in Figure 5-9.

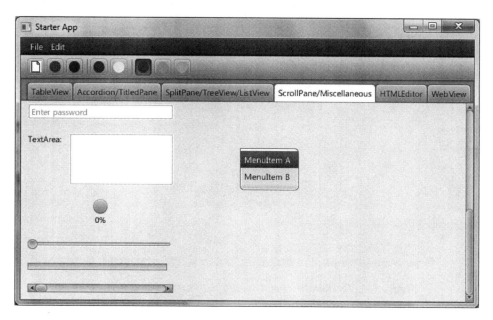

Figure 5-9. *The ContextMenu appearing after the secondary mouse button is clicked*

29. Click the "MenuItem A" menu item in the ContextMenu, noting that the following message appears in the Java console: "ACTION occurred on Menu Item A".

30. Click the tab labeled HTMLEditor, noting that the tab contains a rich text editor and a button labeled View HTML, as shown in Figure 5-10.

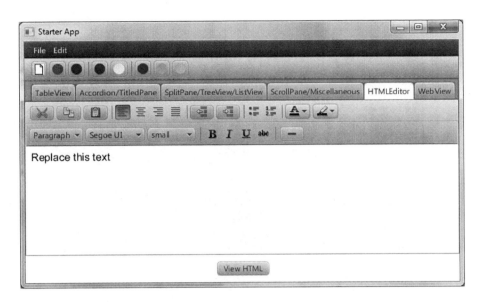

Figure 5-10. The HTMLEditor tab of the StarterApp program

31. Type some text into the editing area, using various tools in the editor's toolbars to style the text. When finished, click the View HTML button to see the HTML in the underlying data model displayed in a Popup, as shown in Figure 5-11.

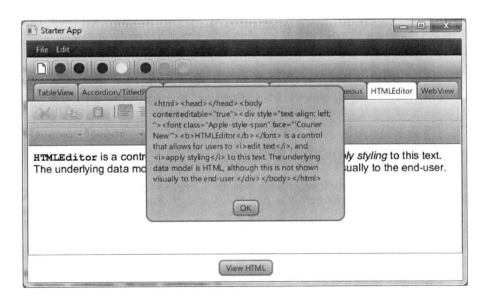

Figure 5-11. After editing text in the HTMLEditor and clicking View HTML

32. Click the OK button to dismiss the popup. Then click the tab labeled WebView, noting that the tab contains a web browser displaying a randomly selected web page (if your computer is connected to the Internet), as shown in Figure 5-12.

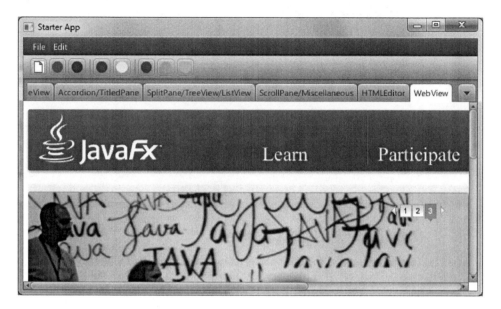

Figure 5-12. *The WebView tab of the StarterApp program*

33. Click on one of the other tabs in the application, and then on the WebVIew tab, noting that the Java console displays a randomly selected URL that the WebView is attempting to load.

Congratulations on sticking with this 33-step exercise! Performing this exercise has prepared you to relate to the code behind it, which we now walk through together.

Leveraging the JavaFX UI Controls

Similar to the Audio Configuration program in Chapter 1, our StarterApp program contains a model class. This class is named StarterAppModel, and is shown in Listing 5-1.

Listing 5-1. *The Source Code for StarterAppModel.java*

```java
package projavafx.starterapp.model;

import javafx.beans.property.DoubleProperty;
import javafx.beans.property.SimpleDoubleProperty;
import javafx.collections.FXCollections;
import javafx.collections.ObservableList;

public class StarterAppModel {
  public ObservableList getTeamMembers() {
    ObservableList teamMembers = FXCollections.observableArrayList();
    for (int i = 1; i <= 10000; i++) {
      teamMembers.add(new Person("FirstName" + i,
                                 "LastName" + i,
                                 "Phone" + i));
    }
    return teamMembers;
  }

  public String getRandomWebSite() {
    String[] webSites = {
      "http://javafx.com",
      "http://fxexperience.com",
      "http://steveonjava.com",
      "http://javafxpert.com",
      "http://pleasingsoftware.blogspot.com",
      "http://www.weiqigao.com/blog",
      "http://google.com"
    };
    int randomIdx = (int)(Math.random() * webSites.length);
    return webSites[randomIdx];
  }

  public ObservableList listViewItems = FXCollections.observableArrayList();

  public ObservableList choiceBoxItems = FXCollections.observableArrayList(
    "Choice A",
    "Choice B",
    "Choice C",
    "Choice D"
  );

  public double maxRpm = 8000.0;
  public DoubleProperty rpm = new SimpleDoubleProperty(0);

  public double maxKph = 300.0;
  public DoubleProperty kph = new SimpleDoubleProperty(0);
}
```

We refer to snippets from this listing as they apply to relevant UI controls that we walk through in the main Java file of the StarterApp program. This file is named StarterAppMain.java and is shown in its entirety one chunk at a time during our imminent discussion of the JavaFX UI controls.

Setting the Stage for the StarterApp Program

Listing 5-2 shows the first portion of the StarterAppMain.java file, in which the Stage and Scene are received and created. In addition, the root of the Scene is assigned a BorderPane, which provides the UI structure in which the MenuBar, ToolBar, and TabPane will reside.

Listing 5-2. *The First Portion of StarterAppMain.java*

```
package projavafx.starterapp.ui;

import javafx.application.Application;
import javafx.beans.value.ChangeListener;
import javafx.beans.value.ObservableValue;
import javafx.event.ActionEvent;
import javafx.event.Event;
import javafx.event.EventHandler;
import javafx.geometry.Insets;
import javafx.geometry.Orientation;
import javafx.geometry.Pos;
import javafx.scene.Node;
import javafx.scene.Scene;
import javafx.scene.SceneBuilder;
import javafx.scene.control.*;
import javafx.scene.control.cell.PropertyValueFactory;
import javafx.scene.image.Image;
import javafx.scene.image.ImageView;
import javafx.scene.input.KeyCombination;
import javafx.scene.input.MouseButton;
import javafx.scene.input.MouseEvent;
import javafx.scene.layout.*;
import javafx.scene.paint.Color;
import javafx.scene.shape.CircleBuilder;
import javafx.scene.shape.RectangleBuilder;
import javafx.scene.web.HTMLEditor;
import javafx.scene.web.HTMLEditorBuilder;
import javafx.scene.web.WebView;
import javafx.scene.web.WebViewBuilder;
import javafx.stage.Popup;
import javafx.stage.PopupBuilder;
import javafx.stage.Stage;
import projavafx.starterapp.model.StarterAppModel;
```

```java
public class StarterAppMain extends Application {

  // A reference to the model
  StarterAppModel model = new StarterAppModel();

  Stage stage;
  CheckBox checkBox;
  ContextMenu contextMenu;
  Label htmlLabel;
  Popup alertPopup;
  Tab webViewTab;

  public static void main(String[] args) {
    Application.launch(args);
  }

  @Override
  public void start(final Stage primaryStage) {
    stage = primaryStage;
    Scene scene = SceneBuilder.create()
      .width(800)
      .height(600)
      .stylesheets(StarterAppMain.class.getResource("starterApp.css")
                                  .toExternalForm())
      .root(
        BorderPaneBuilder.create()
          .top(
            VBoxBuilder.create()
              .children(
                createMenus(),
                createToolBar()
              )
              .build()
          )
          .center(createTabs())
          .build()
      )
      .build();

    stage.setScene(scene);
    stage.setTitle("Starter App");
    stage.show();
  }
```

Of particular note in Listing 5-2:

- The top area of the BorderPane will contain the MenuBar and ToolBar shown in Figure 5-1, created by the createMenus() and createToolBar() methods that we walk through soon.

- The center area of the BorderPane will contain the TabPane shown in Figure 5-1, created by the createTabs() method that we walk through soon as well.

- A style sheet named `starterApp.css` is loaded, which we refer to later when discussing relevant functionality.

Creating a Menu and Defining Menu Items

To create the menu structure, our StarterApp program defines a method that we've arbitrarily named `createMenus()`, shown in Listing 5-3. This method leverages the `MenuBarBuilder`, `MenuBuilder`, and `MenuItemBuilder` classes, and returns a `MenuBar` instance that contains the desired menu structure.

Listing 5-3. The createMenus() Method Located in StarterAppMain.java

```java
MenuBar createMenus() {
  MenuBar menuBar = MenuBarBuilder.create()
    .menus(
      MenuBuilder.create()
        .text("File")
        .items(
          MenuItemBuilder.create()
            .text("New...")
            .graphic((new ImageView(
              new Image(getClass().getResourceAsStream("images/paper.png"))))
            )
            .accelerator(KeyCombination.keyCombination("Ctrl+N"))
            .onAction(new EventHandler<ActionEvent>() {
                @Override public void handle(ActionEvent e) {
                  System.out.println(e.getEventType() +
                                        " occurred on MenuItem New");
                }
              })
            .build(),
          MenuItemBuilder.create()
            .text("Save")
            .build()
        )
        .build(),
      MenuBuilder.create()
        .text("Edit")
        .items(
          MenuItemBuilder.create()
            .text("Cut")
            .build(),
          MenuItemBuilder.create()
            .text("Copy")
            .build(),
          MenuItemBuilder.create()
            .text("Paste")
            .build()
        )
```

```
        .build()
    )
    .build();

  return menuBar;
}
```

As previously shown in Figure 5-2, in addition to a title, menu items often have a graphic and an accelerator key combination. In the snippet below from Listing 5-3, the menu item named New is defined with a title, graphic, and an accelerator key, as well as an action to be performed when the menu item is selected:

```
MenuItemBuilder.create()
  .text("New...")
  .graphic((new ImageView(
    new Image(getClass().getResourceAsStream("images/paper.png"))))
  )
  .accelerator(KeyCombination.keyCombination("Ctrl+N"))
  .onAction(new EventHandler<ActionEvent>() {
      @Override public void handle(ActionEvent e) {
        System.out.println(e.getEventType() +
                                  " occurred on MenuItem New");
      }
  })
  .build(),
```

The recommended size for a menu item graphic is 16 ×16 pixels, which is the size of the graphic used in the New menu item of the StarterApp program. To load the graphic from the file system, the argument supplied to the `graphic()` method in the snippet above causes the same class loader that loaded the `StarterAppMain` class to load the `paper.png` file. This `paper.png` file is loaded from the `images` directory subordinate to the location of the StartAppMain.class file.

To define the Ctrl+N accelerator key combination, the static `keyCombination()` method of the `KeyCombination` class is used to create a `KeyCombination` instance. This instance is passed into the `accelerator()` method of the `MenuItemBuilder`.

The `onAction()` event handler in the snippet above defines an anonymous inner class whose `handle()` method is invoked when the user selects the New menu item. The resulting message printed to the Java console is the one to which Step 2 of the exercise above refers.

Creating a Toolbar

To create the toolbar, our StarterApp program defines a method that we've arbitrarily named `createToolBar()`, shown in Listing 5-4. This method leverages the `ButtonBuilder`, `Separator`, `ToggleButtonBuilder`, and `ToggleGroup` classes, and returns a `ToolBar` instance that contains the desired toolbar buttons.

Listing 5-4. *The createToolBar() Method Located in StarterAppMain.java*

```java
ToolBar createToolBar() {
  final ToggleGroup alignToggleGroup = new ToggleGroup();
  ToolBar toolBar = ToolBarBuilder.create()
    .items(
      ButtonBuilder.create()
        .id("newButton")
        .graphic(new ImageView(
          new Image(getClass().getResourceAsStream("images/paper.png")))
        )
        .tooltip(new Tooltip("New Document... Ctrl+N"))
        .onAction(new EventHandler<ActionEvent>() {
            @Override public void handle(ActionEvent e) {
              System.out.println("New toolbar button clicked");
            }
        })
        .build(),
      ButtonBuilder.create()
        .id("editButton")
        .graphic(
          CircleBuilder.create()
            .fill(Color.GREEN)
            .radius(8)
            .build()
        )
        .build(),
      ButtonBuilder.create()
        .id("deleteButton")
        .graphic(
          CircleBuilder.create()
            .fill(Color.BLUE)
            .radius(8)
            .build()
        )
        .build(),
      new Separator(Orientation.VERTICAL),
      ToggleButtonBuilder.create()
        .id("boldButton")
        .graphic(
          CircleBuilder.create()
            .fill(Color.MAROON)
            .radius(8)
            .build()
        )
        .onAction(new EventHandler<ActionEvent>() {
            @Override public void handle(ActionEvent e) {
              ToggleButton tb = ((ToggleButton)e.getTarget());
              System.out.print(e.getEventType() + " occurred on ToggleButton "
                                + tb.getId());
```

```
          System.out.print(", and selectedProperty is: ");
          System.out.println(tb.selectedProperty().getValue());
        }
      })
    .build(),
ToggleButtonBuilder.create()
  .id("italicButton")
  .graphic(
    CircleBuilder.create()
      .fill(Color.YELLOW)
      .radius(8)
      .build()
  )
  .onAction(new EventHandler<ActionEvent>() {
      @Override public void handle(ActionEvent e) {
        ToggleButton tb = ((ToggleButton)e.getTarget());
        System.out.print(e.getEventType() + " occurred on ToggleButton "
                        + tb.getId());
        System.out.print(", and selectedProperty is: ");
        System.out.println(tb.selectedProperty().getValue());
      }
    })
  .build(),
new Separator(Orientation.VERTICAL),
ToggleButtonBuilder.create()
  .id("leftAlignButton")
  .toggleGroup(alignToggleGroup)
  .graphic(
    CircleBuilder.create()
      .fill(Color.PURPLE)
      .radius(8)
      .build()
  )
  .build(),
ToggleButtonBuilder.create()
  .id("centerAlignButton")
  .toggleGroup(alignToggleGroup)
  .graphic(
    CircleBuilder.create()
      .fill(Color.ORANGE)
      .radius(8)
      .build()
  )
  .build(),
ToggleButtonBuilder.create()
  .id("rightAlignButton")
  .toggleGroup(alignToggleGroup)
  .graphic(
```

```
            CircleBuilder.create()
              .fill(Color.CYAN)
              .radius(8)
              .build()
          )
        .build()
      )
    .build();

    alignToggleGroup.selectToggle(alignToggleGroup.getToggles().get(0));
    alignToggleGroup.selectedToggleProperty().addListener(new ChangeListener() {
      public void changed(ObservableValue ov, Object oldValue, Object newValue) {
        ToggleButton tb = ((ToggleButton)alignToggleGroup.getSelectedToggle());
        if (tb != null) {
            System.out.println(tb.getId() + " selected");
        }
      }
    });

    return toolBar;
  }
```

Defining Graphical Buttons

As shown in Figure 5-1, toolbar buttons often have a graphic rather than a title. They also often have a tooltip that pops up when the mouse cursor hovers over the button, as demonstrated in Step 4 of the exercise. In the snippet below from Listing 5-4, the toolbar button that causes a New Document to be created is defined with a graphic and tooltip, as well as an action to be performed when the toolbar button is selected:

```
        ButtonBuilder.create()
          .id("newButton")
          .graphic(new ImageView(
            new Image(getClass().getResourceAsStream("images/paper.png"))))
          )
          .tooltip(new Tooltip("New Document... Ctrl+N"))
          .onAction(new EventHandler<ActionEvent>() {
              @Override public void handle(ActionEvent e) {
                System.out.println("New toolbar button clicked");
              }
          })
          .build(),
```

Note that the `id()` method of the `ButtonBuilder` is used in the snippet above. This causes the padding in the button to be set to four pixels on all four sides as a result of the following rule in the `starterApp.css` style sheet.

```
#newButton {
    -fx-padding: 4 4 4 4;
}
```

The toolbar button defined in the previous code snippet is a JavaFX `Button`, but there are often use cases in which a JavaFX `ToggleButton` is a more appropriate choice. The following section discusses such cases, and how to implement toggle buttons in a toolbar.

Defining Toggle Buttons

In Steps 5 and 6 of the preceding exercise, you interacted with buttons that have two states: selected and not selected. The buttons in Step 5 are toggle buttons, as are the buttons in Step 6. The buttons in Step 5 operate independently of each other, but only one of the buttons in Step 6 can be in the selected (depressed) state at any given time. The following snippet from Listing 5-4 contains the code behind one of the buttons in Step 5.

```
ToggleButtonBuilder.create()
  .id("boldButton")
  .graphic(
    CircleBuilder.create()
      .fill(Color.MAROON)
      .radius(8)
      .build()
  )
  .onAction(new EventHandler<ActionEvent>() {
      @Override public void handle(ActionEvent e) {
        ToggleButton tb = ((ToggleButton)e.getTarget());
        System.out.print(e.getEventType() + " occurred on ToggleButton "
                        + tb.getId());
        System.out.print(", and selectedProperty is: ");
        System.out.println(tb.selectedProperty().getValue());
      }
  })
  .build(),
```

This use case is the classic Bold button in many document editing applications, where the Bold button is either selected or not selected. The `ToggleButton` shown in the snippet above contains this dual-state functionality, so it is a natural fit for this use case.

The `onAction()` event handler in the snippet above demonstrates how you can ascertain the state of the `ToggleButton` as a result of being clicked. As shown in the snippet, use the `getTarget()` method of the `ActionEvent` to obtain a reference to the `ToggleButton`; then use its `selectedProperty()` method to get a reference to its `selected` property. Finally, use the `getValue()` method to get the value (either true or false) of the selected property.

Using Toggle Groups

As pointed out in the previous section, only one of the buttons in Step 6 of the preceding exercise can be in the selected (depressed) state at any given time. The following snippet from Listing 5-4 contains the code behind one of the buttons in Step 6.

```
    final ToggleGroup alignToggleGroup = new ToggleGroup();
        ...
      ToggleButtonBuilder.create()
        .id("leftAlignButton")
        .toggleGroup(alignToggleGroup)
        .graphic(
          CircleBuilder.create()
            .fill(Color.PURPLE)
            .radius(8)
            .build()
        )
        .build(),
        ...
    alignToggleGroup.selectToggle(alignToggleGroup.getToggles().get(0));
    alignToggleGroup.selectedToggleProperty().addListener(new ChangeListener() {
      public void changed(ObservableValue ov, Object oldValue, Object newValue) {
        ToggleButton tb = ((ToggleButton)alignToggleGroup.getSelectedToggle());
        if (tb != null) {
            System.out.println(tb.getId() + " selected");
        }
      }
    });
```

This use case is the classic Left-Alignment button in many document editing applications, where only one of the Alignment buttons may be selected at any given time. The ToggleGroup instance is passed into the toggleGroup() method of the ToggleButtonBuilder shown in the snippet above to provide this mutually exclusive behavior.

In addition to providing mutual exclusivity, the ToggleGroup instance is used in the snippet above for two purposes:

1. To initially select the first ToggleButton in the group, by using the selectToggle() method of the ToggleGroup instance.

2. To detect when the currently selected ToggleButton changes. This is accomplished by adding a ChangeListener to the selectedToggle property of the ToggleGroup, and then using its getSelectedToggle() method to ascertain which ToggleButton is currently selected. Note that this is generally preferred over putting an onAction event handler in each of the toggle buttons that are participating in a toggle group.

Inserting a Separator into a Toolbar

It is sometimes useful to visually separate toolbar buttons by using the vertical separators shown in Figure 5-3. To accomplish this, use the Separator class as shown in the snippet below from Listing 5-4:

```
    new Separator(Orientation.VERTICAL),
```

Although we didn't make use of separators in the menus of this StarterApp program, Separator objects may be used in menus as well. Of course, separators used in menus typically have a HORIZONTAL Orientation.

Creating a TabPane and Defining Tabs

One of the principles of UI design is called "progressive disclosure," which states that a UI should reveal its functionality progressively rather than inundating the user with all of its functionality at once. The TabPane is a good example of this principle in use, as each tab discloses its functionality while hiding the functionality contained in the other tabs.

To create the TabPane instance, our StarterApp program defines a method that we've arbitrarily named createTabs(), shown in Listing 5-5. This method leverages the TabPaneBuilder and TabBuilder classes, and returns a TabPane instance that contains the desired Tab objects.

Listing 5-5. The createTabs() Method Located in StarterAppMain.java

```
TabPane createTabs() {
  final WebView webView;
  TabPane tabPane = TabPaneBuilder.create()
    .tabs(
      TabBuilder.create()
        .text("TableView")
        .content(createTableDemoNode())
        .closable(false)
        .build(),
      TabBuilder.create()
        .text("Accordion/TitledPane")
        .content(createAccordionTitledDemoNode())
        .closable(false)
        .build(),
      TabBuilder.create()
        .text("SplitPane/TreeView/ListView")
        .content(createSplitTreeListDemoNode())
        .closable(false)
        .build(),
      TabBuilder.create()
        .text("ScrollPane/Miscellaneous")
        .content(createScrollMiscDemoNode())
        .closable(false)
        .build(),
      TabBuilder.create()
        .text("HTMLEditor")
        .content(createHtmlEditorDemoNode())
        .closable(false)
        .build(),
      webViewTab = TabBuilder.create()
        .text("WebView")
        .content(
          webView = WebViewBuilder.create()
            .build()
        )
        .closable(false)
        .onSelectionChanged(new EventHandler<Event>() {
          public void handle(Event evt) {
            String randomWebSite = model.getRandomWebSite();
```

```
            if (webViewTab.isSelected()) {
              webView.getEngine().load(randomWebSite);
              System.out.println("WebView tab is selected, loading: "
                                     + randomWebSite);
            }
          }
        })
        .build()
    )
    .build();

    return tabPane;
  }
```

To define a tab in its simplest form, you need only supply its **text** (which appears on the tab), and **content** (which appears when that tab is selected). The snippet shown below from Listing 5-5 demonstrates some other features of the **TabPane** used in the StarterApp program:

```
webViewTab = TabBuilder.create()
  .text("WebView")
  .content(
    webView = WebViewBuilder.create()
      .build()
  )
  .closable(false)
  .onSelectionChanged(new EventHandler<Event>() {
    public void handle(Event evt) {
      String randomWebSite = model.getRandomWebSite();
      if (webViewTab.isSelected()) {
        webView.getEngine().load(randomWebSite);
        System.out.println("WebView tab is selected, loading: "
                               + randomWebSite);
      }
    }
  })
  .build()
)
.build();
```

In addition to supplying **text** and **content**, we're also specifying that the tab shouldn't be **closable**, and that some processing should occur when the user chooses the tab. The latter is implemented using the **onSelectionChanged()** method shown above, which enables you to implement lifecycle functionality when a tab is exposed or hidden (i.e., selected or not selected). In the snippet above, we're causing the **WebView** (which is covered later) to load a randomly selected site when the tab is selected.

Now that you understand how the menus, toolbar, and tabs were created in the StarterApp program, let's examine the UI controls on each tab. We start with the leftmost tab, labeled TableView, and work our way to the right.

Creating a TableView

As you experienced in Steps 7 and 8 of the exercise, the TableView shown in Figure 5-1 contains 10,000 rows of data, and allows its columns to be rearranged and resized. The code that defines and populates the TableView in the StarterApp program is shown in Listing 5-6.

Listing 5-6. The createTableDemoNode() Method Located in StarterAppMain.java

```
Node createTableDemoNode() {
  TableView table = TableViewBuilder.create()
    .columns(
      TableColumnBuilder.create()
        .text("First Name")
        .cellValueFactory(new PropertyValueFactory("firstName"))
        .prefWidth(180)
        .build(),
      TableColumnBuilder.create()
        .text("Last Name")
        .cellValueFactory(new PropertyValueFactory("lastName"))
        .prefWidth(180)
        .build(),
      TableColumnBuilder.create()
        .text("Phone Number")
        .cellValueFactory(new PropertyValueFactory("phone"))
        .prefWidth(150)
        .build()
    )
    .items(model.getTeamMembers())
    .build();

  table.getSelectionModel().selectedItemProperty()
                           .addListener(new ChangeListener() {
    @Override
    public void changed(ObservableValue observable, Object oldValue,
                        Object newValue) {
      Person selectedPerson = (Person)newValue;
      System.out.println(selectedPerson + " chosen in TableView");
    }
  });
  return table;
}
```

In addition to the code in Listing 5-6, the following code snippet from Listing 5-1 contains a method from our StarterAppModel class that creates the Person instances that will be displayed in the TableView:

```
public ObservableList getTeamMembers() {
  ObservableList teamMembers = FXCollections.observableArrayList();
  for (int i = 1; i <= 10000; i++) {
    teamMembers.add(new Person("FirstName" + i,
                               "LastName" + i,
                               "Phone" + i));
  }
  return teamMembers;
}
```

Assigning Items to a Table

The `items()` method in the `TableViewBuilder` class from Listing 5-6 causes the `ObservableList` containing `Person` instances (returned from the `getTeamMembers()` method) to be associated with the `TableView`. If the contents of the underlying `ObservableList` change, the `TableView` is automatically updated to reflect the changes.

Defining TableView Columns

To define the `columns` in our `TableView` we use the methods of the `TableColumnBuilder` class shown in the snippet below from Listing 5-6:

```
TableColumnBuilder.create()
  .text("First Name")
  .cellValueFactory(new PropertyValueFactory("firstName"))
  .prefWidth(180)
  .build(),
```

The `text()` method specifies the text that should appear in the column header, and the `prefWidth()` method specifies the column's preferred width in pixels.

The argument passed into the `cellValueFactory()` method specifies a property that will be used to populate this column. In this case, the property is the `firstNameProperty` defined in the `Person` model class of our StarterApp program, shown in Listing 5-7.

Listing 5-7. *The Source Code for Person.java*

```
package projavafx.starterapp.model;

import javafx.beans.property.SimpleStringProperty;
import javafx.beans.property.StringProperty;

public final class Person {
  private StringProperty firstName;
  public void setFirstName(String value) { firstNameProperty().set(value); }
  public String getFirstName() { return firstNameProperty().get(); }
  public StringProperty firstNameProperty() {
```

```
    if (firstName == null) firstName = new SimpleStringProperty(this, "firstName");
    return firstName;
  }

  private StringProperty lastName;
  public void setLastName(String value) { lastNameProperty().set(value); }
  public String getLastName() { return lastNameProperty().get(); }
  public StringProperty lastNameProperty() {
    if (lastName == null) lastName = new SimpleStringProperty(this, "lastName");
    return lastName;
  }

  private StringProperty phone;
  public void setPhone(String value) { phoneProperty().set(value); }
  public String getPhone() { return phoneProperty().get(); }
  public StringProperty phoneProperty() {
    if (phone == null) phone = new SimpleStringProperty(this, "phone");
    return phone;
  }

  public Person(String firstName, String lastName, String phone) {
    setFirstName(firstName);
    setLastName(lastName);
    setPhone(phone);
  }

  public String toString() {
    return "Person: " + firstName.getValue() + " " + lastName.getValue();
  }
}
```

Detecting When a Row Is Selected

To detect when the user selects a row in the TableView, the StarterApp program adds a ChangeListener to the selectedItem property of the table view's selection model. The code for accomplishing this is shown in the snippet below from Listing 5-6:

```
    table.getSelectionModel().selectedItemProperty()
                             .addListener(new ChangeListener() {
      @Override
      public void changed(ObservableValue observable, Object oldValue,
                          Object newValue) {
        Person selectedPerson = (Person)newValue;
        System.out.println(selectedPerson + " chosen in TableView");
      }
    });
```

When the user selects a row the changed method of the anonymous inner class is invoked, which prints data from the underlying Person instance represented by that row. This is the behavior you observed in Step 7 of the previous exercise.

Now that we've explored some of the capabilities of the TableView, let's move on to the next tab, labeled "Accordion/TitledPane."

Creating an Accordion and Defining a TitledPane

As you experienced in Step 9 of the exercise, the Accordion shown in Figure 5-4 contains some TitledPane instances, each of which contains nodes and may be expanded/collapsed. The code that defines and populates the Accordion in the StarterApp program is shown in Listing 5-8.

Listing 5-8. The createAccordionTitledDemoNode() Method Located in StarterAppMain.java

```
Node createAccordionTitledDemoNode() {
  TitledPane firstPane;
  Accordion accordion = AccordionBuilder.create()
    .panes(
      firstPane = TitledPaneBuilder.create()
        .text("TitledPane A")
        .content(new TextArea("TitledPane A content"))
        .build(),
      TitledPaneBuilder.create()
        .text("TitledPane B")
        .content(new TextArea("TitledPane B content"))
        .build(),
      TitledPaneBuilder.create()
        .text("TitledPane C")
        .content(new TextArea("TitledPane C content"))
        .build()
    )
    .build();

  accordion.setExpandedPane(firstPane);
  return accordion;
}
```

As shown in the snippet below from Listing 5-8, a TitledPane is typically given the text for its title, and a Node subclass (in this case a TextArea) for its content:

```
      firstPane = TitledPaneBuilder.create()
        .text("TitledPane A")
        .content(new TextArea("TitledPane A content"))
        .build(),
      ...
  accordion.setExpandedPane(firstPane);
```

In addition, we want the first TitledPane in our example initially to be expanded, so the setExpandedPane() method of the Accordion is used to accomplish this.

Now that you know how to create Accordion and TitledPane controls, we move on to the next tab, labeled "SplitPane/TreeView/ListView".

Creating a TreeView

As you experienced in Steps 10 and 11 of the exercise, the TreeView shown in Figure 5-5 contains a hierarchical structure of tree items, each of which may be expanded/collapsed. The code that defines and populates the TreeView in the StarterApp program is shown in Listing 5-9.

Listing 5-9. *The createSplitTreeListDemoNode() Method Located in StarterAppMain.java*

```
Node createSplitTreeListDemoNode() {
  TreeView treeView = TreeViewBuilder.create()
    .minWidth(150)
    .showRoot(false)
    .editable(false)
    .root(
      TreeItemBuilder.create()
        .value("Root")
        .children(
          TreeItemBuilder.create()
            .value("Animal")
            .children(
              TreeItemBuilder.create()
                .value("Lion")
                .build(),
              TreeItemBuilder.create()
                .value("Tiger")
                .build(),
              TreeItemBuilder.create()
                .value("Bear")
                .build()
            )
            .build(),
          TreeItemBuilder.create()
            .value("Mineral")
            .children(
              TreeItemBuilder.create()
                .value("Copper")
                .build(),
              TreeItemBuilder.create()
                .value("Diamond")
                .build(),
              TreeItemBuilder.create()
                .value("Quartz")
                .build()
            )
            .build(),
          TreeItemBuilder.create()
            .value("Vegetable")
            .children(
              TreeItemBuilder.create()
                .value("Arugula")
                .build(),
```

```
                    TreeItemBuilder.create()
                      .value("Broccoli")
                      .build(),
                    TreeItemBuilder.create()
                      .value("Cabbage")
                      .build()
                )
                .build()
            )
          .build()
        )
      .build();

    ListView listView = ListViewBuilder.create()
      .items(model.listViewItems)
      .build();

    SplitPane splitPane = SplitPaneBuilder.create()
      .items(
        treeView,
        listView
      )
      .build();

    treeView.getSelectionModel().setSelectionMode(SelectionMode.SINGLE);
    treeView.getSelectionModel().selectedItemProperty()
                                .addListener(new ChangeListener() {
      @Override
      public void changed(ObservableValue observable, Object oldValue,
                          Object newValue) {
        TreeItem treeItem = (TreeItem)newValue;
        if (newValue != null && treeItem.isLeaf()) {
          model.listViewItems.clear();
          for (int i = 1; i <= 10000; i++) {
            model.listViewItems.add(treeItem.getValue() + " " + i);
          }
        }
      }
    });

    return splitPane;
  }
```

As shown in the snippet below from Listing 5-9, a TreeView may be supplied with values for several properties, including whether the root TreeItem should show and whether the TreeView is editable. In the StarterApp program we're also setting the minWidth so that the user can't hide the TreeView by dragging the SplitPane divider (as you noticed in Step 12 of the previous exercise).

```
TreeView treeView = TreeViewBuilder.create()
  .minWidth(150)
  .showRoot(false)
  .editable(false)
  .root(
    TreeItemBuilder.create()
      ...
```

Defining a TreeItem

Taking a look at the snippet below from Listing 5-9, you see that each `TreeItem` is given the `value` that it represents, and 0 or more `children` `TreeItem` objects:

```
TreeItemBuilder.create()
  .value("Root")
  .children(
    TreeItemBuilder.create()
      .value("Animal")
      .children(
        TreeItemBuilder.create()
          .value("Lion")
          .build(),
        TreeItemBuilder.create()
          .value("Tiger")
          .build(),
```

In addition, you can set properties such as

- `graphic,` which displays a Node in the `TreeItem`
- `expanded,` which controls whether the `TreeItem` is expanded or collapsed

Now that you know how to create a `TreeView` and its `TreeItem` instances, let's examine how to detect when a `TreeItem` has been selected.

Detecting When a TreeItem Is Selected

To detect when the user selects a `TreeItem` in the `TreeView`, the StarterApp program adds a `ChangeListener` to the `selectedItem` property of the tree view's selection model. The code for accomplishing this is shown in this snippet from Listing 5-9:

```
treeView.getSelectionModel().setSelectionMode(SelectionMode.SINGLE);
treeView.getSelectionModel().selectedItemProperty()
                          .addListener(new ChangeListener() {
  @Override
  public void changed(ObservableValue observable, Object oldValue,
                      Object newValue) {
    TreeItem treeItem = (TreeItem)newValue;
```

```
          if (newValue != null && treeItem.isLeaf()) {
            model.listViewItems.clear();
            for (int i = 1; i <= 10000; i++) {
              model.listViewItems.add(treeItem.getValue() + " " + i);
            }
          }
        }
      }
});
```

A TreeView may allow the user to select a single row, or multiple rows, based upon its selection mode. In the first line of the snippet above, we're setting the selection mode of the TableView to SINGLE.

In Step 11 of the exercise, when you clicked on a leaf TreeItem in the TreeView, the ListView on the right side of Figure 5-6 was populated. The code in the snippet above accomplishes this by first checking to see if the selected TreeItem is a leaf, and then populating the model that backs the ListView.

Creating a ListView and Assigning Items to a ListView

The following code snippet, from Listing 5-9, defines and populates the ListView in the StarterApp program:

```
ListView listView = ListViewBuilder.create()
  .items(model.listViewItems)
  .build();
```

In addition to the code in the preceding snippet, the following code snippet from Listing 5-1 contains an instance variable from our StarterAppModel class that contains the objects that will be displayed in the ListView:

```
public ObservableList listViewItems = FXCollections.observableArrayList();
```

Recall that this is the same instance variable that is populated when clicking a leaf TreeItem in the previous section.

The items() method in the ListViewBuilder class causes the ObservableList named listViewItems in the model to be associated with the TableView. As demonstrated in Step 11 of the previous exercise, if contents of the underlying ObservableList change the ListView is automatically updated to reflect the changes.

Creating a SplitPane

As you experienced in Step 12 of the previous exercise, the SplitPane shown in Figure 5-6 contains a TreeView and a ListView, and its divider can be dragged by the user. The following code snippet, from Listing 5-9, defines and populates the SplitPane in the StarterApp program:

```
SplitPane splitPane = SplitPaneBuilder.create()
  .items(
    treeView,
    listView
  )
  .build();
```

In this case there are two nodes in the SplitPane which means that there will be just one divider. Note that a SplitPane may have more than two nodes and therefore more than one divider.

In addition to the functionality shown in the previous snippet, a SplitPane may also have its orientation set to VERTICAL, and its dividerPositions set to given percentages of the pane.

Now that you know how to create TreeView, ListView, and SplitPane controls, we move on to the next tab, labeled "ScrollPane/Miscellaneous".

Defining a ScrollPane

As you experienced in Step 22 of the previous exercise, the ScrollPane shown in Figure 5-8 contains several UI controls, and has a vertical scrollbar so that all of the controls may be accessed.

The code from the StarterApp program that defines the ScrollPane and populates it with UI controls is shown in Listing 5-10.

Listing 5-10. *The createScrollMiscDemoNode() Method Located in StarterAppMain.java*

```java
Node createScrollMiscDemoNode() {
    final ToggleGroup radioToggleGroup = new ToggleGroup();
    ChoiceBox choiceBox;
    final TextField textField;
    final PasswordField passwordField;
    final TextArea textArea;
    Slider slider;
    ProgressIndicator progressIndicator;
    ProgressBar progressBar;
    ScrollBar scrollBar;
    VBox variousControls = VBoxBuilder.create()
      .padding(new Insets(10, 10, 10, 10))
      .spacing(20)
      .children(
        ButtonBuilder.create()
          .text("Button")
          .onAction(new EventHandler<ActionEvent>() {
              @Override public void handle(ActionEvent e) {
                System.out.println(e.getEventType() + " occurred on Button");
              }
            })
          .build(),
        checkBox = CheckBoxBuilder.create()
          .text("CheckBox")
          .onAction(new EventHandler<ActionEvent>() {
              @Override public void handle(ActionEvent e) {
                System.out.print(e.getEventType() + " occurred on CheckBox");
                System.out.print(", and selectedProperty is: ");
                System.out.println(checkBox.selectedProperty().getValue());
              }
            })
          .build(),
```

```
HBoxBuilder.create()
  .spacing(10)
  .children(
    RadioButtonBuilder.create()
      .text("RadioButton1")
      .toggleGroup(radioToggleGroup)
      .build(),
    RadioButtonBuilder.create()
      .text("RadioButton2")
      .toggleGroup(radioToggleGroup)
      .build()
  )
  .build(),
HyperlinkBuilder.create()
  .text("Hyperlink")
  .onAction(new EventHandler<ActionEvent>() {
      @Override public void handle(ActionEvent e) {
        System.out.println(e.getEventType() + " occurred on Hyperlink");
      }
  })
  .build(),
choiceBox = ChoiceBoxBuilder.create()
  .items(model.choiceBoxItems)
  .build(),
MenuButtonBuilder.create()
  .text("MenuButton")
  .items(
    MenuItemBuilder.create()
      .text("MenuItem A")
      .onAction(new EventHandler<ActionEvent>() {
          @Override public void handle(ActionEvent e) {
            System.out.println(e.getEventType() +
                                " occurred on Menu Item A");
          }
      })
      .build(),
    MenuItemBuilder.create()
      .text("MenuItem B")
      .build()
  )
  .build(),
SplitMenuButtonBuilder.create()
  .text("SplitMenuButton")
  .onAction(new EventHandler<ActionEvent>() {
    @Override public void handle(ActionEvent e) {
      System.out.println(e.getEventType() +
                          " occurred on SplitMenuButton");
    }
  })
```

```
        .items(
          MenuItemBuilder.create()
            .text("MenuItem A")
            .onAction(new EventHandler<ActionEvent>() {
                @Override public void handle(ActionEvent e) {
                  System.out.println(e.getEventType() +
                                       " occurred on Menu Item A");
                }
             })
            .build(),
          MenuItemBuilder.create()
            .text("MenuItem B")
            .build()
        )
        .build(),
      textField = TextFieldBuilder.create()
        .promptText("Enter user name")
        .prefColumnCount(16)
        .build(),
      passwordField = PasswordFieldBuilder.create()
        .promptText("Enter password")
        .prefColumnCount(16)
        .build(),
      HBoxBuilder.create()
        .spacing(10)
        .children(
          new Label("TextArea:"),
          textArea = TextAreaBuilder.create()
            .prefColumnCount(12)
            .prefRowCount(4)
            .build()
        )
        .build(),
      progressIndicator = ProgressIndicatorBuilder.create()
        .prefWidth(200)
        .build(),
      slider = SliderBuilder.create()
        .prefWidth(200)
        .min(-1)
        .max(model.maxRpm)
        .build(),
      progressBar = ProgressBarBuilder.create()
        .prefWidth(200)
        .build(),
      scrollBar = ScrollBarBuilder.create()
        .prefWidth(200)
        .min(-1)
        .max(model.maxKph)
        .build()
    )
    .build();
```

```java
radioToggleGroup.selectToggle(radioToggleGroup.getToggles().get(0));
radioToggleGroup.selectedToggleProperty().addListener(new ChangeListener() {
  public void changed(ObservableValue ov, Object oldValue, Object newValue) {
    RadioButton rb = ((RadioButton)radioToggleGroup.getSelectedToggle());
    if (rb != null) {
      System.out.println(rb.getText() + " selected");
    }
  }
});

textField.textProperty().addListener(new ChangeListener() {
  public void changed(ObservableValue ov, Object oldValue, Object newValue) {
    System.out.println("TextField text is: " + textField.getText());
  }
});

passwordField.focusedProperty().addListener(new ChangeListener() {
  public void changed(ObservableValue ov, Object oldValue, Object newValue) {
    if (!passwordField.isFocused()) {
      System.out.println("PasswordField text is: "
                          + passwordField.getText());
    }
  }
});

textArea.focusedProperty().addListener(new ChangeListener() {
  public void changed(ObservableValue ov, Object oldValue, Object newValue) {
    if (!textArea.isFocused()) {
      System.out.println("TextArea text is: " + textArea.getText());
    }
  }
});

slider.valueProperty().bindBidirectional(model.rpm);
progressIndicator.progressProperty().bind(model.rpm.divide(model.maxRpm));

scrollBar.valueProperty().bindBidirectional(model.kph);
progressBar.progressProperty().bind(model.kph.divide(model.maxKph));

choiceBox.getSelectionModel().selectFirst();
choiceBox.getSelectionModel().selectedItemProperty()
                        .addListener(new ChangeListener() {
  @Override
  public void changed(ObservableValue observable, Object oldValue,
                      Object newValue) {
    System.out.println(newValue + " chosen in ChoiceBox");
  }
});
```

```
ScrollPane scrollPane = ScrollPaneBuilder.create()
  .content(variousControls)
  .hbarPolicy(ScrollPane.ScrollBarPolicy.NEVER)
  .vbarPolicy(ScrollPane.ScrollBarPolicy.AS_NEEDED)
  .onMousePressed(new EventHandler<MouseEvent>() {
    public void handle(MouseEvent me) {
      if (me.getButton() == MouseButton.SECONDARY) {
        contextMenu.show(stage, me.getScreenX(), me.getScreenY());
      }
    }
  })
  .build();

contextMenu = ContextMenuBuilder.create()
  .items(
    MenuItemBuilder.create()
      .text("MenuItem A")
      .onAction(new EventHandler<ActionEvent>() {
          @Override public void handle(ActionEvent e) {
            System.out.println(e.getEventType() +
                                    " occurred on Menu Item A");
          }
        })
      .build(),
    MenuItemBuilder.create()
      .text("MenuItem B")
      .build()
  )
  .build();

  return scrollPane;
}
```

As shown in the following snippet from Listing 5-10, the content of a ScrollPane is a Node subclass, in this case a VBox that contains several nodes. When the contents are larger than the viewable area of the ScrollPane, horizontal and/or vertical scroll bars appear according to the specified hbarPolicy and vbarPolicy.

```
ScrollPane scrollPane = ScrollPaneBuilder.create()
  .content(variousControls)
  .hbarPolicy(ScrollPane.ScrollBarPolicy.NEVER)
  .vbarPolicy(ScrollPane.ScrollBarPolicy.AS_NEEDED)
  .onMousePressed(new EventHandler<MouseEvent>() {
    ...
  })
  .build();
```

Other useful ScrollPane properties include:

- pannable, which enables the user to pan the contents of the ScrollPane by dragging it with the mouse

- fitToWidth/fitToHeight, which causes the content node (if resizable) to be stretched to fit the width/height of the ScrollPane

Note that we're using an onMousePressed() event handler in the previous snippet. We walk through that functionality after discussing some of the UI controls that are contained within our ScrollPane, beginning with the CheckBox.

Using a CheckBox

As you experienced in Step 15 of the exercise, the ScrollPane shown in Figure 5-7 contains a CheckBox. When the CheckBox is clicked a message is printed to the Java console indicating the state of its selected property. The following code snippet, from Listing 5-10, implements this functionality in the StarterApp program:

```
checkBox = CheckBoxBuilder.create()
  .text("CheckBox")
  .onAction(new EventHandler<ActionEvent>() {
    @Override public void handle(ActionEvent e) {
      System.out.print(e.getEventType() + " occurred on CheckBox");
      System.out.print(", and selectedProperty is: ");
      System.out.println(checkBox.selectedProperty().getValue());
    }
  })
  .build(),
```

A CheckBox may also represent a third indeterminate state by setting its allowIndeterminate property to true. This third state is typically represented in the CheckBox with a dash, and is useful for indicating that the state represented by the CheckBox is unknown.

Defining a RadioButton

In Step 16 of the previous exercise, you selected each of the RadioButton controls shown in Figure 5-7. As a result, a message was printed to the Java console indicating which RadioButton was selected. The following code snippet, from Listing 5-10, implements this functionality in the StarterApp program:

```
final ToggleGroup radioToggleGroup = new ToggleGroup();
...
        RadioButtonBuilder.create()
          .text("RadioButton1")
          .toggleGroup(radioToggleGroup)
          .build(),
        RadioButtonBuilder.create()
          .text("RadioButton2")
          .toggleGroup(radioToggleGroup)
          .build()
...
```

```
radioToggleGroup.selectToggle(radioToggleGroup.getToggles().get(0));
radioToggleGroup.selectedToggleProperty().addListener(new ChangeListener() {
  public void changed(ObservableValue ov, Object oldValue, Object newValue) {
    RadioButton rb = ((RadioButton)radioToggleGroup.getSelectedToggle());
    if (rb != null) {
      System.out.println(rb.getText() + " selected");
    }
  }
});
```

Because the RadioButton class extends the ToggleButton class, the code in the snippet above is very similar to the code in the Using Toggle Groups section earlier in this chapter. Please review that section if you'd like an explanation of the code in the snippet above.

Creating a Hyperlink

The Hyperlink control is a button that has the appearance of a link seen in a browser. It can have a graphic and/or text, and it responds to mouse rollovers and clicks. In Step 17 of the previous exercise, you clicked the Hyperlink control shown in Figure 5-7. As a result, a message was printed to the Java console indicating that it was clicked. The following code snippet from Listing 5-10 implements this functionality in the StarterApp program:

```
HyperlinkBuilder.create()
  .text("Hyperlink")
  .onAction(new EventHandler<ActionEvent>() {
      @Override public void handle(ActionEvent e) {
        System.out.println(e.getEventType() + " occurred on Hyperlink");
      }
    })
  .build(),
```

Defining a ChoiceBox

When clicked, a ChoiceBox control presents a popup containing a list of items from which to choose. In Step 18 of the previous exercise, you clicked the ChoiceBox control shown in Figure 5-7. As a result, a message was printed to the Java console indicating which item you chose. The following code snippet from Listing 5-10 implements this functionality in the StarterApp program:

```
ChoiceBox choiceBox;
...
    choiceBox = ChoiceBoxBuilder.create()
      .items(model.choiceBoxItems)
      .build(),
...
choiceBox.getSelectionModel().selectFirst();
choiceBox.getSelectionModel().selectedItemProperty()
                              .addListener(new ChangeListener() {
  @Override
```

```
    public void changed(ObservableValue observable, Object oldValue,
                        Object newValue) {
      System.out.println(newValue + " chosen in ChoiceBox");
    }
});
```

To initially select the first item in the ChoiceBox, the preceding snippet invokes the selectFirst() method of the choice box's selectionModel. To detect when the user chooses an item in the ChoiceBox, we add the ChangeListener shown in the snippet to the selectedItem property of the choice box's selection model.

In addition to the code in the snippet above, the following snippet from Listing 5-1 contains an instance variable from our StarterAppModel class that contains the objects that will be displayed in the ChoiceBox:

```
public ObservableList choiceBoxItems = FXCollections.observableArrayList(
  "Choice A",
  "Choice B",
  "Choice C",
  "Choice D"
);
```

Now we move on to a control named MenuButton whose appearance is similar to the ChoiceBox, but whose behavior is similar to a Menu.

Using a MenuButton

When clicked, a MenuButton control pops up a context menu that contains MenuItem instances from which to choose. In Step 19 of the previous exercise, you clicked the MenuButton control shown in Figure 5-7. As a result, a message was printed to the Java console indicating which MenuItem you chose. The following code snippet, from Listing 5-10, implements this functionality in the StarterApp program:

```
MenuButtonBuilder.create()
  .text("MenuButton")
  .items(
    MenuItemBuilder.create()
      .text("MenuItem A")
      .onAction(new EventHandler<ActionEvent>() {
          @Override public void handle(ActionEvent e) {
            System.out.println(e.getEventType() +
                                  " occurred on Menu Item A");
          }
        })
      .build(),
    MenuItemBuilder.create()
      .text("MenuItem B")
      .build()
  )
  .build(),
```

Because of the similarity between the MenuButton and Menu classes, the concepts in the previous snippet are covered in the Creating a Menu section earlier in the chapter. One of the distinguishing features of MenuButton is the popupSide property, which enables you to choose on which side of the MenuButton the ContextMenu should pop up.

Another way to pop up a ContextMenu which doesn't require using a MenuButton, is our next topic of discussion.

Creating a ContextMenu

In Step 28 of the previous exercise, you clicked the secondary mouse button in a blank area of the ScrollPane shown in Figure 5-9, and a ContextMenu popped up from which you chose a MenuItem. The following snippet from Listing 5-10 realizes this behavior:

```
ContextMenu contextMenu;
...
  ScrollPane scrollPane = ScrollPaneBuilder.create()
    ...
    .onMousePressed(new EventHandler<MouseEvent>() {
      public void handle(MouseEvent me) {
        if (me.getButton() == MouseButton.SECONDARY) {
          contextMenu.show(stage, me.getScreenX(), me.getScreenY());
        }
      }
    })
    .build();

  contextMenu = ContextMenuBuilder.create()
    .items(
      MenuItemBuilder.create()
        .text("MenuItem A")
        .onAction(new EventHandler<ActionEvent>() {
          @Override public void handle(ActionEvent e) {
            System.out.println(e.getEventType() +
                               " occurred on Menu Item A");
          }
        })
        .build(),
      MenuItemBuilder.create()
        .text("MenuItem B")
        .build()
    )
    .build();
```

When the user presses the secondary mouse button, the handle() method of the anonymous inner class is invoked. Calling the show() method in the manner used in the snippet causes the ContextMenu to be displayed on the screen at the location in which the mouse was pressed. A ContextMenu must have an owner, either a Node or a Stage, in order for it to be displayed, which is why the Stage object was passed into the show() method.

Creating a SplitMenuButton

Very similar to the MenuButton, the SplitMenuButton pops up a ContextMenu when the down arrow is clicked. In addition, when the main part of the SplitMenuButton is clicked, the behavior is that of a Button. Both of these behaviors are demonstrated in Steps 20 and 21 of the previous exercise when interacting with the SplitMenuButton shown in Figure 5-7. The following snippet from Listing 5-10 realizes these behaviors:

```
SplitMenuButtonBuilder.create()
  .text("SplitMenuButton")
  .onAction(new EventHandler<ActionEvent>() {
    @Override public void handle(ActionEvent e) {
      System.out.println(e.getEventType() +
                            " occurred on SplitMenuButton");
    }
  })
  .items(
    MenuItemBuilder.create()
      .text("MenuItem A")
      .onAction(new EventHandler<ActionEvent>() {
          @Override public void handle(ActionEvent e) {
            System.out.println(e.getEventType() +
                                  " occurred on Menu Item A");
          }
      })
      .build(),
    MenuItemBuilder.create()
      .text("MenuItem B")
      .build()
  )
  .build(),
```

Let's move away from the button-like UI controls and turn our attention to some UI controls that accept text input, starting with the TextField.

Defining a TextField

In Step 23 of the exercise, as you entered text into the TextField shown in Figure 5-8, the contents of the TextField were printed to the Java console each time the contents changed (e.g., as characters were typed into the TextField). The following snippet from Listing 5-10 creates the TextField and implements these behaviors:

```
final TextField textField;
...
    textField = TextFieldBuilder.create()
      .promptText("Enter user name")
      .prefColumnCount(16)
      .build(),
...
```

```
textField.textProperty().addListener(new ChangeListener() {
  public void changed(ObservableValue ov, Object oldValue, Object newValue) {
    System.out.println("TextField text is: " + textField.getText());
  }
});
```

To detect when the **text** property of the **TextField** has changed, the code in the snippet above adds a ChangeListener to the **text** property. The new value of the **text** property is then printed to the Java console in the body of the **changed()** method.

Using a PasswordField

The **PasswordField** extends the **TextField** class, and its purpose is to mask the characters that are typed into it. In Step 24 of the exercise, when you entered text into the **PasswordField** shown in Figure 5-8 and subsequently caused the **PasswordField** to lose focus, the contents of the **PasswordField** were printed to the Java console. The following snippet from Listing 5-10 creates the **PasswordField** and implements these behaviors:

```
final PasswordField passwordField;
...
    passwordField = PasswordFieldBuilder.create()
      .promptText("Enter password")
      .prefColumnCount(16)
      .build(),
...
passwordField.focusedProperty().addListener(new ChangeListener() {
  public void changed(ObservableValue ov, Object oldValue, Object newValue) {
    if (!passwordField.isFocused()) {
      System.out.println("PasswordField text is: "
                         + passwordField.getText());
    }
  }
});
```

To detect when the **PasswordField** has lost focus, the code in the snippet above adds a ChangeListener to the **focused** property. The value of the **text** property is then printed to the Java console in the body of the **changed()** method if the **PasswordField** is indeed not focused.

Creating a TextArea

The **TextArea** control is similar to the TextField control, but allows for multiple lines of text. In Step 25 of the exercise, when you entered text into the **TextArea** shown in Figure 5-8 and subsequently caused the **TextArea** to lose focus, the contents of the **TextArea** were printed to the Java console. The following snippet from Listing 5-10 creates the **TextArea** and implements these behaviors:

```
final TextArea textArea;
...
        textArea = TextAreaBuilder.create()
          .prefColumnCount(12)
          .prefRowCount(4)
          .build()
```

```
...
textArea.focusedProperty().addListener(new ChangeListener() {
  public void changed(ObservableValue ov, Object oldValue, Object newValue) {
    if (!textArea.isFocused()) {
      System.out.println("TextArea text is: " + textArea.getText());
    }
  }
});
```

Some useful TextArea properties not demonstrated in the snippet above are:

- wrapText, which controls whether the text will wrap in the TextArea

- scrollLeft/scrollTop, which are the number of pixels by which the content is horizontally/vertically scrolled

Let's move away from the UI controls that accept text input, and toward ones that graphically represent numeric values in various ranges.

Creating a Slider

The Slider control represents a numeric value with its thumb, and enables the user to choose a numeric value by dragging its thumb. In Step 26 of the exercise you interacted with the Slider, shown in Figure 5-8, to control the value of the ProgressIndicator directly above it. The following snippet from Listing 5-10 contains the code that realizes the Slider-related portions of this behavior:

```
Slider slider;
...
    slider = SliderBuilder.create()
      .prefWidth(200)
      .min(-1)
      .max(model.maxRpm)
      .build(),
...
slider.valueProperty().bindBidirectional(model.rpm);
```

The range of the Slider is set through its min and max properties, which in this case are –1 and the value of the maxRpm instance variable located in the StarterAppModel class. Also, the value property of the Slider is bidirectionally bound to the rpm property in the model, which is used for keeping the ProgressIndicator updated as you experienced in Step 26. The following code snippet from Listing 5-1 contains the relevant instance variables from our StarterAppModel class:

```
public double maxRpm = 8000.0;
public DoubleProperty rpm = new SimpleDoubleProperty(0);
```

Defining a ProgressIndicator

The ProgressIndicator control displays the progress of an operation, either expressed as percent complete or indeterminate. The following snippet contains the code that creates the ProgressIndicator and keeps its progress property updated from the relevant instance variables in the model.

```
ProgressIndicator progressIndicator;
...
    progressIndicator = ProgressIndicatorBuilder.create()
        .prefWidth(200)
        .build(),
...
progressIndicator.progressProperty().bind(model.rpm.divide(model.maxRpm));
```

As a result of the bind shown in the snippet above, when the rpm variable in the StarterAppModel class is negative, the progress property of the ProgressIndicator becomes negative. This causes the ProgressIndicator to assume the indeterminate appearance that you experienced in Step 26 of the exercise. Note that we're using the Fluent API covered in Chapter 3 in the bind expression.

Defining a ScrollBar

The ScrollBar control, like the Slider control discussed earlier, represents a numeric value with its thumb, and enables the user to choose a numeric value by dragging its thumb. The ScrollBar control is typically used in conjunction with other nodes to define a new UI component, the ScrollPane and ListView serving as two examples of this. In Step 27 you interacted with the ScrollBar, shown in Figure 5-8, to control the value of the ProgressBar directly above it. The following snippet from Listing 5-10 contains the code that realizes the ScrollBar-related portions of this behavior:

```
ScrollBar scrollBar;
...
    scrollBar = ScrollBarBuilder.create()
        .prefWidth(200)
        .min(-1)
        .max(model.maxKph)
        .build()
...
scrollBar.valueProperty().bindBidirectional(model.kph);
```

As with the Slider, the range of the ScrollBar is set through its min and max properties, which in this case are –1 and the value of the maxKph instance variable located in the StarterAppModel class. Also, the value property of the ScrollBar is bidirectionally bound to the kph property in the model, which is used for keeping the ProgressBar updated as you experienced in Step 27. The following code snippet from Listing 5-1 contains the relevant instance variables from our StarterAppModel class:

```
public double maxKph = 300.0;
public DoubleProperty kph = new SimpleDoubleProperty(0);
```

Using a ProgressBar

The ProgressBar control is a specialization of the ProgressIndicator that displays the progress of an operation as a bar. The following snippet contains the code that creates the ProgressBar and keeps its progress property updated from the relevant instance variables in the model.

```
ProgressBar progressBar;
...
    progressBar = ProgressBarBuilder.create()
      .prefWidth(200)
      .build(),
...
progressBar.progressProperty().bind(model.kph.divide(model.maxKph));
```

As a result of the bind shown in the snippet above, when the kph variable in the StarterAppModel class is negative, the progress property of the ProgressBar becomes negative. This causes the ProgressBar to assume the indeterminate appearance that you experienced in Step 27.

Now we move away from the UI controls that graphically represent numeric values in various ranges, toward the controls that deal with HTML and other web-related content.

Creating an HTMLEditor

The HTMLEditor control enables users to edit rich text, with its underlying data represented in HTML. As you experienced in Step 30 of the exercise, the HTMLEditor shown in Figure 5-10 contains several tools for editing text, as well as the editing area itself.

To create the HTMLEditor instance, our StarterApp program defines a method that we've arbitrarily named createHtmlEditorDemoNode(), shown in Listing 5-11. This method leverages the BorderPaneBuilder, HTMLEditorBuilder, and ButtonBuilder classes, returning a BorderPane instance that contains the HTMLEditor and a button labeled View HTML.

Listing 5-11. *The createHtmlEditorDemoNode() Method Located in StarterAppMain.java*

```
Node createHtmlEditorDemoNode() {
 final BorderPane htmlEditorDemo;
 final HTMLEditor htmlEditor;
 Button viewHtmlButton;

 htmlEditorDemo = BorderPaneBuilder.create()
   .center(
     htmlEditor = HTMLEditorBuilder.create()
       .htmlText("<p>Replace this text</p>")
       .build()
   )
   .bottom(
     viewHtmlButton = ButtonBuilder.create()
       .text("View HTML")
       .onAction(new EventHandler<ActionEvent>() {
         @Override public void handle(ActionEvent e) {
           Popup alertPopup = createAlertPopup(htmlEditor.getHtmlText());
           alertPopup.show(stage,
             (stage.getWidth() - alertPopup.getWidth()) / 2 + stage.getX(),
             (stage.getHeight() - alertPopup.getHeight()) / 2 + stage.getY());
         }
       })
```

```
        .build()
      )
    .build();

  BorderPane.setAlignment(viewHtmlButton, Pos.CENTER);
  BorderPane.setMargin(viewHtmlButton, new Insets(10, 0, 10, 0));
  return htmlEditorDemo;
}
```

Creating a Popup

As you experienced in Step 31 in the exercise, when the Button is clicked the Popup shown in Figure 5-11 is created and displayed. This Popup displays the HTML that represents the text in the editing area. The snippet above contains the code that calls the show() method of the Popup. The Popup, however, is created by another method in StarterAppMain.java, arbitrarily named createAlertPopup() and shown in Listing 5-12.

Listing 5-12. *The createAlertPopup() Method Located in StarterAppMain.java*

```
Popup createAlertPopup(String text) {
  Button okButton;
  alertPopup = PopupBuilder.create()
    .content(
      StackPaneBuilder.create()
        .children(
          RectangleBuilder.create()
            .width(300)
            .height(200)
            .arcWidth(20)
            .arcHeight(20)
            .fill(Color.LIGHTBLUE)
            .stroke(Color.GRAY)
            .strokeWidth(2)
            .build(),
          BorderPaneBuilder.create()
            .center(
              htmlLabel = LabelBuilder.create()
                .text(text)
                .wrapText(true)
                .maxWidth(280)
                .maxHeight(140)
                .build()
            )
            .bottom(
              okButton = ButtonBuilder.create()
                .text("OK")
```

```
                    .onAction(new EventHandler<ActionEvent>() {
                      @Override public void handle(ActionEvent e) {
                        alertPopup.hide();
                      }
                    })
                    .build()
                )
              .build()
          )
        .build()
      )
    .build();

  BorderPane.setAlignment(okButton, Pos.CENTER);
  BorderPane.setMargin(okButton, new Insets(10, 0, 10, 0));
  return alertPopup;
}
```

Some relevant notes about the createAlertPopup() method code:

- A String argument containing the HTML to be displayed is passed into the method.

- The PopupBuilder class is leveraged to create the Popup.

- The onAction handler in the OK button causes the Popup to hide from view, as you experienced in Step 32 of the exercise.

Let's move on to the final, and arguably the most powerful, UI control in the StarterApp program.

Using a WebView

The WebView control is a web browser that you can embed in JavaFX applications. As you experienced in Steps 32 and 33 of the exercise, the WebView control shown in Figure 5-12 automatically displays a randomly selected web page when the tab labeled PasswordField is selected.

To create the WebView instance, our StarterApp program uses the WebViewBuilder class as shown in the following snippet from Listing 5-5, where the TabPane and its tabs are created.

```
webViewTab = TabBuilder.create()
  .text("WebView")
  .content(
    webView = WebViewBuilder.create()
      .build()
  )
  .closable(false)
  .onSelectionChanged(new EventHandler<Event>() {
    public void handle(Event evt) {
      String randomWebSite = model.getRandomWebSite();
```

```
        if (webViewTab.isSelected()) {
          webView.getEngine().load(randomWebSite);
          System.out.println("WebView tab is selected, loading: "
                                 + randomWebSite);
        }
      }
    })
    .build()
```

The code in the `onSelectionChanged()` method above calls a method in the `StarterAppModel` class to get the URL of a randomly selected website. The `getEngine()` method of the `WebView` is then invoked to get the `WebEngine` instance associated with the `WebView`. The `load()` method of the `WebEngine` is invoked, passing a `String` that contains the randomly selected URL, which causes the `WebView` to display the web page retrieved from that URL. The following snippet contains the relevant code from the `StarterAppModel` class:

```
public String getRandomWebSite() {
  String[] webSites = {
    "http://javafx.com",
    "http://fxexperience.com",
    "http://steveonjava.com",
    "http://javafxpert.com",
    "http://pleasingsoftware.blogspot.com",
    "http://www.weiqigao.com/blog",
    "http://google.com"
  };
  int randomIdx = (int)(Math.random() * webSites.length);
  return webSites[randomIdx];
}
```

The `WebView` control and its `WebEngine` counterpart have additional capabilities documented in the `javafx.scene.web` package of the API that are worth investigating.

Summary

Congratulations, you gained a lot of experience with the UI controls in JavaFX:

- You tried out most of the JavaFX UI controls in the context of the StarterApp program, which also serves as starting point from which you can modify and create an application.

- You explored code examples and explanations for these JavaFX UI controls.

Resources

For some additional information using JavaFX UI controls, consult the following resource.

- *Using JavaFX UI Controls*, developed by Alla Redko, a technical writer for Oracle: http://download.oracle.com/javafx/2.0/ui_controls/jfxpub-ui_controls.htm

CHAPTER 6

Collections and Concurrency

When you know a thing, to hold that you know it; and when you do not know a thing,
to allow that you do not know it;—this is knowledge.

—Confucius

After the fast-paced exploration of JavaFX layouts in Chapter 4 and JavaFX UI controls in Chapter 5, we refocus our attention on some of the lower-level facilities of JavaFX in this chapter.

Recall that in Chapter 3, "Properties and Bindings," you learned about the `Observable` interface and one of its subinterfaces `ObservableValue`. In this chapter, we examine the other two subinterfaces of `Observable`—`ObservableList` and `ObservableMap`—rounding out the story of the `Observable` family of interfaces and classes.

We then cover concurrency in JavaFX. We explain the JavaFX threading model, pointing out the most important threads present in a JavaFX application. We look at the rules that you must follow to ensure your JavaFX application is responsive to user inputs and not locked up by event handlers that take too long to execute. We also show you how the `javafx.concurrent` framework can be used to offload long-running routines to background threads.

We conclude this chapter with two examples that show how a JavaFX scene graph can be embedded into a Swing application using `JFXPanel`, and how it can be embedded into an SWT application using `FXCanvas`, paying attention to how to make the JavaFX event thread play nicely with the Swing event dispatching thread.

Understanding Observable Collections

As we saw in Chapter 3, the `Observable` interface has three direct subinterfaces in JavaFX 2.0—the `ObservableValue` interface, the `ObservableList` interface, and the `ObservableMap` interface. We learned that the `ObservableValue` interface plays a central role in the JavaFX 2.0 Properties and Bindings framework.

The `ObservableList` and `ObservableMap` interfaces reside in the `javafx.collections` package, and are referred to as the JavaFX 2.0 observable collections. In addition to extending the `Observable` interface, `ObservableList` also extends the `java.util.List` interface, and `ObservableMap` extends the `java.util.Map` interface, making both genuine collections in the eyes of the Java collections framework. And you can call all the Java collections framework methods you are familiar with on objects of the JavaFX observable collection interfaces and expect exactly the same results. What the JavaFX observable collections provide in addition to the stock Java collections framework are notifications to registered listeners. Because they are `Observable`s, you can register `InvalidationListener`s with the JavaFX observable collections objects and be notified when the content of the observable collections becomes invalid.

Each of the JavaFX observable collections interfaces supports a change event that conveys more detailed information of the change. We examine the JavaFX observable collections and the change events that they support in the following sections.

Understanding ObservableList

Figure 6-1 is an UML diagram showing the `ObservableList` and supporting interfaces.

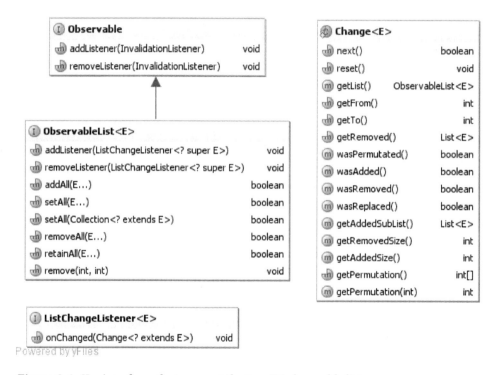

Figure 6-1. *Key interfaces that support the JavaFX observable list*

To prevent clutter, we omitted the `java.util.List` interface from the diagram in Figure 6-1. The `java.util.List` interface is the other super interface of `ObservableList`. The following two methods on the `ObservableList` interface allow you to register and unregister `ListChangeListener`s:

- `addListener(ListChangeListener<? super E> listener)`

- `removeListener(ListChangeListener<? super E> listener)`

The following, additional, six methods on `ObservableList` make working with the interface easier:

- `addAll(E... elements)`
- `setAll(E... elements)`
- `setAll(Collection<? extends E> col)`
- `removeAll(E... elements)`
- `retainAll(E... elements)`
- `remove(int from, int to)`

The `ListChangeListener` interface has only one method: `onChange(ListChangeListener.Change<? extends E> change)`. This method is called back when the content of the `ObservableList` is manipulated. Notice that this method's parameter type is the nested class `Change` that is declared in the `ListChangeListener` interface. We show you how to use the `ListChangeListener.Change` class in the next subsection. For now, we look at a simple example illustrating the firing of invalidation and list change events when an `ObservableList` is manipulated.

Listing 6-1. *ObservableListExample.java*

```
import javafx.beans.InvalidationListener;
import javafx.beans.Observable;
import javafx.collections.FXCollections;
import javafx.collections.ListChangeListener;
import javafx.collections.ObservableList;

import java.util.Arrays;
import java.util.Iterator;
import java.util.List;

public class ObservableListExample {
    public static void main(String[] args) {
        ObservableList<String> strings = FXCollections.observableArrayList();

        strings.addListener(new InvalidationListener() {
            @Override
            public void invalidated(Observable observable) {
                System.out.println("\tlist invalidated");
            }
        });

        strings.addListener(new ListChangeListener<String>() {
            @Override
            public void onChanged(Change<? extends String> change) {
                System.out.println("\tstrings = " + change.getList());
            }
        });
```

```
            System.out.println("Calling add(\"First\"): ");
            strings.add("First");

            System.out.println("Calling add(0, \"Zeroth\"): ");
            strings.add(0, "Zeroth");

            System.out.println("Calling addAll(\"Second\", \"Third\"): ");
            strings.addAll("Second", "Third");

            System.out.println("Calling set(1, \"New First\"): ");
            strings.set(1, "New First");

            final List<String> list = Arrays.asList("Second_1", "Second_2");
            System.out.println("Calling addAll(3, list): ");
            strings.addAll(3, list);

            System.out.println("Calling remove(2, 4): ");
            strings.remove(2, 4);

            final Iterator<String> iterator = strings.iterator();
            while (iterator.hasNext()) {
                final String next = iterator.next();
                if (next.contains("t")) {
                    System.out.println("Calling remove() on iterator: ");
                    iterator.remove();
                }
            }

            System.out.println("Calling removeAll(\"Third\", \"Fourth\"): ");
            strings.removeAll("Third", "Fourth");
        }
    }
```

Unlike the Java collections framework, where the public API contains both the interfaces, such as List and Map, and concrete implementations of the interfaces that you can instantiate, such as ArrayList and HashMap, the JavaFX observable collections framework provides only the interfaces ObservableList and ObservableMap, but not concrete implementation classes. To obtain an object of a JavaFX observable collections interface, you use the utility class FXCollections. In Listing 6-1, we obtain an ObservableList<String> object by calling a factory method on FXCollections:

```
        ObservableList<String> strings = FXCollections.observableArrayList();
```

We then hooked an InvalidationListener and a ListChangeListener to the observable list. The invalidation listener simply prints out a message every time it's called. The list change listener prints out the content of the observable list. The rest of the program simply manipulates the content of the observable list in various ways: by calling methods on the java.util.List interface, by calling some of the new convenience methods added to ObservableList, and by calling the remove() method on an Iterator obtained from the observable list.

When we run the program in Listing 6-1, the following output is printed to the console:

```
Calling add("First"):

        list invalidated

        strings = [First]

Calling add(0, "Zeroth"):

        list invalidated

        strings = [Zeroth, First]

Calling addAll("Second", "Third"):

        list invalidated

        strings = [Zeroth, First, Second, Third]

Calling set(1, "New First"):

        list invalidated

        strings = [Zeroth, New First, Second, Third]

Calling addAll(3, list):

        list invalidated

        strings = [Zeroth, New First, Second, Second_1, Second_2, Third]

Calling remove(2, 4):

        list invalidated

        strings = [Zeroth, New First, Second_2, Third]

Calling remove() on iterator:

        list invalidated

        strings = [New First, Second_2, Third]
```

```
Calling remove() on iterator:

    list invalidated

    strings = [Second_2, Third]

Calling removeAll("Third", "Fourth"):

    list invalidated

    strings = [Second_2]
```

Indeed, every call that we made in the code to change the content of the observable list triggered a callback on both the invalidation listener and the list change listener.

■ **Note** Although it is not specified in the Javadocs, for observable lists obtained by calling FXCollections.observableArrayList() a invalidation event is fired exactly when a list change event is fired. Any invalidation listener you add is wrapped and added as a list change listener. You can verify this by stepping through the code in a debugger.

If an instance of an invalidation listener or a list change listener has already been added as a listener to an observable list, all subsequent addListener() calls with that instance as an argument are ignored. Of course, you can add as many distinct invalidation listeners and list change listeners as you like to an observable list.

Handling Change Events in ListChangeListener

In this section, we take a closer look at the ListChangeListener.Change class and discuss how the onChange() callback method should handle the list change event.

As we saw in the preceding section, for an ObservableList obtained by calling FXCollections.observableArrayList(),each mutator call—that is, each call to a single method that changes the content of the observable list—generates a list change event delivered to each registered observers. The event object, an instance of a class that implements the ListChangeListener.Change interface, can be thought of as representing one or more discrete changes, each of which is of one of four kinds: elements added, elements removed, elements replaced, or elements permuted. The ListChangeListener.Change class provides the following methods that allow you to get at this detailed information about the change:

- boolean next()
- void reset()
- boolean wasAdded()

- `boolean wasRemoved()`
- `boolean wasReplaced()`
- `boolean wasPermutted()`
- `int getFrom()`
- `int getTo()`
- `int getAddedSize()`
- `List<E> getAddedSublist()`
- `int getRemovedSize()`
- `List<E> getRemoved()`
- `int getPermutation(int i)`
- `ObservableList<E> getList()`

The `next()` and `reset()` methods control a cursor that iterates through all the discrete changes in the event object. On entry to the `onChange()` method of `ListChangeListener`, the cursor is positioned before the first discrete change. You must call the `next()` method to move the cursor to the first discrete change. Succeeding calls to the `next()` method will move the cursor to the remaining discrete changes. If the next discrete change is reached, the return value will be `true`. If the cursor is already on the last discrete change, the return value will be `false`. Once the cursor is positioned on a valid discrete change, the methods `wasAdded()`, `wasRemoved()`, `wasReplaced()`, and `wasPermutted()`can be called to determine the kind of change the discrete change represents.

■ **Caution** The `wasAdded()`, `wasRemoved()`, `wasReplaced()`, and `wasPermutted()` methods are not orthogonal. A discrete change is a replacement only if it is both an addition and a removal. So the proper order for testing the kind of a discrete change is to first determine whether it is a permutation or a replacement and then to determine whether it is an addition or a removal.

Once you have determined the kind of discrete change, you can call the other methods to get more information about it. For addition, the `getFrom()` method returns the index in the observable list where new elements were added; the `getTo()` method returns the index of element that is one past the end of the added elements; the `getAddedSize()` method returns the number of elements that were added; and the `getAddedSublist()` method returns a `List<E>` that contains the added elements. For removal, the `getFrom()` and `getTo()` methods both return the index in the observable list where elements were removed; the `getRemovedSize()` method returns the number of elements that were removed; and the `getRemoved()` method returns a `List<E>` that contains the removed elements. For replacement, both the methods that are relevant for addition and the methods that are relevant for removal should be examined, because a replacement can be seen as a removal followed by an addition at the same index. For permutation, the `getPermutation(int i)` method returns the index of an element in the observable list after the permutation whose index in the observable list before the permutation was `i`. In all situations, The `getList()` method always returns the underlying observable list.

In the following example, we perform various list manipulations after attaching a ListChangeListener to an ObservableList. The implementation of ListChangeListener, called MyListener includes a pretty printer for the ListChangeListener.Change object, and prints out the list change event object when an event is fired.

Listing 6-2. ListChangeEventExample.java

```java
import javafx.collections.FXCollections;
import javafx.collections.ListChangeListener;
import javafx.collections.ObservableList;

public class ListChangeEventExample {
    public static void main(String[] args) {
        ObservableList<String> strings = FXCollections.observableArrayList();
        strings.addListener(new MyListener());

        System.out.println("Calling addAll(\"Zero\", \"One\", \"Two\", \"Three\"): ");
        strings.addAll("Zero", "One", "Two", "Three");

        System.out.println("Calling FXCollections.sort(strings): ");
        FXCollections.sort(strings);

        System.out.println("Calling set(1, \"Three_1\"): ");
        strings.set(1, "Three_1");

        System.out.println("Calling setAll(\"One_1\", \"Three_1\", \"Two_1\", \"Zero_1\"): ");
        strings.setAll("One_1", "Three_1", "Two_1", "Zero_1");

        System.out.println("Calling removeAll(\"One_1\", \"Two_1\", \"Zero_1\"): ");
        strings.removeAll("One_1", "Two_1", "Zero_1");
    }

    private static class MyListener implements ListChangeListener<String> {
        @Override
        public void onChanged(Change<? extends String> change) {
            System.out.println("\tlist = " + change.getList());
            System.out.println(prettyPrint(change));
        }

        private String prettyPrint(Change<? extends String> change) {
            StringBuilder sb = new StringBuilder("\tChange event data:\n");
            int i = 0;
            while (change.next()) {
                sb.append("\t\tcursor = ")
                    .append(i++)
                    .append("\n");
```

```java
        final String kind =
            change.wasPermutated() ? "permutted" :
                change.wasReplaced() ? "replaced" :
                    change.wasRemoved() ? "removed" :
                        change.wasAdded() ? "added" : "none";

    sb.append("\t\tKind of change: ")
        .append(kind)
        .append("\n");

    sb.append("\t\tAffected range: [")
        .append(change.getFrom())
        .append(", ")
        .append(change.getTo())
        .append("]\n");

    if (kind.equals("added") || kind.equals("replaced")) {
        sb.append("\t\tAdded size: ")
            .append(change.getAddedSize())
            .append("\n");
        sb.append("\t\tAdded sublist: ")
            .append(change.getAddedSubList())
            .append("\n");
    }

    if (kind.equals("removed") || kind.equals("replaced")) {
        sb.append("\t\tRemoved size: ")
            .append(change.getRemovedSize())
            .append("\n");
        sb.append("\t\tRemoved: ")
            .append(change.getRemoved())
            .append("\n");
    }

    if (kind.equals("permutted")) {
        StringBuilder permutationStringBuilder = new StringBuilder("[");
        for (int k = change.getFrom(); k < change.getTo(); k++) {
            permutationStringBuilder.append(k)
                .append("->")
                .append(change.getPermutation(k));
            if (k < change.getTo() - 1) {
                permutationStringBuilder.append(", ");
            }
        }
        permutationStringBuilder.append("]");
        String permutation = permutationStringBuilder.toString();
        sb.append("\t\tPermutation: ").append(permutation).append("\n");
    }
}
```

```
            return sb.toString();
        }
    }
}
```

In the preceding example, we triggered the four kinds of discrete changes in an observable list. Since no methods on an ObservableList will trigger a permutation event, therefore we used the sort() utility method from the FXCollections class to effect a permutation. We have more to say about FXCollections in a later section. We triggered the replace event twice, once with set(), and once with setAll(). The nice thing about setAll() is that it effectively does a clear() and an addAll() in one operation and generates only one change event.

When we run the program in Listing 6-2, the following output is printed to the console:

```
Calling addAll("Zero", "One", "Two", "Three"):

        list = [Zero, One, Two, Three]

        Change event data:

                cursor = 0

                Kind of change: added

                Affected range: [0, 4]

                Added size: 4

                Added sublist: [Zero, One, Two, Three]


Calling FXCollections.sort(strings):

        list = [One, Three, Two, Zero]

        Change event data:

                cursor = 0

                Kind of change: permutted

                Affected range: [0, 4]

                Permutation: [0->3, 1->0, 2->2, 3->1]
```

Calling set(1, "Three_1"):

      list = [One, Three_1, Two, Zero]

      Change event data:

           cursor = 0

           Kind of change: replaced

           Affected range: [1, 2]

           Added size: 1

           Added sublist: [Three_1]

           Removed size: 1

           Removed: [Three]

Calling setAll("One_1", "Three_1", "Two_1", "Zero_1"):

      list = [One_1, Three_1, Two_1, Zero_1]

      Change event data:

           cursor = 0

           Kind of change: replaced

           Affected range: [0, 4]

           Added size: 4

           Added sublist: [One_1, Three_1, Two_1, Zero_1]

           Removed size: 4

           Removed: [One, Three_1, Two, Zero]

Calling removeAll("One_1", "Two_1", "Zero_1"):

list = [Three_1]

Change event data:

cursor = 0

Kind of change: removed

Affected range: [0, 0]

Removed size: 1

Removed: [One_1]

cursor = 1

Kind of change: removed

Affected range: [1, 1]

Removed size: 2

Removed: [Two_1, Zero_1]

In all but the removeAll() call, the list change event object contains only one discrete change. The reason that the removeAll() call generates a list change event that contains two discrete changes is that the three elements that we wish to remove fall in two disjoint ranges in the list.

In the majority of use cases where we care about list change events, you don't necessarily need to distinguish the kinds of discrete changes. Sometimes you simply want to do something to all added and removed elements. In such a case your ListChangeListener method can be as simple as the following.

```
@Override
public void onChanged(Change<? extends Foo> change) {
    while (change.next()) {
        for (Foo foo : change.getAddedSubList()) {
            // starting up
        }
        for (Foo foo : change.getRemoved()) {
            // cleaning up
        }
    }
}
```

Understanding ObservableMap

Although ObservableMap appears equivalent to ObservableList in the JavaFX observable collections framework hierarchy, it is actually not as sophisticated as ObservableList. Figure 6-2 is an UML diagram showing the ObservableMap and supporting interfaces.

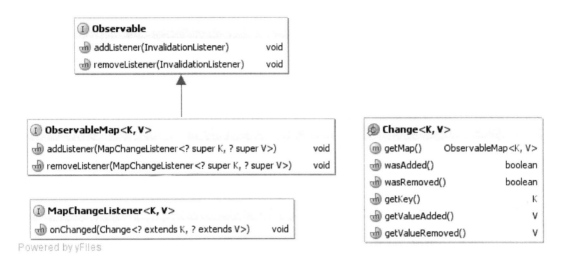

Figure 6-2. *Key interfaces that support the JavaFX observable map*

To prevent clutter, we omitted the java.util.Map interface from the diagram. The java.util.Map interface is the other super interface of ObservableMap, The following methods on the ObservableMap interface allow you to register and unregister MapChangeListeners:

- addListener(MapChangeListener<? super K, ? super V> listener)

- addListener(MapChangeListener<? super K, ? super V> listener)

There are no additional convenience methods on ObservableMap.

The MapChangeListener interface has only one method: onChange(MapChangeListener.Change<? extends K, ? extends V> change). This method is called back when the content of the ObservableMap is manipulated. Notice that this method's parameter type is the nested class Change that is declared in the MapChangeListener interface. Unlike the ListChangeListener.Change class, the MapChangeListener.Change class is geared towards reporting the change of a single key in a map. If a method call on ObservableMap affects multiple keys, as many map change events as the number of affected keys will be fired.

The MapChangeListener.Change class provides the following methods for you to inspect the changes made to a key.

- boolean wasAdded() returns true if a new value was added for the key.

- boolean wasRemoved() returns true if an old value was removed from the key.

- K getKey() returns the affected key.

- V getValueAdded() returns the value that was added for the key.

- V getValueRemoved() returns the value that was removed for the key. (Note that a put() call with an existing key will cause the old value to be removed.)

- ObservableMap<K, V> getMap()

In the following example, we perform various map manipulations after attaching a MapChangeListener to an ObservableMap. The implementation of MapChangeListener, called MyListener includes a pretty printer for the MapChangeListener. Change object, and prints out the map change event object when an event is fired.

Listing 6-3. MapChangeEventExample.java

```java
import javafx.collections.FXCollections;
import javafx.collections.MapChangeListener;
import javafx.collections.ObservableMap;

import java.util.HashMap;
import java.util.Iterator;
import java.util.Map;

public class MapChangeEventExample {
    public static void main(String[] args) {
        ObservableMap<String, Integer> map = FXCollections.observableHashMap();
        map.addListener(new MyListener());

        System.out.println("Calling put(\"First\", 1): ");
        map.put("First", 1);

        System.out.println("Calling put(\"First\", 100): ");
        map.put("First", 100);

        Map<String, Integer> anotherMap = new HashMap<>();
        anotherMap.put("Second", 2);
        anotherMap.put("Third", 3);
        System.out.println("Calling putAll(anotherMap): ");
        map.putAll(anotherMap);

        final Iterator<Map.Entry<String, Integer>> entryIterator = map.entrySet().iterator();
        while (entryIterator.hasNext()) {
            final Map.Entry<String, Integer> next = entryIterator.next();
            if (next.getKey().equals("Second")) {
                System.out.println("Calling remove on entryIterator: ");
                entryIterator.remove();
            }
        }
    }
```

```
            final Iterator<Integer> valueIterator = map.values().iterator();
            while (valueIterator.hasNext()) {
                final Integer next = valueIterator.next();
                if (next == 3) {
                    System.out.println("Calling remove on valueIterator: ");
                    valueIterator.remove();
                }
            }
        }
    }

    private static class MyListener implements MapChangeListener<String, Integer> {
        @Override
        public void onChanged(Change<? extends String, ? extends Integer> change) {
            System.out.println("\tmap = " + change.getMap());
            System.out.println(prettyPrint(change));
        }

        private String prettyPrint(Change<? extends String, ? extends Integer> change) {
            StringBuilder sb = new StringBuilder("\tChange event data:\n");
            sb.append("\t\tWas added: ").append(change.wasAdded()).append("\n");
            sb.append("\t\tWas removed: ").append(change.wasRemoved()).append("\n");
            sb.append("\t\tKey: ").append(change.getKey()).append("\n");
            sb.append("\t\tValue added: ").append(change.getValueAdded()).append("\n");
            sb.append("\t\tValue removed: ").append(change.getValueRemoved()).append("\n");
            return sb.toString();
        }
    }
}
```

When we run the program in Listing 6-3, the following output is printed to the console:

```
Calling put("First", 1):

        map = {First=1}

        Change event data:

                Was added: true

                Was removed: false

                Key: First

                Value added: 1

                Value removed: null
```

245

```
Calling put("First", 100):

        map = {First=100}

        Change event data:

                Was added: true

                Was removed: true

                Key: First

                Value added: 100

                Value removed: 1


Calling putAll(anotherMap):

        map = {Third=3, First=100}

        Change event data:

                Was added: true

                Was removed: false

                Key: Third

                Value added: 3

                Value removed: null


        map = {Third=3, Second=2, First=100}

        Change event data:

                Was added: true

                Was removed: false
```

```
        Key: Second

        Value added: 2

        Value removed: null


Calling remove on entryIterator:

        map = {Third=3, First=100}

        Change event data:

                Was added: false

                Was removed: true

                Key: Second

                Value added: null

                Value removed: 2


Calling remove on valueIterator:

        map = {First=100}

        Change event data:

                Was added: false

                Was removed: true

                Key: Third

                Value added: null

                Value removed: 3
```

In the preceding example, notice that the putAll() call generated two map change events because the other map contains two keys.

Using Factory and Utility Methods from FXCollections

The FXCollections class plays a similar role in the JavaFX observable collections framework that the java.util.Collections class plays in the Java collections framework. The FXCollections class contains ten factory methods for ObservableList:

- ObservableList<E> observableList(List<E> list)

- ObservableList<E> observableArrayList()

- ObservableList<E> observableArrayList(E... items)

- ObservableList<E> observableArrayList(Collection<? extends E> col)

- ObservableList<E> concat(ObservableList<E>... lists)

- ObservableList<E> unmodifiableObservableList(ObservableList<E> list)

- ObservableList<E> checkedObservableList(ObservableList<E> list, Class<E> type)

- ObservableList<E> synchronizedObservableList(ObservableList<E> list)

- ObservableList<E> emptyObservableList()

- ObservableList<E> singletonObservableList(E e)

It contains three factory methods for ObservableMap:

- ObservableMap<K, V> observableMap(Map<K, V> map)

- ObservableMap<K, V> unmodifiableObservableMap(ObservableMap<K, V> map)

- ObservableMap<K, V> observableHashMap()

And it contains nine utility methods that are parallels of methods with the same name in java.util.Collections. They all act on ObservableList objects. And they differ from their java.util.Collections counterpart in that when they act on an ObservableList, care is taken to generate only one list change events whereas their java.util.Collections counterpart would have generated more than one list change event.

- void copy(ObservableList<? super T> dest, java.util.List<? extends T> src)

- void fill(ObservableList<? super T> list, T obj)

- boolean replaceAll(ObservableList<T> list, T oldVal, T newVal)

- void reverse(ObservableList list)

- void rotate(ObservableList list, int distance)

- void shuffle(ObservableList<?> list)

- void shuffle(ObservableList list, java.util.Random rnd)

- void sort(ObservableList<T> list)

- void sort(ObservableList<T> list, java.util.Comparator<? super T> c)

We illustrate the effects of these utility methods in Listing 6-4.

Listing 6-4. *FXCollectionsExample.java*

```java
import javafx.collections.FXCollections;
import javafx.collections.ListChangeListener;
import javafx.collections.ObservableList;

import java.util.Arrays;
import java.util.Comparator;
import java.util.Random;

public class FXCollectionsExample {
    public static void main(String[] args) {
        ObservableList<String> strings = FXCollections.observableArrayList();
        strings.addListener(new MyListener());

        System.out.println("Calling addAll(\"Zero\", \"One\", \"Two\", \"Three\"): ");
        strings.addAll("Zero", "One", "Two", "Three");

        System.out.println("Calling copy: ");
        FXCollections.copy(strings, Arrays.asList("Four", "Five"));

        System.out.println("Calling replaceAll: ");
        FXCollections.replaceAll(strings, "Two", "Two_1");

        System.out.println("Calling reverse: ");
        FXCollections.reverse(strings);

        System.out.println("Calling rotate(strings, 2: ");
        FXCollections.rotate(strings, 2);

        System.out.println("Calling shuffle(strings): ");
        FXCollections.shuffle(strings);

        System.out.println("Calling shuffle(strings, new Random(0L)): ");
        FXCollections.shuffle(strings, new Random(0L));

        System.out.println("Calling sort(strings): ");
        FXCollections.sort(strings);

        System.out.println("Calling sort(strings, c) with custom comparator: ");
        FXCollections.sort(strings, new Comparator<String>() {
            @Override
            public int compare(String lhs, String rhs) {
                // Reverse the order
                return rhs.compareTo(lhs);
            }
        });
```

```
        System.out.println("Calling fill(strings, \"Ten\"): ");
        FXCollections.fill(strings, "Ten");
    }

    // We omitted the nested class MyListener, which is the same as in Listing 6-2
}
```

When we run the program in Listing 6-4, the following output is printed to the console:

```
Calling addAll("Zero", "One", "Two", "Three"):

    list = [Zero, One, Two, Three]

    Change event data:

            cursor = 0

            Kind of change: added

            Affected range: [0, 4]

            Added size: 4

            Added sublist: [Zero, One, Two, Three]


Calling copy:

    list = [Four, Five, Two, Three]

    Change event data:

            cursor = 0

            Kind of change: replaced

            Affected range: [0, 4]

            Added size: 4

            Added sublist: [Four, Five, Two, Three]

            Removed size: 4

            Removed: [Zero, One, Two, Three]
```

Calling replaceAll:

    list = [Four, Five, Two_1, Three]

    Change event data:

        cursor = 0

        Kind of change: replaced

        Affected range: [0, 4]

        Added size: 4

        Added sublist: [Four, Five, Two_1, Three]

        Removed size: 4

        Removed: [Four, Five, Two, Three]

Calling reverse:

    list = [Three, Two_1, Five, Four]

    Change event data:

        cursor - 0

        Kind of change: replaced

        Affected range: [0, 4]

        Added size: 4

        Added sublist: [Three, Two_1, Five, Four]

        Removed size: 4

        Removed: [Four, Five, Two_1, Three]

251

Calling rotate(strings, 2:

    list = [Five, Four, Three, Two_1]

    Change event data:

        cursor = 0

        Kind of change: replaced

        Affected range: [0, 4]

        Added size: 4

        Added sublist: [Five, Four, Three, Two_1]

        Removed size: 4

        Removed: [Three, Two_1, Five, Four]

Calling shuffle(strings):

    list = [Five, Three, Two_1, Four]

    Change event data:

        cursor = 0

        Kind of change: replaced

        Affected range: [0, 4]

        Added size: 4

        Added sublist: [Five, Three, Two_1, Four]

        Removed size: 4

        Removed: [Five, Four, Three, Two_1]

Calling shuffle(strings, new Random(OL)):

    list = [Four, Five, Three, Two_1]

    Change event data:

        cursor = 0

        Kind of change: replaced

        Affected range: [0, 4]

        Added size: 4

        Added sublist: [Four, Five, Three, Two_1]

        Removed size: 4

        Removed: [Five, Three, Two_1, Four]

Calling sort(strings):

    list = [Five, Four, Three, Two_1]

    Change event data:

        cursor = 0

        Kind of change: permutted

        Affected range: [0, 4]

        Permutation: [0->1, 1->0, 2->2, 3->3]

Calling sort(strings, c) with custom comparator:

    list = [Two_1, Three, Four, Five]

```
Change event data:

    cursor = 0

    Kind of change: permutted

    Affected range: [0, 4]

    Permutation: [0->3, 1->2, 2->1, 3->0]


Calling fill(strings, "Ten"):

    list = [Ten, Ten, Ten, Ten]

    Change event data:

        cursor = 0

        Kind of change: replaced

        Affected range: [0, 4]

        Added size: 4

        Added sublist: [Ten, Ten, Ten, Ten]

        Removed size: 4

        Removed: [Two_1, Three, Four, Five]
```

Notice that each invocation of a utility method in FXCollections generated exactly one list change event.

Using the JavaFX Concurrency Framework

It is common knowledge nowadays that almost all GUI platforms use a single-threaded event dispatching model. JavaFX is no exception, and indeed all user interface events in JavaFX are processed in the *JavaFX Application Thread*. However, with multicore desktop machines becoming common in recent years (e.g., I'm writing this chapter on my three-year-old quad-core PC), it is natural for the designers of JavaFX to take advantage of the full power of the hardware by leveraging the excellent concurrency support of the Java programming language.

In this section, we examine important threads that are present in all JavaFX applications. We explain the role they play in the overall scheme of JavaFX applications. We then turn our attention to the JavaFX Application Thread, explaining why executing long-running code in the JavaFX Application Thread makes your application appear to hang. Finally, we look at the `javafx.concurrent` framework and show you how to use it to execute long-running code in a worker thread off the JavaFX Application Thread and communicate the result back to the JavaFX Application Thread to update the GUI states.

■ **Note** If you are familiar with Swing programming, the JavaFX Application Thread is similar to Swing's Event Dispatcher Thread (EDT), usually with the name "AWT-EventQueue-0."

Identifying the Threads in a JavaFX Application

The program in Listing 6-5 creates a simple JavaFX GUI with a `ListView`, a `TextArea` and a `Button`, and populates the ListView with the names of all live threads of the application. When you select an item from the `ListView`, that thread's stack trace is displayed in the `TextArea`. The original list of threads and stack traces is populated as the application is starting up. And you can update the list of threads and stack traces by clicking the Update button.

Listing 6-5. JavaFXThreadsExample.java

```java
import javafx.application.Application;
import javafx.beans.value.ChangeListener;
import javafx.beans.value.ObservableValue;
import javafx.collections.FXCollections;
import javafx.collections.ObservableList;
import javafx.event.ActionEvent;
import javafx.event.EventHandler;
import javafx.geometry.Insets;
import javafx.scene.Scene;
import javafx.scene.SceneBuilder;
import javafx.scene.control.Button;
import javafx.scene.control.ListView;
import javafx.scene.control.TextArea;
import javafx.scene.layout.VBoxBuilder;
import javafx.stage.Stage;

import java.util.Map;

public class JavaFXThreadsExample extends Application
        implements EventHandler<ActionEvent>, ChangeListener<Number> {

    private Model model;
    private View view;

    public static void main(String[] args) {
        Application.launch(args);
    }
```

```java
    public JavaFXThreadsExample() {
        model = new Model();
    }

    @Override
    public void start(Stage stage) throws Exception {
        view = new View(model);
        hookupEvents();
        stage.setTitle("JavaFX Threads Information");
        stage.setScene(view.scene);
        stage.show();
    }

    private void hookupEvents() {
        view.updateButton.setOnAction(this);
        view.threadNames.getSelectionModel().selectedIndexProperty().addListener(this);
    }

    @Override
    public void changed(ObservableValue<? extends Number> observableValue,
                        Number oldValue, Number newValue) {
        int index = (Integer) newValue;
        if (index >= 0) {
            view.stackTrace.setText(model.stackTraces.get(index));
        }
    }

    @Override
    public void handle(ActionEvent actionEvent) {
        model.update();
    }

    public static class Model {
        public ObservableList<String> threadNames;
        public ObservableList<String> stackTraces;

        public Model() {
            threadNames = FXCollections.observableArrayList();
            stackTraces = FXCollections.observableArrayList();
            update();
        }

        public void update() {
            threadNames.clear();
            stackTraces.clear();
            final Map<Thread, StackTraceElement[]> map = Thread.getAllStackTraces();
            for (Map.Entry<Thread, StackTraceElement[]> entry : map.entrySet()) {
                threadNames.add("\"" + entry.getKey().getName() + "\"");
                stackTraces.add(formatStackTrace(entry.getValue()));
            }
        }
```

```java
        private String formatStackTrace(StackTraceElement[] value) {
            StringBuilder sb = new StringBuilder("StackTrace: \n");
            for (StackTraceElement stackTraceElement : value) {
                sb.append("    at ").append(stackTraceElement.toString()).append("\n");
            }
            return sb.toString();
        }
    }

    private static class View {
        public ListView<String> threadNames;
        public TextArea stackTrace;
        public Button updateButton;
        public Scene scene;

        private View(Model model) {
            threadNames = new ListView<>(model.threadNames);
            stackTrace = new TextArea();
            updateButton = new Button("Update");
            scene = SceneBuilder.create()
                .width(440)
                .height(640)
                .root(VBoxBuilder.create()
                    .spacing(10)
                    .padding(new Insets(10, 10, 10, 10))
                    .children(threadNames, stackTrace, updateButton)
                    .build())
                .build();
        }
    }
}
```

This is a pretty minimal JavaFX GUI application. Before letting you run this program, we point out several features of the program.

First of all, make a mental note of the main() method:

```java
public static void main(String[] args) {
    Application.launch(args);
}
```

You have seen this method several times already. This stylized main() method always appears in a class that extends the javafx.application.Application class. There is an overloaded version of the Application.launch() method that takes a Class object as the first parameter that can be called from other classes:

```java
launch(Class<? Extends Application> appClass, String[] args)
```

Therefore you can move the `main()` method to another class:

```
public class Main {
    public static void main(String[] args) {
        Application.launch(JavaFXThreadsExample.class, args);
    }
}
```

to achieve the same result.

Next, notice that the nested class `Model` builds up its data model, which consists of a list of all live threads and the stack traces of each thread, in its `update()` method:

```
public void update() {
    threadNames.clear();
    stackTraces.clear();
    final Map<Thread, StackTraceElement[]> map = Thread.getAllStackTraces();
    for (Map.Entry<Thread, StackTraceElement[]> entry : map.entrySet()) {
        threadNames.add("\"" + entry.getKey().getName() + "\"");
        stackTraces.add(formatStackTrace(entry.getValue()));
    }
}
```

This method is called once in the constructor of `Model`, which is called from the constructor of the `JavaFXThreadsExample`, and once from the event handler of the Update button.

When we run the program in Listing 6-5, the GUI in Figure 6-3 is displayed on the screen. You can explore the threads in this JavaFX program by clicking on each thread name in the list and see the stack trace for that thread in the text area. Here are some interesting observations:

- The "main" thread's call stack includes a call to `com.sun.javafx.application.LauncherImpl.launchApplication()`.

- The "JavaFX-Launcher" thread's call stack includes a call to the constructor `JavaFXThreadsExample.<init>`.

- The "JavaFX Application Thread" thread's call stack includes the native method `com.sun.glass.ui.win.WinApplication._runLoop()`.

- The "QuantumRenderer-0" thread's call stack includes the method `com.sun.javafx.tk.quantum.QuantumRenderer$ObservedRunnable.run()`.

Now when you click the Update button and examine the call stack for the "JavaFX Application Thread" thread, you will discover that the event handler of the Update button is executed on the JavaFX Application Thread.

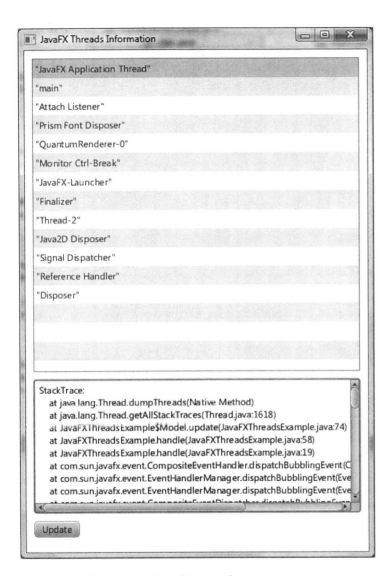

Figure 6-3. The JavaFXThreadsExample program

This little experiment reveals some of the architectural elements of the JavaFX runtime system. Although parts of this information include implementation details represented by, appropriately, classes in the com.sun hierarchy—therefore not to be used in code of normal JavaFX applications—it is nevertheless beneficial to have some knowledge of how the internals work.

■ **Caution** In the discussion that follows, we mention Java classes in packages whose names begin with `com.sun`. These classes are implementation details of the JavaFX runtime system and are not meant to be used in normal JavaFX applications. And they may change in future releases of JavaFX.

The `javafx.application.Application` class provides life-cycle support for JavaFX applications. In addition to the two static `launch()` methods we mentioned earlier in this section, it provides the following life-cycle methods.

- `public void init() throws Exception`

- `public abstract void start(Stage stage) throws Exception`

- `public void stop() throws Exception`

The constructor and the `init()` method are called in the "JavaFX-Launcher" thread. The `start()` and `stop()` methods are called in the "JavaFX Application Thread" thread. The JavaFX application thread is part of the *Glass Windowing Toolkit* in the `com.sun.glass` package hierarchy. JavaFX events are processed on the JavaFX Application Thread. All live scene manipulation must be performed in the JavaFX Application Thread. Nodes that are not attached to a live scene may be created and manipulated in other threads until they are attached to a live scene.

■ **Note** The role the Glass Windowing Toolkit plays in a JavaFX application is similar to that of the AWT in Swing applications. It provides drawing surfaces and input events from the native platform. Unlike in AWT, where the EDT is different from the native platform's UI thread and communication has to occur between them, the JavaFX application thread in the Glass Windowing Toolkit uses the native platform's UI thread directly.

The owner of the "QuantumRenderer-0" thread is the *Quantum Toolkit* that lives in the `com.sun.javafx.tk.quantum` package hierarchy. This thread is responsible for rendering the JavaFX scene graph using the *Prism Graphics Engine* in the `com.sun.prism` package hierarchy. Prism will use a fully accelerated rendering path if the graphics hardware is supported by JavaFX and will fall back to the Java2D rendering path if the graphics hardware is not supported by JavaFX. The Quantum Toolkit is also responsible for coordinating the activities of the event thread and the rendering thread. It does the coordination using `pulse` events.

■ **Note** A *pulse event* is an event that is put on the queue for the JavaFX application thread. When it is processed, it synchronizes the state of the elements of the scene graph down the rendering layer. Pulse events are scheduled if the states of the scene graph change, either through running animation or by modifying the scene graph directly. Pulse events are throttled at 60 frames per second.

Had the `JavaFXThreadsExample` program included media-playing, another thread named "JFXMedia Player EventQueueThread" would have shown up on the list. This thread is responsible for synchronizing the latest frame through the scene graph by using the JavaFX application thread.

Fixing Unresponsive UIs

Event handlers execute on the JavaFX application thread, thus an event handler takes too long to finish its work, the whole UI will become unresponsive because any subsequent user action will simply queue up and won't be handled until the long-running event handler is done.

We illustrate this in Listing 6-6.

Listing 6-6. *UnresponsiveUIExample.java*

```java
import javafx.application.Application;
import javafx.beans.property.ObjectProperty;
import javafx.beans.property.SimpleObjectProperty;
import javafx.event.ActionEvent;
import javafx.event.EventHandler;
import javafx.geometry.Insets;
import javafx.geometry.Pos;
import javafx.scene.Scene;
import javafx.scene.SceneBuilder;
import javafx.scene.control.Button;
import javafx.scene.layout.BorderPaneBuilder;
import javafx.scene.layout.HBox;
import javafx.scene.layout.HBoxBuilder;
import javafx.scene.paint.Color;
import javafx.scene.paint.Paint;
import javafx.scene.shape.Rectangle;
import javafx.scene.shape.RectangleBuilder;
import javafx.stage.Stage;

public class UnresponsiveUIExample extends Application {
    private Model model;
    private View view;

    public static void main(String[] args) {
        Application.launch(args);
    }

    public UnresponsiveUIExample() {
        model = new Model();
    }

    @Override
    public void start(Stage stage) throws Exception {
        view = new View(model);
        hookupEvents();
```

```java
        stage.setTitle("Unresponsive UI Example");
        stage.setScene(view.scene);
        stage.show();
    }

    private void hookupEvents() {
        view.changeFillButton.setOnAction(new EventHandler<ActionEvent>() {
            @Override
            public void handle(ActionEvent actionEvent) {
                final Paint fillPaint = model.getFillPaint();
                if (fillPaint.equals(Color.LIGHTGRAY)) {
                    model.setFillPaint(Color.GRAY);
                } else {
                    model.setFillPaint(Color.LIGHTGRAY);
                }
                // Bad code, this will cause the UI to be unresponsive
                try {
                    Thread.sleep(Long.MAX_VALUE);
                } catch (InterruptedException e) {
                    // TODO properly handle interruption
                }
            }
        });

        view.changeStrokeButton.setOnAction(new EventHandler<ActionEvent>() {
            @Override
            public void handle(ActionEvent actionEvent) {
                final Paint strokePaint = model.getStrokePaint();
                if (strokePaint.equals(Color.DARKGRAY)) {
                    model.setStrokePaint(Color.BLACK);
                } else {
                    model.setStrokePaint(Color.DARKGRAY);
                }
            }
        });
    }

    private static class Model {
        private ObjectProperty<Paint> fillPaint = new SimpleObjectProperty<>();
        private ObjectProperty<Paint> strokePaint = new SimpleObjectProperty<>();

        private Model() {
            fillPaint.set(Color.LIGHTGRAY);
            strokePaint.set(Color.DARKGRAY);
        }

        final public Paint getFillPaint() {
            return fillPaint.get();
        }
```

```
    final public void setFillPaint(Paint value) {
        this.fillPaint.set(value);
    }

    final public Paint getStrokePaint() {
        return strokePaint.get();
    }

    final public void setStrokePaint(Paint value) {
        this.strokePaint.set(value);
    }

    final public ObjectProperty<Paint> fillPaintProperty() {
        return fillPaint;
    }

    final public ObjectProperty<Paint> strokePaintProperty() {
        return strokePaint;
    }
}

private static class View {
    public Rectangle rectangle;
    public Button changeFillButton;
    public Button changeStrokeButton;
    public HBox buttonHBox;
    public Scene scene;

    private View(Model model) {
        rectangle = RectangleBuilder.create()
            .width(200)
            .height(200)
            .strokeWidth(10)
            .build();
        rectangle.fillProperty().bind(model.fillPaintProperty());
        rectangle.strokeProperty().bind(model.strokePaintProperty());

        changeFillButton = new Button("Change Fill");
        changeStrokeButton = new Button("Change Stroke");

        buttonHBox = HBoxBuilder.create()
            .padding(new Insets(10, 10, 10, 10))
            .spacing(10)
            .alignment(Pos.CENTER)
            .children(changeFillButton, changeStrokeButton)
            .build();
```

```
        scene = SceneBuilder.create()
            .root(BorderPaneBuilder.create()
                .padding(new Insets(10, 10, 10, 10))
                .center(rectangle)
                .bottom(buttonHBox)
                .build())
            .build();
    }
  }
}
```

This class stands up a simple UI with a rectangle with a pronounced `Color.DARKGRAY` stroke and a `Color.LIGHTGRAY` fill in the center of a `BorderPane`, and two buttons at the bottom labeled "Change Fill" and "Change Stroke." The "Change Fill" button is supposed to toggle the fill of the rectangle between `Color.LIGHTGRAY` and `Color.GRAY`. The "Change Stroke" button is supposed to toggle the stroke of the rectangle between `Color.DARKGRAY` and `Color.BLACK`. When we run the program in Listing 6-6, the GUI in Figure 6-4 is displayed on the screen.

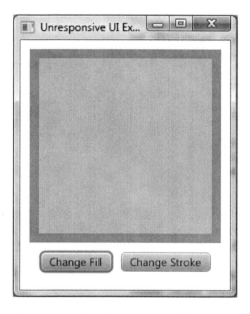

Figure 6-4. *The UnresponsiveUIExample program*

However, this program has a bug in the event handler of the "Change Fill" button:

```
@Override
public void handle(ActionEvent actionEvent) {
    final Paint fillPaint = model.getFillPaint();
    if (fillPaint.equals(Color.LIGHTGRAY)) {
        model.setFillPaint(Color.GRAY);
```

```
        } else {
            model.setFillPaint(Color.LIGHTGRAY);
        }
        // Bad code, this will cause the UI to be unresponsive
        try {
            Thread.sleep(Long.MAX_VALUE);
        } catch (InterruptedException e) {
            // TODO properly handle interruption
        }
    }
}
```

The `Thread.sleep(Long.MAX_VALUE)` simulates code that takes a long time to execute. In real-life applications, this might be a database call, a web service call, or a piece of complicated code. As a result, if you click the "Change Fill" button, the color change is not seen in the rectangle. What is worse, the whole UI appears to be locked up: the "Change Fill" and "Change Stroke" buttons stop working; the close window button that is provided by the operating system will not have the desired effect. The operating system might also mark the program as "Not Responding," and the only way to stop the program is to use the operating system's forced kill functionality.

To fix problems like this, we need to offload long-running code to worker threads and communicate the result of the long computation back to the JavaFX application thread in order to update the states of the UI so that the user can see the result. Depending on when you learned your Java, your answer to the first question of offloading code to worker threads may be different. If you are a long-time Java programmer your instinctive reaction might be to instantiate a `Runnable`, wrap it in a `Thread` and call `start()` on it. If you started with Java after Java 5 and learned the `java.util.concurrent` hierarchy of classes, your reaction might be to stand up a `java.util.concurrent.ExecutorService` and submit `java.util.concurrent.FutureTasks` to it. JavaFX includes a worker threading framework based on the latter approach in the `javafx.concurrent` package.

We examine the interfaces and classes in this framework in the next few sections, but before we do that we use the `Runnable` and `Thread` approach to offload computation to a worker thread. Our intention here is to highlight the answer to the second question of how to cause code to be run on the JavaFX application thread from a worker thread. The complete corrected program can be found in `ResponsiveUIExample.java`. Here is the new code for the event handler of the "Change Fill" button:

```
@Override
public void handle(ActionEvent actionEvent) {
    final Paint fillPaint = model.getFillPaint();
    if (fillPaint.equals(Color.LIGHTGRAY)) {
        model.setFillPaint(Color.GRAY);
    } else {
        model.setFillPaint(Color.LIGHTGRAY);
    }
    Runnable task = new Runnable() {
        @Override
        public void run() {
            try {
                Thread.sleep(3000);
                Platform.runLater(new Runnable() {
                    @Override
                    public void run() {
                        final Rectangle rect = view.rectangle;
```

```
                        double newArcSize =
                            rect.getArcHeight() < 20 ? 30 : 0;
                        rect.setArcWidth(newArcSize);
                        rect.setArcHeight(newArcSize);
                    }
                });
            } catch (InterruptedException e) {
                // TODO properly handle interruption
            }
        }
    };
    new Thread(task).start();
}
```

We have replaced the long sleep with code that executes in a worker thread. After sleeping for three seconds, the worker thread calls the runLater() method of the javafx.application.Platform class, passing it another Runnable that toggles the rounded corners of the rectangle. Because the long-running computation is done in a worker thread, the event handler is not blocking the JavaFX application thread. The change of fill is now reflected immediately in the UI. Because the Platform.runLater() call causes the Runnable to be executed on the JavaFX application thread, the change to the rounded corners is reflected in the UI after three seconds. The reason we have to execute the Runnable on the JavaFX application thread is that it modifies the state of a live scene.

The Platform class includes the following helpful utility methods.

- public static boolean isFxApplicationThread() returns true if it is executed on the JavaFX application thread and false otherwise.

- public static boolean isSupported(ConditionalFeature) tests whether the execution environment supports a ConditionalFeature. Testable ConditionalFeatures include EFFECT, INPUT_METHOD, SCENE3D, and SHAPE_CLIP.

- public static void exit(), if called after the application's start() method has been called, causes the application's stop() method to be executed on the JavaFX application thread before the JavaFX application thread and other JavaFX platform threads are taken down. If the application's start() method has not been called yet, the application's stop() method may not be called.

▓ **Note** If you are familiar with Swing programming, you should see the similarity between JavaFX's Platform.runLater() and Swing's EventQueue.invokerLater(), or SwingUtilities.invokeLater().

Now that we have solved our problem with Runnable and Thread and Platform.runLater(), it is time to see how we can use JavaFX's built-in worker threading framework to solve the problem in a more flexible and elegant way.

Understanding the javafx.concurrent Framework

The JavaFX worker threading framework in the `javafx.concurrent` package combines the versatility and flexibility of the Java concurrency framework introduced in Java 5 with the convenience of the JavaFX properties and bindings framework to produce an easy-to-use tool-set that is aware of the JavaFX application threading rules and also very easy to use. It consists of one interface, `Worker`, and two abstract base classes, `Task<V>` and `Service<V>`, that implement the interface.

Understanding the Worker Interface

The `Worker` interface specifies a JavaFX bean with nine read-only properties, one method named `cancel()`, and a state model and state transition rules. A `Worker` represents a unit of work that runs in one or more background threads yet has some of its internal states safely observable to the JavaFX application thread. The nine read only properties are as follows.

- `title` is a `String` property that represents the title of the task.

- `message` is a `String` property that represents a more detailed message as the task progresses.

- `running` is a `boolean` property that is true only when the `Worker` is in the `Worker.State.SCHEDULED` or `Worker.State.RUNNING` state.

- `state` is an `Object` property that represents the `Worker.State` of the task.

- `totalWork` is a `double` property that represents the total amount of work of the task. Its value is `-1.0` when the total amount of work is not known.

- `workDone` is a `double` property that represents the amount of work that has been done so far in the task. Its value is `-1.0` or a number between 0 and `totalWork`.

- `progress` is a `double` property that represents the percentage of the total work that has been done so far in the task. Its value is `-1.0` or the ratio between `workDone` and `totalWork`.

- `value` is an `Object` property that represents the output of the task. Its value is non-null only when the task has finished successfully, that is, has reached the `Worker.State.SUCCEEDED` state.

- `exception` is an `Object` property that represents a `Throwable` that the implementation of the task has thrown to the JavaFX worker threading framework. Its value is non-null only when the task is in the `Worker.State.FAILED` state.

The preceding properties are meant to be accessed from the JavaFX application thread. It is safe to bind scene graph properties to them because the invalidation events and change events of these properties are fired on the JavaFX application thread. It is helpful to think of the properties through an imaginary task progress message box that you see in many GUI applications. They usually have a title, a progress bar indicating the percentage of the work that has been done, and a message telling the user how many items it has processed already and how many more to go. All of these properties are set by the JavaFX worker threading framework itself or by the actual implementation of the task.

The running, state, value, and exception properties are controlled by the framework and no user intervention is needed for them to be observed in the JavaFX application thread. When the framework wants to change these properties, it does the heavy lifting of making sure that the change is done on the JavaFX application thread. The title, message, totalWork, workDone and progress properties are updatable by the implementation code of the task by calling framework-provided protected methods that do the heavy lifting of making sure that the change is done on the JavaFX application thread.

Worker.State is a nested enum that defines the following six states of a Worker:

- READY (initial state)

- SCHEDULED (transitional state)

- RUNNING (transitional state)

- SUCCEEDED (terminal state)

- CANCELLED (terminal state)

- FAILED (terminal state)

The cancel() method will transition the Worker to the CANCELLED state if it is not already in the SUCCEEDED or FAILED state.

Now that you are familiar with the properties and states of the Worker interface, you can proceed to learn the two abstract classes in the JavaFX worker threading framework that implements this interface, Task<V> and Service<V>.

Understanding the Task<V> Abstract Class

The Task<V> abstract class is an implementation of the Worker interface that is meant to be used for one-shot tasks. Once its state progresses to SUCCEEDED or FAILED or CANCELLED, it will stay in the terminal state forever. The Task<V> abstract class extends the FutureTask<V> class, and as a consequence supports the Runnable, Future<V>, and RunnableFuture<V> interfaces as well as the Worker interface. The Future<V>, RunnableFuture<V>, and FutureTask<V> interfaces and class are part of the java.util.concurrent package. Because of this heritage, a Task<V> object can be used in various ways that befit its parent class. However, for typical JavaFX usage, it is enough to use just the methods in the Task<V> class itself, a list of which can be found in the Javadoc for the class. Here is a listing of these methods, excluding the read-only properties that were discussed in the preceding section:

- protected abstract V call() throws Exception

- public final boolean cancel()

- public boolean cancel(boolean myInterruptIfRunning)

- protected void updateTitle(String title)

- protected void updateMessage(String message)

- protected void updateProgress(long workDone, long totalWork)

Extensions of Task<V> must override the protected abstract call() method to perform the actual work. The implementation of the call() method may call the protected methods updateTitle(), updateMessage(), and updateProgress() to publish its internal state to the JavaFX application thread. The implementation has total control of what the title and message of the task should be. For the updateProgress() call, the workDone and totalWork must either both be -1, indicating indeterminate progress, or satisfy the relations workDone >= 0 and workDone <= totalWork, resulting in a progress value of between 0.0 and 1.0 (0% to 100%).

■ **Caution** The updateProgress() API will throw an exception if workDone > totalWork, or if one of them is <-1. However, it allows you to pass in (0, 0) resulting in a progress of NaN.

The two cancel() methods can be called from any thread, and will move the task to the CANCELLED state if it is not already in the SUCCEEDED or FAILED state. If either cancel() method is called before the task is run, it will move to the CANCELLED state and will never be run. The two cancel() methods differ only if the task is in the RUNNING state, and only in their treatment of the running thread. If cancel(true) is called, the thread will receive an interrupt. For this interrupt to have the desired effect of causing the task to finish processing quickly, the implementation of the call() method has to be coded in a way that will detect the interrupt and skip any further processing. The no-argument cancel() method simply forwards to cancel(true).

Listing 6-7 illustrates the creation of a Task, starting it, and observing the properties of the task from a simple GUI that displays all nine of the properties.

Listing 6-7. WorkerAndTaskExample.java

```
import javafx.application.Application;
import javafx.beans.binding.Bindings;
import javafx.beans.binding.StringBinding;
import javafx.beans.property.ReadOnlyObjectProperty;
import javafx.concurrent.Task;
import javafx.concurrent.Worker;
import javafx.event.ActionEvent;
import javafx.event.EventHandler;
import javafx.geometry.HPos;
import javafx.geometry.Insets;
import javafx.geometry.Pos;
import javafx.scene.Scene;
import javafx.scene.SceneBuilder;
import javafx.scene.control.Button;
import javafx.scene.control.Label;
import javafx.scene.control.ProgressBar;
import javafx.scene.control.ProgressBarBuilder;
import javafx.scene.layout.BorderPaneBuilder;
import javafx.scene.layout.ColumnConstraintsBuilder;
import javafx.scene.layout.GridPane;
import javafx.scene.layout.GridPaneBuilder;
import javafx.scene.layout.HBox;
import javafx.scene.layout.HBoxBuilder;
import javafx.stage.Stage;
```

```java
import java.util.concurrent.atomic.AtomicBoolean;

public class WorkerAndTaskExample extends Application {
    private Model model;
    private View view;

    public static void main(String[] args) {
        Application.launch(args);
    }

    public WorkerAndTaskExample() {
        model = new Model();
    }

    @Override
    public void start(Stage stage) throws Exception {
        view = new View(model);
        hookupEvents();
        stage.setTitle("Worker and Task Example");
        stage.setScene(view.scene);
        stage.show();
    }

    private void hookupEvents() {
        view.startButton.setOnAction(new EventHandler<ActionEvent>() {
            @Override
            public void handle(ActionEvent actionEvent) {
                new Thread((Runnable) model.worker).start();
            }
        });
        view.cancelButton.setOnAction(new EventHandler<ActionEvent>() {
            @Override
            public void handle(ActionEvent actionEvent) {
                model.worker.cancel();
            }
        });
        view.exceptionButton.setOnAction(new EventHandler<ActionEvent>() {
            @Override
            public void handle(ActionEvent actionEvent) {
                model.shouldThrow.getAndSet(true);
            }
        });
    }

    private static class Model {
        public Worker<String> worker;
        public AtomicBoolean shouldThrow = new AtomicBoolean(false);

        private Model() {
            worker = new Task<String>() {
                @Override
                protected String call() throws Exception {
```

```java
                        updateTitle("Example Task");
                        updateMessage("Starting...");
                        final int total = 250;
                        updateProgress(0, total);
                        for (int i = 1; i <= total; i++) {
                            try {
                                Thread.sleep(20);
                            } catch (InterruptedException e) {
                                return "Cancelled at " + System.currentTimeMillis();
                            }
                            if (shouldThrow.get()) {
                                throw new RuntimeException("Exception thrown at " + ↵
System.currentTimeMillis());
                            }
                            updateTitle("Example Task (" + i + ")");
                            updateMessage("Processed " + i + " of " + total + " items.");
                            updateProgress(i, total);
                        }
                        return "Completed at " + System.currentTimeMillis();
                    }
                };
            }
    }

    private static class View {
        public ProgressBar progressBar;

        public Label title;
        public Label message;
        public Label running;
        public Label state;
        public Label totalWork;
        public Label workDone;
        public Label progress;
        public Label value;
        public Label exception;

        public Button startButton;
        public Button cancelButton;
        public Button exceptionButton;

        public Scene scene;

        private View(final Model model) {
            progressBar = ProgressBarBuilder.create()
                .minWidth(250)
                .build();

            title = new Label();
            message = new Label();
            running = new Label();
            state = new Label();
```

271

```java
        totalWork = new Label();
        workDone = new Label();
        progress = new Label();
        value = new Label();
        exception = new Label();

        startButton = new Button("Start");
        cancelButton = new Button("Cancel");
        exceptionButton = new Button("Exception");

        final ReadOnlyObjectProperty<Worker.State> stateProperty =
            model.worker.stateProperty();

        progressBar.progressProperty().bind(model.worker.progressProperty());

        title.textProperty().bind(
            model.worker.titleProperty());
        message.textProperty().bind(
            model.worker.messageProperty());
        running.textProperty().bind(
            Bindings.format("%s", model.worker.runningProperty()));
        state.textProperty().bind(
            Bindings.format("%s", stateProperty));
        totalWork.textProperty().bind(
            model.worker.totalWorkProperty().asString());
        workDone.textProperty().bind(
            model.worker.workDoneProperty().asString());
        progress.textProperty().bind(
            Bindings.format("%5.2f%%", model.worker.progressProperty().multiply(100)));
        value.textProperty().bind(
            model.worker.valueProperty());
        exception.textProperty().bind(new StringBinding() {
            {
                super.bind(model.worker.exceptionProperty());
            }

            @Override
            protected String computeValue() {
                final Throwable exception = model.worker.getException();
                if (exception == null) return "";
                return exception.getMessage();
            }
        });

        startButton.disableProperty().bind(
            stateProperty.isNotEqualTo(Worker.State.READY));
        cancelButton.disableProperty().bind(
            stateProperty.isNotEqualTo(Worker.State.RUNNING));
        exceptionButton.disableProperty().bind(
            stateProperty.isNotEqualTo(Worker.State.RUNNING));
```

```
final HBox topPane = HBoxBuilder.create()
    .padding(new Insets(10, 10, 10, 10))
    .spacing(10)
    .alignment(Pos.CENTER)
    .children(progressBar)
    .build();

final GridPane centerPane = GridPaneBuilder.create()
    .hgap(10)
    .vgap(10)
    .padding(new Insets(10, 10, 10, 10))
    .columnConstraints(
        ColumnConstraintsBuilder.create()
            .halignment(HPos.RIGHT)
            .minWidth(65)
            .build(),
        ColumnConstraintsBuilder.create()
            .halignment(HPos.LEFT)
            .minWidth(200)
            .build()
    )
    .build();
centerPane.add(new Label("Title:"), 0, 0);
centerPane.add(new Label("Message:"), 0, 1);
centerPane.add(new Label("Running:"), 0, 2);
centerPane.add(new Label("State:"), 0, 3);
centerPane.add(new Label("Total Work:"), 0, 4);
centerPane.add(new Label("Work Done:"), 0, 5);
centerPane.add(new Label("Progress:"), 0, 6);
centerPane.add(new Label("Value:"), 0, 7);
centerPane.add(new Label("Exception:"), 0, 8);

centerPane.add(title, 1, 0);
centerPane.add(message, 1, 1);
centerPane.add(running, 1, 2);
centerPane.add(state, 1, 3);
centerPane.add(totalWork, 1, 4);
centerPane.add(workDone, 1, 5);
centerPane.add(progress, 1, 6);
centerPane.add(value, 1, 7);
centerPane.add(exception, 1, 8);

final HBox buttonPane = HBoxBuilder.create()
    .padding(new Insets(10, 10, 10, 10))
    .spacing(10)
    .alignment(Pos.CENTER)
    .children(startButton, cancelButton, exceptionButton)
    .build();
```

```
        scene = SceneBuilder.create()
            .root(BorderPaneBuilder.create()
                .top(topPane)
                .center(centerPane)
                .bottom(buttonPane)
                .build())
            .build();
    }
  }
}
```

The Model nested class for this program holds a worker field of type Worker, and a shouldThrow field of type AtomicBoolean. The worker field is initialized to an instance of an anonymous subclass of Task<String> that implements its call() method by simulating the processing of 250 items at a 20-milliseconds-per-item pace. It updates the properties of the task at the beginning of the call and in each iteration of the loop. If an interrupt to the thread is received while the method is in progress, it gets out of the loop and returns quickly. The shouldThrow field is controlled by the View to communicate to the task that it should throw an exception.

The View nested class of this program creates a simple UI that has a ProgressBar at the top, a set of Labels at the center that display the various properties of the worker, and three buttons at the bottom. The contents of the Labels are bound to the various properties of the worker. The disable properties of the buttons are also bound to the state property of the worker so that only the relevant buttons are enabled at any time. For example, the Start button is enabled when the program starts but becomes disabled after it is pressed and the task execution begins. Similarly, the Cancel and Exception buttons are enabled only if the task is running.

When we run the program in Listing 6-7, the GUI in Figure 6-5 is displayed on the screen.

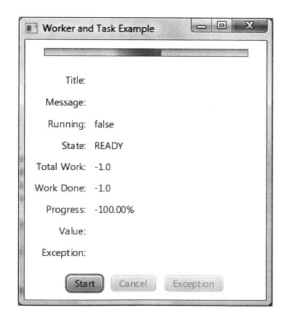

Figure 6-5. *The WorkerAndTaskExample program after starting up*

Notice that the progress bar is in an indeterminate state. The values of Title, Message, Value, and Exception are empty. The value of Running is false. The value of State is READY, and the values of Total Work, Work Done, and Progress are all -1. The Start button is enabled whereas the Cancel and Exception buttons are disabled.

After the Start button is clicked, the task starts to execute and the GUI automatically reflects the values of the properties as the task progresses. Figure 6-6 is a screenshot of the application at this stage. Notice that the progress bar is in a determinate state and reflects the progress of the task. The values of Title and Message reflects what is set to these properties in the implementation of the `call()` method in the task. The value of Running is true. The value of State is RUNNING, and the values of Total Work, Work Done, and Progress reflect the current state of the executing task: 156 of 250 items done. The Value and the Exception fields are empty because neither a value nor an Exception is available from the task. The Start button is disabled now. The Cancel and Exception buttons are enabled, indicating that we may attempt to cancel the task or force an exception to be thrown from the task at this moment.

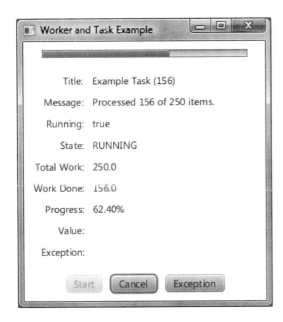

Figure 6-6. *The WorkerAndTaskExample program while a task is in progress*

When the task finishes normally, we arrive at the screenshot in Figure 6-7. Notice that the progress bar is at 100%. The Title, Message, Total Work, Work Done and Progress fields all have values that reflect the fact that the task has finished processing all 250 items. The Running is false. The State is SUCCEEDED. And the Value field now contains the return value from the `call()` method.

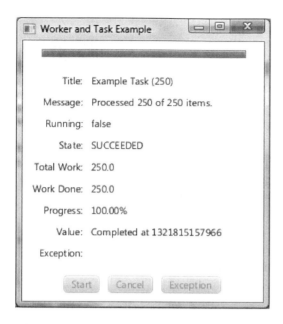

Figure 6-7. *The WorkerAndTaskExample program after the task succeeded*

If, instead of letting the task finish normally, we click the Cancel button, the task will finish immediately and the screenshot in Figure 6-8 results. Notice that the Status field has the value CANCELLED now. The Value field contains the string we returned from the `call()` method when the thread was interrupted. When we catch the `InterruptedException` in the `call()` method, we have two choices of exiting from the method body. In the program in Listing 6-7, we chose to return from the method. That's why we see a Value string. We could also have chosen to exit from the method body by throwing a `RuntimeException`. Had we made that choice, the screenshot would have an empty Value field but with an non-empty Exception field. The state of the worker would have been `CANCELLED` either way.

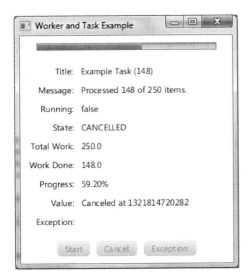

Figure 6-8. *The WorkerAndTaskExample program after the task has been cancelled*

The final screenshot, Figure 6-9, shows what happens when the Exception button is clicked when the task is executing. We simulate an exception in the task by setting an `AtomicBoolean` flag from the JavaFX application, which the task then picks up in the worker thread and throws the exception. Notice that the status field has the value FAILED now. The Value field is empty because the task did not complete successfully. The Exception field is filled with the message of the `RuntimeException` that we threw.

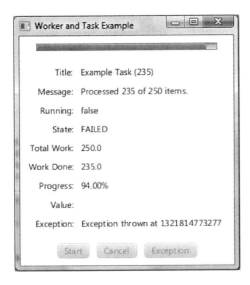

Figure 6-9. *The WorkerAndTaskExample program after the task threw an exception*

■ **Note** The Task<V> class defines one-shot tasks that are executed once and never run again. You have to restart the WorkerAndTaskExample program after each run of the task.

Understanding the Service<V> Abstract Class

The Service<V> abstract class is an implementation of the Worker interface that is meant to be reused. It extends Worker's state model by allowing its state to be reset to Worker.State.READY. Although the Service<V> abstract class does not extend any other class or implement any interface other than Worker, it does include a field of type Task<V> and another one of type java.util.concurrent.Executor. In addition to the nine read only properties of the Worker interface, Service<V> has an additional read write property of type Executor called executor. Here is a listing of the rest of the methods of Service<V>:

- protected abstract Task createTask()

- public void start()

- public void reset()

- public void restart()

- public final boolean cancel()

Extensions of Service<V> must override the protected abstract createTask() method to generate a freshly created Task. The start() method can only be called when the Service<V> object is in the Worker.State.READY state. It calls createTask() to obtain a freshly minted Task, and asks the executor property for an Executor. If the executor property is not set, it creates its own Executor. It binds the Service<V> object's nine Worker properties to that of the Task's. It then transitions the Task to the Worker.State.SCHEDULED state, and executes the Task on the Executor. The reset() method can only be called when the Service<V>'s state is not Worker.State.SCHEDULED or Worker.State.RUNNING. It simply unbinds the nine Service<V> properties from that of the underlying Task and resets their values to fresh start-up values: Worker.State.READY for the state property, and null or "" or false or –1 for the other properties. The restart() method simply cancels the currently executing Task, if any, and then does a reset() followed by a start(). The cancel() method will cancel the currently executing Task, if any; otherwise it will transition the Service<V> to the Worker.State.CANCELLED state.

Listing 6-8 illustrates using an instance of an anonymous subclass of the Service<V> abstract class to execute Tasks repeatedly in its own Executor.

Listing 6-8. ServiceExample.java

```
import javafx.application.Application;
import javafx.beans.binding.Bindings;
import javafx.beans.binding.IntegerBinding;
import javafx.beans.binding.StringBinding;
import javafx.beans.property.IntegerProperty;
import javafx.beans.property.ReadOnlyObjectProperty;
import javafx.beans.property.SimpleIntegerProperty;
import javafx.concurrent.Service;
import javafx.concurrent.Task;
import javafx.concurrent.Worker;
```

```java
import javafx.event.ActionEvent;
import javafx.event.EventHandler;
import javafx.geometry.HPos;
import javafx.geometry.Insets;
import javafx.geometry.Pos;
import javafx.scene.Scene;
import javafx.scene.SceneBuilder;
import javafx.scene.control.Button;
import javafx.scene.control.Label;
import javafx.scene.control.ProgressBar;
import javafx.scene.control.ProgressBarBuilder;
import javafx.scene.control.TextField;
import javafx.scene.control.TextFieldBuilder;
import javafx.scene.layout.BorderPaneBuilder;
import javafx.scene.layout.ColumnConstraintsBuilder;
import javafx.scene.layout.GridPane;
import javafx.scene.layout.GridPaneBuilder;
import javafx.scene.layout.HBox;
import javafx.scene.layout.HBoxBuilder;
import javafx.stage.Stage;

import java.util.concurrent.atomic.AtomicBoolean;

public class ServiceExample extends Application {
    private Model model;
    private View view;

    public static void main(String[] args) {
        Application.launch(args);
    }

    public ServiceExample() {
        model = new Model();
    }

    @Override
    public void start(Stage stage) throws Exception {
        view = new View(model);
        hookupEvents();
        stage.setTitle("Service Example");
        stage.setScene(view.scene);
        stage.show();
    }

    private void hookupEvents() {
        view.startButton.setOnAction(new EventHandler<ActionEvent>() {
            @Override
            public void handle(ActionEvent actionEvent) {
                model.shouldThrow.getAndSet(false);
                ((Service) model.worker).restart();
            }
        });
```

```java
        view.cancelButton.setOnAction(new EventHandler<ActionEvent>() {
            @Override
            public void handle(ActionEvent actionEvent) {
                model.worker.cancel();
            }
        });
        view.exceptionButton.setOnAction(new EventHandler<ActionEvent>() {
            @Override
            public void handle(ActionEvent actionEvent) {
                model.shouldThrow.getAndSet(true);
            }
        });
    }

    private static class Model {
        public Worker<String> worker;
        public AtomicBoolean shouldThrow = new AtomicBoolean(false);
        public IntegerProperty numberOfItems = new SimpleIntegerProperty(250);

        private Model() {
            worker = new Service<String>() {
                @Override
                protected Task createTask() {
                    return new Task<String>() {
                        @Override
                        protected String call() throws Exception {
                            updateTitle("Example Service");
                            updateMessage("Starting...");
                            final int total = numberOfItems.get();
                            updateProgress(0, total);
                            for (int i = 1; i <= total; i++) {
                                try {
                                    Thread.sleep(20);
                                } catch (InterruptedException e) {
                                    return "Canceled at " + System.currentTimeMillis();
                                }
                                if (shouldThrow.get()) {
                                    throw new RuntimeException("Exception thrown at " +↵
System.currentTimeMillis());
                                }
                                updateTitle("Example Service (" + i + ")");
                                updateMessage("Processed " + i + " of " + total + " items.");
                                updateProgress(i, total);
                            }
                            return "Completed at " + System.currentTimeMillis();
                        }
                    };
                }
            };
        }
    }
```

```
private static class View {
    public ProgressBar progressBar;

    public Label title;
    public Label message;
    public Label running;
    public Label state;
    public Label totalWork;
    public Label workDone;
    public Label progress;
    public Label value;
    public Label exception;

    public TextField numberOfItems;
    public Button startButton;
    public Button cancelButton;
    public Button exceptionButton;

    public Scene scene;

    private View(final Model model) {
        progressBar = ProgressBarBuilder.create()
            .minWidth(250)
            .build();

        title = new Label();
        message = new Label();
        running = new Label();
        state = new Label();
        totalWork = new Label();
        workDone = new Label();
        progress = new Label();
        value = new Label();
        exception = new Label();

        numberOfItems = TextFieldBuilder.create()
            .maxWidth(40)
            .build();
        startButton = new Button("Start");
        cancelButton = new Button("Cancel");
        exceptionButton = new Button("Exception");

        final ReadOnlyObjectProperty<Worker.State> stateProperty =
            model.worker.stateProperty();

        progressBar.progressProperty().bind(model.worker.progressProperty());

        title.textProperty().bind(
            model.worker.titleProperty());
        message.textProperty().bind(
            model.worker.messageProperty());
        running.textProperty().bind(
```

```java
        Bindings.format("%s", model.worker.runningProperty())));
state.textProperty().bind(
    Bindings.format("%s", stateProperty));
totalWork.textProperty().bind(
    model.worker.totalWorkProperty().asString());
workDone.textProperty().bind(
    model.worker.workDoneProperty().asString());
progress.textProperty().bind(
    Bindings.format("%5.2f%%", model.worker.progressProperty().multiply(100)));
value.textProperty().bind(
    model.worker.valueProperty());
exception.textProperty().bind(new StringBinding() {
    {
        super.bind(model.worker.exceptionProperty());
    }

    @Override
    protected String computeValue() {
        final Throwable exception = model.worker.getException();
        if (exception == null) return "";
        return exception.getMessage();
    }
});

model.numberOfItems.bind(new IntegerBinding() {
    {
        super.bind(numberOfItems.textProperty());
    }

    @Override
    protected int computeValue() {
        final String text = numberOfItems.getText();
        int n = 250;
        try {
            n = Integer.parseInt(text);
        } catch (NumberFormatException e) {
        }
        return n;
    }
});

startButton.disableProperty().bind(
    stateProperty.isEqualTo(Worker.State.RUNNING));
cancelButton.disableProperty().bind(
    stateProperty.isNotEqualTo(Worker.State.RUNNING));
exceptionButton.disableProperty().bind(
    stateProperty.isNotEqualTo(Worker.State.RUNNING));

final HBox topPane = HBoxBuilder.create()
    .padding(new Insets(10, 10, 10, 10))
    .spacing(10)
    .alignment(Pos.CENTER)
```

```
            .children(progressBar)
            .build();

        final GridPane centerPane = GridPaneBuilder.create()
            .hgap(10)
            .vgap(10)
            .padding(new Insets(10, 10, 10, 10))
            .columnConstraints(
                ColumnConstraintsBuilder.create()
                    .halignment(HPos.RIGHT)
                    .minWidth(65)
                    .build(),
                ColumnConstraintsBuilder.create()
                    .halignment(HPos.LEFT)
                    .minWidth(200)
                    .build()
            )
            .build();
        centerPane.add(new Label("Title:"), 0, 0);
        centerPane.add(new Label("Message:"), 0, 1);
        centerPane.add(new Label("Running:"), 0, 2);
        centerPane.add(new Label("State:"), 0, 3);
        centerPane.add(new Label("Total Work:"), 0, 4);
        centerPane.add(new Label("Work Done:"), 0, 5);
        centerPane.add(new Label("Progress:"), 0, 6);
        centerPane.add(new Label("Value:"), 0, 7);
        centerPane.add(new Label("Exception:"), 0, 8);

        centerPane.add(title, 1, 0);
        centerPane.add(message, 1, 1);
        centerPane.add(running, 1, 2);
        centerPane.add(state, 1, 3);
        centerPane.add(totalWork, 1, 4);
        centerPane.add(workDone, 1, 5);
        centerPane.add(progress, 1, 6);
        centerPane.add(value, 1, 7);
        centerPane.add(exception, 1, 8);

        final HBox buttonPane = HBoxBuilder.create()
            .padding(new Insets(10, 10, 10, 10))
            .spacing(10)
            .alignment(Pos.CENTER)
            .children(new Label("Process"), numberOfItems, new Label("items"),
                startButton, cancelButton, exceptionButton)
            .build();

        scene = SceneBuilder.create()
            .root(BorderPaneBuilder.create()
                .top(topPane)
                .center(centerPane)
```

```
                            .bottom(buttonPane)
                            .build())
                    .build();
            }
        }
    }
```

The preceding program is derived from the WorkerAndTaskExample class that we studied in the previous section. The Model nested class for this program holds a worker field of type Worker, a shouldThrow field of type AtomicBoolean, and a numberOfItems field of type IntegerProperty. The worker field is initialized to an instance of an anonymous subclass of Service<String> that implements its createTask() method to return a Task<String> whose call() method is implemented almost exactly like the Task<String> implementation in the last section, except that instead of always processing 250 items, it picks up the number of items to process from the numberOfItems property from the Model class.

The View nested class of this program creates a UI that is almost identical to that in the previous section but with some additional controls in the button panel. One of the controls added to the button panel is a TextField named numberOfItems. The model's numberOfItems IntegerProperty is bound to an IntegerBinding created with the textProperty() of the view's numberOfItems field. This effectively controls the number of items each newly created Task will process. The Start button is disabled only if the service is in the Worker.State.RUNNING state. Therefore you can click on the Start button after a task has finished.

The action handler of the Start button now resets the shouldThrow flag to false and calls restart() of the service.

The screenshots in Figures 6-10 to 6-14 are taken with the ServiceExample program under situations similar to those for the screenshots in Figures 6-5 to 6-9 for the WorkerAndTaskExample program.

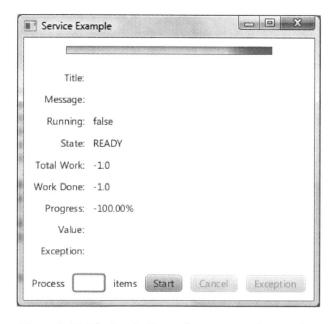

Figure 6-10. The ServiceExample program after starting up

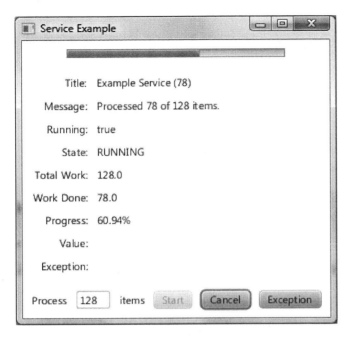

Figure 6-11. The ServiceExample program while a task is in progress

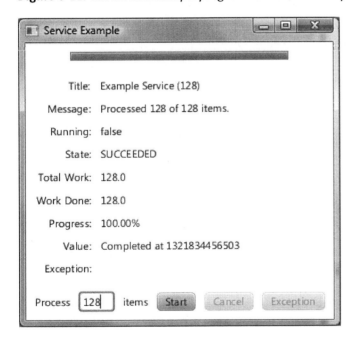

Figure 6-12. The ServiceExample program after the task succeeded

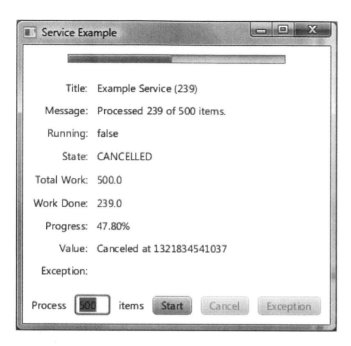

Figure 6-13. The ServiceExample program after the task has been cancelled

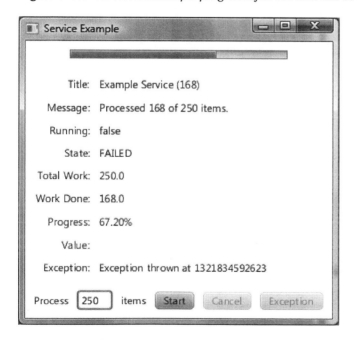

Figure 6-14. The ServiceExample program after the task threw an exception

As you can see from the preceding screenshots, the number that is entered into the text field does indeed influence the number of items processed in each run of the service, as is evidenced by the messages reflected in the UI in the screenshots.

■ **Caution**   Because the task that is started with the JavaFX worker threading framework executes in background threads, it is very important not to access any live scenes in the task code.

Embedding JavaFX Scenes in Swing and SWT Applications

Having examined the threading paradigm of the JavaFX runtime and ways to execute code from the JavaFX application thread, we now look at how to make use of JavaFX scenes in Swing and SWT applications. JavaFX 2.0 supports embedding a JavaFX scene into a Swing application through the `javafx.embed.swing` package of classes. This is a pretty small package that includes two public classes: `JFXPanel`, and `JFXPanelBuilder`. The `JFXPanel` class extends `javax.swing.JComponent`, and as such can be placed in a Swing program just as any other Swing component. `JFXPanel` can also host a JavaFX scene, and as such can add a JavaFX scene to a Swing program.

However, this Swing program with a JavaFX scene embedded in it needs both the Swing runtime to make its Swing portion function correctly, and the JavaFX runtime to make the JavaFX portion function correctly. Therefore it has both the Swing Event Dispatching Thread (EDT) and the JavaFX Application Thread. The `JFXPanel` class does a two-way translation of all the user events between Swing and JavaFX.

Just as JavaFX has the rule that requires all access to live scenes to be done in the JavaFX Application Thread, Swing has the rule that requires all access to Swing GUIs to be done in the EDT. You still need to jump the thread if you want to alter a Swing component from a JavaFX event handler or *vice versa*. The proper way to execute a piece of code on the JavaFX Application Thread, as we saw earlier, is to use `Platform.runLater()`. The proper way to execute a piece of code on the Swing EDT is to use `EventQueue.invokeLater()`.

In the rest of this section, we will convert a pure Swing program into a Swing and JavaFX hybrid program, and a pure SWT program into a SWT and JavaFX hybrid program. We start off with the Swing program in Listing 6-9, which is very similar to the `ResponsiveUIExample` program.

Listing 6-9. *NoJavaFXSceneInSwingExample.java*

```java
import javax.swing.*;
import java.awt.*;
import java.awt.event.ActionEvent;
import java.awt.event.ActionListener;

public class NoJavaFXSceneInSwingExample {
    public static void main(final String[] args) {
        EventQueue.invokeLater(new Runnable() {
            @Override
            public void run() {
                swingMain(args);
            }
        });
    }
```

```
    private static void swingMain(String[] args) {
        Model model = new Model();
        View view = new View(model);
        Controller controller = new Controller(model, view);
        controller.mainLoop();
    }

    private static class Model {
        public Color fillColor = Color.LIGHT_GRAY;
        public Color strokeColor = Color.DARK_GRAY;
    }

    private static class View {
        public JFrame frame;
        public JComponent canvas;
        public JButton changeFillButton;
        public JButton changeStrokeButton;

        private View(final Model model) {
            frame = new JFrame("No JavaFX in Swing Example");
            canvas = new JComponent() {
                @Override
                public void paint(Graphics g) {
                    g.setColor(model.strokeColor);
                    g.fillRect(0, 0, 200, 200);
                    g.setColor(model.fillColor);
                    g.fillRect(10, 10, 180, 180);
                }

                @Override
                public Dimension getPreferredSize() {
                    return new Dimension(200, 200);
                }
            };
            FlowLayout canvasPanelLayout = new FlowLayout(FlowLayout.CENTER, 10, 10);
            JPanel canvasPanel = new JPanel(canvasPanelLayout);
            canvasPanel.add(canvas);

            changeFillButton = new JButton("Change Fill");
            changeStrokeButton = new JButton("Change Stroke");
            FlowLayout buttonPanelLayout = new FlowLayout(FlowLayout.CENTER, 10, 10);
            JPanel buttonPanel = new JPanel(buttonPanelLayout);
            buttonPanel.add(changeFillButton);
            buttonPanel.add(changeStrokeButton);

            frame.add(canvasPanel, BorderLayout.CENTER);
            frame.add(buttonPanel, BorderLayout.SOUTH);
            frame.setDefaultCloseOperation(JFrame.EXIT_ON_CLOSE);
            frame.setLocationByPlatform(true);
            frame.pack();
        }
    }
```

```
private static class Controller {
    private View view;

    private Controller(final Model model, final View view) {
        this.view = view;
        this.view.changeFillButton.addActionListener(new ActionListener() {
            @Override
            public void actionPerformed(ActionEvent e) {
                if (model.fillColor.equals(Color.LIGHT_GRAY)) {
                    model.fillColor = Color.GRAY;
                } else {
                    model.fillColor = Color.LIGHT_GRAY;
                }
                view.canvas.repaint();
            }
        });
        this.view.changeStrokeButton.addActionListener(new ActionListener() {
            @Override
            public void actionPerformed(ActionEvent e) {
                if (model.strokeColor.equals(Color.DARK_GRAY)) {
                    model.strokeColor = Color.BLACK;
                } else {
                    model.strokeColor = Color.DARK_GRAY;
                }
                view.canvas.repaint();
            }
        });
    }

    public void mainLoop() {
        view.frame.setVisible(true);
    }
}
```

When the program in Listing 6-9 is run, the UI in Figure 6-15 is displayed. It is a JFrame holding three Swing components, a JComponent with overridden paint() and getPreferredSize() methods that makes it look like the rectangle we saw in the earlier program, and two JButtons that will change the fill and the stroke of the rectangle.

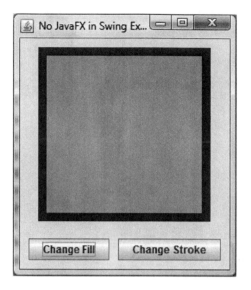

Figure 6-15. *The NoJavaFXSceneInSwingExample program*

Inasmuch as the custom-painted `JComponent` in `NoJavaFXSceneInSwingExample` is hard to maintain over the long run, we replace it with the JavaFX `Rectangle`. This is done by replacing the Swing code with the equivalent `JFXPanel` code. Here is the Swing code:

```
canvas = new JComponent() {
    @Override
    public void paint(Graphics g) {
        g.setColor(model.strokeColor);
        g.fillRect(0, 0, 200, 200);
        g.setColor(model.fillColor);
        g.fillRect(10, 10, 180, 180);
    }

    @Override
    public Dimension getPreferredSize() {
        return new Dimension(200, 200);
    }
};
```

And here is the `JFXPanel` code:

```
canvas = new JFXPanel();
canvas.setPreferredSize(new Dimension(210, 210));
Platform.runLater(new Runnable() {
    @Override
    public void run() {
        final Rectangle rectangle = RectangleBuilder.create()
            .width(200)
            .height(200)
            .strokeWidth(10)
```

```
                    .build();
            rectangle.fillProperty().bind(model.fillProperty());
            rectangle.strokeProperty().bind(model.strokeProperty());
            canvas.setScene(SceneBuilder.create()
                .root(VBoxBuilder.create()
                    .children(rectangle)
                    .build())
                .build());
        }
    });
```

The JFXPanel constructor bootstraps the JavaFX runtime system. We set the preferred size to the JFXPanel in order for it to be laid out correctly in Swing containers. We then constructed the scene graph on the JavaFX application thread and bound it to the model, which we changed into a JavaFX bean. Another set of changes that need to be made are in the ActionListeners of the two JButtons. Modifying the model triggers a change to the JavaFX rectangle, therefore the following code needs to be run on the JavaFX application thread:

```
this.view.changeFillButton.addActionListener(new ActionListener() {
    @Override
    public void actionPerformed(ActionEvent e) {
        Platform.runLater(new Runnable() {
            @Override
            public void run() {
                final javafx.scene.paint.Paint fillPaint = model.getFill();
                if (fillPaint.equals(Color.LIGHTGRAY)) {
                    model.setFill(Color.GRAY);
                } else {
                    model.setFill(Color.LIGHTGRAY);
                }
            }
        });
    }
});
```

The completed Swing JavaFX hybrid program is shown in Listing 6-10.

Listing 6-10. *JavaFXSceneInSwingExample.java*

```
import javafx.application.Platform;
import javafx.beans.property.ObjectProperty;
import javafx.beans.property.SimpleObjectProperty;
import javafx.embed.swing.JFXPanel;
import javafx.scene.SceneBuilder;
import javafx.scene.layout.VBoxBuilder;
import javafx.scene.paint.Color;
import javafx.scene.paint.Paint;
import javafx.scene.shape.Rectangle;
import javafx.scene.shape.RectangleBuilder;

import javax.swing.*;
import java.awt.*;
```

```java
import java.awt.event.ActionEvent;
import java.awt.event.ActionListener;

public class JavaFXSceneInSwingExample {
    public static void main(final String[] args) {
        EventQueue.invokeLater(new Runnable() {
            @Override
            public void run() {
                swingMain(args);
            }
        });
    }

    private static void swingMain(String[] args) {
        Model model = new Model();
        View view = new View(model);
        Controller controller = new Controller(model, view);
        controller.mainLoop();
    }

    private static class Model {
        private ObjectProperty<Color> fill = new SimpleObjectProperty<>(Color.LIGHTGRAY);
        private ObjectProperty<Color> stroke = new SimpleObjectProperty<>(Color.DARKGRAY);

        public final Color getFill() {
            return fill.get();
        }

        public final void setFill(Color value) {
            this.fill.set(value);
        }

        public final Color getStroke() {
            return stroke.get();
        }

        public final void setStroke(Color value) {
            this.stroke.set(value);
        }

        public final ObjectProperty<Color> fillProperty() {
            return fill;
        }

        public final ObjectProperty<Color> strokeProperty() {
            return stroke;
        }

    }
```

```java
private static class View {
    public JFrame frame;
    public JFXPanel canvas;
    public JButton changeFillButton;
    public JButton changeStrokeButton;

    private View(final Model model) {
        frame = new JFrame("JavaFX in Swing Example");
        canvas = new JFXPanel();
        canvas.setPreferredSize(new Dimension(210, 210));
        Platform.runLater(new Runnable() {
            @Override
            public void run() {
                final Rectangle rectangle = RectangleBuilder.create()
                    .width(200)
                    .height(200)
                    .strokeWidth(10)
                    .build();
                rectangle.fillProperty().bind(model.fillProperty());
                rectangle.strokeProperty().bind(model.strokeProperty());
                canvas.setScene(SceneBuilder.create()
                    .root(VBoxBuilder.create()
                        .children(rectangle)
                        .build())
                    .build());
            }
        });
        FlowLayout canvasPanelLayout = new FlowLayout(FlowLayout.CENTER, 10, 10);
        JPanel canvasPanel = new JPanel(canvasPanelLayout);
        canvasPanel.add(canvas);

        changeFillButton = new JButton("Change Fill");
        changeStrokeButton = new JButton("Change Stroke");
        FlowLayout buttonPanelLayout = new FlowLayout(FlowLayout.CENTER, 10, 10);
        JPanel buttonPanel = new JPanel(buttonPanelLayout);
        buttonPanel.add(changeFillButton);
        buttonPanel.add(changeStrokeButton);

        frame.add(canvasPanel, BorderLayout.CENTER);
        frame.add(buttonPanel, BorderLayout.SOUTH);
        frame.setDefaultCloseOperation(JFrame.EXIT_ON_CLOSE);
        frame.setLocationByPlatform(true);
        frame.pack();
    }
}

private static class Controller {
    private View view;

    private Controller(final Model model, final View view) {
        this.view = view;
        this.view.changeFillButton.addActionListener(new ActionListener() {
```

```
                    @Override
                    public void actionPerformed(ActionEvent e) {
                        Platform.runLater(new Runnable() {
                            @Override
                            public void run() {
                                final Paint fillPaint = model.getFill();
                                if (fillPaint.equals(Color.LIGHTGRAY)) {
                                    model.setFill(Color.GRAY);
                                } else {
                                    model.setFill(Color.LIGHTGRAY);
                                }
                            }
                        });
                    }
                });
                this.view.changeStrokeButton.addActionListener(new ActionListener() {
                    @Override
                    public void actionPerformed(ActionEvent e) {
                        Platform.runLater(new Runnable() {
                            @Override
                            public void run() {
                                final Paint strokePaint = model.getStroke();
                                if (strokePaint.equals(Color.DARKGRAY)) {
                                    model.setStroke(Color.BLACK);
                                } else {
                                    model.setStroke(Color.DARKGRAY);
                                }
                            }
                        });
                    }
                });
            }

        public void mainLoop() {
            view.frame.setVisible(true);
        }
    }
}
```

When the program in Listing 6-10 is run, the GUI in Figure 9-16 is displayed. You can't tell from the screenshot, but the rectangle in the center of the JFrame is a JavaFX rectangle.

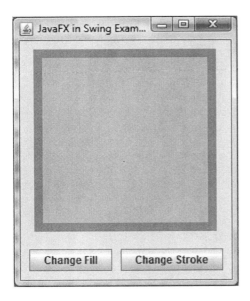

Figure 6-16. *The JavaFXSceneInSwingExample program*

JavaFX 2.0.2 introduced the capability of embedding JavaFX scene into an SWT application through the `javafx.embed.swt` package of classes. It contains one public class `FXCanvas`. The `FXCanvas` class extends `org.eclipse.swt.widgets.Canvas`, and can be placed in an SWT program just like any other SWT widget. `FXCanvas` can also host a JavaFX scene, and can add a JavaFX scene to an SWT program.

Since both SWT and JavaFX uses the native platform's UI thread as their own event dispatching thread, the SWT UI thread (where a Display object is instantiated and where the main loop is started and where all other UI widgets must be created and accessed) and the JavaFX application thread are one and the same. Therefore there is no need to use `Platform.runLater()` or its SWT equivalent `display.asyncExec()` in your SWT and JavaFX event handlers.

The SWT program in Listing 6-11 is an SWT port of the Swing program in Listing 6-9.

■ **Note** You need to add the jar file that contains the SWT classes to your classpath in order to compile the programs in Listings 6-11 and 6-12. On my development machine the SWT jar is located in %ECLIPSE_HOME%\plugins\org.eclipse.swt.win32.win32.x86_64_3.7.1.v3738a.jar, where %ECLIPSE_HOME% is my Eclipse (Indigo) installation directory.

Listing 6-11. *NoJavaFXSceneInSWTExample.java*

```java
import org.eclipse.swt.SWT;
import org.eclipse.swt.events.MouseEvent;
import org.eclipse.swt.events.MouseMoveListener;
import org.eclipse.swt.events.MouseTrackAdapter;
import org.eclipse.swt.events.PaintEvent;
```

```java
import org.eclipse.swt.events.PaintListener;
import org.eclipse.swt.events.SelectionAdapter;
import org.eclipse.swt.events.SelectionEvent;
import org.eclipse.swt.graphics.Color;
import org.eclipse.swt.graphics.GC;
import org.eclipse.swt.graphics.RGB;
import org.eclipse.swt.layout.RowData;
import org.eclipse.swt.layout.RowLayout;
import org.eclipse.swt.widgets.Button;
import org.eclipse.swt.widgets.Canvas;
import org.eclipse.swt.widgets.Composite;
import org.eclipse.swt.widgets.Display;
import org.eclipse.swt.widgets.Label;
import org.eclipse.swt.widgets.Shell;

public class NoJavaFXSceneInSWTExample {
    public static void main(final String[] args) {
        Model model = new Model();
        View view = new View(model);
        Controller controller = new Controller(model, view);
        controller.mainLoop();
    }

    private static class Model {
        public static final RGB LIGHT_GRAY = new RGB(0xd3, 0xd3, 0xd3);
        public static final RGB GRAY = new RGB(0x80, 0x80, 0x80);
        public static final RGB DARK_GRAY = new RGB(0xa9, 0xa9, 0xa9);
        public static final RGB BLACK = new RGB(0x0, 0x0, 0x0);
        public RGB fillColor = LIGHT_GRAY;
        public RGB strokeColor = DARK_GRAY;
    }

    private static class View {
        public Display display;
        public Shell frame;
        public Canvas canvas;
        public Button changeFillButton;
        public Button changeStrokeButton;
        public Label mouseLocation;
        public boolean mouseInCanvas;

        private View(final Model model) {
            this.display = new Display();
            frame = new Shell(display);
            frame.setText("No JavaFX in SWT Example");
            RowLayout frameLayout = new RowLayout(SWT.VERTICAL);
            frameLayout.spacing = 10;
            frameLayout.center = true;
            frame.setLayout(frameLayout);
```

```
        Composite canvasPanel = new Composite(frame, SWT.NONE);
        RowLayout canvasPanelLayout = new RowLayout(SWT.VERTICAL);
        canvasPanelLayout.spacing = 10;
        canvasPanel.setLayout(canvasPanelLayout);

        canvas = new Canvas(canvasPanel, SWT.NONE);
        canvas.setLayoutData(new RowData(200, 200));
        canvas.addPaintListener(new PaintListener() {
            @Override
            public void paintControl(PaintEvent paintEvent) {
                final GC gc = paintEvent.gc;
                final Color strokeColor = new Color(display, model.strokeColor);
                gc.setBackground(strokeColor);
                gc.fillRectangle(0, 0, 200, 200);
                final Color fillColor = new Color(display, model.fillColor);
                gc.setBackground(fillColor);
                gc.fillRectangle(10, 10, 180, 180);
                strokeColor.dispose();
                fillColor.dispose();
            }
        });

        Composite buttonPanel = new Composite(frame, SWT.NONE);
        RowLayout buttonPanelLayout = new RowLayout(SWT.HORIZONTAL);
        buttonPanelLayout.spacing = 10;
        buttonPanelLayout.center = true;
        buttonPanel.setLayout(buttonPanelLayout);

        changeFillButton = new Button(buttonPanel, SWT.NONE);
        changeFillButton.setText("Change Fill");
        changeStrokeButton = new Button(buttonPanel, SWT.NONE);
        changeStrokeButton.setText("Change Stroke");
        mouseLocation = new Label(buttonPanel, SWT.NONE);
        mouseLocation.setLayoutData(new RowData(50, 15));

        frame.pack();
    }
}

private static class Controller {
    private View view;

    private Controller(final Model model, final View view) {
        this.view = view;
        view.changeFillButton.addSelectionListener(new SelectionAdapter() {
            @Override
            public void widgetSelected(SelectionEvent e) {
                if (model.fillColor.equals(model.LIGHT_GRAY)) {
                    model.fillColor = model.GRAY;
```

```java
                } else {
                    model.fillColor = model.LIGHT_GRAY;
                }
                view.canvas.redraw();
            }
        });
        view.changeStrokeButton.addSelectionListener(new SelectionAdapter() {
            @Override
            public void widgetSelected(SelectionEvent e) {
                if (model.strokeColor.equals(model.DARK_GRAY)) {
                    model.strokeColor = model.BLACK;
                } else {
                    model.strokeColor = model.DARK_GRAY;
                }
                view.canvas.redraw();
            }
        });
        view.canvas.addMouseMoveListener(new MouseMoveListener() {
            @Override
            public void mouseMove(MouseEvent mouseEvent) {
                if (view.mouseInCanvas) {
                    view.mouseLocation.setText("(" + mouseEvent.x + ", " + mouseEvent.y +
")");
                }
            }
        });
        this.view.canvas.addMouseTrackListener(new MouseTrackAdapter() {
            @Override
            public void mouseEnter(MouseEvent e) {
                view.mouseInCanvas = true;
            }

            @Override
            public void mouseExit(MouseEvent e) {
                view.mouseInCanvas = false;
                view.mouseLocation.setText("");
            }
        });

    }

    public void mainLoop() {
        view.frame.open();
        while (!view.frame.isDisposed()) {
            if (!view.display.readAndDispatch()) {
                view.display.sleep();
            }
        }
        view.display.dispose();
    }
}
```

When the program in Listing 6-11 is run, the UI in Figure 6-17 is displayed. It is a SWT `Shell` holding four SWT widgets, a `Canvas` with a `PaintListener` that makes it look like the rectangle we saw earlier, two `Buttons` that will change the fill and the stroke of the rectangle, and a `Label` widget that will show the location of the mouse pointer when the mouse is inside the rectangle.

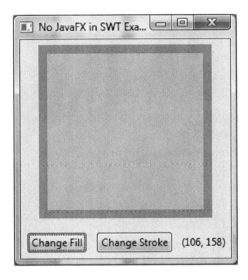

Figure 6-17. *The NoJavaFXSceneInSWTExample program*

As we did with the Swing example, we replace the custom painted Canvas widget in the program NoJavaFXSceneInSWTExample with a JavaFX Rectangle. This is done by replacing the SWT code with the equivalent FXCanvas code. Here is the SWT code:

```
canvas = new Canvas(canvasPanel, SWT.NONE);
canvas.setLayoutData(new RowData(200, 200));
canvas.addPaintListener(new PaintListener() {
    @Override
    public void paintControl(PaintEvent paintEvent) {
        final GC gc = paintEvent.gc;
        final Color strokeColor = new Color(display, model.strokeColor);
        gc.setBackground(strokeColor);
        gc.fillRectangle(0, 0, 200, 200);
        final Color fillColor = new Color(display, model.fillColor);
        gc.setBackground(fillColor);
        gc.fillRectangle(10, 10, 180, 180);
        strokeColor.dispose();
        fillColor.dispose();
    }
});
```

And here is the FXCanvas code:

```
canvas = new FXCanvas(canvasPanel, SWT.NONE);
canvas.setScene(SceneBuilder.create()
    .width(210)
    .height(210)
    .root(VBoxBuilder.create()
        .children(rectangle = RectangleBuilder.create()
            .width(200)
            .height(200)
            .strokeWidth(10)
            .build())
        .build())
    .build());
rectangle.fillProperty().bind(model.fillProperty());
rectangle.strokeProperty().bind(model.strokeProperty());
```

We also changed the model into a JavaFX bean. The event listeners are changed in a natural way. The complete SWT JavaFX hybrid program is shown in Listing 6-12.

Listing 6-12. *JavaFXSceneInSWTExample.java*

```
import javafx.beans.property.ObjectProperty;
import javafx.beans.property.SimpleObjectProperty;
import javafx.embed.swt.FXCanvas;
import javafx.event.EventHandler;
import javafx.scene.SceneBuilder;
import javafx.scene.input.MouseEvent;
import javafx.scene.layout.VBoxBuilder;
import javafx.scene.paint.Color;
import javafx.scene.paint.Paint;
import javafx.scene.shape.Rectangle;
import javafx.scene.shape.RectangleBuilder;
import org.eclipse.swt.SWT;
import org.eclipse.swt.events.SelectionAdapter;
import org.eclipse.swt.events.SelectionEvent;
import org.eclipse.swt.layout.RowData;
import org.eclipse.swt.layout.RowLayout;
import org.eclipse.swt.widgets.Button;
import org.eclipse.swt.widgets.Composite;
import org.eclipse.swt.widgets.Display;
import org.eclipse.swt.widgets.Label;
import org.eclipse.swt.widgets.Shell;

public class JavaFXSceneInSWTExample {
    public static void main(final String[] args) {
        Model model = new Model();
        View view = new View(model);
        Controller controller = new Controller(model, view);
        controller.mainLoop();
    }
```

```java
private static class Model {
    private ObjectProperty<Color> fill = new SimpleObjectProperty<>(Color.LIGHTGRAY);
    private ObjectProperty<Color> stroke = new SimpleObjectProperty<>(Color.DARKGRAY);

    public Color getFill() {
        return fill.get();
    }

    public void setFill(Color value) {
        this.fill.set(value);
    }

    public Color getStroke() {
        return stroke.get();
    }

    public void setStroke(Color value) {
        this.stroke.set(value);
    }

    public ObjectProperty<Color> fillProperty() {
        return fill;
    }

    public ObjectProperty<Color> strokeProperty() {
        return stroke;
    }
}

private static class View {
    public Display display;
    public Shell frame;
    public FXCanvas canvas;
    public Button changeFillButton;
    public Button changeStrokeButton;
    public Label mouseLocation;
    public boolean mouseInCanvas;
    public Rectangle rectangle;

    private View(final Model model) {
        this.display = new Display();
        frame = new Shell(display);
        frame.setText("JavaFX in SWT Example");
        RowLayout frameLayout = new RowLayout(SWT.VERTICAL);
        frameLayout.spacing = 10;
        frameLayout.center = true;
        frame.setLayout(frameLayout);

        Composite canvasPanel = new Composite(frame, SWT.NONE);
        RowLayout canvasPanelLayout = new RowLayout(SWT.VERTICAL);
        canvasPanelLayout.spacing = 10;
        canvasPanel.setLayout(canvasPanelLayout);
```

```java
        canvas = new FXCanvas(canvasPanel, SWT.NONE);
        canvas.setScene(SceneBuilder.create()
            .width(210)
            .height(210)
            .root(VBoxBuilder.create()
                .children(rectangle = RectangleBuilder.create()
                    .width(200)
                    .height(200)
                    .strokeWidth(10)
                    .build())
                .build())
            .build());
        rectangle.fillProperty().bind(model.fillProperty());
        rectangle.strokeProperty().bind(model.strokeProperty());

        Composite buttonPanel = new Composite(frame, SWT.NONE);
        RowLayout buttonPanelLayout = new RowLayout(SWT.HORIZONTAL);
        buttonPanelLayout.spacing = 10;
        buttonPanelLayout.center = true;
        buttonPanel.setLayout(buttonPanelLayout);

        changeFillButton = new Button(buttonPanel, SWT.NONE);
        changeFillButton.setText("Change Fill");
        changeStrokeButton = new Button(buttonPanel, SWT.NONE);
        changeStrokeButton.setText("Change Stroke");
        mouseLocation = new Label(buttonPanel, SWT.NONE);
        mouseLocation.setLayoutData(new RowData(50, 15));

        frame.pack();
    }
}

private static class Controller {
    private View view;

    private Controller(final Model model, final View view) {
        this.view = view;
        view.changeFillButton.addSelectionListener(new SelectionAdapter() {
            @Override
            public void widgetSelected(SelectionEvent e) {
                final Paint fillPaint = model.getFill();
                if (fillPaint.equals(Color.LIGHTGRAY)) {
                    model.setFill(Color.GRAY);
                } else {
                    model.setFill(Color.LIGHTGRAY);
                }
            }
        });
        view.changeStrokeButton.addSelectionListener(new SelectionAdapter() {
            @Override
            public void widgetSelected(SelectionEvent e) {
                final Paint strokePaint = model.getStroke();
```

```java
                    if (strokePaint.equals(Color.DARKGRAY)) {
                        model.setStroke(Color.BLACK);
                    } else {
                        model.setStroke(Color.DARKGRAY);
                    }
                }
            });
            view.rectangle.setOnMouseEntered(new EventHandler<MouseEvent>() {
                @Override
                public void handle(MouseEvent mouseEvent) {
                    view.mouseInCanvas = true;
                }
            });
            view.rectangle.setOnMouseExited(new EventHandler<MouseEvent>() {
                @Override
                public void handle(final MouseEvent mouseEvent) {
                    view.mouseInCanvas = false;
                    view.mouseLocation.setText("");
                }
            });
            view.rectangle.setOnMouseMoved(new EventHandler<MouseEvent>() {
                @Override
                public void handle(final MouseEvent mouseEvent) {
                    if (view.mouseInCanvas) {
                        view.mouseLocation.setText("(" + (int) mouseEvent.getSceneX() + ", " +
(int) mouseEvent.getSceneY() + ")");
                    }
                }
            });
        }

        public void mainLoop() {
            view.frame.open();
            while (!view.frame.isDisposed()) {
                if (!view.display.readAndDispatch()) view.display.sleep();
            }
            view.display.dispose();
        }
    }
}
```

When the program in Listing 6-12 is run, the GUI in Figure 6-18 is displayed. The rectangle in the center of the SWT Shell is a JavaFX rectangle.

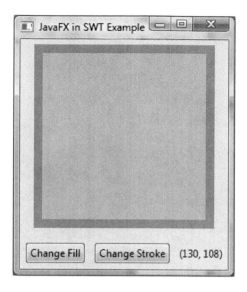

Figure 6-18. *The JavaFXSceneInSWTExample program*

Summary

In this chapter, we looked at JavaFX observable collections, the JavaFX worker threading framework, and embedding JavaFX scene in Swing and SWT applications to help you understand the following principles and techniques.

- JavaFX 2.0 supports two observable collection classes: `ObservableList` and `ObservableMap`.

- `ObservableList` fires `Change` events through `ListChangeListener`. `ListChangeListener.Change` may contain one or more discrete changes.

- `ObservableMap` fires `Change` events through `MapChangeListener`. `MapChangeListener.Change` represents the change of only one key.

- The `FXCollections` class contains factory methods to create observable collections, and utility methods to work on them.

- The main event processing thread in JavaFX applications is the JavaFX application thread. All access to live scenes must be done through the JavaFX application thread.

- Other important threads such as the prism rendering thread and the media event thread collaborate with the JavaFX application thread to make graphics rendering and media playback possible.

- Long-running computations on the JavaFX application thread make JavaFX GUIs unresponsive. They should be farmed out to background, or worker, threads.

- The `Worker` interface defines nine properties that can be observed on the JavaFX application thread. It also defines a `cancel()` method.

- `Task<V>` defines a one-time task for offloading work to background, or worker, threads and communicates the results or exceptions to the JavaFX application thread.

- `Service<V>` defines a reusable mechanism for creating and running background tasks.

- The `JFXPanel` class is a `JComponent` that can put a JavaFX scene into a Swing application.

- In a Swing JavaFX hybrid program, use `Platform.runLater()` in Swing event listeners to access the JavaFX scene, and use `EventQueue.invokeLater()`, or `SwingUtilities.invokeLater()` in JavaFX event handlers to access Swing widgets.

- The `FXCanvas` class is an SWT widget that can put a JavaFX scene into a SWT application.

- In an SWT JavaFX hybrid program, the SWT UI thread and the JavaFX application thread is one and the same.

Resources

Here are some useful resources for understanding this chapter's material:

- *The JavaFX architecture page on the JavaFX tutorials site:* `http://docs.oracle.com/javafx/2.0/architecture/jfxpub-architecture.htm`

- *The original JavaFX worker threading framework write up on FX Experience:* `http://fxexperience.com/2011/07/worker-threading-in-javafx-2-0/`

- *The original JavaFX and SWT interoperability write up on FX Experience:* `http://fxexperience.com/2011/12/swt-interop/`

- *The JavaOne 2011 site has links to all presentation slides, including many about JavaFX:* `http://www.oracle.com/javaone/index.html`

CHAPTER 7

Creating Charts in JavaFX

Any sufficiently advanced technology is indistinguishable from magic.

—Arthur C. Clarke

Reporting is an important aspect in many business applications. The JavaFX Platform contains an API for creating charts. Because a chart is basically a node, integrating charts with other parts of a JavaFX application is straightforward. As a consequence, reporting is an integral part of the typical JavaFX Business Application.

Designing an API is often a compromise between a number of requirements. Two of the most common requirements are "make it easy" and "make it easy to extend." The JavaFX Chart API fulfills both of these. The Chart API contains a number of methods that allow developers to change the look and feel as well as the data of the chart, making it a flexible API that can be easily extended. The default values for the settings are very reasonable though, and make it easy to integrate a chart with a custom application, with only a few lines of code.

The JavaFX Chart API in JavaFX 2.0 has six concrete implementations that are ready to be used by developers, and this number is expected to grow in subsequent releases. Also, developers can add their own implementations by extending one of the abstract classes.

Structure of the JavaFX Chart API

Different types of charts exist, and there are a number of ways to categorize them. The JavaFX Chart API distinguishes between two-axis charts and charts without an axis. The JavaFX 2.0 release contains one implementation of a no-axis chart, which is the PieChart. There are a number of two-axis charts, which all extend the abstract class XYChart, as shown in Figure 7-1.

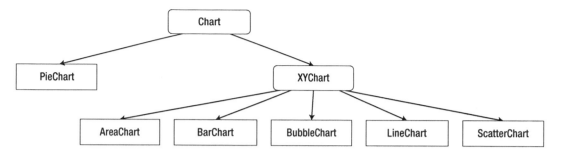

Figure 7-1. *Overview of the charts in the JavaFX Chart API*

The abstract Chart class defines the setup for all charts. Basically, a chart consists of three parts: the title, legend, and content. The content is specific for each implementation of the chart, but the legend and the title concepts are similar across the implementations. Therefore, the Chart class has a number of properties with corresponding getter and setter methods that allow the manipulation of those concepts. The javadoc of the Chart class mentions the following properties.

```
BooleanProperty animated
ObjectProperty<Node> legend
BooleanProperty legendVisible
StringProperty title
ObjectProperty<Side> titleSide
```

We use some of these properties in the upcoming examples, but we also show that even without setting values for these properties, the Chart API allows you to create nice charts.

Inasmuch as Chart extends Region, Parent, and Node, all of the properties and methods available on these classes can be used on a Chart as well. One of the benefits is that the same CSS styling techniques that are used to add style information to JavaFX Nodes also apply to JavaFX Charts.

The *JavaFX CSS Reference Guide*, available at `http://docs.oracle.com/javafx/2.0/api/javafx/scene/doc-files/cssref.html`, contains an overview of CSS properties that can be altered by designers and developers. By default, the caspian stylesheet that comes with the JavaFX 2.0 Runtime is used to skin JavaFX Charts. For more information on using CSS styles in JavaFX Chart, we refer to the Oracle Chart tutorial at `http://docs.oracle.com/javafx/2.0/charts/css-styles.htm`.

Using the JavaFX PieChart

A PieChart renders information in a typical pie structure, where the sizes of the slices are proportional to the values of the data. Before diving into the details, we show a small application that renders a PieChart.

The Simple Example

Our example shows the "market share" of a number of programming languages, based on the TIOBE index in December 2011. The TIOBE Programming Community Index is available at `www.tiobe.com/index.php/content/paperinfo/tpci/index.html`, and it provides an indication of the popularity of programming languages, based on search engine traffic. A screenshot of the ranking in December 2011 is shown in Figure 7-2.

Position Dec 2011	Position Dec 2010	Delta in Position	Programming Language	Ratings Dec 2011	Delta Dec 2010	Status
1	1	=	Java	17.561%	-0.44%	A
2	2	=	C	17.057%	+0.98%	A
3	3	=	C++	8.252%	-0.76%	A
4	5	↑	C#	8.205%	+1.52%	A
5	8	↑↑↑	Objective-C	6.805%	+3.56%	A
6	4	↓↓	PHP	6.001%	-1.51%	A
7	7	=	(Visual) Basic	4.757%	-0.36%	A
8	6	↓↓	Python	3.492%	-2.99%	A
9	9	=	Perl	2.472%	+0.14%	A
10	12	↑↑	JavaScript	2.199%	+0.69%	A
11	11	=	Ruby	1.494%	-0.29%	A
12	10	↓↓	Delphi/Object Pascal	1.245%	-0.93%	A
13	13	=	Lisp	1.175%	+0.11%	A
14	23	↑↑↑↑↑↑↑↑↑	PL/SQL	0.803%	+0.24%	A
15	14	↓	Transact-SQL	0.746%	-0.03%	A
16	16	=	Pascal	0.734%	-0.03%	A
17	18	↑	Ada	0.632%	-0.02%	B
18	35	↑↑↑↑↑↑↑↑↑↑	Logo	0.619%	+0.26%	B
19	17	↓↓	Assembly	0.563%	-0.10%	B
20	25	↑↑↑↑↑	ABAP	0.560%	+0.01%	B

Figure 7-2. Screenshot of the TIOBE index in December 2011, taken from www.tiobe.com/index.php/content/paperinfo/tpci/index.html

---

▨ **Note** The algorithm used by TIOBE is described at www.tiobe.com/index.php/content/paperinfo/tpci/tpci_definition.htm. The scientific value of the numbers is out of scope for our examples.

Listing 7-1 contains the code for the example.

Listing 7-1. *Rendering the TIOBE Index in a PieChart*

```
import javafx.application.Application;
import javafx.collections.FXCollections;
import javafx.collections.ObservableList;
import javafx.scene.Scene;
import javafx.scene.chart.PieChart;
import javafx.scene.chart.PieChart.Data;
import javafx.scene.layout.StackPane;
import javafx.stage.Stage;

public class ChartApp1 extends Application {

    public static void main(String[] args) {
        launch(args);
    }

    @Override
    public void start(Stage primaryStage) {
        PieChart pieChart = new PieChart();
        pieChart.setData(getChartData());

        primaryStage.setTitle("PieChart");
        StackPane root = new StackPane();
        root.getChildren().add(pieChart);
        primaryStage.setScene(new Scene(root, 400, 250));
        primaryStage.show();
    }

    private ObservableList<PieChart.Data> getChartData() {
        ObservableList<PieChart.Data> answer = FXCollections.observableArrayList();
        answer.addAll(new PieChart.Data("java", 17.56),
                new PieChart.Data("C", 17.06),
                new PieChart.Data("C++", 8.25),
                new PieChart.Data("C#", 8.20),
                new PieChart.Data("ObjectiveC", 6.8),
                new PieChart.Data("PHP", 6.0),
                new PieChart.Data("(Visual)Basic", 4.76),
                new PieChart.Data("Other", 31.37));
        return answer;
    }
}
```

The result of running this example is shown in Figure 7-3.

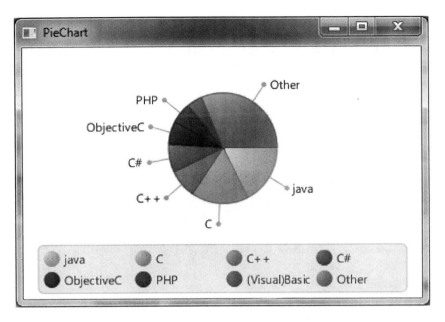

Figure 7-3. *Rendering the TIOBE index in a PieChart*

With only a limited amount of code, we can render data in a PieChart. Before we make modifications to this example, we explain the different parts.

The code required for setting up the Application, the Stage, and the Scene is covered in Chapter 1. A PieChart extends a Node, so we can easily add it to the scene graph. The first two lines of code in the start method create the PieChart, and add the required data to it:

```
PieChart pieChart = new PieChart();
pieChart.setData(getChartData());
```

The data, which are of type ObservableList<PieChart.Data> are obtained from the getChartData() method and for our example, it contains static data. As the return type of the getChartData() method specifies, the returned data are an ObservableList of PieChart.Data.

An instance of PieChart.Data, which is a nested class of PieChart, contains the information required to draw one slice of the pie. PieChart.Data has a constructor that takes the name of the slice and its value:

```
PieChat.Data(String name, double value)
```

We use this constructor to create data elements containing the name of a programming language and its score in the TIOBE index.

```
new PieChart.Data("java", 17.56)
```

And we add those elements to the ObservableList<PieChart.Data> we need to return.

Some Modifications

Although the result of the simple example already looks good, we can tweak both the code and the rendering. First of all, the example uses two lines of code for creating the PieChart and populating it with data:

```
PieChart pieChart = new PieChart();
pieChart.setData(getChartData());
```

Because PieChart has a single argument constructor as well, the preceding code snippets can be replaced as follows.

```
PieChart pieChart = new PieChart(getChartData());
```

We can also use the builder pattern, using the PieChartBuilder class:

```
PieChart pieChart = PieChartBuilder.create().data(getChartData()).build();
```

These modifications do not alter the output, and it is up to the developer to choose whether to use the builder pattern or to manipulate the properties using the JavaBeans pattern.

Apart from the properties defined on the abstract Chart class, a PieChart has the following properties.

- BooleanProperty clockwise

- ObjectProperty<ObservableList<PieChart.Data>> data

- DoubleProperty labelLineLength

- BooleanProperty labelsVisible

- DoubleProperty startAngle

We covered the data property in the previous section. Some of the other properties are demonstrated in the next code snippet. Listing 7-2 contains a modified version of the start() method.

Listing 7-2. *Modified Version of the PieChart Example*

```
public void start(Stage primaryStage) {
    PieChart pieChart = new PieChart();
    pieChart.setData(getChartData());
    pieChart.setTitle("Tiobe index");
    pieChart.setLegendSide(Side.LEFT);
    pieChart.setClockwise(false);
    pieChart.setLabelsVisible(false);

    primaryStage.setTitle("Chart App 2");


    StackPane root = new StackPane();
    root.getChildren().add(pieChart);
    primaryStage.setScene(new Scene(root, 300, 250));
    primaryStage.show();
}
```

Running this modified version results in the modified output in Figure 7-4.

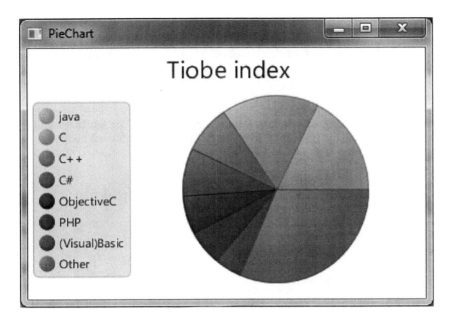

Figure 7-4. *The output of the modified PieChart example*

By changing a few lines of code, the output looks very different. We go over the changes we made in a bit more detail. First, we added a title to the chart. That was done using the call

```
pieChart.setTitle("Tiobe index");
```

We could also have used the builder pattern.

```
PieChartBuilder.create().title("Tiobe index")
```

Or we could have used the titleProperty:

```
pieChart.titleProperty().set("Tiobe index");
```

The three approaches result in the same output.

■ **Note** The upcoming modifications could also be done using the same patterns. We only document the approach with setter methods, but it is easy to replace this with the builder pattern or with a property-based approach.

The next line of code in our modified example changing the location of the legend:

```
pieChart.setLegendSide(Side.LEFT);
```

When the legendSide is not specified, the legend is shown at the default location, which is below the chart. The title and the legendSide are both properties that belong to the abstract Chart class. As a consequence, they can be set on any chart. The next line in our modified example modifies a property that is specific to a PieChart:

```
pieChart.setClockwise(false);
```

By default, the slices in a PieChart are rendered clockwise. By setting this property to false, the slices are rendered counterclockwise. We also disabled showing the labels in the PieChart. The labels are still shown in the legend, but they do not point to the individual slices anymore. This is achieved by the following line of code:

```
pieChart.setLabelsVisible(false);
```

All layout changes so far are done programmatically. It is also possible to style applications in general and charts in particular using a CSS stylesheet.

We remove the layout changes from the Java code, and add a stylesheet containing some layout instructions. Listing 7-3 shows the modified code of the start() method and Listing 7-4 contains the stylesheet we added.

Listing 7-3. *Remove Programmatic Layout Instructions*

```
public void start(Stage primaryStage) {
    PieChart pieChart = new PieChart();
    pieChart.setData(getChartData());
    pieChart.titleProperty().set("Tiobe index");
    pieChart.setLegendSide(Side.LEFT);

    primaryStage.setTitle("PieChart");
    StackPane root = new StackPane();
    root.getChildren().add(pieChart);
    Scene scene = new Scene (root, 400, 250);

scene.getStylesheets().add(ChartApp2css.class.getResource("chartapp2.css").toExternalForm());

    primaryStage.setScene(scene);
    primaryStage.show();
}
```

Listing 7-4. *Stylesheet for PieChart Example*

```
.chart {
    -fx-clockwise: false;
    -fx-pie-label-visible: true;
    -fx-label-line-length: 5;
    -fx-start-angle: 90;
}

.default-color0.chart-pie {
    -fx-pie-color: blue;
}
```

```
.default-color1.chart-pie {
    -fx-pie-color: yellow;
}

.chart-legend {
    -fx-background-color: #f0e68c;
    -fx-stroke: #696969;
}
```

Running this code results in the output shown in Figure 7-5.

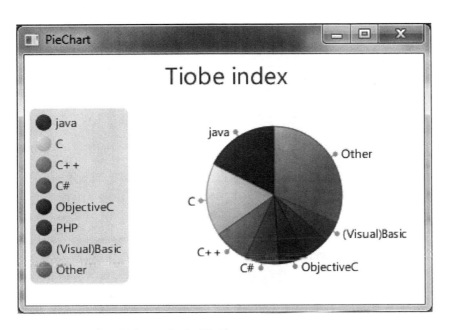

Figure 7-5. *Using CSS to style the PieChart*

We now go over the changes we made. Before we go over the individual changes in detail, we show how we include the CSS with our application. This is achieved by adding the stylesheet to the scene, which is done as follows.

```
scene.getStylesheets().add(ChartApp2css.class.getResource("chartapp2.css").toExternalForm());
```

In Listing 7-2, we set the clockwise configuration using

```
pieChart.setClockwise(false)
```

We removed that line from the code in Listing 7-3, and instead defined the -fx-clockwise-property on the chart class in the stylesheet:

```
.chart {
    -fx-clockwise: false;
    -fx-pie-label-visible: true;
    -fx-label-line-length: 5;
    -fx-start-angle: 90;
}
```

In that same .chart class definition, we make the labels on the pie visible by setting -fx-pie-label-visible property to true, and we specify the length of the lines for each label to be 5.

Also, we rotate the whole pie by 90 degrees, which is achieved by defining the -fx-start-angle property. The labels are now defined in the stylesheet, and we remove the corresponding definition from the code by omitting the following line.

```
pieChart.setLabelsVisible(false)
```

By default, a PieChart uses the default colors defined in the caspian stylesheet. The first slice is filled with default-color0, the second slice with default-color1, and so on. The easiest way to change the color of the different slices is by overriding the definitions of the default color. In our stylesheet, this is done by

```
.default-color0.chart-pie {
    -fx-pie-color: blue;
}
```

The same can be done for the other slices.

Finally, we changed the background and the stroke of the legend. This is achieved by overriding the chart-legend class as follows.

```
.chart-legend {
    -fx-background-color: #f0e68c;
    -fx-stroke: #696969;
}
```

Again, we refer the reader to http://docs.oracle.com/javafx/2.0/charts/css-styles.htm for more information about using CSS with JavaFX charts.

Using the XYChart

The XYChart class is an abstract class with five direct known subclasses. The difference between these classes and the PieChart class is that an XYChart has two axes and an optional alternativeColumn or alternativeRow. This translates to the following list of additional properties on an XYChart.

- BooleanProperty alternativeColumnFillVisible

- BooleanProperty alternativeRowFillVisible

- ObjectProperty<ObservableList<XYChart.Series<X,Y>>> data

- BooleanProperty horizontalGridLinesVisible

- BooleanProperty horizontalZeroLineVisible

- BooleanProperty verticalGridLinesVisible

- BooleanProperty verticalZeroLineVisible

Data in an XYChart are ordered in series. How these series are rendered is specific to the implementation of the subclass of XYChart. In general, a single element in a series contains a number of pairs. The following examples use a hypothetical projection of market share of three programming languages in the future. We start with the TIOBE index for Java, C, and C++ in 2011, and add random values (between –2 and +2) to them for each year until 2020. The resulting (year, number) pairs for Java constitute the Java Series, and the same holds for C and C++. As a result, we have three series, each containing 10 pairs.

A major difference between a PieChart and an XYChart is the presence of an x axis and a y axis in the XYChart. These axes are required when creating an XYChart, as can be observed from the following constructor.

```
XYChart (Axis<X> xAxis, Axis<Y> yAxis)
```

The Axis class is an abstract class extending Region (hence also extending Parent and Node) with two subclasses: CategoryAxis and ValueAxis. The CategoryAxis is used to render labels that are in the String format, as can be observed from the class definition:

```
public class CategoryAxis extends Axis<java.lang.String>
```

The ValueAxis is used to render data entries that represent a Number. It is an abstract class itself, defined as follows.

```
public abstract class ValueAxis <T extends java.lang.Number> extends Axis<T>
```

The ValueAxis class has one concrete subclass, which is the NumberAxis:

```
public final class NumberAxis extends ValueAxis<java.lang.Number>
```

The differences between those Axis classes become clear throughout the examples.

We now show some examples of the different XYChart implementations, starting with the ScatterChart. Some features common to all XYCharts are also explained in the section on ScatterChart.

Using the ScatterChart

An instance of the ScatterChart class is used to render data where each data item is represented as a symbol in a two-dimensional area. As mentioned in the previous section, we will render a chart containing 3 series of data, representing the hypothetical evolution of the TIOBE index for, respectively, Java, C, and C++. We first show the code of a naive implementation, and refine that to something more useful.

A Simple Implementation

A first implementation of our application using a ScatterChart is shown in Listing 7-5.

Listing 7-5. First Implementation of Rendering Data in a ScatterChart

```
import javafx.application.Application;
import javafx.collections.FXCollections;
import javafx.collections.ObservableList;
import javafx.scene.Scene;
import javafx.scene.chart.NumberAxis;
import javafx.scene.chart.ScatterChart;
```

```java
import javafx.scene.chart.XYChart;
import javafx.scene.chart.XYChart.Series;
import javafx.scene.layout.StackPane;
import javafx.stage.Stage;

public class ChartApp3 extends Application {

    public static void main(String[] args) {
        launch(args);
    }

    @Override
    public void start(Stage primaryStage) {
        NumberAxis xAxis = new NumberAxis();
        NumberAxis yAxis = new NumberAxis();
        ScatterChart scatterChart = new ScatterChart(xAxis, yAxis);
        scatterChart.setData(getChartData());
        primaryStage.setTitle("Chart App 3");

        StackPane root = new StackPane();
        root.getChildren().add(scatterChart);
        primaryStage.setScene(new Scene(root, 400, 250));
        primaryStage.show();
    }

    private ObservableList<XYChart.Series<Integer, Double>> getChartData() {
        double javaValue = 17.56;
        double cValue = 17.06;
        double cppValue = 8.25;
        ObservableList<XYChart.Series<Integer, Double>> answer =
FXCollections.observableArrayList();
        Series<Integer, Double> java = new Series<Integer, Double>();
        Series<Integer, Double> c = new Series<Integer, Double>();
        Series<Integer, Double> cpp = new Series<Integer, Double>();
        for (int i = 2011; i < 2021; i++) {
            java.getData().add(new XYChart.Data(i, javaValue));
            javaValue = javaValue + 4 * Math.random() - 2;
            c.getData().add(new XYChart.Data(i, cValue));
            cValue = cValue + Math.random() - .5;
            cpp.getData().add(new XYChart.Data(i, cppValue));
            cppValue = cppValue + 4 * Math.random() - 2;
        }
        answer.addAll(java, c, cpp);
        return answer;
    }
}
```

Executing this application results in the image shown in Figure 7-6.

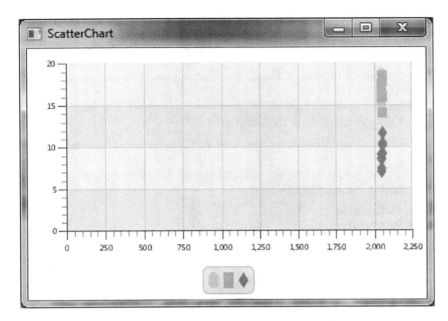

Figure 7-6. *The result of the naive implementation of the ScatterChart*

Although the chart shows the required information, it is not very readable. We add a number of enhancements, but we first have a deeper look at the different parts of the code.

Similar to the PieChart example, we created a separate method for obtaining the data. One of the reasons for this is that in real-world applications, it is unlikely to have static data. By isolating the data retrieval in a separate method, it becomes easier to change the way data are obtained.

A single data point is defined by an instance of XYChart.Data<Integer, Double>, created with the constructor XYChart.Data(Integer i, Double d) where the parameters have the following definitions.

```
i: Integer, representing a specific year (between 2011 and 2020)
d: Double, representing the hypothetical TIOBE index for the particular series in the year
specified by I
```

The local variables javaValue, cValue, and cppValue are used for keeping track of the scores for the different programming languages. They are initialized with the real values from 2011. Each year, an individual score is incremented or decremented by a random value between –2 and +2. Data points are stacked into a series. In our examples, we have three series each containing 10 instances of XYChart.Data<Integer, Double>. Those series are of type XYChart.Series<Integer, Double>.

The data entries are added to the respective series by calling

```
java.getData().add (...)
c.getData().add(...)
```

and

```
cpp.getData().add(...)
```

Finally, all series are added to the ObservableList<XYChart.Series<Integer, Double>> and returned. The start() method of the application contains the functionality required for creating and rendering the ScatterChart, and for populating it with the data obtained from the getChartData method.

■ **Note**   As discussed earlier in the PieChart section, we can use different patterns here. We used the JavaBeans pattern in the examples, but we could also use properties or the Builder pattern.

In order to create a ScatterChart, we need to create an xAxis and a yAxis. In our first, simple, implementation, we use two instances of NumberAxis for this:

```
NumberAxis xAxis = new NumberAxis();
NumberAxis yAxis = new NumberAxis();
```

Apart from calling the following ScatterChart constructor, there is nothing different in this method than in the case of the PieChart.

```
ScatterChart scatterChart = new ScatterChart(xAxis, yAxis);
```

Improving the Simple Implementation

One of the first observations when looking at Figure 7-5 is that all data plots in a series are almost rendered on top of each other. The reason for this is clear: the x-Axis starts at 0 and ends at 2250. By default, the NumberAxis determines its range automatically. We can overrule this behavior by setting the autoRanging property to false, and by providing values for the lowerBound and the upperBound. If we replace the constructor for the xAxis in the original example by the following code snippet,

```
NumberAxis xAxis = new NumberAxis();
xAxis.setAutoRanging(false);
xAxis.setLowerBound(2011);
xAxis.setUpperBound(2021);
```

the resulting output will look as shown in Figure 7-7.

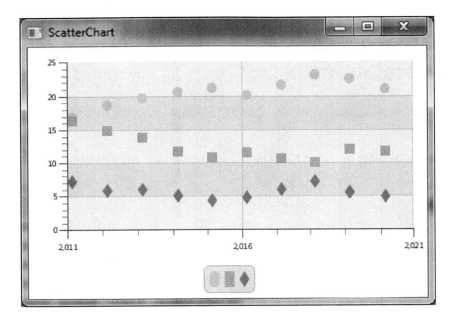

Figure 7-7. *Defining the behavior of the xAxis*

Next, we want to add a title to the chart, and we want to have names near the symbols in the legend node. Adding a title to the chart is no different from adding a title to the PieChart and is achieved by the code:

```
scatterChart.setTitle("Speculations");
```

By adding a name to the three instances of XYChart.Series, we add labels to the symbols in the legend node. The relevant part of the getChartData method becomes

```
Series<Integer, Double> java = new Series<Integer, Double>();
Series<Integer, Double> c = new Series<Integer, Double>();
Series<Integer, Double> cpp = new Series<Integer, Double>();
java.setName("java");
c.setName("C");
cpp.setName("C++");
```

Running the application again after applying both changes results in the output shown in Figure 7-8.

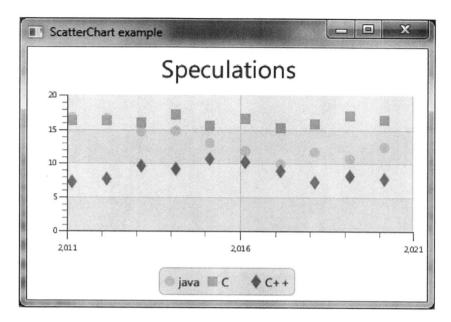

Figure 7-8. *ScatterChart with a title and named symbols*

Until now, we used a NumberAxis for the xAxis. Inasmuch as years can be represented as Number instances, that works. However, because we don't do any numerical operation on the years, and because the distance between consecutive data entries is always one year, we can as well use a String value to represent this information.

We now modify the code in order to work with a CategoryAxis for the xAxis. Changing the xAxis from a NumberAxis to a CategoryAxis also implies that the getChartData() method should return an instance of ObservableList<XYChart.Series<String, Double>> and that implies that the different elements in a single Series should have the type XYChart.Data<String, Double>.

In Listing 7-6, the original code has been modified to use the CategoryAxis.

Listing 7-6. *Using CategoryAxis Instead of NumberAxis for the xAxis*

```
import javafx.application.Application;
import javafx.collections.FXCollections;
import javafx.collections.ObservableList;
import javafx.scene.Scene;
import javafx.scene.chart.CategoryAxis;
import javafx.scene.chart.NumberAxis;
import javafx.scene.chart.ScatterChart;
import javafx.scene.chart.XYChart;
import javafx.scene.chart.XYChart.Series;
import javafx.scene.layout.StackPane;
import javafx.stage.Stage;
```

```java
public class ChartApp6 extends Application {

    public static void main(String[] args) {
        launch(args);
    }

    @Override
    public void start(Stage primaryStage) {
        CategoryAxis xAxis = new CategoryAxis();
        NumberAxis yAxis = new NumberAxis();
        ScatterChart scatterChart = new ScatterChart(xAxis, yAxis);
        scatterChart.setData(getChartData());
        scatterChart.setTitle("speculations");
        primaryStage.setTitle("ScatterChart example");

        StackPane root = new StackPane();
        root.getChildren().add(scatterChart);
        primaryStage.setScene(new Scene(root, 400, 250));
        primaryStage.show();
    }

    private ObservableList<XYChart.Series<String, Double>> getChartData() {
        double javaValue = 17.56;
        double cValue = 17.06;
        double cppValue = 8.25;
        ObservableList<XYChart.Series<String, Double>> answer =
FXCollections.observableArrayList();
        Series<String, Double> java = new Series<String, Double>();
        Series<String, Double> c = new Series<String, Double>();
        Series<String, Double> cpp = new Series<String, Double>();
        java.setName("java");
        c.setName("C");
        cpp.setName("C++");

        for (int i = 2011; i < 2021; i++) {
            java.getData().add(new XYChart.Data(Integer.toString(i), javaValue));
            javaValue = javaValue + 4 * Math.random() - .2;
            c.getData().add(new XYChart.Data(Integer.toString(i), cValue));
            cValue = cValue + 4 * Math.random() - 2;
            cpp.getData().add(new XYChart.Data(Integer.toString(i), cppValue));
            cppValue = cppValue + 4 * Math.random() - 2;
        }
        answer.addAll(java, c, cpp);
        return answer;
    }
}
```

Running the modified application results in the output shown in Figure 7-9.

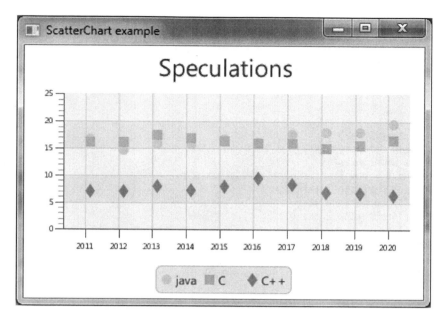

Figure 7-9. *Using a ScatterChart with a CategoryAxis on the xAxis*

Before we move on to the LineChart, we show how to use the alternativeRowFillVisible and alternativeColumnVisible properties. As you can observe from Figure 7-9, two consecutive horizontal rows (between the major tickmarks on the axis) have slightly different colors. No such difference is observed in the columns, though. By adding the following lines of code to Listing 7-6, that behavior will be reversed.

```
scatterChart.setAlternativeRowFillVisible(false);
scatterChart.setAlternativeColumnFillVisible(true);
```

These two statements define that there should not be a difference between consecutive rows, but there should be a difference in the background color of consecutive columns. Running the example again after adding those two lines of code gives the output shown in Figure 7-10.

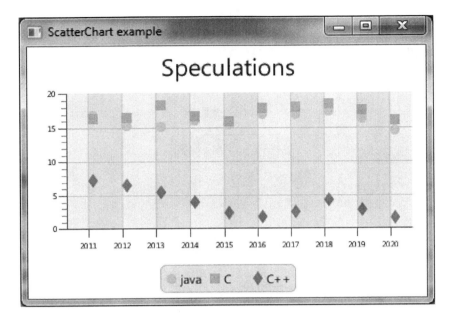

Figure 7-10. Using similar fill values for rows and different fill values for columns

---

■ **Note** The appearance of the alternative rows can be defined by overriding the chart-alternative-row-fill class in a CSS stylesheet.

Using the LineChart

The example in the previous section resulted in data entries being represented by single dots or symbols. Often, it is desirable to have the dots connected by a line because this helps in seeing trends. The JavaFX LineChart is well suited for this.

The API for the LineChart has many methods in common with the API for the ScatterChart. In fact, we can reuse most of the code in Listing 7-6, and just replace the ScatterChart occurrences with LineChart. The data stay exactly the same, so we only show the new start() method in Listing 7-7.

Listing 7-7. Using a LineChart Instead of a ScatterChart

```
public void start(Stage primaryStage) {
    CategoryAxis xAxis = new CategoryAxis();
    NumberAxis yAxis = new NumberAxis();
    LineChart lineChart = new LineChart(xAxis, yAxis);
    lineChart.setData(getChartData());
    lineChart.setTitle("speculations");
    primaryStage.setTitle("LineChart example");
```

```
        StackPane root = new StackPane();
        root.getChildren().add(lineChart);
        primaryStage.setScene(new Scene(root, 400, 250));
        primaryStage.show();
    }
```

Running this application gives the output shown in Figure 7-11.

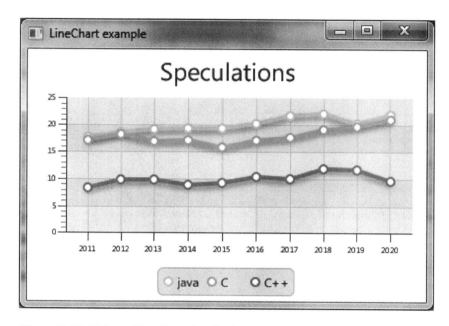

Figure 7-11. *Using a LineChart for displaying trends*

Most of the functionality available for the ScatterChart is also available for the LineChart. Changing the location of the legend, adding or removing a title, and using a NumberAxis instead of a CategoryAxis are very well possible using the LineChart.

Using the BarChart

A BarChart is capable of rendering the same data as a ScatterChart and a LineChart, but it looks different. In a BarChart, the focus is often more on showing the relative differences between the different series for a given category. In our case, that means that we focus on the differences between the values for Java, C, and C++.

Again, we do not need to modify the method that returns our data. Indeed, a BarChart requires a CategoryAxis for its xAxis, and we already modified the getChartData() method to return an ObservableList containing XYChart.Series<String, double>. Starting from Listing 7-6, we change only the occurrences of ScatterChart with BarChart and we obtain Listing 7-8.

Listing 7-8. *Using a BarChart Instead of a ScatterChart*

```
public void start(Stage primaryStage) {
    CategoryAxis xAxis = new CategoryAxis();
    NumberAxis yAxis = new NumberAxis();
    BarChart barChart = new BarChart(xAxis, yAxis);
    barChart.setData(getChartData());
    barChart.setTitle("speculations");
    primaryStage.setTitle("BarChart example");

    StackPane root = new StackPane();
    root.getChildren().add(barChart);
    primaryStage.setScene(new Scene(root, 400, 250));
    primaryStage.show();
}
```

The result of this application is shown in Figure 7-12.

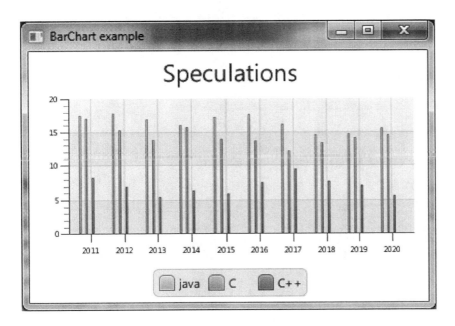

Figure 7-12. *Using BarChart for highlighting differences between the values*

Although the result indeed shows the differences between the values for each year, it is not very clear because the bars are rather small. With a total scene width at 400 pixels, there is not much space to render large bars. However, the BarChart API contains methods to define the inner gap between bars, and the gap between categories. In our case, we want a smaller gap between the bars, for example, one pixel. This is done by calling

```
barChart.setBarGap(1);
```

Adding this single line of code to the start method and rerunning the application results in the output shown in Figure 7-13.

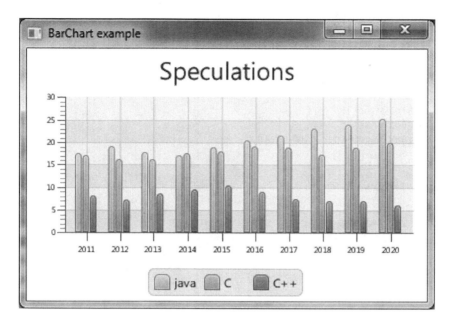

Figure 7-13. *Setting the gap between bars to one pixel*

Clearly, this one line of code leads to a huge difference in readability.

Using the AreaChart

In some cases, it makes sense to fill the area under the line connecting the dots. Although the same data are rendered as in the case of a LineChart, the result looks different. Listing 7-9 contains the modified start() method that uses an AreaChart instead of the original ScatterChart. As in the previous modifications, we didn't change the getChartData() method.

Listing 7-9. *Using an AreaChart Instead of a ScatterChart*

```
@Override
  public void start(Stage primaryStage) {
      CategoryAxis xAxis = new CategoryAxis();
      NumberAxis yAxis = new NumberAxis();
      AreaChart areaChart = new AreaChart(xAxis, yAxis);
      areaChart.setData(getChartData());
      areaChart.setTitle("speculations");
      primaryStage.setTitle("AreaChart example");
```

```
    StackPane root = new StackPane();
    root.getChildren().add(areaChart);
    primaryStage.setScene(new Scene(root, 400, 250));
    primaryStage.show();
}
```

Running this application results in the output shown in Figure 7-14.

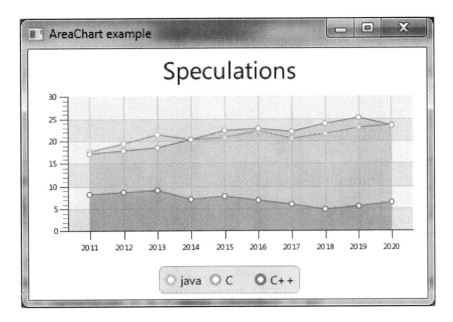

Figure 7-14. *Rendering area plots using AreaChart*

Using the BubbleChart

The last implementation of the XYChart is a special one. The BubbleChart does not contain properties that are not already on the XYChart class, but it is the only direct implementation in the current JavaFX Chart API that uses the additional parameter on the XYChart.Data class.

We first modify the code in Listing 7-6 to use the BubbleChart instead of the ScatterChart. Because by default, bubbles are stretched when the span on the xAxis is much different from the span on the yAxis, we do not use years, but a tenth of a year as the value on the xAxis. Doing so, we have a span of 100 units on the xAxis (10 years) compared with a span of about 30 units on the yAxis. This is also more or less the ratio between the width and the height of our chart. As a consequence, the bubbles are relatively circular.

Listing 7-10 contains the code for rendering a BubbleChart.

Listing 7-10. *Using the BubbleChart*

```java
import javafx.application.Application;
import javafx.collections.FXCollections;
import javafx.collections.ObservableList;
import javafx.scene.Scene;
import javafx.scene.chart.*;
import javafx.scene.chart.XYChart.Series;
import javafx.scene.layout.StackPane;
import javafx.stage.Stage;
import javafx.util.StringConverter;

public class ChartApp10 extends Application {

    public static void main(String[] args) {
        launch(args);
    }

    @Override
    public void start(Stage primaryStage) {
        NumberAxis xAxis = new NumberAxis();
        NumberAxis yAxis = new NumberAxis();
        yAxis.setAutoRanging(false);
        yAxis.setLowerBound(0);
        yAxis.setUpperBound(30);
        xAxis.setAutoRanging(false);
        xAxis.setAutoRanging(false);
        xAxis.setLowerBound(20110);
        xAxis.setUpperBound(20201);
        xAxis.setTickUnit(10);
        xAxis.setTickLabelFormatter(new StringConverter<Number>() {

            @Override
            public String toString(Number n) {
                return String.valueOf(n.intValue() / 10);
            }

            @Override
            public Number fromString(String s) {
                return Integer.valueOf(s) * 10;
            }
        });
        BubbleChart bubbleChart = new BubbleChart(xAxis, yAxis);
        bubbleChart.setData(getChartData());
        bubbleChart.setTitle("Speculations");
        primaryStage.setTitle("BubbleChart example");
```

```
            StackPane root = new StackPane();
            root.getChildren().add(bubbleChart);
            primaryStage.setScene(new Scene(root, 400, 250));
            primaryStage.show();
        }

    private ObservableList<XYChart.Series<Integer, Double>> getChartData() {
            double javaValue = 17.56;
            double cValue = 17.06;
            double cppValue = 8.25;
            ObservableList<XYChart.Series<Integer, Double>> answer =
FXCollections.observableArrayList();
            Series<Integer, Double> java = new Series<Integer, Double>();
            Series<Integer, Double> c = new Series<Integer, Double>();
            Series<Integer, Double> cpp = new Series<Integer, Double>();
            java.setName("java");
            c.setName("C");
            cpp.setName("C++");
            for (int i = 20110; i < 20210; i = i + 10) {
                double diff = Math.random();
                java.getData().add(new XYChart.Data(i, javaValue));
                javaValue = Math.max(javaValue + 4 * diff - 2, 0);
                diff = Math.random();
                c.getData().add(new XYChart.Data(i, cValue));
                cValue = Math.max(cValue + 4 * diff - 2, 0);
                diff = Math.random();
                cpp.getData().add(new XYChart.Data(i, cppValue));
                cppValue = Math.max(cppValue + 4 * diff - 2, 0);
            }
            answer.addAll(java, c, cpp);
            return answer;
        }

}
```

The xAxis ranges from 20110 till 20210, but of course we want to show the years at the axis. This can be achieved by calling

```
xAxis.setTickLabelFormatter(new StringConverter<Number>() {

...
}
```

where the StringConverter we supply converts the numbers we use (e.g., 20150) to Strings (e.g., 2015) and vice versa. Doing so, we are able to use whatever quantity we want for calculating the bubbles and still have a nice way of formatting the labels. Running this example results in the code shown in Figure 7-15.

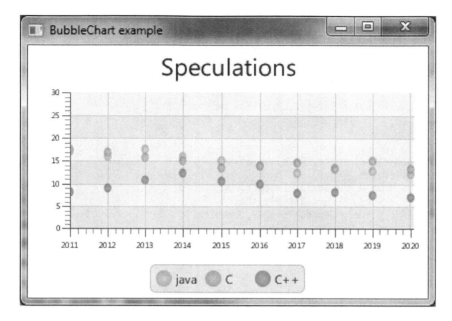

Figure 7-15. *Using a BubbleChart with fixed radius*

Until now, we didn't leverage the three-argument constructor of XYChart.Data. Apart from the two-argument constructor that we are already familiar with,

```
XYChart.Data (X xValue, Y yValue)
```

XYChart.Data also has a three-argument constructor:

```
XYChart.Data (X xValue, Y yValue, Object extraValue)
```

The extraValue argument can be of any type. This allows for developers to implement their own subclasses of XYChart that take advantage of additional information that can be enclosed inside a single data element. The BubbleChart implementation uses this extraValue for deciding how large the bubbles should be rendered.

We now modify the getChartData() method to use the three-argument constructor. The xValue and yValue parameters are still the same as in the previous listing, but we now add a third parameter that indicates an upcoming trend. The larger this parameter is, the bigger the rise in the next year. The smaller the parameter is, the bigger the drop in the next year. The modified getChartData() method is shown in Listing 7-11.

Listing 7-11. *Using a Three-Argument Constructor for XYChart.Data Instances*

```
    private ObservableList<XYChart.Series<Integer, Double>> getChartData() {
        double javaValue = 17.56;
        double cValue = 17.06;
        double cppValue = 8.25;
        ObservableList<XYChart.Series<Integer, Double>> answer =
FXCollections.observableArrayList();
        Series<Integer, Double> java = new Series<Integer, Double>();
```

```
        Series<Integer, Double> c = new Series<Integer, Double>();
        Series<Integer, Double> cpp = new Series<Integer, Double>();
        java.setName("java");
        c.setName("C");
        cpp.setName("C++");
        for (int i = 20110; i < 20210; i =  i+10) {
            double diff = Math.random();
            java.getData().add(new XYChart.Data(i, javaValue, 2*diff));
            javaValue = Math.max(javaValue + 4*diff - 2,0);
            diff = Math.random();
            c.getData().add(new XYChart.Data(i, cValue,2* diff));
            cValue = Math.max(cValue + 4*diff - 2,0);
            diff = Math.random();
            cpp.getData().add(new XYChart.Data(i, cppValue, 2*diff));
            cppValue = Math.max(cppValue + 4*diff - 2,0);
        }
        answer.addAll(java, c, cpp);
        return answer;
    }
```

Integrating this method with the start() method in Listing 7-10 results in the output shown in Figure 7-16.

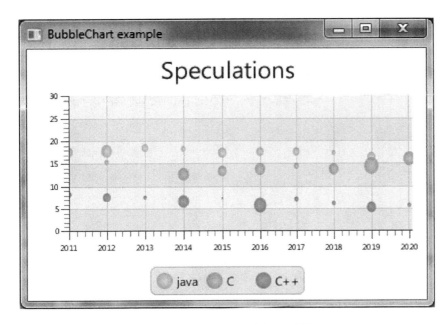

Figure 7-16. *Adding variations in the size of the Bubbles*

Summary

The JavaFX Chart API provides a number of ready-to-use implementations for different chart types. Each of these implementations serves a different purpose, and it is up to the developer to choose the most appropriate Chart.

Modifying a Chart and tuning it for a specific application can be done by applying CSS rules or by using Chart-specific methods or properties. If you prefer to use the Builder pattern, you can use this as well because a corresponding Builder class exists for all existing concrete subclasses of Chart.

In case you need a more customized Chart, you can extend the abstract Chart class and take advantage of the existing properties on that class, or you can extend the abstract XYChart class in case your chart requires two axes.

Resources

For more information on the JavaFX Chart API, consult the following resources.

- http://docs.oracle.com/javafx/2.0/charts/jfxpub-charts.htm

- http://docs.oracle.com/javafx/2.0/api/javafx/scene/doc-files/cssref.html

CHAPTER 8

Using the Media Classes

We keep moving forward, opening new doors, and doing new things, because we're curious and curiosity keeps leading us down new paths.

—Walt Disney

In the previous chapters you have learned how to create applications using the JavaFX library. Now we make good use of that knowledge while creating applications that explore the audio and video capabilities of the JavaFX platform.

The Foundation

The media classes in JavaFX are based on an open source multimedia framework named GStreamer.[1] This is a big change from the media library in previous versions of JavaFX where the native media capabilities of the various supported platforms were used directly. In comparison, the new GStreamer-based library provides better stability and more consistency across platforms. The downside is that, at least in JavaFX 2.0, the new library is slightly more limited in some of its capabilities and in its support for media containers and codecs. For example, there is no support for streaming media and only video encoded with the VP6 format is currently supported. As compensation there are a few new features as well, which we cover in the following sections.

It should be noted that the limitations mentioned above are not limitations of GStreamer itself. We remain optimistic that these features will appear in future releases. In the meantime, the changeover to the GStreamer library provides a solid foundation for the media capabilities of JavaFX 2.0 and beyond.

Supported Media Formats

Table 8-1 shows the file formats that are supported by the JavaFX media classes. Three audio formats and two identical video formats are supported. The three audio formats supported in JavaFX (MP3, WAV,

---

[1] http://gstreamer.freedesktop.org/

and AIFF) are very common and are all well supported by most audio tools on the market. You should have no trouble obtaining your source audio files in, or converting them to, one of the formats supported by JavaFX.

FXM is the "native" JavaFX video format. It consists of VP6 encoded video and MP3 audio, a combination that is also used in Flash Video (FLV) files. An FLV container can host several different options for video and audio encoding other than VP6 and MP3. Therefore, it is not correct to say that JavaFX can play any FLV file. However, the VP6/MP3 combination is very common and so it is fair to say that JavaFX should be able to play most FLV files that can be found on the Internet. FLV video is widely supported by tools from Adobe and others so you should have no trouble converting or authoring video in this format.

Table 8-1. *Media Formats Supported by JavaFX*

File Extension	Type	Format	Mime Type
.mp3	Audio	MP3: MPEG-1, 2, 2.5 audio with ID3 v2.3, v2.4 metadata	audio/mpeg
.aif, .aiff	Audio	Audio Interchange File Format: uncompressed audio	audio/x-aiff
.wav	Audio	Waveform Audio Format: uncompressed audio	audio/x-wav
.fxm	Video	FX Media: VP6 video with MP3 audio	video/x-javafx
.flv	Video	Flash Video: VP6 video with MP3 audio	video/x-flv

■ **Note** As this book goes to press, Oracle has announced that support for AAC audio and H.264 video will be added to JavaFX 2.1.

Working with Audio Clips

In previous versions of JavaFX, there was no way to play low latency audio. This much-needed feature is now available in version 2.0 using the new AudioClip class. Audio clips are not suitable for large or lengthy sounds because the audio data associated with these sounds are decompressed and stored completely in memory. If you need to play a song or other lengthy audio file, you should use a Media object instead, which is discussed in the next section.

An AudioClip is ideal for playing short sounds in response to user actions in a game or other rich-media application. An AudioClip instance is constructed by passing a URI string as the only parameter to the constructor. This URI can point to a resource on the Internet, the local file system, or within the jar file by using the http:, file:, and jar: schemes, respectively. Once constructed, you can adjust several properties that affect the playback of the clip such as the volume, playback rate, panning, and balance. Calling its play method will begin playback of an AudioClip. You may call the play method repeatedly to begin multiple overlapping playbacks of a given clip.

There are actually three overloaded versions of the play method in the AudioClip class. Calling the method with no arguments will use the current properties of the AudioClip instance for the playback. There is also a variant of the play method that takes a volume argument, which allows you to override the volume of the clip for that playback only. The final variant of the play method allows you to specify the volume, balance, rate, pan, and priority of that playback. Specifying these parameters as arguments of the play methods does not cause them to be saved permanently; they are a one-time-only override of the AudioClip's instance data. There is also a stop method that stops all playback of the AudioClip.

Listing 8-1 illustrates the simple steps required to create and play an AudioClip. This source code is part of the BasicAudioClip example project in the Chapter08 directory of the book's source code.

Listing 8-1. Playing an Audio Clip

```
public class BasicAudioClip extends Application {

    public static void main(String[] args) {
        launch(args);
    }

    @Override
    public void start(Stage primaryStage) {
        final URL resource = getClass().getResource("resources/beep.wav");
        final AudioClip clip = new AudioClip(resource.toString());

        final Button button = new Button("Bing Zzzzt!");
        button.setOnAction(new EventHandler<ActionEvent>() {
            @Override
            public void handle(ActionEvent event) {
                clip.play(1.0);
            }
        });

        final StackPane stackPane = new StackPane();
        stackPane.setPadding(new Insets(10));
        stackPane.getChildren().add(button);

        final Scene scene = new Scene(stackPane, 200, 200);
        final URL stylesheet = getClass().getResource("media.css");
        scene.getStylesheets().add(stylesheet.toString());

        primaryStage.setTitle("Basic AudioClip Example");
        primaryStage.setScene(scene);
        primaryStage.show();
    }
}
```

The prerequisite to creating an AudioClip is to create the URI string for the resource to be loaded. In Listing 8-1, we use the getResource method to return the URI for an audio file embedded in the jar file. The URI is converted to a String and then passed to the AudioClip constructor. As previously mentioned, the AudioClip constructor loads the entire sound into memory, decoding it if necessary. If your sound effect files are small you can store them in an uncompressed format such as the .wav file we use in this example to avoid the overhead of decoding them. Once a sound file grows larger than 100 kB or so, you should consider storing it as a compressed MP3 file instead because the smaller size of the file can more than make up for the overhead of decoding the sound. This is especially true if you are loading your sound files from a server on the Internet. You should also keep in mind that the AudioClip constructor will block the current thread until the sound is completely loaded. For this reason, you should consider loading your sound effects on a background thread if you are loading a lot of files or if the files are large. See the section titled *Using the JavaFX Concurrency Framework* in Chapter 6 for details on using JavaFX's concurrency classes.

Once the AudioClip is constructed, you simply need to call one of its play methods to start a playback. The sound in Listing 8-1 is played in response to a button click by calling the play method and passing it a volume parameter of 1.0, which causes the sound to be played at maximum volume. The Button is then added to a StackPane so that it will automatically remain centered in the Scene. Finally, the Scene is added to the Stage and shown to the user. Note that the *media.css* style sheet is applied to the scene. This style sheet is used by all of the sample applications in this chapter. The style sheet is shown in Listing 8-2.

Listing 8-2. The First Version of the Style Sheet Used by the Applications in This Chapter

```
.root {
  -fx-base: #606060;
  -fx-background-color: radial-gradient(center 50% 50%, radius 60%,
                                        #666a6b, #2b2f32);
  -fx-background-image: url("resources/cross.png");
  -fx-background-position: left top;
}

.button {
  -fx-text-fill: #E0E0E0;
  -fx-font-size: 20pt;
  -fx-pref-width: 300px;
}

.label {
  -fx-text-fill: #E0E0E0;
}

#clipLabel {
  -fx-font-size: 24pt;
}

.hyperlink {
  -fx-text-fill: #808080;
}
```

Figure 8-1 shows how this simple AudioClip example should look when it is running. A new playback of the AudioClip is started each time the button is clicked. If you're very quick, you might get two or three playing at a time.

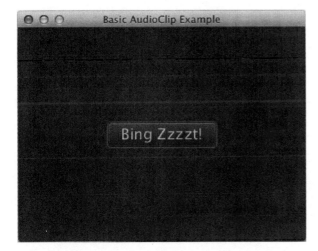

Figure 8-1. *The BasicAudioClip application*

Controlling the Playback Parameters of an AudioClip

We now build on the preceding example to show how AudioClip allows a sound effect to be played at differing volumes and rates. We also show how the balance of an audio clip can be adjusted to control the volume of the left and right channels. This can be useful when you want to achieve a bit of 2D spatialization in your sound effects. The application we end up with is shown in Figure 8-2.

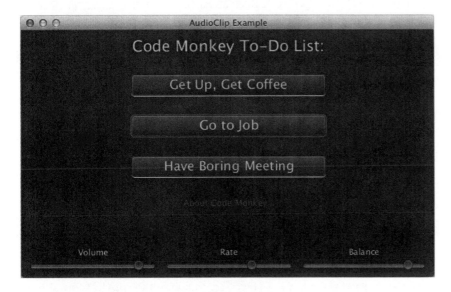

Figure 8-2. *The CodeMonkeyToDo application*

We start by examining the `Application` class and look at how the sounds are loaded. Listing 8-3 shows the application with the scene construction code removed. This allows you to see more easily that we are loading MP3 files from the jar file using the `getResource` method again. In this case, our sound effects are in a different location relative to our application class. Therefore we use a path such as "resources/coffee.mp3" to locate them. These clips are a little longer, so the decision was made to use MP3 files to keep the size of the jar file to a minimum at the expense of a little extra decoding time during startup.

The audio clips are all loaded in the constructor of the `CodeMonkeyToDo` class. Loading them in the constructor guarantees that they are loaded at the very start of the program before the `start` method is called. Alternatively, we could have overridden the `init` method of the `Application` class and loaded our clips there. Notice that the three `AudioClip`s and the three `Slider` controls are declared as fields in the Application class. This allows convenient access later when the `AudioClip` is played using the current values from the `Slider` controls shown in Figure 8-2.

Listing 8-3. The Application Class of the CodeMonkeyToDo Example Program

```
public class CodeMonkeyToDo extends Application {

  private final AudioClip coffeeClip;
  private final AudioClip jobClip;
  private final AudioClip meetingClip;

  private Slider volumeSlider;
  private Slider rateSlider;
  private Slider balanceSlider;

  public static void main(String[] args) {
    CodeMonkeyToDo.launch(args);
  }

  public CodeMonkeyToDo() {
    coffeeClip = new AudioClip(getClipResourceString("resources/coffee.mp3"));
    jobClip = new AudioClip(getClipResourceString("resources/job.mp3"));
    meetingClip =
        new AudioClip(getClipResourceString("resources/meeting.mp3"));
  }

  // Scene construction code removed for now...

  private String getClipResourceString(String clipName) {
    return getClass().getResource(clipName).toString();
  }
}
```

Constructing the Scene

We now take a brief look at the scene construction code for the application shown in Figure 8-2. The application is organized as a vertical column of buttons that play the audio clips with a row of controls at the bottom of the window. We use a `GridPane` as the top-level layout container for the application. You can see the `GridPane` created in the application's `start` method, which is shown in Listing 8-4. Once the

GridPane is created and configured, it is passed as an argument to the createControls and createClipList methods. The createClipList method is responsible for creating the vertical column of buttons and is shown and discussed later in this section. The createControls method creates Labels and the corresponding Slider controls that allow the user to set the volume, rate, and balance of the next clip to be played. The Sliders and their Labels are then added to the GridPane before the method returns. After the grid has been populated with its controls, it is used as the root node of a new Scene. The Scene is then styled with our *media.css* style sheet and added to the primaryStage, which is then shown to the user.

Listing 8-4. Constructing the Scene and the Volume, Balance, and Rate Controls

```
@Override
public void start(Stage primaryStage) {
    final GridPane grid = new GridPane();
    grid.setPadding(new Insets(10));
    grid.setHgap(10);
    grid.setVgap(5);

    createControls(grid);
    createClipList(grid);   // Shown later...

    final Scene scene = new Scene(grid, 640, 380);
    scene.getStylesheets()
        .add(getClass().getResource("media.css").toString());

    primaryStage.setTitle("AudioClip Example");
    primaryStage.setScene(scene);
    primaryStage.show();
}

private void createControls(GridPane grid) {
    final Label volumeLabel = new Label("Volume");
    final Label rateLabel = new Label("Rate");
    final Label balanceLabel = new Label("Balance");

    GridPane.setHalignment(volumeLabel, HPos.CENTER);
    GridPane.setHalignment(rateLabel, HPos.CENTER);
    GridPane.setHalignment(balanceLabel, HPos.CENTER);

    volumeSlider = new Slider(0.0, 1.0, 1.0);
    rateSlider = new Slider(0.25, 2.5, 1.0);
    balanceSlider = new Slider(-1.0, 1.0, 0.0);

    GridPane.setHgrow(volumeSlider, Priority.ALWAYS);
    GridPane.setHgrow(rateSlider, Priority.ALWAYS);
    GridPane.setHgrow(balanceSlider, Priority.ALWAYS);
```

```
        grid.add(volumeLabel, 0, 2);
        grid.add(volumeSlider, 0, 3);
        grid.add(rateLabel, 1, 2);
        grid.add(rateSlider, 1, 3);
        grid.add(balanceLabel, 2, 2);
        grid.add(balanceSlider, 2, 3);
    }
```

Listing 8-5 shows the `createClipList` method. This method creates a `VBox` to hold a `Label`, the three `Buttons` that play the `AudioClips`, and a `Hyperlink` that triggers the display of the Code Monkey web page at jonathancoulton.com in a separate window. The `VBox` is then added to the `GridPane` such that it spans all remaining columns in the first row. The `VBox` is always centered horizontally in the grid and grows in both the horizontal and vertical directions, taking up whatever extra space is available in the layout.

Listing 8-5. Constructing the Buttons That Play the AudioClips

```
    private void createClipList(GridPane grid) {
        final VBox vbox = new VBox(30);
        vbox.setAlignment(Pos.TOP_CENTER);

        final Label clipLabel = new Label("Code Monkey To-Do List:");
        clipLabel.setId("clipLabel");

        final Button getUpButton = new Button("Get Up, Get Coffee");
        getUpButton.setPrefWidth(300);
        getUpButton.setOnAction(createPlayHandler(coffeeClip));

        final Button goToJobButton = new Button("Go to Job");
        goToJobButton.setPrefWidth(300);
        goToJobButton.setOnAction(createPlayHandler(jobClip));

        final Button meetingButton = new Button("Have Boring Meeting");
        meetingButton.setPrefWidth(300);
        meetingButton.setOnAction(createPlayHandler(meetingClip));

        final Hyperlink link = new Hyperlink("About Code Monkey...");
        link.setOnAction(new EventHandler<ActionEvent>() {
          @Override
          public void handle(ActionEvent event) {
            WebView wv = new WebView();
            wv.getEngine().load("http://www.jonathancoulton.com/2006/04/14/" +
                                "thing-a-week-29-code-monkey/");

            Scene scene = new Scene(wv, 720, 480);

            Stage stage = new Stage();
            stage.setTitle("Code Monkey");
            stage.setScene(scene);
            stage.show();
          }
        });
```

```
    vbox.getChildren().addAll(clipLabel, getUpButton, goToJobButton,
                             meetingButton, link);

    GridPane.setHalignment(vbox, HPos.CENTER);
    GridPane.setHgrow(vbox, Priority.ALWAYS);
    GridPane.setVgrow(vbox, Priority.ALWAYS);
    grid.add(vbox, 0, 0, GridPane.REMAINING, 1);
}

private EventHandler<ActionEvent> createPlayHandler(final AudioClip clip) {
    return new EventHandler<ActionEvent>() {
      @Override
      public void handle(ActionEvent event) {
        clip.play(volumeSlider.getValue(), balanceSlider.getValue(),
                  rateSlider.getValue(), 0, 0);
      }
    };
}
```

As each Button is created, a new EventHandler is also created that plays the appropriate AudioClip for that Button. The play method in the EventHandler uses the current values of the volume, rate, and balance sliders as its arguments. The last two arguments of the play method are set to zero, but these can be used to specify the pan and priority of the AudioClip when it is played. We discuss these two properties in the next section.

AudioClip Wrap-Up

There are two properties of an AudioClip that we have not shown in the preceding examples: pan and priority. The pan property allows you to move the center of your clip. Setting it to 1.0 moves the clip completely to the left channel, and setting it to 1.0 moves it completely to the right. The default setting of 0.0 leaves the clip as it was originally. Unlike the balance property, which merely adjusts the relative volumes of the left and right channels, the pan property actually remixes the two channels. This allows you to introduce some or all of the left channel into the right channel and vice versa. It really only makes sense to use the pan property on actual stereo sound effects whose right and left channels differ. Setting the pan on a mono sound has the exact same outcome as adjusting the balance, and balance is much less computationally expensive. You can set or retrieve a clip's current pan setting using the setPan and getPan methods and the property is exposed by the panProperty method.

You can optionally assign a priority to your AudioClips. This is an IntegerProperty that specifies the relative priority of your sound effects. The higher the number, the more importance you are assigning to that AudioClip. If you exceed the limit of AudioClip playbacks that the system can handle, the priorities are used to determine which clips are stopped. The number of clips that can be played is not specified precisely, nor can it be queried in the current version of JavaFX. Therefore, if you play a lot of AudioClips at once, as might be the case for a game, you should consider assigning priorities to your sound effects.

AudioClips are very useful for playing short, low-latency sound effects. If you need to play songs or background music instead, the JavaFX media classes are a better choice.

Working with Media

The JavaFX media classes make it very easy to work with audio and video files by simply treating them as two different types of media. Therefore, the basic playback of an audio or video file can be accomplished using only a few lines of (nearly identical) code. On the other hand, there is also some depth to the API that allows you to go beyond simple playback to enhance the experience for your users. In the remainder of this chapter, we start with simple audio playback and then show you how to tap into the power of this API and take your media-based applications to the next level.

The JavaFX media classes are located in the javafx.scene.media package. There are three main classes named `Media`, `MediaPlayer`, and `MediaView` as well as a number of supporting classes. The `Media` class encapsulates the audio or video resource to be played. The string representation of the URI identifying this resource is passed to the `Media` constructor as its only argument. The Media object exposes properties that describe the media's width and height (when dealing with video), its duration, and two properties related to error handling. Once constructed, a `Media` object can be passed to the constructor of a `MediaPlayer` instance, which provides a set of methods for controlling the playback of the audio or video resource. And finally, a `MediaPlayer` can be passed to the constructor of a `MediaView` node in order for the video to be displayed in the scene graph. The relationship among these three classes is illustrated in Figure 8-3.[2]

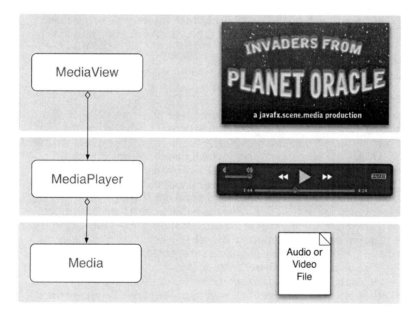

Figure 8-3. *The JavaFX 2.0 media classes*

---

[2] Naturally the invaders are initially greeted with fear and distrust. In a surprise plot twist, they turn out to be a competent and helpful group of people.

It bears repeating that of these three classes, only `MediaView` *is-a* `Node` and therefore capable of being inserted into the scene graph. This means we have taken a slight liberty in showing a set of visual controls associated with the `MediaPlayer` class in Figure 8-3. In reality you will have to create your own buttons and sliders, wired to `MediaPlayer` methods, to allow the user to control the playback of the media in your application. We have plenty of opportunity to show you how to do this in the examples that follow in this chapter. Let's begin our in-depth look at these media classes by creating an application that plays audio files.

Playing Audio

Playing audio files involves only the `Media` and `MediaPlayer` classes. There is no video to deal with, thus no MediaView is needed. Listing 8-6 shows the minimum amount of code needed to play audio with JavaFX.

Listing 8-6. *A Very Simple Application That Plays an Audio File*

```
public class AudioPlayer1 extends Application {

    public static void main(String[] args) {
        launch(args);
    }

    @Override
    public void start(Stage primaryStage) {
        URL resource = getClass().getResource("resources/keeper.mp3");
        Media media = new Media(resource.toString());
        MediaPlayer mediaPlayer = new MediaPlayer(media);
        mediaPlayer.play();

        primaryStage.setTitle("Audio Player 1");
        primaryStage.setWidth(200);
        primaryStage.setHeight(200);
        primaryStage.show();
    }
}
```

This simplistic application starts by finding the URL of an audio file resource that is packaged within its jar file. The String form of the resource URL is passed as the `source` parameter to the `Media` constructor. The `Media` class can also load resources from the Internet or from the local filesystem just like an `AudioClip`. Once the `Media` object is constructed, it is used to construct a new `MediaPlayer` and the `MediaPlayer`'s `play` method is called to begin playback. This application has no actual scene to display so the width and height of the `Stage` are set to 200 so that the resulting window will be visible. If your audio needs are no more complicated than loading a sound file and starting it playing, your job is now finished. However, the code in Listing 8-6 is not exactly production quality yet.

■ **Note** Once a MediaPlayer is created, its Media object cannot be changed. If you wish to change the song or video that is currently playing, you must create a new MediaPlayer for the new Media object. Multiple MediaPlayers can share one Media object.

Error Handling

The Media class has two properties, error and onError, that help you deal with any errors that occur during playback. You can manually check for errors by calling the getError method, which will return a MediaException object. This method will return a nonnull value from the underlying errorProperty if an error has occurred. You can listen for errors by attaching an InvalidationListener or ChangeListener to the errorProperty of the Media class. As a convenience, you can simply pass a Runnable to the setOnError method in order to achieve the same result. The Runnable's run method will be called if an error occurs. It is safe to update the scene graph from the run method inasmuch as it is called on the JavaFX application thread.

Media instances are rarely used on their own. Normally they will be passed to a MediaPlayer as a constructor argument. The MediaPlayer class replicates the error and onError properties of Media, and all Media errors are forwarded to the error property and the onError callback of the enclosing MediaPlayer instance. Therefore, you only need to use the MediaPlayer error properties to catch errors from both the MediaPlayer and its underlying Media object all in one place.

Exceptions, including MediaExceptions, can also occur during the construction of a Media or MediaPlayer instance. Obviously these exceptions will not be available in the object's error property because the object does not exist yet. If you want to be thorough in your error handling, you should also enclose your constructors in try-catch blocks in addition to setting MediaPlayer's onError handler. This error-handling technique is demonstrated in Listing 8-7.

Listing 8-7. Error Handling with the Media Classes

```
try {
  final URL resource = getClass().getResource("resources/keeper.mp3");
  final Media media = new Media(resource.toString());

  final MediaPlayer mediaPlayer = new MediaPlayer(media);
  mediaPlayer.setOnError(new Runnable() {
    @Override
    public void run() {
      // Handle Media and MediaPlayer errors during playback...
      final String errorMessage = media.getError().getMessage();
    }
  });

  mediaPlayer.play();

} catch (RuntimeException re) {
  // Handle Media and MediaPlayer construction errors...
}
```

Displaying Metadata

Most media file formats have the ability to embed *metadata*, data that describe the song or video. MP3 files, for instance, have ID3 tags that can be used to identify the artist, album, track number, and even the year that the song was released. Many MP3 files also have embedded images of the artist, the album cover, or a logo (in the case of podcasts and such). The JavaFX Media class reads these metadata and presents them to the developer in the form of an ObservableMap of key-value pairs. The keys are Strings that identify the metadata and the values are Objects, most likely a String or an Image.

Although there is no guarantee as to which metadata are present in any given media file, there are a few fields that are very common: artist, title, album, and year. In addition, if any image is embedded in a file's metadata, the Media class will give you access to it using the "image" key. Listing 8-8 shows you how to add the ability to receive metadata notifications when a new Media object is created.

In the listing we are loading an episode of the Java Posse podcast from an Internet URL. Immediately after the Media instance is created, we get a reference to its metadata map by calling the getMetadata method. We then attach a MapChangeListener to the metadata map that makes a check to see if a new key-value pair was added to the map. If so, the new key and value are passed to the handleMetadata helper method, which checks to see if it is a piece of metadata that we are interested in handling. This is the code that is shown in bold in Listing 8-8.

Listing 8-8. *Listening for Metadata from the Media Class*

```
private Label artist;
private Label album;
private Label title;
private Label year;
private ImageView albumCover;

private void createMedia() {
  try {
    media = new Media("http://traffic.libsyn.com/dickwall/JavaPosse373.mp3");
    media.getMetadata().addListener(new MapChangeListener<String, Object>() {
      @Override
      public void onChanged(Change<? extends String, ? extends Object> ch) {
        if (ch.wasAdded()) {
          handleMetadata(ch.getKey(), ch.getValueAdded());
        }
      }
    });

    mediaPlayer = new MediaPlayer(media);
    mediaPlayer.setOnError(new Runnable() {
      @Override
      public void run() {
        final String errorMessage = media.getError().getMessage();
        // Handle errors during playback
        System.out.println("MediaPlayer Error: " + errorMessage);
      }
    });

    mediaPlayer.play();
```

```
    } catch (RuntimeException re) {
      // Handle construction errors
      System.out.println("Caught Exception: " + re.getMessage());
    }
  }

  private void handleMetadata(String key, Object value) {
    if (key.equals("album")) {
      album.setText(value.toString());
    } else if (key.equals("artist")) {
      artist.setText(value.toString());
    } if (key.equals("title")) {
      title.setText(value.toString());
    } if (key.equals("year")) {
      year.setText(value.toString());
    } if (key.equals("image")) {
      albumCover.setImage((Image)value);
    }
  }
}
```

If the handleMetadata method determines that the new metadata are of interest to the program, it sets the metadata's value as either the string of a Label control or the Image of an ImageView node. Listing 8-9 shows the rest of this application's code wherein these controls are created and placed into a GridPane for display to the user. There have also been some minor additions to the *media.css* style sheet to set the size of the fonts used in the Labels. You can view these changes in the source files for the AudioPlayer2 example application in the book's example code.

Listing 8-9. *Displaying the Metadata Information in the Scene Graph*

```
public class AudioPlayer2 extends Application {
  private Media media;
  private MediaPlayer mediaPlayer;

  private Label artist;
  private Label album;
  private Label title;
  private Label year;
  private ImageView albumCover;

  public static void main(String[] args) {
    launch(args);
  }

  @Override
  public void start(Stage primaryStage) {
    createControls();
    createMedia();

    final Scene scene = new Scene(createGridPane(), 800, 400);
    final URL stylesheet = getClass().getResource("media.css");
    scene.getStylesheets().add(stylesheet.toString());
```

```
    primaryStage.setScene(scene);
    primaryStage.setTitle("Audio Player 2");
    primaryStage.show();
}

private GridPane createGridPane() {
    final GridPane gp = new GridPane();
    gp.setPadding(new Insets(10));
    gp.setHgap(20);
    gp.add(albumCover, 0, 0, 1, GridPane.REMAINING);
    gp.add(title, 1, 0);
    gp.add(artist, 1, 1);
    gp.add(album, 1, 2);
    gp.add(year, 1, 3);

    final ColumnConstraints c0 = new ColumnConstraints();
    final ColumnConstraints c1 = new ColumnConstraints();
    c1.setHgrow(Priority.ALWAYS);
    gp.getColumnConstraints().addAll(c0, c1);

    final RowConstraints r0 = new RowConstraints();
    r0.setValignment(VPos.TOP);
    gp.getRowConstraints().addAll(r0, r0, r0, r0);

    return gp;
}

private void createControls() {
    artist = new Label();
    artist.setId("artist");
    album = new Label();
    album.setId("album");
    title = new Label();
    title.setId("title");
    year = new Label();
    year.setId("year");

    final Reflection reflection = new Reflection();
    reflection.setFraction(0.2);

    final URL url = getClass().getResource("resources/defaultAlbum.png");
    final Image image = new Image(url.toString());

    albumCover = new ImageView(image);
    albumCover.setFitWidth(240);
    albumCover.setPreserveRatio(true);
    albumCover.setSmooth(true);
    albumCover.setEffect(reflection);
}
```

```
    private void createMedia() {
      // As previously shown...
    }

    private void handleMetadata(String key, Object value) {
      // As previously shown...
    }
}
```

The AudioPlayer2 application with the Java Posse podcast's metadata on display is shown in Figure 8-4. You can see from the code in Listing 8-9 and the image in Figure 8-4 that we have also added a subtle reflection to the image that was read from the metadata. Although we don't want to abuse these types of effects, it is really nice that JavaFX allows us to create them so easily.

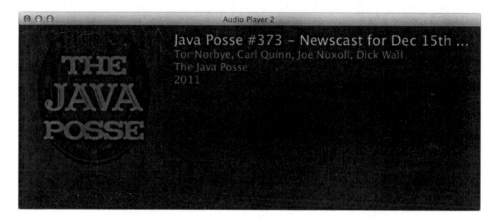

Figure 8-4. *Displaying media metadata in the second version of the audio player*

Loading Media

Loading media files from a predetermined jar resource or Internet URL is limiting if this audio player is going to grow into a reasonably useful application. We support two ways of selecting content. First, we allow the user to select files from the local filesystem using the JavaFX **FileChooser**. We also support dragging and dropping a file or URL onto the audio player. Another issue that requires attention is scaling the application's source code. It is growing too large to be contained in a single file and a single class. It is time to inflict a bit of architecture upon our sample application.

We begin by isolating the code that deals with the **Media**, its associated metadata, and its **MediaPlayer** into a separate class named **SongModel**. This class will expose a set of JavaFX properties (refer back to Chapter 3, *Properties and Bindings,* if you need a refresher) that represent the metadata of the current media and one that exposes the **MediaPlayer** instance. It also defines a method for setting a media URL, which will trigger the creation of new **Media** and **MediaPlayer** instances. This class is shown in Listing 8-10.

Listing 8-10. *The SongModel Class*

```
public final class SongModel {
  private static final String DEFAULT_IMG_URL =
      SongModel.class.getResource("resources/defaultAlbum.png").toString();
  private static final Image DEFAULT_ALBUM_COVER =
      new Image(DEFAULT_IMG_URL);

  private final StringProperty album =
      new SimpleStringProperty(this, "album");
  private final StringProperty artist =
      new SimpleStringProperty(this,"artist");
  private final StringProperty title =
      new SimpleStringProperty(this, "title");
  private final StringProperty year =
      new SimpleStringProperty(this, "year");

  private final ObjectProperty<Image> albumCover =
      new SimpleObjectProperty<Image>(this, "albumCover");

  private final ReadOnlyObjectWrapper<MediaPlayer> mediaPlayer =
      new ReadOnlyObjectWrapper<MediaPlayer>(this, "mediaPlayer");

  public SongModel() {
    resetProperties();
  }

  public void setURL(String url) {
    if (mediaPlayer.get() != null) {
      mediaPlayer.get().stop();
    }

    initializeMedia(url);
  }

  public String getAlbum() { return album.get(); }
  public void setAlbum(String value) { album.set(value); }
  public StringProperty albumProperty() { return album; }

  // The three methods above are repeated for the artist, title,
  // year, and albumCover properties...

  public MediaPlayer getMediaPlayer() { return mediaPlayer.get(); }
  public ReadOnlyObjectProperty<MediaPlayer> mediaPlayerProperty() {
    return mediaPlayer.getReadOnlyProperty();
  }
```

```java
    private void resetProperties() {
      setArtist("");
      setAlbum("");
      setTitle("");
      setYear("");

      setAlbumCover(DEFAULT_ALBUM_COVER);
    }

  private void initializeMedia(String url) {
      resetProperties();

      try {
        final Media media = new Media(url);
        media.getMetadata().addListener(new MapChangeListener<String,Object>() {
          @Override
          public void onChanged(Change<? extends String, ? extends Object> ch) {
            if (ch.wasAdded()) {
              handleMetadata(ch.getKey(), ch.getValueAdded());
            }
          }
        });

        mediaPlayer.setValue(new MediaPlayer(media));
        mediaPlayer.get().setOnError(new Runnable() {
          @Override
          public void run() {
            String errorMessage = mediaPlayer.get().getError().getMessage();
            // Handle errors during playback
            System.out.println("MediaPlayer Error: " + errorMessage);
          }
        });
      } catch (RuntimeException re) {
        // Handle construction errors
        System.out.println("Caught Exception: " + re.getMessage());
      }
    }

    private void handleMetadata(String key, Object value) {
      if (key.equals("album")) {
        setAlbum(value.toString());
      } else if (key.equals("artist")) {
        setArtist(value.toString());
      } if (key.equals("title")) {
        setTitle(value.toString());
      } if (key.equals("year")) {
        setYear(value.toString());
      } if (key.equals("image")) {
        setAlbumCover((Image)value);
      }
    }
}
```

The `MediaPlayer` property is exposed as a `ReadOnlyObjectProperty` inasmuch as we don't want users of the class to be able to set the `MediaPlayer` instance to a new value. Now that we have a nicely encapsulated class for our media, we turn our attention to separating our user interface code into more manageable chunks, or *views*. A new AbstractView base class is created to eliminate duplication by holding some code that is common to all of our views. This small class is shown in Listing 8-11.

Listing 8-11. *The AbstractView Base Class*

```
public abstract class AbstractView {
  protected final SongModel songModel;
  protected final Node viewNode;

  public AbstractView(SongModel songModel) {
    this.songModel = songModel;
    this.viewNode = initView();
  }

  public Node getViewNode() {
    return viewNode;
  }

  protected abstract Node initView();
}
```

This class ensures that all of the views have access to the application's `SongModel` instance. It also provides a pattern for easily writing new views. Each new view only has to provide a concrete implementation of the `initView` method. This method returns a top-level `Node` that is the root node of a scene graph for that view.

With those two pieces of infrastructure in place, we can proceed to create some actual views. The obvious place to start is to move the GridPane, Labels, and ImageView that display the metadata in AudioPlayer2 into a new view class named `MetadataView`. The source code for this class is not presented here because it is virtually the same user interface code that was shown in the `createGridPane` and `createControls` methods of Listing 8-9. If you are curious, the view can be found in the source code of the AudioPlayer3 project.

We now return to the original goal of letting the user select a media resource to play by means of a `FileChooser` dialog box or by dragging and dropping a file or URL onto the application. A new view is created to hold controls for our audio player. Its first component is a button that shows the `FileChooser` when clicked. The button's event handler will get the file chosen by the user and pass the file's URL to the `SongModel`. This view, called PlayerControlsView, is shown in Listing 8-12.

Listing 8-12. *The PlayerControlsView Class*

```
class PlayerControlsView extends AbstractView {

  public PlayerControlsView(SongModel songModel) {
    super(songModel);
  }

  @Override
  protected Node initView() {
    final HBox hbox = new HBox();
```

353

```
      hbox.setPadding(new Insets(10));

      final Button openButton = new Button();
      openButton.setId("openButton");
      openButton.setOnAction(new OpenHandler());
      openButton.setPrefWidth(32);
      openButton.setPrefHeight(32);

      hbox.getChildren().addAll(openButton);
      return hbox;
    }

    private class OpenHandler implements EventHandler<ActionEvent> {
      @Override
      public void handle(ActionEvent event) {
        FileChooser fc = new FileChooser();
        fc.setTitle("Pick a Sound File");
        File song = fc.showOpenDialog(viewNode.getScene().getWindow());
        if (song != null) {
          songModel.setURL(song.toURI().toString());
          songModel.getMediaPlayer().play();
        }
      }
    }
  }
}
```

The code fragment shown below sets the **openButton**'s icon from the CSS style sheet.

```
#openButton {
  -fx-graphic: url("resources/music_note.png");
}
```

The next step is to add the drag and drop support. The drag event handlers are added to the Scene because we want to support the dropping of a file or URL anywhere on the application. Listing 8-13 shows the **initSceneDragAndDrop** method that creates these event handlers.

Listing 8-13. The DragEvent Handlers for the Scene

```
private void initSceneDragAndDrop(Scene scene) {
    scene.setOnDragOver(new EventHandler<DragEvent>() {
      @Override
      public void handle(DragEvent event) {
        Dragboard db = event.getDragboard();
        if (db.hasFiles() || db.hasUrl()) {
          event.acceptTransferModes(TransferMode.ANY);
        }
        event.consume();
      }
    });
```

```
    scene.setOnDragDropped(new EventHandler<DragEvent>() {
      @Override
      public void handle(DragEvent event) {
        Dragboard db = event.getDragboard();
        String url = null;

        if (db.hasFiles()) {
          url = db.getFiles().get(0).toURI().toString();
        } else if (db.hasUrl()) {
          url = db.getUrl();
        }

        if (url != null) {
          songModel.setURL(url);
          songModel.getMediaPlayer().play();
        }

        event.setDropCompleted(url != null);
        event.consume();
      }
    });
  }
```

The handler for the `DRAG_OVER` event checks to make sure that this drag contains either files or a URL. If so, it calls `DragEvent`'s `acceptTransferModes` method to set which types of `TransferModes` are supported. In this case we indicate that any type of transfer is supported. Other options are `COPY`, `LINK`, and `MOVE`. Because we are interested only in the string form of the file's URL or in an actual URL string, we can accept any type of transfer. It is important to call the `acceptTransferModes` method in your `DRAG_OVER` handler because on many platforms that will affect the visual feedback the user receives as she moves her drag cursor over your window.

The `DRAG_DROPPED` handler gets the URL of the first file in the list of dropped files or the URL itself if that is what is being dragged. Just as with the file chooser code, it then passes this URL to the `SongModel` and begins playback of the song. The final step in the drag operation is to call the `setDropCompleted` method of the `DragEvent` to inform it that the drop was successfully completed.

Listing 8-14 shows the new `Application` class that creates the views and initializes the drag and drop handling. The `SongModel` instance is created in the constructor of the `AudioPlayer3` class and gets passed to the application's views later in the start method. The code that creates and initializes the `Scene`, loads the style sheets, and initializes the `Stage` is mostly unchanged from AudioPlayer2, with the minor addition of calling the `initSceneDragAndDrop` method that was shown in Listing 8-13. Another difference is that we are now using a BorderPane layout node to keep our metadata view on top of the controls view.

Listing 8-14. *The AudioPlayer3 Application Class*

```
public class AudioPlayer3 extends Application {
  private final SongModel songModel;

  private MetadataView metaDataView;
  private PlayerControlsView playerControlsView;
```

```
    public static void main(String[] args) {
      launch(args);
    }

    public AudioPlayer3() {
      songModel = new SongModel();
    }

    @Override
    public void start(Stage primaryStage) {
      songModel.setURL("http://traffic.libsyn.com/dickwall/JavaPosse373.mp3");
      metaDataView = new MetadataView(songModel);
      playerControlsView = new PlayerControlsView(songModel);

      final BorderPane root = new BorderPane();
      root.setCenter(metaDataView.getViewNode());
      root.setBottom(playerControlsView.getViewNode());

      final Scene scene = new Scene(root, 800, 400);
      initSceneDragAndDrop(scene);

      final URL stylesheet = getClass().getResource("media.css");
      scene.getStylesheets().add(stylesheet.toString());

      primaryStage.setScene(scene);
      primaryStage.setTitle("Audio Player 3");
      primaryStage.show();
      songModel.getPlayer().play();
    }

  private void initSceneDragAndDrop(Scene scene) {
    // Shown in Listing 8.13.
  }
}
```

We now have a good beginning to an audio player application, but it's pretty annoying when you can't control the playback of the songs. It's time to remedy that.

Controlling Playback

There are three main methods in the MediaPlayer class that are used to control the playback of Media objects: play, pause, and stop. None of these methods takes any parameters, but they do affect the MediaPlayer's status and currentTime properties. The play method is used to begin the playback of the media. As the media are played, MediaPlayer's currentTime property is continuously updated to indicate the progress of the playback. Because currentTime is of type Duration, it can give you the position of the playback in milliseconds, seconds, minutes, or hours. The pause method will cause the playback to pause and a subsequent call to play will restart the playback from where it was paused. Calling the stop method stops playback and resets the currentTime variable to the start of the Media.

When a MediaPlayer object is first created, its status property is initialized to MediaPlayer.Status.UNKNOWN. Once the Media resource begins loading and there are no other errors, the status will change to MediaPlayer.Status.READY. Calling the play method causes the status variable to change to MediaPlayer.Status.PLAYING. Calling stop or pause will reset the status to MediaPlayer.Status.STOPPED or MediaPlayer.Status.PAUSED, respectively. Other possible values for status include MediaPlayer.Status.HALTED and MediaPlayer.Status.STALLED. The halted state means that a critical unrecoverable error has occurred. Once entered, the MediaPlayer will never exit the halted state. The stalled status will occur when a media stream runs out of data during playback and must wait until more data become available. You can call the play method on the MediaPlayer at any time, even when its status is UNKNOWN. In that case, playback will begin as soon as the MediaPlayer is in the READY state.

Laying Out the Player Controls

It is time to revisit the PlayerControlsView that we created in Listing 8-12. In addition to the openButton we currently have, we add the ability to control playback, volume, and playback position as well as display the media's current time, total duration, and the status of the MediaPlayer. That is a lot to display in one layout, so we use JavaFX's most flexible layout node, the GridPane, to keep track of it all. The GridPane layout that we end up with is shown in Figure 8-5.

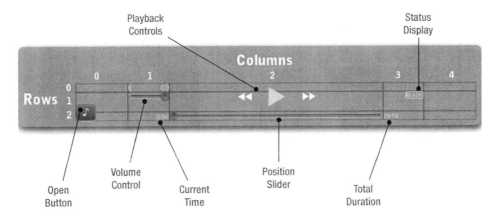

Figure 8-5. *The GridPane layout of the media player controls*

Some controls in Figure 8-5, such as the playback controls and the open button, span multiple rows. Others use special alignment constraints. Listing 8-15 shows the new initView method of the PlayerControlsView that creates this layout.

Listing 8-15. *The GridPane Layout for the Player Controls*

```
@Override
protected Node initView() {
  final Button openButton = createOpenButton();
  controlPanel = createControlPanel();
  volumeSlider = createSlider("volumeSlider");
  statusLabel = createLabel("Buffering", "statusDisplay");
  positionSlider = createSlider("positionSlider");
```

```
    totalDurationLabel = createLabel("00:00", "mediaText");
    currentTimeLabel = createLabel("00:00", "mediaText");

    final ImageView volLow = new ImageView();
    volLow.setId("volumeLow");

    final ImageView volHigh = new ImageView();
    volHigh.setId("volumeHigh");

    final GridPane gp = new GridPane();
    gp.setHgap(1);
    gp.setVgap(1);
    gp.setPadding(new Insets(10));

    final ColumnConstraints buttonCol = new ColumnConstraints(100);
    final ColumnConstraints spacerCol = new ColumnConstraints(40, 80, 80);
    final ColumnConstraints middleCol = new ColumnConstraints();
    middleCol.setHgrow(Priority.ALWAYS);

    gp.getColumnConstraints().addAll(buttonCol, spacerCol, middleCol,
                                     spacerCol, buttonCol);

    GridPane.setValignment(openButton, VPos.BOTTOM);
    GridPane.setHalignment(volHigh, HPos.RIGHT);
    GridPane.setValignment(volumeSlider, VPos.TOP);
    GridPane.setHalignment(statusLabel, HPos.RIGHT);
    GridPane.setValignment(statusLabel, VPos.TOP);
    GridPane.setHalignment(currentTimeLabel, HPos.RIGHT);

    gp.add(openButton, 0, 0, 1, 3);
    gp.add(volLow, 1, 0);
    gp.add(volHigh, 1, 0);
    gp.add(volumeSlider, 1, 1);
    gp.add(controlPanel, 2, 0, 1, 2);
    gp.add(statusLabel, 3, 1);
    gp.add(currentTimeLabel, 1, 2);
    gp.add(positionSlider, 2, 2);
    gp.add(totalDurationLabel, 3, 2);

    return gp;
}

private Slider createSlider(String id) {
    final Slider slider = new Slider(0.0, 1.0, 0.1);
    slider.setId(id);
    slider.setValue(0);
    return slider;
}
```

```
private Label createLabel(String text, String styleClass) {
  final Label label = new Label(text);
  label.getStyleClass().add(styleClass);
  return label;
}
```

The method starts by creating the controls and `ImageView`s that will be placed in the layout. We have already seen the code that creates the `openButton` in Listing 8-12. The `createControlPanel` method is presented later in this section. The next step is to create the `GridPane` and its `ColumnConstraints`. Three different column constraints are created. The first, `buttonCol`, is for the open button and has a fixed width of 100 pixels. The buttons are smaller than 100 pixels, so the width of this column creates a nice buffer between the buttons and the actual player controls. The second column constraint is the `spacerCol` and can vary in width from a minimum of 40 pixels to a maximum of 80 pixels, with a preferred width that is also 80 pixels. This constraint is used for the columns that mainly contain the volume slider and the status display. And finally we have the `middleCol` constraint. The column having this constraint is allowed to grow to fill the remaining space left over from the other columns. It will contain the position slider and the playback controls.

The constraints are added in the following order: `buttonCol`, `spacerCol`, `middleCol`, `spacerCol`, and `buttonCol`. We added the last buttonCol constraint even though we don't have any controls to put in that last column. This keeps the layout symmetrical and keeps the player controls centered in the window.

Several of the controls also have special alignments that are set using the `setHalignment` and `setValignment` methods to control their horizontal and vertical alignment. For example, the openButton is aligned to the bottom of the three cells that it spans. As previously mentioned, this is to create "white space" between the button and the actual player controls. Another example is the `volHigh` `ImageView`. It is aligned to the right of its cell. The reason is that we add the volLow and volHigh images to the same GridPane cell. Because volLow is left-aligned (the default) and volHigh is right-aligned, they don't overlap and automatically maintain their proper positions above the volume slider even when the layout is resized.

The final step, of course, is actually to add the controls to the `GridPane`. We used GridPane's add methods in Listing 8-15. There are two different variants of the method. The first allows you to specify the Node to be added along with its column index and its row index. The second version of the add method additionally allows you to specify the number of columns and rows that the `Node` should span. This latter version is used for the player controls (the `controlPanel` Node and the `openButton`) to allow them to span multiple rows.

With its ability to specify row and column sizing constraints, custom alignments, and even display multiple nodes per cell, the GridPane is by far the most powerful and flexible layout in your JavaFX toolkit. It really pays to become familiar with all of its abilities.

Creating Playback Controls

Now that you have a basic knowledge of controlling playback with a MediaPlayer and our layout is now in place, let's consider the implementation of a play/pause button. This simple control will show a play icon if the `MediaPlayer` is not currently in the `PLAYING` state. If the `MediaPlayer` is `PLAYING`, the button will show a pause icon. If pressed while the MediaPlayer is in the PLAYING state, the button's event handler will call the MediaPlayer's pause method. Otherwise, the MediaPlayer's play method will be called. The code that loads the play and pause icons, creates the button, and attaches the event handler that implements this logic is shown in Listing 8-16.

Listing 8-16. *The Logic Behind the Play/Pause Button*

```
private Button createPlayPauseButton() {
  URL url = getClass().getResource("resources/pause.png");
  pauseImg = new Image(url.toString());

  url = getClass().getResource("resources/play.png");
  playImg = new Image(url.toString());

  playPauseIcon = new ImageView(playImg);

  final Button playPauseButton = new Button(null, playPauseIcon);
  playPauseButton.setId("playPauseButton");
  playPauseButton.setOnAction(new EventHandler<ActionEvent>() {
    @Override
    public void handle(ActionEvent arg0) {
      final MediaPlayer mediaPlayer = songModel.getMediaPlayer();
      if (mediaPlayer.getStatus() == MediaPlayer.Status.PLAYING) {
        mediaPlayer.pause();
      } else {
        mediaPlayer.play();
      }
    }
  });
  return playPauseButton;
}
```

The first step in creating the playPauseButton is to load the two images that will serve as the button's icons. The playPauseIcon, an ImageView, is then initialized with the play Image. This ImageView serves as the playPauseButton's graphic node. The two Images and the ImageView are private members of the PlayerControlsView class because we need to access them later to set the button's icon according to the state of the media player.

The playPauseButton is also given an ID that is used by the application's style sheet to apply additional styles to the button. These styles make the button's background completely transparent unless the mouse is currently hovering over it. In that case, a translucent background is applied to give the user some visual feedback that the button is live. These styles are shown in the code fragment below.

```
#playPauseButton {
  -fx-background-color: transparent;
}
#playPauseButton:hover {
  -fx-background-color: rgb(255, 255, 255, 0.1);
}
```

To switch the icon of the playPauseButton based on the state of the MediaPlayer, we need to listen to the MediaPlayer's status property. Unfortunately, the status property is not updated on the JavaFX application thread, so we cannot bind the button's icon directly to the property. Doing so would violate JavaFX's threading rules and could lead to "undefined behavior."

▪ **Caution** The status and currentTime properties are updated by the MediaPlayer and, as of JavaFX version 2.0.2, these updates do not occur on the JavaFX application thread. Therefore, you cannot bind to these properties or use them in binding expressions that affect live scene graph nodes. Doing so will result in strange bugs or exceptions because this violates the threading conventions of JavaFX.

The solution is to attach a listener to the property and use the Platform.runLater method to trigger updates on the application thread. This code is shown in Listing 8-17.

Listing 8-17. *Listening to Status Property Changes to Update the Scene Graph*

```
private class StatusListener implements InvalidationListener {
  @Override
  public void invalidated(Observable observable) {
    Platform.runLater(new Runnable() {
      @Override public void run() {
        updateStatus(songModel.getMediaPlayer().getStatus());
      }
    });
  }
}

private void updateStatus(Status newStatus) {
  if (newStatus == Status.UNKNOWN || newStatus == null) {
    controlPanel.setDisable(true);
    positionSlider.setDisable(true);
    statusLabel.setText("Buffering");
  } else {
    controlPanel.setDisable(false);
    positionSlider.setDisable(false);
    statusLabel.setText(newStatus.toString());

    if (newStatus == Status.PLAYING) {
      playPauseIcon.setImage(pauseImg);
    } else {
      playPauseIcon.setImage(playImg);
    }
  }
}
```

The StatusListener inner class is an InvalidationListener that, once added to a MediaPlayer's status property, will be notified whenever the status property changes. Its job is to call out to the private updateStatus method of its enclosing class on the JavaFX application thread. This makes it safe to update live scene graph nodes from within the updateStatus method. One of those updates is to set the image of the playPauseIcon (an ImageView node) as shown by the code that is highlighted within the updateStatus method.

We also update the text of the statusLabel that is used as the status display (refer back to Figure 8-5) as well as enable or disable the playback controls and the position slider any time the status changes. If the MediaPlayer's status is UNKNOWN or null, the player is not ready to begin playback and we indicate this status by displaying the "Buffering" string and disabling the playback controls. Any other MediaPlayer status will result in its name being displayed and the playback controls being enabled.

The status display is shown as a text string with a border around it. This is accomplished simply by using a Label control with some extra styling, which is shown in the following code.

```
.statusDisplay {
  -fx-border-color: white;
  -fx-border-radius: 2;
  -fx-border-width: 1;
  -fx-text-fill: white;
  -fx-font-size: 10pt;
}
```

The final piece of the playback puzzle is to stop the playback once the media end. MediaPlayer does not stop playback automatically when the end of the media is reached (technically, when the stopTime is reached; more on that in the *Seeking* section). You can stop playback explicitly by setting the MediaPlayer's onEndOfMedia callback property to a Runnable that invokes the stop method on the MediaPlayer.

```
songModel.getMediaPlayer().setOnEndOfMedia(new Runnable() {
  @Override
  public void run() {
    songModel.getMediaPlayer().stop();
  }
});
```

Calling MediaPlayer's stop method will set the status to STOPPED and reset the playback position to the start of the media by setting currentTime to 0.

■ **Note** It may seem a little odd that all of the MediaPlayer callback properties such as onEndOfMediaProperty, onError, and onReadyProperty are Runnables rather than EventHandlers as is done in the rest of the JavaFX API. The JavaFX team at Oracle has indicated that this was merely an oversight and that it will likely be changed in a future version.

As a final note on playback, MediaPlayer also contains a property named autoPlay. This Boolean property will cause playback to start as soon as possible if it is set to true. Occasionally it is a little too aggressive and we have found that playback will sometimes pause or even restart after a second or two when using this feature with audio files. Therefore we recommend that the play method be used in normal circumstances and that autoPlay only be used in situations where potential glitches in playback are not a serious concern and you just want to "fire and forget" the playback.

Seeking

The read-only property named currentTime always contains the MediaPlayer's current playback position. This property is of type Duration and can be set only by using the seek method. You can use the seek method to move the playback position to any time between the current startTime and stopTime. MediaPlayer's startTime and stopTime properties are initialized to 0 and totalDuration, respectively, where the totalDuration property, also read-only, specifies the total length of the media. The seek method has no effect if the MediaPlayer is currently in the STOPPED state.

Three controls in the audio player application make use of the seek functionality of the MediaPlayer. Perhaps the most obvious are the "seek to beginning" and "seek to end" buttons that are located on each side of the playPauseButton. These buttons show icons that consist of double triangles pointing to the left (seek to beginning) and right (seek to end). Listing 8-18 shows the createControlPanel method from the PlayerControlsView class in which these buttons are created.

Listing 8-18. Creating the Panel Containing the Play/Pause Button and the Seek Buttons

```java
private Node createControlPanel() {
  final HBox hbox = new HBox();
  hbox.setAlignment(Pos.CENTER);
  hbox.setFillHeight(false);

  final Button playPauseButton = createPlayPauseButton();

  final Button seekStartButton = new Button();
  seekStartButton.setId("seekStartButton");
  seekStartButton.setOnAction(new EventHandler<ActionEvent>() {
    @Override
    public void handle(ActionEvent event) {
      seekAndUpdatePosition(Duration.ZERO);
    }
  });

  final Button seekEndButton = new Button();
  seekEndButton.setId("seekEndButton");
  seekEndButton.setOnAction(new EventHandler<ActionEvent>() {
    @Override
    public void handle(ActionEvent event) {
      final MediaPlayer mediaPlayer = songModel.getMediaPlayer();
      final Duration totalDuration = mediaPlayer.getTotalDuration();
      final Duration oneSecond = Duration.seconds(1);
      seekAndUpdatePosition(totalDuration.subtract(oneSecond));
    }
  });

  hbox.getChildren().addAll(seekStartButton, playPauseButton, seekEndButton);
  return hbox;
}

private void seekAndUpdatePosition(Duration duration) {
  final MediaPlayer mediaPlayer = songModel.getMediaPlayer();

  if (mediaPlayer.getStatus() == Status.STOPPED) {
    mediaPlayer.pause();
  }
```

```
    mediaPlayer.seek(duration);

    if (mediaPlayer.getStatus() != Status.PLAYING) {
        updatePositionSlider(duration);
    }
}
```

Recall that Listing 8-16 showed the code for the `createPlayPauseButton` method. Listing 8-18 shows the creation of the rest of the playback control panel, namely the `seekStartButton` and the `seekEndButton`. These two buttons specify a seek time as the argument to the `seekAndUpdatePosition` helper method. For the `seekStartButton`, the seek time is `Duration.ZERO,` which will always seek to the start of the media. The seekEndButton actually seeks to one second prior to the end of the media, which is specified by the `MediaPlayer`'s `totalDuration` property. There is no reason that you cannot seek all the way to the `totalDuration` value. We arbitrarily decided to seek to one second prior to the end in order to let the user hear the very end of the song rather than just silence.

The assignment of the buttons' icons can be handled easily by the application's style sheet because these icons are static. The buttons also share some of the styling of the play/pause button as shown here.

```css
#seekStartButton {
  -fx-graphic: url("resources/prev.png");
}

#seekEndButton {
  -fx-graphic: url("resources/next.png");
}

#playPauseButton, #seekEndButton, #seekStartButton {
  -fx-background-color: transparent;
}

#playPauseButton:hover, #seekEndButton:hover, #seekStartButton:hover {
  -fx-background-color: rgb(255, 255, 255, 0.1);
}
```

The logic that controls the actual seek operation is encapsulated in the `seekAndUpdatePosition` method. Remember that the `seek` method has no effect if the player is in the `STOPPED` state. If that is the case, we need to call the `pause` method before the `seek` method is called or the seek will not work. Also note that after `seek` is called, we manually update the position slider if the `MediaPlayer` is not playing. This is necessary because the `MediaPlayer`'s `currentTime` property is not updated automatically by the call to seek. If the `MediaPlayer` is playing, this is not noticeable because playback will immediately continue from the new seek position, causing the `currentTime` to be quickly updated as well. On the other hand, if the MediaPlayer is not playing then the currentTime will not be updated, causing the position slider (which listens to and displays `currentTime` updates) to become out of sync with the new playback position. This is noticeable the next time the play button is pressed; the position slider will suddenly skip ahead or back to the position of the last seek.

This discussion has led nicely to the third control in the audio player that makes use of the seek function: the aforementioned position slider. The position slider does double duty; it displays the `currentTime` value but can also be dragged to a new position resulting in a call to the `seek` method. As you can probably guess, there are some subtleties to account for when getting this to work properly. Listing 8-19 shows the code required to implement the first part of this functionality: displaying the `currentTime` value on the position slider.

Listing 8-19. *Displaying the Value of currentTime on the Position Slider*

```
private class CurrentTimeListener implements InvalidationListener {
  @Override
  public void invalidated(Observable observable) {
    Platform.runLater(new Runnable() {
      @Override
      public void run() {
        final MediaPlayer mediaPlayer = songModel.getMediaPlayer();
        final Duration currentTime = mediaPlayer.getCurrentTime();
        currentTimeLabel.setText(formatDuration(currentTime));
        updatePositionSlider(currentTime);
      }
    });
  }
}

private void updatePositionSlider(Duration currentTime) {
  if (positionSlider.isValueChanging())
    return;

  final MediaPlayer mediaPlayer = songModel.getMediaPlayer();
  final Duration total = mediaPlayer.getTotalDuration();

  if (total == null || currentTime == null) {
    positionSlider.setValue(0);
  } else {
    positionSlider.setValue(currentTime.toMillis() / total.toMillis());
  }
}
```

Like the `status` property, `MediaPlayer`'s `currentTime` property is updated on a different thread than the main JavaFX application thread. Therefore we cannot bind to it directly and must instead attach an `InvalidationListener` that utilizes `Platform.runLater` in order to perform updates to live scene graph nodes such as the position slider. Listing 8-19 above shows the implementation of the `CurrentTimeListener` inner class that accomplishes this for us. The `Runnable`'s `run` method is called on the JavaFX application thread. Inside the `run` method we get the `currentTime` from the `MediaPlayer` and pass it as a parameter to the `updatePositionSlider` method. The `updatePositionSlider` method, also shown in Listing 8-19, first checks to see if the positionSlider's value is currently changing and, if so, returns without doing anything. We do this to make sure we don't change the slider's position while the user is currently dragging it. Doing so would make the slider's thumb bar flicker back and forth between the drag position and the position indicated by the `currentTime` value. Needless to say, this is an unwanted effect that we are careful to avoid. If the user is not currently changing the position slider's value, we are free to update it based on the value of currentTime and totalDuration. The position slider is created with minimum and maximum values of 0.0 and 1.0. The currentTime value is therefore divided by the media's `totalDuration` to calculate the correct value for the slider. If either `totalDuration` or `currentValue` is null, the slider is simply positioned at 0.

You probably noticed that the `CurrentTimeListener` also formats the value of `currentTime` and displays it as the text of the `currentTimeLabel`. If you refer back to Figure 8-5 you can see that the position slider is bracketed by two `Label` controls. On the left is a label that displays the `currentTime` value, and the `totalDuration` is displayed by a label to the right of the slider. The label displaying the `totalDuration` is set by a listener that is attached to `MediaPlayer`'s `totalDuration` property much like the

CurrentTimeListener shown above. Whenever the value of totalDuration changes, the listener calls the formatDuration method to create a String to use as the label's text. The formatDuration method used to format both of these values is shown in Listing 8-20.

Listing 8-20. *The formatDuration Method*

```java
private String formatDuration(Duration duration) {
    double millis = duration.toMillis();
    int seconds = (int) (millis / 1000) % 60;
    int minutes = (int) (millis / (1000 * 60));
    return String.format("%02d:%02d", minutes, seconds);
}
```

The formatDuration method takes a Duration as a parameter and returns a String with the format *mm:ss* where *mm* is minutes and *ss* is seconds. The minutes and seconds values will be zero-padded if they are only one digit long.

The second part of the position slider's job is to allow the user to set the playback position by dragging the slider back and forth. This is accomplished by listening for changes to the Slider's valueChangingProperty as shown in Listing 8-21.

Listing 8-21. *Listening to Position Slider Changes and Seeking*

```java
@Override
protected Node initView() {
  // Controls are created as was shown in Listing 8-15.

  positionSlider = createSlider("positionSlider");
  positionSlider.valueChangingProperty().addListener(new PositionListener());

  // Lay out the GridPane as was shown in Listing 8-15.
}

private class PositionListener implements ChangeListener<Boolean> {
  @Override
  public void changed(ObservableValue<? extends Boolean> observable,
                      Boolean oldValue, Boolean newValue) {
    if (oldValue && !newValue) {
      double pos = positionSlider.getValue();
      final MediaPlayer mediaPlayer = songModel.getMediaPlayer();
      final Duration seekTo = mediaPlayer.getTotalDuration().multiply(pos);
      seekAndUpdatePosition(seekTo);
    }
  }
}
```

PositionListener is a ChangeListener that waits for an old value of true (the value was changing) and a new value of false (the value is not changing anymore). When those conditions exist, we know the user has finished dragging the slider and it is time to seek the new position. The new position is calculated by multiplying the slider's new value, which you recall can range from 0.0 to 1.0, by the MediaPlayer's totalDuration to give the new Duration we pass to the seek method. This value is passed to the same seekAndUpdatePosition helper method that was shown in Listing 8-18, which handles the details of the call to the seek method.

Controlling Volume

The MediaPlayer class has two properties that control the volume of the audio playback. The volume property has a range that goes from 0.0 (mute) to 1.0 (maximum volume). This volume setting does not affect the master volume of the computer on which the audio is playing; it controls only the volume used by the MediaPlayer. The default value for the volume property is 1.0. There is also a Boolean property named mute. When this variable is set to true, the volume of the playback will be muted. Although playback continues, no sound will be heard. This is effectively equivalent to setting the volume property to 0.0, but muting playback allows you to cut out the sound and easily restore it later to its previous level without needing to read and reset the volume value.

The volume control in the audio player application is a Slider whose value can range from 0.0 to 1.0. Simply establishing a bidirectional binding between the Slider's value property and the MediaPlayer's volume property will allow the user to control the volume of the playback.

```
volumeSlider.valueProperty().bindBidirectional(mediaPlayer.volumeProperty());
```

That concludes our look at the player controls in our sample application. We have not shown the code that listens to changes in the mediaPlayer property itself in order to add and remove listeners cleanly. If you are interested in viewing the full source of the PlayerControlsView, it can be found in the AudioPlayer3 project in the book's Chapter 8 example code. Figure 8-6 shows what the audio player looks like at this point.

MediaPlayer also exposes a balance property, which controls the left-to-right balance of the audio. The range of the variable is from –1.0 (playing from the left speakers only) to 1.0 (playing from the right speakers only). If the audio that is playing has only one track (mono), that track will be played on both speakers and the balance control will act as a volume control allowing you to adjust how loud the left or right speaker is playing. If the audio has two tracks (stereo), the left track is played on the left speaker and the right track is played on the right speaker. In this case the balance control will allow you to fade back and forth between the left and right audio tracks. The default value of the balance variable is 0.0. The audio player application does not provide any controls to adjust the balance; we have mentioned it here only for completeness.

Figure 8-6. *The audio player's playback controls. "Just take a point called z in the complex plane. . . ."*

Repetition

Another MediaPlayer feature not used by the audio player sample application, but that certainly bears mentioning, is the ability to repeat the playback of your media. You can set the playback to repeat itself a certain number of times or to repeat forever. This behavior is controlled by the cycleCount property. The number of playback cycles that have been completed is available in the currentCount property. When the end of the media is reached, currentCount is incremented and, if it is less than cycleCount, playback will begin again automatically. The onRepeat callback function is called whenever playback is repeated. The usual call to onEndOfMedia will not be made until after the final repetition. Setting cycleCount to the value MediaPlayer.INDEFINITE will cause the playback to loop indefinitely.

The startTime and stopTime properties in the MediaPlayer class can affect where the media start and stop playing. As their names indicate, both of these properties are Duration types. The startTime property is initialized to 0 milliseconds whereas stopTime is initialized to the value of totalDuration. If a stopTime is set, playback will stop or repeat when that time is reached. On a related note, the cycleDuration property is a read-only property that gives you the current difference between the startTime and stopTime.

The ability to set the playback to repeat would be a handy feature for the audio player to have. It is not currently implemented in the sample application, but adding it would be a good exercise for the enthusiastic reader.

Audio Equalization

Two very cool new features of the JavaFX media API are the abilities to create an audio equalizer and to view the live spectrum of the audio as it's being played. The equalizer allows you to boost or attenuate the audio at certain frequencies. This change is then visible if you are visualizing the audio's frequency spectrum; the two features work together to give you or your users ultimate control of the playback experience.

Each MediaPlayer creates an AudioEqualizer instance that you can access using the getAudioEqualizer method. The AudioEqualizer class has an enabled property that you can use to enable or disable the equalizer. It also exposes an ObservableList of EqualizerBand instances. Each EqualizerBand has bandwidth, centerFrequency, and gain properties. The bandwidth and centerFrequency properties let you define the range of frequencies that are affected by the band, and the gain property boosts or attenuates those frequencies. All three of those properties are mutable. When you get a reference to the MediaPlayer's equalizer, it will already have a number of EqualizerBands defined. You can modify the settings of those bands, or remove some or all of them and replace them with your own bands.

Listing 8-22 shows the start of the EqualizerView class. This new view is used to display an audio equalizer and a live spectrum. It is added in the AudioPlayer4 example project in the book's source code.

Listing 8-22. The EqualizerView Class

```
public class EqualizerView extends AbstractView {
  private static final double START_FREQ = 250.0;
  private static final int BAND_COUNT = 7;
```

```
public EqualizerView(SongModel songModel) {
    super(songModel);
    createEQInterface();
}

@Override
protected Node initView() {
    final GridPane gp = new GridPane();
    gp.setPadding(new Insets(10));
    gp.setHgap(20);

    RowConstraints middle = new RowConstraints();
    RowConstraints outside = new RowConstraints();
    outside.setVgrow(Priority.ALWAYS);

    gp.getRowConstraints().addAll(outside, middle, outside);
    return gp;
}

private void createEQInterface() {
    final GridPane gp = (GridPane) getViewNode();
    final MediaPlayer mp = songModel.getMediaPlayer();

    createEQBands(gp, mp);
}

// To be continued...
}
```

Here we have the first portion of our new view. As with all of our custom `AbstractView` classes, we need to override the `initView` method so that we can create and return the view's "root" node. The equalizer view eventually shows the live audio spectrum above the equalizer controls. The `GridPane` is once again the natural choice for displaying content that consists of several rows of nodes. The top row contains our spectrum display, the middle row contains a set of labels identifying the center frequency of each `EqualizerBand`, and the bottom row consists of a row of sliders to adjust the gain of each `EqualizerBand`. We therefore create two row constraints to control the sizing behavior of these rows. Finally, the new GridPane instance is returned so that it can become the view's root node.

Because `initView` is called from the superclass constructor, it is called before the rest of `EqualizerView`'s constructor runs. Therefore, by the time that `createEQInterface` is called in the constructor, `initView` will already have completed. This is why we can call the `getViewNode` method in `createEQInterface` to retrieve the `GridPane` that was just created in `initView`. The `createEQInterface` method also retrieves the current `MediaPlayer` instance from `songModel` and passes them both to the `createEQBands` method, which creates the `EqualizerBand` instances and the `Slider` controls that are used to manipulate the gain of each band. This method is shown in Listing 8-23.

Listing 8-23. *Creating Equalizer Bands*

```
private void createEQBands(GridPane gp, MediaPlayer mp) {
    final ObservableList<EqualizerBand> bands =
            mp.getAudioEqualizer().getBands();
```

```
    bands.clear();

    double min = EqualizerBand.MIN_GAIN;
    double max = EqualizerBand.MAX_GAIN;
    double mid = (max - min) / 2;
    double freq = START_FREQ;

    // Create the equalizer bands with the gains preset to
    // a nice cosine wave pattern.
    for (int j = 0; j < BAND_COUNT; j++) {
      // Use j and BAND_COUNT to calculate a value between 0 and 2*pi
      double theta = (double)j / (double)(BAND_COUNT-1) * (2*Math.PI);

      // The cos function calculates a scale value between 0 and 0.4
      double scale = 0.4 * (1 + Math.cos(theta));

      // Set the gain to be a value between the midpoint and 0.9*max.
      double gain = min + mid + (mid * scale);

      bands.add(new EqualizerBand(freq, freq/2, gain));
      freq *= 2;
    }

    for (int i = 0; i < bands.size(); ++i) {
      EqualizerBand eb = bands.get(i);
      Slider s = createEQSlider(eb, min, max);

      final Label l = new Label(formatFrequency(eb.getCenterFrequency()));
      l.getStyleClass().addAll("mediaText", "eqLabel");

      GridPane.setHalignment(l, HPos.CENTER);
      GridPane.setHalignment(s, HPos.CENTER);
      GridPane.setHgrow(s, Priority.ALWAYS);

      gp.add(l, i, 1);
      gp.add(s, i, 2);
    }
  }

  private Slider createEQSlider(EqualizerBand eb, double min, double max) {
    final Slider s = new Slider(min, max, eb.getGain());
    s.getStyleClass().add("eqSlider");
    s.setOrientation(Orientation.VERTICAL);
    s.valueProperty().bindBidirectional(eb.gainProperty());
    s.setPrefWidth(44);
    return s;
  }
```

```
private String formatFrequency(double centerFrequency) {
  if (centerFrequency < 1000) {
    return String.format("%.0f Hz", centerFrequency);
  } else {
    return String.format("%.1f kHz", centerFrequency / 1000);
  }
}
```

The `createEQBands` method begins by getting the list of `EqualizerBands` from the `AudioEqualizer` associated with the current `MediaPlayer`. The list is then cleared to make way for the bands that we want to create. The minimum and maximum gains for an `EqualizerBand` on the current platform are accessible through the `EqualizerBand.MIN_GAIN` and `EqualizerBand.MAX_GAIN` constants. These constants should always be used in calculations involving the range of valid gain values. We use them to define the min, max, and mid (the midpoint of the gain range) variables. A `for` loop then creates the number of `EqualizerBands` defined by the `BAND_COUNT` constant, setting their gain values in a nice cosine wave pattern. This pattern emphasizes the bass and high-range frequencies, which makes a nice set of default values.

Afterward, a second `for` loop iterates through the list of `EqualizerBand` instances we just created and creates a corresponding `Slider` control and frequency `Label` for each one. Each Slider is created by the createEQSlider method. The new `Slider`'s `value` property is bidirectionally bound to the `EqualizerBand`'s `gain` property inside this method. This is the crucial part that gives the user control of the band's gain. Note that each `Slider` is also given a style class of `eqSlider`. We use this class later to add some nice styling to our equalizer display.

The final step in the `createEQBands` method is to set the alignment and grow constraints of the `Slider` and Label and add them to the `GridPane` layout node. The `Sliders` are set to grow horizontally so that the `GridPane` will expand to fill the width of the window. Of course, the same result could have been achieved by setting the `Labels` to grow, but then we would also have had to reset the `Label`'s maximum size because all `Labels`, by default, have their maximum size set equal to their preferred size. The `Labels` and `Sliders` populate rows one and two in the `GridPane`, leaving row zero for the spectrum display.

`MediaPlayer` has four properties that deal with the frequency spectrum of the current audio track: `audioSpectrumListener`, `audioSpectrumInterval`, `audioSpectrumNumBands`, and `audioSpectrumThreshold`. The `audioSpectrumListener` property is an instance of the `AudioSpectrumListener` interface. You use `MediaPlayer`'s `setAudioSepctrumListener` method to attach the listener, which then enables the computation of spectrum data and sends periodic updates to the listener's `spectrumDataUpdate` method. Calling setAudioSpectrumListener again with a null value turns off audio spectrum calculations and updates.

The `audioSpectrumInterval` property lets you control the interval at which updates are sent to the `AudioSpectrumListener`. The value is specified in seconds, and its default value is 0.1 seconds, which means that by default your listener will receive 10 spectrum updates per second. The number of spectrum bands that will be reported to the listener is controlled by the `audioSpectrumNumBands` property. And the `audioSpectrumThreshold` property defines the minimum value that will be reported for a given spectral band. This value has a unit of decibels and must be less than zero.

Listing 8-24 highlights the additions that need to be made to the `createEQInterface` method to create the controls that display the audio frequency spectrum.

Listing 8-24. Creating the Frequency Spectrum Display

```
private void createEQInterface() {
  final GridPane gp = (GridPane) getViewNode();
  final MediaPlayer mp = songModel.getMediaPlayer();

  createEQBands(gp, mp);
  createSpectrumBars(gp, mp);
  spectrumListener = new SpectrumListener(START_FREQ, mp, spectrumBars);
}

private void createSpectrumBars(GridPane gp, MediaPlayer mp) {
  spectrumBars = new SpectrumBar[BAND_COUNT];

  for (int i = 0; i < spectrumBars.length; i++) {
    spectrumBars[i] = new SpectrumBar(100, 20);
    spectrumBars[i].setMaxWidth(44);
    GridPane.setHalignment(spectrumBars[i], HPos.CENTER);
    gp.add(spectrumBars[i], i, 0);
  }
}
```

The createSpectrumBars method creates a new array of SpectrumBar controls, one for each equalizer band that was previously created. SpectrumBar is a custom control class that extends VBox to arrange a series of Rectangle nodes in a vertical stack. The constructor parameters determine the maximum value of the bar, 100 in this case, and the number of Rectangle nodes in the stack, which we have set to 20. The control has a setValue method that determines how many of the bars are lit. For example, if we set a value of 50 (out of a maximum of 100), half of the bars, 10 in this case, will be lit. The maximum width of each SpectrumBar is set to 44 to match the width of the equalizer sliders. Each bar is then added to the GridPane layout in row zero where they are each centered horizontally within their GridPane cell. Several examples of the control are shown in Figure 8-7. We do not list the code for SpectrumBar because creating a custom control is not the focus of this chapter. If you would like to view the source code for this control, it is in SpectrumBar.java in the AudioPlayer4 example project.

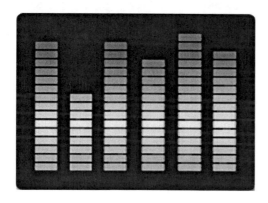

Figure 8-7. A row of six SpectrumBar controls

Listing 8-24 also shows a new line in the `createEQInterface` method that instantiates a new instance of the `SpectrumListener` class. This class is an implementation of the `AudioSpectrumListener` interface. Its job is to listen for spectrum data updates, calculate the magnitude of the frequencies that lie within each of the equalizer bands we have defined, and update the corresponding `SpectrumBar` with this calculated value. Listing 8-25 shows the class and its initialization code.

Listing 8-25. *The SpectrumListener Class*

```
class SpectrumListener implements AudioSpectrumListener {
  private final SpectrumBar[] bars;
  private double minValue;
  private double[] norms;
  private int[] spectrumBucketCounts;

  SpectrumListener(double startFreq, MediaPlayer mp, SpectrumBar[] bars) {
    this.bars = bars;
    this.minValue = mp.getAudioSpectrumThreshold();
    this.norms = createNormArray();

    int bandCount = mp.getAudioSpectrumNumBands();
    this.spectrumBucketCounts = createBucketCounts(startFreq, bandCount);
  }

  public void spectrumDataUpdate(double timestamp, double duration,
                                 float[] magnitudes, float[] phases) {
    // Shown in Listing 8-26.
  }

  private double[] createNormArray() {
    double[] normArray = new double[bars.length];
    double currentNorm = 0.05;
    for (int i = 0; i < normArray.length; i++) {
      normArray[i] = 1 + currentNorm;
      currentNorm *= 2;
    }
    return normArray;
  }

  private int[] createBucketCounts(double startFreq, int bandCount) {
    int[] bucketCounts = new int[bars.length];

    double bandwidth = 22050.0 / bandCount;
    double centerFreq = bandwidth / 2;
    double currentSpectrumFreq = centerFreq;
    double currentEQFreq = startFreq / 2;
    double currentCutoff = 0;
    int currentBucketIndex = -1;
```

```
      for (int i = 0; i < bandCount; i++) {
        if (currentSpectrumFreq > currentCutoff) {
          currentEQFreq *= 2;
          currentCutoff = currentEQFreq + currentEQFreq / 2;
          ++currentBucketIndex;
          if (currentBucketIndex == bucketCounts.length) {
            break;
          }
        }

        ++bucketCounts[currentBucketIndex];
        currentSpectrumFreq += bandwidth;
      }

      return bucketCounts;
    }
}
```

The SpectrumListener constructor takes three parameters. The first is the center frequency of the first equalizer band. The second is the MediaPlayer instance to which this listener will be attached. The third is the array of SpectrumBar controls that the listener will update. This array is saved in the class's instance data for later use. The MediaPlayer instance is used to gain access to the data needed by the listener during initialization. This includes the value of the audioSpectrumNumBands property as well as the value of audioSpectrumThreshold. The listener's calculations would be slightly off if either of these two values were changed after the SpectrumListener constructor was called. We know that AudioPlayer4 does not do this, but if you have to deal with that situation, you would need to either bind or attach listeners to those properties to be notified of the changes.

The constructor then initializes a normalization array named normArray. This is an array of double values used to normalize the magnitude values that are later computed for each equalizer band's frequency range. The normalization factor attempts to compensate for the fact that the bandwidth doubles in each successive equalizer band, but we still want to display all of them on the same scale in our SpectrumBar controls.

The final piece of initialization code called from our constructor is the createBucketCounts method. This method's job is to figure out how many spectrum bands fall within each of our equalizer bands. It creates "buckets" into which we can later sum the magnitudes of each of the spectrum bands, thus easily figuring out to which equalizer band they correspond. The bucket counts are stored in an int array that is the same length as the SpectrumBar array, that is, one bucket for each SpectrumBar.

To begin the bucket calculation, we assume that the spectrum data will cover frequencies of up to 22.05 kHz, which is a good assumption for music. Spoken audio (voices only) will typically cover a much smaller range of frequencies, but the spectrum data provided by the media engine will cover all 22.05 kHz. We divide this maximum frequency by the number of audio spectrum bands to yield the bandwidth of each band. Half of the bandwidth gives us the center frequency of the first band. We then proceed to set the initial values of the variables used inside the for loop. These are set such that the first time through the loop, the value of currentSpectrumFreq (which was initialized to the center frequency of the first spectrum band) is greater than the currentCutoff frequency (which was initialized to zero) thus triggering a recalculation of our loop variables. We do this so that we don't have to treat the first iteration of the loop differently than the following iterations.

After the first iteration, the loop variables are all set up as expected and the count of the first bucket is incremented. The loop then proceeds to check the center frequency of each spectrum band. If it is greater than the cutoff frequency of the current equalizer band, the bucket index is incremented and the bucket corresponding to the next equalizer frequency begins to be incremented. When finished, we have an array that tells us how many spectrum bands are contained in each equalizer band.

This bucket array allows us to sum the magnitudes of each spectrum band quickly and assign them to the correct equalizer band during the listener's `spectrumDataUpdate` method. This optimization is a good idea because the `spectrumDataUpdate` takes place 10 times per second. The code for the listener's `spectrumDataUpdate` method is shown in Listing 8-26.

Listing 8-26. *SpectrumListener's spectrumDataUpdate Method*

```
@Override
public void spectrumDataUpdate(double timestamp, double duration,
                              float[] magnitudes, float[] phases) {
  int index = 0;
  int bucketIndex = 0;
  int currentBucketCount = 0;
  double sum = 0.0;

  while (index < magnitudes.length) {
    sum += magnitudes[index] - minValue;
    ++currentBucketCount;

    if (currentBucketCount >= spectrumBucketCounts[bucketIndex]) {
      bars[bucketIndex].setValue(sum / norms[bucketIndex]);
      currentBucketCount = 0;
      sum = 0.0;
      ++bucketIndex;
    }

    ++index;
  }
}
```

The `spectrumDataUpdate` method takes four parameters. The timestamp parameter gives the time of the update in seconds. The duration is the number of seconds for which the spectrum was computed. The duration should normally be approximately equal to the value of `MediaPlayer`'s `audioSpectrumInterval` property. The `magnitudes` array will hold the floating-point values corresponding to the magnitude of each spectrum band. The array length will always equal the value of `MediaPlayer`'s `audioSpectrumNumBands` property. The value is in decibels and will be between `audioSpectrumThreshold` and zero. It is always less than zero. Similarly, the `phases` array contains the phase offset of each spectrum band. These arrays should be treated as read-only by the listener because the MediaPlayer may reuse them between updates.

For our purposes, we are only trying to give the user a general idea of the spectrum content in each of the equalizer bands. Therefore we need to be concerned only with the `magnitudes` array. We iterate through the array and use the bucket counts to sum the magnitudes of the bands that correspond to each equalizer band. When we reach the count for each bucket, the current sum is divided by the normalization factor and then passed as the value to the corresponding `SpectrumBar`. Then the values are reset and the sum for the next band is calculated.

We now have the ability to create a custom set of `EqualizerBand`s and to display the magnitude of the frequencies in each band as calculated from the audio signal that is currently being played. This gives a pretty nice equalizer interface for the users of the application. We do need to ensure that we reinitialize our equalizer interface whenever a new MediaPlayer is created (a new song is loaded). A listener attached to SongModel's mediaPlayer property handles this and is shown in Listing 8-27.

Listing 8-27. EqualizerView's MediaPlayer Listener

```java
private class MediaPlayerListener implements ChangeListener<MediaPlayer> {
  @Override
  public void changed(ObservableValue<? extends MediaPlayer> observable,
                      MediaPlayer oldValue, MediaPlayer newValue) {
    if (oldValue != null) {
      oldValue.setAudioSpectrumListener(null);
      clearGridPane();
    }

    createEQInterface();
  }

  private void clearGridPane() {
    for (Node node : ((GridPane)getViewNode()).getChildren()) {
      GridPane.clearConstraints(node);
    }
    ((GridPane)getViewNode()).getChildren().clear();
  }
}
```

This inner class resides in EqualizerView. If the oldValue is not null, we set its spectrum listener to null to turn off the spectrum calculations. Then we clear the GridPane and recreate the equalizer interface. This is necessary because each MediaPlayer has its own AudioEqualizer instance that cannot be initialized or set from the outside. It would also be wasteful to have the MediaPlayer compute the audio spectrum when it is not visible, such as when the metadata view is being shown. We can attach another listener to our GridPane's scene property to ensure that this does not happen. Listing 8-28 shows the final version of the EqualizerView constructor with this addition highlighted.

Listing 8-28. The EqualizerView Constructor with the Scene Listener Declared

```java
public EqualizerView(SongModel songModel) {
  super(songModel);

  songModel.mediaPlayerProperty().addListener(new MediaPlayerListener());
  createEQInterface();

  getViewNode().sceneProperty().addListener(new ChangeListener<Scene>() {
    @Override
    public void changed(ObservableValue<? extends Scene> observable,
                        Scene oldValue, Scene newValue) {
      final MediaPlayer mp = EqualizerView.this.songModel.getMediaPlayer();
      if (newValue != null) {
        mp.setAudioSpectrumListener(spectrumListener);
      } else {
```

```
          mp.setAudioSpectrumListener(null);
        }
      }
  });
}
```

Whenever EqualizerView's GridPane is not part of the scene (whenever `newValue` is null), we make sure to set `MediaPlayer`'s `audioSpectrumListener` to null in order to disable the spectrum calculations, which begs the question of how and when to add the equalizer view to the application. We created an EQ button and added it to the far right side of the player controls view. Whenever this button is clicked, the metadata and controls views are hidden and the equalizer view is shown. We have also added a "Back" button to the equalizer view that returns the application to the metadata and controls views. To facilitate the changing of views, a new listener field has been added to the `AbstractView` class. It lets us specify one event handler per view that can be used to indicate that the "next" view should be shown. The new version of the AbstractView class is shown in Listing 8-29.

Listing 8-29. Adding the setNextHandler Method to AbstractView

```
public abstract class AbstractView {
  protected final SongModel songModel;
  protected final Node viewNode;

  public AbstractView(SongModel songModel) {
    this.songModel = songModel;
    this.viewNode = initView();
  }

  // other methods removed...

  public void setNextHandler(EventHandler<ActionEvent> nextHandler) {
  }
}
```

As you can see, the `setNextHandler` does nothing by default, so existing views are free to ignore it. Any view that needs to support this new functionality can override the method and pass along the `nextHandler` argument to whichever control is the source of the next action. In our case, this is the "EQ" button in the player controls view and the "Back" button in the equalizer view. Naturally, the `AudioPlayer4` application class also needs to be modified to create the event handlers that are capable of switching between the two "pages" of our final application. We do not detail those changes here, but you can consult the AudioPlayer4 example code if you are curious.

The final version of the audio player application is shown in Figure 8-8. The top image shows the "page" containing the metadata and controls views, and the bottom image shows the final version of the equalizer view.

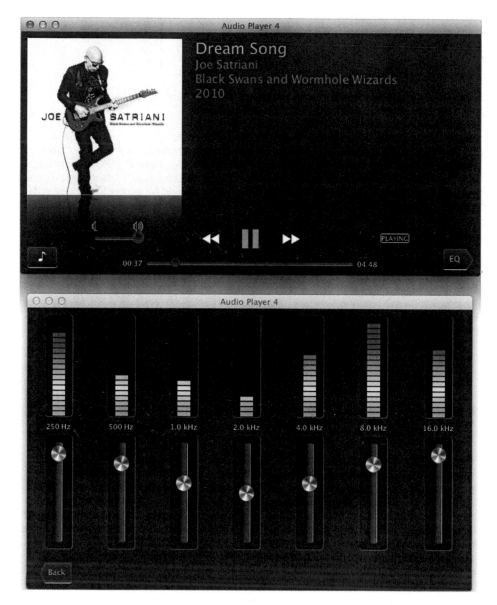

Figure 8-8. *The final version of AudioPlayer 4 with the metadata/controls view (top) and equalizer view (bottom)*

The bottom image of Figure 8-8 shows the special styling that was applied to the `Slider` and `SpectrumBar` controls of the `EqualizerView`. You may also have noticed that the Back and EQ buttons are shaped like arrows. This was also done via the application's style sheet. Those styles are shown in Listing 8-30.

Listing 8-30. Styling the Equalizer and Buttons

```
#eqButton {
  -fx-shape: "M 1,0 L 10,0 13,5 10,10 1,10 Q 0 10 0 9 L 0,1 Q 0 0 1 0";
  -fx-font-size: 12pt;
  -fx-alignment: center-left;
}

#backButton {
  -fx-shape: "M 3,0 L 12,0 Q 13,0 13,1 L 13,9 Q 13,10 12,10 L 3,10 1,5";
  -fx-font-size: 12pt;
  -fx-alignment: center-right;
}

.eqSlider {
  -fx-background-radius: 5;
  -fx-background-color: #222, #888, black;
  -fx-background-insets: 0, 1 0 0 1, 1;
  -fx-padding: 2 10;
}

.eqSlider .thumb {
  -fx-background-image: url("resources/thumb.png");
  -fx-padding: 12;
}

.eqSlider:vertical .track{
  -fx-padding: 5;
}

.spectrumBar {
  -fx-background-radius: 5;
  -fx-background-color: #222, #888, black;
  -fx-background-insets: 0, 1 0 0 1, 1;
  -fx-padding: 2 10;
}
```

MediaPlayer Wrap-Up

Playing media files over the Internet happens automatically with the JavaFX media API. All you have to do is point a Media object to an HTTP resource and attach it to a MediaPlayer with autoPlay set to true. If, however, you are interested in monitoring the progress of the download buffer, you can use the bufferProgressTime property in the MediaPlayer class. When data are loaded from a stream or from disk, the amount of time those data will take to play is calculated and this time is regularly updated as the value of bufferProgressTime. By binding to this property, you can receive these updates and effectively monitor the media's buffer.

The final two MediaPlayer properties we discuss are the rate and currentRate properties. Calling setRate allows you to control the rate of the playback. Passing a parameter of 1.0 will cause playback to proceed at the normal rate. A parameter of 2.0 would cause your media to be played at twice the normal rate. You can pass any value between 0.0 and 8.0. The currentRate property always reflects the actual rate of playback, regardless of the value of the rate property. For example, if playback is currently stalled, currentRate will be 0.0 even though rate may be set to 4.0.

Playing Video

From an API standpoint, playing video instead of audio is as simple as wrapping a MediaPlayer with a MediaView and adding the MediaView to the scene graph. Listing 8-31 shows how this is done. You simply point a Media object at a valid source (a Flash movie in this case) and wrap it with an auto-playing MediaPlayer, which, in turn, is wrapped with a MediaView. The final step is to add the MediaView to the scene and set the size of the scene to match the size of the movie.

Listing 8-31. A Minimalist but Functional Movie Player

```
public class VideoPlayer1 extends Application {

  public static void main(String[] args) {
    launch(args);
  }

  @Override
  public void start(Stage primaryStage) {
    String workingDir = System.getProperty("user.dir");
    File f = new File(workingDir, "../media/omgrobots.flv");

    Media m = new Media(f.toURI().toString());
    MediaPlayer mp = new MediaPlayer(m);
    MediaView mv = new MediaView(mp);

    StackPane root = new StackPane();
    root.getChildren().add(mv);

    primaryStage.setScene(new Scene(root, 960, 540));
    primaryStage.setTitle("Video Player 1");
    primaryStage.show();

    mp.play();
  }
}
```

This example loads the video file from the filesystem. Loading video from the Internet using an http URL will work just as well, but it is not advisable to package movies of any significant size inside your jar file because that will drastically increase the size of the download (assuming you are deploying to the browser or with webstart). Once we have our file URL, everything becomes familiar. You use the URL to create the Media object and wrap that Media object in a MediaPlayer. The only new step is to construct a MediaView node using the MediaPlayer as the constructor argument and add it to the root of our scene graph, a StackPane in this case. We create a Scene that is sized to fit the dimensions of our movie, then pass it to the stage and show it. The final step is to start the movie playing with the same familiar call to MediaPlayer's play method. Figure 8-9 shows this simple movie player in action.

Figure 8-9. *Playing a robot movie in JavaFX*

Everything you've learned up to this point about playing audio with Media and MediaPlayer also applies to playing video with MediaView. There are only a few extra concepts that you need to know.

Controlling the Size of a MediaView

MediaView is just another node in the scene graph, therefore it is possible to scale its content using the usual transforms or the scaleX and scaleY properties of the Node class. There are more convenient ways to get the job done when dealing with MediaViews, however. The properties fitWidth and fitHeight can be used to make the MediaView stretch or shrink to the desired size. Using only one of them at a time will make the MediaView scale only in that dimension while the size in the other dimension remains unchanged.

If you want to maintain the movie's original aspect ratio as you scale it to fit your application, you can set the preserveRatio property to true. If you specify a fit size in one dimension along with setting preserveRatio to true, the other dimension will be automatically scaled to match the movie's original aspect ratio as it's being fit along your specified dimension. For example, let's say our movie's size is originally 640 × 352 pixels, which gives an aspect ratio of 640 ÷ 352, or approximately 1.82. If you specify a fitWidth of 400 and enable preserveRatio, the final height of the movie will be changed from 352 pixels to 400 ÷ 1.82 = 220 pixels. Note that the aspect ratio is preserved because 400 ÷ 220 is also 1.82.

You can also choose to scale in both dimensions by specifying both a fitWidth and a fitHeight value along with enabling preserveRatio. In this case the best fit for the movie will be calculated and the other dimension will be scaled to preserve the original aspect ratio. For example, if the fit area and the movie are both wider than they are tall (the common case), the movie will be scaled to fit horizontally and the height will be determined by using the aspect ratio to calculate the height needed to match the new width.

One last property that is worth knowing about in relation to resizing a movie is the smooth property. This is a **Boolean** property that controls the quality of the resulting image after the scale. If smooth is true, the scaling algorithm will produce a higher-quality image at the cost of some extra computation time. If false, the scaling will be done faster but the result will not look as good. This lets the developer make a time versus quality trade-off. When making a movie smaller, there is not a large difference in quality between the smooth and nonsmooth options. Although the difference in quality while upscaling is noticeable, it still may be acceptable for some applications. Therefore, if you need to generate and show thumbnails of movies, this can be a worthwhile option to consider. By default, smooth is usually set to true but this can depend on the platform on which you are running.

Listing 8-32 shows a full-screen movie player that uses the fitWidth, fitHeight, and preserveRatio to scale a movie to play using the entire screen. This is accomplished by using the Stage's fullScreen property to ensure that only the movie can be seen on the screen. Pressing the Escape key will restore the application to its normal window.

Listing 8-32. *A Full-Screen Movie Player*

```
public class FullScreenVideoPlayer extends Application {

  public static void main(String[] args) {
    launch(args);
  }

  @Override
  public void start(Stage primaryStage) {
    String workingDir = System.getProperty("user.dir");
    final File f = new File(workingDir, "../media/omgrobots.flv");

    final Media m = new Media(f.toURI().toString());
    final MediaPlayer mp = new MediaPlayer(m);
    final MediaView mv = new MediaView(mp);

    final DoubleProperty width = mv.fitWidthProperty();
    final DoubleProperty height = mv.fitHeightProperty();

    width.bind(Bindings.selectDouble(mv.sceneProperty(), "width"));
    height.bind(Bindings.selectDouble(mv.sceneProperty(), "height"));

    mv.setPreserveRatio(true);

    StackPane root = new StackPane();
    root.getChildren().add(mv);

    final Scene scene = new Scene(root, 960, 540);
    scene.setFill(Color.BLACK);

    primaryStage.setScene(scene);
    primaryStage.setTitle("Full Screen Video Player");
    primaryStage.setFullScreen(true);
    primaryStage.show();
```

```
    mp.play();
  }
}
```

The highlighted code in Listing 8-32 shows that `MediaView`'s `fitWidth` and `fitHeight` properties are bound to the `width` and `height` properties of the MediaView's `Scene` object. `Bindings.selectDouble` is used to make sure `fitWidth` and `fitHeight` are updated when the `MediaView` is added to the active scene graph. For the movie to scale properly, the `preserveRatio` property must be set to true.

MediaView and Effects

All of the normal effects that can be applied to a `Node` can also be applied to a `MediaView`. Some care must be taken to ensure that the effects are not so expensive as to interfere with the smooth playback of the movie. With that caveat in place, we go over some of the effects that are commonly in use with media player applications. Reflections (see javafx.scene.effect.Reflection) are a popular effect, specifically in demos that are meant to show off a platform's graphical horsepower. A reflection can make the movie look as if it is sitting on a shiny surface. The effect is very compelling because the reflection is updated in real-time to match the movie. JavaFX's ColorAdjust effect can be used to alter the colors in the movie for a fun and visually interesting effect. If you're in a more artsy kind of mood, the SepiaTone effect may be just the thing. And of course there is the old reliable DropShadow effect to make the movie look as if it is floating over the background. We encourage you to use the example programs and experiment with the different effects in the javafx.scene.effect package. It is a fun and interesting way to learn about them.

Using Markers

The JavaFX 2.0 media API also includes support for media markers. These markers can be used to trigger events during media playback. Every `Media` object contains an `ObservableMap` whose keys are `String`s and whose values are `Duration`s. During playback, these markers trigger `MediaMarkerEvent`s at the `Duration` specified by the marker. These events can be caught by passing an `EventHandler` to the `MediaPlayer`'s `setOnMarker` method. Listing 8-33 contains the code for the VideoPlayer2 application that sets and then displays the text of these markers during video playback. Although we show them here during video playback, the marker functionality is available during audio playback as well.

Listing 8-33. *Displaying Media Markers in a Movie*

```
public class VideoPlayer2 extends Application {

  public static void main(String[] args) {
    launch(args);
  }

  @Override
  public void start(Stage primaryStage) {
    final Label markerText = new Label();
    StackPane.setAlignment(markerText, Pos.TOP_CENTER);

    String workingDir = System.getProperty("user.dir");
    final File f = new File(workingDir, "../media/omgrobots.flv");
```

```
    final Media m = new Media(f.toURI().toString());

    final ObservableMap<String, Duration> markers = m.getMarkers();
    markers.put("Robot Finds Wall", Duration.millis(3100));
    markers.put("Then Finds the Green Line", Duration.millis(5600));
    markers.put("Robot Grabs Sled", Duration.millis(8000));
    markers.put("And Heads for Home", Duration.millis(11500));

    final MediaPlayer mp = new MediaPlayer(m);
    mp.setOnMarker(new EventHandler<MediaMarkerEvent>() {
      @Override
      public void handle(final MediaMarkerEvent event) {
        Platform.runLater(new Runnable() {
          @Override public void run() {
            markerText.setText(event.getMarker().getKey());
          }
        });
      }
    });

    final MediaView mv = new MediaView(mp);

    final StackPane root = new StackPane();
    root.getChildren().addAll(mv, markerText);
    root.setOnMouseClicked(new EventHandler<MouseEvent>() {
      @Override
      public void handle(MouseEvent event) {
        mp.seek(Duration.ZERO);
        markerText.setText("");
      }
    });

    final Scene scene = new Scene(root, 960, 540);
    final URL stylesheet = getClass().getResource("media.css");
    scene.getStylesheets().add(stylesheet.toString());

    primaryStage.setScene(scene);
    primaryStage.setTitle("Video Player 1");
    primaryStage.show();

    mp.play();
  }
}
```

A Label is used to display the text of each marker centered at the top of the screen by setting its alignment to be Pos.TOP_CENTER. Then, after creating the Media object, four markers are inserted into the ObservableMap starting with the message "Robot Finds Wall" at 3.1 seconds and ending with "And Heads for Home" at 11.5 seconds. Once the MediaPlayer is instantiated, a new MediaMarkerEvent handler is created and passed to the setOnMarker method. This event will occur on the JavaFX media thread, so we must use Platform.runLater to set the text of the markerText label on the JavaFX application thread. One other change we've made to this version of the video player is to add an onMouseClicked handler, which seeks back to the beginning of the media and clears the markerText label. This lets you simply click on the window to restart playback. The running application displaying the "And Heads for Home" marker text is shown in Figure 8-10. The styling of the messageLabel text is included in the *media.css* style sheet that is loaded by the Scene after it is created.

Figure 8-10. Displaying markers during movie playback

One Player, Multiple Views

Each MediaView supports the concept of a viewport. This is a Rectangle2D that defines which part of the movie to view. Multiple MediaViews can share the same MediaPlayer, and through the use of viewports, they can all be displaying different views of the same media. Because they all share the same player, all views will be showing the same frame of video at the same time. The viewport will become your view of the player's content. If you specify a fitWidth or fitHeight, any transforms or effects, they will be applied to the viewport just as they would have been applied to the view as a whole. The code in Listing 8-34 shows how to define multiple MediaViews and viewports for a single MediaPlayer.

The listing starts by defining a Label to hold a "secret" message, which is initially set invisible. After the Media object is created, two markers are defined that will tell us when it is time to split and join the two viewports that we create. Next, two MediaViews are created and each is given one half of the video to view. The arguments to the Rectangle2D constructor specify, in order, the minimum x coordinate, the minimum y coordinate, the width, and the height of the viewport's rectangle. Therefore, you can see that the first MediaView will contain a viewport into the left side of the movie and the second MediaView will view the right side of the movie. A StackPane is created to hold the message behind the two MediaViews; the message is added as the first child. When the "split" marker is triggered, the two viewports will slide apart revealing our message. The "join" marker will trigger the two viewports to slide back together, hiding the message once again.

Listing 8-34. Defining Viewports for MediaViews

```java
public class VideoPlayer3 extends Application {
  public static void main(String[] args) {
    launch(args);
  }

  @Override
  public void start(Stage primaryStage) {
    final Label message = new Label("I \u2764 Robots");
    message.setVisible(false);

    String workingDir = System.getProperty("user.dir");
    final File f = new File(workingDir, "../media/omgrobots.flv");

    final Media m = new Media(f.toURI().toString());
    m.getMarkers().put("Split", Duration.millis(3000));
    m.getMarkers().put("Join", Duration.millis(9000));

    final MediaPlayer mp = new MediaPlayer(m);

    final MediaView mv1 = new MediaView(mp);
    mv1.setViewport(new Rectangle2D(0, 0, 960 / 2, 540));
    StackPane.setAlignment(mv1, Pos.CENTER_LEFT);

    final MediaView mv2 = new MediaView(mp);
    mv2.setViewport(new Rectangle2D(960 / 2, 0, 960 / 2, 540));
    StackPane.setAlignment(mv2, Pos.CENTER_RIGHT);

    StackPane root = new StackPane();
    root.getChildren().addAll(message, mv1, mv2);
    root.setOnMouseClicked(new EventHandler<MouseEvent>() {
      @Override public void handle(MouseEvent event) {
        mp.seek(Duration.ZERO);
        message.setVisible(false);
      }
    });

    final Scene scene = new Scene(root, 960, 540);
    final URL stylesheet = getClass().getResource("media.css");
    scene.getStylesheets().add(stylesheet.toString());

    primaryStage.setScene(scene);
    primaryStage.setTitle("Video Player 3");
    primaryStage.show();

    mp.setOnMarker(new EventHandler<MediaMarkerEvent>() {
      @Override public void handle(final MediaMarkerEvent event) {
```

```
        Platform.runLater(new Runnable() {
          @Override public void run() {
            if (event.getMarker().getKey().equals("Split")) {
              message.setVisible(true);
              buildSplitTransition(mv1, mv2).play();
            } else {
              buildJoinTransition(mv1, mv2).play();
            }
          }
        });
      }
    });
    mp.play();
  }
}
```

The last step in showing our hidden message is to set a handler for the MediaMarkerEvents that lets us know when it is time to split the two viewports and when it is time to rejoin them. As in the last example, the Platform.runLater method is required because we manipulate the visibility of the message Label as well as apply translations to the two MediaView nodes. The methods that build and return the two transitions are shown in Listing 8-35.

Listing 8-35. *Building the Split and Join Transitions*

```
private ParallelTransition buildJoinTransition(Node one, Node two) {
  return ParallelTransitionBuilder.create().children(
          TranslateTransitionBuilder.create().
            duration(Duration.millis(1000)).
            node(one).
            byX(200).build(),
          TranslateTransitionBuilder.create().
            duration(Duration.millis(1000)).
            node(two).
            byX(-200).build()).
        build();
}

private ParallelTransition buildSplitTransition(Node one, Node two) {
  return ParallelTransitionBuilder.create().children(
          TranslateTransitionBuilder.create().
            duration(Duration.millis(1000)).
            node(one).
            byX(-200).build(),
          TranslateTransitionBuilder.create().
            duration(Duration.millis(1000)).
            node(two).
            byX(200).build()).
        build();
}
```

This example demonstrates that there are many uses for media markers other than simply displaying captions. They can be used to trigger all kinds of events in your applications. A screen shot of the running application with our hidden message revealed is shown in Figure 8-11.

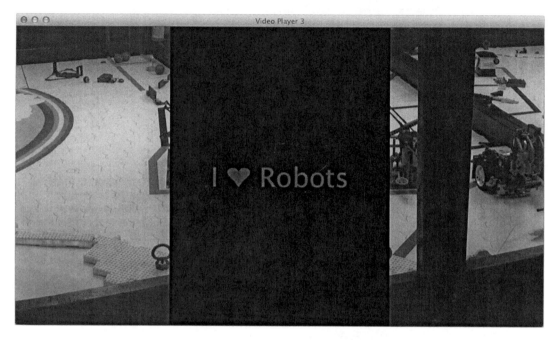

Figure 8-11. *The MediaViews slide apart to reveal the hidden message.*

Converting AudioPlayer into a VideoPlayer

Based on what you have learned so far, you may think that converting the AudioPlayer application to play video is a straightforward task, and you would be right. The first step is simply to rename the SongModel class to the more appropriate MediaModel. No code changes are required. Although movies do not typically contain metadata, it does not hurt to leave in the code that looks for them. Rather than display metadata, we create a new view that displays the MediaView instead. This VideoView class is shown in Listing 8-36.

Listing 8-36. *A View That Displays the MediaView Node*

```
public class VideoView extends AbstractView {

  public VideoView(MediaModel mediaModel) {
    super(mediaModel);
  }

  @Override
  protected Node initView() {
```

```
        MediaView mv = new MediaView();
        mv.mediaPlayerProperty().bind(mediaModel.mediaPlayerProperty());
        return mv;
    }
}
```

This simple class uses its `initView` method to create a `MediaView` and bind the `MediaView`'s `mediaPlayerProperty` to the `mediaPlayerProperty` we created in our `MediaModel` (formerly `SongModel`) class.

The next step is to replace the MetadataView with this new VideoView. Listing 8-37 shows the modified code from the `VideoPlayer4` class (formerly `AudioPlayer4`). Instead of creating the `MetadataView`, we now create the `VideoView`, passing it the `mediaModel` instance. The `VideoView`'s view node is then retrieved and set as the center node of the `BorderPane` in place of the `MetadataView`'s view node. That is literally all there is to it!

Listing 8-37. Creating the VideoView and Adding It to the Application's First Page

```
private Parent createPageOne() {
    videoView = new VideoView(mediaModel);
    playerControlsView = new PlayerControlsView(mediaModel);
    playerControlsView.setNextHandler(new EventHandler<ActionEvent>() {
        @Override
        public void handle(ActionEvent arg0) {
            rootNode.getChildren().setAll(page2);
        }
    });

    final BorderPane bp = new BorderPane();
    bp.setCenter(videoView.getViewNode());
    bp.setBottom(playerControlsView.getViewNode());

    return bp;
}
```

One final finishing touch is to change the music note icon on the open button to something more appropriate. We therefore created a filmstrip icon and replaced the name of the image file used by the button in the application's style sheet.

```
#openButton {
    -fx-graphic: url("resources/filmstrip.png");
}
```

The final result of our conversion is shown in Figure 8-12 playing a promotional video from Oracle's web site. All of the controls work exactly the same as they did in the version that played audio files, right down to the equalizer. You just have to love JavaFX, don't you?

Figure 8-12. *The converted video player in action*

Summary

In this chapter, you learned about a very important aspect of the JavaFX platform: the media classes. We showed you how to accomplish the following.

- Use the `AudioClip` class to play low-latency sound effects.

- Load the various media types supported by JavaFX into a `Media` object.

- Use the `MediaPlayer` class to play audio files from .jar files, from disk, and by loading them over the Internet.

- Build a simple media player that contains a graphical user interface that can be used to control playback of the audio files.

- Take advantage of the MediaPlayer's equalizer and audio frequency spectrum capabilities.

- Play video files using the `MediaView` class.

- Use media markers to trigger events during media playback.

- Split your video playback into multiple viewports.

CHAPTER 9

Accessing Web Services

An expert is a man who has made all the mistakes which can be made, in a narrow field.

— Niels Bohr

The modern application paradigm is clear: nothing lives in an isolated environment. Client applications interact with data obtained from a wide array of resources, both physical and logical. Whether data are retrieved from a hard disk, a remote database, or an exposed network resource, we expect our applications to be flexible, provide a wide array of data retrieval options, and, in general, work well with others.

So far, we've explained how the JavaFX Platform can be used both for rendering information and for interactively manipulating data. In this chapter, we provide a brief overview of the options available for integrating JavaFX applications with enterprise systems, and then continue with some specific examples of that process.

Our examples are constructed to demonstrate how easily a JavaFX application can access a REST resource and then translate the response (from either JSON or XML format) into a format understandable by JavaFX Controls. As our example external data source, the Twitter REST APIs are ideal, as they are publicly available, easy to understand, and widely used on the Internet.

Front-end and Back-end Platforms

JavaFX is often considered a front-end platform. Although that statement does not do justice to the APIs in the JavaFX platform that are not related to a user interface, it is true that most JavaFX applications focus on the rich and interactive visualization of "content."

One of the great things about Java is the fact that a single language can be used within a wide range of devices, desktops, and servers. The same Java language that creates the core of JavaFX is also the fundamental core of the Java Platform, Enterprise Edition (Java EE).

The Java Platform is the number one development platform for enterprise applications. The combination of the JavaFX platform providing a rich and interactive user interface with enterprise applications running on the Java Platform creates huge possibilities. In order to achieve this, it is required to have JavaFX applications and Java enterprise applications exchanging data.

Exchanging data can happen in a number of ways, and depending on the requirements (from the front end as well as from the back end), one way might be more suited than another way.

Basically, there are two different approaches:

- The JavaFX application can leverage the fact that it runs on the same infrastructure as typical enterprise applications, and can deeply integrate with these enterprise components. This is illustrated in Figure 9-1.

- JavaFX applications live in a relatively simple Java Platform, and exchange data with enterprise servers using standard protocols that are already supported by Java enterprise components. This is shown in Figure 9-2.

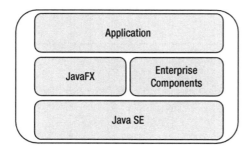

Figure 9-1. *JavaFX and enterprise components on a single system*

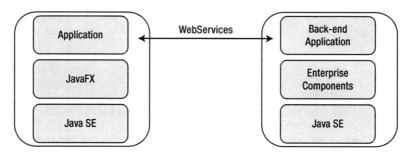

Figure 9-2. *JavaFX application communicates with enterprise components on a remote server*

The first approach is mentioned and briefly touched upon, but the focus of this chapter is on the second approach, where the JavaFX client communicates with Java enterprise components on a remote server.

It should also be stressed here that as long as a standard, well-defined protocol (e.g., SOAP/REST) is used, it is very possible to connect a JavaFX application to a non-Java back-end application. The decoupling between client and server indeed allows for different programming languages to be used on the client and on the server.

Merging JavaFX and Java Enterprise Modules in the Same Environment

JavaFX 2 is built on top of the Java Platform, Standard Edition. As a consequence, all functionality provided by this platform can be leveraged in JavaFX 2. The Java Platform, Enterprise Edition is also built on top of the Java Platform, Standard Edition. As a consequence, JavaFX applications can live in the same environment as applications using the Java Platform, Enterprise Edition.

By doing so, the JavaFX developer can use his or her favorite enterprise tools to create applications. There are a number of advantages in doing so. Enterprise components offer tools that allow developers to focus on a specific domain layer, while shielding them away from, for example, database resources and transactions.

Java is a popular platform in the enterprise environment, and a number of enterprise components and libraries have been developed by companies, organizations, and individuals.

The Java Platform, Enterprise Edition is defined by specifications that are standardized via the Java Community Process (JCP) program. For the different constituting parts, individual Java Specification Requests (JSRs) are filed. The current version of the Java Platform, Enterprise Edition, Java EE 6 contains the following JSRs.

Java API for RESTful Web Services (JAX-RS) 1.1 (JSR 311)

Implementing Enterprise Web Services 1.3 (JSR 109)

Java API for XML-Based Web Services (JAX-WS) 2.2 (JSR 224)

Java Architecture for XML Binding (JAXB) 2.2 (JSR 222)

Web Services Metadata for the Java Platform (JSR 181)

Java API for XML-Based RPC (JAX-RPC) 1.1 (JSR 101)

Java APIs for XML Messaging 1.3 (JSR 67)

Java API for XML Registries (JAXR) 1.0 (JSR 93)

Java Servlet 3.0 (JSR 315)

JavaServer Faces 2.0 (JSR 314)

JavaServer Pages 2.2/Expression Language 2.2 (JSR 245)

Standard Tag Library for JavaServer Pages (JSTL) 1.2 (JSR 52)

Debugging Support for Other Languages 1.0 (JSR 45)

Contexts and Dependency Injection for Java (Web Beans 1.0) (JSR 299)

Dependency Injection for Java 1.0 (JSR 330)

Bean Validation 1.0 (JSR 303)

Enterprise JavaBeans 3.1 (JSR 318)

Java EE Connector Architecture 1.6 (JSR 322)

Java Persistence 2.0 (JSR 317)

Common Annotations for the Java Platform 1.1 (JSR 250)

Java Message Service API 1.1 (JSR 914)

Java Transaction API (JTA) 1.1 (JSR 907)

JavaMail 1.4 (JSR 919)

Java Authentication Service Provider Interface for Containers (JSR 196)

Java Authorization Contract for Containers 1.3 (JSR 115)

Java EE Application Deployment 1.2 (JSR 88)

J2EE Management 1.1 (JSR 77)

Java API for XML Processing (JAXP) 1.3 (JSR 206)

Java Database Connectivity 4.0 (JSR 221)

Java Management Extensions (JMX) 2.0 (JSR 255)

JavaBeans Activation Framework (JAF) 1.1 (JSR 925)

Streaming API for XML (StAX) 1.0 (JSR 173)

Most of these individual JSRs are implemented by a number of companies, and implementations are often grouped into a product. Typical enterprise components implement one or more JSRs, and they might include additional product-specific functionality. Among the most popular enterprise components we count the Spring Framework, Guice, Tomcat, Hibernate, JBoss, RestEasy, and Glassfish. A number of products implement all JSRs, and those products are then called implementations of the Java Platform, Enterprise Edition, often referred to as Java EE Platforms.

Technically, there are no restrictions in the JavaFX platform that prevent Java enterprise components from being used. However, enterprise development differs from client development in a number of ways:

- Enterprise infrastructure is shifting towards the cloud. Specific tasks (e.g., storage, mail, etc.) are outsourced to components in a "cloud" that offer specific functionality. Enterprise servers are often located in a cloud environment, allowing fast and seamless interaction with cloud components.

- Resource requirements: enterprise systems focus on computing resources (CPU, cache, and memory) where desktop computers and laptops focus instead on visual resources (e.g., graphical hardware acceleration).

- Startup time is hardly an issue in servers, but is critical in many desktop applications. Also, servers are supposed to be up and running 24/7, which is not the case with most clients.

- Deployment and lifecycle management are often specific to a server-product or a client-product. Upgrading servers or server software is often a tedious process. Downtime has to be minimized because client applications might have open connections to the server. Deploying a client application can happen in a number of ways such as via JNLP.

- Enterprise development uses a number of patterns (e.g., Inversion of Control, container-based initialization) that can be useful in client development, but that often require a different architecture than traditional clients.

Using JavaFX to Call Remote (Web) Services

Enterprise components are often accessed via web resources. Some specifications clearly describe how web-based frameworks should interact with enterprise components for rendering information. However, there are other specifications that allow enterprise components (written in Java or in another language) to be accessed from non-web resources as well. Because those specifications allow for a decoupling between enterprise development and any other development, they have been defined by a number of stakeholders.

In 1998, SOAP was invented by Microsoft and subsequently used as "the" exchange format between Java applications and .Net applications. The SOAP protocol is based on XML, and the current version 1.2 became a W3C recommendation in 2003. Java provides a number of tools that allow developers to exchange data with SOAP.

Although powerful and relatively readable, SOAP is often considered to be rather verbose. With the rise of mashups and simple services offering specific functionality, a new protocol emerged: the representational state transfer (REST). The REST protocol allows server and client developers to exchange data in a loosely coupled way, where the protocol can be XML, JSON, Atom, or any other format.

SOAP

A number of Enterprise applications use SOAP at the back end, and thus require SOAP to be supported on the client as well. Fortunately, SOAP is supported in Java. The examples in this chapter use the REST protocol inasmuch as this is more comprehensive, but using the javax.xml.soap package is perfectly possible in JavaFX applications, because this package is available in the Java 2 Standard Platform.

REST

The remainder of this chapter is about calling REST-based web services. Plenty of resources and documentation about REST and REST-based web services can be found on the Internet. Web-based REST services expose a number of URIs (uniform resource identifiers) that can be accessed using the HTTP protocol. Typically, different HTTP request methods (get, post, put, delete) are used to indicate different operations on resources.

REST-based web services can be accessed using standard HTTP technologies, and the Java Platform comes with a number of APIs (mainly in java.io and java.net) that facilitate the access to REST-based web services.

One of the major advantages of JavaFX being written on top of the Java 2 Platform, Standard Edition is the ability to use all of these APIs in JavaFX applications. This is what we do in the first examples in this chapter. We show how we can use Java APIs for consuming REST-based web services, and how we can integrate the result in a JavaFX application.

Next, we show how to leverage the JavaFX APIs to avoid common pitfalls (e.g., unresponsive applications, no dynamic update, etc.). Finally, we give a brief overview of third-party libraries that make it easy for JavaFX developers to access REST-based web services.

Setting Up the Application

First of all, we create the framework for our samples. We want to obtain tweets and render them in a JavaFX Control. For most of the samples, we use a ListView, but we also demonstrate how we can leverage the TableView APIs.

A single tweet contains information about the author (screenname, full name, picture), the timestamp, the content, and some meta-information. The goal of our samples is not to create a complete client for the Twitter API, so we only take into account a few important fields of a tweet: the name of the author, the timestamp, and the content.

Initially, we represent a tweet by a Java Object with getters and setters. This is shown in Listing 9-1.

Listing 9-1. *Tweet Class*

```
public class Tweet {

    private String author;
    private String title;
    private String timeStamp;

    public Tweet() {
    }

    public Tweet(String a, String t, String s) {
        this.author = a;
        this.title = t;
        this.timeStamp = s;
    }

    public String getAuthor() {
        return author;
    }

    public void setAuthor(String author) {
        this.author = author;
    }

    public String getTitle() {
        return title;
    }

    public void setTitle(String title) {
        this.title = title;
    }

    public String getTimeStamp() {
        return timeStamp;
    }
```

```
        public void setTimeStamp(String timeStamp) {
            this.timeStamp = timeStamp;
        }
}
```

Our Tweet class has two constructors. The zero-arg constructor is needed in one of the following examples and we come back to this later. The constructor that takes three arguments is used for convenience in other examples.

In Listing 9-2, we show how to display tweets. In this first example, the tweets are not obtained via the Twitter API, but they are hard-coded in the example.

Listing 9-2. *Framework for Rendering Tweets in a ListView*

```
import javafx.application.Application;
import javafx.collections.FXCollections;
import javafx.collections.ObservableList;
import javafx.scene.Scene;
import javafx.scene.control.ListView;
import javafx.scene.layout.StackPane;
import javafx.stage.Stage;

public class TweetApp1 extends Application {

    public static void main(String[] args) {
        launch(args);
    }

    @Override
    public void start(Stage primaryStage) {
        primaryStage.setTitle("TweetList");
        ListView<Tweet> listView = new ListView<Tweet>();
        listView.setItems(getObservableList());
        StackPane root = new StackPane();
        root.getChildren().add(listView);
        primaryStage.setScene(new Scene(root, 500, 300));
        primaryStage.show();
    }

    ObservableList<Tweet> getObservableList() {
        ObservableList<Tweet> answer = FXCollections.observableArrayList();
        Tweet t1 = new Tweet("JavaFXFan", "I love JavaFX!!", "today");
        Tweet t2 = new Tweet("JavaDeveloper", "Developing \"Hello World\" in JavaFX...",↩
 "yesterday");
        answer.addAll(t1, t2);
        return answer;
    }
}
```

If you have read the previous chapters, this code does not contain anything new. We create a ListView, add it to a StackPane, create a Scene, and render the Stage.

The ListView is populated with an ObservableList containing Tweets. This ObservableList is obtained by calling the getObservableList() method. In the following samples, we modify this method and show a number of ways for retrieving Tweets from the Twitter API.

■ **Note** The getObservableList returns an ObservableList. The ListView automatically observes this ObservableList. As a consequence, changes in the ObservableList are immediately rendered in the ListView control. In a later sample, we leverage this functionality.

Running this example results in the window shown in Figure 9-3.

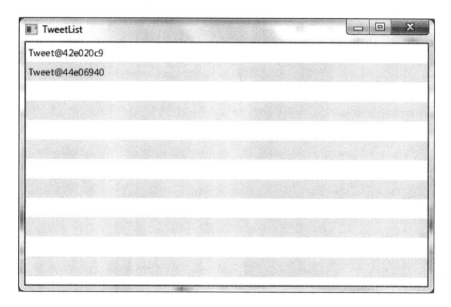

Figure 9-3. *The result of the first example*

The resulting window contains a ListView with two entries. Those entries correspond to the two tweets that are created in the getObservableList() method at the bottom of Listing 9-2.

The information about the tweets that is shown in the window is not very useful. Indeed, we told the ListView that it should display some instances of Tweet, but we did not tell how those should be displayed. The latter can be achieved by specifying a CellFactory. In this chapter, our goal is not to create a fancy user interface; rather, we want to show how to retrieve data and render these data in the user interface. Hence, we briefly show how the developer can alter the visualization of data by using the CellFactory concept. For an overview of the UI Controls that we use in our examples (ListView and TableView), we refer to Chapter 5, "Using the JavaFX UI Controls."

In Listing 9-3, we create a TweetCell class that extends ListCell and that defines how to lay out a cell.

Listing 9-3. Define TweetCell

```java
import javafx.scene.control.ListCell;

public class TweetCell extends ListCell<Tweet> {

    @Override
    protected void updateItem(Tweet tweet, boolean b) {
        if (tweet != null) {
            StringBuilder sb = new StringBuilder();
            sb.append("[").append(tweet.getTimeStamp()).append("]").
                    append(tweet.getAuthor()).append(": ").append(tweet.getTitle());
            setText(sb.toString());
        }
    }
}
```

When a cell item has to be updated, we tell it to show some text containing the timestamp between square brackets, followed by the author and the content or title of the Tweet. Next, the ListView needs to be told that it should render TweetCells. We do this by calling the ListView.setCellFactory() method. In Listing 9-4, we show the modified version of the start method of our TweetApplication.

Listing 9-4. Use CellFactory on the ListView

```java
public void start(Stage primaryStage) {
        primaryStage.setTitle("TweetList");
        ListView<Tweet> listView = new ListView<Tweet>();
        listView.setItems(getObservableList());
        listView.setCellFactory(new Callback<ListView<Tweet>, ListCell<Tweet>>() {

            @Override
            public ListCell<Tweet> call(ListView<Tweet> listview) {
                return new TweetCell();
            }
        });
        StackPane root = new StackPane();
        root.getChildren().add(listView);
        primaryStage.setScene(new Scene(root, 500, 30));
        primaryStage.show();
}
```

If we now run the application, the output appears as in Figure 9-4.

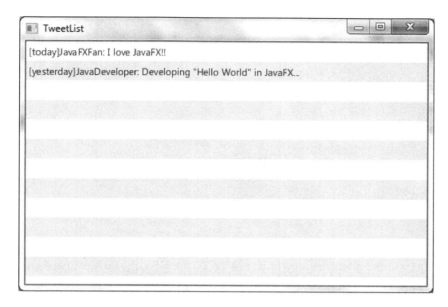

Figure 9-4. *The result of adding a TweetCell*

For every tweet that is in the items of the ListView, the output is now what we expected it to be. We can do a lot more with CellFactories (e.g., we can use graphics instead of just text), but that is beyond the scope of this chapter.

We now replace the hard-coded tweets with real information obtained via the Twitter API.

Using the Twitter API

Twitter (`http://twitter.com`) allows third-party developers to browse and access tweets using a REST-based interface. Twitter maintains a number of REST-based APIs, but for our examples we limit ourselves to the Search API. Detailed information on the Search API is obtained from `https://dev.twitter.com/docs/api/1/get/search` or `https://dev.twitter.com/docs/using-search` .

The resource URL—the endpoint for the REST service—is very simple:

```
http://search.twitter.com/search.format?q=searchterm
```

The search.format defines the format of the response. Currently, JSON, atom, and RSS are valid formats. Atom and RSS are both XML-based formats. The JSON (JavaScript Object Notation) format is also a human-readable text format that is very popular in REST services. In our examples, we use the JSON and the RSS format. The searchterm defines the search query. Apart from the format and the search query, there are a number of additional optional parameters that can be supplied with the request. For our examples, those two parameters are sufficient though.

If we want to retrieve tweets on "javafx" in JSON format, we call the following url.

```
http://search.twitter.com/search.json?q=javafx
```

The result is something like the JSON-text in Listing 9-5.

Listing 9-5. *JSON Response Obtained from the Twitter Search API*

```
{"completed_in":0.032,
"max_id":156099093272346624,
"max_id_str":"156099093272346624",
"next_page":"page=2&max_id=156099093272346624&q=javafx",
"page":1,
"query":"javafx",
"refresh_url":"?since_id=156099093272346624&q=javafx",
"results":[
{"created_at":"Sun, 08 Jan 2012 19:44:58+0000",
"from_user":"ITfacto",
"from_user_id":435927432,
"from_user_id_str":"435927432",
"from_user_name":"ITfacto",
"geo":null,
"id":156099093272346624,
"id_str":"156099093272346624",
"iso_language_code":"fr",
"metadata":{"result_type":"recent"},
"profile_image_url":"http://a1.twimg.com/profile_images/1704224541/ITfacto_mini_normal.JPG",
"profile_image_url_https":"https://si0.twimg.com/profile_images/1704224541/↵
ITfacto_mini_normal.JPG",
"source":"&lt;a href=&quot;http://twitterfeed.com&quot;↵
rel=&quot;nofollow&quot;&gt;twitterfeed&lt;/a&gt;",
"text":"#J2EE NetBeans IDE 7.1 : Oracle met en avant JavaFX 2.0 et PHP - Journal du Net↵
http://t.co/j9GK25ET",
"to_user":null,
"to_user_id":null,
"to_user_id_str":null,
"to_user_name":null
},
{ <other tweets omitted> }
],"results_per_page":15,"since_id":0,"since_id_str":"0"}
```

If we would rather have the result in the XML-based RSS format, we call the following url.

```
http://search.twitter.com/search.rss?q=javafx.
```

This query results in the XML response in Listing 9-6.

Listing 9-6. *RSS Response Obtained from the Twitter Search API*

```
<?xml version="1.0" encoding="UTF-8"?>
<rss version="2.0" xmlns:google="http://base.google.com/ns/1.0"↵
 xmlns:openSearch="http://a9.com/-/spec/opensearch/1.1/"↵
 xmlns:media="http://search.yahoo.com/mrss/" xmlns:twitter="http://api.twitter.com/">
    <channel>
        <title>javafx - Twitter Search</title>
        <description>javafx - Twitter Search</description>
        <link>http://search.twitter.com/search?q=javafx</link>
        <twitter:refresh_url>http://search.twitter.com/search.rss?since_id=↵
```

```
156099093272346624&amp;q=javafx</twitter:refresh_url>
        <pubDate>Sun, 08 Jan 2012 19:44:58 +0000
</pubDate>
        <openSearch:itemsPerPage>15</openSearch:itemsPerPage>
        <item>
                <title>#J2EE NetBeans IDE 7.1 : Oracle met en avant JavaFX 2.0 et PHP -↵
Journal du Net http://t.co/j9GK25ET</title>
                <link>http://twitter.com/ITfacto/statuses/156099093272346624</link>
                <description>&lt;a href="http://search.twitter.com/search?q=%23J2EE"↵
title="#J2EE" class=" "&gt;#J2EE&lt;/a&gt; NetBeans IDE 7.1 : Oracle met en avant↵
&lt;em&gt;JavaFX&lt;/em&gt; 2.0 et PHP - Journal du Net &lt;a↵
href="http://t.co/j9GK25ET"&gt;http://t.co/j9GK25ET&lt;/a&gt;</description>
                <pubDate>Sun, 08 Jan 2012 19:44:58 +0000</pubDate>
                <guid>http://twitter.com/ITfacto/statuses/156099093272346624</guid>
                <author>ITfacto@twitter.com (Itfacto)</author>
                <media:content type="image/jpg" height="48" width="48"↵
url="http://a1.twimg.com/profile_images/1704224541/ITfacto_mini_normal.JPG"/>
                <google:image_link>http://a1.twimg.com/profile_images/↵
1704224541/ITfacto_mini_normal.JPG</google:image_link>
                <twitter:metadata>
                        <twitter:result_type>recent</twitter:result_type>
                </twitter:metadata>
        </item>
    <Other items omitted>
    </channel>
</rss>
```

Although the data in the JSON response contain the same information as the data in the RSS/XML response, the format is of course very different. JSON and XML are both widely used on the Internet, and a large number of web services offer responses in both formats.

Depending on the use-case and the developer, one format may be preferred over the other. In general, JavaFX applications should be able to work with both formats, because they have to connect with third-party data, and the JavaFX developer cannot always influence the data format used by the back end.

■ **Note** Many applications allow a number of formats, and by specifying the HTTP "Accept" Header, the client can choose between the different formats.

In the next example, we show how to retrieve and parse the JSON response used in the Twitter Search API.

JSON Response Format

JSON is a very popular format on the Internet, especially in web applications where incoming data are parsed with JavaScript. JSON data are rather compact and more or less human readable.

A number of tools exist in Java for reading and writing JSON data. Unfortunately, at the time of writing there is no standard specification in Java that describes how to read and write JSON data. However, a Java Specification Request regarding JSON has been filed recently at `www.jcp.org/en/jsr/detail?id=353` with the title "JSR 353: Java API for JSON Processing."

The description of this JSR reads as follows.

> *The Java API for JSON Processing (JSON-P) JSR will develop a Java API to process (for e.g. parse, generate, transform and query) JSON.*

Once this JSR is accepted, there will be a uniform way in Java for dealing with JSON data. Until then, developers have to choose an existing JSON library or parse the data in their own code.

Each JSON library comes with its own set of tools, patterns, and advantages. Among the popular Java JSON libraries are

json.org (`www.json.org/java/index.html`)

jackson (`http://jackson.codehaus.org/`)

jsonmarshaller (`http://code.google.com/p/jsonmarshaller/`)

json.simple (`http://code.google.com/p/json-simple/`)

In our examples, we use the jackson library. The other tools are able to achieve the same result, though. The Jackson JSON Processor is also used in a number of frameworks (e.g., Jersey, RESTeasy, Apache Camel, etc.).

We now replace the hard-coded list containing two fake tweets with real Tweets obtained via the REST-Twitter API with JSON response format. We keep the existing code, but we modify the getObservableList() method as shown in Listing 9-7.

Listing 9-7. *Obtain Tweets Via the Twitter REST API, JSON Format and Parse the JSON*

```
ObservableList<Tweet> getObservableList() throws IOException {
    ObservableList<Tweet> answer = FXCollections.observableArrayList();

    String url = "http://search.twitter.com/search.json?q=javafx";
    JsonFactory f = new JsonFactory();
    JsonParser jp = f.createJsonParser(new URL(url));

    JsonToken token = jp.nextToken();
    while (token != JsonToken.START_ARRAY) {
        token = jp.nextToken();
    }
    while (token != JsonToken.END_ARRAY) {
        token = jp.nextToken();
        if (token == JsonToken.START_OBJECT) {
            Tweet tweet = parseTweet(jp);
            answer.add(tweet);
        }
    }
    return answer;
}
```

```
private Tweet parseTweet(JsonParser jp) throws IOException {
    Tweet tweet = new Tweet();
    JsonToken token = jp.nextToken();

    while (token != JsonToken.END_OBJECT) {
        if (token == JsonToken.START_OBJECT) {
            while (token != JsonToken.END_OBJECT) {
                token = jp.nextToken();
            }
        }
        if (token == JsonToken.FIELD_NAME) {
            String fieldname = jp.getCurrentName();

            if ("created_at".equals(fieldname)) {
                jp.nextToken();
                tweet.setTimeStamp(jp.getText());
            }
            if ("from_user".equals(fieldname)) {
                jp.nextToken();
                tweet.setAuthor(jp.getText());
            }
            if ("text".equals(fieldname)) {
                jp.nextToken();
                tweet.setTitle(jp.getText());
            }
        }
        token = jp.nextToken();
    }
    return tweet;
}
```

The code is a bit longer than in the case of the hard-coded tweets, and that is mainly because we do the JSON parsing ourselves. Later, we show how we can reduce the amount of code by using existing tools and libraries.

Before we dive into the code, we show the result of the modified application in Figure 9-5.

Figure 9-5. The result of the TweetApplication retrieving JSON data

The code in Listing 9-7 can be divided into four parts:

1. Call the REST endpoint.

2. Obtain the raw JSON data.

3. Convert each item into a tweet.

4. Add the Tweets to the result.

Calling the REST endpoint is very straightforward:

```
String url = "http://search.twitter.com/search.json?q=javafx";
JsonFactory f = new JsonFactory();
JsonParser jp = f.createJsonParser(new URL(url));
```

We create a URL Object that refers to the desired location, and pass that URL to the JsonFactory.createJsonParser method.

Note JsonFactory and JsonParser are specific to the Jackson JSON Parser. Other JSON libraries have other (factory) methods for calling endpoints.

We now have a JSON parser that contains a link to the data we want to have. Parsing these JSON data manually requires specific code for a specific case.

■ **Note**   It is not our intention to deliver an exhaustive JSON parsing guide. We only try to show how JSON data can be parsed for our specific use case. You can easily find a number of tutorials on JSON on the Internet. For example, the Jackson JSON parser we are using here already comes with a number of tutorials and examples.

In Listing 9-5, we observe that the tweets are in an array named "results," starting with the left square bracket "[". By calling the JsonParser.next() method, we jump from one token to the next one. The following loop causes the JsonParser to jump until the first occurrence of an Array element.

```
while (token!= JsonToken.START_ARRAY) {
        token = jp.nextToken();
}
```

As long as we don't encounter the STOP_ARRAY token (the right square bracket "]") at this level, we know that we are processing the tweet results. Because parsing the individual tweets is a separate process, we isolated that in a specific parseTweet method.

In the parseTweet method, we create a Tweet instance and fill its fields based on what the JsonParser reads in the JSON data. We keep reading tokens until we encounter an END_OBJECT token at the same level at which we started. Our response contains nested elements inside a single tweet result, and thus we have to be careful not to stop parsing on the first END_OBJECT token. Listing 9-5 indeed shows a metadata field that contains an object as well. In order to make sure we keep parsing until we reach the end of the tweet information, we include the following loop.

```
if (token == JsonToken.START_OBJECT) {
        while (token != JsonToken.END_OBJECT) {
                token = jp.nextToken();
        }
}
```

As you can see, there is a lot of information about individual tweets in the JSON response. For our example, we only need the author, the timestamp, and the content of the tweet. This information is present in the JSON response in the following format.

```
...
"created_at":"Sun, 18 Dec 2011 02:16:28 +0000",
"from_user":"bieroduwysm9",

...
"text":"@KGWiley83 http://t.co/pbAAmhjg",
...
```

In the parseTweet() method, once we know we are not processing nested elements (e.g., the metadata element), we check the type of the current token. If that type is JsonToken.FIELD_NAME, we obtain the name of the field by calling

```
String fieldname = jp.getCurrentName();
```

The token following the FIELD_NAME contains the information about the token. Hence, if the fieldName is "created_at", the next token will contain the value. Because we have all information in text format, we can call jp.getText() to obtain the information as a String.

The result of the parseTweet() method is a single Tweet. This tweet is added to the ObservableList by the following snippet.

```
Tweet tweet = parseTweet(jp);
answer.add(tweet);
```

This example shows that it is relatively easy to retrieve and parse JSON data obtained from a REST endpoint. However, the parsing is a bit cumbersome and error prone. Good-enough tools exist that help us out in this area. The Jackson JSON parser contains a JSON – Object mapper that directly binds text in JSON format to a Java Object.

Jackson supports Full Data Binding and Simple Data Binding. Full Data Binding allows the developer to read the incoming JSON data and automatically create a POJO. Simple Data Binding also reads and parses the incoming data, but the result is put in a Map rather than in a specific dedicated POJO.

▩ **Note** The word "binding" in the jackson documentation should not be confused with the Binding concept in JavaFX.

Our next example uses the Simple Data Binding. Again, the only part of the code we have to change is the getObservableList() method. Listing 9-8 introduces the Simple Data Binding.

Listing 9-8. *Obtain Tweets from JSON Response Using Simple Data Binding*

```
ObservableList<Tweet> getObservableList() throws IOException {
    ObservableList<Tweet> answer = FXCollections.observableArrayList();
    String url = "http://search.twitter.com/search.json?q=javafx";
    ObjectMapper mapper = new ObjectMapper();
    Map<String, Object> rawMap = mapper.readValue(new URL(url), Map.class);
    List<Map<String, Object>> results = (List) rawMap.get("results");
    for (Map<String, Object> entry : results) {
        Tweet tweet = new Tweet();
        tweet.setTimeStamp((String) entry.get("created_at"));
        tweet.setAuthor((String) entry.get("from_user"));
        tweet.setTitle((String) entry.get("text"));
        answer.add(tweet);
    }
    return answer;
}
```

As you can observe, the code has become much simpler, mainly because we don't have to do the manual token processing anymore. The class that is helping us here is the org.codehaus.jackson.map.ObjectMapper.

The following code snippet creates a key-value Map based on the JSON response.

```
ObjectMapper mapper = new ObjectMapper();
Map<String, Object> rawMap = mapper.readValue(new URL(url), Map.class);
```

Each key in the Map points to an element in the response. The value corresponding to a key can be the simple value of the element, a list of elements, or a nested element.

We know that the element with key "results" is a list of tweets.

```
List<Map<String, Object>> results = (List) rawMap.get("results");
```

Therefore, the preceding snippet creates a list of tweets, with the information about a specific tweet in a specific Map<String, Object>.

We iterate over this list in order to obtain the specific information on the specific tweets. Each entry in the list contains a Map<String, Object> with the tweet-specific information (e.g., "created_at", "from_user", "text"). After parsing each individual tweet, we add it to the result.

The examples that we analyzed in this section show that we can easily call REST-based endpoints, and convert the resulting JSON response into a ListView. In the next section, we demonstrate a similar process for XML responses.

XML Response Format

The XML format is widely used in the Java platform. As a consequence, standardization of XML-based operations in Java already happened years ago. There are a number of XML tools built into the Java Platform, Standard Edition, and we can use these APIs and tools in JavaFX without any external dependency. In this section, we first use a DOM processor for parsing the XML response obtained from the Twitter API. Next, we use the JAXB standard to automatically obtain Java Objects.

Changing our application from JSON-input to XML-input requires only the getObservableList method to be changed. The new implementation is shown in Listing 9-9.

Listing 9-9. Obtaining Tweets from the XML-Based Response

```
ObservableList<Tweet> getObservableList() throws IOException,⤸
ParserConfigurationException, SAXException {
    ObservableList<Tweet> answer = FXCollections.observableArrayList();
    String url = "http://search.twitter.com/search.rss?q=javafx";

    DocumentBuilderFactory dbf = DocumentBuilderFactory.newInstance();
    DocumentBuilder db = dbf.newDocumentBuilder();
    Document doc = db.parse(url);
    NodeList tweetNodes = doc.getElementsByTagName("item");
    int count = tweetNodes.getLength();
    for (int i = 0; i < count; i++) {
        Tweet tweet = new Tweet();
        Node tweetNode = tweetNodes.item(i);
        NodeList childNodes = tweetNode.getChildNodes();
        int cnt2 = childNodes.getLength();
        for (int j = 0; j < cnt2; j++) {
            Node me = childNodes.item(j);
            String nodeName = me.getNodeName();
            if ("pubDate".equals(nodeName)) {
                tweet.setTimeStamp(me.getTextContent());
            }
            if ("author".equals(nodeName)) {
                tweet.setAuthor(me.getTextContent());
            }
```

```
            if ("title".equals(nodeName)) {
                tweet.setTitle(me.getTextContent());
            }
        }
        answer.add(tweet);
    }
    return answer;
}
```

Again, the goal of this section is not to give a comprehensive overview of the DOM APIs. There are a large number of resources available on the Internet that provide information about XML in general, or DOM in particular.

In order to be able to compile the code in Listing 9-9, the following import statements had to be added.

```
import javax.xml.parsers.DocumentBuilder;
import javax.xml.parsers.DocumentBuilderFactory;
import javax.xml.parsers.ParserConfigurationException;
import org.w3c.dom.Document;
import org.w3c.dom.Node;
import org.w3c.dom.NodeList;
import org.xml.sax.SAXException;
```

Before we go into detail about the code, we show the output of this example in Figure 9-6.

Figure 9-6. *The result of the tweet application using XML response*

The code in Listing 9-9 shows some similarities to the code in Listing 9-7. In both cases, we process data available in a text format (JSON or XML/RSS) and convert the data into Tweet instances. In Listing 9-8, the DOM approach is used to inspect the received response.

An org.w3c.dom.Document instance is obtained using the following code snippet.

```
DocumentBuilderFactory dbf = DocumentBuilderFactory.newInstance();
DocumentBuilder db = dbf.newDocumentBuilder();
Document doc = db.parse(url);
```

The resulting Document can now be queried. From the XML response shown in Listing 9-6, we learn that the individual tweets are enclosed in XML Elements named "item". We use the following to obtain a list of those XML Elements.

```
NodeList tweetNodes = doc.getElementsByTagName("item");
```

We then iterate over this list, and obtain the tweet-specific fields by inspecting the childNodes in the respective XML Elements. Finally, we add the resulting tweet to the answer.

This approach is rather simple, but we still have to do some manual XML parsing. Although this allows for flexibility, parsing becomes harder and more error prone with increasing complexity of the datastructure.

Fortunately, the Java 2 Standard Edition APIs contain tools for converting XML directly into Java Objects. The specification for these APIs is defined by the JAXB standard, and is available in the javax.xml.bind package. The process of converting XML data into Java Objects is called unmarshalling.

We now modify our example and make it use a mix of DOM parsing and JAXB unmarshalling. Again, we only change the getObservableList() method. The modified implementation is shown in Listing 9-10.

Listing 9-10. *Combining XML Parsing and JAXB*

```
ObservableList<Tweet> getObservableList() throws IOException, ↵
ParserConfigurationException, SAXException {
    ObservableList<Tweet> answer = FXCollections.observableArrayList();
    String url = "http://search.twitter.com/search.rss?q=javafx";

    DocumentBuilderFactory dbf = DocumentBuilderFactory.newInstance();
    DocumentBuilder db = dbf.newDocumentBuilder();
    Document doc = db.parse(url);
    NodeList tweetNodes = doc.getElementsByTagName("item");
    int count = tweetNodes.getLength();
    for (int i = 0; i < count; i++) {
        Node tweetNode = tweetNodes.item(i);
        DOMSource source = new DOMSource(tweetNode);
        final Tweet tweet = (Tweet) JAXB.unmarshal(source, Tweet.class);
        answer.add(tweet);
    }
    return answer;
}
```

The only difference between this approach and the approach used in Listing 9-9 is the parsing of the individual tweets. Instead of using DOM parsing for obtaining the specific fields of the individual tweets, we use the unmarshal method in JAXB. The JAXB specifications allow for lots of flexibility and configuration, and the JAXB.unmarshal method is only a convenience method. However, in many cases, this method is sufficient. The JAXB.unmarshal method takes two parameters: the input source and the class that is the result of the conversion.

We want to convert the XML source into instances of our Tweet class, but how does the JAXB framework know how to map the fields? In many cases, the mapping is straightforward and does not require changes to existing code, but in other cases, the mapping is a bit more complex. Good enough, a whole package with annotations exists that we can use to help JAXB determine the conversion between XML and the Java Object.

In order to make the code in Listing 9-10 work, we made some minor modifications to the Tweet class. The new code for the Tweet class is shown in Listing 9-11.

Listing 9-11. *Tweet Class with JAXB Annotations*

```
import javax.xml.bind.annotation.XmlAccessType;
import javax.xml.bind.annotation.XmlAccessorType;
import javax.xml.bind.annotation.XmlElement;

@XmlAccessorType(XmlAccessType.FIELD)
public class Tweet {

    private String author;
    private String title;
    @XmlElement(name = "pubDate")
    private String timeStamp;

    public Tweet() {
    }

    public Tweet(String a, String t, String s) {
        this.author = a;
        this.title = t;
        this.timeStamp = s;
    }

    public String getAuthor() {
        return author;
    }

    public void setAuthor(String author) {
        this.author = author;
    }

    public String getTitle() {
        return title;
    }

    public void setTitle(String title) {
        this.title = title;
    }

    public String getTimeStamp() {
        return timeStamp;
    }
}
```

```
    public void setTimeStamp(String timeStamp) {
        this.timeStamp = timeStamp;
    }

}
```

We added two annotations to the original Tweet class. First, we annotated the class itself with

```
@XmlAccessorType(XmlAccessType.FIELD)
```

This annotation tells the JAXB framework to map XML data on the fields of this class, as opposed to on the JavaBean properties (getter/setter methods) of this class. The second annotation is added to the timeStamp field:

```
@XmlElement(name = "pubDate")
private String timeStamp;
```

This indicates that the timeStamp field corresponds to an XML element named "pubDate". Indeed, if we look at Listing 9-6, it shows that the creationDate is in an element with the name "pubDate". We have to instruct the JAXB runtime to map this element with our timeStamp field, and this is what we do with the @XmlElement annotation.

Using the JAXB annotations made it easy to convert the XML tweet elements into individual Tweet instances, but we still had some manual XML processing in our main class. However, we can completely remove the manual XMLParsing and convert the whole XML response into a Java Object. Doing so, the getObservableList() method becomes very simple, as shown in Listing 9-12.

Listing 9-12. *Parsing Incoming XML Data Using JAXB*

```
ObservableList<Tweet> getObservableList() throws MalformedURLException {
    String loc = "http://search.twitter.com/search.rss?q=javafx";
    URL url = new URL(loc);
    TwitterResponse response = JAXB.unmarshal(url, TwitterResponse.class);
    List<Tweet> raw = response.getTweets();
    ObservableList<Tweet> answer = FXCollections.observableArrayList(raw);
    return answer;
}
```

In this example, we use JAXB to convert the XML response into an instance of TwitterResponse, and the tweets are then obtained via this TwitterResponse instance. Note that we convert the tweets from a regular List Object into an ObservableList object, as required by the method signature. We later show an example where we don't have to do that additional conversion.

The TwitterResponse class has two goals: map the XML response on a Java Object and make the tweet items available as a List of Tweet instances. This is achieved by the code in Listing 9-13.

Listing 9-13. *TwitterResponse Class, Enabling Conversion Between XML Response and Java Objects*

```
import java.util.LinkedList;
import java.util.List;
import javax.xml.bind.annotation.*;
```

```
@XmlRootElement(name="rss")
@XmlAccessorType(XmlAccessType.FIELD)
public class TwitterResponse {

  public List<Tweet> getTweets() {
    return channel.getItem();
  }

  private TwitterResponse.Channel channel = new Channel();

  @XmlAccessorType(XmlAccessType.FIELD)
  private static class Channel {

    private String title;
    @XmlElement(name="item")
    private List<Tweet> item = new LinkedList<Tweet>();

    public Channel() {
    }

    public List<Tweet> getItem() {
      return item;
    }

    public void setItem(List<Tweet> item) {
      this.item = item;
    }
  }

}
```

The TwitterResponse class itself has two annotations:

```
@XmlAccessorType(XmlAccessType.FIELD)
```

was already discussed before and

```
@XmlRootElement(name="rss")
```

indicates that this class corresponds to a root object in the XML structure, with the name "rss". This indeed corresponds to the syntax of the XML response of the Twitter API shown in Listing 9-6.

The TwitterResponse has a field named channel (defined by an inner class named Channel). This field corresponds to the "channel" XML element in the response in Listing 9-6. The Channel class contains a List of Tweet instances, annotated with the @XmlElement(name="item") in order to map those on the respective XML elements.

The previous examples show how existing technologies available in the Java 2 Platform, Standard Edition, can be used to obtain data from web services and inject these data in JavaFX controls. We now modify the example code in order to take advantage of some specific features of the JavaFX Platform.

Asynchronous Processing

A major problem with the examples so far is that they block the user interface during the process of data retrieval and parsing. In many real-world situations, this is unacceptable. Calls to external web services might take longer than expected due to network or server issues. Even when the external calls are fast, a temporarily unresponsive user interface decreases the overall quality of the application.

Fortunately, the JavaFX Platform allows for concurrency and asynchronous tasks. The concepts of Task, Worker, and Service have already been discussed in Chapter 6. In this section, we show how to leverage the javafx.concurrent package when accessing web services. We also leverage the fact that the ListView watches the ObservableList that contains its items.

The basic idea is that, when creating the ListView, we immediately return an empty ObservableList, while retrieving the data in a background Thread. Once we retrieve and parse the data, we add it to the ObservableList and the result will immediately be visible in the ListView.

The main class for this example is shown in Listing 9-14. We started with the code of the previous example, using an XML response and a TwitterResult class containing the response. With some minor modifications, we could use the JSON response as well, though.

Listing 9-14. Use a Background Thread for Retrieving Tweets ListView

```
import java.net.MalformedURLException;
import javafx.application.Application;
import javafx.beans.InvalidationListener;
import javafx.beans.Observable;
import javafx.collections.FXCollections;
import javafx.collections.ObservableList;
import javafx.concurrent.Worker.State;
import javafx.scene.Scene;
import javafx.scene.control.ListCell;
import javafx.scene.control.ListView;
import javafx.scene.layout.StackPane;
import javafx.stage.Stage;
import javafx.util.Callback;

public class TweetApp8 extends Application {

    public static void main(String[] args) {
        launch(args);
    }

    @Override
    public void start(Stage primaryStage) throws MalformedURLException {
        primaryStage.setTitle("TweetList");
        ListView<Tweet> listView = new ListView<Tweet>();
        listView.setItems( getObservableList());
        listView.setCellFactory(new Callback<ListView<Tweet>, ListCell<Tweet>>() {

            @Override
            public ListCell<Tweet> call(ListView<Tweet> listview) {
                return new TweetCell();
            }
        });
```

```
        StackPane root = new StackPane();
        root.getChildren().add(listView);
        primaryStage.setScene(new Scene(root, 500, 300));
        primaryStage.show();
        System.out.println("Setup complete");
    }

    ObservableList<Tweet> getObservableList() throws MalformedURLException {
        final ObservableList<Tweet> tweets = FXCollections.observableArrayList();

        String loc = "http://search.twitter.com/search.rss?q=javafx";
        final TwitterRetrievalService twitterRetrievalService = new↵
TwitterRetrievalService(loc);
        twitterRetrievalService.start();
        twitterRetrievalService.stateProperty().addListener(new InvalidationListener() {

            @Override
            public void invalidated(Observable arg0) {
                State now = twitterRetrievalService.getState();
                System.out.println("State of service = " + now);
                if (now == State.SUCCEEDED) {
                    tweets.setAll(twitterRetrievalService.getValue());
                }
            }
        });

        return tweets;
    }
}
```

The main method is not different from the previous example, apart from the addition of a System.out log message that will print a message when we are done with the setup.

The getObservableList method will first create an instance of ObservableList, and this instance is returned upon method completion. Initially, this instance will be an empty list. In this method, an instance of TwitterRetrievalService is created and the location of the REST endpoint is passed in the constructor. The TwitterRetrievalService, which extends javafx.concurrent.Service, is started, and we listen for changes in the State of the Service. When the state of the Service changes to State.SUCCEEDED, we add the retrieved tweets to the ObservableList. Note that on every state change in the instance of the TwitterRetrievalService, we log a message to System.out.

We now take a closer look at the TwitterRetrievalService in order to understand how it starts a new Thread, and how it makes sure that the retrieved tweets are added to the ListView control using the JavaFX Thread. The code of the TwitterRetrievalService is shown in Listing 9-15.

Listing 9-15. *TwitterRetrievalService*

```
import java.net.URL;
import java.util.List;
import javafx.collections.FXCollections;
import javafx.collections.ObservableList;
import javafx.concurrent.Service;
import javafx.concurrent.Task;
import javax.xml.bind.JAXB;
```

```
public class TwitterRetrievalService extends Service<ObservableList<Tweet>> {

    private String loc;

    public TwitterRetrievalService(String loc) {
        this.loc = loc;
    }

    @Override
    protected Task createTask() {
        Task task = new SingleRetrieverTask(this.loc);
        return task;
    }

    private static class SingleRetrieverTask extends Task<ObservableList<Tweet>> {

        private String location;

        public SingleRetrieverTask(final String loc) {
            location = loc;
        }

        @Override
        protected ObservableList<Tweet> call() throws Exception {
            URL url = new URL(location);
            TwitterResponse response = JAXB.unmarshal(url, TwitterResponse.class);
            List<Tweet> raw = response.getTweets();
            ObservableList<Tweet> answer = FXCollections.observableArrayList(raw);
            return answer;
        }
    }
}
```

The TwitterRetrievalService extends Service and thus has to implement a createTask method. When the Service is started, this task is executed in a separate Thread. For clarity, we created an implementation of Task as an innerclass named SingleRetrieverTask. The createTask method on the TwitterRetrievalService creates a new SingleRetrieverTask and returns it. The location of the URL endpoint is passed in the constructor.

The signature of the SingleRetrieverTask,

```
private static class SingleRetrieverTask extends Task<ObservableList<Tweet>>
```

ensures that the return value of the SingleRetrieverTask has the type

```
ObservableList<Tweet>
```

which is needed in the getObservableList method in the main class.

Indeed, the following code snippet states that the twitterRetrievalService.getValue() should return an ObservableList<Tweet>

```
if (now == State.SUCCEEDED) {
    tweets.setAll(twitterRetrievalService.getValue());
}
```

Because SingleRetrieverTask implements Task, we have to implement the call method. This method is actually doing what the getObservableList method in the previous examples was doing: retrieving the data and parsing them.

Although the real work in a Service (the Task created by createTask) is done in a background Thread, all methods on the Service, including the getValue() call, should be accessed from the JavaFX Thread. The internal implementation makes sure that all changes to the available properties in the Service are executed on the JavaFX application Thread.

Running the example gives the exact same visual output as running the previous example. However, we added some System.out messages for clarity. If we run the example, the following messages can be seen on the console.

```
Setup complete
State of service = RUNNING
State of service = SUCCEEDED
```

This shows that the getObservable method returns before the tweets are obtained and added to the list.

■ **Note** In theory, you could notice a different behavior inasmuch as the background thread might be completed before the other initialization has been done. In practice, however, this behavior is unlikely when network calls are involved.

Converting Web Services Data to TableView

So far, all our examples showed tweets in a ListView. The ListView is an easy and powerful JavaFX Control, however, there are other controls that are in some cases more suitable to render information.

We can show the Tweet data in a TableView as well, and that is what we do in this section. The retrieval and parsing of the data stay the same as in the previous example. However, we now use a TableView to render the data, and we have to define which columns we want to see. For each column, we have to specify the origination of the data. The code in Listing 9-16 shows the start method used in the example.

Listing 9-16. *The Start Method in the Application Rendering Tweets in a TableView*

```
@Override
  public void start(Stage primaryStage) throws MalformedURLException {
      primaryStage.setTitle("TweetTable");
      TableView<Tweet> tableView = new TableView<Tweet>();
      TableColumn<Tweet, String> dateColumn = new TableColumn<Tweet, String>("Date");
      TableColumn<Tweet, String> authorColumn = new TableColumn<Tweet, String>("Author");
      TableColumn<Tweet, String> textColumn = new TableColumn<Tweet, String>("Text");
      textColumn.setPrefWidth(400);
      dateColumn.setCellValueFactory(new Callback<CellDataFeatures<Tweet, String>, ↵
ObservableValue<String>>() {
```

```
                @Override
                public ObservableValue<String> call(CellDataFeatures<Tweet, String> cdf) {
                    Tweet tweet = cdf.getValue();
                    return new SimpleStringProperty(tweet.getTimeStamp());
                }
            });
            authorColumn.setCellValueFactory(new Callback<CellDataFeatures<Tweet, String>,↵
        ObservableValue<String>>() {

                @Override
                public ObservableValue<String> call(CellDataFeatures<Tweet, String> cdf) {
                    Tweet tweet = cdf.getValue();
                    return new SimpleStringProperty(tweet.getAuthor());
                }
            });
            textColumn.setCellValueFactory(new Callback<CellDataFeatures<Tweet, String>,↵
        ObservableValue<String>>() {

                @Override
                public ObservableValue<String> call(CellDataFeatures<Tweet, String> cdf) {
                    Tweet tweet = cdf.getValue();
                    return new SimpleStringProperty(tweet.getTitle());
                }
            });


            tableView.getColumns().addAll(dateColumn, authorColumn, textColumn);
            tableView.setItems(getObservableList());

            StackPane root = new StackPane();
            root.getChildren().add(tableView);
            primaryStage.setScene(new Scene(root, 500, 300));
            primaryStage.show();
        }
```

Clearly, this example requires more code than the example showing a ListView. Setting up a table is slightly more complex, due to the different columns that are involved. There is not much difference between setting the contents of the ListView and setting contents of the TableView. This is achieved doing

```
            tableView.setItems(getObservableList());
```

where the getObservableList() method is the same implementation as in the previous example.

When using a TableView, we have to define a number of TableColumns. This is done in the following code snippet.

```
        TableColumn<Tweet, String> dateColumn = new TableColumn<Tweet, String>("Date");
        TableColumn<Tweet, String> authorColumn = new TableColumn<Tweet, String>("Author");
        TableColumn<Tweet, String> textColumn = new TableColumn<Tweet, String>("Text");
```

Using the TableColumn constructor, we create one TableColumn with title "Date", one with title "Author", and a third one titled "Text". The Generics <Tweet, String> indicate that each entry in a row represents a Tweet, and the individual cells in the specified column are of type String.

Next, the instances of TableColumn that we created need to know what data they should render. This is done using CellFactories, as shown in the following snippet.

```
        dateColumn.setCellValueFactory(new Callback<CellDataFeatures<Tweet, String>,↵
ObservableValue<String>>() {

            @Override
            public ObservableValue<String> call(CellDataFeatures<Tweet, String> cdf) {
                Tweet tweet = cdf.getValue();
                return new SimpleStringProperty(tweet.getTimeStamp());
            }
        });
```

A detailed description of the setCellValueFactory method is beyond the scope of this chapter. As can be observed from the example, we have to specify a Callback class with a call method that returns an ObservableValue containing the content of the specific cell. The tweet we are displaying in this row can be obtained via the CellDataFeatures instance that is passed in the call method. Because we want to show the timestamp, we return a SimpleStringProperty whose content is set to the timeStamp of the specified Tweet.

The same technique has to be used for the other TableColumns (containing the author and the title of the Tweet).

Finally, we have to add the columns to the TableView:

```
        tableView.getColumns().addAll(dateColumn, authorColumn, textColumn);
```

Running this example results in the visual output shown in Figure 9-7.

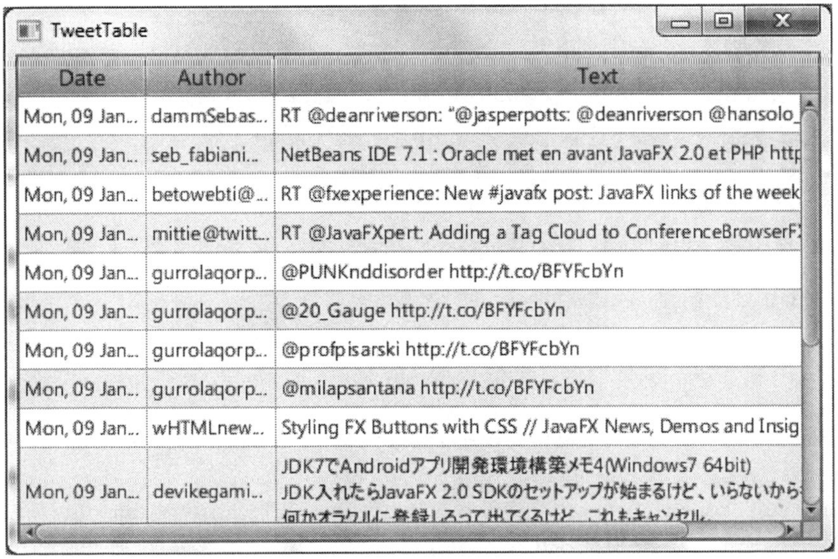

Figure 9-7. *Using a TableView for rendering tweets*

This sample requires lots of boilerplate code for a simple table, but fortunately the JavaFX Platform contains a way to reduce the amount of code. Manually setting the CellValueFactory instances for each column is cumbersome, but we can use another method for doing this, by using JavaFX Properties. Listing 9-17 contains a modified version of the start method of the main class, where we leverage the JavaFX Properties concept.

Listing 9-17. *Rendering Data in Columns Based on JavaFX Properties*

```java
@Override
public void start(Stage primaryStage) throws MalformedURLException {
    primaryStage.setTitle("TweetList");
    TableView<Tweet> tableView = new TableView<Tweet>();
    TableColumn<Tweet, String> dateColumn = new TableColumn<Tweet, String>("Date");
    dateColumn.setCellValueFactory(new PropertyValueFactory<Tweet, String>("timeStamp"));
    TableColumn<Tweet, String> authorColumn = new TableColumn<Tweet, String>("Author");
    authorColumn.setCellValueFactory(new PropertyValueFactory<Tweet, String>("author"));
    TableColumn<Tweet, String> textColumn = new TableColumn<Tweet, String>("Text");
    textColumn.setCellValueFactory(new PropertyValueFactory<Tweet, String>("title"));

    textColumn.setPrefWidth(400);

    tableView.getColumns().addAll(dateColumn, authorColumn, textColumn);
    tableView.setItems(getObservableList());

    StackPane root = new StackPane();
    root.getChildren().add(tableView);
    primaryStage.setScene(new Scene(root, 500, 300));
    primaryStage.show();
}
```

This code is clearly shorter than the code in the previous sample. We actually replaced

```java
dateColumn.setCellValueFactory(new Callback<CellDataFeatures<Tweet, String>, ↵
ObservableValue<String>>() {

    @Override
    public ObservableValue<String> call(CellDataFeatures<Tweet, String> cdf) {
        Tweet tweet = cdf.getValue();
        return new SimpleStringProperty(tweet.getTimeStamp());
    }
});
```

by

```java
dateColumn.setCellValueFactory(new PropertyValueFactory<Tweet, String>("timeStamp"));
```

The same holds for the authorColumn and the textColumn.

We are using instances of javafx.scene.control.cell.PropertyValueFactory<S,T>(String name) for defining what specific data should be rendered in which cell.

The PropertyValueFactory searches for a JavaFX property with the specified name and returns the ObservableValue of this property when called. In case no property with such a name can be found, the JavaDoc says the following.

In this example, the "firstName" string is used as a reference to an assumed `firstNameProperty()` method in the `Person` class type (which is the class type of the TableView items list). Additionally, this method must return a `Property` instance. If a method meeting these requirements is found, then the `TableCell` is populated with this ObservableValue. In addition, the TableView will automatically add an observer to the returned value, such that any changes fired will be observed by the TableView, resulting in the cell immediately updating.

If no method matching this pattern exists, there is fall-through support for attempting to call get<property>() or is<property>() (that is, `getFirstName()` or `isFirstName()` in the example above). If a method matching this pattern exists, the value returned from this method is wrapped in a `ReadOnlyObjectWrapper` and returned to the TableCell. However, in this situation, this means that the TableCell will not be able to observe the ObservableValue for changes (as is the case in the first approach above).

From this, it is clear that JavaFX Properties are the preferred way for rendering information in a TableView. So far, we used the POJO Tweet class with JavaBean getter and setter methods as the value object for being displayed in both a ListView and a TableView.

Although the example above also works without using JavaFX Properties, as stated by the JavaDoc, we now modify the Tweet class to use Properties for the author information. The timeStamp and the text fields could have been modified to use JavaFX Properties as well, but the mixed example shows that the fall-through scenario described in the JavaDoc really works. The modified Tweet class is shown in Listing 9-18.

Listing 9-18. *Implementation of Tweet Class Using JavaFX Properties for the Author Field*

```java
import javafx.beans.property.SimpleStringProperty;
import javafx.beans.property.StringProperty;
import javax.xml.bind.annotation.XmlAccessType;
import javax.xml.bind.annotation.XmlAccessorType;
import javax.xml.bind.annotation.XmlElement;

@XmlAccessorType(XmlAccessType.PROPERTY)
public class Tweet {

    private final StringProperty authorProperty = new SimpleStringProperty();

    public final StringProperty authorProperty() {
        return authorProperty;
    }
    private String title;
    private String timeStamp;

    public Tweet() {
    }
```

```
    public Tweet(String a, String t, String s) {
        this.authorProperty.set(a);
        this.title = t;
        this.timeStamp = s;
    }

    public String getAuthor() {
        return authorProperty.get();
    }

    public void setAuthor(String author) {
        authorProperty.set(author);

    }

    public String getTitle() {
        return title;
    }

    public void setTitle(String title) {
        this.title = title;
    }

    public String getTimeStamp() {
        return timeStamp;
    }

    @XmlElement(name = "pubDate")
    public void setTimeStamp(String timeStamp) {
        this.timeStamp = timeStamp;
    }
}
```

The authorProperty follows the standard JavaFX Convention, as explained in Chapter 3, "Understanding the JavaFX Bean Convention."

Apart from the introduction of JavaFX Properties, there is another major change in the implementation of the Tweet class. The class is now annotated with

```
@XmlAccessorType(XmlAccessType.PROPERTY)
```

The reason for this is that when doing so, the setter methods will be called by the JAXB.unmarshal method when it creates an instance of the Tweet with some specific information. Now that we are using JavaFX Properties instead of primitive types, this is required. The JAXB framework could easily assign the value of the XML Element "author" to the author String field, but it cannot assign a value to a JavaFX Property object by default.

By using XmlAccessType.PROPERTY, the setAuthor(String v) method will be called by the JAXB framework, supplying the value of the XML Element to the setAuthor method. The implementation of this method

```
        authorProperty.set(author);
```

will then update the JavaFX Property that is subsequently being used by the TableColumn and the TableView.

The examples we have shown so far in this chapter demonstrate that the Java Platform, Standard Edition, already contains a number of APIs that are very useful when accessing Web services. We also showed how to use the JavaFX Concurrent Framework, the ObservableList pattern, JavaFX Properties, and the PropertyValueFactory class in order to enhance the flow between calling the web service and rendering the data in the JavaFX Controls.

Although there is no rocket science involved in the examples, additional requirements will make things more complex, and more boilerplate code will be required. Fortunately, a number of initiatives already popped up in the JavaFX community, with the goal of making our lives easier.

Using External Libraries

With the exception of the JSON parser used in the first examples, all our examples so far did not require any additional external library. The Java 2 Platform, Standard Edition and the JavaFX Platform offer a great environment that can be used for accessing web services. In this section, we use three external libraries and show how they make accessing web services easier.

RestFX

The RestFX project is hosted at `http://code.google.com/p/restfx/` and that web site mentions the following mission statement.

> *REST/FX provides a set of classes for producing and consuming REST services in a JavaFX application.*

RestFX contains implementations of Services that allow asynchronous access to web services, with Listeners that are notified when the State of the Service is changed. As such, it resembles Listing 9-15 where we created a primitive implementation of such a Service.

Using RestFX in our examples is very easy. Again, we only have to change the getObservableList() method, but for clarity we show the complete code of the main class here. Listing 9-19 shows how to retrieve tweets from the Twitter API with JSON output, and render them in a ListView.

Listing 9-19. *Obtaining Tweets Using RestFX*

```
import java.net.MalformedURLException;
import java.util.List;
import java.util.Map;
import javafx.application.Application;
import javafx.collections.FXCollections;
import javafx.collections.ObservableList;
import javafx.scene.Scene;
import javafx.scene.control.ListCell;
import javafx.scene.control.ListView;
import javafx.scene.layout.StackPane;
import javafx.stage.Stage;
import javafx.util.Callback;
import restfx.web.GetQuery;
import restfx.web.Query;
import restfx.web.QueryListener;
```

```java
public class TweetAppRestFX extends Application {

    public static void main(String[] args) {
        launch(args);
    }

    @Override
    public void start(Stage primaryStage) throws MalformedURLException {
        primaryStage.setTitle("TweetAppRestFX");
        ListView<Tweet> listView = new ListView<Tweet>();
        listView.setItems(getObservableList());
        listView.setCellFactory(new Callback<ListView<Tweet>, ListCell<Tweet>>() {

            @Override
            public ListCell<Tweet> call(ListView<Tweet> listview) {
                return new TweetCell();
            }
        });

        StackPane root = new StackPane();
        root.getChildren().add(listView);
        primaryStage.setScene(new Scene(root, 500, 300));
        primaryStage.show();
        System.out.println("Setup complete");
    }

    ObservableList<Tweet> getObservableList() throws MalformedURLException {
        final ObservableList<Tweet> tweets = FXCollections.observableArrayList();
        GetQuery getQuery = new GetQuery("search.twitter.com", "/search.json");
        getQuery.getParameters().put("q", "javafx");
        getQuery.execute(new QueryListener<Object>() {

            @Override
            @SuppressWarnings("unchecked")
            public void queryExecuted(Query<Object> task) {
                Map<String, Object> value = (Map<String, Object>) task.getValue();
                List<Object> results = (List<Object>) value.get("results");
                for (Object target : results) {
                    Map<String, String> tweetMap = (Map<String, String>) target;
                    String timeStamp = tweetMap.get("created_at");
                    String author = tweetMap.get("from_user");
                    String title = tweetMap.get("text");
                    Tweet tweet = new Tweet(author, title, timeStamp);
                    tweets.add(tweet);
                }
            }
        });
        return tweets;
    }
}
```

The ObservableList creates a GetQuery and supplies the required information about the web services Endpoint. RestFX supports GetQuery, PostQuery, PutQuery, and DeleteQuery and as such it aligns very well with the REST specifications. When we want to execute the query, we have to specify an implementation of the QueryListener interface with a callback method that is called once execution is completed.

In our example, the result of the rest call is a JSON response, and similar to the jackson API we used in a previous example, the result is contained in a Map<String, Object>.

The "results" key in this Map corresponds with a List of Map<String, String> that contains information about a specific tweet. Querying this map allows us to construct a Tweet instance, and add it to the ObservableMap.

Being very much aligned with the REST/HTTP protocol, RESTFX provides APIs for easy manipulation of HTTP headers for Authentication, and for supplying query and form parameters. RESTFX uses the concept of "serializers" for translating content of a specific format into Java objects (e.g., Map). We used the JSON Serializer in our example, but RESTFX contains a number of other serializers (e.g., a CSVSerializer).

DataFX

The DataFX library is described at `http://javafxdata.org` and it provides an end-to-end toolkit for retrieving, parsing, massaging, populating, viewing, and rendering data. These data might be obtained using REST-based web services, but can also be obtained from a local filesystem, a database, or a number of other datasources.

DataFX consists of two integrated parts:

- Cell Factories, providing a number of useful CellFactories and hence reducing the boilerplate code that is often required in projects

- DataSources, providing a level of abstraction about the origin of the data, both regarding the physical location (file, network resources) and the format (JSON, XML, JDBC, etc.)

In the next example, we integrate DataFX with our Twitter example. Once again, the only change is in the getObservableList method, but for clarity, we show the whole main class in Listing 9-20.

Listing 9-20. *Obtaining Tweets Using DataFX*

```
import java.io.IOException;
import java.net.MalformedURLException;
import javafx.application.Application;
import javafx.collections.ObservableList;
import javafx.concurrent.Service;
import javafx.scene.Scene;
import javafx.scene.control.ListCell;
import javafx.scene.control.ListView;
import javafx.scene.layout.StackPane;
import javafx.stage.Stage;
import javafx.util.Callback;
import org.javafxdata.datasources.io.NetworkSource;
import org.javafxdata.datasources.protocol.ObjectDataSource;
```

```java
public class TweetAppDataFX extends Application {

    public static void main(String[] args) {
        launch(args);
    }

    @Override
    public void start(Stage primaryStage) throws MalformedURLException, IOException {
        primaryStage.setTitle("TweetList");
        ListView<Tweet> listView = new ListView<Tweet>();
        listView.setItems(getObservableList());
        listView.setCellFactory(new Callback<ListView<Tweet>, ListCell<Tweet>>() {

            @Override
            public ListCell<Tweet> call(ListView<Tweet> listview) {
                return new TweetCell();
            }
        });

        StackPane root = new StackPane();
        root.getChildren().add(listView);
        primaryStage.setScene(new Scene(root, 500, 300));
        primaryStage.show();
        System.out.println("Setup complete");
    }

    ObservableList<Tweet> getObservableList() throws MalformedURLException, IOException {
        String url = "http://search.twitter.com/search.rss?q=javafx";
        NetworkSource reader = new NetworkSource(url);
        ObjectDataSource objectDataSource = new↵
 ObjectDataSource().reader(reader).tag("item").clazz(Tweet.class);
        Service service = objectDataSource.retrieve();
        return objectDataSource.getData();
    }
}
```

The relevant part, the implementation of the getObservableList method, is very simple. We first construct a NetworkSource that points to the required REST endpoint. Next, we create an ObjectDataSource and use the builder pattern to do the following:

1. Assign the NetworkSource as the source of the data.

2. Indicate that we are interested in items that are defined as "item" elements.

3. Convert these items into instances of the Tweet class.

By calling the ObjectDataSource.retrieve method, an asynchronous Service is started. Instead of waiting for the result, we can immediately return the result object to our visual controls. The DataFX framework will update the result object while it reads and parses incoming data. For large chunks of data, this is very useful, because this approach allows developers to already render parts of the data while other parts are still coming in, or are still being processed.

Apart from the ObjectDataSource, DataFX has a number of other DataSources, including an XMLDataSource. Developers familiar with the Java XML APIs can use this DataSource and use xpath expressions in order to define what columns in a TableColumn should render what parts of the incoming XML.

Jersey-Client

Jersey is the reference implementation of JAX-RS. Although Jersey itself has no direct link to JavaFX, we mention it here for two reasons:

- Jersey-client provides some useful tools for calling REST-based web services.

- JAX-RS 2.0 will contain a client specification.

The JAX-RS 2.0 specification work is done in JSR 339 and the final release is expected in the second quarter of 2012. Jersey will provide the reference implementation for this JSR. At this moment, Jersey already provides the Reference Implementation for JAX-RS 1.x, which mainly defines the Server components of a REST implementation, but the client components will only be standardized in JAX-RS 2.0. Jersey uses the same principles we have shown in the examples in this chapter (support for both JSON and XML, unmarshalling data to Objects, etc.).

Once the JAX-RS 2.0 specification is approved and the Jersey-Client reference implementation is available, it will provide useful tools for reducing the amount of boilerplate code. At this moment, one of the flavors of DataFX already uses Jersey-Client, and it is expected that more JavaFX Frameworks will leverage the standard Java 2 REST retrieving and parsing APIs that are defined in JAX-RS 2.0.

In the next example, we modify the TwitterRetrievalService of Listing 9-15 to use the Jersey-Client API. This is shown in Listing 9-21.

Listing 9-21. *Using Jersey-Client for Retrieving Tweets*

```
import com.sun.jersey.api.client.Client;
import com.sun.jersey.api.client.WebResource;
import java.util.List;
import javafx.collections.FXCollections;
import javafx.collections.ObservableList;
import javafx.concurrent.Service;
import javafx.concurrent.Task;

public class TwitterRetrievalService extends Service<ObservableList<Tweet>> {

        private String host;
        private String path;
        private String search;

        public TwitterRetrievalService(String h, String p, String s) {
                this.host = h;
                this.path = p;
                this.search = s;
        }

        @Override
        protected Task createTask() {
                Task task = new SingleRetrieverTask(host, path, search);
                return task;
        }
```

```
        private static class SingleRetrieverTask extends Task<ObservableList<Tweet>> {

                private String host;
                private String path;
                private String search;

                public SingleRetrieverTask(final String host, final String path, final⏎
    String search) {
                        this.host = host;
                        this.path = path;
                        this.search = search;
                }

                @Override
                protected ObservableList<Tweet> call() throws Exception {
                        try {
                                Client client = new Client();
                                WebResource wr =⏎
    client.resource(host).path(path).queryParam("q", search);
                                TwitterResponse response = wr.get(TwitterResponse.class);
                                List<Tweet> raw = response.getTweets();
                                ObservableList<Tweet> answer =⏎
    FXCollections.observableArrayList(raw);
                                return answer;
                        } catch (Exception e) {
                                e.printStackTrace();
                        }
                        return null;
                }
        }
}
```

In order to show one of the nice tools of Jersey, we slightly modified the constructor of the TwitterRetrievalService to take three parameters:

```
        public TwitterRetrievalService(String host, String path, String search);
```

This is because Jersey allows us to use the Builder pattern to construct REST resources, allowing a distinction among hostname, path, query parameters, and others.

As a consequence, we have to make a slight modification in Listing 9-14:

```
String loc = "http://search.twitter.com/search.rss?q=javafx";
final TwitterRetrievalService twitterRetrievalService = new TwitterRetrievalService(loc);
```

is replaced by

```
final TwitterRetrievalService twitterRetrievalService = new⏎
 TwitterRetrievalService("http://search.twitter.com", "search.rss", "javafx");
```

The hostname, path, and search parameter are used to create a Jersey WebResource:

```
Client client = new Client();
WebResource wr = client.resource(host).path(path).queryParam("q", search);
```

On this WebResource, we can call the get(Class clazz) method, and supply a class parameter. The result of the REST call will then be parsed into an instance of the supplied class, which is also what we did using JAXB in our example in Listing 9-15.

```
TwitterResponse response = wr.get(TwitterResponse.class);
```

The response now contains a list of Tweets, and we can use the exact same code as in Listing 9-15 to render the tweets.

Summary

In this chapter, we explained briefly two options for integrating JavaFX applications and enterprise applications. We demonstrated a number of techniques for retrieving data available via web services, and also showed how to render the data in typical JavaFX controls as ListView and TableView.

We used a number of third-party tools that facilitate the process of retrieving, parsing, and rendering data. We demonstrated some JavaFX-specific issues related to remote web services (i.e., updating the user interface should happen on the JavaFX application thread).

It is important to realize that the decoupling between JavaFX client applications and web services allows for a large degree of freedom. There are different tools and techniques for dealing with web services, and developers are encouraged to use their favorite tools in their JavaFX application.

CHAPTER 10

JavaFX Languages and Markup

Computer programming is tremendous fun. Like music, it is a skill that derives from an unknown blend of innate talent and constant practice. Like drawing, it can be shaped to a variety of ends—commercial, artistic, and pure entertainment. Programmers have a well-deserved reputation for working long hours, but are rarely credited with being driven by creative fevers. Programmers talk about software development on weekends, vacations, and over meals not because they lack imagination, but because their imagination reveals worlds that others cannot see.

—Larry O'Brien and Bruce Eckel

JavaFX provides a rich set of capabilities for building applications that lets you create immersive user interfaces that go beyond what you can accomplish with traditional UI toolkits. However, it does not stop there, because by sitting on top of the Java language, you can also take full advantage of all the languages and tools that have been developed for the Java platform. Also, JavaFX comes with its own UI declaration language written in XML, which is quite powerful in its own right.

In this chapter we show how you can leverage different languages and markup to create great-looking JavaFX user interfaces with less code. The wonderful thing about all the languages and capabilities discussed in this chapter is that it is your choice. You can continue to build JavaFX applications in pure Java using the imperative or builder style, or you can take advantage of your favorite JVM language. Who knows, you may even become a convert to one of the languages discussed in this chapter based on its usage for JavaFX alone.

A Quick Comparison of Alternative Languages

To give you an idea of the power and expressiveness of using different JVM languages, we start out by taking a simple example and showing it in six different representations. The example is an extension of the Colorful Circles application designed by Jasper Potts from the JavaFX team. It is a great example of shapes, animation, and effects in a very small amount of code, and we have adapted it to show binding and interactivity as well.

The running Vanishing Circles application is shown in Figure 10-1.

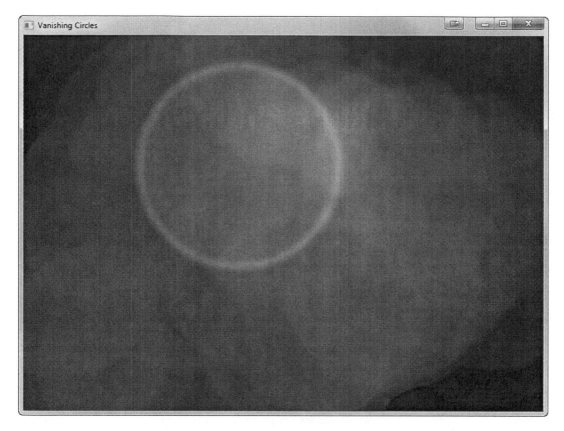

Figure 10-1. *The Vanishing Circles application demonstrating JavaFX effects, animation, and interaction*

Vanishing Circles in Java

To start with, let's show the code in standard Java imperative style. This is the most verbose way of writing JavaFX code, but it is also the most straightforward for anyone familiar with the Java programming language and earlier UI toolkits such as Swing. The full code listing for writing this example is shown in Listing 10-1.

Listing 10-1. *Vanishing Circles Application Written in Imperative Java Style*

```
public class VanishingCircles extends Application {

  public static void main(String[] args) {
    Application.launch(args);
  }

  @Override
  public void start(Stage primaryStage) {
```

```
    primaryStage.setTitle("Vanishing Circles");
    Group root = new Group();
    Scene scene = new Scene(root, 800, 600, Color.BLACK);
    List<Circle> circles = new ArrayList<Circle>();
    for (int i = 0; i < 50; i++) {
      final Circle circle = new Circle(150);
      circle.setCenterX(Math.random() * 800);
      circle.setCenterY(Math.random() * 600);
      circle.setFill(new Color(Math.random(), Math.random(), Math.random(), .2));
      circle.setEffect(new BoxBlur(10, 10, 3));
      circle.addEventHandler(MouseEvent.MOUSE_CLICKED, new EventHandler<MouseEvent>() {
        public void handle(MouseEvent t) {
          KeyValue collapse = new KeyValue(circle.radiusProperty(), 0);
          new Timeline(new KeyFrame(Duration.seconds(3), collapse)).play();
        }
      });
      circle.setStroke(Color.WHITE);
      circle.strokeWidthProperty().bind(Bindings.when(circle.hoverProperty())
        .then(4)
        .otherwise(0));
      circles.add(circle);
    }
    root.getChildren().addAll(circles);
    primaryStage.setScene(scene);
    primaryStage.show();

    Timeline moveCircles = new Timeline();
    for (Circle circle : circles) {
      KeyValue moveX = new KeyValue(circle.centerXProperty(), Math.random() * 800);
      KeyValue moveY = new KeyValue(circle.centerYProperty(), Math.random() * 600);
      moveCircles.getKeyFrames().add(new KeyFrame(Duration.seconds(40), moveX, moveY));
    }
    moveCircles.play();
  }
}
```

Although the code is fairly easy to understand, it is also quite verbose at 40 lines and 1,299 characters, excluding imports. The basic functionality can be summarized as follows.

- Fifty circles of varying colors are overlaid with a transparent fill.

- Those circles are animated in a semirandom pattern around the window.

- When the mouse hovers over a circle, the circle gets surrounded by a white border.

- Upon clicking a circle, it slowly shrinks and vanishes.

In a very short amount of code this lets us demonstrate many different JavaFX features, including shapes, effects, animation, binding, and event listeners. In the next few examples we convert this exact application to several different languages and representations, letting you see how these features vary in each of the choices available to you.

First, let's convert this code to use the JavaFX builders. This allows for a more fluent API, but also comes with its own boilerplate that is required to do this pattern in Java. As a result, it can sometimes take more code to produce the same result; however, you gain some additional expressiveness in the process. This is also a great segue into other languages, such as Groovy, where we can take advantage of the same builder pattern without the boilerplate required to do this in Java.

The builder version of the Vanishing Circles application is shown in Listing 10-2.

Listing 10-2. *Vanishing Circles Application Written in JavaFX Builder Style*

```java
public class VanishingCirclesBuilder extends Application {

  public static void main(String[] args) {
    Application.launch(args);
  }

  @Override
  public void start(Stage primaryStage) {
    primaryStage.setTitle("Vanishing Circles");
    List<Circle> circles = new ArrayList<Circle>();
    for (int i = 0; i < 50; i++) {
      Circle circle = CircleBuilder.create()
        .radius(150)
        .centerX(Math.random() * 800)
        .centerY(Math.random() * 600)
        .stroke(Color.WHITE)
        .fill(new Color(Math.random(), Math.random(), Math.random(), .2))
        .effect(new BoxBlur(10, 10, 3))
        .onMouseClicked(new EventHandler<MouseEvent>() {
          public void handle(MouseEvent t) {
            TimelineBuilder.create().keyFrames(
              new KeyFrame(Duration.seconds(3),
                new KeyValue(((Circle) t.getSource()).radiusProperty(), 0))
            ).build().play();
          }
        })
        .build();
      circle.strokeWidthProperty().bind(Bindings.when(circle.hoverProperty())
        .then(4)
        .otherwise(0));
      circles.add(circle);
    }
    primaryStage.setScene(SceneBuilder.create()
      .width(800)
      .height(600)
      .fill(Color.BLACK)
      .root(GroupBuilder.create()
        .children(
          circles
        ).build()
      ).build());
    primaryStage.show();
```

```
    List<KeyFrame> keyFrames = new ArrayList<KeyFrame>();
    for (Circle circle : circles) {
      keyFrames.add(new KeyFrame(Duration.seconds(40),
        new KeyValue(circle.centerXProperty(), Math.random() * 800),
        new KeyValue(circle.centerYProperty(), Math.random() * 600)));
    }
    TimelineBuilder.create()
      .keyFrames(keyFrames)
      .build().play();
  }
}
```

At 51 lines and 1,285 characters, the character count for the builder pattern is slightly less than that of the earlier imperative style, whereas the line count is actually higher. The main advantage of using the builder pattern is that it allows you to nest the UI elements in a hierarchy matching the UI scene graph, which at a quick glance makes it much easier to understand what the code will produce.

In practice, you will probably find a mix of the imperative and builder styles to be the best choice. Notice that we did not bother using builders for the Color or BlurEffect, because the constructors were much more concise and the number of arguments was reasonable. Also, due to the present lack of closures in Java, it is difficult to construct nested iterating structures, which forced a certain style of construction. Similarly, it was not possible to create the binding in the builder clause; however, most other JVM languages have closures and other advanced language features that get around these limitations in the builder syntax.

Vanishing Circles in Alternative JVM Languages

Now we move on to different JVM languages and show what is possible by using Groovy, Scala, and Visage. For the first two languages we make use of an inner domain-specific language (DSL) written on top of the JavaFX APIs. Visage requires no DSL, because it is a language specifically designed for writing UIs, so it has built-in features that mirror what you would want a DSL to show.

Groovy is a great choice for those getting started with JVM languages, because its syntax most closely matches the Java language. In fact, with a few minor changes all Java programs are also valid Groovy programs! However, to get the full advantage of the language features in Groovy you need to make use of a DSL written for your target use case, such as GroovyFX. GroovyFX is an open source project that lets you write JavaFX code in the Groovy language that looks like the code in Listing 10-3.

***Listing 10-3.** Vanishing Circles Application Written in Groovy Using the GroovyFX DSL*

```
GroovyFX.start { primaryStage ->
  def sg = new SceneGraphBuilder()
  def rand = new Random().&nextInt
  def circles = []

  sg.stage(title: 'Vanishing Circles', show: true) {
    scene(fill: black, width: 800, height: 600) {
      50.times {
        circles << circle(centerX: rand(800), centerY: rand(600), radius: 150, stroke: white,
              strokeWidth: bind('hover', converter: {val -> val ? 4 : 0})) {
          fill rgb(rand(255), rand(255), rand(255), 0.2)
          effect boxBlur(width: 10, height: 10, iterations: 3)
```

```groovy
            onMouseClicked { e ->
              timeline {
                at(3.s) { change e.source.radiusProperty() to 0 }
              }.play()
            }
          }
        }
      }
    }

    timeline(cycleCount: Timeline.INDEFINITE, autoReverse: true) {
      circles.each { circle ->
        at (40.s) {
          change circle.centerXProperty() to rand(800)
          change circle.centerYProperty() to rand(600)
        }
      }
    }.play()
  }
}
```

This GroovyFX code has the same functionality as the earlier JavaFX examples, but is significantly shorter and more expressive. The GroovyFX version of the Vanishing Circles application is only 29 lines and 671 characters, which saves you 639 keystrokes from the initial Java version. Also, as your application grows you will get even more benefit from using a DSL such as this, allowing you to write more complex and feature-rich applications with less code.

Some of the Groovy language features that this code takes advantage of include:

- Groovy Builder Pattern: Groovy makes it particularly easy to build powerful and concise builder code, as demonstrated with the GroovyFX SceneGraphBuilder.

- Name Parameters: Remembering the order of arguments to methods and constructors with long argument lists is hard, but named parameters allow you to be explicit and change the order for your convenience.

- Class Extension: Groovy allows you to add new methods and functionality to existing classes, as demonstrated by the creation of duration objects with syntax 40.s where "s" is a method on integers.

- Closures: The event handlers are greatly simplified by creating anonymous single method interface extensions via closures.

All of this contributes to a very concise and readable syntax with very little boilerplate code. We dig into the features of how each of the JavaFX features translates to Groovy syntax in the later section entitled, "Making Your JavaFX Groovy."

The second JVM language we cover is Scala. It provides a lot of the same benefits as Groovy, but has the additional benefit of being fully type safe. This means that the compiler will catch bugs and type errors before you even run your application, which can be a huge boon to productivity, and shorten your development and testing cycle.

Again, we take advantage of an inner DSL written in the Scala language called ScalaFX, which is another open-source project that provides a full wrapper library for the JavaFX 2.0 APIs. The code listing for the Vanishing Circles application written using ScalaFX is shown in Listing 10-4.

Listing 10-4. *Vanishing Circles Application Written in Scala Using the ScalaFX DSL*

```scala
object VanishingCircles extends JFXApp {
  var circles: Seq[Circle] = null
  stage = new Stage {
    title = "Vanishing Circles"
    width = 800
    height = 600
    scene = new Scene {
      fill = BLACK
      circles = for (i <- 0 until 50) yield new Circle {
        centerX = random * 800
        centerY = random * 600
        radius = 150
        fill = color(random, random, random, .2)
        effect = new BoxBlur(10, 10, 3)
        strokeWidth <== when (hover) then 4 otherwise 0
        stroke = WHITE
        onMouseClicked = {
          Timeline(at (3 s) {radius -> 0}).play()
        }
      }
      content = circles
    }
  }

  new Timeline {
    cycleCount = INDEFINITE
    autoReverse = true
    keyframes = for (circle <- circles) yield at (40 s) {
      Set(
        circle.centerX -> random * stage.width,
        circle.centerY -> random * stage.height
      )
    }
  }.play();
}
```

The ScalaFX code above is four lines longer than the Groovy code at 33 lines; it is only 591 characters, saving you an additional 76 keystrokes.

The Scala example makes use of an object literal pattern for constructing the scene graph, which gives the same benefits as the Java and Groovy builders. It also benefits from the powerful binding support that is built into the ScalaFX libraries. Some of the Scala language features that this code takes advantage of include:

- Operator Overloading: Scala lets you overload the existing operators and create entirely new ones. This is used in several places, including the bind and animation syntax.

- Implicits: Scala's answer to class extension is via the implicit conversions. This makes it possible to extend the JavaFX API classes with convenience methods for object literal construction, giving you all the power of builders with the core classes.

- Closures: Scala also supports closures, which makes event handlers much more concise, and allows powerful looping constructs such as the for…yield syntax.

- DSL-Friendly Syntax: The usual code punctuation, such as dots and parentheses, is optional in most situations, making it possible to build fluent APIs that read like language keywords.

Although the code ends up being fairly short and easy to understand, there is quite a bit of depth to the Scala language. We show how you can take advantage of some of the built-in features of Scala to further improve your applications in the section entitled, "Scala and JavaFX."

The final language we explore is called Visage. It is the successor to JavaFX Script, which was the language in which all JavaFX applications were written prior to version 2. As a result, its syntax is ideal for expressing UI applications and it integrates seamlessly with many of the JavaFX 2 platform features, such as binding, observable sequences, and animation. The code for the Vanishing Circles application written in the Visage language is shown in Listing 10-5.

Listing 10-5. Vanishing Circles Application Written in the Visage UI Language

```
var circles:Circle[];
Stage {
  title: "Vanishing Circles"
  Scene {
    width: 800
    height: 600
    fill: BLACK
    Group {
      circles = for (i in [1..50]) {
        def c:Circle = Circle {
          centerX: random() * 800
          centerY: random() * 600
          radius: 150
          fill: color(random(), random(), random(), .2)
          effect: BoxBlur {
            height: 10
            width: 10
            iterations: 3
          }
          stroke: WHITE
          strokeWidth: bind if (c.hover) 5 else 0
          onMouseClicked: function(e) {
            Timeline {at (3s) {c.radius => 0}}.play()
          }
        }
      }
    }
  }
}
```

```
Timeline {
  for (circle in circles) at (40s) {
    circle.centerX => random() * 800;
    circle.centerY => random() * 600
  }
}.play()
```

At 35 lines and 487 characters, this is the shortest of all the DSLs available to write your JavaFX application, which should not be a surprise inasmuch as this was a language written specifically for JavaFX. Also, Visage comes with direct support for accessing the JavaFX APIs as well as a very efficient compiled bind capability, giving you the best performance possible from a JVM language. Some of the Visage language features that we are taking advantage of include the following.

- Object Literal Syntax: Visage has a native syntax for creating hierarchical user interfaces, including auto-flattening sequences and built-in for comprehensions that make it easy to build complicated UI elements inline.

- Compile Bind Support: Binding is an API feature in JavaFX 2.0, however, Visage retains the elegance and performance of bind support built into the language.

- Closures: As do Groovy and Scala, Visage also supports closures, which lets you simplify your event listeners.

- Animation Syntax: Visage has a custom animation syntax that makes it easy to create timeline-based animations, but sits on top of the JavaFX animation subsystem.

As you have seen, using a domain-specific language to write your JavaFX code can produce significant benefits over what you would have to write in Java using either the imperative or builder styles. Also, because all of these languages sit on top of the same underlying JavaFX APIs, they have the same functionality as applications written in pure Java. Therefore, the choice is yours as to which language you want to use to write your JavaFX applications.

In the next few sections we go into each of these three languages in more detail to help you get started with developing your JavaFX applications using them. Also, it is possible to use virtually any JVM language to write JavaFX applications with, so if you have a favorite language that is not listed here, it is worth a try!

Making Your JavaFX Groovy

According to job trends, Groovy is the most popular language that runs on the JVM other than Java.[1] This is helped by the fact that Groovy is extremely easy to get started with; other than a few minor differences,[2] any Java program is also a valid Groovy application. This makes it very easy for Java

---

[1] Scala, Groovy, Clojure, Jython, JRuby, and Java: Jobs by Language, `http://bloodredsun.com/2011/10/04/scala-groovy-clojure-jython-jruby-java-jobs/`, October 2011.

[2] Differences from Java, `http://groovy.codehaus.org/Differences+from+Java`, 2011.

developers to start using it, even before they appreciate all the power and convenience that Groovy brings to the Java ecosystem.

Groovy source files compile directly to Java bytecodes and can run anywhere you have a Java Virtual Machine. As a result, you can access any Java libraries directly, including the JavaFX APIs. A well-written Groovy application will almost always be shorter than the equivalent Java version, because of all the conveniences built into the language. Some of the features of the Groovy language that make it attractive as a replacement for Java and JavaFX code include:

- Closures: The most requested feature for the Java language, closures are particularly important for GUI programming, because they make it much simpler to write code that gets called when an event happens.

- Operator Overloading: Groovy lets you overload existing operators or define new ones, which is important for writing a readable DSL.

- Dynamic Typing: Types are optional in Groovy code, which makes it easier to write succinct code.

- Getter/Setter Access: Groovy will automatically convert direct field access to getters and setters, which shortens this very common pattern for accessing Java APIs.

- Named Constructor Parameters: When initializing an object with a constructor, you can also set fields on the class by referring to them by name. This pattern is used quite a bit in our GroovyFX code later.

- Built-In Data Structure Syntax: Many commonly used data structures, such as Lists and Maps, have a built-in syntax in Groovy, which makes it much more convenient to work with them and build them dynamically.

Using JavaFX directly from Groovy is possible; however, you are missing out on a lot of the benefits of Groovy without using a dedicated DSL library, such as GroovyFX. In the next few sections we show you some of the benefits of writing JavaFX code using the Groovy language and GroovyFX library.

Introduction to GroovyFX

GroovyFX is a library for developing JavaFX applications in Groovy that lets you build your application in a more Groovy-like fashion. It was started by Jim Clarke and Dean Iverson, one of the coauthors of this title, and is being developed as an open-source Groovy module. The main landing page for GroovyFX is on GitHub at the following URL:

```
http://groovyfx-project.github.com/
```

Some of the benefits of writing code using GroovyFX, rather than simply coding directly against the JavaFX APIs include:

- Builder Pattern: GroovyFX has Groovy builders for all the major JavaFX classes, making it easy and convenient to declaratively construct a scene graph.

- Property Generation: The JavaFX property pattern for writing your own properties is quite long-winded, but is replaced with a one-line annotation in GroovyFX.

- Timeline DSL: GroovyFX has a convenient short-hand syntax for animation.

- Convenient Bind Syntax: GroovyFX makes creating bindings much more terse and readable than the equivalent Java code.

- API Improvements: A lot of the JavaFX APIs have been tweaked and enhanced to make them easier to use.

To get you started using GroovyFX, we walk you through setting up a small GroovyFX project from scratch. These directions assume that you already have a current Java and JavaFX 2.0 SDK installed on your system. Also, we have chosen to tailor the instructions for the IntelliJ Community Edition, which is a free, open-source IDE with a long track record of excellent Groovy support. There is also Groovy support for Eclipse, NetBeans, and many other IDEs, so if you have a preference for a different IDE, you can easily adapt these instructions to work with your IDE of choice.

To start with, download and install the latest version of IntelliJ IDEA. The community edition comes with Groovy support, so there is no need to purchase the Ultimate Edition. The IntelliJ web site can be found here:

`http://www.jetbrains.com/idea`

After installing and launching IntelliJ, you need to create a new Java project with Groovy language support enabled. On the landing page you can click "Create New Project," or if you are on a different screen you can get to the same wizard by selecting "New Project…" from the "File" menu. This will present you with the new Project Wizard shown in Figure 10-2.

Figure 10-2. IntelliJ new project wizard dialog

Name your project "HelloGroovyFX," make sure that the project type is set to "Java Module," and then click Next. For the next page of the wizard, you can simply accept the default src folder location and continue, which will take you to the extension screen shown in Figure 10-3.

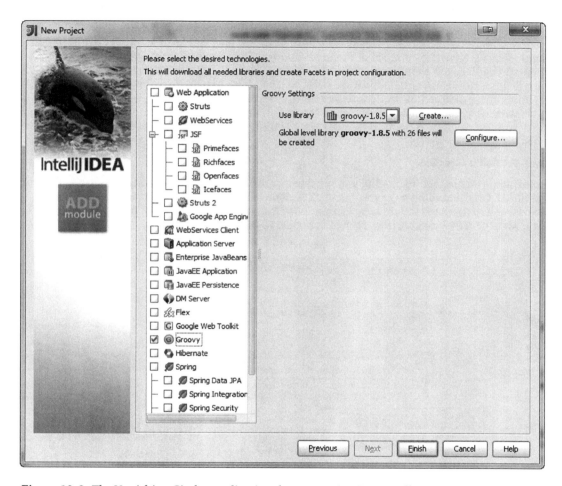

Figure 10-3. *The Vanishing Circles application demonstrating JavaFX effects, animation, and interaction*

This is where you can select and enable Groovy support for your project. Find Groovy from the list on the left and select the checkbox. You also need to configure a Groovy runtime for it to work with on the right-hand pane. If you don't already have a current Groovy runtime installation, you can grab the latest from the Groovy site:

```
http://groovyfx-project.github.com/
```

The binary zip release should work fine. Extract this to a folder on your hard drive, and then go back to IntelliJ and set up the Groovy library by clicking on the "Create…" button and selecting the folder to where you just finished extracting Groovy. To complete the project creation, click "Finish" and your new project will be opened in the current window.

We are almost done with the project setup, but are missing the dependent libraries for JavaFX and GroovyFX. To add these in, open the "Project Structure…" dialog from the "File" menu, and navigate to the "Modules" section. This lets you configure the project settings in more detail than the new project wizard allows.

Click on the "Dependencies" tab on the right side and the screen shown in Figure 10-4 appears.

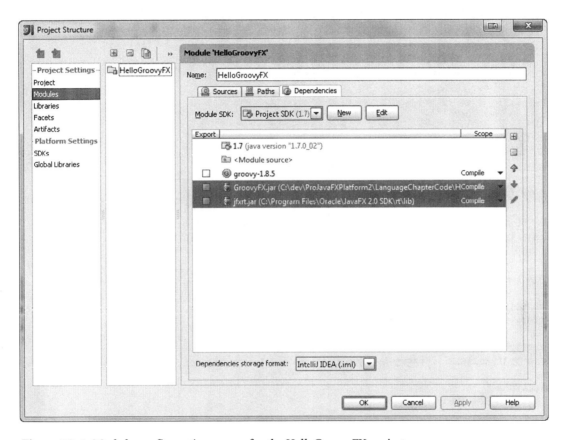

Figure 10-4. *Module configuration screen for the HelloGroovyFX project*

In the Dependencies tab you need to configure two additional jar references, both of which are highlighted in the illustration. The first is the GroovyFX jar file, which you can download from the GroovyFX site. Again, the URL for the GroovyFX site is:

`http://groovyfx-project.github.com/`

The second dependency is the jfxrt.jar, which is in the lib folder of your JavaFX runtime. On the Windows operating system, this is typically located under "Program Files/Oracle/JavaFX/JavaFX 2.0 Runtime/lib" (for 64-bit) or "Program Files (x86)/Oracle/JavaFX/JavaFX 2.0 Runtime/lib" (for 32-bit).

Now to create the HelloGroovyFX application, we need to add a new Groovy script to the project. Right-click on the src directory of your project and choose "New" > "Groovy Script" from the context menu. This pops up a script creation dialog where you can type the name of your script file and click "OK" to create it, as shown in Figure 10-5.

Figure 10-5. *Groovy Class creation dialog*

Now you are finally ready to get started with some coding. The HelloGroovyFX application is very short, so you can grab the code from the source bundle that comes with the book, or just type in the code shown in Listing 10-6 yourself.

Listing 10-6. *Hello GroovyFX Code*

```
import groovyx.javafx.GroovyFX
import groovyx.javafx.SceneGraphBuilder

GroovyFX.start {
  new SceneGraphBuilder().stage(visible: true) {
    scene {
      stackPane {
        text("Hello GroovyFX")
      }
    }
  }
}
```

To run the application, simply right-click on the class and choose 'Run "HelloGroovyFX"' from the context menu. This gives you the application shown in Figure 10-6.

Figure 10-6. *Output from running the Hello GroovyFX application in IntelliJ*

Congratulations, you have created and run your very first JavaFX application in Groovy! In the next few sections we go into more detail on the features and capabilities of GroovyFX, but remember that anything you can do in JavaFX is possible in GroovyFX, because it wraps the full JavaFX APIs.

Properties in GroovyFX

One of the features that would most benefit UI development in Java with JavaFX is having a notion of first-class, observable properties in the language. Because this does not exist today, the JavaFX team added properties at an API level, which is sufficient, but much more verbose than a native syntax can provide.

Fortunately, with dynamic languages such as Groovy, it is quite easy to add in powerful features including a native property syntax. Groovy already has a built-in notion of simplified getter/setter access, so you can retrieve and store JavaFX properties just as if they were normal variables. For example, to set the width of a Rectangle in Groovy, all you need to write is:

```
rectangle.width = 500
```

And this will be automatically translated to a setter call, such as the following.

```
rectangle.setWidth(500);
```

The other part of the JavaFX property pattern that is even more tedious is the creation of new properties. To define a new property on your class in the same way that the JavaFX APIs define properties, you need a total of one field and three methods per property. The standard boilerplate for creating a name property on a Person object is shown in Listing 10-7.

Listing 10-7. JavaFX Property Pattern to Create New Properties in Java

```
import javafx.beans.property.SimpleStringProperty
import javafx.beans.property.StringProperty

public class Person {
  private StringProperty name;
  public final void setName(String val) { nameProperty().set(val); }
  public final String getName() { return nameProperty().get(); }
  public StringProperty nameProperty() {
    if (name == null) {
      name = new SimpleStringProperty(this, "name");
    }
    return name;
  }
}
```

▓ **Note** The above code can be further optimized by checking whether the property has been created in the getName method, and returning null if it has not been created (and thus not initializing the name property).

Although this code is only a bit more verbose than the standard Java property bean pattern, multiply it by the number of properties you need to define in your application, and you have quite a bit of code to maintain and debug when there is something that is not working as expected.

GroovyFX has a very elegant solution to this using a compiler hook for AST transformations. Rather than copying and pasting the property boilerplate each time you want to define a new property, you can simply annotate a variable with the @FXBindable annotation, and GroovyFX will take care of the rest. It generates exactly the same optimized code you would write by hand, but does it behind the scenes during the compile phase so that your source code is not cluttered with the additional logic.

Listing 10-8 shows what the name property would look like in Groovy.

Listing 10-8. JavaFX Property Pattern to Create New Properties in Java

```
import groovyx.javafx.beans.FXBindable

class Person {
  @FXBindable String name
}
```

The GroovyFX @FXBindable annotation also supports handling the case where a property has a default initialization value:

```
class Person {
  @FXBindable String name = "Guillaume Laforge"
}
```

And has a convenient shortcut syntax for converting all the variables in a class to properties:

```
@FXBindable
class Person {
    String name;
    int age;
    String gender;
    Date dob;
}
```

■ **Caution** There is a bug in Groovy 1.8.5 that will give you a compiler error when using FXBindable with Dates. If this bug has not been fixed by the time this is published, you can roll back to Groovy 1.8.2 to fix this.

GroovyFX Binding

Binding in JavaFX is an extremely powerful feature, but the API-based syntax in JavaFX 2.0 can often get in the way of understanding what the bind code is doing. GroovyFX solves this problem by taking advantage of the operator overloading feature of the Groovy language to provide an infix notation for common bind expressions.

For example, to bind one rectangle's width to the width of a second rectangle, you can write the following code in GroovyFX.

```
rect1.widthProperty.bind(rect2.widthProperty)
```

There is also an alternate version of the same code that you can use instead:

```
rect1.widthProperty.bind(rect2, 'width')
```

However, the real power of GroovyFX binding comes into play when you are combining multiple properties in a bind statement. As a second example, let's say that you want to bind one rectangle's width to the sum of two others. In GroovyFX you can write the following code.

```
rect1.widthProperty.bind(rect2.widthProperty + rect3.widthProperty)
```

This would translate to the following, much longer, JavaFX Java code.

```
rect1.getWidthProperty().bind(rect2.getWidthProperty().add(rect3.getWidthProperty()));
```

The GroovyFX distribution comes with an example of some binding code to animate the hands of an analog clock. This example was written by Jim Clark, and the relevant code showing properties and binding is shown in Listing 10-9.

Listing 10-9. Analog Clock Excerpt from the GroovyFX Demo Package

```
@FXBindable
class Time {
  Integer hours
  Integer minutes
  Integer seconds

  Double hourAngle
  Double minuteAngle
  Double secondAngle

  public Time() {
    // bind the angle properties to the clock time
    hourAngleProperty.bind((hoursProperty * 30.0) + (minutesProperty * 0.5))
    minuteAngleProperty.bind(minutesProperty * 6.0)
    secondAngleProperty.bind(secondsProperty * 6.0)
    ...
  }
}
```

The combination of automatic properties expansion via AST transforms and infix notation binding lets you express fairly complex logic without much code. The resulting Groovy Analog clock graphic UI that you get when running the example is shown in Figure 10-7.

Figure 10-7. *Groovy analog clock demo*

GroovyFX API Enhancements

In addition to the core language benefits of using Groovy instead of JavaFX, GroovyFX has taken many of the JavaFX APIs and Groovy-ized them to make them easier to use from a dynamic language. We cover three major ones in this section: the GroovyFX custom DSL for animation, a simplified table construction pattern, and streamlined JavaFX layouts. All of these provide significant benefits over the core JavaFX APIs, allowing you to write less code and do more.

Animation

GroovyFX supports building animations using a special DSL that has syntax for creating Durations, KeyFrames, and KeyValues, all with a concise syntax. We showed an example of the Groovy animation syntax earlier in the Vanishing Circles application, which looked like this:

```
timeline {
  at(3.s) { change e.source.radiusProperty() to 0 }
}.play()
```

The basic pattern is as follows, where you can have multiple at expressions in a timeline and multiple change expressions within an at.

```
timeline {
  at(duration) {
    [change property to value]
  }
}
```

Similar to binding, there is also a second format for referring to the property that makes up the change expression:

```
timeline {
  at(3.s) { change(e.source, 'radius') to 0 }
}.play()
```

And the syntax also supports an optional tween that lets you provide a curve for the speed at which the animation proceeds:

```
timeline {
  at(3.s) { change e.source.radiusProperty() to 0 tween ease_both }
}.play()
```

With the above change, the animation would start out slow and speed up to its normal rate, and then slow down at the end the same way.

Compared to the full Java code, the Groovy animation syntax is a huge savings in characters and makes it much easier to see what your animation is actually doing.

Tables

Between the extra syntactic sugar for builders or imperative Java, and the need to specify Generic at multiple levels, building simple data tables in Java code can be quite a lot of code. Groovy simplifies this with a fairly intuitive builder format for creating tables, along with some conveniences, such as a built-in type converter that lets you specify a closure to change the output type for a field.

As a result, you can write fairly complex tables with very little code. The following example builds from the Person class that we created earlier to display a list of people in a tabular format. The full code is shown in Listing 10-10.

Listing 10-10. *Code Demonstrating a Table in Groovy with Strings, ints, and Dates*

```
import groovyx.javafx.GroovyFX
import groovyx.javafx.SceneGraphBuilder
import binding.Person
import java.text.SimpleDateFormat

def dateFormat = new SimpleDateFormat("MM/dd/yyyy")

def persons = [
  new Person(name: "Ada Lovelace", age: 36, gender: "Female",
          dob: dateFormat.parse("10/10/1815")),
  new Person(name: "Henrietta Swan Leavitt", age: 53, gender: "Female",
          dob: dateFormat.parse("7/4/1868")),
  new Person(name: "Grete Hermann", age: 83, gender: "Female",
          dob: dateFormat.parse("3/2/1901"))
]

GroovyFX.start {
  new SceneGraphBuilder().stage(visible: true) {
    scene {
      tableView(items: persons) {
        tableColumn(property: "name", text: "Name", prefWidth: 160)
```

```
        tableColumn(property: "age", text: "Age", prefWidth: 70)
        tableColumn(property: "gender", text: "Gender", prefWidth: 90)
        tableColumn(property: "dob", text: "Birth", prefWidth: 100,
          type: Date,
          converter: { d -> return dateFormat.format(d) })
      }
    }
  }
}
```

Notice that the code to display the table is almost as short as the code to set up the data. The converter in the last column to format the Date is a one-line operation in Groovy, but requires a CellValueFactory with an implementation of a Callback interface, which is several lines of Java code saved.

Figure 10-8 displays the result of running this table application in Groovy.

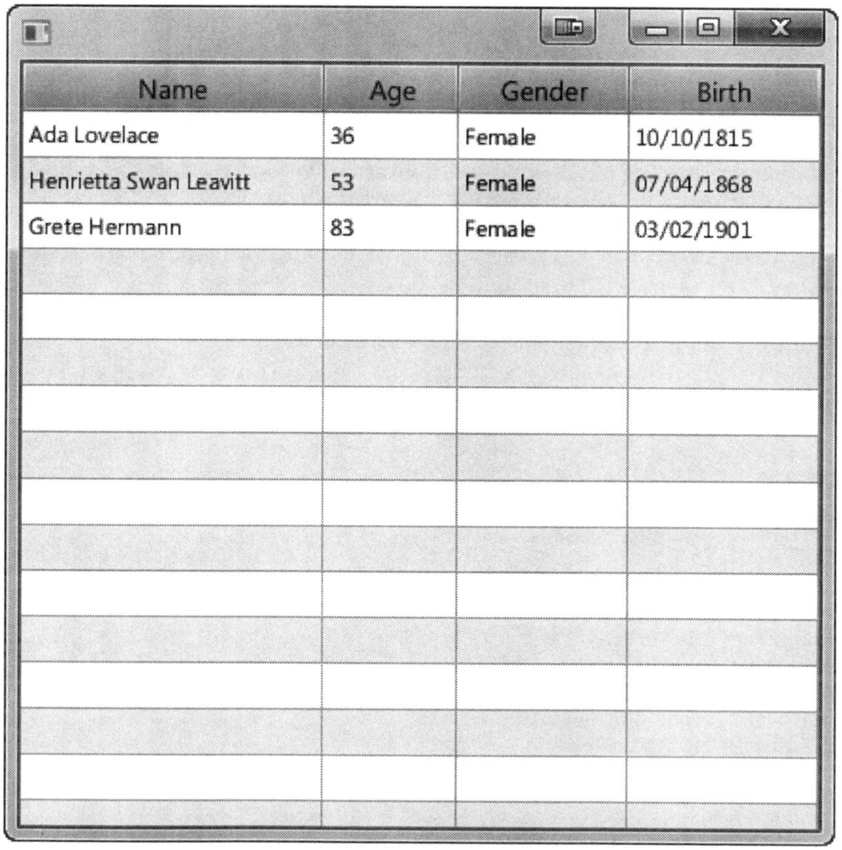

Figure 10-8. *Groovy Table demo with famous women in computers listed*

Layouts

Another set of APIs that are relatively challenging to use in a declarative fashion are the JavaFX layouts. They have a powerful constraint system that you can use to give Nodes special layout behavior on a per-layout basis, but this also means that adding a Node to a layout involves two steps: (1) adding it to the container and (2) assigning constraints.

The GroovyFX APIs solve the layout problem with a very clean solution that involves annotating the node object with additional pseudo-properties for layout constraints. This allows you to define the constraints as you construct the scene graph, and then during the layout phase, the JavaFX layout system uses the constraints to control how the Nodes are positioned and sized.

Listing 10-11 shows an example of one of the more complicated layouts, GridPaneLayout, with the entire application written in a declarative style.

Listing 10-11. Example Code of a GridPane Layout in GroovyFX

```
import groovyx.javafx.GroovyFX
import groovyx.javafx.SceneGraphBuilder
import javafx.scene.layout.GridPane
import javafx.scene.text.Font

GroovyFX.start {
  def sg = new SceneGraphBuilder()

  sg.stage(title: "GridPane Demo", width: 400, height: 500, visible: true) {
    scene {
      stackPane {
        imageView {
          image("puppy.jpg", width: 1100, height: 1100, preserveRatio: true)
          effect colorAdjust(brightness: 0.C, input: gaussianBlur())
        }
        gridPane(hgap: 10, vgap: 10, padding: 20) {
          columnConstraints(minWidth: 60, halignment: "right")
          columnConstraints(prefWidth: 300, hgrow: "always")

          label("Dog Adoption Form", font: new Font(24), margin: [0, 0, 10, 0],
              halignment: "center", columnSpan: GridPane.REMAINING)

          label("Size: ", row: 2)
          textField(promptText: "approximate size in pounds", row: 2, column: 1)

          label("Breed:", row: 3)
          textField(promptText: "pet breed", row: 3, column: 1)

          label("Sex:", row: 4)
          choiceBox(items: ['Male', 'Female', 'Either'], row: 4, column: 1)

          label("Additional Info:", wrapText: true, textAlignment: "right",
              row: 5, valignment: "baseline")
          textArea(prefRowCount: 8, wrapText: true, row: 5, column: 1, vgrow: 'always')
```

```
                button("Submit", row: 6, column: 1, halignment: "right")
            }
        }
    }
}
}
```

Notice that the code is succinct, clean, and closely models the UI that it is trying to build. The result of running this application looks exactly like what you would expect from a typical UI form, as shown in Figure 10-9.

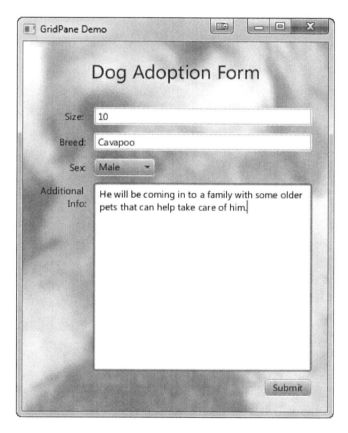

Figure 10-9. *Running Dog Adoption Form example with a Cavapoo (cross between Cavalier King Charles Spaniel and Poodle) in the background*[3]

---

[3] Public domain picture from Wikimedia Commons: `http://commons.wikimedia.org/wiki/File:Image-Cavapoo_puppy.JPG`

Scala and JavaFX

Scala is a powerful JVM language combining the best features of functional and object-oriented programming in a single language. As do the other JVM languages discussed in this chapter, it compiles source files directly to Java bytecodes and all the existing Java language libraries commonly used are compatible with it. However, Scala adds powerful, type-safe collections, an elegant actor model for concurrency, and functional language features including closures, pattern matching, and currying.

Scala was started by Martin Odersky in 2001 at the École Polytechnique Fédérale de Lausanne (EPFL), and has grown in maturity and popularity over the years. Martin has actually been the genius behind the scenes working on Java compilers for many years, including the Pizza language that extended Java and GJ, which is the grandfather of the modern Java compiler after its adoption by Sun in Java 1.3. By developing an entirely new language on the JVM, Martin was able to overcome several of the inherent design limitations of Java.

Scala is used today in many large enterprises such as Twitter, LinkedIn, Foursquare, and Morgan Stanley. There is also commercial support available from the creators of the language via TypeSafe, a Scala language company. Also, Scala has been hailed as the successor to Java by James Gosling, the father of Java, James Strachan, creator of Groovy, and Charles Nutter, JRuby Core Developer, among others. So with all this support behind the Scala language, it makes a great candidate for also providing superior APIs for JavaFX development!

Although you can code in Scala directly against the JavaFX APIs, the end result will look very similar to the Java code we have been writing up to this point and will be unable to take full advantage of the language. The ScalaFX project was started to provide a more Scala-friendly API for doing JavaFX development and is what we use in all the examples throughout this book.

ScalaFX is an open-source project created by Stephen Chin, one of the authors of this book, and has numerous additional contributors who have helped with the design and testing of the library. It is very similar to the GroovyFX library described earlier in this chapter, because it is also an open-source library that constitutes a bridge between a JVM language and the JavaFX APIs. However, ScalaFX is different in that it prioritizes type safety and consistent semantics, which is in spirit with the design goals of the Scala language.

Many of the constructs in the ScalaFX library were inspired by the JavaFX Script language that was used in JavaFX releases prior to 2.0, so for those of you familiar with JavaFX Script, the syntax will feel quite comfortable. It takes advantage of many of the advanced features available in Scala, but does not expose or burden the end user with understanding these to build great-looking UI applications.

Making you an expert Scala developer is beyond the scope of this book, but we do describe the Scala features as we use them in our ScalaFX code, so this should also serve as a gentle introduction to Scala for anyone who is already a proficient Java developer.

Getting Started with ScalaFX

To write your first ScalaFX application you need to download and install Scala as well as the ScalaFX library. Because ScalaFX code is a DSL written in the Scala language, you can use any IDE that supports Scala development, such as IntelliJ, Eclipse, or NetBeans, although you may want to start with the Scala IDE for Eclipse inasmuch as that is the one supported by the Scala language team at TypeSafe. We demonstrate the basic setup of an Eclipse environment for ScalaFX in this chapter, although the concepts apply to other IDEs as well.

To start with, install the latest version of Eclipse and launch it. From the Help menu choose "Install New Software…" and paste the Scala IDE update URL into the "Work with" field. You can get the latest update URL for Scala IDE from their web site:

`http://scala-ide.org/download/current.html`

This lets you select the Scala IDE for the Eclipse plug-in as shown in Figure 10-10.

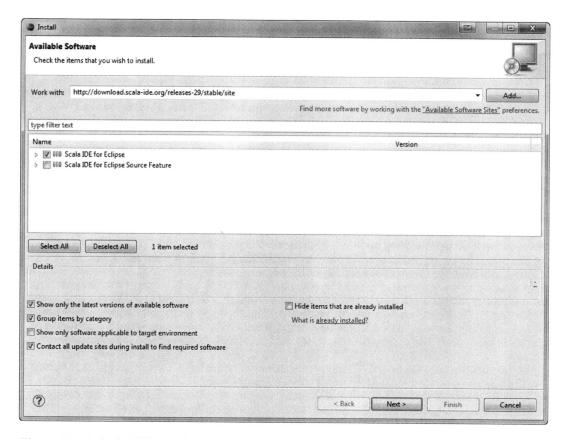

Figure 10-10. *Scala IDE installation in Eclipse*

Continue with the wizard, accepting the license agreement and default settings, and after downloading and installing the plug-in and restarting Eclipse, you will be ready to begin Scala development.

To start with, we create a new Scala project. Go to the File menu and choose "New" > "Project…" to open the project creation wizard shown in Figure 10-11. Choose "Scala Wizards"/"Scala Project" from the list of choices and click Next….

Figure 10-11. *Scala project creation in Eclipse*

We name our project "Hello ScalaFX" and use the default project settings. When asked to switch to the Scala Perspective, choose yes and you will be in the proper view for editing Scala code.

In addition to the standard project setup, we also need to add in the ScalaFX and JavaFX libraries to code using this DSL. ScalaFX can be downloaded from the Google Code web site here:

`http://code.google.com/p/scalafx/`

And you already have the JavaFX libraries installed as part of the JavaFX runtime and SDK. To install ScalaFX, simply download the latest distribution as a jar and add it in to your project as a dependent library. The easiest way to do this is as follows.

1. Copy the ScalaFX.jar file to a lib folder under your project root.

2. Right-click on your project and choose "Properties…" from the context menu.

3. Navigate to the "Java Build Path" entry, select the "Libraries" tab, and click "Add Jars…".

4. Select the ScalaFX.jar file you added to your project in Step 1.

Steps 2 through 4 are illustrated in Figure 10-12.

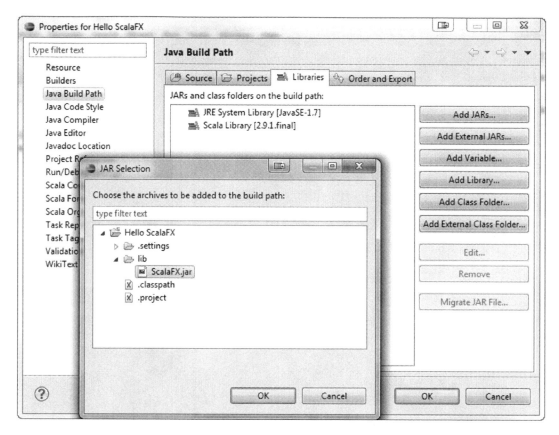

Figure 10-12. *Adding the ScalaFX jar file to your project*

In the same dialog you can also add in the JavaFX runtime library by clicking on "Add External JARs…" and navigating to the JavaFX Runtime or SDK folder. The one jar file you need is called jfxrt.jar and is located in the lib folder under the root of the JavaFX installation.

Now you are ready to create your first ScalaFX application. To start, we create a very simple ScalaFX application that shows a Stage and Scene with a single Label inside it. This is the Hello World of JavaFX applications, and will ensure that all your project settings are correct and you are ready to build larger applications.

To create a new ScalaFX class, choose "New" > "Scala Object" from the "File" menu. This opens a wizard where you can set the name of your class to HelloScalaFX and select the scalafx.application.JFXApp class from which it should extend. Upon completing the wizard, Eclipse will create a stub class for you.

To complete the example, you need to add in a Stage, Scene, and Label to your application. The full code for the Hello ScalaFX application is shown in Listing 10-12.

Listing 10-12. *Hello ScalaFX Application to Test Your Newly Created Project*

```
import scalafx.Includes._
import scalafx.application.JFXApp
import scalafx.stage.Stage
import scalafx.scene.Scene
import scalafx.scene.control.Label

object HelloScalaFX extends JFXApp {
  stage = new Stage {
    scene = new Scene {
      content = new Label {
        text = "Hello ScalaFX"
      }
    }
  }
}
```

You probably noticed some obvious differences from Java code. In Scala, semicolons are almost always optional where a line break would otherwise indicate that a statement has ended. This is why there is no semicolon on the import statements or the assignment to text. Also, Scala has both classes and objects, either or both of which can be defined in a given file. In this case we are creating an object that subclasses scalafx.application.JFXApp, which serves as a way of both defining our application and launching it in one step.

Creating an Object that extends scalafx.application.JFXApp is the fundamental pattern for building JavaFX applications using ScalaFX. This base class has all the core functionality to instantiate a JavaFX application, freeing you from the usual boilerplate required. All you have to do is take care of whatever initialization you need and override the stage variable with your own ScalaFX stage object.

This same pattern is followed for the Stage, Scene, and Label, all of which are ScalaFX objects that have properties on them for each of the available JavaFX properties of the same class. If you notice from the imports, we are not actually referring to JavaFX classes, but instead working with proxy classes in a parallel set of ScalaFX classes. These proxies are interchangeable with the equivalent JavaFX classes using a feature in Scala called implicits, but have additional functionality that supports this nested object-literal-like syntax.

To run this application, right-click on the file and choose "Run As" > "Scala Application". Upon execution, this application opens a window with the words Hello ScalaFX as shown in Figure 10-13.

Figure 10-13. *Hello ScalaFX application launched from Eclipse*

Congratulations, you have successfully run your first ScalaFX application! We now dig more into the design and features of ScalaFX, showing you how you can build more complex JavaFX applications in Scala.

ScalaFX Proxies and Implicit Conversions

For almost every JavaFX API class, there is an equivalent ScalaFX proxy class. The ScalaFX proxy classes are in a parallel package structure where javafx is replaced by scalafx and provides additional functionality on top of the JavaFX APIs. The proxy classes each include one or more of the following.

- Delegate Object: Each proxy contains a reference back to the JavaFX class that it extends and wraps.

- Property Aliases: For all properties, rather than referring to them as fooProperty, you can instead directly access them as foo.

- Property Assignment: To support an object-literal-like syntax, the assignment operator is overloaded to allow you to set writeable properties directly.

- List Access: All JavaFX ObservableLists are wrapped with a property to access the list that lets you treat it as a Scala collection.

- API Enhancements: Some of the JavaFX APIs were not designed with the Scala language and object-literal construction in mind, so the API authors have taken some liberties in adding strategic enhancements.

For most uses, you can actually ignore the fact that there is a parallel set of classes, because the Scala implicits feature allows you to use them interchangeably. Anywhere you have an API that expects a JavaFX class, you can pass in the ScalaFX proxy and it will automatically get converted back to the JavaFX version. Similarly, if you have an API that expects the ScalaFX version, there is a Scala implicit conversion that will automatically wrap the JavaFX class in a ScalaFX proxy.

For example, you can change the Hello ScalaFX code to use a JavaFX label directly and the code will compile and run fine. The modified version is shown in Listing 10-13.

Listing 10-13. *Hello ScalaFX Application to Test Your Newly Created Project*

```
import scalafx.Includes._
import scalafx.application.JFXApp
import scalafx.stage.Stage
import scalafx.scene.Scene
import javafx.scene.control.Label

object HelloScalaFXImplicits extends JFXApp {
  stage = new Stage {
    scene = new Scene {
      content = new Label("Hello ScalaFX Implicits")
    }
  }
}
```

Notice that we have changed the import to the normal JavaFX one and used the standard constructor with a String argument. Even though the Scene content is defined as a collection of ScalaFX Nodes, the Scala implicit kicks in and automatically converts the JavaFX object to a ScalaFX proxy.

The ScalaFX implicit conversions require that you import scalafx.Includes._, which has been the first line in all the programs we have shown. This is a special syntax for Scala that is equivalent to a static import in Java, and will automatically include several utility methods and all the JavaFX to ScalaFX implicit conversions. For the purposes of ScalaFX development, you should simply treat it as a preamble and include it on all your ScalaFX source files.

JavaFX Properties in Scala

Although we have been using ScalaFX properties directly, we have not directly shown how they work. In particular, notice the absence of the usual getter/setter pattern found in JavaFX. This is possible because ScalaFX lets us override the behavior of operators and assignment to substitute more efficient versions of the same operations. To understand this, let's take a look at the JavaFX property pattern again.

When creating properties for JavaFX in Java, each property definition consists of one variable and three different accessor methods as shown again in Listing 10-14.

Listing 10-14. *JavaFX Property Pattern to Create New Properties in Java*

```
import javafx.beans.property.SimpleStringProperty
import javafx.beans.property.StringProperty

public class Person {
  private StringProperty name;
  public public void setName(String val) { nameProperty().set(val); }
  public public String getName() { return nameProperty().get(); }
  public StringProperty nameProperty() {
    if (name == null) {
      name = new SimpleStringProperty(this, "name");
    }
    return name;
  }
}
```

Direct access to the property is restricted in order to allow it to be lazily created upon the first use. The initialization occurs in the nameProperty method if it is null, and then the get and set simply delegate the call to the same named method on the property.

In ScalaFX, you get the same benefits of lazy initialization in a single line as shown in Listing 10-15.

Listing 10-15. *Simplified JavaFX Property Pattern Adapted Using ScalaFX APIs*

```
import scalafx.beans.property.StringProperty

class Person {
  lazy val name = new StringProperty(this, "name")

  // this is optional, but supports the object-literal construction pattern:
  def name_=(v: String) {
    name() = v
  }
}
```

The first line that defines the property is sufficient to do everything that the Java code above does. By declaring "name" as a "val", this tells Scala that it is a constant variable. The "lazy" keyword that precedes the declaration indicates that it should not be initialized until the first use. As a result, you can directly access this variable from user code and the initialization logic is automatically invoked when needed.

■ **Tip**   Scala supports three different types of variable definitions: val, var, and def. The var keyword behaves most closely to what you are familiar with in Java, and defines a variable that can be modified in place. The val keyword, which we used above, declares a constant variable, and is most similar to final variables in Java. The last keyword, def, declares an expression that is re-evaluated each time it is called, so it behaves just like a method in Java.

The second definition of a "name_=" method is special syntax for overloading the assignment operator in Scala. This is how the object-literal-like syntax we used earlier works; however, it is just a shortcut for accessing the property and assigning the value. It also demonstrates the basic pattern for how properties are used in ScalaFX.

Table 10-1 compares all the different combinations of how you access and set properties in Java and ScalaFX.

Table 10-1. Property Operations in ScalaFX Versus Java

Operation	Java	ScalaFX	Description
Get Property	getFooProperty()	foo	Get the raw property (typically used for setting up binds or listeners)
Get Property Value	1: getFoo() 2: getFooProperty.get() [long form]	1: foo() 2: foo.get() [long form]	Vertical offset of the Node for layout positioning
Set Property Value	1: setFoo(val) 2: getFooProperty.set(val) [long form]	1: foo() = val 2: foo.set(val) [long form] 3: obj.foo = val [object literal shortcut]	Preferred width of the Node (when given the passed-in height)

Once you get used to the ScalaFX syntax, it is quite natural. In general, if you refer to a property directly, you will be accessing the full property object, which has all the methods for binding, listeners, and so on. However, if you follow the property name with parentheses, you will get (or set) the property value.

■ **Tip**   This use of parentheses is supported via the Scala apply and update syntax, which is commonly used for Arrays and Lists, but in ScalaFX is used to differentiate between the raw properties and their values.

One exception to this rule is in the object literal case (third example of Set Property Value), where you can use the assignment operator directly to set the value of a property (no parentheses needed). An unambiguous case, this is allowed because JavaFX properties references are read-only, and it significantly cleans up the syntax of the user code.

If you ever get confused between properties and values, Scala's type system will come to the rescue. In general, the ScalaFX APIs have been designed to preserve strong typing and produce type errors anywhere the developer's intent is ambiguous. Therefore, if you use a property where a type is expected, or vice versa, the compiler will most likely catch the error before you even run the application.

ScalaFX Bind APIs

Binding is arguably one of the most innovative features in the JavaFX library, however, the APIs can be a bit cumbersome to use, especially in cases where you have complicated bind logic. The fluent API provided is quite powerful and expressive given the constraints of the Java language, but lacks a lot of the elegance that made bind so powerful with JavaFX Script.

The ScalaFX Bind APIs sit on top of the JavaFX binding support, but wrap them in a programming language syntax that is natural to write and understand. By taking advantage of operator overloading and infix notation, you can write complex ScalaFX bind expressions without even knowing all of the bind API methods that come with JavaFX.

For example, here is how you bind the height of one Rectangle to the sum of the heights of two others:

```
rect1.height <== rect2.height + rect3.height
```

Other than the special bind operator (<==), and lack of parentheses to convert from properties to values, this is the same code that you would write to add up the heights statically. However, once the bind is in place, any updates to rect2 or rect3 will dynamically change the height of rect1.

What this expression actually translates to is the following JavaFX code in Java.

```
rect1.heightProperty().bind(rect2.heightProperty().add(rect3.heightProperty()));
```

Even for a simple bind expression such as this, it is easy to get lost in all the parentheses and method calls that Java requires.

You can also do aggregate operators in ScalaFX. Rather than having to use the static methods on the JavaFX Bindings class, the ScalaFX Includes import gives you all these functions as methods you can call directly, such as the following code to bind the width of one rectangle to the max width of three others.

```
rect1.width <== max(rect2.width, rect3.width, rect4.width)
```

The other type of bind expression that is extremely common is conditional statements. Creating conditionals with the JavaFX APIs is possible, again by using the static Bindings class, but much simpler using the ScalaFX APIs. The following code changes the strokeWidth based on whether the cursor is hovering (just as we did in the Vanishing Circles application earlier).

```
strokeWidth <== when (hover) then 4 otherwise 0
```

The expressions passed in for the conditional value and result clauses can be arbitrarily complicated. The following example combines Boolean logic, String concatenation, and a conditional expression.

```
text <== when (rect.hover || circle.hover && !disabled) then textField.text + " is enabled"
otherwise "disabled"
```

In all of the above examples, because you are writing code that sits directly on top of the JavaFX bind APIs, you get all the same benefits, such as lazy evaluation. Also, because Scala is a statically typed language like Java, you get these benefits without giving up type safety as you do with other dynamic languages. In fact, you get better type safety with the ScalaFX APIs, because it also supports type-safe dereferencing of subproperties. For example, in ScalaFX to bind a rectangle to the width of a Scene you would simply write:

```
rect1.width <== stage.scene.width
```

This works even if the Scene has not been created yet, such as during initialization of the Stage object. You can also accomplish the same thing in Java, but it requires a non-type-safe property selector:

```
rect.widthProperty().bind(Bindings.selectDouble(stage, "scene.width"));
```

Underneath the covers, the ScalaFX calls this exact JavaFX API, but it protects the application developer from accessing a property that may be misspelled or of the wrong type.

Finally, a discussion of binding would not be complete without an example of bidirectional binding. This is similarly easy in ScalaFX, and can be accomplished using a slight variation on the bind operator as shown in the following example.

```
textField.text <==> model.name
```

This creates a bidirectional binding between the name property in the model and a TextField, such that if the user edits the text field, the model object will automatically be updated too.

Although most of the ScalaFX operators are fairly intuitive, there are a few cases where it was not possible to use the standard operators. These include:

- if/else: These are Scala language keywords, so as demonstrated earlier, these have been replaced with when/otherwise, just as in the corresponding JavaFX APIs.

- ==/!=: Directly using the equality and inequality operators produces some unwanted interactions with the same operations on the core Scala object base class. Instead use === and =!=, both of which were carefully chosen to have the same precedence rules as the operators they are replacing.

As an added bonus, you can specify the precision of the === and =!= operators for numeric comparison by using the following syntax.

```
aboutFiveHundred <== value1 === 500+-.1
```

This would test that value1 is less than .1 away from 500.

API Enhancements

By this time, you should have a pretty good feel for how the JavaFX applications you have been building translate to equivalent ScalaFX code. In general the ScalaFX APIs mirror the JavaFX APIs, providing equivalent functionality. However, in some cases it was actually possible to provide an improved API or alternative choice that matches the declarative style of programming that ScalaFX encourages. In this section we cover a few different areas in which ScalaFX improves on the JavaFX APIs.

Closures

One of the features that Java developers have been waiting eagerly to see introduced into the language is closures. This simplifies the case where you are creating event listeners or similar callbacks where you need to implement an interface that contains a single method.

Fortunately, most modern JVM languages include closures as a core language feature, as does the Scala language. This means that anywhere you would normally have to implement an event or property listener, you can instead use a closure to simplify your code.

Earlier in the Vanishing Circles application we showed an example of a closure to set a mouse click handler:

```
onMouseClicked = {
  Timeline(at (3 s) {radius -> 0}).play()
}
```

The closure part is really that simple; all you have to do is surround your method logic with curly braces and assign it to the property for the event handler. There is another variant of this if you also need access to some of the variables passed in, such as the MouseEvent:

```
onMouseClicked = { (e: MouseEvent) =>
  Timeline(at (3 s) {radius -> 0}).play()
}
```

Layout Constraints

The layout constraint mechanism introduced in JavaFX 2.0 is very flexible, because it lets layout authors define their own constraints that get stored on Node, but is also not ideal from an application developer standpoint. It forces your code into an imperative pattern where you add children in one step and then set constraints following that.

Because the set of interesting layout constraints is fairly small, the ScalaFX APIs simply add the common ones onto the Node class directly. This lets you specify constraints such as alignment, margin, and grow declaratively as you are creating your object tree.

For example, to add a margin to the Label in our Hello ScalaFX example, it is as easy as setting the margin property on the Label:

```
object HelloScalaFXMargin extends JFXApp {
  stage = new Stage {
    scene = new Scene {
      content = new Label {
        text = "Hello ScalaFX Margin"
        margin = new Insets(20)
      }
    }
  }
}
```

And this adds 20 pixels around the Label to space it out in the window. Without this ScalaFX feature, you would have been required to save a reference to the Label and later call the following.

```
StackPane.setMargin(new Insets(20));
```

An added benefit of the ScalaFX Node Layout Constraints is that they apply across all JavaFX layouts regardless of which type of container you are using. With the normal JavaFX Layout Constraints, you need to use the static method from the right layout type, otherwise the constraint will not work.

■ **Tip**   For layout authors who want to make use of the ScalaFX Node Layout Constraints, ScalaFX also stores the layout constraint in an unprefixed form that you can directly access. For example, to get the margin constraint, simply call node.getProperties().get("margin"). For alignment you get your choice of accessing it as "alignment," "halignment," or "valignment," all of which get updated anytime the user sets the alignment property.

Animation

ScalaFX provides a shortcut syntax for expressing timelines that was inspired by the same syntax in JavaFX Script. It lets you specify the duration, keyframes, keyvalues, and tweens in a shortcut syntax that fits on a single line. We used this earlier in the Vanishing Circles example to specify an animation that shrinks the circles when they are clicked:

```
Timeline(at (3 s) {radius -> 0}).play()
```

This code is equivalent to the following Java code using the JavaFX animation API.

```
KeyValue collapse = new KeyValue(circle.radiusProperty(), 0);
new Timeline(new KeyFrame(Duration.seconds(3), collapse)).play();
```

As you can see, the ScalaFX variant is much more concise and readable even in this simple example. The basic syntax for animations in ScalaFX is:

```
at (duration) {[property -> value]}
```

This statement translates to a KeyFrame that can be added to a Timeline directly. You can pass in multiple KeyFrames to a Timeline or use multiple property->value pairs in the above syntax, giving you the flexibility to specify arbitrarily complex animations.

Breaking down this example further, notice that we used a shortcut syntax to create the Duration and the KeyValue. For the former, ScalaFX has an implicit conversion that adds a function to Doubles for ms(), s(), m(), and h(), allowing you to create a new Duration simply by calling the respective function. By using the postfix operator shortcut syntax in Scala, rather than calling "3.s()" or "3.s," you can further abbreviate it to "3 s" (where the space between 3 and s is required).

For the latter, ScalaFX properties have an overloaded operator of "->" that takes a value and returns a KeyValue object. In fact, not only can you specify the target value, but you can also add in a tween expression as shown here:

```
radius -> 0 tween EASE_OUT
```

This addition causes the animation to slow down as it approaches the end, resulting in a smoother transition.

Visage, the JavaFX Language

Most programming languages have their basis in computation and mathematics, and grow towards their most common use case. For some languages, such as LISP, this is artificial intelligence. For others, such as Java, the predominant use case has become backend business applications. However, there are very few languages that are designed and tailored specifically for UI development.

Visage is an exception, inasmuch as it was originally conceived by Christopher Oliver as a UI language called F3 for Form Follows Function, specifically targeted at making it easier to program graphic user interfaces. It was renamed JavaFX Script and served as the UI programming language for all JavaFX applications prior to the release of JavaFX 2.0. Currently it is being developed as an independent UI programming language called Visage, available as open-source, and can be used with JavaFX and other UI toolkits.

Advantages of Using Visage

So what is it about Visage that makes it better suited for UI development than other programming languages? Here are some of the unique features of Visage that make it a superior environment for developing GUIs.

- Null Safety: Visage applications never throw Null Pointer Exceptions. This is important for UI applications, because getting an NPE in your Java code grinds your application to a halt giving a very poor user experience.

- Binding: Visage provides powerful compiled bind capabilities. Although you have seen the power of the JavaFX binding library, this goes beyond by allowing you to integrate data and interaction with a natural syntax.

- Static Typing: Having a language that is specified with strong typing allows better tooling for IDEs and also avoids runtime errors that could blow up on your user unexpectedly.

- Object Literals: Having a built-in construct for creating object trees allows you to create hierarchical UIs quickly with no external mark-up needed.

- Built-in Animation: Visage has its own animation syntax for defining quick timeline-based animation with adapters to plug directly into the JavaFX animation library.

- UI Types: In Visage, Colors, Lengths, Durations, and Angles are built-in types with a shorthand literal syntax. This allows you to have extremely concise UI code.

Some of these concepts are available in other languages or mirrored in APIs and DSLs, but it is the combination of these features when put together that give Visage its power. Visage is also a first-class JVM language with a compiler engineered by the Java compiler team at Sun Microsystems. This means you get the same power and polish that you have come to expect from the Java compiler toolchain, including reliable compiler errors and warnings, efficient byte-code generation, and fast compiler performance for large projects. In the next section we show you how to use these tools to get started with using Visage in your own projects.

Getting Started with Visage

To use Visage you need to download the latest version of the Visage compiler and JavaFX libraries from the Visage open-source web site. The project is currently hosted on Google Code and can be downloaded from the project home page at:

http://code.google.com/p/visage/

The file you need to download is the latest version of the Visage project, version 2.0 or higher. The distribution zip file contains everything you need to start writing JavaFX applications, including the compiler, core libraries, and runtime. We show you how to compile your code and run it from the command line. However, there is work in progress on updating the plug-ins for NetBeans, Eclipse, and IntelliJ to work with the latest release, so by the time you read this you can likely choose your favorite IDE.

Here is a short description of the package contents that come with Visage.

- bin/visagec[.exe]: This is the compiler that you use to generate Java class files from the Visage source. It has similar command line switches to javac.

- bin/visage[w][.exe]: This is an executable that bootstraps your Visage application, doing initialization and setup required by the JavaFX APIs. It is analogous to the java and javaw commands you use to run Java applications.

- bin/visagedoc[.exe]: Creates HTML API documentation from javadoc-style code comments in your source. This is analogous to the javadoc command for Java source.

- doc/index.html: The visagedoc documentation for all of the core Visage classes.

- lib/*: This contains the jar files you need to execute your Visage application, including core libraries as well as JavaFX specific adapters.

Our first Visage application is a single file that is compiled and executed from the command line. You can build on this to create more complicated applications or to integrate Visage with existing projects, but it should be enough to demonstrate the fundamentals.

Start by creating a file called HelloVisage.visage and type the code in Listing 10-16 into the file.

Listing 10-16. *Hello Visage Application Demonstrating How to Build a Simple Visage App*

```
import visage.javafx.stage.Stage;
import visage.javafx.scene.Scene;
import visage.javafx.scene.control.Label;

Stage {
  Scene {
    Label {text: "Hello Visage"}
  }
}
```

Writing a Visage JavaFX application is that simple; this same code would be over seven times as long if written in standard Java, but with Visage can be accomplished in only 39 characters (not including imports).

▓ **Note** For readers familiar with JavaFX Script, notice that we have left off the labels for the Stage and Scene's contents. This is a new feature introduced in Visage called default variables that you can read more about in Appendix A.

To compile the application all you need to do is invoke the visagec compiler on this file. The command to run the compiler is shown in Listing 10-17.

Listing 10-17. *Command to Run the visagec Compiler*

```
visagec HelloVisage.visage
```

▓ **Note** The command line examples here assume that you have added %VISAGE_SDK%\bin (windows) or $VISAGE_SDK/bin (unix/mac) to your path, where VISAGE_SDK is the location to which you unzipped the Visage distribution. You can also simply prefix the commands with the path to the Visage SDK bin folder.

Notice that we did not need to specify the location of Java or the JavaFX Runtime. The Visage wrapper scripts automatically detect the location of these based on your platform and set up the classpath with all the necessary jars. Running your Visage application is similarly easy. To execute the Visage runtime wrapper, simply execute the command shown in Listing 10-18.

Listing 10-18. *Command to Execute a Visage Application*

```
visage HelloVisage
```

Running your application results in the output shown in Figure 10-14.

Figure 10-14. *Output of the Hello Visage application*

Writing and running Visage applications is really that simple. All the examples in this book can easily be rewritten in Visage and compiled and run in the same fashion. As an exercise, try porting some of the GUI examples from earlier chapters into the Visage language.

By using a UI-focused language such as Visage, you will find that your JavaFX code will be easier to write and more maintainable in the future. For more details about the Visage language, see Appendix A, which is a full language reference that includes plenty of examples.

Constructing UIs with FXML Markup

The last language we cover is not actually a language, but instead a type of markup. With the JavaFX 2.0 release, they added in an additional XML-based markup called FXML that provides a declarative way of creating your user interface.

FXML is particularly useful if you want to be able to treat your user interface as data. This may be the case if you need to load portions of the scene graph dynamically from disk or network without restarting. Also, if you are using a UI builder tool, it is highly likely that it will generate an FXML-based UI that you can load in your application to which to bind behavior. To teach the fundamentals of how FXML works, we show you how to handcode the XML format and load it into your application.

■ **Note** In practice you will probably find that one of the alternative languages discussed earlier or even plain old Java is a better language for handwriting user interfaces.

Learning FXML by Example

To build a JavaFX application using FXML, you require at least two files. The first one is a JavaFX application, and the second is the FXML file you want to load into the scene graph. The JavaFX application file is typically written in Java, although any of the JVM languages we covered earlier in this chapter can be used to load an FXML file. The FXML file is always written in XML, and must conform to a specific format used by JavaFX.

To illustrate the use of FXML, we have converted the Dog Adoption Form from the GroovyFX section earlier in this chapter to Java and FXML. The first file in the project is a Java language file that extends the JavaFX Application class and builds the scene graph by loading an FXML file. The full source code is shown in Listing 10-19.

Listing 10-19. *Java Source Code for Loading an FXML File*

```
package com.projavafx.fxml;

import javafx.application.Application;
import javafx.fxml.FXMLLoader;
import javafx.scene.Parent;
import javafx.scene.Scene;
import javafx.stage.Stage;

public class FXMLAdoptionForm extends Application {
    public static void main(String[] args) {
        launch(args);
    }
```

```
    @Override
    public void start(Stage stage) throws Exception {
        stage.setTitle("FXML GridPane Demo");
        Parent root = FXMLLoader.load(getClass().getResource("AdoptionForm.fxml"));
        stage.setScene(new Scene(root));
        stage.show();
    }
}
```

■ **Note** Due to a NetBeans bug, you may get an NullPointerException caused by a missing resource. If this happens, simply clean and rebuild your project to have the resources copied over properly.

Other than the line that calls the static load method on FXMLLoader, this could be the start of any of the JavaFX examples throughout this book. In this case we are loading the FXML file via a relative classpath reference to a local resource, but you can also load FXML from the network or generate it programmatically.

The second file needed in any FXML application is the XML file that contains the UI markup. FXML is expressive enough to let you build up an entire scene graph, just as you would normally have done via either imperative or builder code in Java. In fact, FXML relies upon method lookups in the Java builder classes, so the property names exactly match what you would normally call when using the builder pattern.

The full source code for the converted Pet Adoption application is shown in Listing 10-20. Just to keep things interesting, we have swapped the test and graphics for a cat-themed UI instead.

Listing 10-20. FXML Markup for the Cat Adoption Form UI

```
<?xml version="1.0" encoding="UTF-8"?>

<?import java.lang.*?>
<?import javafx.collections.*?>
<?import javafx.scene.*?>
<?import javafx.scene.control.*?>
<?import javafx.scene.effect.*?>
<?import javafx.scene.image.*?>
<?import javafx.scene.layout.*?>

<StackPane prefWidth="400" prefHeight="500" xmlns:fx="http://javafx.com/fxml">
    <children>
        <ImageView>
            <image>
                <Image url="@cat.jpg" requestedWidth="800" requestedHeight="800"
                    preserveRatio="true"/>
            </image>
```

```
                <effect>
                    <ColorAdjust brightness="0.1">
                        <input>
                            <GaussianBlur/>
                        </input>
                    </ColorAdjust>
                </effect>
            </ImageView>
            <GridPane hgap="10" vgap="10" style="-fx-padding: 20">
                <columnConstraints>
                    <ColumnConstraints minWidth="60" halignment="right"/>
                    <ColumnConstraints prefWidth="300" hgrow="always"/>
                </columnConstraints>
                <children>
                    <Label text="Cat Adoption Form" style="-fx-font-size: 24"
                      GridPane.halignment="center" GridPane.columnSpan="2147483647"/>

                    <Label text="Size: " GridPane.rowIndex="2"/>
                    <TextField promptText="approximate size in pounds"
                      GridPane.rowIndex="2" GridPane.columnIndex="1"/>

                    <Label text="Breed: " GridPane.rowIndex="3"/>
                    <TextField promptText="pet breed"
                      GridPane.rowIndex="3" GridPane.columnIndex="1"/>

                    <Label text="Sex: " GridPane.rowIndex="4"/>
                    <ChoiceBox GridPane.rowIndex="4" GridPane.columnIndex="1">
                        <items>
                            <FXCollections fx:factory="observableArrayList">
                                <String fx:value="Male"/>
                                <String fx:value="Female"/>
                                <String fx:value="Either"/>
                            </FXCollections>
                        </items>
                    </ChoiceBox>

                    <Label text="Additional Info: " wrapText="true" textAlignment="right"
                      GridPane.rowIndex="5" GridPane.valignment="baseline"/>
                    <TextArea prefRowCount="8" wrapText="true"
                      GridPane.rowIndex="5" GridPane.columnIndex="1" GridPane.vgrow="always"/>

                    <Button text="Submit" GridPane.rowIndex="6" GridPane.columnIndex="1"
                      GridPane.halignment="right""/>
                </children>
            </GridPane>
        </children>
    </StackPane>
```

Although the FXML is not nearly as succinct as the earlier GroovyFX code, it retains a lot of the benefits of the declarative style by nesting XML elements. By reading through this code, you should have gotten the hang of the basic FXML file format:

- All FXML files should start with an XML preamble (<?xml version =" 1.0" encoding="UTF-8"?>

- Any JavaFX imports you require should also be declared as processing instructions following the preamble.

- The body of the XML document contains a hierarchical scene definition, the root of which gets returned when the FXML document is loaded.

From here, you should see all the class names (elements) and properties (attributes) that you recognize from writing JavaFX code in Java. There are, however, a few important exceptions that let you declare a complete UI declaratively:

1. Complex properties (lists, Nodes, or other structures that cannot easily be represented as attribute values) can be declared as nested child elements.

2. Layout constraints (e.g., margin, alignment, grow) can be declared inline by prefacing them with a static reference to the layout class.

3. To declare an ObservableList inline, you can use the special factory attribute to refer to a static list constructor, such as those found in FXCollections (see the ChoiceBox list initialization above).

4. To reference a relative file, you can prefix filenames with an "@" symbol (see the Image loading code above).

Also, for the most part FXML is namespace-free, which makes writing documents much less tedious, but there are a few important tags that require the "http://javafx.com/fxml" namespace, so it is a good idea to declare this on the root element of your document.

Running the completed application will give you very similar output to the earlier Dog Adoption Form example as shown in Figure 10-15, except you have now accomplished this with dynamic XML instead of compiled code.

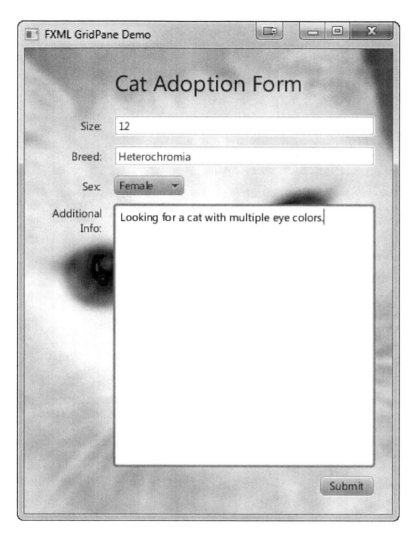

Figure 10-15. Completed Cat Adoption Form application showing a cat with heterochromia in the background[4]

_____

[4] Public domain picture from Wikimedia Commons: http://commons.wikimedia.org/
wiki/File:Cat_Eyes.jpg

Controlling FXML Applications

We showed how you can declaratively build applications with FXML, however, this does not let you control and interact with the FXML-generated scene graph from your Java code very easily. To make this interaction more straightforward, FXML also supports a controller class that you can hook up to the generated user interface.

To demonstrate the use of a controller in FXML applications, we augment the previous example to add a controller that shows or hides grid lines when the submit button is clicked. The first step is to write the controller code, which must implement the FXML Initializable interface as shown in Listing 10-21.

Listing 10-21. Java Source Code for an FXML Controller

```java
package com.projavafx.fxml;

import java.net.URL;
import java.util.ResourceBundle;
import javafx.event.ActionEvent;
import javafx.fxml.FXML;
import javafx.fxml.Initializable;
import javafx.scene.layout.GridPane;

public class AdoptionFormController implements Initializable {
    @FXML
    private GridPane grid;

    @FXML
    private void handleSubmit(ActionEvent event) {
        grid.setGridLinesVisible(!grid.isGridLinesVisible());
    }

    @Override
    public void initialize(URL url, ResourceBundle rb) {
        // no init action required
    }
}
```

Notice that we have made use of the FXML annotation on both the grid variable and the handleSubmit method. This tells the FXML support that these methods correspond to ids and references in the FXML document. To complete the example, let's add these references.

The first change to the FXML document is to add in a reference to the FXML controller by modifying the root element as shown here:

```
<StackPane prefWidth="400" prefHeight="500" xmlns:fx="http://javafx.com/fxml"
  fx:controller="com.projavafx.fxml.AdoptionFormController">
```

The second change is to add in an id reference to the grid that we want to have access to from our Java code:

```
<GridPane fx:id="grid" hgap="10" vgap="10" style="-fx-padding: 20">
```

Notice that we have used the namespace prefixed fx:id attribute, rather than just id.

Finally, we have to hook up the event listener to call our handleSubmit method by adding in a reference in the FXML:

```
<Button text="Submit" GridPane.rowIndex="6" GridPane.columnIndex="1"
GridPane.halignment="right" onAction="#handleSubmit"/>
```

With these three changes to the FXML, plus the controller code we wrote earlier, we have created interaction between the FXML and Java code. If you rerun the application and click the Submit button, you get some helpful gridlines that you can use to debug your layout code in the future as shown in Figure 10-16.

Figure 10-15. Modified Cat Adoption Form application that shows grid lines when you click Submit

Summary

As we have shown you in the chapter, you have a lot more options for writing JavaFX code than just using the Java language. You can declare your UI as markup using FXML, there are already several DSLs available written in popular JVM languages such as Groovy and Scala, and you can even use a dedicated UI programming language, such as Visage.

The great thing is that you have the choice to use the language and markup that best suits your project needs. All of these technologies integrate cleanly with JavaFX code written in Java, and have their own benefits that you can take advantage of based on the needs of your project.

If you are interested in learning more about the different JVM languages and markup for JavaFX that we have discussed in this chapter, please refer to the resources section. Also, make sure to check out the final chapter of this book, "Appendix A : The Visage Language Guide," to find out more about this great UI language in detail.

Resources

For more information about Groovy and GroovyFX, consult the following resources.

- Groovy Home Page: `http://groovy.codehaus.org/`

- GroovyFX Home Page: `http://groovyfx-project.github.com/`

- GroovyFX Announcement Blog Entry: `http://pleasingsoftware.blogspot.com/2011/08/introducing-groovyfx-it-about-time.html`

Additional information on Scala and ScalaFX can be found here:

- Scala Home Page: `http://www.scala-lang.org/`

- ScalaFX Home Page: `http://code.google.com/p/scalafx/`

- ScalaFX Announcement Blog Entry: `http://javafx.steveonjava.com/javafx-2-0-and-scala-like-milk-and-cookies/`

Here is a resource on the Visage Language:

- Visage Project Home Page: `http://code.google.com/p/visage/`

And finally some FXML resources:

- FXML Getting Started Guide: `http://docs.oracle.com/javafx/2.0/fxml_get_started/jfxpub-fxml_get_started.htm`

- API Documentation for FXML: `http://docs.oracle.com/javafx/2.0/api/javafx/fxml/doc-files/introduction_to_fxml.html`

The Visage Language in Depth

…a lot my of opinions about what makes programming languages "expressive" comes from my observations and opinions about what allows us effective expression in natural languages.

—Christopher Oliver

The Visage language stands out from other languages you can use with the JavaFX Platform because it was designed and engineered specifically for that platform. Visage's origins date back to the F3 language designed by Christopher Oliver while he was working at SeeBeyond. With the purchase of SeeBeyond by Sun Microsystems, F3 was renamed JavaFX Script and went on to be the primary language of the JavaFX Platform up to version 1.3. At that time, Sun also made JavaFX Script open source, releasing it to the development community to enhance and extend. With the acquisition of Sun by Oracle, JavaFX Script was dropped as the language of JavaFX in favor of pure Java APIs. The JavaFX Script language was subsequently adopted by several members of the JavaFX community under the name Visage and continues to be developed and maintained for use with JavaFX and other UI toolkits.

In this appendix, we will cover the Visage language in greater detail, describing the full syntax, programming model, and language features. This will help you to understand the language at a fundamental level, enabling you to efficiently build rich user interfaces for the JavaFX Platform.

> **Note** Although Visage is a programming language for the Java platform, our coverage does not require any prior Java programming experience. Because of the close relationship between Visage and Java, using Java concepts to explain corresponding Visage concepts is sometimes inevitable. We will fully explain these Java concepts when the need arises.

An Overview of Visage

The Visage programming language was designed specifically for UI programming with the JavaFX platform. It has the following characteristics:

- It is an object-oriented language. It supports classes, instance variables, instance functions, and inheritance.

- It is a functional language. Functions are first-class entities that can be assigned to variables, passed in, and returned from functions.

- It is an expression language. All executable code in Visage consists of expressions.

- It supports a declarative style suitable for GUI programming. Its object literal syntax and sequence syntax make describing GUIs easy.

- It supports data binding. It allows for easy separation of GUI views and models, which gives rise to "the way of Visage."

- It is a statically typed, compiled language with basic type inference capabilities. It compiles source code into Java classes.

- It can leverage the vast number of Java libraries. Visage classes can extend Java classes and interfaces, and Visage code can instantiate Java objects and call Java methods.

We will use Visage data types as guideposts in our coverage of the programming language. There are four kinds of data types in Visage: primitive, sequence, class, and function. We concentrate on primitive and sequence types in the first half of this appendix. In the second half, we build up to function and class types, followed by advanced features like reflection and Java interoperability.

Variables, Values, and Their Types

The simplest construct in Visage is the *variable*. A variable can be assigned *values*. Values can be *literals* or *expressions*. Each variable has a *declared type*. Each value has a *runtime type*. An assignment is valid only if the runtime type of the value is compatible with the declared type of the variable.

As you can see in Listing A-1, variable declarations are introduced by the var keyword, followed by the name of the variable, an optional type specifier, and an optional initializer, and are terminated by a semicolon (;).

Listing A-1. *Variable Declarations*

```
var b: Boolean = true;
var i: Integer = 1024;
var n: Number = 3.14;
var str: String = "Hello, World";
var dur: Duration = 60s;
var col: Color = #E01B4C
```

In Listing A-1, we declare six variables:

- The variable b is of type Boolean and is initialized to the literal value true.

- The variable i is of type Integer and is initialized to the literal value 1024.

- The variable n is of type Number and is initialized to the literal value 3.14.

- The variable str is of type String and is initialized to the literal value "Hello, World".

- The variable dur is of type Duration and is initialized to the literal value 60s, meaning "60 seconds."

- The variable col is of type Color and is initialized to the literal value #E01B4C, which is the hexadecimal RGB string for a shade of red.

Variable Names

Visage variable names follow the Visage *identifier* syntax. A Visage identifier starts with a letter, followed by letters, digits, or both. For the purpose of forming Visage identifiers, letters include the uppercase and lowercase ASCII letters and other Unicode letters, the underscore (_), and the dollar character ($), and other currency characters. Digits include digits 0 through 9 and other Unicode digits.

The following are valid Visage identifiers:

```
i
x2
Builtins
toString
_tmp$getter
```

The following are invalid Visage identifiers:

```
2x
package-info
Hello, World
```

Visage identifiers are case sensitive. Therefore count, Count, and COUNT are considered three distinct identifiers.

Variable Types

Visage variables may be declared with an explicit type, as we did in Listing A-1. The type of a variable follows the variable name and is separated from the name by a colon (:). The colon is not considered a part of the variable name or a part of the type name. The type of a variable dictates the kind of values that can be assigned to the variable. For example, it is illegal to assign a String value to an Integer variable.

Visage has a *type inference* facility that allows you to declare a variable without an explicit type. The Visage compiler will infer the variable's type from the initializer in the declaration or, if no initializer is given in the declaration, the first subsequent assignment.

Therefore, you can safely rewrite the variable declarations from Listing A-1 as shown in Listing A-2.

Listing A-2. *Variable Declarations with Inferred Types*

```
var b = true;
var i = 1024;
var n = 3.14;
```

```
var str = "Hello, World";
var dur = 60s;
var color = #E01B4C
```

Visage's type system consists of various kinds of types. These include the primitive, sequence, function, and class types.

Primitive Types

Visage intrinsically understands a few data types. These are called the *primitive types*. The core primitive types in Visage are: Boolean, Integer, Character, Byte, Short, Long, Number, Float, Double, and String. These types allow Visage programs to integrate seamlessly with class libraries written in Java. There are also several extended types that let you succinctly express UI specific concepts. These are Duration, Length, Angle, and Color. Both the core and extended primitive types share some common characteristics:

- Each primitive type—except the three "small" types, Character, Byte, and Short—has its own literal syntax so that you can put values directly into a Visage program.

- Each primitive type has a default value that a variable of the type gets if it is declared without an initializer.

- Each primitive type supports a set of operations that are appropriate for the type.

- Each primitive type is backed by a class that provides more capabilities for working with variables of the type.

▓ **Caution** If you are familiar with the Java programming language, you should notice that primitive types in Visage differ from those in Java. For example, String is a primitive type in Visage but is a reference type in Java, and Java primitive types are not backed by classes.

Boolean Type

The Boolean type has two possible values: true and false. You can use a Boolean variable to denote a condition in a Visage program. Boolean values are used in conditional and looping expressions.

Boolean Literals and the Default Value

To specify an explicit boolean value in Visage, you use the literals true and false. The default value of a Boolean variable is false.

Boolean Operators

Visage's boolean operators allow you to build new Boolean values from existing ones.

The not operator is a unary operator. Its operand must evaluate to a Boolean value, and it negates its operand.

The and operators and the or operators are binary infix operators. An infix operator is an operator that appears between its operands. Both operands must evaluate to Boolean values. The and operator produces true if both operands are true, and false otherwise; the or operator produces true if at least one operand is true, and false otherwise. Both operators perform their evaluations in a short-circuit fashion. If the first operand of an and expression is false, the and expression's value will be false, and the second operand is not evaluated. Similarly, if the first operand of an or expression is true, the or expression's value will be true, and the second operand is not evaluated.

The Backing Class of the Boolean Type

The Boolean type is backed by the Java class java.lang.Boolean. This means that you can call any Java methods, including static methods, in java.lang.Boolean on a Visage Boolean value.

Since java.lang.Boolean is a small class and most of its methods are geared toward supporting Java functionality, the fact that it is the backing class of the Visage Boolean type is rarely used.

In Listing A-3, you can see Visage Boolean variables at work.

Listing A-3. Boolean Variables at Work

```
var a = true;
var b = false;

println("a = {a}");
println("b = {b}");

println("not a = {not a}");
println("not b = {not b}");

println("a and a = {a and a}");
println("a and b = {a and b}");
println("b and a = {b and a}");
println("b and b = {b and b}");

println("a or a = {a or a}");
println("a or b = {a or b}");
println("b or a = {b or a}");
println("b or b = {b or b}");
```

In Listing A-3 presents two features of Visage that we have not covered in detail yet. The println() function prints its argument to the console; it is a built-in function. The curly braces embedded in a String allow us to put the String representation of an arbitrary Visage expression in a String.

Integer Type

The Integer type represents 32-bit signed integral values, with valid values ranging from –2,147,483,648 to 2,147,483,647. You can use Integer values as counters and sequence indexes.

Integer Literals and the Default Value

Visage supports three forms of *integral type literals*. *Decimal literals* consist of a leading nonzero decimal digit (1 through 9) followed by a series of decimal digits (0 through 9). *Octal literals* consist of a leading digit zero (0) followed by a series of octal digits (0 through 7). *Hexadecimal literals* consist of a leading digit zero (0) followed by the character x or X, and then a series of hexadecimal digits (0 through 9, a through f, and A through F). The default value of an Integer variable is 0.

Here are some examples of integral type literals:

```
2009
03731
0x07d9
0X07D9
```

An integral type literal whose value falls within the range of the Integer type is an Integer literal. It has an inferred type of Integer. An integral type literal can also be a Long literal, as you'll see shortly.

■ **Caution** When you're initializing or assigning to an Integer variable, the integral type literal that you use must be an Integer literal. Using an integral type literal outside the range of the Integer type will cause a compilation error. Catching errors early is one of the benefits of a compiled language.

Arithmetic Operators

Visage's arithmetic operators operate on Character, Byte, Short, Integer, and Long values as well as Number, Float, Double, and Duration values. These operators are the addition (+), subtraction (-), multiplication (*), division (/), and modulo (mod) operators. Notice that not all arithmetic operations are meaningful for Duration values. For example, you cannot multiply two Duration values.

When applied to Integer operands, these operators always produce Integer values. They associate from left to right. The multiplication, division, and modulo operators have higher precedence over the addition and subtraction operators. The addition, subtraction, and multiplication operators are capable of overflowing the legal limits of the Integer type. In such cases, Visage will silently produce an inaccurate result. Dividing an Integer value by zero causes an exception to be thrown at runtime. You will learn more about exceptions in the section entitled "Exceptions" later in this appendix.

Visage supports the preincrement operator (++i), the postincrement operator (i++), the predecrement operator (--i), and the postdecrement operator (i--). Visage also supports the negation operator (-x).

The Backing Class of the Integer Type

The Integer type is backed by the Java class java.lang.Integer. This means that you can call any Java methods, including static methods in java.lang.Integer, on a Visage Integer value.

Again, since most methods of java.lang.Integer are geared toward supporting Java functionality, you will rarely call these methods on Visage Integer values.

Listing A-4 shows Visage Integer variables at work.

Listing A-4. *Integer Variables at Work*

```
var i = 1024;
var j = 2048;
var k = 15625;

println("i = {i}");
println("j = {j}");
println("k = {k}");

println("i + j = {i + j}");
println("i - j = {i - j}");
println("i * k = {i * k}");
println("k / i = {k / i}");
println("k mod j = {k mod j}");

var max = Integer.MAX_VALUE;
var min = Integer.MIN_VALUE;

println("max = {max}");
println("min = {min}");

println("max + 1 will overflow to {max + 1}");
println("min - 1 will overflow to {min - 1}");
println("max * min will overflow to {max * min}");

println("i = {i}, ++i = {++i}");
println("j = {j}, --j = {--j}");
println("k = {k}, k++ = {k++}");
println("k = {k}, k-- = {k--}");
```

Listing A-4 uses a Visage feature that allows us to access Java classes and their members directly. We access the static fields MAX_VALUE and MIN_VALUE of the Visage Integer, backed by the java.lang.Integer class. You will learn how to access Java programming language features from Visage in the section entitled "Leveraging Java from Visage" later in this appendix.

Running this example will produce the following output:

```
i = 1024

j = 2048

k = 15625

i + j = 3072

i - j = -1024
```

```
i * k = 16000000

k / i = 15

k mod j = 1289

max = 2147483647

min = -2147483648

max + 1 will overflow to -2147483648

min - 1 will overflow to 2147483647

max * min will overflow to -2147483648

i = 1024, ++i = 1025

j = 2048, --j = 2047

k = 15625, k++ = 15625

k = 15626, k-- = 15626
```

Character Type

The Character type represents 16-bit unsigned character values, with valid values in the range from 0 to 65,535. You can use Character values to represent Unicode characters.

Sources of Character Values and the Default Value

Visage does not support Character literals. The main source of Character values is from Java code that contains fields and returns values of the Java char type or the java.lang.Character wrapper type. You can assign Integer literals that fall within the Character range to Character type variables. The default value of a Character variable is 0.

You can also assign values of other numeric types to variables of the Character type. However, doing so will result in a loss of precision and a compilation warning will be generated.

Here is an example:

```
var ch: Character = 100;
println("ch={ch}.");
```

This will print ch=d to the console, since 100 is the Unicode value, as well as the ASCII value, of the character "d."

■ **Caution** If you are familiar with Java, you might be tempted to try to assign `'d'` to a variable of `Character` type. This will generate a compilation error because `'d'` is a `String` value in Visage and cannot be assigned to a `Character` variable.

Arithmetic Operations

`Character` values may participate in arithmetic operations. The type of the result of an arithmetic operation involving a `Character` value depends on the type of the other operand:

- It is `Integer` if the other operand is a `Character`, `Byte`, `Short`, or `Integer` value.

- It is `Long` if the other operand is a `Long` value.

- It is `Float` if the other operand is a `Float` value.

- It is `Double` if the other operand is a `Double` value.

The Backing Class of the Character Type

The Character type is backed by the Java class `java.lang.Character`. This means that you can call any Java methods, including static methods in `java.lang.Character`, on a Visage `Character` value. Many of the methods are geared toward supporting Java functionality and will rarely be called from Visage.

Byte, Short, and Long Types

The `Byte` type represents 8-bit signed integer values, with valid values ranging from –128 to 127. The `Short` type represents 16-bit signed integer values, with valid values ranging from –32,768 to 32,767. The `Long` type represents 64-bit signed integer values, with valid values ranging from $–2^{63}$ to $2^{63}–1$.

Sources of Byte and Short Values, Long Literals, and the Default Values

Visage does not support Byte or Short literals. The main source of values of `Byte` and `Short` types is from Java code that contains fields and returns values of the corresponding Java primitive types, byte and short, and their wrapper types, `java.lang.Byte` and `java.lang.Short`. You can assign integral type literals that fall within their range to `Byte` or `Short` variables.

An integral type literal whose value falls outside the range of the `Integer` type but within the range of the `Long` type is a `Long` literal. It has an inferred type of `Long`. You can assign any `Integer` or `Long` literals to `Long` variables.

■ **Caution** An integral type literal whose value falls outside the range of the `Long` type will generate a compilation error.

The default value of a Byte, Short, or Long variable is 0.

You can also assign values of other numeric types to variables of Byte, Short, or Long types. A compilation warning is generated if you are assigning a wider typed value to a narrower typed variable, such as assigning an Integer value to a Short variable.

Arithmetic Operations

Values of Byte, Short, or Long types may participate in arithmetic operations with other numeric values. The general rules governing the type of the result of arithmetic operations of numeric values are the same as those in the Java programming language:

- If one of the operands is a Double value, the result is a Double value.

- If one of the operands is a Float value, the result is a Float value.

- If one of the operands is a Long value, the result is a Long value.

- Otherwise, the result is an Integer value.

The Backing Classes of the Byte, Short, and Long Types

The Byte, Short, and Long types are backed by the Java classes java.lang.Byte, java.lang.Short, and java.lang.Long, respectively. This means that you can call any Java methods, including static methods in their backing classes on Visage Byte, Short, or Long values.

Float and Number Types

In Visage, the Float type is synonymous with the Number type. They have the same behavior under all circumstances. The Number type represents 32-bit floating-point numeric values, with valid absolute values between approximately 1.4×10^{-45} and 3.40×10^{38}. Not every real number can be represented by a floating-point number. Therefore, floating-point arithmetic is only an approximation.

■ **Caution** If you are familiar with the Java programming language, notice that the Visage Number type is distinct from the java.lang.Number abstract class in Java. In Visage, it represents 32-bit floating-point values backed by java.lang.Float.

Number Literals and the Default Value

Visage supports two forms of *floating-point type literals*. In the *decimal notation*, you specify a floating-point type literal as an integral part followed by the decimal point (.) and then the fractional part. Either the integral part or the fractional part, but not both, may be omitted. In the *scientific notation*, you specify a floating-point type literal as a magnitude followed by the letter "E" or "e" and then an exponent. The magnitude may be an integral number or a decimal number. The exponent may be a positive or a negative integer. The default value for a Number variable is 0.0.

The following are some examples of floating-point type literals:

```
3.14
2.
.75
3e8
1.380E-23
```

A floating-point type literal whose value falls within the range of the Number type is a Number literal. It has an inferred type of Number. A floating-point type literal can also be a Double literal, as you will see shortly.

Arithmetic Operations

All the arithmetic operators you learned in the section "Integer Type" apply to the Number type. Moreover, you can use the binary arithmetic operators on mixed Integer and Number values producing Number values. In such calculations, the Integer value is first promoted to a Number value before the arithmetic operation is performed.

Arithmetic operations on Number values may overflow the legal limits of the Number type and become positive infinity or negative infinity. Certain operations may produce results so small that they underflow the legal limits of the Number type and become zero (0.0). Certain invalid expressions, such as dividing infinity by infinity, produces a NaN (not a number) value.

The Backing Class of the Number Type

The Number type is backed by the Java class java.lang.Float. This means that you can call any Java methods, including static methods, in java.lang.Float on a Visage Number value.

You can use the isInfinite() and isNaN() methods of java.lang.Float to test whether a Number value is infinity or a NaN value.

Listing A-5 shows Visage Number variables at work.

Listing A-5. *Number Variables at Work*

```
var x = 3.14159;
var y = 2.71828;

println("x = {x}");
println("y = {y}");

println("x + y = {x + y}");
println("x - y = {x - y}");
println("x * y = {x * y}");
println("x / y = {x / y}");
println("x mod y = {x mod y}");

var max = Float.MAX_VALUE;
var min = Float.MIN_VALUE;
```

```
println("max = {max}");
println("min = {min}");

println("max * 2 will overflow to {max * 2}");
println("min / 2 will underflow to {min / 2}");

var inf = max * max;

println("inf = {inf}");
println("inf.isInfinite() = {inf.isInfinite()}");
println("inf / inf = {inf / inf}");

var nan = inf / inf;

println("nan = {nan}");
println("nan.isNaN() = {nan.isNaN()}");
```

Double Types

The Double type represents 64-bit floating-point numeric values, with valid absolute values between approximately 4.9×10^{324} and 1.79×10^{308}.

Double Literals and the Default Value

A floating-point type literal whose value falls outside the range of the Float type but within the range of the Double type is a Double literal. It has an inferred type of Double. You can assign any Number (Float) or Double literals to Double variables.

The Backing Class of the Double Type

The Double type is backed by the Java class java.lang.Double. This means that you can call any Java methods, including static methods, in java.lang.Double on a Visage Double value.

String Type

The String type represents a sequence of Unicode characters. You have seen Visage String values in use in previous examples.

String Literals and the Default Value

Visage supports String literals enclosed in double-quote (") or single-quote (') characters. The two notations are interchangeable with two exceptions:

- The double-quote character itself can appear without being escaped in a single-quoted string but must be escaped by a backslash (\) prefix in a double-quoted string.

- The single-quote character itself can appear without being escaped in a double-quoted string but must be escaped by a backslash prefix in a single-quoted string.

`String` literals may not span multiple lines. However, the Visage compiler will automatically merge adjacent `String` literals and `String` expressions into one at compile time, which allows you to split a string across multiple lines.

Open and close brace characters ({, }) that are not escaped have special meaning in `String` literals. They are used to form `String` expressions, which we will cover in the upcoming section.

The backslash character is an escape character. Visage understands the following escape sequences in its `String` literals:

- \udddd: A Unicode character, with each d a hexadecimal digit

- \ddd: An octal character, with each d an octal digit

- \b: Backspace (\u0008)

- \f: Form feed (\u000C)

- \n: Newline (\u000A)

- \r: Return (\u000D)

- \t: Tab (\u0009)

- \': Single quote

- \": Double quote

- \{: Open brace

- \}: Close brace

The default value of a `String` variable is "" (an empty string). Here are some examples of `String` literals:

```
"Hello, World."
"It's raining."
'The string "abc" has three characters'
```

String Expressions

You can include a string representation of any Visage expression in a Visage string by forming *string expressions*. A string expression is formed by adding brace-delimited segments into a string literal, with each brace-delimited segment containing a Visage expression.

You have seen string expressions at work in Listings A-3, A-4, and A-5.

The Backing Class of the String Type

The `String` type is backed by the Java class `java.lang.String`. This means that you can call any Java methods, including static methods, in `java.lang.String` on a Visage `String` value.

The java.lang.String class is a fairly extensive class, and you can take advantage of many of its methods in your Visage code. Here's a sampling of the methods that are of interest to Visage programmers:

- length()
- startsWith(prefix)
- startsWith(prefix, offset)
- endsWith(suffix)
- indexOf(str)
- indexOf(str, fromIndex)
- lastlndexOf(str)
- lastlndexOf(str, fromlndex)
- substring(beginlndex)
- substring(beginlndex, endlndex)
- matches(regex)
- contains(s)
- replaceFirst(regex, replacement)
- replaceAll(regex, replacement)
- replace(target, replacement)
- toLowerCase()
- toUpperCase()
- trim()

These methods do what their names suggest. Each character in a string has an index, which is zero based. Thus the first character has index 0, the second character has index 1, and so forth. Visage strings are immutable. None of the methods modify the string on which they are called. Some of the methods, such as trim(), return a new string. Therefore, if the variable str has the value " Hello ", calling str.trim() will not change what's stored in the str variable. To capture the trimmed string, you must assign the return value of the call to a variable.

In Listing A-6, you can see Visage String variables at work.

Listing A-6. *String Variables at Work*

```
var greeting = "Hello, World.";

println("greeting = {greeting}");
println("greeting.length() = {greeting.length()}");
println("greeting.startsWith(\"H\") = {greeting.startsWith("H")}");
println("greeting.endsWith(\".\") = {greeting.endsWith(".")}");
```

```
println("greeting.indexof(\",\") = {greeting.indexOf(",")}");
println("greeting.substring(3, 5) = {greeting.substring(3, 5)}");
println("greeting.toUpperCase() = {greeting.toUpperCase()}");
println("greeting.toLowerCase() = {greeting.toLowerCase()}");

var multiLine = "To construct a multi-line string in Visage,\n"
           "you can use its string literal and string expression\n"
           "concatenation capabilities.";
println(multiLine);

var str = "abcabc";
println("str = {str}");
println("str.indexOf('b') = {str.indexOf('b')}");
println("str.lastIndexOf('b') = {str.lastIndexOf('b')}");
println("str.contains('cab') = {str.contains('cab')}");
println("str.replaceFirst('a', 'x') = {str.replaceFirst('a', 'x')}");
println("str.replaceAll('a', 'x') = {str.replaceAll('a', 'x')}");
```

One thing from Listing A-6 that bears mentioning is that in the embedded expression region of a string expression, you do not need to escape the single-quote or double-quote characters even if they are the same ones used in the surrounding string expression.

Duration Type

The Duration type represents an amount of time. Duration values are used in Visage's keyframe animation facilities.

Duration Literals and the Default Value

Duration literals are formed by appending a time unit to an integer or decimal literal. Visage understands four time units: hour (h), minute (m), second (s), and millisecond (ms). The default value of a Duration variable is 0.0ms.

The following are some examples of Duration literals:

```
0.1h
2m
30s
1000ms
```

Arithmetic Operations Involving Durations

By their nature, Duration values can enter into arithmetic operations. Visage supports adding two Duration values, subtracting one Duration value from another, multiplying a Duration value by a numeric value, and dividing a Duration value by a numeric value. The results of these operations are Duration values. Visage also supports dividing one Duration value by another Duration value, resulting in a Number value. The negation operator also applies to Duration values.

The Backing Class of the Duration Type

Unlike the other four primitive types, which are backed by Java classes, the Duration type is backed by a Visage class, visage.lang.Duration. Here are the instance functions of the visage.lang.Duration class that should be of interest to you:

- toMillis()

- toSeconds()

- toMinutes()

- toHours()

- valueOf(ms)

Internally, Visage keeps track of Duration values in terms of numbers of milliseconds since midnight Greenwich mean time (GMT) January 1, 1970. The first four functions convert a Duration value to the specified unit and return a Number value.

The valueOf(ms) function is a factory function and should be called on the Duration class instead of on any Duration values. It returns a newly constructed Duration value that represents the supplied number of milliseconds.

▓ **Note** We will show you the usage of Visage classes in much more detail in the "Object Literals" section and how to write Visage classes in the "Working with Classes" section.

Listing A-7 shows the Visage Duration variables at work.

Listing A-7. Duration Variables at Work

```
var oneHour = 1h;
var oneMinute = 1m;
var oneSecond = 1s;
var oneMillisecond = 1ms;

println("oneHour = {oneHour}");
println("oneMinute = {oneMinute}");
println("oneSecond = {oneSecond}");
println("oneMillisecond = {oneMillisecond}");

println("oneHour + 30 * oneMinute = {oneHour + 30 * oneMinute}");
println("oneMinute - 20 * oneSecond = {oneMinute - 20 * oneSecond}");
println("oneSecond / 2 = {oneSecond / 2}");
println("-oneMillisecond = {-oneMillisecond}");
```

```
println("oneHour.toHours() = {oneHour.toHours()}");
println("oneHour.toMinutes() = {oneHour.toMinutes()}");
println("oneMinute.toSeconds() = {oneMinute.toSeconds()}");
println("oneSecond.toMillis() = {oneSecond.toMillis()}");

var now = Duration.valueOf(1229923309734.0);
println("now = {now}");
```

Length Type

Lengths represent a scalar unit of measurement. They are used in Visage to specify lengths and distances and are commonly used in specifying layouts and widths.

Length Literals and the Default Value

Length literals are formed by appending a length unit to an integer or decimal literal. Visage understands ten types of length units: inches (in), centimeters (cm), millimeters (mm), pixels (px), points (pt), picas (pc), ems (em), density-independent pixels (dps), scale-independent pixels (sps), and percentage (%). The default value of a Length variable is 0px.

The following are some examples of Length literals:

```
12px
5mm
2cm
1.5em
10dp
20%
```

Core Types of Length Literals

Visage supports five core types of length literals. Each of the core types has different properties and suggested uses based on the type of API you are using and the target device. Using the right type of length will make your application look good on different devices regardless of the screen size and resolution.

- *Exact screen pixels*: This is an exact measurement in device pixels (px) of the screen and should be used wherever you need pixel-perfect alignment. Be careful using pixels directly, because doing so will reduce the portability of your application across devices.

- *Density-independent lengths*: These are lengths that scale based on the target device. The reference measurement is called a density-independent pixel (dp) and has a one-to-one ratio with pixels on a 96dpi (dots-per-inch) device held at arm's length. Other units of this type include centimeters (cm), millimeters (mm), inches (in), points (pt), and picas (pc), all of which are converted for a 96dpi screen. This type of unit is ideal to use when you want your application to be easily portable.

- *Scale-independent lengths:* These are adjusted pixel measures based on the density of the screen and scale factor of the application. This type is most often used to update the font sizes based on user scaling but can also be used for layout and to scale graphics. The only unit of this type, the scale-independent pixel, is suffixed with sp.

- *Typographic length:* This length unit is based on the size of fonts and ligatures. Historically this is the height of the "M" ligature in the given font, but in practice will be the same as the reference font height. Em literals are suffixed with "em".

- *Percentage:* This relative length unit is expressed as a percentage, suffixed with %. This is context-sensitive based on the use of the length, but it usually refers to a fraction of the parent length.

Length Arithmetic and Conversions

By their nature, Length values can enter into arithmetic operations. Visage supports adding two Length values, subtracting one Length value from another, multiplying a Length value by a numeric value, and dividing a Length value by a numeric value. The results of these operations are Length values. Visage also supports dividing one Length value by another Length value, resulting in a Number value. The negation operator also applies to Length values.

Arithmetic involving lengths of the same core type will result in a length value of the same type. Arithmetic involving lengths of different types will result in a compound type that contains the constituent length components in their unconverted forms. This value can then be converted back into a simple length by calling one of the conversions functions on the backing Length class.

The Backing Class of the Length Type

The Length type is backed by the Visage class visage.lang.Length. Here are the instance functions of the visage.lang.Length class that should be of interest to you:

- toInches()

- toCentimeters()

- toMillimeters()

- toPoints()

- toPicas()

- toEms()

- toPixels()

- toDensityIndependentPixels()

- toScaleIndependentPixels()

- toPercentage()

- valueOf(length, unit)

Internally, Visage keeps track of Length values as a compound structure containing the five length types discussed earlier. The core types are pixels, density-independent pixels, scale-independent pixels, ems, and percentage, each expressed as Double values.

Each of the first ten conversion functions will return a Double containing the magnitude of the length in the requested units. If the length has a different core type than the requested unit, you will get an UncovertableLengthException unless you pass in the optional conversion parameters. There is also an alternate variant of these ten functions that ends in Length and returns a wrapped Length type instead of a Double.

The valueOf(length, unit) function is a factory function and should be called on the Length class instead of on any Length values. It returns a newly constructed Length value that represents the supplied length in the given units. The units correspond to the ten supported length types and are enumerated in the LengthUnit class.

Listing A-8 shows the Visage Length variables at work.

Listing A-8. *Length Variables at Work*

```
var onePixel = 1px;
var onePoint = 1pt;
var onePica = 1pc;
var oneDensityIndependentPixel = 1dp;
var oneMillimeter = 1mm;
var oneCentimeter = 1cm;
var oneInch = 1in;
var oneScaleIndependentPixel = 1sp;
var oneEm = 1em;
var onePercent = 1%;

println("onePixel = {%#s onePixel}");
println("onePoint = {%#s onePoint}");
println("onePica = {%#s onePica}");
println("oneDensityIndependentPixel = {oneDensityIndependentPixel}");
println("oneMillimeter = {%#s oneMillimeter}");
println("oneCentimeter = {%#s oneCentimeter}");
println("oneInch = {%#s oneInch}");
println("oneScaleIndependentPixel = {oneScaleIndependentPixel}");
println("oneEm = {oneEm}");
println("onePercent = {onePercent}");

println("3mm + 2mm = {%#s 3mm + 2mm}");
println("5mm - 2mm = {%#s 5mm - 2mm}");
println("3mm * 2 = {%#s 3mm * 2}");
println("2 * 3mm = {%#s 2 * 3mm}");
println("2cm * 2.5 = {%#s 2cm * 2.5}");
println("2.5 * 2cm = {%#s 2.5 * 2cm}");
println("3mm / 2 = {%#s 3mm / 2}");
println("2.5cm / 2.5 = {%#s 2.5cm / 2.5}");
println("2.5mm / 5.0mm = {2.5mm/5.0mm}");

println("oneInch.toCentimeters() = {oneInch.toCentimeters()}");
println("oneInch.toMillimeters() = {oneInch.toMillimeters()}");
println("oneInch.toDensityIndependentPixels() = {oneInch.toDensityIndependentPixels()}");
```

```
println("onePica.toPoints() = {onePica.toPoints()}");
println("onePoint.toDensityIndependentPixels() = {onePoint.toDensityIndependentPixels()}");

var tenInches = Length.valueOf(10, visage.lang.LengthUnit.INCH);
println("tenInches = {%#s tenInches}");
```

In Listing A-8, we made use of one of the special features of length literal formatting. By specifying the alternative formatting using %#s, the output will automatically be converted to the closest matching unit. This provides a much more readable program result than having all the output in density independent pixels.

Angle Type

Angles represent a rotational unit of measurement. They are commonly used in Visage to specify rotation of objects, such as in transformations.

Angle Literals and the Default Value

Angle literals are formed by appending an angle unit to an integer or decimal literal. Visage understands 3 angle units: degrees (deg), radians (rad), and turns (turn). The default value of an Angle variable is 0rad.

The following are some examples of Angle literals:

```
45deg
1rad
.3turn
```

Angle Arithmetic and Conversions

By their nature, Angle values can enter into arithmetic operations. Visage supports adding two Angle values, subtracting one Angle value from another, multiplying an Angle value by a numeric value, and dividing an Angle value by a numeric value. The results of these operations are Angle values. Visage also supports dividing one Angle value by another Angle value, resulting in a Number value. The negation operator also applies to Angle values.

When you perform arithmetic on two angles of the same type, it will be done in the original units reducing rounding errors. However, if the types differ they will first be converted to radians as the common unit and then the arithmetic will be performed.

The Backing Class of the Angle Type

The Angle type is backed by the Visage class visage.lang.Angle. Here are instance functions of the visage.lang.Angle class that should be of interest to you:

- toDegrees()

- toRadians()

- toTurns()

- valueOf(angle, unit)

Internally, Visage keeps track of Angle values as a double and unit pair. This reduces loss of precision when storing angles in any of the three types.

Each of the first three conversion functions will return a Double containing the magnitude of the angle in the requested units. An alternate variant of these functions ends in Angle and returns a wrapped Angle type instead of a Double.

The valueOf(angle, unit) function is a factory function and should be called on the Angle class instead of on any Angle values. It returns a newly constructed Angle value that represents the supplied angle in the given units. The units correspond to the three supported angle types and are enumerated in the AngleUnit class.

Listing A-9 shows the Visage Angle variables at work.

Listing A-9. *Angle Variables at Work*

```
var oneDegree = 1deg;
var oneRadian = 1rad;
var oneTurn = 1turn;

println("oneDegree = {oneDegree}");
println("oneRadian = {oneRadian}");
println("oneTurn = {oneTurn}");

println("3deg + 2deg = {3deg + 2deg}");
println("5deg - 2deg = {5deg - 2deg}");
println("3deg * 2 = {3deg * 2}");
println("2 * 3deg = {2 * 3deg}");
println("2rad * 2.5 = {2rad * 2.5}");
println("2.5 * 2rad = {2.5 * 2rad}");
println("3deg / 2 = {3deg / 2}");
println("2.5rad / 2.5 = {2.5rad / 2.5}");
println("2.5deg / 5.0deg = {2.5deg / 5.0deg}");

println("oneRadian.toDegrees() = {oneRadian.toDegrees()}");
println("oneTurn.toDegrees() = {oneTurn.toDegrees()}");
println("oneDegree.toTurns() = {oneDegree.toTurns()}");

var ninetyDegrees = Angle.valueOf(10, visage.lang.AngleUnit.DEGREE);
println("ninetyDegrees = {ninetyDegrees}");
```

Color Type

The Color type lets you specify different visual pigments in your application using a shorthand literal syntax. It is commonly used for fill and line color of shapes or gradients and color themes used in user interface components.

Color Literals and the Default Value

Color literals are formed by appending a list of hexadecimal red, green, and blue values to a hash symbol (#). You can also specify the alpha or opacity of the color as an optional fourth hexadecimal value separated by a pipe (I). The default value of a Color variable is #000000|FF, which is black with full opacity.

There are a few different syntax options you can use when specifying colors. If you do not need a high degree of precision, you can use single hexadecimal values (4-bit) instead of double hexadecimal values (8-bit). If you use 4-bit color values, you must use them for all the component values, and these will be automatically repeated to fill an 8-bit value.

Also, the alpha component is optional, and if omitted, will be assumed to be fully opaque with a value of FF. Finally, the case of the hexadecimal symbols is irrelevant.

The following are some examples of Color literals:

```
#BF40BF
#b5d
#000|C
#ba55d3|5d
```

Color Arithmetic

Using the regular infix arithmetic operators, you can perform simple blending and adjustment of colors. Visage supports adding two Color values, subtracting one Color value from another, multiplying a Color value by a numeric value, and dividing a Color value by a numeric value. The results of these operations are Color values. Visage also supports dividing one Color value by another Color value, resulting in a Number value. The negation operator also applies to Color values.

The arithmetic operations will behave the same as if you individually applied the same operation to each of the red, green, and blue component values individually. Since these values are stored as floats internally, you can freely overflow or underflow the color range while performing arithmetic. However, most uses will clip the value to the visible color range.

The Backing Class of the Color Type

The Color type is backed by the Visage class visage.lang.Color. Here are the instance functions of the visage.lang.Color class that should be of interest to you:

- clip()

- valueOf(hex:Integer, hasAlpha:Boolean)

- color(red:Float, green:Float, blue:Float, opacity:Float)

- hsb(hue:Float, saturation:Float, brightness:Float, opacity:Float)

- hsl(hue:Float, saturation:Float, lightness:Float, opacity:Float)

- rgb(red:Integer, blue:Integer, green:Integer, opacity:Float)

Internally, Visage keeps track of Color values as individual red, green, blue, and opacity values of type Float. This allows arithmetic to temporarily overflow or underflow the visible range. However, the clip() function can be used to return a Color with its values in the range from 0 to 1.

The remaining functions are factories that should be called on the Color class instead of on any Color values. They provide different methods of specifying colors in alternate encodings and color models. The valueOf(hex, hasAlpha) function accepts its argument in the form of an integer hexadecimal value that can optionally have the alpha component stored in the lower 8 bits. The color(red, green, blue, opacity) function is the closest to the internal representation, and should be used where precise color values need to be specified. The hsb and hsl functions allow you to specify colors using these two alternative color models. Finally, the rgb function is similar to the valueOf but takes its inputs in separate integer components. For all of the functions, the opacity argument is optional and will be assumed to be fully opaque if not specified.

In addition to these functions, the Visage Color class also contains constants for all of the Web "X11 Colors" from the CSS3 specification, which can be a convenient way of finding web-safe colors to use in your application.

Listing A-10 shows the Visage Color variables at work.

Listing A-10. *Color Variables at Work*

```
var a = Color.MAGENTA;
var b = Color.YELLOW;

println("Magenta = {a}");
println("Yellow = {b}");

println("Magenta + Yellow = {a + b}");
println("Magenta - Yellow = {a - b}");
println("Magenta * 2 = {a * 2}");
println("2 * Magenta = {2 * a}");
println("Magenta * 2.5 = {a * 2.5}");
println("2.5 * Magenta = {2.5 * a}");
println("Magenta / 2 = {a / 2}");
println("Magenta / 2.5 = {a / 2.5}");
println("Magenta / Yellow = {a / b}");

var navy = Color.valueOf(0x000080, false);
println("navy = {navy}");
var silver = Color.rgb(0xC0, 0xC0, 0xC0);
println("silver = {silver}");
var red = Color.color(1, 0, 0);
println("red = {red}");
```

Working with Sequences

In the previous section, you learned about Visage primitive types. Primitive types represent indivisible pieces of data. However, sometimes you need to aggregate individual data together and manipulate that data as a unit. Visage provides two mechanisms for data aggregation. First, you can group dissimilar data into classes, create objects of classes, and manipulate the objects in your code. Second, you can group similar data into a construct called a sequence and manipulate the sequence and its values in your code.

You will learn how to create objects of existing classes in the "Object Literals" section and how to create classes in the "Working with Classes" section, both later in this appendix.

In this section, we will teach you the Visage sequence concept, how to create sequences, and how to manipulate sequences.

Sequence Types

A Visage *sequence* represents an ordered list of data of the same type. Each individual piece of data in a sequence is an *element* of the sequence. The type of elements of a sequence is called the sequence's *element type.* The type of a sequence is written as its element type followed by a pair of square brackets ([]).

Here are some examples of sequences of primitive types:

```
var booleans: Boolean[] = [true, false, true, true, false];
var integers: Integer[] = [1, 3, 5, 7, 9];
var numbers: Number[] = [3.14159, 2.71828];
var strings: String[] = ["hello", "hello again", "goodbye"];
var durations: Duration[] = [0.5m, 1.0m, 1.5m, 2.0m];
```

In these examples, the variables are of sequence types. With the help of Visage's type inference facility, you can omit the data types:

```
var booleans = [true, false, true, true, false];
var integers = [1, 3, 5, 7, 9];
var numbers = [3.14159, 2.71828];
var strings = ["hello", "hello again", "goodbye"];
var durations = [0.5m, 1.0m, 1.5m, 2.0m];
```

The element type of a sequence can be one of the primitive types, a class type, or a function type. We will cover class types and function types in detail later in this appendix. In this section, we will use one small example of the class type to illustrate the interaction between sequence types and class types. For the rest of this section, we will use the following class:

```
class Point {
  var x: Number;
  var y: Number;
}
```

This defines a class type Point. You can declare a variable of type Point (called an object) and initialize it with an object literal as follows:

```
var p: Point = Point { x: 3.0, y: 4.0 }
```

Once again, you can omit the type specifier for the variable and let Visage's type inference facility deduce the type:

```
var p = Point { x: 5.0, y: 12.0 }
```

You can also declare a variable of a class type without giving it an initializer:

```
var p: Point;
```

In this case, the variable will get the default value for class types: null.

You are now ready to declare a variable of type Point[], a sequence of Point objects:

```
var points: Point[] = [Point {x: 3.0, y: 4.0}, Point {x: 5.0, y: 12.0}];
```

With the help of type inference, you can omit the type specifier:

```
var points = [Point {x: 3.0, y: 4.0}, Point {x: 5.0, y: 12.0}];
```

As is the case with primitive types, if a variable is declared to be of a sequence type but without an explicit initializer, it gets the default value of the sequence type. The default value of a sequence type is a sequence with zero elements in it. This sequence is called the *empty sequence.*

Constructing Sequences Using Explicit Sequence Expressions

In the previous section, all variables of sequence types are initialized with explicit sequence expressions. An *explicit sequence expression* is constructed by enclosing its elements within a pair of brackets. The elements in an explicit sequence expression are separated by commas. The comma may be omitted after an element that is an object literal or other expression that ends with a closing brace. Thus, the declaration

```
var points = [Point {x: 3.0, y: 4.0}, Point {x: 5.0, y: 12.0}];
```

can be written as

```
var points = [
  Point {x: 3.0, y: 4.0}
  Point {x: 5.0, y: 12.0}
];
```

You cannot create a sequence with "holes" in it. In other words, every element in a sequence must be a non-null value of the element type. Since primitive values are always non-null, this rule applies only to sequences of nonprimitive types.

The empty sequence can be constructed with the [ ] expression.

Constructing Numeric Sequences Using Range Expressions

When creating numeric sequences—that is, sequences of Integer or Number values—you can use range expressions in addition to explicit sequence expressions. A Visage *range expression* allows you to create an arithmetic progression from a start value, an end value, and an optional step value. The step value defaults to 1 or 1.0, depending on whether the element type is Integer or Number. Here are a few examples:

```
var oneToTen = [1..10];
var oneToTenOdd = [1..10 step 2];
var ticks = [3.0 .. 5.0 step 0.5];
var decreasing = [10..1 step -1];
```

▓ **Tip** Visage represents range expressions internally in an efficient manner. When you use a range expression like [0..1000000], Visage will not actually build a sequence with a million elements and therefore will not take up megabytes of memory.

In the previous range expressions, the start value and the end value are separated with two dots (..), and the step value, if present, is separated from the end value with step. This notation produces sequences that may include the end value itself. To obtain a sequence that does not include the end value, two dots and a less-than sign (..<) may be places between the start value and the end value. Here is an example of this form of range expression:

```
var oneToNine = [1 ..< 10];
```

▓ **Caution** If the step value is negative while the end value is greater than the start value, or if the step value is positive while the end value is less than the start value, the range expression produces an empty sequence. This may happen when you try to construct a decreasing sequence, one in which the end value is less than the start value, but you fail to specify a negative step value. For example, the range expression [10..1] will produce an empty sequence. The Visage compiler will generate a warning for such expressions.

In Listing A-11, you can see explicit sequence expressions and range expressions at work.

Listing A-11. *Constructing Sequences with Explicit Sequence Expressions and Range Expressions*

```
var booleans = [true, false, true, true, false];
var integers = [1, 3, 5, 7, 9];
var numbers = [3.14159, 2.71828];
var strings = ["hello", "hello again", "goodbye"];
var durations = [0.5m, 1.0m, 1.5m, 2.0m];

print("booleans = "); println(booleans);
print("integers = "); println(integers);
print("numbers = "); println(numbers);
print("strings = "); println(strings);
print("durations = "); println(durations);

class Point {
  var x: Number;
  var y: Number;
  override function toString() {
    "Point \{ x: {x}, y: {y} \}"
  }
}

var points = [Point {x: 3.0, y: 4.0}, Point {x: 5.0, y: 12.0}];

print("points = "); println(points);

integers = [1, 3, 5, 7, 9];
print("integers = "); println(integers);
```

```
var oneToTen = [1..10];
var oneToTenOdd = [1..10 step 2];
var ticks = [3.0 .. 5.0 step 0.5];
var decreasing = [10..1 step -1];
var oneToNine = [1 ..< 10];

print("oneToTen = "); println(oneToTen);
print("oneToTenOdd = "); println(oneToTenOdd);
print("ticks = "); println(ticks);
print("decreasing = "); println(decreasing);
print("oneToNine = "); println(oneToNine);

print("[10..1] = "); println([10..1]);
```

In Listing A-11, we used another Visage built-in function, print(). The print() function differs from println() in that it does not append a new line at the end of its output.

▒ **Note** In Visage, converting a sequence to a string via "{seq}" will produce a string without the surrounding brackets and separators between elements. For example, println("{[1, 2, 3]}") prints 123, while println([1, 2, 3]) prints [1, 2, 3].

Manipulating Sequences

Visage provides a rich set of built-in facilities for you to easily manipulate sequences:

- You can access the size of a sequence, a single element of a sequence, a slice or a segment of consecutive elements of a sequence, or a subset of nonconsecutive elements that satisfy certain criteria.

- You can reverse a sequence.

- You can insert an element into a sequence.

- You can insert another sequence into a sequence.

- You can delete an element from a sequence.

- You can delete a slice from a sequence.

Each element in a sequence has an index and sequence indexes are zero-based. The first element has index 0, the second element has index 1, and so on.

Accessing the Size of a Sequence

You can use the size of operator to access the size of a sequence. The size of a sequence is the number of elements in the sequence. The size of an empty sequence is zero. In the following example

```
var integers = [1, 3, 5, 7, 9];
var s = sizeof integers;
```

the value of s would be 5.

▨ **Note** Although the size of operator is primarily used with sequences, you can use it with nonsequence variables and values. A primitive value always has size 1. A variable of class type has size 1 if it holds an object of the class, and it has size 0 if it is null.

Accessing an Element in a Sequence

To access a single element of a sequence, you use the *sequence indexing* expression. It consists of the sequence name or another expression that evaluates to a sequence followed by a pair of brackets that encloses the index of the element. Here are some examples:

```
var integers = [1, 3, 5, 7, 9];
var a = integers[0];
var b = integers[4];
var c = integers[-1];
var d = integers[5];
```

If the index is within the range between zero and one less than the size of the sequence, the appropriate element will be produced. If the index is outside of that range, the default value of the element type of the sequence will be produced. Thus in this example, a would be 1, b would be 9, and both c and d would be 0, the default value for the Integer type.

▨ **Note** Although indexing a variable of sequence type is the most common use of sequence indexing expressions, the Visage syntax allows you to index any expression that evaluates to a sequence. For example, [1, 3, 5, 7, 9][2] is a valid sequence indexing expression. Its value is 5. This is also the case for the sequence slice expression and the sequence select expression that you will learn in the next two sections.

Accessing a Slice of a Sequence

To access a consecutive subset of elements of a sequence, you use the *sequence slice* expression. It consists of the sequence name or another expression that evaluates to a sequence, followed by a pair of brackets that encloses a starting index and an optional ending index separated by two dots (..) or two dots and a less-than sign (..<). If the ending index is not specified, it is understood to be the index of the last element of the sequence, namely, the size of the sequence minus one. This expression produces a *slice* of the original sequence. Here are some examples:

```
var integers = [1, 3, 5, 7, 9];
var seq1 = integers[0..2];
var seq2 = integers[0..<2];
var seq3 = integers[2..];
var seq4 = integers[-3..10];
var seq5 = integers[2..<2];
var seq6 = integers[2..0];
var seq7 = integers[-2..-1];
var seq8 = integers[5..6];
```

If the two-dot notation is used, all elements of the original sequence whose index is greater than or equal to the starting index and less than or equal to the ending index are elements of the slice. If two dots and a less-than sign are used, all elements of the original sequence whose index is greater than or equal to the starting index and less than the ending index are elements of the slice. The elements in the slice appear in the same order as they appear in the original sequence.

If no element of the original sequence satisfies the slice's condition, the slice is an empty sequence. This is the case, for example, if the slice's ending index is less than the slice's starting index, if the slice's starting index is greater than or equal to the size of the sequence, or if the slice's ending index is less than zero. Notice that it is okay for the starting index to be less than zero or for the ending index to be greater than or equal to the size of the sequence.

Thus in the previous example, seq1 is [1, 3, 5], seq2 is [1, 3], seq3 is [5, 7, 9], and seq4 is [1, 3, 5, 7, 9]. And seq5, seq6, seq7, and seq8 are equal to the empty sequence [ ]. The conditions in seq5 and seq6 are not satisfied by any indexes. The condition in seq7 is satisfied only by -2 and -1, but integers does not contain elements with indexes -2 or -1. Similarly, the condition in seq8 is satisfied by 5 and 6, but integers does not contain elements with indexes 5 or 6.

Accessing a Subset of a Sequence Through a Predicate

To access a not-necessarily-consecutive subset of elements of a sequence, you use the *sequence select* expression. It consists of

- The sequence name or another expression that evaluates to a sequence

- A pair of brackets that encloses a predicate in the form of a *selection variable*

- A pipe (|)

- A Boolean expression involving the selection variable

Here are some examples:

```
var integers = [1, 3, 5, 7, 9];
var seq1 = integers[x | x > 4];
var seq2 = integers[x | indexof x <2];
var seq3 = integers[x | x > 10];
```

The resulting sequence will contain all elements of the original sequence whose values satisfy the predicate. A value satisfies a predicate if the Boolean expression in the predicate is true when the value is substituted for the selection variable. The indexof operator can be used inside the predicate to obtain the index of the selection variable x in the original sequence. If no elements of the original sequence satisfy the predicate, the resulting sequence is the empty sequence. The elements in the resulting sequence appear in the same order as they appear in the original sequence.

Thus, in the previous example seq1 is [5, 7, 9], seq2 is [1, 3], and seq3 is the empty sequence.

Reversing a Sequence

Visage provides a reverse operator to reverse a sequence. The reverse operator does not modify the original sequence but produces a new sequence that contains the same elements as the original sequence in the reverse order. Here is an example:

```
var integers = [1, 3, 5, 7, 9];
var seq1 = reverse integers;
```

In this example, seq1 is [9, 7, 5, 3, 1].

Inserting an Element into a Sequence

So far, you've learned four methods of accessing the elements of a sequence. One thing that these methods have in common is that they do not change the original sequence in any way. Coming up, we will show you methods for altering an existing sequence.

To add one element to a sequence, you use the insert expression. Only a value of a compatible type may be inserted into a sequence. The only time you are allowed to insert a value of one primitive type into a sequence of a different type is when you are inserting a numeric value into a sequence of a different numeric type. You may lose precision when the sequence's element type is narrower than the type of the value being inserted. For example, inserting a Number value into an Integer sequence will cause the Number value's fractional part to be dropped. For class types, you are allowed to insert an object of class type into a sequence of its superclass type. You will learn about superclasses in the section entitled "Extending Classes" later in this appendix.

There are three forms of insert expressions: the insert-into form, the insert-before form, and the insert-after form. Here are some examples:

```
var numbers = [3.14159, 2.71828];
insert 0.57722 into numbers;
insert 1.618 before numbers[0];
insert 1.4142 after numbers[2];
```

The insert-into form takes two pieces of information as its input: the value to be inserted and the sequence variable to insert the value into. It then appends the value to the end of the sequence. Thus, after the first insert expression in the previous example, numbers will be [3.14159, 2.71828, 0.57722].

The insert-before form takes three pieces of information as its input: the value to be inserted, the sequence variable to insert the value into, and an index. It then inserts the value into the sequence at a position just before the index. Thus, after the second insert expression, numbers will be [1.618, 3.14159, 2.71828, 0.57722].

The insert-after form takes the same three pieces of information as the insert-before form as its input and inserts the value into the sequence at a position just after the index. Thus, after the third insert expression, numbers will be [1.618, 3.14159, 2.71828, 1.4142, 0.57722].

Attempting to insert an element after an invalid index will keep the sequence unchanged. Attempting to insert an element before an invalid index will also keep the sequence unchanged, except when the index is equal to the size of the sequence (in that case, the element is appended to the sequence).

■ **Caution** The way you provide the requisite information to the three insert forms is somewhat unconventional. It is designed to make the whole expression easy to remember. Although the last part of the insert-before and insert-after forms looks identical to an element access expression, it is not one.

Inserting Another Sequence into a Sequence

In addition to inserting a single element into a sequence, Visage supports inserting another sequence into a sequence. To do so, you can use the same three forms of insert expressions you just learned As with a single element insertion, the element type of the other sequence must be compatible with the target sequence.

Notice that after the insertion, the original sequence is still a flat sequence, only with more elements. Visage does not support nested sequences.

Attempting to insert an empty sequence will keep the original sequence unchanged. Attempting to insert null into a sequence will also keep the original sequence unchanged.

Here is an example:

```
var strings = ["hello", "hello again", "goodbye"];
insert ["how are you", "see you"] after strings[1];
```

After this insertion, the sequence strings will be ["hello", "hello again", "how are you", "see you", "goodbye"].

Deleting Elements from a Sequence

To delete elements from a sequence, you use the delete expression. There are four forms of delete expressions, as you can see here:

```
var strings = ["hello", "hello again", "how are you", "see you", "goodbye"];
delete "see you" from strings;
delete strings[2];
delete strings[0..1];
delete strings;
```

The delete from form takes two pieces of information as its input: the value to be deleted and the sequence variable to delete the value from. It then deletes all occurrences of the value from the sequence. The type of the value must be compatible with the element type of the sequence. If the value does not occur in the sequence, the sequence is unchanged. Thus, after the first delete expression in the previous example, strings will be ["hello", "hello again", "how are you", "goodbye"].

The other three forms are variants of the delete form. The first variant takes two pieces of information as its input: a sequence variable and an index. It then deletes the element at the index from the sequence. If the index is not valid, the sequence remains unchanged. Thus, after the second delete expression, strings will be ["hello", "hello again", "goodbye"].

The second variant takes three pieces of information as its input: a sequence variable, a starting index, and an optional ending index. It then deletes the slice from the sequence. The information is arranged in a form reminiscent of a sequence slice expression. Both the .. and the ..< forms are supported. If the ending index is not specified, it is understood to be the index of the last element of the sequence. Thus, after the third delete expression in the previous example, the string will be ["goodbye"].

The third variant takes only one piece of information, a sequence variable, and deletes all elements from the sequence. Thus, after the fourth delete expression, the string will be the empty sequence, [ ].

■ **Caution** Although the last part of the first and the second variants of the delete form looks identical to a sequence indexing expression or a sequence slice expression, it is not one.

Sequence Manipulation Example

Listing A-12 shows sequence manipulation constructs at work.

Listing A-12. Manipulating Sequences

```
var integers = [1, 3, 5, 7, 9];

print("integers = "); println(integers);
print("sizeof integers = "); println(sizeof integers);
print("integers[0] = "); println(integers[0]);
print("integers[4] = "); println(integers[4]);
print("integers[-1] = "); println(integers[-1]);
print("integers[5] = "); println(integers[5]);

print("integers[0..2] = "); println(integers[0..2]);
print("integers[0..<2] = "); println(integers[0..<2]);
print("integers[2..] = "); println(integers[2..]);
print("integers[-3..10] = "); println(integers[-3..10]);

print("integers[2..<2] = "); println(integers[2..<2]);
print("integers[2..0] = "); println(integers[2..0]);
print("integers[-2..-1] = "); println(integers[-2..-1]);
print("integers[5..6] = "); println(integers[5..6]);

print("integers[x | x > 4] = "); println(integers[x | x > 4]);
print("integers[x | indexof x < 2] = "); println(integers[x | indexof x < 2]);
print("integers[x | x > 10] = "); println(integers[x | x > 10]);

print("reverse integers = "); println(reverse integers);

var numbers = [3.14159, 2.71828];
print("numbers = "); println(numbers);

insert 0.57722 into numbers;
print("numbers = "); println(numbers);

insert 1.618 before numbers[0];
print("numbers = "); println(numbers);
```

```
insert 1.4142 after numbers[2];
print("numbers = "); println(numbers);

var strings = ["hello", "hello again", "goodbye"];
print("strings = "); println(strings);

insert ["how are you", "see you"] after strings[1];
print("strings = "); println(strings);

delete "see you" from strings;
print("strings = "); println(strings);

delete strings[2];
print("strings = "); println(strings);

delete strings[0..1];
print("strings = "); println(strings);

delete strings;
print("strings = "); println(strings);
```

Comprehending Sequences

Sequences play an important role in Visage. They are a versatile container of application objects. The explicit sequence expression syntax, together with the object literal syntax, form the basis of the declarative GUI programming style that is a distinguishing characteristic of Visage applications.

Visage allows you to do more with sequences using the for *expression*, which produces new sequences based on one or more existing sequences. Following the functional programming language tradition, syntaxes for generating new sequences from existing ones are called *sequence comprehension*.

The for expression starts with the for keyword, which is followed by one or more comma-separated in clauses enclosed in a pair of parentheses (()). Each in clause may have an optional where clause. The in clauses are followed by the body of the for expression. The following is a simple example of a for expression:

```
for (x in [1..4]) x*x
```

Its in clause has the form x in [1..4] and its body is the expression x*x. It produces the sequence [1, 4, 9, 16].

An in clause starts with a variable name followed by the in keyword and a sequence expression. The variable named in the in clause is called the *iteration variable*. The optional where clause, if present, follows the in clause with the where keyword and a Boolean expression involving the iteration variable of the in clause. The following example shows a for expression with a where clause:

```
for (x in [1..4] where x > 2) x*x
```

Its in clause has the form x in [1..4] where x > 2. The where clause serves to filter out some of the elements from the sequence in the in clause. This for expression produces the sequence [9, 16].

When a for expression has multiple in clauses, the iteration variable names of the in clauses must be distinct. The elements of the resulting sequence are ordered as if an iteration variable in a later in clause varies faster than iteration variables in earlier in clauses. Therefore, in the following example:

```
var rows = ["A", "B"];
var columns = [1, 2];
var matrix = for (row in rows, column in columns) "{row}{column}";
```

the resulting sequence matrix will be ["A1", "A2", "B1", "B2"]. The sequences iterated by the different in clauses need not be different sequences, as shown here:

```
var digits = [1, 2, 3];
var seq = for (x in digits, y in digits) "{x}{y}";
```

The resulting sequence seq will be ["11", "12", "13", "21", "22", "23", "31", "32", "33"].

In a for expression with multiple in clauses, the where clause associated with a later in clause may refer to iteration variables of earlier in clauses. However, the where clause associated with an earlier in clause cannot refer to iteration variables of later in clauses. In other words, the *scope* of an iteration variable of an in clause is its own where clause, the where clause of later in clauses, and the body of the for expression. You will learn more about scopes of variables in Visage later in this appendix when we talk about Visage expressions. In the following example, the where clause of the second in clause refers to the iteration variable of both the first and the second in clauses:

```
var digits = [1, 2, 3];
var seq = for (x in digits where x > 1, y in digits where y >= x) {
  "{x}{y}"
}
```

The resulting sequence seq will be ["22","23","33"]. This example also illustrates the use of a block expression as the body of a for expression. You will learn more about block expressions in the "Visage Expressions" section later in this appendix.

In Listing A-13, you can see sequence comprehension at work.

Listing A-13. *Sequence Comprehension*

```
var seq = for (x in [1..4]) x*x;
print("seq = "); println(seq);

seq = for (x in [1..4] where x > 2) x*x;
print("seq = "); println(seq);

var rows = ["A", "B"];
var columns = [1, 2];
var matrix = for (row in rows, column in columns) "{row}{column}";
print("matrix = "); println(matrix);

var digits = [1, 2, 3];
var seq1 = for (x in digits, y in digits) "{x}{y}";
print("seq1 = "); println(seq1);

var seq2 = for (x in digits where x > 1, y in digits where y >= x) {
  "{x}{y}"
}
print("seq2 = "); println(seq2);
```

Using Utility Functions in visage.util.Sequences

The Visage runtime includes the class `visage.util.Sequences`, which provides some useful sequence manipulation functions. It includes the following functions:

- `binarySearch(seq, key)`
- `binarySearch(seq, key, comparator)`
- `indexByIdentity(seq, key)`
- `indexOf(seq, key)`
- `isEqualByContentIdentity(seql, seq2)`
- `max(seq)`
- `max(seq, comparator)`
- `min(seq)`
- `min(seq, comparator)`
- `nextIndexByIdentity(seq, key, pos)`
- `nextIndexOf(seq, key, pos)`
- `reverse(seq)`
- `shuffle(seq)`
- `sort(seq)`
- `sort(seq, comparator)`

All of the functions take at least one argument of the sequence type. A sequence that is passed in as a parameter is not modified by the functions. A new sequence is returned instead if necessary.

Some functions have a variant that takes an additional comparator argument. The variant that takes a comparator is necessary only if the element type of the sequence does not have its own natural ordering or if you want to override the natural ordering. All Visage primitive types have a natural ordering. A *comparator* is an object of a Visage or Java class that implements the `java.util.Comparator` Java interface. We will explain how to define Visage classes and how to use Visage's Java interoperability later in this appendix.

A few of the methods deal with identities of elements in sequences. You will learn about identities of Visage objects in the "Relational Operators" section later in this appendix. For now, it suffices to say that every Visage object has an identity and a value, and object comparisons in Visage are usually carried out by comparing object values. However, under some special circumstances it is necessary to compare object identities. Values of primitive types have values but not identities.

The `binarySearch()` function takes a sorted sequence and a key (and an optional comparator) and uses a binary search algorithm to find the index of the key in the sequence. The result is a meaningless integer if the sequence is not sorted. The result is the index of the key in the sequence if the key appears in the sequence. If the key appears multiple times, one of the indexes is returned, but you cannot tell which one. If the key does not appear in the sequence, a negative integer is returned.

The `indexOf()` and `indexByIdentity()` functions take a sequence and a key and find the index of the first occurrence of the key in the sequence. If the key does not appear in the sequence, -1 is returned.

The `nextIndexOf()` and `nextIndexByIdentity()` functions take a sequence, a key, and a starting position and find the index of the first occurrence of the key in the sequence on or after the specified position. If the key does not appear on or after the specified position, -1 is returned.

The `isEqualByContentIdentity()` takes two sequences and determines if the sequences contain the same elements according to object identity.

The `max()`, `min()`, `reverse()`, `shuffle()`, and `sort()` functions work as their names suggest. A runtime exception will be thrown if an empty sequence is passed to the `max()` and `min()` functions.

Listing A-14 uses some of the utility functions.

Listing A-14. *Sequence Utility Functions*

```
import visage.util.Sequences.*;

var seq = [1, 4, 2, 8, 5, 7];
print("seq = "); println(seq);

println("The index of 4 in seq = {indexOf(seq, 4)}");
println("The max value of seq = {max(seq)}");
println("The min value of seq = {min(seq)}");

print("reverse(seq) = "); println(reverse(seq));
print("shuffle(seq) = "); println(shuffle(seq));

var sorted = sort(seq);
print("sortd = "); println(sorted);

var index = binarySearch(sorted, 4);
println("Found 4 in sorted at index {index}");

var integers = [1, 3, 5, 3, 1];
print("integers = "); println(integers);
println("indexOf(integers, 3) = {indexOf(integers, 3)}");
println("nextIndexOf(integers, 3, 2) = {nextIndexOf(integers, 3, 2)}");
```

In Listing A-14, the `import` statement `import visage.util.Sequences.*;` allows you to call the functions of the class. We will cover `import` statements in more detail in the section entitled "Import Directives" later in this appendix.

Visage Expressions

A Visage *expression* is a chunk of Visage code that the Visage compiler understands. The compiler will generate code that evaluates Visage expressions into Visage values. The values are fed into yet more expressions, which evaluate to more values, leading eventually to the solution to your problem.

Expressions and Their Types

Visage understands many kinds of expressions, and all executable Visage code is composed of expressions. Every expression has some expectation for its constituent parts and makes certain guarantees for the value it produces. If these expectations are not met, the compiler will reject the program and report an error. For example, the expression a and b expects its operands to be values of type Boolean and produces a Boolean value as a result. The compiler will flag the expression 3 and 4 as an error. As another example, consider the variant of the delete expression that deletes all elements from a sequence. This expression expects the operand following delete to be a variable of the sequence type and produces no results. The compiler will flag the expression delete 5; as an error. The expression delete [1, 3, 5, 7, 9]; is similarly in error because its operand, although a sequence, is not a variable of the sequence type but rather an explicit sequence expression. These checks are called *type checks*.

And because the Visage compiler performs type checks at compile time, Visage falls into the category of *statically typed* programming languages. In Visage, all variables have a static type: it is either explicitly specified or inferred. The type of a variable cannot be changed during the lifetime of the variable. This is another benefit of type checking.

Expressions such as the delete expression that produce no results are said to be of the *void type*. The void type is a special type. There could never be a value of the void type, and you cannot declare a variable to be of the void type. You can use Void as a function's return type to indicate that the function returns nothing. Expressions that are not of the void type are called *value expressions*.

▨ **Note** There is a difference between an expression being of the void type and having the value null. An expression of the void type can never have a value, not even null. On the other hand, if an expression is capable of having a null value, it is capable of having a non-null value.

Block Expression

A block expression is formed by enclosing a number of other expressions within a pair of braces ({}). The type of the block expression is the type of the last expression it encloses. If the last expression is not of the void type, then the value of the last expression is the value of the block expression. Here is an example:

```
var x = {
  var a = 3;
  var b = 4;
  a*a + b*b
}
```

The block in the example contains three expressions: two variable declaration expressions and an arithmetic expression. After execution, the variable x will have the value 25.

Blocks introduce a new *scope*. Variables declared inside the block are not visible to code outside the block. You cannot declare a variable with the same name as another variable in the current block level or the surrounding level, up to the enclosing function or class.

In the next example, we use a block of the void type:

```
var a = 3;
var b = 4;
{
  var s = a*a + b*b;
  println("s = {s}");
}
```

Since the block is of the void type, we cannot assign it to a variable. The block only serves to confine the scope of the variable s.

Precedence and Groupings

When presented with a compound expression that involves multiple operators, Visage will carry out the operations in accordance with the precedence assigned to each operator. For operators of the same precedence, Visage will carry out the operations in accordance to the associativity assigned to the operators. For example, the well-known precedence rules for arithmetic operators are observed in Visage. Thus, the value of 1 + 2 * 3 is 7 rather than 9, and the value of 6 / 2 * 3 is 9 rather than 1.

A pair of parentheses can be used to force the operations to be done in a different order. Thus, the value of (1 + 2) * 3 is 9, and the value of 6 / (2 * 3) is 1. Only value expressions can be surrounded by parentheses.

Expression Separator

The semicolon (;) serves as an expression terminator. You have seen its use in all the example programs in this book so far. Some expressions have a natural termination point. For example, both the block expression you learned in this section and the for expression you learned in the previous section naturally terminate at the closing brace. For such expressions, the semicolon is optional; in other words, the compiler will not specifically look for a semicolon at these locations, but if a semicolon is present, the compiler will not complain either. A few expressions that you will learn later in this appendix—such as the while expression, one form of the if expression, and the object literal expression—also fall into this category.

The semicolon is also optional after the last expression in a block. For all other expressions, a semicolon is required.

Variable and Constant Declarations

In Visage, variable declarations are expressions. They are called *variable declaration expressions*. Here are examples of the basic forms of variable declaration expressions:

```
var a;
var b: Integer;
var c: Number = 3.14;
var d = "Hello, World.";
var e = bind c;
var f = d on replace { println("f changed.") }
```

Here we declared six variables:

- Variable a is declared with neither a type nor an initializer.

- Variable b is declared to be of type Integer but without an initializer.

- Variable c is declared to be of type Number and initialized to the value 3.14.

- Variable d is declared without a type specifier and initialized to the string "Hello, World.".

- Variable e is declared without a type but with a binding.

- Variable f is declared without a type but with an initializer and a trigger.

A variable declaration is introduced by the keyword var followed by a variable name and an optional type specifier, an optional value expression or bind expression, and an optional trigger. We will provide an in-depth coverage of bind expressions in the section entitled "Working with Data Bindings" and cover triggers in more detail in the section entitled "Triggers," both later in this appendix.

Notice that the colon that separates the variable name and the type is omitted if the type is omitted. If a type is not specified, the type of the variable is determined by Visage's type inference facility. If an initializer is given in the variable declaration, the type of the initial value is taken as the type of the variable. Otherwise, the type of the variable is determined by the first subsequent assignment to the variable. If the variable is never assigned a value in the program, the variable is taken to be of type Object, which is a class type.

Once the compiler determines the type of a variable that is declared without a type, it will treat the variable as if it is declared with the inferred type.

If the type is specified, the type of the initializer value or the binding expression must be compatible with the specified type.

▦ **Caution** It is generally a good idea to either specify a type or an initializer in a variable declaration. If neither is specified, only nonsequence values can be assigned to the variable.

Constants are named values that cannot be subsequently assigned. They are declared in *constant declaration expressions*. A constant declaration is introduced by the keyword def followed by a constant name and an optional type specifier, a required value expression or bind expression, and an optional trigger. Here are some examples:

```
def PI = 3.14159;
def GREETING = "Hello";
var x = 1024;
def y = bind x;
```

Although a constant can never be assigned a new value, its value may change if it is declared with a data binding and the expression it binds to changes.

Variable and constant names cannot be keywords and must be unique within the same function.

Assignment Operator

The *assignment expression* assigns a new value to a previously declared variable. The second line in the following example is an assignment expression:

```
var x: Integer = 1024;
x = 2048;
```

The assignment expression consists of a variable name followed by the equal sign (=) and an expression. The value on the right-hand side must have a type that is compatible with the type of the variable. After the assignment expression, the value of the variable will be the value on the right-hand side.

If the variable is declared without a type and without an initializer or binding, the first subsequent assignment will determine the variable's type.

The assignment expression itself, considered as an expression, has a value that is the same as the value that is assigned to the variable. You can chain several assignments together, as shown in the following code:

```
var a;
var b;
a = b = 3;
```

The assignment operator is right associative. Thus, the third line in the previous code is equivalent to a = (b = 3). Therefore, b is assigned the value 3, and then a is assigned the value of the expression b = 3, which is also 3.

Compound Assignment Operators

The *compound assignment expression* performs an arithmetic operation between the value of the left-side variable and the value of the right-side expression and assigns the result to the variable. The second to the fifth lines of the following example are compound assignment expressions:

```
var x: Integer = 1024;
x += 1;
x -= 2;
x *= 3;
x /= 4;
```

The compound assignment expression consists of a variable name followed by one of the compound assignment operators (+=, -=, *=, /=) and an expression. The value of the variable and the value of the expression must be numeric or duration values. The appropriate arithmetic operations indicated by the compound assignment operator are performed and the result assigned to the variable. Thus, x += 1 behaves the same as x = x + 1, and x will be 1025 after it. Similarly, x -= 2 behave the same as x = x - 2, and x will be 1023 after it. And x will be 3069 after x *= 3, and 767 after x /= 4.

Compound assignment operations play the same role as the regular assignment operation in inferring variable types.

The compound assignment expression itself has a value that is the same as the value assigned to the variable. The compound assignment operators are right associative and can be chained together, although such chaining is rarely used.

Relational Operators

Visage supports six relational operators: the equals operator (==), the not-equals operator (!=), the less-than operator (<), the less-than or equal operator (<=), the greater-than operator (>), and the greater-than or equal operator (>=).

The *relational expression* consists of a left-side expression followed by a relational operator and a right-side expression. The equals and the not-equals operators can be used to compare values of any types, whereas the other four operators can be used only to compare values of numeric or duration types.

The Visage equals operator performs value comparisons. For primitive types, this gives you intuitive results. For example, the expressions true == true, 3 == 3, 4 == 4.0, 5.5 == 5.5, "hello" == "hello", and 1m == 60s all evaluate to true.

For class types, value comparison is done using the equals() instance function of the class. You will learn more about classes later in this appendix. For now it is enough to know that value comparison for class types can be controlled by the programmer. The default behavior of the equals() instance function is to perform object identity comparisons. In this comparison, each newly created object is not equal to any previously created objects.

▨ **Caution** If you are familiar with the Java programming language, you should recognize that the semantics of the == operator in Visage is different from that of the == operator in Java, where the former performs value comparisons and the latter performs object identity comparisons.

Two sequences are equal if they have the same size and if, for each valid index, the corresponding elements are equal.

Listing A-15 shows some of the expressions you have learned in this section at work.

Listing A-15. Basic Expressions

```
// block expressions
var x = {
  var a = 3;
  var b = 4;
  a*a + b*b
};
println("The value of x is {x}");

// precedence and groupings
println("1 + 2 * 3 = {1 + 2 * 3}");
println("(1 + 2) * 3 = {(1 + 2) * 3}");
println("6 / 2 * 3 = {6 / 2 * 3}");
println("6 / (2 * 3) = {6 / (2 * 3)}");

// var and def
var o;
var i: Integer;
var n: Number = 3.14;
var str = "Hello, World.";
var j = bind i;
var greeting = str on replace { println("greeting changed") };

def PI = 3.14159;
def k = bind i;
```

```
// assignment and type inference
var v1;
println("Before: v1 = {v1}");
v1 = 42;
println("After: v1 = {v1}");

class Point {
  var x: Number;
  var y: Number;
  override function toString() {
    "Point \{ x: {x}, y: {y} \}"
  }
}
var v2;
println("Before: v2 = {v2}");
v2 = Point {x: 3, y: 4};
println("After: v2 = {v2}");

// compound assignment
x = 1024;
println("x = {x}");
x += 1;
println("x = {x}");
x -= 2;
println("x = {x}");
x *= 3;
println("x = {x}");
x /= 4;
println("x = {x}");

// relational operators
println("true == true is {true == true}");
println("3 == 3.0 is {3 == 3.0}");
println('"hello" == "hello" is {"hello" == "hello"}');

println("3.14159 > 2.71828 is {3.14159 > 2.71828}");
println("1h < 100m is {1h < 100m}");

var p1 = Point {x: 3, y: 4};
var p2 = Point {x: 3, y: 4};
println("p1 == p1 is {p1 == p1}");
println("p1 == p2 is {p1 == p2}");
```

While Expression

A while *expression* is introduced by the while keyword, followed by a pair of parentheses that encloses a *condition*, which must be an expression of type Boolean, and a *body* expression after the closing parenthesis. Although the syntax allows any expression to be the body, a block is the most common body of while expressions. A semicolon is required to terminate the while expression if the body is not a block.

First, the condition is checked. If it is true, the body of the while expression is evaluated, and the condition is checked again. As long as the condition is true, the body is executed repeatedly. The while expression itself is of the void type, so you cannot assign a while expression to a variable as you can with blocks.

The following code prints the squares of the first ten natural numbers:

```
var i = 1;
while (i <= 10) {
  println("{i} squared: {i * i}");
  i += 1;
}
```

You can use the keyword break to break out of a while expression. The keyword continue can be used to skip the rest of the code in one iteration. If there are multiple nested loops in your code, these keywords only affect the innermost loop that encloses them. In the following code, the first loop prints natural numbers up to 7, and the second prints only the even ones:

```
var i = 1;
while (i <= 10) {
  if (i > 7) {
    break;
  } else {
    println(i);
  }
  i += 1;
}

var j = 1;
while (j <= 10) {
  if (j mod 2 != 0) {
    j += 1;
    continue;
  } else {
    println(j); j += 1;
  }
}
```

Revisiting the for Expression

Because of its close relationship with sequence comprehension, we covered the for expression in the "Working with Sequences" section earlier in this appendix. Recall that a for expression is introduced by the for keyword, followed by a pair of parentheses that enclose one or more comma-separated in clauses, and an expression after the closing parenthesis.

Strictly speaking, a for expression is sequence comprehension only if its body is a value expression. If the body of a for expression is of the void type, the for expression is more like the while expression and exhibits a loop behavior. Here is an example that prints the first ten natural numbers:

```
for (x in [1..10]) {
  println(i);
}
```

As is the case for while loops, the keywords break and continue can be used in for loops. Again, you can use the break keyword to break out of a for loop and the continue keyword to skip the rest of the code in one iteration. In the following code, the first for loop prints natural numbers up to 7, and the second prints only the even ones:

```
for (x in [1..10]) {
  if (x > 7) {
    break;
  } else {
    println(x);
  }
}

for (x in [1..10]) {
  if (x mod 2 != 0) {
    continue;
  } else {
    println(x);
  }
}
```

■ **Caution** The syntax of the for expression allows the break and continue keywords to be used in any kind of for expression. However, with the current Visage compiler, using these keywords in sequence comprehension will cause either a compiler crash or a runtime exception.

If Expression

The if *expression* is introduced by the if keyword, followed by a pair of parentheses that enclose a *condition*, which must be an expression of type Boolean; a then clause after the closing parenthesis; and an optional else clause. The then clause has two forms: it can either be an expression or the then keyword followed by an expression. The else clause is the else keyword followed by an expression. The then keyword is customarily used in short if expressions where both the then and else clauses contain simple nonblock expressions. Here are some examples:

```
// short form if expression
var x = if (i == j) then 1 else 0;
// long form if expression
if (x < 0) {
  println("{x} < 0");
} else {
  println("{x} >= 0");
}
```

In the short-form if expression, the expressions for the then and else clauses are simple Integer values. Thus, the entire if expression is of type Integer. In the long-form if expression, the expressions for the then and else clauses are both block expressions of the void type. Consequently, the entire if expression is of the void type and cannot be assigned to another variable.

In general, the type of an if expression is determined by the types of the two expressions in the then and else clauses. If both expressions are of the same type, the entire if expression is of that type. If one of them is of the void type, the entire if expression is of the void type. If the else clause is omitted, the if expression is of the void type.

The situation becomes more complicated if the two expressions are of different types. In such situations, Visage will attempt to find a type that will accommodate both expressions. Consider the following examples:

```
var x = if (true) then 3 else "4";
var y = if (true) then 5 else [6];
```

After the assignments, the variable x will have the type Object and value 3, and y will have the type Integer[] and value [5]. In practice, if expressions with dissimilar then and else clause expressions are rarely needed.

The else clause of one if expression can be another if expression. This joined if expression allows you to test for multiple conditions, as shown here:

```
if (x <0) {
  println("{x} < 0");
} else if (x == 0) {
  println("{x} = 0");
} else {
  println("{x} > 0");
}
```

Listing A-16 shows the looping and conditional expressions at work.

Listing A-16. *Looping and Conditional Expressions*

```
// while loop
var i = 1;
while (i <= 10) {
  println("{i} squared: {i * i}");
  i += 1;
}

// break from while loop
var j = 1;
while (j <= 10) {
  if (j mod 2 != 0) {
    j += 1;
    continue;
  } else {
    println(j);
    j += 1;
  }
}
```

```
// continue in for loop
for (x in [1..10]) {
  if (x > 7) {
    break;
  } else {
    println(x);
  }
}

// if expressions
var k = if (i == j) then 1 else 0;

if (k < 0) {
  println("{k} < 0");
} else {
  println("{k} >= 0");
}

for (x in [-1..1]) {
  if (x < 0) {
    println("{x} < 0");
  } else if (x == 0) {
    println("{x} = 0");
  } else {
    println("{x} > 0");
  }
}

// if expression with dissimilar then and else clauses
var a = if (true) then 3 else "4";
println("a = {a}");
// assign an Integer to a
a = 5;
println("a = {a}");
// assign a Stirng to a
a = "hi";
println("a = {a}");

var b = if (true) then 7 else [8];
print("b = "); println(b);
```

In this section, we covered some of the most basic expressions in Visage. These expressions are building blocks for larger pieces of code.

Object Literals

This section examines class types and their objects. We'll begin with using Visage classes since it is easier to use them than to write them, and there are plenty of classes already written for you in the Visage JavaFX API. Writing your own classes is covered in the section entitled "Working with Classes" later in this appendix.

Classes and Objects

The *class* is a unit of code that encapsulates a data model and functions that manipulate the data model. A class contains *instance variables, instance functions*, and *initialization blocks*. The instance variables represent the data modeled by the class, and the instance functions perform computations based on the values of the instance variables. The initialization blocks set up the initial values of the instance variables in a way that is meaningful to the class.

To use a class, you must instantiate it. When you instantiate a class, the Visage runtime system allocates memory to hold all the instance variables of the class and initialize the memory according to the initializers and initialization blocks. This properly initialized memory is called an *object* of the class. It is also called an *instance* of the class.

The runtime system may also perform some other housekeeping chores before it hands you an *object reference*. The object reference allows you to read from and write to its instance variables that are accessible to you as specified by the class. It also allows you to call its instance functions that are accessible to you as specified by the class.

When you are finished with an object reference, you don't have to do anything special. You simply let it go out of scope. The runtime system will figure out that you will never use that object reference again and reclaim the memory that it occupies. This process is called *garbage collection.*

You can instantiate a class multiple times to create multiple objects of the class. Different objects of the same class may have the same set of instance variables, but each object's instance variable values are independent of every other object's instance variable values.

The Object Literal Expression

To instantiate a Visage class, you use an *object literal expression*. Unlike some of the expressions you encountered in the previous section, the object literal expression is quite involved and sometimes occupies numerous program lines.

To illustrate this point, we'll pick a class from the Visage JavaFX API whose fully qualified name is `visage.javafx.scene.shape.Circle` and try to instantiate it in various ways. We will refer to it by its simple name, `Circle`. Since this class represents an onscreen circle, when you compile and run the snippets of codes in this section, a window will pop up with a circle drawn in it. You will need to close the window manually when you are finished examining its content.

To instantiate a class, you must know what the class offers. You get that information by reading the Visagedoc of the class. "Visagedoc" is the documentation that is generated directly from the source code using the Visagedoc tool, which comes with the Visage distribution.

Initializing Instance Variables

According to the API documentation, the `Circle` class defines three instance variables: `centerX`, `centerY`, and `radius`, all of type `Number` and all having a default value of 0.0. We can read, write, and initialize all three instance variables. In the following example, we instantiate a circle of radius 100.0 centered at the point (100.0, 100.0):

```
import visage.javafx.scene.shape.Circle;
var circle = Circle { centerX: 100.0, centerY: 100.0, radius: 100.0 }
```

An object literal expression starts with the name of the class, followed by a pair of braces that encloses the following parts:

- Instance variable initializers

- Variable declarations

- Instance variable overrides

- Instance function overrides

- Default instance variable initializer

In the previous example, we supplied three instance variable initializers. An *instance variable initializer* consists of the instance variable name followed by a colon and a value or a bind expression. You will learn about bind expressions in the next section. The expression must be of a type that is compatible with the type of the instance variable. If multiple instance variable initializers are present, they can be separated by commas, semicolons, or spaces. Commas are typically used when the initializers all appear on the same line, and white spaces are typically used when the initializers contain complicated expressions and must be presented one per line. We could have written this example in a multiline form:

```
import visage.javafx.scene.shape.Circle;
var circle = Circle {
  centerX: 100.0
  centerY: 100.0
  radius: 100.0
}
```

Default Instance Variables

Some classes mark one of the variables as being the default. For example, the `Circle` class has the radius property marked as the default. In an object literal expression, you can initialize the default instance variable by simply including a value with no label:

```
import visage.javafx.scene.shape.Circle;
var circle = Circle {100.0}
```

This is a shorthand form to create a circle that has a radius of 100 centered at (0, 0).

In addition, you can use this together with the instance variable initializers to do more complex initialization:

```
import visage.javafx.scene.shape.Circle;
var circle = Circle {
  centerX: 100.0
  centerY: 100.0
  100.0
}
```

This will create a circle of radius 100 centered at (100, 100), producing identical results to the same example at the end of the last section with the radius label explicitly called out. For more information about how to set variables in your own classes as the default, see the section entitled "Declaring Default Instance Variables."

Declaring Constants and Variables

You can declare constants and variables in an object literal expression to aid the initialization process. Constant and variable declarations in an object literal must be separated from other parts of the object literal by a semicolon. Constants and variables defined in an object literal expression are confined to the scope of the object literal expression. In Listing A-17, we've introduced a variable r to help initialize the Circle instance.

Listing A-17. *Declaring a Variable in an Object Literal Expression*

```
import visage.javafx.scene.shape.Circle;

var circle = Circle {
  var r = 100.0;
  centerX: r
  centerY: r
  radius: r
}
```

Overriding Instance Functions and Instance Variables

You can override instance variables and instance functions in an object literal expression to change the behavior of the class just for the instance. Such overrides must be separated from other parts of the object literal by a semicolon if they do not end with a closing brace. You may want to override an instance variable to add a trigger. We will cover instance variable overrides and instance function overrides, as well as triggers, in more detail later in this appendix.

Listing A-18 illustrates both an instance variable and an instance function overriding in object literal expressions. We overrode the instance variable x to add a replace trigger. We also overrode the toString() instance function to give our point p a nicer printed representation.

Listing A-18. *Overriding Instance Variables and Functions in an Object Literal Expression*

```
class Point {
  var x: Number;
  var y: Number;
}

var p = Point {
  override var x on replace {
    println("x is now {x}");
  }
  override function toString(): String {
    "Point({x}, {y})"
  }
  x: 3.0
  y: 4.0
}

println(p);
```

The instance function `toString()` in `Point` is inherited from the `java.lang.Object` class. The `println()` function uses an object's `toString()` instance function to generate a string representation of the object. When the code in Listing A-18 is run, the following output is printed to the console:

```
x is now 3.0

Point(3.0, 4.0)
```

Manipulating Objects

Once you obtain an object reference by instantiating a Visage class using an object literal notation, you can manipulate the object through the object reference. You can also assign the object reference to a variable and manipulate the object through the object variable. You can pass the object reference or the object variable as function parameters. In general, you can use object references and object variables the same way you use primitive values and variables or sequence values and variables.

To take advantage of the functionality the class provides, you need to access the instance variables and instance functions of the class.

Manipulating Object States

The values of all instance variables of an object are called the object's *state*. You access an object's instance variables using a *member access expression*. The member access expression consists of a left side, a dot (.), and a right side. The left side of the dot must be an expression that evaluates to an object reference. The right side of the dot must be the name of an instance variable or an instance function of the class. Assume p is a variable of type `Point` and is assigned a valid instance of `Point`; then `p.x` and `p.y` are member access expressions that refer to the state of the object.

It is the class writer's job to decide what kind of access rights you have regarding instance variables and instance functions of its instances. Access rights are granted based on whether your code is in the same script file, in the same package, or in a different package than the class you are accessing. Using access modifiers to specify instance variable and instance function access rights is explained in the section entitled "Access Modifiers" later in this appendix. For now, assume that any code that is in the same file as the class has full access rights to all its instance variables and instance functions. Listing A-19 shows code in the same file reading from and writing to instance variables x and y of the class `Point`.

Listing A-19. *Accessing Instance Variables*

```
class Point {
  var x: Number;
  var y: Number;
  override function toString(): String {
    "Point({x}, {y})"
  }
}
```

```
// reading instance variables
var p = Point { x: 3.0, y: 4.0 };
println("p.x = {p.x}");
println("p.y = {p.y}");
println("p = {p}");

// writing to instance variables
p.x = 5.0;
p.y = 12.0;
println("p = {p}");
```

Invoking Instance Functions

The dot notation also allows you to access instance functions of a class. Functions play an important role in the Visage language. Not only can you define and call functions and instance functions, you can assign functions to variables, pass functions into other functions, and use functions as return values in another function. Variables that refer to functions have function types. Function types, along with primitive, sequence, and object types, are the only four kinds of types of Visage. We will fully explore this functional programming aspect of Visage later in this appendix.

The *function invocation expression* consists of a function name or an expression of the function type followed by a pair of parentheses that encloses a comma-separated list of *arguments*. The number of arguments must agree with the number of arguments in the function's definition. The type of each argument must be compatible with the type that is specified for that argument in the function definition. The function invocation expression's type is the return type of the function it invokes. If that type is not the void type, the function invocation expression's value is the return value of the function.

You have seen function invocation expressions at work throughout this appendix. We have used the println() function in our examples.

As is the case for instance variables, it is the class writer's job to decide what kind of access rights you have regarding instance functions. Listing A-20 shows several instance function invocations.

Listing A-20. *Invoking Instance Functions import java.lang.Math.*;*

```
import java.lang.Math.*;

class Point {
  var x: Number;
  var y: Number;
  function distanceFromOrigin(): Number {
    sqrt(x*x + y*y)
  }
  function translate(dx: Number, dy: Number) {
    x += dx;
    y += dy;
  }
  override function toString(): String {
    "Point({x}, {y})"
  }
}
```

```
var p = Point { x: 3.0, y: 4.0 };
println("p = {p}");
println("Distance between p and the origin = {p.distanceFromOrigin()}");

p.translate(2.0, 8.0);
println("p = {p}");
println("Distance between p and the origin = {p.distanceFromOrigin()}");

print("Distance between Point \{x: 8.0, y: 15.0\} and the origin = ");
println(Point {x: 8.0, y: 15.0}.distanceFromOrigin());
```

The first line in Listing A-20 imports a number of methods, including sqrt(), from the Java class java.lang.Math into the program. We used sqrt() in the distanceFromOrigin() instance function to calculate the distance from the point to the origin. In the second line from the last, we escaped the brace characters in the string literal to turn off the special meaning of braces. The last line of the code demonstrates invoking an instance function directly on an object literal, without assigning the object reference to a variable.

Handling Nulls in Visage

In the previous examples, we ensured that all the variables we accessed and objects we invoked functions on were initialized before we used them. However, in a complicated program there are often times when we might get passed in an object that has a null value and inadvertently try to access a member variable or function.

In these cases, Visage will gracefully proceed. For a variable, it will return the default value for the variable type, and for a function call, it will skip the invocation and return the default value for the expected function result.

Listing A-21 demonstrates the result of calling methods and accessing variables on a null object.

Listing A-21. *Null Safe Handling in Visage*

```
class A {
  var objVar:Object;
  var intVar:Integer;
  var stringVar:String;

  function retObj():Object {
    println("should not get called");
    objVar
  }
}

var nullA:A = null;

println("nullA.objVar = {nullA.objVar}");
println("nullA.intVar = {nullA.intVar}");
println("nullA.stringVar = {nullA.stringVar}");
println("nullA.retObj() = {nullA.retObj()}");
```

Running this code will return the default object types as shown in the following output:

```
nullA.objVar = null

nullA.intVar = 0

nullA.stringVar =

nullA.retObj() = null
```

For user interface code, this graceful handling of nulls prevents exceptions or other interruptions that would take away from the user experience. However, there are times when you want to fail immediately if the variable you are accessing is null. This can be accomplished by using the null-check operator (!.), which will throw a `java.lang.NullPointerException` if the operand is null.

In the following example, we expect a `NullPointerException` to result from accessing a null object:

```
var nullA:A = null;
nullA!.objVar;
```

Checking null on dereference is handy for debugging code and happens to be the default behavior in Java. You can find more information about handling exceptions, such as the `NullPointerException` that the null-check operator throws, in the section entitled "Exceptions."

Creating Java Objects with the new Operator

The new *expression* consists of the keyword new, followed by the name of a Java class and an optional pair of parentheses that encloses a comma-separated list of constructor arguments. It calls the constructor of the Java class that matches the number and type of the arguments and results in an object reference. If the constructor without any arguments (also called the *no-arg* or *default constructor*) is intended, you can either use a pair of empty parentheses or omit the parentheses altogether.

In the following example, we instantiate the `java.util.Date` class and call its `getTime()` method:

```
import java.util.Date;
var date = new Date();
var time = date.getTime();
```

> ■ **Note**   Visage allows you to use a new expression to instantiate a Visage class. The effect of the new expression for a Visage class is the same as an object literal expression with an empty pair of braces. For consistency, you should always use object literal expressions to instantiate Visage classes.

Making of a Declarative Syntax

One characteristic of object literal expressions is that they are self-explanatory. You can understand what is being instantiated by reading the object literal expression without having to refer to the class definition. If an instance variable in a class is itself of the class type or the sequence type, its instance variable initializer can be another nested object literal expression or an explicit sequence expression.

This combination gives object literal expressions a hierarchical feel, which makes it ideal for describing GUIs.

Working with Data Bindings

Visage's data binding facility allows any variable to be bound to a value expression. When any constituent part of the bound expression is changed, the bound expression is recalculated and the variable's value is also changed. The data binding capability is at the center of the Visage approach for GUI development, in which onscreen UI controls' properties are bound to a model object and the GUI is controlled through state changes in the model object.

Bind Expression

A *bind expression* is introduced by the bind keyword, followed by a value expression and optionally the with inverse keywords. Bind expressions are automatically reevaluated when their dependencies change. Unlike all the other expressions that you've learned so far, bind expressions are not true stand-alone expressions. A bind expression must appear on the right-hand side of constant declarations, variable declarations, or instance variable initializers in object literal expressions. It also puts restrictions on the value expression that appears on its right-hand side. The constant, variable, or instance variable is said to be *bound* to the expression.

Here are some examples of bind expressions:

```
var a = 3.14159;
def b = bind a;
var c = bind a;
var p = Point { x: bind a, y: bind a }
```

The constant b, variable c, and instance variables p.x and p.y are all bound to the bind expression bind a. Any value assigned to a after the binding will also become the new value of b, c, p.x, and p.y.

A bound variable or a bound instance variable (except for bindings with inverse, which we will explain shortly) cannot be assigned another value. The following lines will cause a compilation error:

```
var a = 1024;
var b = bind a;
b = 2048;
```

▓ **Caution**   The compiler cannot effectively detect all assignments to bound variables at compile time. Assignments to bound variables will cause a runtime exception to be thrown.

What Does the Data Binding Remember?

With a regular (nonbinding) assignment or initialization, the right-hand side expression is evaluated and its value is assigned to the left-hand side variable. With a binding assignment or initialization, the Visage runtime system not only evaluates the expression and assigns the value to the variable but also remembers the entire expression, figuring out which variables the expression depends on and keeping an eye on the *dependent variables*. When any one of them gets a new value, the saved expression is *updated in a bind context* and its value becomes the new value of the bound variable.

In the following example, the variable z becomes a bound variable in the third line. It gets the value 7. The Visage also remembers that z is bound to x + y, which depends on the variables x and y. When the value of x or y is changed, the expression x + y is updated, and its new value becomes the new value of z.

```
var x = 3;
var y = 4;
var z = bind x + y;
```

A bind expression cannot contain assignments, pre- or postincrement or decrement expressions, or while expressions.

Binding to if Expressions

When a variable is bound to an if expression, its dependencies are the union of the dependencies of the condition, the then clause, and the else clause. To update an if expression in a bind context, the if expression is simply reevaluated. Here is an example:

```
var b = true;
var x = 3;
var y = 4;
def z = bind if (b) then x else y;
```

In this example, z depends on b, x, and y. When any one of them changes, the value of z is updated by reevaluating the if expression.

Binding to for Expressions

Since for expressions of the void type are not value expressions, the only kind of for expressions that can appear in a bind expression are sequence comprehensions. When a variable is bound to a for expression, its dependencies are the union of the dependencies of the sequences specified in the in clauses and the dependencies of the where clauses, excluding the iteration variables. To update a for expression in the bind context, the body of the for expression is reevaluated for a minimal number of element tuples in the sequences.

```
var a = 1;
var b = 10;
var m = 4;
def c = bind for (x in [a..b] where x < m) { x * x }
```

In the preceding example, the dependencies of c are the union of the dependencies of [a..b], which is a and b, and the dependencies of x < m, which is x and m. Excluding the iteration variable x, that gives us the dependencies a, b, and m. With the given values of a, b, and m, the qualified x values are 1, 2, 3. If m is changed to 7, the qualified x values will also include 4, 5, and 6. The body of the for expression is only evaluated for the new x values of 4, 5, and 6.

Binding to a Block

Visage restricts the expressions that can appear in a block in a binding context. The block can have only a certain number of constant declarations and a final value expression. The constant declarations are treated as if they are binding declarations. When a variable is bound to a block, its dependencies are the dependencies of the last expression in the block, which may, in turn, depend on the constant declarations in the block or variables outside the block.

```
var a = 3;
var b = 4;
def c = bind {
  def d = a;
  def e = b;
  d * d
}
```

In the preceding example, the dependencies of c are the same as the dependencies of d * d, which are the same as the dependencies of d, which is a. Therefore, the value of c is updated when the value of a is changed but not when the value of b is changed.

The restrictions on the content of blocks under a binding context apply also to blocks in if and for expressions.

▓ **Note** The compiler allows you to include variable declarations in a block in the bind context. However, since no assignments can appear in the block, these variable declarations are effectively constant declarations. They are also treated as if they are binding declarations.

Binding to Function Invocation Expressions

Visage has two kinds of functions: functions and bound functions. Both kinds of functions behave the same way except when their invocation is under a binding context. You will learn how to define functions and bound functions in the section entitled "Bound Functions" later in this appendix.

When a variable is bound to a (nonbound) function invocation expression, its dependencies are the union of the dependencies of the arguments. When a variable is bound to a bound function invocation expression, its dependencies are the dependencies of the bound function body treated like a block. The update rule for functions is that the function is reinvoked when the dependencies change. The update rule for bound functions is the same as the update rule for blocks.

```
function sumOfSquares(x, y) { x * x + y * y }
var a = 3;
def c = bind sumOfSquares(a + 5, a + 6);
```

In the preceding example, the dependency of c is the union of that of a + 5 and a + 6, which is a. Therefore, the value of c is updated when the value of a is changed. The function is reinvoked with the new arguments.

Binding to Object Literal Expressions

When a variable is bound to an object literal expression, its dependencies are the union of the dependencies of the right-hand side expressions of those instance variable initializers whose right-hand side expression is not already a bound expression. When a dependency changes, a new object is instantiated.

```
var a = 3;
var b = 4;
def p = bind Point { x: a, y: b };
def q = bind Point { x: bind a, y: b };
def r = bind Point { x: bind a, y: bind b };
```

In the preceding example, the dependencies of p are a and b, the dependency of q is b, and the dependency of r is empty. When a is changed, a new instance of Point is created for p, but not for q and r. However, since q.x and r.x are bound to a, their values will be updated. Similarly, when b is changed, a new instance of Point is created for p and q, but not for r. However, r.y is updated. Since the dependencies of r are empty, binding r to the object literal expression is unnecessary.

■ **Caution**   Two levels of binding are at work in the preceding example: one at the object level and one at the instance variable level. Changes in dependencies of bound instance variables will not cause a new instance of Point to be created; only the value of the instance variable is updated. Changes in dependencies of bound object literal will cause the creation of a new instance of Point. This subtle difference may not be readily differentiated when you print out the values of p, q, or r with println().

Bidirectional Bindings and Lazy Bindings

Visage supports bidirectional bindings. A *bidirectional binding* is specified by appending the with inverse keywords to the end of a bind expression. The only expression allowed is a variable name. The following trivial example illustrates this construct:

```
var a = 3;
var b = bind a with inverse;
```

A value can be assigned to a bidirectionally bound variable, and its new value will also become the new value of its peer. Bidirectional bindings are useful in GUI programs where several onscreen elements are used to edit the same underlying quantity, such as when you want the user to change the RGB settings of a color using sliders and text fields.

Visage supports lazy bindings. A *lazy binding* is specified by adding the lazy keyword after bind. Both regular bindings and bidirectional bindings can be lazy bindings. Lazy bindings have the same meaning as regular bindings with the exception that the bound variable is not updated until its value is needed. This may reduce the number of recalculations to the minimum and therefore boost the performance of the code.

In Listing A-22, you can see Visage bindings at work.

Listing A-22. *Data Bindings*

```
var pointInstance = 1;
class Point {
  var instance = pointInstance++;
  var x: Number;
  var y: Number;
  override public function toString() {
    "Point({x}, {y})@{instance}"
  }
}

// data bindings
var a = 3.14159;
def b = bind a;
var c = bind a;
var p = Point { x: bind a, y: bind a };
println("a = {a}, b = {b}, c = {c}, p.x = {p.x}, p.y = {p.y}");

a = 2.17828;
println("a = {a}, b = {b}, c = {c}, p.x = {p.x}, p.y = {p.y}");

// binding to arithmetic expressions
var x1 = 3;
var y1 = 4;
var z1 = bind x1 + y1;
println("x1 = {x1}, y1 = {y1}, z1 = {z1}");
x1 = 5;
println("x1 = {x1}, y1 = {y1}, z1 = {z1}");
y1 = 12;
println("x1 = {x1}, y1 = {y1}, z1 = {z1}");

// binding to if expression
var b2 = true;
var x2 = 3;
var y2 = 4;
def z2 = bind if (b2) then x2 else y2;
println("b2 = {b2}, x2 = {x2}, y2 = {y2}, z2 = {z2}");
b2 = false;
println("b2 = {b2}, x2 = {x2}, y2 = {y2}, z2 = {z2}");
x2 = 5;
println("b2 = {b2}, x2 = {x2}, y2 = {y2}, z2 = {z2}");
y2 = 12;
println("b2 = {b2}, x2 = {x2}, y2 = {y2}, z2 = {z2}");

// binding to for expression
var a3 = 1;
var b3 = 10;
var m3 = 4;
def c3 = bind for (x in [a3..b3] where x < m3) { x * x };
print("a3 = {a3}, b3 = {b3}, m3 = {m3}, c3 = "); println(c3);
m3 = 7;
```

```
print("a3 = {a3}, b3 = {b3}, m3 = {m3}, c3 = "); println(c3);
a3 = 2;
print("a3 = {a3}, b3 = {b3}, m3 = {m3}, c3 = "); println(c3);
b3 = 5;
print("a3 = {a3}, b3 = {b3}, m3 = {m3}, c3 = "); println(c3);

// binding to block
var a4 = 3;
var b4 = 4;
def c4 = bind {
  def d4 = a4;
  def e4 = b4;
  d4 * d4
};
println("a4 = {a4}, b4 = {b4}, c4 = {c4}");
a4 = 5;
println("a4 = {a4}, b4 = {b4}, c4 = {c4}");
b4 = 12;
println("a4 = {a4}, b4 = {b4}, c4 = {c4}");

// binding to function invocation expression
function sumOfSquares(x, y) { x * x + y * y }
var a5 = 3;
var b5 = 4;
def c5 = bind sumOfSquares(a5 + 5, a5 + 6);
println("a5 = {a5}, b5 = {b5}, c5 = {c5}");
a5 = 5;
println("a5 = {a5}, b5 = {b5}, c5 = {c5}");
b5 = 12;
println("a5 = {a5}, b5 = {b5}, c5 = {c5}");

// binding to object literals
var a6 = 3;
var b6 = 4;
def p6 = bind Point { x: a6, y: b6 };
def q6 = bind Point { x: bind a6, y: b6 };
def r6 = bind Point { x: bind a6, y: bind b6 };
println("a6 = {a6}, b6 = {b6}, p6 = {p6}, q6 = {q6}, r6 = {r6}");
a6 = 5;
println("a6 = {a6}, b6 = {b6}, p6 = {p6}, q6 = {q6}, r6 = {r6}");
b6 = 12;
println("a6 = {a6}, b6 = {b6}, p6 = {p6}, q6 = {q6}, r6 = {r6}");

// bidirectional binding
var a7 = 3;
var b7 = bind a7 with inverse;
println("a7 = {a7}, b7 = {b7}");
a7 = 4;
println("a7 = {a7}, b7 = {b7}");
b7 = 5;
println("a7 = {a7}, b7 = {b7}");
```

Working with Functions

In Visage, functions serve to break long and complicated code into manageable pieces. Once written, functions can be invoked multiple times with different arguments, so they also provide a code reuse mechanism. Additionally, functions are one of the ingredients of the two programming paradigms: functional programming and object-oriented programming.

Functions come into being in two ways: as function definitions or as anonymous function expressions. The following sections explore how to create functions each way.

Function Definitions

A *function definition* is introduced by the function keyword, followed by the name of the function, a pair of parentheses that encloses zero or more argument specifications (if more than one, the arguments will appear in a comma-separated list), an optional return type specifier, and a *body* block.

In Listing A-23, we define a function that calculates the nth value of the recursively defined Fibonacci series. The first two numbers in the series are 0 and 1, and any subsequent number in the series is the sum of the two preceding numbers.

Listing A-23. *The Fibonacci Series*

```
function fib(n:Integer):Integer {
  if (n <= 0) then 0 else
    if (n == 1) then 1 else
      fib(n - 1) + fib(n - 2)
}
println("fib(6) = {fib(6)}");
```

When you run the program in Listing A-23, the following output is printed to the console:

```
fib(6) = 8
```

In the preceding definition, we defined a function named fib. It takes one argument of type Integer named n. It returns an Integer value. And its body is a block that contains a single if expression. Both the parameter type and the return type are explicitly specified.

Function definitions are not expressions. They can appear in only two places: at the top level of a Visage source file or within the scope of a Visage class. Function definitions that appear at the top level of a Visage source file are called *script functions*. Those that appear within the scope of a class are called *instance functions*. They cannot appear inside other expressions, such as in a block. You will learn about classes and instance functions in the "Working with Classes" section later in this appendix.

In Visage, function names introduced by function definitions live in their own space, which is different from the space where variable and constant names introduced by variable or constant declarations live. As a result, in a Visage file, you can define both a function foo and a variable foo, and the compiler will happily compile your source file.

Return Types

In Visage, the return type of a function is specified after the closing parenthesis of the argument list, separated from the argument list by a colon (:). Any Visage types, including primitive types, sequence types, function types, and class types, can serve as the return type of a function. A special type specifier, Void, can also be used as the return type of functions. As a matter of fact, the only legitimate use of Void is as the return type of a function. Listing A-24 shows some examples of function definitions.

Listing A-24. Function Definitions with Explicit Return Types

```
class Point {
  var x: Number;
  var y: Number;
}

function primes(n:Integer):Integer[] {
  [2..n][k | sizeof [2..<k][d | k mod d == 0] == 0];
}

function midpoint(p1:Point, p2:Point):Point {
  Point { x: (p1.x + p2.x) / 2, y: (p1.y + p2.y) / 2 }
}

function printSquaresTable(n:Integer):Void {
  for (x in [1..n]) {
    println("{x} squared = {x*x}");
  }
}
```

The function primes returns a sequence of integers consisting of all prime numbers less than or equal to the parameter value n. Its body is a block that contains a sequence comprehension consisting of all ks in the range from 2 to *n* for which a condition is true. The condition involves another sequence comprehension that contains all factors of k, between 2 and k-1, and the condition is true only if the size of the factor sequence is zero.

The midpoint function calculates the midpoint between its two arguments.

The printSquaresTable function prints a table of squares of integers between 1 and the function parameter n. It has a return type of Void, which means that this function does not return any values.

■ **Note** One subtlety of the Void return type is that it does not prevent the body of the function from implicitly returning a value as the last expression of its body. The value will simply be ignored, and any function invocation expressions cannot be used in contexts where a value expression is expected. For example, var x = printSquareTables() will generate a compilation error.

As is the case for variable declarations, under certain restrictions, Visage's type inference facility can infer the return type of a function if an explicit type specifier is not given. Three of the four functions that you have seen earlier can also be defined without explicit return types, as demonstrated in Listing A-25.

Listing A-25. *Function Definitions with Implicit Return Types*

```
function primes(n:Integer) {
  [2..n][k | sizeof [2..<k][d | k mod d == 0] == 0];
}

function midpoint(p1:Point, p2:Point) {
  Point { x: (p1.x + p2.x) / 2, y: (p1.y + p2.y) / 2 }
}

function printSquaresTable(n:Integer) {
  for (x in [1..n]) {
    println("{x} squared = {x*x}");
  }
}
```

A restriction on inferring the return types of functions is that the function definition cannot have cycles. The fib function cannot be defined with implicit return types because it is recursively defined. This restriction also applies to two or more functions that reference each other in their bodies in such a way as to cause a cycle. For example, if function f calls function g, function g calls function h, and function h calls back to function f, all three functions need to have explicit return types.

Parameters and Their Types

A Visage function can have zero or more parameters. In function definitions, the function parameters appear after the function name as a comma-separated list enclosed in a pair of parentheses. In the four examples from the last section, the functions fib, primes, and printSquaresTable have one parameter, and the midpoint function has two parameters.

Each parameter is specified as a parameter name followed by an optional type specifier. If more than one parameter is specified, they all must have distinct names.

When a parameter's type is not explicitly specified, the type inference facility will infer the type of the parameter. However, the power of Visage's type inference facility for implicitly typed function parameters is weaker than that for either variables or return types. The inferred type will be either Object or Double depending on whether the parameter participates in arithmetic operations inside the function body.

None of the four functions from the last section is a good candidate for type inference on parameter types. Because the parameter n in the function fib participates in arithmetic operations, its inferred type is Double, not Integer as we intended. Because the function bodies of primes, midpoint, and printSquaresTable do not contain any arithmetic operations on their parameters, the inferred types of the parameters will be Object, which is not specific enough for these functions to compile successfully.

Naturally, function definitions that are candidates for type inference on parameter types are ones that perform numerical calculations. Listing A-26 gives an example.

Listing A-26. Function Definitions with Implicit Parameter Types

```
import java.lang.Math.*;

function hypot(x, y) {
  sqrt(x*x + y*y)
}

println("hypot(3, 4) = {hypot(3, 4)}");
```

This function calculates the hypotenuse of a right triangle given the other two sides. When you run the program in Listing A-26, the following output is printed to the console:

```
hypot(3, 4) = 5.0
```

Note that we used the `import java.lang.Math.*;` statement to bring all the functions in the Java class `java.lang.Math` into our program. We used the `sqrt()` function in our calculations. We will cover import statements in the "Import Directives" section later in this appendix.

Function Bodies and the Return Expression

The body of a function is a block. Everything that you've learned about blocks also applies to function bodies. Additionally, function bodies may contain *return expressions*. When a function is invoked, its function body is executed until the end of the body or a return expression is reached. The execution of a function body may also end because of exceptions. We will cover exceptions in the "Exceptions" section.

A return expression is introduced by the `return` keyword, followed optionally by an expression. If the `return` keyword is not followed by an expression, the return expression is a stand-alone return expression. A stand-alone return expression is of the void type and has no value. If the `return` keyword is followed by an expression, the return expression is of the same type as the following expression, and its value is the value of the following expression.

Here is a stand-alone return expression:

```
return;
```

And here is a return expression that returns an integer value of 1024:

```
return 1024;
```

Return expressions may appear only inside a function body. If the function definition has an explicit return type that is not `Void`, all the return expressions inside the function body as well as the last expression of the function body must be compatible with the specified return type. If the function definition has an explicit return type of `Void`, all return expressions inside the function body must be stand-alone return expressions. If the function definition has no explicit return type, the return type of the function is inferred from the last expression of the function body and all the return expressions. The inferred return type will be a type that can accommodate all the return expressions.

Listing A-27 presents some examples of function definitions whose bodies contain return expressions.

Listing A-27. *Function Definitions with Return Expressions*

```
function gcd(a:Integer, b:Integer):Integer {
  if (b == 0) {
    return a;
  } else {
    return gcd(b, a mod b);
  }
}

function ampm(hour:Integer, minute:Integer):Void {
  if (hour == 0 and minute == 0) {
    println("midnight");
    return;
  }
  if (hour < 12) {
    println("a.m.");
    return;
  }
  if (hour == 12 and minute == 0) {
    println("noon");
    return;
  }
  println("p.m.");
}

function onClick(n:Integer) {
  if (n == 0) {
    return "No click";
  }
  if (n == 1) {
    return "Single click";
  }
  if (n == 2) {
    return "Double click";
  }
  return "Multiple click";
}

println("gcd(24, 18) = {gcd(24, 18)}");
ampm(0, 0);
ampm(6, 0);
ampm(12, 0);
ampm(18, 0);
println(onClick(0));
println(onClick(1));
println(onClick(2));
println(onClick(3));
```

The function gcd() calculates the greatest common divisor of parameters a and b using the Euclidean algorithm. It has an explicit return type of Integer, and both return expressions in the function body are of type Integer. The function ampm() prints out midnight, a.m., noon, or p.m.

depending on the hour and minute parameters. It has an explicit return type of Void, and all three return expressions in the function body are stand-alone return expressions. The function onClick() attempts to return a string that describes the type of click based on the parameter n. It does not have an explicit return type, and since all return expressions in the function body are of type String, the return type of the function is inferred to be String.

When you run the program in Listing A-27, the following output is printed to the console:

```
gcd(24, 18) = 6

midnight

a.m.

noon

p.m.

No click

Single click

Double click

Multiple click
```

Function Body Scope

Within the body of a script function, you can access three kinds of variables:

- *Script variables and constants* declared in the same Visage source file
- *Function parameters* that are passed into the function invocation expression
- *Local variables and constants* that are declared in the function body

You also have access to other script functions in the same Visage source file. This list of accessible entities to script functions will grow when you see how to organize your Visage code into multiple files and how to make entities from one file accessible from other files in the "Organizing Visage Code" section later in this appendix.

Listing A-28 illustrates the accessibility of script variables from script functions.

Listing A-28. *Accessing Script Variables from Function Definitions*

```
var q:Integer[];

function enqueue(i:Integer):Void {
  insert i into q;
  println("Enqueued {i}.  Size of q is {sizeof q} now.");
}

function dequeue():Integer {
  if (sizeof q == 0) {
    println("Size of q is {sizeof q} now. Returning -1.");
    return -1;
  } else {
    var i = q[0];
    delete q[0];
    println("Dequeued {i}.  Size of q is {sizeof q} now.");
    return i;
  }
}

enqueue(1);
enqueue(2);
enqueue(3);
println(dequeue());
println(dequeue());
enqueue(4);
println(dequeue());
println(dequeue());
println(dequeue());
```

The script variable q is a sequence of Integer values. The two script functions enqueue() and dequeue() manipulate q in their bodies. The enqueue() function uses the insert statement to add the parameter i at the end of the sequence q and prints a message to the console. The dequeue() function first checks whether q is empty. If q is empty, the function prints a message and returns –1. Otherwise, it saves q[0] into a local variable i, uses the delete statement to remove the first element from q, prints a message, and returns the local variable i.

When you run the program in Listing A-28, the following output is printed to the console:

```
Enqueued 1.  Size of q is 1 now.

Enqueued 2.  Size of q is 2 now.

Enqueued 3.  Size of q is 3 now.

Dequeued 1.  Size of q is 2 now.
```

```
1
```

```
Dequeued 2.  Size of q is 1 now.
```

```
2
```

```
Enqueued 4.  Size of q is 2 now.
```

```
Dequeued 3.  Size of q is 1 now.
```

```
3
```

```
Dequeued 4.  Size of q is 0 now.
```

```
4
```

```
Size of q is 0 now. Returning -1.
```

```
-1
```

Function parameters and local variables and constants can be seen only in the body of the function where they are defined. One function cannot see the parameters and local variables of another function. Function parameters are read-only. You cannot change the values of a function's parameters in the body of that function.

The following function will generate the compilation error message "You cannot change the value(s) of 'x' because it is a parameter":

```
// Won't compile
function f(x:Number):Void {
  x = 1024;
}
```

Overloaded Functions

In Visage, you can have several function definitions with the same name, as long as they can be distinguished by differences in either the number or types of parameters. Multiple functions with the same name but different parameters are called *overloaded functions.*

The definitions of overloaded functions are no different from the definitions of non-overloaded functions. You simply use the same function name in two or more function definitions.

Listing A-29 shows an example of some overloaded functions.

Listing A-29. *Overloaded Function Definitions*

```
function f(i:Integer):Void {
  println("Integer version of f is called with i = {i}.");
}
```

```
function f(n:Number):Void {
  println("Number version of f is called with n = {n}.");
}

function f(str:String):Void {
  println("String version of f is called with str = {str}.");
}

f(1024);
f(3.14);
f("Hello, World");
```

When these functions are invoked, the function invocation expression will look like f(exp), where exp is some expression. The Visage compiler determines which of the overloaded functions is called by examining the type of the expression exp and selects the most appropriate function to call. In the three function invocation expressions in Listing A-29, because 1024 is of type Integer, 3.14 is of type Number, and "Hello, World" is of type String, f(1024) invokes the version of f that takes a single Integer parameter, f(3.14) invokes the version of f that takes a single Number parameter, and f("Hello, World") invokes the version of f that takes a single String parameter.

When you run the program in Listing A-29, the following output is printed to the console:

```
Integer version of f is called with i = 1024.

Number version of f is called with n = 3.14.

String version of f is called with str = Hello, World.
```

Without adding a version of f for a single Boolean parameter, the function invocation expression f(false) would cause a compilation error because the compiler cannot find an appropriate version of f to call.

■ **Caution** To cut down the confusion of the program that calls overloaded functions, you should overload a function name only with functions that logically perform the same task, with slight differences in the parameters passed in.

Implicit Type Conversions

Up to this point, we have used the term *compatible* when we referred to the ability to assign a value to a variable or to pass a value into a function invocation expression as a parameter.

Visage will allow a value of one type to be assigned to a variable of a different type in three situations:

- Numeric conversions

- Sequence conversions

- Class hierarchies

Numeric conversions happen when a value of one numeric type is assigned to a variable of a different numeric type. Here is an example:

```
var n:Number = 1024;
```

This code looks normal, yet it does involve an implicit numeric conversion. The literal value 1024, which is of type Integer, is assigned to the variable n, which is of type Number. This assignment succeeds because Visage allows Integer values to be converted to Number values.

Sequence conversions happen when a value of a nonsequence type is assigned to a variable of the corresponding sequence type. Visage allows this conversion to simplify sequence manipulation code, because in many cases, a sequence variable contains only one element. Therefore, the two assignments in the following snippet of code are equivalent:

```
var strs:String[];
strs = ["Hello, World"];
strs = "Hello, World";
```

As this conversion demonstrates, if a sequence contains only one element, the brackets are optional. There is no implicit conversion from a sequence type to its element type. The following code will cause a compilation error:

```
// Won't compile
var str:String = ["Hello, World"];
```

Defining class hierarchies is discussed further in the "Creating Class Hierarchies" section later in this appendix; for now, you just need to understand the rule for assignability regarding such hierarchies: if class Bar extends class Foo, an instance of Bar can be assigned to a variable of type Foo. Here is a simple example:

```
class Foo {}
class Bar extends Foo {}
var foo:Foo = Bar {};
```

In the third line, we created a new instance of Bar with an object literal expression and assigned the resulting instance of Bar to the variable foo, which is declared with type Foo. Notice that no conversion on the instance is performed nor is it needed. An instance of a subclass is naturally also an instance of its superclasses. This is different from numeric or sequence conversions.

For the purposes of assignment and function parameter passing, the primitive and function types are considered assignable to the Object type. Sequence types are not considered assignable to the Object type.

Resolving Overloaded Functions

The rules the Visage compiler uses to find the function to invoke for a function invocation expression are as follows:

1. Find all functions with the given name, with the same number of parameters as in the function invocation expression, and with compatible types for each parameter. If only one function matches, invoke that function.

2. If more than one function remains, and if one function in the set has parameter types that are more specific than another function in the set, eliminate the less-specific function. Repeat this process until no more eliminations can be made.

3. If exactly one function remains, invoke that function. If more than one function remains, the function invocation expression cannot be resolved, and a compilation error results.

Listing A-30 presents an example of an ambiguous invocation of overloaded functions.

Listing A-30. *Resolving Overloaded Function Definitions*

```
function f(i:Integer, n:Number):Void {
  println("Integer, Number version of f is called with ({i}, {n}).");
}

function f(n:Number, i:Integer):Void {
  println("Number, Integer version of f is called with ({n}, {i}).");
}

f(1024, 3.14);
f(6.28, 2048);
// f(1024, 2048); // Won't compile
```

Both overloaded functions match the third (commented out) invocation. However, because the first function definition is more specific in the first parameter and the second function definition is more specific in the second parameter, neither function can be eliminated in the second step of the resolution rules.

When you run the program in Listing A-30, the following output is printed to the console:

```
Integer, Number version of f called with (1024, 3.14).

Number, Integer version of f called with (6.28, 2048).
```

Function Types and Anonymous Functions

Although Visage's function definition facility allows you to define functions at the script and class level, Visage's *anonymous function expression* allows you to create functions anywhere an expression can appear.

Because an anonymous function expression is an expression, you may naturally ask two questions of any Visage expressions: What is the type of the expression? And what is the value of the expression? The answers are straightforward. Visage anonymous function expressions have *function types*, and they evaluate to *closures*.

The concepts of anonymous function expressions, closures, and function types are intricately related, so we will first present a simple example in Listing A-31, which involves all of these concepts. We will then point to portions of the example when we explain the relevant concepts.

Listing A-31. *Anonymous Function Example*

```
import java.lang.Math.*;

{
  var hypot: function(:Number, :Number):Number;

  hypot = function(x, y) {
    sqrt(x*x + y*y);
  };

  println("hypot(3, 4) = {hypot(3, 4)}");
}
```

We deliberately put all the code inside a block, where a function definition is not allowed but anonymous function expressions are allowed.

We first declare a variable, hypot, with the type specifier function(:Number, :Number):Number. This specifies a function type representing all functions that takes two Number parameters and returns a Number value. We then assign an anonymous function expression to the variable hypot. The anonymous function expression, which is shown in bold type, resembles an ordinary function definition without the function name. After the assignment, the variable hypot has as its value a closure that is the result of evaluating the anonymous function expression. We finally invoke the closure, which performs the calculation specified in the anonymous function expression, in this case calculating the hypotenuse of a right triangle, which will output the following:

```
hypot(3, 4) = 5.0
```

More Details on Function Type Specifiers

The format of a function type specifier is simple. It starts with the function keyword, followed by a pair of parentheses enclosing a comma-separated list of parameter type specifiers, and then the return type specifier. You define the parameter type specifier by including a colon (:) followed by the type name or by including a parameter name followed by another colon and the type name. You provide the return type specifier using a colon followed by the type name.

Because no function body is associated with a function type specifier, all parameter types must be provided. You can omit the return type specifier. However, if you do so, the return type is assumed to be Void.

The following is a list of function type specifiers that are found in the Visage JavaFX API documentation:

```
function(:Duration):Void
function(:Event):Void
function(:Exception):Void
function(:InputStream):Void
function(:KeyEvent):Void
```

```
function(:MediaError):Void
function(:MediaTimer):Void
function(:MouseEvent):Void
function(:MouseEvent):Boolean
function(:OutputStream):Void
function(:Sequence):Void
function(:String):Void
function(:String):Boolean
function(:Boolean):Void
function(:Integer):Void
```

These are the data types of various event handlers in Visage JavaFX API classes. The `function(:MouseEvent):Void` type, for example, is the type of instance variables named `onMousePressed`, `onMouseReleased`, and `onMouseMoved` in the `visage.javafx.scene.CustomNode` class.

You can build more complicated function types. Here is an example:

```
function(:Integer):function(:Integer):Integer
```

This is the type of a function that takes an `Integer` parameter and returns a function. The function it returns takes an `Integer` parameter and returns an `Integer`.

More Details on Anonymous Function Expressions

As you saw in Listing A-31, an anonymous function expression is almost identical with a function definition in form. In that program, we used a form of anonymous function expression that relied on Visage's type inference facility to determine the function type of the resulting closure.

You can also use the form of anonymous function expression that explicitly specifies the parameter and return types, as shown in Listing A-32.

Listing A-32. *Anonymous Function with Explicit Types*

```
{
  var primes = function(n:Integer):Integer[] {
    [2..n][k | sizeof [2..<k][d | k mod d == 0] == 0]
  };
  println(primes(64));
}
```

In this example, we redefine our earlier `primes` function as an anonymous function expression with explicitly specified types. Because we do not explicitly specify the type of `primes`, it gets the type of the first value that is assigned to it. In this case, the value is the closure resulting from evaluating the anonymous function expression.

If you attempt to assign a closure to an explicit function type variable and the type of the closure is different from the type of the variable, a compilation error will be generated.

More Details on Closures

One of the benefits of supporting function types in a language is that functions can be assigned to variables, passed into functions, and returned from functions. Programming languages that support such features are usually said to support *first-class functions*. And you can use a style of programming that relies heavily on first-class functions called *functional programming*.

Listing A-33 shows a typical first example of functional programming.

Listing A-33. *Functional Programming*

```
{
  var addN: function(:Integer):function(:Integer):Integer;
  addN = function(n) {
    function(i:Integer) {
      i + n
    }
  };

  var addTen = addN(10);
  println("addTen(4) = {addTen(4)}.");
}
```

We declare addN as a function type variable that takes an Integer parameter and returns a function, which, in turn, takes an Integer parameter and returns an Integer. We then assign a closure to it: any Integer parameter will return a function that adds the Integer to its parameter. We then assign addN(10) to the variable addTen. The variable addTen is, therefore, of the function type function(:Integer):Integer, which is the return type of addN, and the closure that is assigned to addTen will simply add 10 to its parameter. Finally, we invoke addTen with a parameter of 4, which should produce the result 14.

When we run the program in Listing A-33, the following output is printed to the console:

```
addTen(4) = 14.
```

In the "Function Body Scope" section earlier in this appendix, we showed that the function definition's body can access all script variables and constants and all script functions. In much the same way, the body of an anonymous function expression can also access all the functions, variables, and constants that are in scope when the anonymous function expression is evaluated. The resulting closure will capture these functions, variables, and constants.

Much of the power of closure comes from the fact that the environment that it captures remains available even after the original environment is gone. In Listing A-33, for example, by the time addTen(4) is invoked, the earlier invocation addN(10) has already returned, yet addTen can still access the parameter 10 that is passed into the invocation of addN(10).

Bound Functions

A *bound function* is a function definition decorated with the bound modifier whose body is restricted to a number of variable and constant declarations followed by one final expression.

When a variable is bound to a function invocation expression that includes a bound function, its dependency is the dependency of the last expression of the bound function, traced transitively to either a parameter of the function or a script variable. Listing A-34 shows an example of a bound function.

Listing A-34. Binding to a Bound Function

```
var x = 3;

bound function f(y:Number, z:Number):Number {
  var u = y;
  var v = z;
  x + u
}

var a = 4;
var b = 5;
var c = bind f(a, b) on replace {
  println("x = {x}, a = {a}, b = {b}, c = {c}.");
};

println("About to change x...");
x = 5;
println("About to change a...");
a = 6;
println("About to change b...");
b = 7;
```

In Listing A-34, the dependency of c is the dependency of x + u, the last expression of the bound function f. Because x is a script variable and u depends on the first parameter y, the dependency of c is the script variable x and the first parameter of the function invocation expression, a. We add an on replace trigger to monitor the update of c. We will cover triggers in the "Triggers" section later in this appendix.

When we run the program in Listing A-34, the following output is printed to the console:

```
x = 3, a = 4, b = 5, c = 7.0.

About to change x...

x = 5, a = 4, b = 5, c = 9.0.

About to change a...

x = 5, a = 6, b = 5, c = 11.0.

About to change b...
```

As you can see, the value of c is indeed updated when x and a changed but not when b changed.

When a bound function is invoked in a bind expression, its function body is also evaluated in a bound context, which causes each assignment in the body to behave as if it were a binding assignment.

This allows complicated expressions to be bound to a variable through a series of simpler bound functions.

Handling Exceptions

As your Visage code base grows, systematically handling errors becomes more important. The exception facility is Visage's way of dealing with exceptional conditions.

The Call Stack

As your program runs, the code will call into and exit from functions. Every time the code calls into a function, the Visage runtime creates a *stack frame*. The stack frame for each function call contains the parameters that are passed into the function as well as local variables and constants declared within the function. The *call stack* is the accumulation of stack frames of all active function calls. As the code makes deeper and deeper function calls, the call stack grows. As the code exits the called functions, the call stack shrinks.

As you saw earlier, reaching a return expression inside a function body and reaching the end of the function body are two ways to return from function calls. These are called *normal exits* from function calls.

If your code encounters an exceptional condition or an error condition and cannot complete the calculation the function is designed to do, you can use Visage's exception facility to throw an exception. If your code calls functions that may throw exceptions, you can use a `try-catch-finally` expression to install handlers for the exceptions that it is prepared to handle. When an exception is thrown, the Visage runtime will look for a handler for the exception. If one cannot be found in the current function, it will exit the function and continue looking for one in the calling function. The runtime may exit several levels of function calls before a handler is found. These are called *abnormal exits* from function calls. The process of exiting functions abnormally in search of an exception handler is called *unwinding of the call stack*.

Throwing Exceptions

You throw an exception using a *throw expression*. A throw expression is introduced by the `throw` keyword, followed by an instance of a class that extends the Java class `java.lang.Throwable`. When a throw expression is evaluated, the Visage exception handling facility is started.

The class `java.lang.Throwable` is the root of the exception class hierarchy for Java, which include many exception classes that can be used directly in Visage. You can also define your own exception classes for use in your code. However, for the majority of Visage programs, the Java exceptions are adequate.

Listing A-35 shows an example of a function that throws an exception.

Listing A-35. Throwing an Exception

```
import java.lang.IllegalArgumentException;

function weekday(i:Integer):String {
  if (i == 0) then "Sunday" else
  if (i == 1) then "Monday" else
  if (i == 2) then "Tuesday" else
  if (i == 3) then "Wednesday" else
  if (i == 4) then "Thursday" else
  if (i == 5) then "Friday" else
  if (i == 6) then "Saturday" else
```

```
    throw new IllegalArgumentException("Invalid weekday: {i}.");
}

for (i in [0..7]) {
  println("weekday({i}) = {weekday(i)}.");
}
```

In Listing A-35, we define a simple function that translates numeric representations of weekdays into their corresponding string representations. When the parameter is not in the correct range, we throw a newly constructed instance of java.lang.IllegalArgumentException. We then called the function eight times in a for loop, the last time with an illegal argument. Because java.lang.IllegalArgumentException is a Java class, we use the new keyword to create an instance of it for use in our thrown exception. You will find out more about instantiating Java classes in the "Leveraging Java from Visage" section later in this appendix.

When we run the program in Listing A-35, the following output is printed to the console:

```
weekday(0) = Sunday.

weekday(1) = Monday.

weekday(2) = Tuesday.

weekday(3) = Wednesday.

weekday(4) = Thursday.

weekday(5) = Friday.

weekday(6) = Saturday.

java.lang.IllegalArgumentException: Invalid weekday: 7.

at ThrowingException.weekday(ThrowingException.visage:11) at
ThrowingException.visage$run$(ThrowingException.visage:15)
```

We call the function without a custom exception handler, so when Visage unwinds the stack, it exits not only the weekday() function but also the calling code into the default exception handler, which simply prints the stack trace to the console.

The following are general-purpose exception classes that can be used when appropriate in your Visage code:

```
java.lang.Exception
java.lang.IllegalArgumentexception
java.lang.IllegalStateException
java.lang.RuntimeException
java.lang.UnsupportedOperationException
```

Handling Exceptions

To handle potential exceptions that may be thrown from a piece of code, use a try-catch-finally expression.

A try-catch-finally *expression* starts with a try *block*, which is introduced by the try keyword and encloses the code that may throw exceptions. This, in turn, is followed by zero or more catch clauses and an optional finally block. A catch *clause* is introduced by the catch keyword, followed by a pair of parentheses that encloses an exception specification in the same format as an explicitly or implicitly typed function parameter, and a block that is the *handler* for the specified exception. Only subclasses of java.lang.Throwable are allowed in exception specifications of catch clauses. If a type is not specified, the inferred type of an exception specification is java.lang.Throwable. A finally *block* is introduced by the finally keyword followed by a block.

At least one catch clause or finally block must be present in a try-catch-finally expression.

When a try-catch-finally expression is evaluated, the try block is executed. If no exception is thrown, the finally block, if present, is executed, and execution continues past the try-catch-finally expression. If an exception is thrown, the catch blocks are checked one by one for compatibility with the thrown exception. If a compatible catch clause is found, the exception is handled by the try-catch-finally expression. If the exception is handled, its handler and the finally block, if present, are executed, and execution continues past the try-catch-finally expression. If the exception is not handled, the finally block, if present, is executed, and the exception is propagated outside the try-catch-finally expression.

In Listing A-36, we define a wheelOfException() function that throws the five general-purpose exceptions you learned in the last section and then call the function through several levels of function calls in a try-catch-finally expression.

Listing A-36. *Handling Exceptions*

```
import java.lang.*;

function wheelOfException(i:Integer):Void {
  if (i == 0) throw new Exception("Zero");
  if (i == 1) throw new IllegalArgumentException("One");
  if (i == 2) throw new IllegalStateException("Two");
  if (i == 3) throw new RuntimeException("Three");
  if (i == 4) throw new UnsupportedOperationException("Four");
  println("Out of exceptions for i = {i}");
}

function catchExceptions(i:Integer):Void {
  try {
    wheelOfException(i);
  } catch (iae:IllegalArgumentException) {
    println("Caught IllegalArgumentException with message: "
            "{iae.getMessage()}.");
  } catch (ise:IllegalStateException) {
    println("Caught IllegalStateException with message: "
            "{ise.getMessage()}.");
  } catch (uoe:UnsupportedOperationException) {
    println("Caught UnsupportedOperationException with message: "
            "{uoe.getMessage()}.");
  } catch (re:RuntimeException) {
```

```
      println("Caught RuntimeException with message: "
              "{re.getMessage()}.");
  } catch (e:Exception) {
    println("Caught Exception with message: "
            "{e.getMessage()}.");
  } finally {
    println("Reached finally block.");
  }
}

function callWheelOfException() {
  for (i in [0..5]) {
    catchExceptions(i);
  }
}

callWheelOfException ();
```

When we run the program in Listing A-36, the following output is printed to the console:

```
Caught Exception with message: Zero.

Reached finally block.

Caught IllegalArgumentException with message: One.

Reached finally block.

Caught IllegalStateException with message: Two.

Reached finally block.

Caught RuntimeException with message: Three.

Reached finally block.

Caught UnsupportedOperationException with message: Four.

Reached finally block.

Out of exceptions for i = 5

Reached finally block.
```

Two points from the preceding example are worth noting:

- The catch clauses in the try-catch-finally expression are ordered from the most specific to the least specific. Because RuntimeException extends Exception, and the other three exceptions extend RuntimeException, we have to put the catch clauses for the other three exceptions before that of RuntimeException, and we also have to put the catch clause for RuntimeException before that of Exception. Had the order been reversed, the catch clause for Exception would have caught all the exceptions because all five exceptions are compatible with Exception.

- The finally block is always executed regardless of whether an exception is thrown.

Working with Classes

You create class types by defining classes. Visage's class facility supports instance variables and instance functions, member access control, and inheritance. Classes can be instantiated at runtime to create objects. Objects are linked together to form a network of objects that communicate by calling each other's instance functions. Such systems of well-behaved communicating objects are called *object-oriented software systems*. Visage's class facilities make it an object-oriented programming language, just like its function facilities make it a functional programming language.

Class Definitions

A *class definition* is introduced by the class keyword, followed by the name of the class, an optional superclass and mix-in list, and a pair of braces that encloses zero or more class members. The superclass and mix-in list, if present, start with the keyword extends, followed by a comma-separated list of names of classes that serve as the superclasses and mix-ins of the class being defined. Four kinds of members may be included in a class definition: instance variables and constants, instance functions, the init block, and the postinit block. *Instance variable and constant* declarations have the same form as script variable and constant declarations. *Instance function* definitions have the same form as script function definitions but may use two more kinds of expressions in their function bodies: this and super. The init *block* is introduced by the init keyword, followed by a block. The postinit *block* is introduced by the postinit keyword, followed by a block. A class definition may include zero or more instance variables and constants, zero or more instance functions, an optional init block, and an optional postinit block.

In this section and the next, we examine class definitions to see how each part of a class definition works. In the example in Listing A-37, we define a class that keeps track of coins in a piggy bank. For simplicity, we consider only pennies (1 cent) and nickels (5 cents). The class has tree instance variables and two instance functions. After the class definition, we create two instances of the class using object literal expressions and invoke instance functions on the object references.

Listing A-37. *A PiggyBank Class*

```
import java.lang.*;

class PiggyBank {
  var name: String;
  var pennies: Integer;
  var nickels: Integer;
```

```
    function putInPennies(count: Integer):Void {
      if (count <= 0) {
        throw new IllegalArgumentException("count must be positive.");
      } else {
        pennies += count;
        println("You put {count} pennies into {name}.");
      }
    }

    function putInNickels(count: Integer):Void {
      if (count <= 0) {
        throw new IllegalArgumentException("count must be positive.");
      } else {
        nickels += count;
        println("You put {count} nickels into {name}.");
      }
    }

    function total():Integer {
      pennies + nickels * 5
    }
}

var myPiggyBank = PiggyBank { name: "My Piggy Bank" };
myPiggyBank.putInPennies(7);
myPiggyBank.putInNickels(3);
myPiggyBank.putInNickels(1);
println("{myPiggyBank.name} has {myPiggyBank.total()} cents:  "
  "{myPiggyBank.pennies} pennies and {myPiggyBank.nickels} nickels.");

var yourPiggyBank = PiggyBank { name: "Your Piggy Bank" };
yourPiggyBank.putInPennies(4);
yourPiggyBank.putInNickels(6);
yourPiggyBank.putInPennies(9);
println("{yourPiggyBank.name} has {yourPiggyBank.total()} cents:  "
  "{yourPiggyBank.pennies} pennies and {yourPiggyBank.nickels} nickels.");
```

When we run the program from Listing A-37, the following output is printed to the console:

```
You put 7 pennies into My Piggy Bank.

You put 3 nickels into My Piggy Bank.

You put 1 nickels into My Piggy Bank.

My Piggy Bank has 27 cents:  7 pennies and 4 nickels.

You put 4 pennies into Your Piggy Bank.
```

```
You put 6 nickels into Your Piggy Bank.

You put 9 pennies into Your Piggy Bank.

Your Piggy Bank has 43 cents:  13 pennies and 6 nickels.
```

One thing to note in this example is that we instantiated the class twice to get two distinct instances of the same class. Even though the two instances are created from the same class, they are independent of each other. You can contrast this with the queue example in Listing A-28, where we use a script variable to represent the queue, and consequently, only one queue exists in the program. You can think of classes as molds out of which we make instances.

Class definitions are not expressions. They can appear only at the top level of a Visage source file. Visage does not support anonymous class expressions, which would be analogous to anonymous function expressions. A class definition does, however, introduce a new type, called a *class type*, which you can use in your programs. The class name is also the name of the class type introduced by the class. Object references created by object literal expressions have class types. In Listing A-37, the variables myPiggyBank and yourPiggyBank are both of type PiggyBank.

In Visage, each class name introduced by class definitions live in its own space, which is different from the space where names of variables and constants live, as well as the space where function names live. As a result, in a Visage source file, you can define a class foo, a function foo, and a variable foo, and the compiler will happily compile your source file. However, by convention (not enforced by the compiler), Visage class names start with an uppercase letter, whereas variable names and function names start with lowercase letters.

Instance Variables

In Listing A-37, we defined the class PiggyBank with three instance variables. Here is how they are declared:

```
var name: String;
var pennies: Integer;
var nickels: Integer;
```

Although these look like ordinary script-level variable declarations and local variable declarations in a function body or a block, they mean quite different things. For one thing, script-level and local variable declarations are expressions that, when executed, create the variable right there and then. Instance variable declarations in a class are not expressions and therefore are not executed immediately. The effects of instance variable declarations are felt when an instance of the class is created with an object literal expression.

An object literal expression may include initializers for instance variables of the class. Both the instance variable declaration in the class definition and the instance variable initializer in the object literal expression have influence on the instance variable.

Like ordinary variable declarations, instance variable declarations may include information about the variable's name, type, default initializer, and trigger. Here is an example of a class with a fuller-featured instance variable declaration:

```
class A {
  var i: Integer = 1024 on replace {
    println("Trigger in class definition: i = {i}.");
  }
}
```

This class declares an instance variable i of type Integer, with a default initializer of 1024 and a trigger that fires when the instance variable's value changes.

In object literal expressions, you can override instance variables, and you can provide initializers for instance variables. Instance variable overrides must include the override modifier before the var keyword and can override the default initializer or the trigger. Here are some examples of object literal expressions that create instances of class A:

```
var a1 = A {}
var a2 = A { i: 2048 }
var a3 = A {
  override var i = 3072 on replace {
    println("Trigger in object literal override: i = {i}.");
  }
}
var a4 = A {
  override var i = 4096 on replace {
    println("Trigger in object literal override: i = {i}.");
  }
  i: 5120
}
```

The type of the instance variable is dictated by the instance variable declaration in the class. You cannot change the type of the instance variable in an object literal. So naturally a1.i, a2.i, a3.i, and a4.i are Integer variables, just as the class definition indicates.

The value of the instance variable may come from three sources: the instance variable initializer in the object literal expression, the default initializer of the instance variable override in the object literal expression, and the default initializer of the instance variable declaration in the class definition. These sources are searched in this order until a value is found. In the case of a1, neither an instance variable initializer nor an instance variable override is found in the object literal expression, so the value of a1.i comes from the instance variable declaration in the class definition, which gives a1.i a value of 1024. For a2, the instance variable initializer in the object literal gives a2.i the value of 2048. For a3, no instance variable initializer exists, but it does have an instance variable override, so a3.i gets its value 3072 from the override. And finally, a4.i gets its value 5120 from the instance variable initializer.

Triggers will be covered in the "Triggers" section later in this appendix. For now, just understand that triggers are blocks of code that can be attached to a variable so that they are executed every time the variable changes its value. The on replace triggers that we use in the preceding example are the simplest triggers. When you override an instance variable in an object literal, the trigger you provide does not replace the trigger in the instance variable declaration in the class definition. Instead, both triggers are added to the instance variable, and both will fire when the instance variable's value changes. Therefore, a1.i and a2.i each have one trigger attached, whereas a3.i and a4.i each have two triggers attached.

■ **Note** Triggers are cumulative with instance variable overrides because one of the uses for triggers is to maintain some invariants on a variable. For example, instance variables that represent the red, green, and blue values of a color may have triggers that keep their values within the legal range. These triggers will remain in effect even if the instance variable is overridden.

In the program presented in Listing A-38, you can see the forces that influence the instance variables at work.

Listing A-38. *Instance Variable Initializations*

```
class A {
  var i: Integer = 1024 on replace {
    println("Trigger in class definition: i = {i}.");
  }
}

var a1 = A {};
var a2 = A { i: 2048 };
var a3 = A {
  override var i = 3072 on replace {
    println("Trigger in object literal override: i = {i}.");
  }
};
var a4 = A {
  override var i = 4096 on replace {
    println("Trigger in object literal override: i = {i}.");
  }
  i: 5120
};

println("a1.i = {a1.i}");
println("a2.i = {a2.i}");
println("a3.i = {a3.i}");
println("a4.i = {a4.i}");
```

When we run the program in Listing A-38, the following output is printed to the console:

```
Trigger in class definition: i = 1024.

Trigger in class definition: i = 2048.

Trigger in class definition: i = 3072.

Trigger in object literal override: i = 3072.
```

```
Trigger in class definition: i = 5120.

Trigger in object literal override: i = 5120.

a1.i = 1024

a2.i = 2048

a3.i = 3072

a4.i = 5120
```

Notice that the triggers are fired because when the initial values of the instance variables took effect, they all changed their values from 0 to the new value.

Declaring Default Instance Variables

You can mark one of the member variables in a class as the default. This makes it possible to initialize it in an object literal without the use of a label, offering a convenient shorthand. To declare a variable as default you use the default keyword as shown here:

```
class A {
  default var i: Integer = 1024;
}
```

You can then instantiate instances of this object by simply including the value in the object literal constructor with no label required:

```
var a = A { 2056 }
```

Each class can only have one default member variable. It is a compiler error to define multiple default variables. Default variables are inherited from superclasses but can be overridden by explicitly marking another variable as default in the subclass.

Instance Functions

Instance function definitions are function definitions that appear inside a class definition. Aside from the top level of a Visage source file, this is the only other place where function definitions may appear. You saw examples of instance functions in the PiggyBank class in Listing A-37.

Instance function definitions have the same form as script function definitions, and two more keywords may be used in instance function bodies: this and super.

A natural question to ask is, "What can instance function bodies see?" The body of an instance function definition has access to four kinds of variables:

- Script variables and constants declared in the same Visage source file

- Instance variables declared in the same class as the instance function

- Function parameters that are passed into the function invocation expression

- Local variables and constants that are defined in the instance function body

The instance function body also has access to other instance functions in the same class, and script functions and other classes in the same source file. This list of accessible entities to instance functions will grow when you learn how to organize your Visage code into multiple files and how to make entities from one file accessible from other files in the "Organizing Visage Code" section later in this appendix.

Listing A-39 illustrates the accessibility of the aforementioned variables.

Listing A-39. *Instance Functions Example*

```
var total: Integer = 0;

function displayTotal() {
  println("The total in all piggy banks is {total} cents now.");
}

class PiggyBank {
  var name: String;
  var pennies: Integer = 0;

  function putInPennies(n: Integer) {
    println("Putting {n} pennies into {name}.");
    pennies += n;
    total += n;
    displayTotal();
  }
}

var myPiggyBank = PiggyBank { name: "My Piggy Bank" };
var yourPiggyBank = PiggyBank { name: "Your Piggy Bank" };

myPiggyBank.putInPennies(15);
yourPiggyBank.putInPennies(22);
myPiggyBank.putInPennies(6);

println("{myPiggyBank.name} has {myPiggyBank.pennies} cents.");
println("{yourPiggyBank.name} has {yourPiggyBank.pennies} cents.");
```

Listing A-39 contains a script variable, total; a script function, displayTotal(); a class, PiggyBank, that has two instance variables, name and pennies; and an instance function, putInPennies(). The instance function putInPennies() uses the script variable total, the instance variable pennies, and the parameter n, and calls the script function displayTotal(). This program allows you to maintain any number of piggy banks, and it knows the total amount in all the piggy banks created in the program.

When we run the program in Listing A-39, the following output is printed to the console:

```
Putting 15 pennies into My Piggy Bank.

The total in all piggy banks is 15 cents now.

Putting 22 pennies into Your Piggy Bank.

The total in all piggy banks is 37 cents now.

Putting 6 pennies into My Piggy Bank.

The total in all piggy banks is 43 cents now.

My Piggy Bank has 21 cents.

Your Piggy Bank has 22 cents.
```

In the last section, you learned that instance variables live only within instances of the class. Because instance functions make use of instance variables, the invocation of instance functions must also be done through instances of the class. In Listing A-39, we invoke the instance function putInPennies() as follows:

```
myPiggyBank.putInPennies(15);
```

In this instance function invocation expression, the myPiggyBank instance of the PiggyBank class supplies the instance variables used in the putInPennies() function. The object through which an instance function is invoked is also called the *target* of the invocation.

■ **Note** You can override instance functions in object literal expressions. Examples of instance function overrides can be found in the "Object Literals" section earlier in this appendix.

The this Expression

The target of an instance function invocation is available to the instance function body as the this *expression*. It is perhaps the simplest Visage expression, consisting of the this keyword only. Its type is the type of the class, and it evaluates to the target of the invocation. The this expression can be used just like any other expression in the instance function body. It can be passed to other functions as parameters, and it can be used as the return value of the instance function. You can also use the this expression to access the instance variables and functions of the target object, although you already have a simpler way of accessing them by using their names directly. The putInPennies() instance function from Listing A-39 can be rewritten as follows:

```
function putInPennies(n: Integer) {
  println("Putting {n} pennies into {this.name}.");
  this.pennies += n;
  total += n;
  displayTotal();
}
```

The target of an instance function invocation is not necessarily of the class where the instance function is defined. An instance function can be invoked on objects of derived classes.

The this expression can also appear in other parts of the class definition, including in instance variable declarations, init blocks, and postinit blocks.

init Blocks

Class definitions can also include init and postinit blocks. An init *block* is introduced by the init keyword, followed by a block. A postinit block is introduced by the postinit keyword, followed by a block. The init and postinit blocks of a class are executed as an object is being created.

Both the init and postinit blocks of a class are executed during the evaluation of object literal expressions. They are guaranteed to execute after all the instance variable initializers are evaluated.

The postinit block is further guaranteed to execute after the instance initializers of the most derived class are evaluated. This feature is useful when designing object hierarchies.

The simple example shown in Listing A-40 illustrates the relative order in which the various parts of an object literal expression are executed. We will also use some nonconventional expressions as instance variable initializers. Most Visage classes do not have to be written this way.

Listing A-40. init Blocks

```
var counter = 0;

class Base {
  var i: Integer;
  init {
    println("Step {counter}: Base init block.  i = {i}.");
    counter++;
  }
  postinit {
    println("Step {counter}: Base postinit block.  i = {i}.");
    counter++;
  }
}

class Derived extends Base {
  var str: String;
  init {
    println("Step {counter}: Derived init block.  i = {i}, str = {str}.");
    counter++;
  }
}
```

563

```
  postinit {
    println("Step {counter}: Derived postinit block.  i = {i}, str = {str}.");
    counter++;
  }
}

var o = Derived {
  i: {
    println("Step {counter}: i initialized to 1024.");
    counter++;
    1024;
  }
  str: {
    println('Step {counter}: str initialized to "Hello, World".');
    counter++;
    "Hello, World";
  }
}
```

The initializers in the object literal expression might look a little bit strange, but rest assured that they are legitimate Visage expressions.

When we run the program in Listing A-40, the following output is printed to the console:

```
Step 0: i initialized to 1024.

Step 1: str initialized to "Hello, World".

Step 2: Base init block.  i = 1024.

Step 3: Derived init block.  i = 1024, str = Hello, World.

Step 4: Base postinit block.  i = 1024.

Step 5: Derived postinit block.  i = 1024, str = Hello, World.
```

Notice that the init and postinit blocks are executed after the instance variable initializers. Notice also that the postinit block of Base is executed after the init block of Derived.

Creating Class Hierarchies

Visage supports object-oriented programming through its class facilities. It supports such concepts as data abstraction, encapsulation, polymorphism, and inheritance. In this section, we teach you how to extend Visage classes and point out the important features of the language such as dynamic dispatch that make object-oriented programming possible.

Mix-in Classes

Visage supports a form of inheritance called *mix-in inheritance*. A Visage class can optionally extend one Visage class and any number of Visage mix-in classes. A *mix-in class* is a class whose primary purpose is to be extended by other classes and cannot be instantiated directly. Such a class is defined by using the mix-in modifier before the class keyword. Like regular classes, mix-in classes may contain instance variable and constant declarations, instance function definitions, init blocks, and postinit blocks. Here is an example:

```
mixin class Locatable {
  var x: Number;
  var y: Number;

  function moveToOrigin() {
    x = 0.0;
    y = 0.0;
  }

  function setLocation(x: Number, y: Number) {
    this.x = x;
    this.y = y;
  }
}
```

The mix-in class Locatable will cause classes that extend it to have instance variables x and y and instance functions moveToOrigin() and setLocation().

Extending Classes

You extend Visage classes by including a superclass and mix-in list in a class definition. The superclass and mix-in list appear after the class name and consist of the extends keyword followed by a comma-separated list of class names. The list may contain an optional regular (non-mix-in) class and any number of mix-in classes. The regular class in the superclass and mix-in list is called a *superclass* of the class. The mix-in classes in the superclass and mix-in list are called *parent mix-ins* of the class. A class is called a *subclass* of its superclass and a *mixee* of its parent mix-ins.

A class inherits its superclass's instance variables, instance constants, and instance functions to which the writer of the superclass has allowed access. The smallest unit of access rights in Visage is the Visage source file. Therefore, if a subclass is in the same file as the superclass, it inherits all of its instance variables, instance constants, and instance functions.

A mixee will inherit its parent mix-in's instance variables, instance constants, and instance functions to which the writer of the parent mix-in has allowed access.

Up to this point in the appendix, we have used single-source-file programs to demonstrate language features. As you might imagine, this approach will soon become inadequate because restricted access rights can only be demonstrated with multifile programs. And most real-world applications consist of more than one file; some may have hundreds of files. We will cover code organization in the "Organizing Visage Code" section, which discusses the details of access modifiers and access control. For the remainder of this section, we will operate under the single-source-file model, where everything is accessible by everything else.

In Listing A-41, class C extends classes A and mix-in class B. It inherits instance variables and instance functions from both A and B.

Listing A-41. *Inheritance*

```
class A {
  var b: Boolean;
  function f() {
    println("A.f() called: b is {b}.");
  }
}

mixin class B {
  var i: Integer;
  function g() {
    println("B.g() called: i is {i}");
  }
}

class C extends A, B {
  var n: Number;
  function h() {
    println("C.h() called: b = {b}, i = {i}, n = {n}.");
  }
}

var c = C { b: true, i: 1024, n: 3.14 };
c.f();
c.g();
c.h();
```

When we run the program in Listing A-41, the following output is printed to the console:

```
A.f() called: b is true.

B.g() called: i is 1024

C.h() called: b = true, i = 1024, n = 3.14.
```

Notice that in the object literal expression we initialize three instance variables, b, i, and n. The resulting object reference is assigned to the variable c, which the code will infer is type C. And we invoke three instance functions, f(), g(), h(), through c. Regarding the code that uses class C, the instance variables and instance functions C inherited from A and B can be used the same way as those defined directly in C.

▧ **Note** A mix-in class itself can extend other mix-in classes, but a mix-in class cannot extend a regular class. If you are familiar with Java programming, the distinction between Visage classes and mix-in classes is analogous to that between Java classes and interfaces.

Overriding Instance Variables

An *instance variable override* is an instance variable declaration that has the same name as an instance variable of one of its direct or indirect superclasses. It must include override as one of its modifiers and can have other access modifiers, as well as a default initializer and/or a trigger. It must not include the type specifier.

The overriding default initializer will be used instead of the superclass default initializer as the initializer for the instance variable if an initializer is not provided in an object literal expression. The overriding trigger will be added to the set of triggers of the instance variable so that both the superclass triggers, and the overriding triggers will fire when the value of the instance variable is changed. Listing A-42 shows a simple example of an instance variable override.

Listing A-42. Instance Variable Override

```
class A {
  var i: Integer = 1024;
}

class B extends A {
  override var i = 2048;
}

var a = A {};
var b = B {};

println("a.i = {a.i}.");
println("b.i = {b.i}.");
```

When we run the program in Listing A-42, the following output is printed to the console:

```
a.i = 1024.

b.i = 2048.
```

Because we do not provide an initializer in the object literal expressions, the instance variable a.i is initialized by the default initializer of i in the class A, which is 1024, and the instance variable b.i is initialized by the default initializer of i in the class B, which is 2048.

Overriding Instance Functions

An *instance function override* is an instance function definition that has the same name, number, and type of variables as an instance function in the superclass or the parent mix-in. It must include override as one of its modifiers and may have other access modifiers. The overriding instance function must have the same return type as the overridden instance function.

When an overridden instance function is invoked through an object of the subclass type, the overriding instance function's body is executed. If the instance function is invoked through an object of the superclass type, the body of the original version of the instance function is executed. Listing A-43 shows an example of an instance function override.

Listing A-43. *Instance Function Override*

```
class A {
  function f(i:Integer):Integer {
    println("A.f() is invoked with parameter i = {i}.");
    i + 3
  }
}

class B extends A {
  override function f(i:Integer):Integer {
    println("B.f() is invoked with parameter i = {i}.");
    i * 5;
  }
}

var a = A {};
var b = B {};
var ra = a.f(4);
var rb = b.f(7);
println("a.f(4) = {ra}.");
println("b.f(7) = {rb}.");
```

When we run the program in Listing A-43, the following output is printed to the console:

```
A.f() is invoked with parameter i = 4.

B.f() is invoked with parameter i = 7.

a.f(4) = 7.

b.f(7) = 35.
```

Because a is an instance of A and not an instance of B, a.f(4) invokes the version of f() defined in class A. Similarly, because b is an instance of B, b.f(7) invokes the version of f() defined in class B.

If you accidentally leave out the override modifier when overriding an instance function, the Visage compiler will issue an error message telling you so.

Notice that when the Visage compiler tries to figure out whether an instance function is an override of a superclass or parent mix-in instance function, it checks the name, the number of the parameters, and the type of each parameter. The names of the parameters are not considered. Having determined that an instance function definition is an override of a superclass instance function, the compiler will further check whether they have the same return type and reports an error if the overriding instance function has a different return type.

The super Keyword

When one class extends another class or mix-in class, you can use the super keyword in the subclass or mixee's instance function bodies, but only as the target of instance function invocations. The super keyword will find a matching instance function from the instance functions of the superclasses or parent mix-ins. Although it can be used for any instance functions of any superclass or parent mix-in, its use is necessary only if the instance function in the superclass or parent mix-in is overridden in the subclass or mixee. Nonoverridden instance functions of the superclass and parent mix-ins may be invoked directly without using the super target.

The technique of invoking an overridden instance function is useful in certain programming tasks. Listing A-44 presents a fun example that illustrates the use of the super keyword.

Listing A-44. *Using the super Keyword*

```
class Hamburger {
  function whatsInIt() {
    "Beef patties"
  }
}

class HamburgerWithCheese extends Hamburger {
  override function whatsInIt() {
    "{super.whatsInIt()} and cheese"
  }
}

var hamburger = Hamburger {};
var cheeseburger = HamburgerWithCheese {};
println("hamburger.whatsInIt() = {hamburger.whatsInIt()}.");
println("cheeseburger.whatsInit() = {cheeseburger.whatsInIt()}.");
```

Simple as this example is, it illustrates one principle of object-oriented programming: information ought to be stored in one place. By calling super.whatsInIt(), the HamburgerWith-Cheese class can avoid its listing of what's in it ever going out of sync with that of Hamburger.

When we run the program in Listing A-44, the following output is printed to the console:

```
hamburger.whatsInIt() = Beef patties.

cheeseburger.whatsInit() = Beef patties and cheese.
```

Using Abstract and Mix-in Classes

One style of object-oriented programming calls for the separation of the interfaces of an object from the implementation details. Under this context, an *interface* of a class consists of the function types of its important instance functions and *implementation details* of a class consists of the bodies of these instance functions.

Visage supports the concept of interfaces through its abstract instance function, abstract class, and mix-in facilities.

An *abstract instance function* in a class or a mix-in class is an instance function definition without a body, prefaced with the keyword abstract. A class that includes an abstract instance function is automatically an abstract class and must be marked by the abstract keyword. A class that does not include any abstract instance functions can also be made abstract by marking it with this keyword. A mix-in class is implicitly abstract. In the following discussion, we focus on abstract classes. However, the principles discussed also apply to mix-in classes.

You cannot create instances of abstract classes with object literal expressions. So how are abstract classes useful? The answer is twofold. Obviously, you have to extend the abstract classes to fill in the missing function bodies by overriding the abstract instance functions. This is sometimes called *implementing the interface.* On the other hand, you can hide the implementation details from the code that uses the class by using only the abstract class. The calling code will not create instances of the implementing classes directly using object literal expressions because that will defeat the purpose of hiding the implementation detail from the calling code. A client will get its instance using some other means.

Listing A-45 illustrates this separation of interface from the implementation detail by using abstract classes.

Listing A-45. *Separating an Interface from Implementation Details with an Abstract Class*

```
// The interface
abstract class Food {
  abstract function getName():String;
  abstract function whatsInIt():String;
}

// The implementation
class Hamburger extends Food {
  override function getName() {
    "Hamburger"
  }
  override function whatsInIt() {
    "beef patties"
  }
}

// A function that gives the calling code an instance of Food
function getTodaysSpecial():Food {
  Hamburger {}
}

// The calling code, no direct mentioning of Hamburger is made here
var food = getTodaysSpecial();
println("Today's special is {food.getName()}.   "
        "It has {food.whatsInIt()} in it.");
```

In practice, one group develops the interface, the implementation, and the function that hands out the instance, and another group develops the calling code. The calling code never directly uses the name of the implementation detail class.

When we run the program in Listing A-45, the following output is printed to the console:

```
Today's special is Hamburger.   It has beef patties in it.
```

Another important detail to learn from Listing A-45 has to do with the type of the variable food. Because it does not have an explicit type, it gets its type from its initializer. In our case, the initializer is a function invocation expression, which would have a type that is the same as its return type. So food is a variable of type Food. However, when the compiler sees the instance function invocation expressions food.getName() and food.whatsInIt(), it does not merely determine that the instance functions are abstract, and therefore, the calls are invalid. It will instead wait until runtime to choose which version of these instance functions to execute based on the type of the value of the variable. When we run the program, the food variable will contain an instance of the Hamburger subclass, and the instance function overrides in that class are executed.

This way of choosing which instance function to execute based on the type of the value at runtime is called *dynamic dispatch*. (You may be familiar with the same concept being referred to as dynamic binding or late binding in other languages. However, because the term *binding* means something quite different in Visage, we will stick to the term *dynamic dispatch* here.)

Conflict Resolution in Mix-in Inheritance

Visage supports a restricted version of multiple inheritance using mix-ins. Mix-in inheritance is designed to support the common use cases of multiple inheritance while reducing the complexity and error-prone nature of full-blown multiple inheritance.

The key to the simplification of mix-in inheritance lies in the way conflicts are resolved when a mixee extends multiple parent mix-ins that have competing public instance variable names. In mix-in inheritance, a parent mix-in will cause the mixee to have the parent mix-in's instance variables, if the mixee does not already have them. This process is applied for all the parent mix-ins in the order that they appear in the superclass and mix-ins list of the mixee. As a consequence, if two parent mix-ins have the same public instance variable with the same type, the mixee gets only one copy of the variable, not two.

This can be illustrated with the following example:

```
mixin class A {
  public var i:Integer;
  function f():Void {
    println("f() called: i = {i}.");
    i++;
  }
}

mixin class B {
  public var i: Integer;
  function f():Void {
    println("shadowed!");
  }
  function g() {
    println("g() called: i = {i}.");
    i++;
  }
}
```

```
class C extends A, B { }

var o = C { i: 1024 }
o.f();
o.g();
o.f();
```

Since both parent mix-in A and parent mix-in B have a public instance variable i of Integer type, the mixee C gains the instance variable i as mix-in inheritance processes A. By the time the parent mix-in B is processed, C already has instance variable i, so parent mix-in B's requirement that its mixee have instance variable i is met, and C does not gain an additional copy of i.

When this program is run, you should see the following result:

```
f() called: i = 1024.

g() called: i = 1025.

f() called: i = 1026.
```

Understanding that all parent mix-ins share the same set of public instance variables makes sense when you think of them as part of the public interface to the class. If you are using variables instead as part of the internal implementation of your class, leave off the public modifier to declare them as script-private. This will change the mix-in behavior to variable shadowing, where each mix-in gets its own unique copy of the variable.

A compilation error results if two parent mix-ins have instance variables of the same name but different types. A compilation error also results if the mixee has, or inherits from its superclass, an instance variable with the same name as an instance variable of a parent mix-in but with different types. Similarly, if an instance function is declared in multiple parent mix-ins, or a parent mix-in and a mixee, or a parent mix-in and a superclass with the same name but with non-override-compatible function types, a compilation error results.

Casting and the instanceof and as Operators

The ability to assign an instance of a subclass or a mixee to a variable of a superclass or a parent mix-in type is a fundamental feature of the Visage language. It is what makes dynamic dispatching possible.

Sometimes, a situation may arise that necessitates your code to test whether a value in a superclass or a parent mix-in type variable is indeed an instance of a subclass or a mixee type. This is done with the instanceof operator. The instanceof *expression* consists of a value expression, the instanceof keyword, and a type name.

Here are some examples:

```
class A {}
class B extends A {}

var a:A;
a = A {}
println(a instanceof B);
```

```
a = B {}
println(a instanceof B);
```

The variable a is of static type A. We first assign an instance of A to it and print out the value of a `instanceof B`, which should be false. We then assign an instance of B to a and print out the value of the same expression, which this time should be true.

Once you have ascertained that a superclass or parent mix-in variable is holding an instance of a subclass or a mixee type, you can *cast* it to the subclass or mixee type. The *cast expression* consists of a value expression, the as keyword, and a type name. You may want to cast an expression to a subclass or a mixee type so that you can assign it to a variable of the subclass or mixee type or use it to access instance variables and instance functions that are defined in the subclass or mixee but not in the superclass or the parent mix-in. The compiler will not allow you to do these things without a cast, because the compiler has no knowledge of the dynamic type of values. Listing A-46 shows some examples of casting.

Listing A-46. *Casting Examples*

```
class A {
  function f() {
    println("A.f() called.");
  }
}

class B extends A {
  function g() {
    println("B.g() called.");
  }
}

var a: A;
a = B {}
a.f();
(a as B).g();
```

We assign an instance of subclass B to the variable a of superclass type A. We can call instance function f() of A directly, but we have to cast a into B to call the instance function g() of B.

If you try to cast a value to a wrong type, a java.lang.ClassCastException will be thrown.

This concludes our coverage of class types. You now know the four kinds of data types in Visage—primitive types, sequence types, function types, and class types—and can implement expressions involving these data types.

Organizing Visage Code

The single-file programs you have been writing and experimenting with so far do not represent an efficient way to develop larger Visage applications. Fortunately, Visage has some code organization features that help you to split your code into multiple files and create a hierarchical structure:

- *Scripts*: A script is a single Visage source file that can be run as a program.
- *Modules:* A module is a single Visage source file whose main purpose is to be used by other Visage source files.

- *Packages*: A Visage source file can be declared to belong to a named package. Packages make it much easier to avoid name conflicts when you use libraries of different origins together.

- *Access modifiers:* Access modifiers can be applied to classes, functions, class members, and so forth to make them visible to the outside world. Some access modifiers also control what can be done to a variable from the outside world.

The concepts examined in this section open up the single Visage file model for access from other Visage files.

Scripts

All the programs that you have seen up to this point are examples of scripts in Visage. A *script* is a Visage source file that can be compiled and then run and may contain class definitions, function definitions, variable and constant declarations, and loose expressions. *Loose expressions* are expressions that appear at the top level of a script.

Scripts are saved in files on a file system. Visage files use the .visage file name extension, which the Visage compiler visagec requires. The file name without the .visage extension will become the script's name. A script is run with the visage command followed by the script name.

Following is a traditional Hello World example, presented as a script named HelloWorld that is saved in the HelloWorld.visage file; as you can see, it contains a comment line and a loose function invocation expression:

```
// HelloWorld.visage
println("Hello, World")
```

We compile and run the script with the following command lines:

```
$ visagec HelloWorld.visage
$ visage HelloWorld
```

Here the $ character represents the operating system command prompt. This prompt may be something different on your operating system. The compilation step will compile the script file into a Java class file, HelloWorld.class.

Of course, the traditional greeting appears when we run the script:

```
Hello, World
```

An alternative way of organizing a script is to define a function named run that takes either no arguments or a sequence of String values as arguments and move all the loose expressions into it. The run() function is the entry point to the script. And if you use a run() function that takes a sequence of Strings as arguments, the arguments sequence will contain any command-line arguments that you specify on the Visage command line after the name of the script. The Visage compiler actually transforms a script with loose expressions into a script with a run() function automatically. As far as the Visage runtime system knows, all scripts are of the neater form containing class definitions, function definitions, and variable and constant definitions, and one of the function definitions just happens to have the name run().

Here is an example script that prints out the command-line arguments, one per line:

```
function run(args: String[]) {
  for (arg in args) {
    println(arg);
  }
}
```

Modules

A *module* is a Visage source file that contains class definitions, function definitions, and variable and constant declarations that are intended for use in other Visage source files.

You make a class, a function, a variable, or a constant usable by other Visage source files by prefacing its definition or declaration with an access modifier. Without an access modifier, such items can be used only by the source file in which they appear. This is called *script-level access*. Two access modifiers are available that widen the scope of these entities. The public modifier enables any Visage source file anywhere to use these entities. This level of access is called *public access*. The package modifier allows any Visage source file that is tagged to be in the same package as the module itself to use the functions, classes, variables, and constants within that module. This is *package-level access*.

A module is said to *export* the entities it contains that have either package-level or public access. The Visage compiler does not allow source files that export their entities to also contain loose expressions. So the only way that a module can also be a script is to have a run() function. And in most cases, your modules will not also be scripts.

A module's name is its file name without the .visage extension. An exported entity from a module is known to the outside world by a *qualified name*, which is the module name followed by a dot (.) and the entity name.

Listing A-47 shows an example of a module, and Listing A-48 presents a script that makes use of the module.

Listing A-47. *A Queue Module*

```
// Queue.visage
public var q:Integer[];

public function enqueue(i:Integer):Void {
  insert i into q;
  println("Enqueued {i}.  Size of q is {sizeof q} now.");
}

public function dequeue():Integer {
  if (sizeof q == 0) {
    println("Size of q is {sizeof q} now. Returning -1.");
    return -1;
  } else {
    var i = q[0];
    delete q[0];
    println("Dequeued {i}.  Size of q is {sizeof q} now.");
    return i;
  }
}
```

Listing A-48. *A Program That Uses the Queue Module*

```
// QueueDemonstration.visage
Queue.enqueue(1);
Queue.enqueue(2);
Queue.enqueue(3);
println(Queue.dequeue());
println(Queue.dequeue());
Queue.enqueue(4);
println(Queue.dequeue());
println(Queue.dequeue());
println(Queue.dequeue());
```

This is the same queue implementation provided in the "Function Body Scope" section earlier in this appendix, in Listing A-28. Here, we simply pull the queue implementation into its own module, export the functions by giving them public access, and modify the demonstration part by qualifying the function calls with the module name. Notice that the variable that holds the content of the queue is kept at the script level of access. This prevents it from being accidentally modified by foreign code.

■ **Tip**   Although you can create modules with unconventional characters in its names, doing so may render the module unusable within Visage programs. We recommend using module names that are valid Visage identifiers.

A Special Provision for Classes

Because of its Java heritage, Visage supports a special arrangement for classes that are defined in Visage source files that also bear the name of the class. This is, by far, the most popular code organization for Java projects.

If a class is defined in a source file bearing its name, the class is referred to using the class name just once, not twice. Other entities defined in the source file, such as other classes, functions, and variables and constants, are still referred to as before. Listings A-49 and A-50 illustrate this.

Listing A-49. *A Class Defined in a File with the Same Name*

```
// Car.visage
public class Car {
  public var make: String;
  public var model: String;
  override function toString() {
    "Car \{make: {make}, model: {model}\}"
  }
}

public function getACar() {
  Car { make: "BMW", model: "Z5" }
}
```

Listing A-50. *A Class Defined in a File with a Different Name*

```
// Parts.visage
public class Wheel {
  public var diameter: Number;
  override function toString() {
    "Wheel \{diameter: {diameter}\}"
  }
}
```

Because the Car class is defined in a file named Car.visage, the outside world can refer to it just by the name Car. The getACar() function in Car.visage is still referred to as Car.getACar(). The Wheel class is not defined in a file with the same name, so Parts is considered to be a regular module, and Wheel must be referred to by the outside world as Parts.Wheel. Listing A-51 shows the different treatment for these classes.

Listing A-51. *Usage of Classes*

```
var car = Car { make: "Ford", model: "Taurus" }
var anotherCar = Car.getACar();
var wheel = Parts.Wheel { diameter: 16 }

println(car);
println(anotherCar);
println(wheel);
```

■ **Caution** Because of the special treatment of classes defined in a file with the same name, some conflicts may result. For example, in such a file, you cannot define a script function that has the same name as an instance function of the class.

Running this program will print out the car and wheel instance variables:

```
Car {make: Ford, model: Taurus}

Car {make: BMW, model: Z5}

Wheel {diameter: 16.0}
```

Packages

Visage's package facility is a mechanism for separating source files into logical name spaces. Source files belonging to the same package are considered to be more closely related than source files in different packages. Access can be granted to source files in the same package with the package modifier.

To tag a source file as belonging to a package, you put a package *directive* at the beginning of the source file. A package directive consists of the package keyword followed by one or more identifiers connected by dots (.) and terminated by a semicolon. The package directive must be the first noncomment, non-whitespace line in the source file. Source files that do not contain a package directive are said to belong to the *unnamed package*. That's the package all of our example code in this appendix belong to so far.

■ **Caution**   The unnamed package is provided as a place to experiment with your code and is not meant to be the permanent home of your code. In Visage, as in Java, code in named packages cannot access code in unnamed packages.

Following the recommendation of the Java platform, if your Visage code will have worldwide exposure, you should use the Internet domain name of your organization in reverse order as the starting portions of package names for your code. For smaller-scale projects, a simpler package name is sufficient.

The package name becomes the leading portion of an entity's fully qualified name.

Listings A-52 and A-53 demonstrate the use of packages.

Listing A-52. Drinks Module in a Food Package

```
// Drinks.visage
package food;

public class Coffee {
  public var brand: String;
}

public class Tea {
  public var kind: String;
}
package var drinksOffered:Integer;

public function getCoffee():Coffee {
  drinksOffered++;
  Coffee { brand: "Folgers" }
}
public function getTea():Tea {
  drinksOffered++;
  Tea { kind: "Iced" }
}
public function numberOfDrinksOffered() {
  drinksOffered
}
```

Listing A-53. Consuming Drinks from the Food Package

```
// ConsumeDrinks.visage
package consumer;

var coffee = food.Drinks.getCoffee();
println("Good coffee.  It's {coffee.brand}.");
var tea = food.Drinks.getTea();
println("Good tea.  It's {tea.kind} tea.");
println("Number of drinks offered = {food.Drinks.numberOfDrinksOffered()}.");
```

In Listing A-53, we invoke public functions getCoffee(), getTea(), and numberOfDrinksOffered() in the Drinks module of the food package through their fully qualified names, shown in bold. The drinksOffered variable in the Drinks module has package-level access and cannot be used from the calling code because it is in a different package.

The recommended way of organizing Visage source files is to use a directory hierarchy that mirrors the package hierarchy. Thus to store the code shown in Listings A-51 and A-52 into source files, we need to create two directories, food and consumer, and put Drinks.visage in the food directory and ConsumeDrinks.visage in the consumer directory. From the directory where we have created the food and consumer directories, we can compile and run the program with the following command line:

```
$ visagec food/Drinks.visage consumer/ConsumerDrinks.visage
$ visage consumer.ConsumeDrinks
```

When we invoke the visagec compiler without an explicit -d command-line argument, it will leave the compiled class files in the same directory where the source file is found. Because we start with a source directory hierarchy that mirrors the package hierarchy, this will leave the class files in the same hierarchy, which is exactly where the Visage runtime expects them. Notice also that when we finally run the program, we have to use the fully qualified module name on the visage command line.

▪ **Caution** The package keyword is used in two contexts in Visage. It is used at the beginning of a source file to tag the file as belonging to a package. It is also used as a modifier on an entity in a module to make it visible to other modules and scripts in the package.

Import Directives

Modules and packages are great ways of organizing Visage code into a structure that's easier to maintain. However, they involve names that are longer and with more parts. Visage's import facility will help you regain the ability to use simple names in your code, even for entities from foreign modules, classes, and packages.

The import *directive* consists of the import keyword, an indication of what is to be imported, and a semicolon. Four variants exist for the import directive:

- A package name followed by .*, which imports all module names of the package

- A package name followed by a dot (.) and a module name, which imports just that one module name from the package

- A package name followed by a dot, a module name, and .*, which imports all the entities defined in that module

- A package name followed by a dot, a module name, a dot, and an entity name, which imports just that entity name from the module

When modules from the same package import each other's names, the package name may be omitted from the import directives.

Listings A-54 through A-57 show the four versions of the program in Listing A-53 we get when we applying the four import variants to it.

Listing A-54. *Importing All Modules in a Package*

```
// ConsumeDrinksImportPackageStar.visage
package consumer;

import food.*;

var coffee = Drinks.getCoffee();
println("Good coffee.  It's {coffee.brand}.");
var tea = Drinks.getTea();
println("Good tea.  It's {tea.kind} tea.");
println("Number of drinks offered = {Drinks.numberOfDrinksOffered()}.");
```

Listing A-55. *Importing One Module in a Package*

```
// ConsumeDrinksImportPackageModule.visage
package consumer;

import food.Drinks;

var coffee = Drinks.getCoffee();
println("Good coffee.  It's {coffee.brand}.");
var tea = Drinks.getTea();
println("Good tea.  It's {tea.kind} tea.");
println("Number of drinks offered = {Drinks.numberOfDrinksOffered()}.");
```

Listing A-56. *Importing All Entities from a Module*

```
// ConsumeDrinksImportModuleStar.visage
package consumer;

import food.Drinks.*;

var coffee = getCoffee();
println("Good coffee.  It's {coffee.brand}.");
var tea = getTea();
println("Good tea.  It's {tea.kind} tea.");
println("Number of drinks offered = {numberOfDrinksOffered()}.");
```

Listing A-57. Importing Specific Entities from a Module

```
// ConsumeDrinksImportModuleEntities.visage
package consumer;

import food.Drinks.getCoffee;
import food.Drinks.getTea;
import food.Drinks.numberOfDrinksOffered;

var coffee = getCoffee();
println("Good coffee.  It's {coffee.brand}.");
var tea = getTea();
println("Good tea.  It's {tea.kind} tea.");
println("Number of drinks offered = {numberOfDrinksOffered()}.");
```

The style of import directive used depends mostly on taste. You should pick a style that makes the development and maintenance of your Visage project easy and hassle free.

▓ **Caution** The Visage compiler actually allows import directives to appear anywhere below the package directive. Because the effect of import directives is for the entire file and not merely the source lines below the directive, there is no good reason to put the import directives anywhere but just below the package directive.

Access Modifiers

This section describes the access modifiers for class-level entities (i.e., instance variable and constant declarations and instance function definitions). The usage scenarios of class-level entities are more complex than script-level entities, so the access modifiers for them are naturally more complex.

You can apply the public and package modifiers to instance variables and instance functions, and they mean the same thing as when they are applied to script-level entities. A public instance variable can be read from or written to from anywhere in the application. A public instance function can be invoked from anywhere in the application. An instance variable with a package modifier can be read from and written to from any code in the same package. An instance function with a package modifier can be invoked from any code in the same package.

Protected Modifiers

You can apply the protected modifier to both instance variables and instance functions. A protected instance variable can be read from and written to by code in the same package or in subclasses or mixees. A protected instance function can be invoked by code in the same package or in subclasses or mixees. The protected level of access implies package level of access.

One subtlety of protected level of access is that a subclass or a mixee that is not in the same package as the superclass or parent mix-in may access a protected instance variable or an instance function in that superclass or parent mix-in only through an object of the subclass type.

Protected instance variables and instance functions are often used to delegate implementation detail decisions to subclasses.

The simple examples in Listings A-58 and A-59 show what is and is not permitted when a subclass accesses a protected instance variable or instance function in the superclass.

Listing A-58. *A Class with a Protected Variable*

```
// a/A.visage
package a;

public class A {
  protected var i: Integer;
  public function getI() {
    i
  }
}
```

Listing A-59. *Accessing a Protected Instance Variable*

```
// b/B.visage
package b;

import a.A;

public class B extends A {
  public function adjustI(adj: Integer) {
    i += adj;   // OK.
  }
  public function adjustI(a: A, adj: Integer) {
    // a.i += adj; // Not allowed
  }
}
```

We define class A in package a with a protected instance variable i. We then define a subclass B of a.A that resides in a different package b. In the first adjustI() instance function in B, we modify a simple variable reference i, which refers to the i in the target of the invocation. This access is allowed because the target of the invocation is the class B. In the second adjustI() instance function in B, we try to modify the instance variable i of an instance a of A that is passed in as a function parameter. Because a is not of the subclass type, access is not allowed.

public-init and public-read Modifiers

You can apply the public-init and public-read modifiers to instance variables. A public-init variable can be initialized in object literal expressions from anywhere in the application. A public-read variable can be read from anywhere in the application.

Listings A-60 and A-61 illustrate public-init and public-read instance variables.

Listing A-60. Instance Variables with public-init and public-read Access

```
// Sandwiches.visage
package food;

public class Club {
  public-init var kind: String;
  public-read var price: Number;
}

public function calculatePrice(club: Club) {
  if (club.kind == "Roast Beef") {
    club.price = 7.99;
  } else if (club.kind == "Chicken") {
    club.price = 6.99;
  }
}
```

Listing A-61. Uses of public-init and public-read Instance Variables

```
package consumer;

import food.Sandwiches.*;

var club = Club { kind: "Roast Beef" };
calculatePrice(club);
println("The price of the {club.kind} club sandwich is {club.price}.");
```

The public-init modifier for the kind instance variable in Club allows us to provide an initializer to the kind instance variable in the object literal expression for Club. The public-read modifier for the price instance variable in Club allows us to read the value of the price variable out of the club object.

When used in conjunction with the package or protected modifiers, the public-init and public-read modifiers open the scope of write access.

Triggers

Triggers are an integral part of the Visage variable and constant declaration expression syntax. The trigger is the optional last part of variable declaration expressions and constant declaration expressions. A trigger is introduced by the on replace keywords, followed by a (possibly empty) *variable modification specification* and a block called the *trigger block*. The variable or constant to which the trigger is attached is called the *observed variable* or *observed constant*.

The trigger block is executed once after every change to the variable or constant being declared. A variable is considered changed when a different value is assigned to it, or, if it is initialized to a bound expression, when its bound expression is reevaluated and the new value is different from the old value. A variable of sequence type is considered changed also when elements are inserted into or deleted from the sequence or when elements of the sequence change. Because it is impossible to assign to constants, only a constant initialized to a bind expression can change, and this occurs when its bind expression is reevaluated.

The variable modification specification provides information to the trigger block. Six forms of variable modification specification exist, and these provide zero, one, two, three, or four pieces of information to the trigger block. Two of the six forms apply to sequence-type and nonsequence-type variables and constants. The other four forms make sense only for sequence-type variables and constants.

Accessing the Old and New Values in Trigger Blocks

The first form is the *empty form*. In this form, the trigger block has access to the variables in the surrounding scope, including the variable or constant itself, as shown in Listing A-62.

Listing A-62. *A Trigger with an Empty Variable Modification Specification*

```
var i = 1024 on replace {
  println("Variable i changed to {i}.");
}
i = 2048;
i = 2048;
```

The trigger in this example will be executed twice: once when the variable i is initialized, which counts as a change from the default value of 0 to the initializer value of 1024, and once when the variable i is assigned the value 2048 for the first time. The second assignment is not considered a change because the new value is the same as the old value. Within the trigger block, the variable i has the newly changed value.

When we run the program in Listing A-62, the following output is printed to the console:

```
Variable i changed to 1024.

Variable i changed to 2048.
```

Visage allows you to further modify the observed variable in a trigger. This is useful when some invariants must be maintained for the observed variable, as shown in Listing A-63.

Listing A-63. *A Trigger That Further Modifies the Observed Variable to Maintain Invariants*

```
// Using a trigger to keep the value of i to be between 0 and 9999.
var i = 1024 on replace {
  println("Variable i changed to {i}.");
  if (i < 0) {
    println("Since {i} < 0, setting i to 0.");
    i = 0;
  } else if (i > 9999) {
    println("Since {i} > 9999, setting i to 9999.");
    i = 9999;
  }
};
```

```
i = -100;
i = 20000;
```

The trigger in this example will be executed five times: when i is initialized to 1024, when i is assigned the value –100, when i is modified to 0 inside the trigger because –100 is less than 0, when i is assigned the value 20000, and when i is modified to 9999 inside the trigger because 20000 is greater than 9999.

When we run the program in Listing A-63, the following output is printed to the console:

```
Variable i changed to 1024.

Variable i changed to -100.

Since -100 < 0, setting i to 0.

Variable i changed to 0.

Variable i changed to 20000.

Since 20000 > 9999, setting i to 9999.

Variable i changed to 9999.
```

▓ **Caution** It is your responsibility to make sure that triggers are not executed in an infinitely recursive fashion. Programs that contain such triggers will cause a `java.lang.StackOverflowError`. The simplest such erroneous program is `var x = 0 on replace { x++; }`. However, with more complicated models and data bindings, the error may not be so obvious.

The second form of variable modification specification in a trigger consists of just a variable name. A variable so named can be accessed from within the trigger block in a read-only fashion, and it would contain the value of the observed variable just prior to the change. Listing A-64 presents an example.

Listing A-64. *Accessing the Old Value from a Trigger*

```
var i = 1024 on replace oldValue {
  println("Variable i changed from {oldValue} to {i}.");
}

i = 2048;
```

When we run the program in Listing A-64, the following output is printed to the console:

```
Variable i changed from 0 to 1024.

Variable i changed from 1024 to 2048.
```

The meaning of the variable name in this form of variable modification specification is not apparent from the syntax alone, so we recommend you use a name that reminds you of its role of providing the old value of the observed variable to the trigger block, such as oldValue, as we have done in the example.

For nonsequence type variables, the old values and the new values of the variables are all we are interested in, and the first two forms of the variable modification specification suffice for all their triggers.

Accessing Sequence Modification Information in Trigger Blocks

For sequence type variables, the modification scenarios are more complicated, and the other four forms of the modification specification are designed to provide the relevant information to their trigger blocks.

The third form of variable modification specification consists of a variable name, a pair of brackets ([]) enclosing a pair of variable names separated by two dots (..), an equal sign (=), and another variable name. The four variable names so designated can be accessed from within the trigger block in a read-only fashion. The first variable, the one before the brackets, contains the old value of the observed variable. The two variables between the brackets contain the low index and the high index of the portion of the sequence that has changed. The last variable, the one after the equal sign, is a sequence that contains any newly inserted elements to the observed variable. See Listing A-65 for an example.

Listing A-65. *A Trigger for a Sequence Variable with Access to the Complete Set of Modification Information*

```
println("Initializing seq...");
var seq = [1, 3, 5, 7, 9] on replace oldValue[lo..hi] = newSlice {
  print("  Variable seq changed from ");
  print(oldValue);
  print(" to ");
  println(seq);
  println("  The change occurred at low indexe {lo} and high index {hi}.");
  print("  The new slice is ");
  println(newSlice);
}

println('Executing "insert [2, 4, 6] before seq[3]"...');
insert [2, 4, 6] before seq[3];

println('Executing "delete seq [1..2]"...');
delete seq [1..2];

println('Executing "seq[4..5] = [8, 10]"...');
seq[4..5] = [8, 10];
```

This form of the variable modification specification is designed to resemble an assignment to a slice of a sequence to remind you of the meaning of the four variable names inside the trigger block. However, because the meaning of these variable names is still not apparent, we recommend that you use descriptive names such as the ones we used in the example: oldValue, lo, hi, and newSlice.

In Listing A-65, we attach a trigger with the third form of variable modification specification to a sequence of Integer variable seq. The trigger will be executed four times: when the variable is initialized, when a sequence is inserted, when a slice is deleted, and when a slice is replaced with another slice.

When we run the program in Listing A-65, the following output is printed to the console:

```
Initializing seq...

  Variable seq changed from [ ] to [ 1, 3, 5, 7, 9 ]

  The change occurred at low indexe 0 and high index -1.

  The new slice is [ 1, 3, 5, 7, 9 ]

Executing "insert [2, 4, 6] before seq[3]"...

  Variable seq changed from [ 1, 3, 5, 7, 9 ] to [ 1, 3, 5, 2, 4, 6, 7, 9 ]

  The change occurred at low indexe 3 and high index 2.

  The new slice is [ 2, 4, 6 ]

Executing "delete seq [1..2]"...

  Variable seq changed from [ 1, 3, 5, 2, 4, 6, 7, 9 ] to [ 1, 2, 4, 6, 7, 9 ]

  The change occurred at low indexe 1 and high index 2.

  The new slice is [ ]

Executing "seq[4..5] = [8, 10]"...

  Variable seq changed from [ 1, 2, 4, 6, 7, 9 ] to [ 1, 2, 4, 6, 8, 10 ]

  The change occurred at low indexe 4 and high index 5.

  The new slice is [ 8, 10 ]
```

This output should pretty much match your intuitive ideas of what the four variables should contain under each of the triggering conditions. The only thing that we would like to point out is that the values of the high index are one less than the values of the low index under insertions.

The remaining forms of the variable modification specification are shortened versions of the third form, which is also known as the *full form*.

The fourth form omits the old value portion from the third form, offering only the low and high indexes and the new slice, as is shown in the following example:

```
var seq = [1, 3, 5, 7, 9] on replace [lo..hi] = newSlice {
  // ...
}
```

The fifth form omits the low and high indexes portion from the third form, offering only the old value and the new slice, as is shown in the following example:

```
var seq = [1, 3, 5, 7, 9] on replace oldValue = newSlice {
  // ...
}
```

The sixth form omits the old value and the low and high indexes portion from the third form, offering only the new slice, as is shown in the following example:

```
var seq = [1, 3, 5, 7, 9] on replace = newSlice {
  // ...
}
```

By far, the most popular forms of variable modification specifications are the empty form and the full form.

Debugging with Triggers

Aside from their uses in production code, triggers are surprisingly useful tools for tracing the values of variables throughout the life of a program. Although the Visage debugger in the NetBeans plug-in is quite powerful, in certain situations, you need a little bit of println debugging to help you understand the behavior of your Visage program.

When used in conjunction with data binding, you don't even have to attach triggers to the module variables or instance variables that you want to monitor. You can simply declare a variable that binds to the module variable or instance variable you want to monitor and attach a trigger to your variable. Listing A-66 presents a simple example of this.

Listing A-66. Using Triggers to Monitor States of Another Object

```
class Gcd {
  var a: Integer;
  var b: Integer;
  function gcd(): Integer {
    if (b == 0) {
      return a;
    } else {
      var tmp = a mod b;
      a = b;
      b = tmp;
      return gcd();
    }
  }
}
```

```
var o = Gcd { a: 165, b: 105 };

var x = bind o.b on replace {
  println("Iterating: o.a={o.a}, o.b = {x}.");
}

var result = o.gcd();
println("The gcd of 106 and 105 is {result}.");
```

The class Gcd uses the Euclidean algorithm to calculate the greatest common divisor of its two instance variables, a and b. We are able to hook into the internal states of instance o of class Gcd without making any changes to the class itself. All we have to do is to declare a variable, x, that binds to o.b so that whenever o.b changes x is updated accordingly. Then, we attach a trigger to x that prints out the value of o.a, which we know is updated before o.b is updated, and prints out the value of x, which we know reflects the value of o.b.

When we run the program in Listing A-66, the following output is printed to the console:

```
Iterating: o.a=165, o.b = 105.

Iterating: o.a=105, o.b = 60.

Iterating: o.a=60, o.b = 45.

Iterating: o.a=45, o.b = 15.

Iterating: o.a=15, o.b = 0.

The gcd of 106 and 105 is 15.
```

String Formatting and Internationalization

This section examines two more features of strings: the fine-grained formatting of numerical, date/time, and other types of values using format specifiers and the internationalization and localization of Visage applications.

Using String Format Specifications

Visage supports another, more versatile, form of string expression in which each brace-delimited segment may contain a string format specification and a Visage expression. Listing A-67 shows some examples of this form of string expression.

Listing A-67. *Format Specifiers in String Expressions*

```
var b = true;
var i = 1024;
var n = 3.14;
var str = "Hello, World";

println("Display b in a 15 character field    [{%15b b}].");
println("Display i in a 15 character field    [{%15d i}].");
println("Display n in a 15 character field    [{%15f n}].");
println("Display str in a 15 character field [{%15s str}].");
```

A *string format specification* starts with a percent character (%), followed by an optional set of *flags*, an optional *field-width specifier*, an optional *precision specifier*, and a mandatory *conversion character*. The conversion character determines how the accompanying Visage expression is to be formatted into a resulting string. The optional flags, field-width specifier, and precision specifier control some detailed aspects of the conversion.

In Listing A-67, we use four string format specifications, %15b, %15d, %15f, and %15s, with conversion characters b (Boolean), d (integer), f (floating), and s (string). They all have a field width of 15. We surrounded the braces with brackets to illustrate the field into which the expressions are rendered.

When we run the program in Listing A-67, the following output is printed to the console:

```
Display b in a 15 character field    [           true].

Display i in a 15 character field    [           1024].

Display n in a 15 character field    [       3.140000].

Display str in a 15 character field [    Hello, World].
```

Visage relies on the Java class `java.util.Formatter` to perform the conversions. This class draws its inspirations from the C programming language `printf()` format specifications. Table A-1 summarizes some of the most useful conversion characters and their flags. Note that the double-character conversion specifications, starting from tH in the table, convert `java.util.Date` values.

Table A-1. *Visage String Format Specifications*

Conversion Character	Effect
s	Format as string. Its use is necessary only with nontrivial flags and field-width and precision specifiers. The - flag causes the string to be flush left in the field. The precision specifier limits the number of characters in the output.
d	Format as decimal integer. The - flag causes the number to be flush left in the field. The + flag causes the sign to be included. The 0 flag causes the number to be zero padded. The , (comma) flag causes locale-specific grouping separators to be included. The ((open parenthesis) flag causes negative numbers to be surrounded with parentheses.

Conversion Character	Effect
o	Format as octal integer. The - and 0 flags work the same way as with decimal integers.
x, X	Format as hexadecimal integer. The - and 0 flags work the same way as with decimal integers.
f	Format as floating-point number. The -, +, 0, ,, and (flags work the same way as with decimal integers.
e, E	Format as scientific notation. The -, +, 0, and (flags work the same way as with decimal integers.
g, G	Format as either floating-point number or scientific notation depending on the value of the expression. The -, +, 0, and (flags work the same way as with decimal numbers.
tH	Format a java.util.Date value to hour of the day (24-hour clock). Valid values: 00–23.
tI	Format as hour (12-hour clock). Valid values: 01–12.
tk	Format as hour (24-hour clock). Valid values: 0–23.
tl	Format as hour (12-hour clock). Valid values: 1–12.
tM	Format as minutes. Valid values: 00–59.
tS	Format as seconds. Valid values: 00–59.
tL	Format as milliseconds within seconds. Valid values: 000–999.
tN	Format as nanoseconds within seconds. Valid values: 000000000– 999999999.
tp, Tp	Format as am, AM or pm, PM.
tz	Format as time zone offset from GMT (e.g., –0600).
tZ	Format as time zone abbreviation (e.g., CST).
tB	Format as full month name (e.g., March).
tb	Format as abbreviated month name (e.g., Mar).
tA	Format as full day of the week (e.g., Monday).

Continued

Conversion Character	Effect
ta	Format as abbreviated day of the week, (e.g., Mon).
tC	Format as century number. Valid values: 00–99.
tY	Format as four-digit year (e.g., 2009).
ty	Format as two-digit year (e.g., 09).
tj	Format as day of the year. Valid values: 001–366.
tm	Format as month. Valid values: 01–12.
td	Format as day of the month. Valid values: 01–31.
te	Format as day of the month. Valid values: 1–31.
tR	Format as HH:MM time (24-hour clock, e.g., 20:42).
tT	Format as HH:MM:SS time (24-hour clock, e.g., 20:42:51).
tr	Format as HH:MM:SS AM/PM time (12-hour clock, e.g., 08:42:51 PM).
td	Format as mm/dd/yy date (e.g., 03/02/09).
tF	Format as yyyy-mm-dd date (e.g., 2009-03-02).
tc	Format as full date/time (e.g., Mon Mar 02 20:42:51 CST 2009).

The string and number conversions are similar but not identical to the conversions found in C programming language. The date/time conversions can be somewhat overwhelming because of the many components making up a date/time value. However, the last six composite conversions should cover many use cases. Some of the conversions, for example, the character used as the decimal point and the month and weekday names, are locale-sensitive.

Internationalizing Visage Programs

Internationalization is the process of extracting user-visible strings out of a program written in one language or culture to be translated into other languages and cultures. *Localization* is the process of translating an internationalized program into one or several specific languages or cultures.

Visage provides an internationalization and localization mechanism that is easy to use. To internationalize a program, you go through the string literals and string expressions of the program and prepend a double hash mark (##) before the ones that you wish to be translated. The double hash mark may optionally be followed by a pair of brackets ([]) that encloses a *key* to the string literal or string expression.

Listing A-68 shows a simple Visage program that contains several string literals and string expressions that are marked for translation.

Listing A-68. *A Visage Program with Strings Marked for Translations*

```
var name = "Weiqi";
var i = 1024;
var j = 9765625.0;
println(##[greeting]"Hello, {name}.");
println(##[trivia]"Do you know that "
  "{i} * {j} = {%,.1f i * j}?");
println(##"1024 is the 10th power of 2, "
  "and 9765625 is the 10th power of 5.");
```

The program in Listing A-68 contains two string expressions and a string literal that are marked for internationalization. The first string expression is given the key greeting. The second string expression is given the key trivia. The string literal is not given a key. If a string literal is marked for internationalization without a key, Visage will take the entire string literal as the key. Notice also that adjacent string literals and string expressions merged into one string literal or string expression are treated as one for the purposes of internationalization. Therefore, you need to put a double hash mark in front of only the first component.

If a string expression is marked for internationalization without a key, Visage will use a transformed version of the string expression as the key. This transformation replaces each embedded, brace-enclosed expression with its string format specification augmented with its position in the string. An embedded expression that does not have a string format specification is considered to have an implicit %s specification. The position numbers, which start with 1, are inserted after the % character and separated from the rest of the string format specification with an inserted $ character.

These transformed versions of the strings are also candidates for translation. For the program in Listing A-68, the strings to translate are as follows:

```
Hello, %1$s.
Do you know that %1$s * %2$s = %3$,.1f?
1024 is the 10th power of 2, and 9765625 is the 10th power of 5.
```

To localize a program for a particular language or a language and culture combination, you create a set of translation files, one for each Visage source file that contains strings marked for translation. The translation files must have the .visageproperties file name extension. The names of these files are derived from the Visage source file names by appending a language suffix or a language and culture suffix.

Listing A-69 shows a translation file in Simplified Chinese for the program in Listing A-68.

Listing A-69. *Translation File for GreetingTrivia.visage*

```
// GreetingTrivia_zh_CN.visageproperties
"greeting" = "%1$s你好."

"trivia" = "你知道%1$s*%2$s=%3$,.1f吗?"

"1024 is the 10th power of 2, and 9765625 is the 10th power of 5." =
"1024是2的10次方, 9765625是5的10次方."
```

When we run the program in Listing A-68 in a non-Chinese locale, the following output is printed to the console:

```
Hello, Weiqi

Do you know that 1024 * 9765625.0 = 10,000,000,000.0?

1024 is the 10th power of 2, and 9765625 is the 10th power of 5.
```

When we run this program in a Simplified Chinese locale or with command-line options that set the user.language property to zh (Chinese) and user.country to CN (China), as in the following command line (the .visageproperties file is saved in UTF-8, so we also need to set the file.encoding property to utf-8):

```
visage -Dfile.encoding=utf-8 -Duser.language=zh -Duser.country=CN GreetingTrivia
```

we get this output:

```
Weiqi你好.
你知道1024*9765625.0=10,000,000,000.0吗?
1024是2的10次方,9765625是5的10次方.
```

The translation files must be in the class path when the program is run. If the Visage source file belongs to a package, the translation files must also be in a directory structure that reflects the package.

There is far more to internationalization and localization than merely having strings translated, but Visage's translation mechanism gets you started very quickly.

Leveraging Java from Visage

Visage is built on top of the Java platform, so it can leverage the vast number of available Java libraries. In the following sections, we show you how to take advantage of Java libraries in Visage.

Instantiating Java Classes

Concrete Java classes can be instantiated in Visage using *new expressions*. A new expression is introduced by the new keyword, followed by a Java class name and a pair of parentheses that encloses a comma-separated list of zero or more expressions. The Java class must have a constructor with the same number of parameters, and each expression in the expression list must be convertible to the corresponding type of the Java constructor. Here are some examples of instantiating Java objects:

```
var now = new java.util.Date();
var fw = new java.io.FileWriter("output.txt");
```

The Visage string that we pass to the FileWriter constructor will be converted to a Java string when the Java constructor is called.

▓ **Note** The Visage syntax allows you to use an object literal expression to create objects of Java reference types that have a default constructor (i.e., a constructor that takes no arguments). Thus you can also use `var now = java.util.Date {};` to create a new `java.lang.Date` object. Similarly, the new expression without any arguments allows you to create objects of Visage class types with the same effect as an object literal expression without any initializers. As a best practice, we recommend using new expressions for creating Java objects and using object literal expressions for creating Visage objects.

Accessing Java Object Fields

Accessing fields of a Java object is achieved using the same member access expression (the dot notation) for accessing instance variables of Visage objects. Exposing public fields is not a common practice in Java API design, so this feature is not used as often as some of the other features.

Calling Java Methods

Once you create a Java object, you can call its methods using function invocation expressions. The parameters are converted from Visage types to Java types on the invocation, and the return values, if any, are converted back to Visage types.

Visage Boolean and numerical primitive types are converted to the corresponding Java primitive types. The Visage `String` type is converted to `java.lang.String`. The Visage `Duration` type is converted to `visage.lang.Duration`. Visage class types are not converted but are checked for the ability to be assigned to Java class types. Visage sequence types are converted to Java arrays.

In the following example, we create a `java.util.HashMap` instance and insert several key value pairs into it:

```
var map = new java.util.HashMap();
map.put("b", true);
map.put("i", 1024);
map.put("n", 3.14159);
map.put("str", "Hello, World");
```

While support for a built-in `Map` construct is on the roadmap for Visage, until it is added the `java.util.HashMap` is a very handy class to have at your disposal.

▓ **Note** Visage does not yet support Java generics. Therefore, when you use a Java generic class or method, you have to use it in the raw type form.

Accessing Static Fields and Methods

Static fields in a Java class are shared across all instances of the Java class. Static methods in a Java class do not receive an implicit `this` parameter when invoked. Visage does not support static variables and static functions in its classes. However, static fields and static methods in Java are very similar to Visage's script variables and script functions in a module. You can use the same syntax for accessing script-level entities in a module to access static members of a Java class.

In the following example, we access some static members of the `java.lang.Math` class:

```
var pi = java.lang.Math.PI;
var x = java.lang.Math.sin(pi/6);
```

After the calculation, the variable x has value `sin(pi/6)`, which is 0.5.

You can also use the following import directive to access all static members of a Java class:

```
import java.lang.Math.*;
var pi = PI;
var x = sin(pi/6);
```

This Visage import directive has the same power as Java's static import directive.

Quoting Visage Keywords

Visage does not come with its own input/output facilities aside from the `println()` function that you have seen in our examples. Therefore, it is natural to use Java's input/output facilities. For example, instead of printing something to the console, you might want to read some user input from the console. The `java.lang.System` class contains a static field called in that represents the standard input.

However, if you try to compile the following line of code

```
java.lang.System.in.read();
```

you will get a compilation error because in is a Visage keyword. Visage allows you to *quote* such keywords by surrounding them with <<and >>. Thus the preceding line of code could be rewritten as

```
java.lang.System.<<in>>.read();
```

Other Visage keywords that are often quoted include insert, delete, and reverse, which are legitimate method names in Java.

Accessing Nested Classes

In Java, a class may contain other classes as members. A *static nested class* is a class that is declared inside another class with a static modifier. Static nested classes can be accessed from Visage using the same strategy for accessing static fields and static methods. Here is an example of how to access a Java class with a static nested class from Visage:

```
// Outer.java
package food;

public class Outer {
  public static class Nested {
  }
}
// Main.visage
import food.Outer.*;
var o = new Nested();
```

An *inner class* is a class that is declared inside another class without the static modifier. Instances of inner classes must have access to an instance of the containing class. Visage does not provide a way to directly create an inner class. For the odd case where you need to directly create an instance of an inner class from a parent class reference, you can write the code in Java and call it from Visage.

Accessing Java Enums

Java enums can be accessed from Visage the same way as in Java. Here is an example:

```
// Suit.java public enum Suit {
  CLUBS, DIAMONDS, HEARTS, SPADES
}

// Main.visage
var a = Suit.CLUBS;
var c = Suit.DIAMONDS;
var b = Suit.HEARTS;
var d = Suit.SPADES;
```

You can also access methods that you define in Java enums.

Extending Java Classes and Interfaces

A Visage class can extend Java classes and interfaces. Visage does not have an implements keyword, as Java does. And the extends keyword is used for both Java classes and interfaces. As far as extending Java classes and interfaces is concerned, Visage counts Java classes (including abstract classes) as regular classes and Java interfaces as mix-in classes. Therefore, the rule for Visage inheritance, which you learned in the "Extending Classes" section earlier in this appendix, can be restated as follows: Visage classes can extend zero or one Java or Visage class, any number of Java interfaces, and any number of Visage mix-in classes.

In Listing A-70, we define a Java interface, Sum, with two methods: addInts, which takes two ints and returns an int; and addDoubles, which takes two doubles and returns a double. We implement addInts and addDoubles in the Visage class VisageSum, which extends Sum. The SumClient Java class holds an instance of Sum and contains methods that exercise Sum's methods.

Listing A-70. *Extending Java Classes*

```
// Sum.java
public interface Sum {
  int addInts(int a, int b);
  double addDoubles(double x, double y);
}
```

```
// VisageSum.visage
public class VisageSum extends Sum {
  public override function addInts(a:Integer, b:Integer):Integer {
    a + b
  }
  public override function addDoubles(x:Double, y:Double):Double {
    x + y
  }
}
```

```
// SumClient.java
public class SumClient {
  private Sum sum;
  public SumClient(Sum sum) {
    this.sum = sum;
  }
  public int addUpInts(int[] ints) {
    int result = 0;
    for (int i = 0; i < ints.length; i++) {
      result = sum.addInts(result, ints[i]);
    }
    return result;
  }
  public double addUpDoubles(double[] doubles) {
    double result = 0.0;
    for (int i = 0; i < doubles.length; i++) {
      result = sum.addDoubles(result, doubles[i]);
    }
    return result;
  }
}
```

```
// ExercisingSum.visage
var visageSum = VisageSum {};
var sumClient = new SumClient(visageSum);
var sumOfInts = sumClient.addUpInts([1, 3, 5, 7, 9]);
var sumOfDoubles = sumClient.addUpDoubles([3.14159, 2.71828]);
println("sumOfInts={sumOfInts}.");
println("sumOfDoubles={sumOfDoubles}.");
```

When we run the program in Listing A-70, the following output is printed to the console:

```
sumOfInts=25.
```

```
sumOfDoubles=5.859870195388794.
```

Even though Java classes can be extended by Visage classes, some differences between Java classes and Visage classes remain. One important difference is between Java fields and Visage instance variables. Some of the most powerful things that you can do with Visage instance variables, such as using them on the right-hand side of bind expressions or attaching a trigger using an instance variable override, cannot be done to fields in Java objects because Java lacks the facilities to track the changes made to fields.

Dealing with Java Arrays

Visage supports a native array type that allows it to efficiently handle Java APIs that either require a Java array parameter or return a Java array.

A *native array type* is declared as the keywords nativearray of followed by a Java class type or a Visage class type or primitive type. To illustrate its usage, we use the java.lang.Package.getPackages() API. This method returns an array of java.lang.Package objects that represent all the Java packages that are already loaded into the JVM.

```
import java.lang.Package; import java.lang.Package.*;

var b = getPackages();
for (i in [0..b.length - 1]) {
  println(b[i]);
}
```

The getPackages() call is a static method call on the java.lang.Package class. It returns a Java array of type Package[]. To avoid the conversion to a Visage sequence, it will use nativearray of Package to represent this return type. Since the return value is used as an initializer for the variable b, the type of variable b is also nativearray of Package. Just like with Java arrays, you can access its length field, and you can access the array elements using bracket notation: b[i].

It is possible to declare native array types for multidimensional Java arrays. For example, the Java type int[][] corresponds to the Visage native array type nativearray of nativearray of Integer.

Iterating Through Java Collections

Objects of Java classes that implement the java.lang.Iterable interface can be iterated over using the Visage for expression. Because the Java collection interfaces java.util.List, java.util.Set, and java.util.Queue all implement java.lang.Iterable, objects of any concrete Java collection classes that implement these interfaces (e.g., java.util.ArrayList, java. util.HashSet, and java.util.ArrayDeque) can be iterated over using for expressions, as demonstrated in Listing A-71.

Listing A-71. *Iterating Through Java Collections*

```
import java.util.*;

var list = new java.util.ArrayList();
list.add("One");
list.add("Two");
list.add("Three");

for (elem in list) {
  println("index: {indexof elem}, element: {elem}.");
}
```

When we run the program in Listing A-71, the following output is printed to the console:

```
index: 0, element: One.

index: 1, element: Two.

index: 2, element: Three.
```

Visage Reflection

Visage includes a reflection API that allows you to perform certain metaprogramming tasks. *Metaprogramming* is the act of manipulating a programming facility using a language rather than using the programming facility itself.

The Visage provides its reflection API as a set of Java classes in the Visage runtime library. The fact that the Visage reflection API is written in Java rather than in Visage means that you can use it in either Visage code or Java code. We will show you its usage mostly in Visage.

Because the reflection API is written in Java, we will use Java's terminology to describe its parts. Therefore, in the upcoming text we will talk about fields and methods instead of instance functions and instance variables.

Mirror-Based Reflection

Visage's reflection facility follows a design principle called *mirrors*, which seek to separate conventional programming facilities from metaprogramming facilities and at the same time achieve symmetry between the conventional and metaprogramming facilities.

■ **Note** The Java reflection facility does not follow the mirrors principle. This is mostly manifested through code like `employee.getClass()`, where `employee` is an object of an `Employee` class. Although methods like `getEmployeeId()` or `getName()` have a legitimate place in an `Employee` class, one can argue that `getClass()` does not.

The interfaces and abstract classes in the `visage.reflect` package presented in Table A-2 provide the fundamental abstractions of the reflection facilities of the Visage programming language.

Table A-2. Interfaces and Abstract Classes of the Visage Reflection API

Name	Visage Concept
VisageType	A Visage type
VisageValue	A Visage value
VisageMember	A member of a class or a module
VisageLocation	The location of a variable, used in data binding
VisageContext	A reflection context, the entryway into reflection

Concrete subclasses of the VisageType abstract class include VisagePrimitiveType, VisageSequenceType, VisageFunctionType, VisageClassType, and VisageJavaArrayType. This reflects the four kinds of Visage types plus the native array types that we covered earlier.

Implementations of the VisageValue interface include VisagePrimitiveValue, VisageSequenceValue, VisageFunctionValue, and VisageObjectValue. VisagePrimitiveValue has additional subclasses: VisageBooleanValue, VisageIntegerValue, VisageLongValue, VisageFloatValue, and VisageDoubleValue.

Implementations of the VisageMember interface include VisageFunctionMember and VisageVarMember. They reflect instance functions and instance variables as well as script functions and script variables. Script functions and script variables are considered members of the script or module to which they belong.

Concrete subclasses of the VisageLocation abstract class include VisageVarMemberLocation.

Entering the Reflection World

By design, the Visage reflection API can support reflections in a local Java virtual machine as well as remote Java virtual machines. Visage ships with a concrete implementation for local Java virtual machine reflections called VisageLocal. Its getContext() method returns a VisageLocal.Context object, which is an implementation of VisageContext.

The VisageLocal.Context class has a family of overloaded mirrorOf() methods that bridges the conventional programming and metaprogramming world. To get a VisagePrimitiveValue or VisageObjectValue value from a primitive value or an object, you use a version of mirrorOf() that takes one parameter. To get a VisageSequenceValue or VisageFunctionValue value from a sequence or a function, you use a version of mirrorOf() that takes two parameters, the second parameter being the type of the sequence or the function.

The VisageValue objects are where further reflection tasks are performed. Its getType() method returns an appropriate VisageType subclass. Its asObject() method returns the original Visage value.

Listing A-72 shows an example of obtaining and examining the mirror reflections of the four kinds of Visage values.

Listing A-72. *Examining the Mirrors of Conventional Visage Types*

```
import java.lang.Math.*;
import visage.reflect.*;

public class Point {
  public var x: Number;
  public var y: Number;

  public function dist() {
    sqrt(x * x + y * y);
  }

  public override function toString() {
    "Point \{ x: {x}, y: {y} \}"
  }
}

public function run() {
  var i = 1024;
  var o = Point { x: 3, y: 4 };
  var seq = [3.14159, 2.71828];
  var func = o.dist;

  var context: VisageLocal.Context = VisageLocal.getContext();

  println("Examining...");
  var mirrorOfI = context.mirrorOf(i);
  print("  original: "); println({i});
  print("  mirror: "); println(mirrorOfI);
  print("  type: "); println({mirrorOfI.getType()});
  print("  back from mirror: "); println({mirrorOfI.asObject()});

  println("Examining...");
  var mirrorOfO = context.mirrorOf(o);
  print("  original: "); println({o});
  print("  mirror: "); println(mirrorOfO);
  print("  type: "); println({mirrorOfO.getType()});
  print("  back from mirror: "); println({mirrorOfO.asObject()});

  println("Exemining...");
  var seqType = context.getNumberType().getSequenceType();
  var mirrorOfSeq = context.mirrorOf(seq, seqType);
  print("  original: "); println({seq});
  print("  mirror: "); println(mirrorOfSeq);
  print("  type: "); println({mirrorOfSeq.getType()});
  print("  back from mirror: "); println({mirrorOfSeq.asObject()});
```

```
    println("Exemining...");
    var classType = context.findClass("MirrorsOfValues.Point");
    var funcMember = classType.getFunction("dist");
    var funcType = funcMember.getType();
    var mirrorOfFunc = context.mirrorOf(func, funcType);
    print("  original: "); println({func});
    print("  mirror: "); println(mirrorOfFunc);
    print("  type: "); println({mirrorOfFunc.getType()});
    print("  back from mirror: "); println({mirrorOfFunc.asObject()});
}
```

Notice that, to obtain the mirrors of the sequence and function values, we have to construct their types beforehand and pass them into the mirrorOf() method as the second parameter. To obtain the type of a Number sequence, we call getNumberType() on context and then getSequenceType() on the result. The VisageLocal.Context class has methods that return the VisagePrimitiveType object of every primitive type. To obtain the function type, we call findClass() on context to get the VisageClassType, getFunction() on classType to get the VisageFunctionMember, and finally getType() on funcMember to get the VisageFunctionType.

When we run the program in Listing A-72, the following output is printed to the console:

```
Examining...

  original: 1024

  mirror: IntegerValue(1024)

  type: Integer

  back from mirror: 1024

Examining...

  original: Point { x: 3.0, y: 4.0 }

  mirror: visage.reflect.VisageLocal$ObjectValue@37a786c3

  type: class MirrorsOfValues.Point

  back from mirror: Point { x: 3.0, y: 4.0 }

Exemining...

  original: [ 3.14159, 2.71828 ]

  mirror: visage.reflect.VisageLocal$SequenceValue@b32e13d
```

```
  type: Float[]

  back from mirror: [ 3.14159, 2.71828 ]

Exemining...

  original: MirrorsOfValues$1Local$1.function<0>

  mirror: visage.reflect.VisageLocal$FunctionValue@182d9c06

  type: function():Double

  back from mirror: MirrorsOfValues$1Local$1.function<0>
```

Notice that the type of the Number sequence is reported as Float[], which is the backing class of the Visage Number type.

Programming Through Reflection

In this section, we show you a series of small code snippets that can be used to perform some common programming tasks using reflection. Reflection code is always considerably longer than nonreflection code. However, its length depends on the classes and functions being programmed.

The idiomatic way of creating a new instance of a Visage class is as follows:

```
// CreatingInstance.visage
import visage.reflect.*;

public class Point {
  public var x: Number;
  public var y: Number;
  public override function toString() {
    "Point \{ x: {x}, y: {y} \}"
  }
}

public function run() {
  var context = VisageLocal.getContext();
  var classType = context.findClass("CreatingInstance.Point");
  var classValue = classType.allocate();
  classValue.initVar("x", context.mirrorOf(3.0));
  classValue.initVar("y", context.mirrorOf(4.0));
  classValue.initialize();
  var p = (classValue as VisageLocal.ObjectValue).asObject();
  println(p);
}
```

Here, classType is of type VisageLocal.ClassType, a subclass of VisageClassType, and objectValue is of type VisageLocal.ObjectValue, a subclass of VisageObjectValue. The allocate() call allocates the memory for an instance of the class. The initVar() call supplies the initial values of instance variables of the object. Another version of initVar() takes an VisageVarMember object as the first parameter instead of a string. The initialize() call performs the actual setting of the instance variables to their initial values and the running of the init and postinit blocks that the class may have.

Getting and Setting Values of Instance and Script Variables

The following code works with instance variables of Visage classes and script variables of Visage modules:

```
// GettingSettingVariables.visage
import visage.reflect.*;

public class Point {
  public var x: Number;
  public var y: Number;
}

public var a:String;

public function run() {
  var p = Point { x: 3, y: 4 };

  // Working with instance variable x
  var context = VisageLocal.getContext();
  var classType = context.findClass("GettingSettingVariables.Point");
  var xVar = classType.getVariable("x");
  xVar.setValue(context.mirrorOf(p), context.mirrorOf(7.0));
  println("p.x={p.x}.");

  // Working with script variable a
  var moduleType = context.findClass("GettingSettingVariables");
  var aVar = moduleType.getVariable("a");
  aVar.setValue(context.mirrorOf(p), context.mirrorOf("Hello, World"));
  println("a={a}.");
}
```

Here, we obtain the mirror of an instance variable in a class using the getVariable() call on classType, passing in the variable name. Two other methods exist for getting instance variables. One version of the overloaded getVariables() call takes a Boolean parameter and returns a java.util.List<VisageVarMember>. If the parameter is false, only instance variables declared in the class are included in the list. If the parameter is true, all instance variables, including those declared in the superclasses, are included. Another version of the getVariables() call takes an extra first parameter of type VisageMemberFilter, which allows you to get only those instance variables that pass the filter.

The type of xVar is VisageVarMember. It represents the instance variable x of class Point. The setValue() call on xVar takes two parameters: the first is a mirror of p and the second is a mirror of the new value of x. VisageVarMember has a corresponding getValue() call, which takes one parameter, the mirror of an instance of the class, and returns a mirror of the value of the instance variable.

> ■ **Note** The Visage compiler compiles Visage modules into Java classes and Visage classes in a module into nested Java classes. Therefore, the reflection facility represents both classes and modules as `VisageLocal.ClassType`. The `getVariable()` and `getVariables()` calls on a module class type will return information related to script variables in the module. The `setValue()` and `getValue()` calls on instances of `VisageVarMember` that represent script variables will ignore the first parameter, and we usually pass in `null`.

Invoking Instance and Script Functions

The reflection code for invoking instance functions and script functions is very similar to the code for accessing instance variables and script variables, as shown here:

```
// InvokingFunctions.visage
import visage.reflect.*;

public class A {
  public function f(i:Integer):Integer {
    i * i
  }
}

public function g(str:String):String {
  "{str} {str}"
}

public function run() {
  var o = A {};

  var context = VisageLocal.getContext();

  // Working with instance function f() of A
  var classType = context.findClass("InvokingFunctions.A");
  var fFunc = classType.getFunction("f", context.getIntegerType());
  var fVal = fFunc.invoke(context.mirrorOf(o), context.mirrorOf(4));
  println("o.f(4)={(fVal as VisagePrimitiveValue).asObject()}.");

  // Working with script function g()
  var moduleClassType = context.findClass("InvokingFunctions");
  var gFunc = moduleClassType.getFunction("g", context.getStringType());
  var gVal = gFunc.invoke(null, context.mirrorOf("Hello"));
  println('g("Hello")={(gVal as VisageLocal.ObjectValue).asObject()}.');
}
```

Here, we call the `getFunction()` method on `classType` to obtain a mirror of an instance function. This method can take a variable number of parameters. The first parameter is the name of the function. The rest of the parameters are mirrors of the types of the instance function. Two other methods are available for getting instance functions. One version of the overloaded `getFunctions()` call takes a Boolean parameter and returns a `java.util.List<VisageVarFunction>`. If the parameter is false, only instance functions defined in the class are included in the list. If the parameter is true, all instance functions, including those defined in the superclasses, are included. Another version of a `getFunctions()` call takes an extra first parameter of type `VisageMemberFilter`, which allows you to get only those instance functions that pass the filter.

The type of `fFunc` in the preceding code is `VisageFunctionMember`. It represents the instance function `f` of class `A`. The `invoke()` call on `fFunc` takes a variable number of parameters, in this case two: the first parameter is a mirror of `o`, an instance of `A`, and the second parameter is the mirror of the instance function parameter. It returns an instance `fVal` of type `VisageValue` that represents a mirror of the value of the function invocation expression.

The situation with the script function g is analogous to the situation for instance functions, except that we search for the script function in the module class type, and that we pass a null as the first parameter to the `invoke()` call.

Other Reflection Capabilities

The reflection API also provides the following capabilities:

- The `VisageLocal.ClassType` class has `getMember(String, VisageType)`, `getMembers(boolean)`, and `getMembers(VisageMemberFilter, boolean)` methods to get at member functions and member variables through the same API.

- The `VisageLocal.ClassType` class has a `getSuperClasses(boolean)` method to get a list of direct or indirect superclasses.

- The `VisageLocal.ObjectValue` class has overloaded `bindVar(String, VisageLocation)` and `bindVar(VisageVarMember, VisageLocation)` methods to bind member variables to `VisageLocations` associated to other `VisageVarMembers`.

- The `VisageVarMember` class has a `getLocation(VisageObjectvalue)` method that gets the location of member variables for use in `bindVar()` calls.

Resources

The best place for more information about the Visage language is the official Visage compiler home page at `http://visage-lang.org`.

Index

T